THE BROADVIEW
ANTHOLOGY OF
EXPOSITORY
PROSE

THE BROADVIEW ANTHOLOGY OF EXPOSITORY
PROSE

edited by

Tammy Roberts | Mical Moser
Don LePan | Craig Lawson
Julia Gaunce | Jane Britton

broadview press

Library and Archives Canada Cataloguing in Publication

Roberts, Tammy, 1975–
    The Broadview anthology of expository prose

ISBN-13: 978-1-55111-426-2
    1. Essays. 2. Exposition (Rhetoric) 3. College readers.

PN6142.B76 2002   808.84   C2002-900909-7

Broadview Press is an independent, international publishing house, incorporated in 1985. Broadview believes in shared ownership, both with its employees and with the general public; since the year 2000 Broadview shares have traded publicly on the Toronto Venture Exchange under the symbol BDP.

We welcome comments and suggestions regarding any aspect of our publications—please feel free to contact us at the addresses below or at broadview@broadviewpress.com.

North America
PO Box 1243, Peterborough, Ontario Canada K9J 7H5
PO Box 1015, 3576 California Road, Orchard Park, NY, USA 14127
Tel: (705) 743-8990; Fax: (705) 743-8353
email: customerservice@broadviewpress.com

UK, Ireland, and continental Europe
NBN International, Estover Road, Plymouth, UK PL6 7PY
Tel: 44 (0) 1752 202300; Fax: 44 (0) 1752 202330
email: enquiries@nbninternational.com

Australia and New Zealand
UNIREPS, University of New South Wales
Sydney, NSW, Australia 2052
Tel: 61 2 9664 0999; Fax: 61 2 9664 5420
email: info.press@unsw.edu.au

Broadview Press gratefully acknowledges the financial support of the Government of Canada through the Book Publishing Industry Development Program for our publishing activities.

www.broadviewpress.com

Cover design by Rachel Hershfield with Thinkinc.

PRINTED IN CANADA

PREFACE

This anthology has its origin in the space between two books. For many years the Broadview Press list has included two outstanding readers designed for first-year composition and literature courses at post-secondary institutions: *The Broadview Reader* (edited by Herbert Rosengarten and Jane Flick), comprising an excellent selection of every sort of non-fiction prose except scholarly writing; and *Academic Reading* (edited by Janet Giltrow), comprising an excellent selection of purely scholarly writing. An attractive third option, it seemed to us, would be an anthology combining a wide range of literary and other non-scholarly essays with a good selection of academic writing.

Central to the idea of this anthology, then, is the inclusion of a substantial selection of academic writing. Very frequently, anthologies which make a stab at including academic writing end up selecting journalistic writing by academics rather than "real" academic writing. Granted, it is not easy to find examples of purely academic discourse that are at all accessible to a first- or second-year student who is unlikely to be familiar with the conventions of the given discipline. But it is not impossible. One guideline we have followed in searching out such essays has been to look for academic pieces which have ended up exerting considerable influence on a public much broader than that within the discipline. Essays such as that by Milgram on obedience and conformity; Wilson on continental drift (written at a time when the idea was regarded by most as a crackpot theory); Putnam on social capital in modern American society; and Harris on the importance of peer influence to the formation of personality have all presented ideas that have ended by being widely discussed and widely influential outside academia. Also included here are many pieces which, while they may not have reached the general public in any form, have been widely influential within their discipline.

A second central principle of the book is variety. At the heart of the anthology are a wide range of essays that attempt in one way or another to persuade the reader of something. But a variety of other modes of prose writing are also included. The reader will find personal essays, occasional pieces, letters, and humourous sketches. Selections range from less than a page in length to more than twenty pages. In some essays the writing is almost transparent in its simplicity; in others the reader may be challenged by complex syntax as well as by difficulty of material. In many cases the intended audience is clearly the general reader, but some selections aim at a much narrower readership. And the anthology includes a wide range of subject matter, with a number of essays on scientific subjects in addition to many on subjects in the humanities and social sciences. Most of the selections are of course written in English, but we have also included a handful of pieces first written in other languages either because (as in the case of Montaigne) they have been extraordinarily influential in shaping the history of the essay, or because of the central position of their authors in shaping intellectual discourse in Western society (as in the case of Barthes).

One category of expository writing that is not represented in this anthology is the student essay. For instructors who would like to include discussion of student work in their courses, however, we have posted on an associated website a selection of excellent student essays; simply go to www.broadviewpress.com and follow the links to the website designed to accompany both this book and *The Broadview Guide to Writing*.

Most essay anthologies designed for university use are arranged either by broad subject category ("Nature," "Science," and so on) or by rhetorical category ("Descriptive essays," "Persuasive essays," etc.). On the good advice of the majority of academics we consulted on this matter, we have instead adopted a chronological arrangement, in the interests both of simplicity and of flexibility. In an anthology where the grouping is by subject or by rhetorical category each essay must of necessity appear as part of only one grouping—whereas in reality, of course, many of the finest and most interesting essays will have two or more subjects, many of the best persuasive essays also employ description or narration, and so on. The chronological approach, by contrast, allows the instructor to group the essays in whatever combinations seem most interesting or appropriate, and to change those groupings as desired each time a course is taught. (Tables of contents by subject category and by rhetorical category—in both of which each essay is likely to appear two or three times—appear following this preface.) A chronological organization is flexible in another respect too; it lends itself to use in courses on the history of the essay or on non-fiction prose as a genre as well as in courses on composition and rhetoric.

One issue in assembling almost any anthology is whether or not to excerpt. If the book is to be essentially an anthology of essays, does the integrity of the form demand that all essays selected for inclusion be included in their entirety? Should selections taken from full-length books be excluded on the grounds of their provenance? To both these questions we have answered in the negative. If an anthology such as this is to do the best possible job of presenting the widest possible range within a manageable compass, practical and pedagogical concerns seem to us to justify the occasional decision to excerpt a very long essay, or to select a discrete section from a full-length book. We have, however, included a considerable number of longer essays in their entirety.

We should say something, finally, about the book's title. There may be no satisfactory solution to naming a book of this sort. "Anthology of Prose" is obviously inappropriate, since prose fiction is excluded. "Anthology of Essays" becomes unsuitable once the decision has been made to include selections from longer works as well. "Anthology of Non-Fiction Prose" is clunky, and would argue for the inclusion of a much wider variety of forms of non-fiction prose than are presented here (among them interview transcripts, car maintenance manuals, and truthful advertising copy); conversely, it would argue for the exclusion of pieces such as the "essays" in this collection by George Eliot and by Stephen Leacock, both of which hover on the border between fiction and non-fiction.

In the end we have settled on "Anthology of Expository Prose." That too is a title that if taken narrowly would argue for the exclusion of certain of the selections in the anthology. Defined according to traditional rhetorical categories, expository writing is an umbrella category of writing that involves explanation. It has been taken to include writing engaged in comparison or contrast, definition, analysis, and persuasion or argument—but not to include purely descriptive or narrative forms of non-fiction prose. More broadly, though, "expository prose" is often used nowadays as a short form for "non-fiction prose that aims to set something forth for a public readership." There are good grounds on which to base this more inclusive meaning; "exposition" may refer simply to "setting forth," and that is certainly what descriptive and even some narrative prose may fairly be said to do, quite as much as prose that attempts to argue or persuade sets something forth. (Though much argument attempts to explain, often the line between explanation and assertion is exceedingly thin—a good deal thinner in many cases than that separating, say, description from explanation.) In any case, writing that falls within the traditional criteria of expository prose constitutes the overwhelming majority of the prose that appears in these pages; we beg the indulgence of the purist who would have it approach more nearly to one hundred per cent.

* * *

Tammy Roberts has been the central coordinating force for the anthology, and to her goes pride of place in the list of the book's editors. We would also like to acknowledge the work of a number of others who under Roberts' supervision have helped very substantially in the preparation of the book: Lynne Churchill-Frail, Chris Enright, Jennifer Ford, Trevor Rueger, Christine Schill, Janet Sisson, Shari Wattling (who is responsible for much of the material in the Biographical Notes as well as many of the questions), and Nicole Zylstra. Kathryn Brownsey is to be thanked for her excellent work designing and setting the book, and both Brownsey and Eileen Eckert for their sharp editorial eyes. Finally, we would particularly like to thank the following for the helpful advice they provided along the way: Candace Fertile, Camosun College; Richard Harrison, Mount Royal College; David McNeil, Dalhousie University; Kenneth Phillips, Okanagan University College; Susan Willens, George Washington University; Michael John Martin, San Francisco State University; Alison Wariner, California State University, Hayward; and four academics at Malaspina University College: Terri Doughty, Gwyneth Evans, Craig Tapping, and Deborah Torkko.

* * *

We welcome the comments and suggestions of all readers—instructors or students—about any and all aspects of this book, from the selections themselves to the book's organization, questions, and ancillary material; please feel free to email us at <u>broadview@broadviewpress.com.</u> We hope you will enjoy the book as it stands—but we also want to think of possible improvements for a second edition.

Tammy Roberts, Mical Moser, Don LePan, Craig Lawson,
Julia Gaunce, Jane Britton, July 14, 2001

CONTENTS

CONTENTS BY SUBJECT

Children and Students / Culture(s) and Race(s) / Death and Life / The Earth, Humans, and Other Animals / History, and Other Ways of Looking at the Past / The Human Psyche / Issues of Ethics and Conscience / Language and Communication / Literature and the Arts / Personal Experience / Philosophical Perspectives / Religion / Science, Technology, Change / Social Patterns, Social Issues / Sport/ Women in Society / Work and Business

Note: Many selections deal with two or more of these subjects.

Children and Students

Culture(s) and Race(s)

Death and Life

The Earth, Humans, and other Animals

History, and Other Ways of Looking at the Past

The Human Psyche

Issues of Ethics and Conscience

Language and Communication

Literature and the Arts

Personal Experience

Philosophical Perspectives

Religion

Science, Technology, and Change

Social Patterns, Social Issues

Sport

Women in Society

Work and Business

CONTENTS BY RHETORICAL CATEGORY

Essays that employ:
Analysis / Cause and Effect / Comparison and Contrast /
Classification / Definition / Description / Humor and Satire /
Narration / Persuasion and Argument

Note: Many selections employ two or more of these modes.

Analysis

Cause and Effect

Comparison and Contrast

Classification

Definition

Description

Humor and Satire

Narration

Persuasion and Argument

Michel de Montaigne

Of Democritus and Heraclitus

Montaigne, a sixteenth-century French aristocrat, is commonly regarded as the originator of the essay form. The following selections are from the 1603 English edition translated by John Florio; it was in this form that Montaigne's essays became widely read in the English-speaking world.

∾

The judgment is an utensil proper for all subjects, and will have an oar in everything: which is the reason, that in these essays I take hold of all occasions where, though it happen to be a subject I do not very well understand, I try however, sounding it at a distance, and finding it too deep for my stature, I keep me on the shore; and this knowledge that a man can proceed no further, is one effect of its virtue, yea, one of those of which it is most proud. One while in an idle and frivolous subject, I try to find out matter whereof to compose a body, and then to prop and support it; another while, I employ it in a noble subject, one that has been tossed and tumbled by a thousand hands, wherein a man can scarce possibly introduce anything of his own, the way being so beaten on every side that he must of necessity walk in the steps of another: in such a case, 'tis the work of the judgment to take the way that seems best, and of a thousand paths, to determine that this or that is the best. I leave the choice of my arguments to fortune, and take that she first presents to me; they are all alike to me, I never design to go through any of them; for I never see all of anything: neither do they who so largely promise to show it to others. Of a hundred members and faces that everything has, I take one, one while to look it over only, another while to ripple up the skin, and sometimes to pinch it to the bones: I give a stab, not so wide but as deep as I can, and am for the most part tempted to take it in hand by some new light I discover in it. Did I know myself less, I might perhaps venture to handle something or other to the bottom, and to be deceived in my own inability; but sprinkling here one word and there another, patterns cut from several pieces and scattered without design and without engaging myself too far, I am not responsible for them, or obliged to keep close to my subject, without varying at my own liberty and pleasure, and giving up myself to doubt and uncertainty, and to my own gover[n]ing method, ignorance.

All motion discovers us: the very same soul of Caesar, that made itself so conspicuous in marshaling and commanding the battle of Pharsalia, was also seen as solicitous and busy in the softer affairs of love and leisure. A man makes a judgment of a horse, not only by seeing him when he is showing off his paces, but by his very walk, nay, and by seeing him stand in the stable.

Among the functions of the soul, there are some of a lower and meaner form; he who does not see her in those inferior offices as well as in those of nobler note, never fully discovers her; and, peradventure, she is best shown where she moves her simpler pace. The winds of passions take most hold of her in her highest flights; and the rather by reason that she wholly applies herself to, and exercises her whole virtue upon, every particular subject, and never handles more than one thing at a time, and that not according to it, but according to herself. Things in respect to themselves have, peradventure, their weight, measures and conditions; but when we once take them into us, the soul forms them as she pleases. Death is terrible to Cicero, coveted by Cato, indifferent to Socrates. Health, conscience, authority, knowledge, riches, beauty, and their contraries, all strip themselves at their entering into us, and receive a new robe, and of another fashion, from the soul; and of what color, brown, bright, green, dark, and of what quality, sharp, sweet, deep, or superficial, as best pleases each of them, for they are not agreed upon any common standard of forms, rules, or proceedings; every one is a queen in her own dominions. Let us, therefore, no more excuse ourselves upon the external qualities of things; it belongs to us to give ourselves an account of them. Our good or ill has no other dependence but on ourselves. 'Tis there that our offerings and our vows are due, and not to fortune: she has no power over our manners; on the contrary, they draw and make her follow in their train, and cast her in their own mold. Why should not I judge of Alexander at table, ranting and drinking at the prodigious rate he sometimes used to do? Or, if he played at chess? what string of his soul was not touched by this idle and childish game? I hate and avoid it, because it is not play enough, that it is too grave and serious a diversion, and I am ashamed to lay out as much thought and study upon it as would serve to much better uses. He did not more pump his brains about his glorious expedition into the Indies, nor than another in unraveling a passage upon which depends the safety of mankind. To what a degree does this ridiculous diversion molest the soul, when all her faculties are summoned together upon this trivial account! and how fair an opportunity she herein gives every one to know and to make a right judgment of himself? I do not more thoroughly sift myself in any other posture than this: what passion are we exempted from in it? Anger, spite, malice, impatience, and a vehement desire of getting the better in a concern wherein it were more excusable to be ambitious of being overcome; for to be eminent, to excel above the common rate in frivolous things, nowise befits a man of honor. What I say in this example may be said in all others. Every particle, every employment of man manifests him equally with any other.

Democritus and Heraclitus were two philosophers, of whom the first, finding human condition ridiculous and vain, never appeared abroad but with a jeering and laughing countenance; whereas Heraclitus commiserating that same condition of ours, appeared always with a sorrowful look, and tears in his eyes:

> *Alter*
> *Ridebat, quoties a limine moverat unum*
> *Protuleratque pedem; flebat contrarius alter.*[1]

I am clearly for the first humor: not because it is more pleasant to laugh than to weep, but because it expresses more contempt and condemnation than the other, and I think we can never be despised according to our full desert. Compassion and bewailing seem to imply some esteem of and value for the thing bemoaned; whereas the things we laugh at are by that expressed to be of no moment. I do not think that we are so unhappy as we are vain, or have in us so much malice as folly; we are not so full of mischief as inanity; nor so miserable as we are vile and mean. And therefore Diogenes, who passed away his time in rolling himself in his tub, and made nothing of the great Alexander esteeming us no better than flies, or bladders puffed up with wind, was a sharper and more penetrating, and, consequently in my opinion, a juster judge than Timon, surnamed the Man-hater; for what a man hates he lays to heart. This last was an enemy to all mankind, who passionately desired our ruin, and avoided our conversation as dangerous, proceeding from wicked and depraved natures: the other valued us so little

---

[1] "The one was always laughing whenever he put a foot outside the door, the other, his opposite, was always weeping" (Juvenal *Satires* X. 28ff).

that we could neither trouble nor infect him by our example; and left us to herd one with another, not out of fear, but from contempt of our society: concluding us incapable of doing good as ill.

Of the same strain was Statilius' answer, when Brutus courted him into the conspiracy against Caesar; he was satisfied that the enterprise was just, but he did not think mankind worthy of a wise man's concern; according to the doctrine of Hegesias, who said, that a wise man ought to do nothing but for himself, forasmuch as he only was worthy of it: and to the saying of Theodorus, that it was not reasonable a wise man should hazard himself for his country, and endanger wisdom for a company of fools. Our condition is as ridiculous as risible.[2]

(1603)

from OF EXPERIENCE

There is no desire more natural than that of knowledge. We try all ways that can lead us to it; where reason is wanting, we therein employ experience.

> Per varios usus artem experientia fecit,
> Exemplo monstrante viam,[3]

which is a means much more weak and cheap; but truth is no great thing, that we ought not to disdain any mediation that will guide us to it. Reason has so many forms, that we know not to which to take; experience has no fewer; the consequence we would draw from the comparison of events is unsure, by reason they are always unlike. There is no quality so universal in this image of things, as diversity and variety. Both the Greeks and the Latins, and we, for the most express example of similitude, employ that of eggs: and yet there have been men, particularly one at Delphos, who could distinguish

---

[2] The story of Statilius comes from Plutarch's *Lives*, life of Brutus 12.3. The doctrines of Hegisias and Theodorus can be found in Diogenes Laertius' life of Aristippus, *Lives of the Eminent Philosophers* II. 8; the views of Hegesias are stated at §95, and those of Theodorus at §98.

[3] "Through various exercises, experience produces art, with example showing the way" (Minilius *Astronomica* I. 61–2).

marks of difference among eggs so well, that he never mistook one for another; and, having many hens, could tell which had laid it. Dissimilitude intrudes itself of itself in our works; no art can arrive at perfect similitude: neither Perrozet, nor any other cardmarker, can so carefully polish and blanch the backs of his cards, that some gamesters will not distinguish them by seeing them only shuffled by another. Resemblance does not so much make one, as difference makes another. Nature has obliged herself to make nothing other, that was not unlike.

And yet I am not much pleased with his opinion, who thought by the multitude of laws to curb the authority of judges, in cutting out for them their several parcels; he was not aware that there is as much liberty and latitude in the interpretation of laws, as in their form; and they but fool themselves, who think to lessen and stop our disputes by recalling us to the express words of the Bible: forasmuch as our mind does not find the field less spacious wherein to controvert the sense of another, than to deliver his own; and as if there were less animosity and tartness in commentary than in invention. We see how much he was mistaken; for we have more laws in France than all the rest of the world put together, and more than would be necessary for the government of all the worlds of Epicurus: *Ut olim flagitiis, sic nunc legibus laboramus*[4]: and yet we have left so much to the opinions and decisions of our judges, that there never was so full a liberty or so full a license. What have our legislators gained by culling out a hundred thousand particular cases, and by applying to these a hundred thousand laws? This number holds no manner of proportion with the infinite diversity of human actions; the multiplication of our inventions will never arrive at the variety of examples; add to these a hundred times as many more, it will still not happen, that of events to come, there shall one be found that, in this vast number of millions of events so chosen and recorded, shall so tally with any other one, and be so exactly coupled and matched with it, that there will not remain some circumstance and diversity which will require a diverse judgment. There is little relation between our actions, which are in perpetual mutation, and fixed and immutable laws; the most to be desired, are those that are the most rare, the most simple and general: and I am even of opinion, that we had better have none at all, than to have them in so prodigious a number as we have.

Nature always gives them better and happier than those we make ourselves. Witness the picture of the Golden Age of the poets, and the state

---

[4] "Previously we suffered from crimes, now we suffer from laws" (Tacitus *Annals* III. 25).

wherein we see nations live, who have no other: some there are, who for their only judge, take the first passer-by that travels along their mountains, to determine their cause: and others who, on their market day, choose out some one among them upon the spot to decide their controversies. What danger would there be, that the wisest among us should so determine ours, according to occurrences, and at sight, without obligation of example and consequence? For every foot, its own shoe. King Ferdinand, sending colonies[5] to the Indies, wisely provided that they should not carry along with them any students of the long-robe,[6] for fear lest suits should get footing in that new world, as being a science in its own nature, the mother of altercation and division: judging with Plato, "that lawyers and physicians are the pests of a country."

Whence does it come to pass that our common language, so easy for all other uses, becomes obscure, and unintelligible in wills and contracts? and that he who so clearly expresses himself, in whatever else he speaks or writes, cannot find in these, any way of declaring himself that does not fall into doubt and contradiction? if it be not that the princes of that art, applying themselves with a peculiar attention to cull out portentous words and to contrive artificial sentences, have so weighed every syllable, and so thoroughly sifted every sort of quirking connection, that they are now confounded and intangled in the infinity of figures and minute divisions, and can no more fall within any rule or prescription, nor any certain intelligence: *Confusum est, quidquid usque in pulverem sectum est.*[7] As you see children trying to bring a mass of quicksilver to a certain number of parts; the more they press and work it, and endeavour to reduce it to their own will, the more they irritate the liberty of this generous metal; it evades their endeavor, and sprinkles itself into so many separate bodies as frustrate all reckoning; so is it here; for in subdividing these subtleties, we teach men to increase their doubts; they put us into a way of extending and diversifying difficulties, and lengthen and disperse them. In sowing and retailing questions, they make the world fructify and increase in uncertainties and disputes, as the earth is made fertile by being crumbled and dug deep: *Difficultatim facit doctrina.*[8] We doubted of Ulpian,[9] and are now still more perplexed with Bartolus and

---

[5] *colonies*   colonists

[6] *students of the long-robe*   those knowledgeable in the law

[7] "Whatever is ground to dust becomes confused" (Seneca *Letters* 89, 3).

[8] "Learning creates a problem" (Quintilian *Institutiones Oratoriae* (or else *Declamationes*) X, iii. 16).

[9] *Ulpian*   Roman jurist

Baldus.[10] We should efface the trace of this innumerable diversity of opinions; not adorn ourselves with it, and fill posterity with crotchets. I know not what to say to it; but experience makes it manifest, that so many interpretations dissipate truth, and break it. Aristotle wrote to be understood; if he could not do this, much less will another that is not so good at it; and a third than he who expressed his own thoughts. We open the matter, and spill it in pouring out: of one subject we make a thousand, and in multiplying and subdividing them, fall again into the infinity of atoms of Epicurus. Never did two men make the same judgment of the same thing; and 'tis impossible to find two opinions exactly alike, not only in several men, but in the same man, at diverse hours. I often find matter of doubt in things of which the commentary has disdained to take notice; I am most apt to stumble in an even country, like some horses that I have known, that make most trips in the smoothest way.

5   Who will not say that glosses augment doubts and ignorance, since there's no one book to be found, either human or divine, which the world busies itself about, whereof the difficulties are cleared by interpretation. The hundredth commentator passes it on to the next, still more knotty and perplexed than he found it. When were we ever agreed among ourselves: "this book has enough; there is now no more to be said about it?" This is most apparent in the law; we give the authority of law to infinite doctors, infinite decrees, and as many interpretations: yet do we find any end of the need of interpreting? is there, for all that, any progress or advancement toward peace, or do we stand in need of any fewer advocates and judges, than when this great mass of law was yet in its first infancy? On the contrary, we darken and bury intelligence; we can no longer discover it, but at the mercy of so many fences and barriers. Men do not know the natural disease of the mind; it does nothing but ferret and inquire, and is eternally wheeling, juggling, and perplexing itself like silkworms, and then suffocates itself in its work; *Mus in pice.*[11] It thinks it discovers at a great distance, I know not what glimpse of light and imaginary truth; but while running to it, so many difficulties, hindrances and new inquisitions cross it, that it loses its way, and is made drunk with the motion: not much unlike Aesop's dogs, that seeing something like a dead body floating in the sea, and not being able to approach it, set to work to drink the water and lay the passage dry, and so choked themselves. To which, what one Crates said of the writings of

---

[10] *Bartolus and Baldus*   medieval scholars of the law

[11] "a mouse [stuck] in pitch"

Heraclitus, falls pat enough, "that they required a reader who could swim well," so that the depth and weight of his doctrine might not overwhelm and stifle him. 'Tis nothing but particular weakness that makes us content with what others or ourselves have found out in this chase after knowledge: one of better understanding will not rest so content; there is always room for one to follow, nay, even for ourselves; and another road: there is no end of our inquisitions; our end is in the other world. 'Tis a sign either that the mind has grown short-sighted when it is satisfied, or that it has got weary. No generous mind can stop in itself; it will still tend further, and beyond its power; it has sallied beyond its effects; if it do not advance and press forward, and retire, and rush and wheel about, 'tis but half alive: its pursuits are without bound or method; its aliment is admiration, the chase, ambiguity, which Apollo sufficiently declared in always speaking to us in a double, obscure, and oblique sense; not feeding, but amusing and puzzling us. 'Tis an irregular and perpetual motion, without model and without aim; its inventions heat, pursue, and interproduce one another.

(1603)

from OF THE EDUCATION OF CHILDREN

I happened the other day upon this piece of fortune; I was reading a French book, where after I had a long time run dreaming over a great many words, so dull, so insipid, so void of all wit or common sense, that indeed they were only French words; after a long and tedious travel, I came at last to meet with a piece that was lofty, rich, and elevated to the very clouds; of which, had I found either the declivity easy or the ascent gradual, there had been some excuse; but it was so perpendicular a precipice, and so wholly cut off from the rest of the work, that, by the six first words, I found myself flying into the other world, and thence discovered the vale whence I came so deep and low, that I have never had since the heart to descend into it any more. If I should set out one of my discourses with such rich spoils as these, it would but too evidently manifest the imperfection of my own writing. To reprehend the fault in others that I am guilty of myself, appears to me no more unreasonable, than to condemn, as I often do, those of others in myself: they are to be everywhere reproved, and ought to have no sanctuary allowed them. I know very well how audaciously I myself, at every turn, attempt to equal myself to my thefts, and to make my style go hand in hand with them, not without a temerarious hope of deceiving the eyes of my reader from discerning the difference; but withal, it is as much by the benefit of my application, that I hope to do it, as by that of my invention or any force of my own. Besides, I do not offer to contend with the whole body of these champions, nor hand to hand with any one of them: 'tis only by flights and little light attempts that I engage them; I do not grapple with them, but try their strength only, and never engage so far as I make a show to do. If I could hold them in play, I were a brave fellow; for I never attack them, but where they are most sinewy and strong. To cover a man's self (as I have seen some do) with another man's armor, so as not to discover so much as his fingers' ends; to carry on a design (as it is not hard for a man that has anything of a scholar in him, in an ordinary subject to do) under old inventions, patched up here and there with his own trumpery, and then to endeavor to conceal the theft, and to make it pass for his own, is first injustice and meanness of spirit in those who do it, who having nothing in them of their own fit to procure them a reputation, endeavor to do it by attempting to impose things upon the world in their own name, which they have no manner of title to; and, next, a ridiculous folly to content themselves with acquiring the ignorant approbation of the vulgar by such a pitiful cheat, at the price at the same time of degrading themselves in the eyes of men of understanding, who turn up their noses at all this borrowed incrustation, yet whose praise alone is worth the having. For my own part, there is nothing I would not sooner do than that, neither have I said so much of others, but to get a better opportunity to explain myself. Nor in this do I glance at the composers of centos, who declare themselves such; of which sort of writers I have in my time known many very ingenious, and particularly one under the name of Capilupus, besides the ancients. These are really men of wit, and that make it appear they are so, both by that and other ways of writing; as for example, Lipsius, in that learned and laborious contexture of his politics.

But, be it how it will, and how inconsiderable soever these essays of mine may be, I will say I never intended to conceal them, no more than my old bald grizzled pate before them, where the painter has presented you not with a perfect face, but with mine. For these are my own particular opinions and fancies, and I deliver them as only what I myself believe, and not for what is to be believed by others. I have no other end in this writing, but only to discover myself, who, also, shall, peradventure, be another thing tomorrow, if I chance to meet any new instruction to change me. I have no authority to be believed, neither do I desire it, being too conscious of my own inerudition to be able to instruct others.

(1603)

QUESTIONS:

1. "Of Democritus and Heraclitus" is the essay in which Montaigne first referred to "essais"— literally, "attempts." Express in your own words what Montaigne thinks of himself as attempting in these "essais."

2. Is the topic of "Of Democritus and Heraclitus" really Democritus and Heraclitus? What other title(s) might be given to this piece?

3. To what extent are the various ideas that Montaigne throws out in "Of Democritus and Heraclitus" connected?

4. Whereas "Of Democritus and Heraclitus" is reprinted here in its entirety, the passages from "Of Experience" and "Of the Education of Children" are selections from much longer essays. To what extent do these passages provide a fuller sense of Montaigne's notions of intellectual endeavour?

5. As you sift through Montaigne's wide variety of observations and assertions, which strike you as being particularly astute? Which (if any) strike you as being no longer relevant, and which (if any) strike you as being unhelpful or simply wrong?

FRANCIS BACON

OF STUDIES

*Bacon was one of the first to try in English the form that had been
pioneered by Montaigne. "Of Studies" remains one of the most
widely quoted essays in English.*

~~

Studies serve for delight, for ornament, and for ability. Their chief use for delight is in privateness and retiring; for ornament, is in discourse; and for ability, is in the judgment and disposition of business. For expert men can execute, and perhaps judge of particulars, one by one; but the general counsels, and the plots and marshalling of affairs, come best from those that are learned. To spend too much time in studies is sloth; to use them too much for ornament is affectation; to make judgment wholly by their rules is the humour of a scholar. They perfect nature, and are perfected by experience, for natural abilities are like natural plants, that need pruning by study; and studies themselves do give forth directions too much at large, except they be bounded in by experience. Crafty men contemn studies, simple men admire them, and wise men use them, for they teach not their own use; but that is a wisdom without them and above them, won by observation. Read not to contradict and confute, nor to believe and take for granted, nor to find talk and discourse, but to weigh and consider. Some books are to be tasted, others to be swallowed, and some few to be chewed and digested; that is, some books are to be read only in parts, others to be read, but not curiously,[1] and some few to be read wholly, and with diligence and attention. Some books also may be read by deputy, and extracts made of them by others; but that would be only in the less important arguments and the meaner sort of books; else distilled books are, like common distilled

---

[1] *curiously* with curiosity and care

waters, flashy things. Reading maketh a full man, conference[2] a ready man, and writing an exact man. And therefore if a man write little, he had need have a great memory; if he confer little, he had need have a present wit; and if he read little, he had need have much cunning, to seem to know that he doth not. Histories make men wise; poets, witty; the mathematics, subtle; natural philosophy, deep; moral, grave; logic and rhetoric, able to contend.[3] *Abeunt studia in mores.*[4] Nay, there is no stond[5] or impediment in the wit but may be wrought out by fit studies, like as diseases of the body may have appropriate exercises. Bowling is good for the stone and reins,[6] shooting for the lungs and breast, gentle walking for the stomach, riding for the head, and the like. So if a man's wit be wandering, let him study the mathematics, for in demonstrations, if his wit be called away never so little, he must begin again. If his wit be not apt to distinguish or find differences, let him study the Schoolmen,[7] for they are *cymini sectores.*[8] If he be not apt to beat over matters,[9] and to call up one thing to prove and illustrate another, let him study the lawyers' cases. So every defect of the mind may have a special receipt.

(1613)

QUESTIONS:

1. Comment on the organization (or lack thereof) in this essay. What are some of the ways in which the essay has evolved as a form since Bacon's time? This essay is filled with confident generalizations. Which of these in particular seem to you to be well founded? Are there any that you would strongly disagree with? How much value do you see in generalizing to the extent that Bacon does?

---

[2] *conference* discussion

[3] *contend* argue effectively

[4] *Abeunt studia in mores* study affects one's habits (and character)

[5] *stond* obstacle

[6] *reins* kidneys

[7] *the Schoolmen* theologians of the late-medieval period (eg., St. Thomas Aquinas) known for making fine distinctions

[8] *cymini sectores* splitters of seeds, hair-splitters

[9] *not apt to beat over matters* not skilled at discussion

2. Comment on the use by Bacon of parallelism and balance in structuring his sentences. To what extent does the effectiveness of this essay stem from stylistic matters such as this (as opposed to the strength of the ideas themselves)?

JOHN DONNE

from FOR WHOM THIS BELL TOLLS (MEDITATION XVII)

In this famous meditation, the dean of St. Paul's in London reflects on the significance of the tolling of church bells.

⌇

NUNC LENTO SONITU DICUNT, MORIERIS[1]

Perchance he for whom this bell tolls may be so ill, as that he knows not it tolls for him; and perchance I may think myself so much better than I am, as that they who are about me, and see my state, may have caused it to toll for me, and I know not that. The church is Catholic, universal, so are all her actions; all that she does belongs to all. When she baptizes a child, that action concerns me; for that child is thereby connected to that body which is my head too, and ingrafted into that body whereof I am a member. And when she buries a man, that action concerns me: all mankind is of one author, and is one volume; when one man dies, one chapter is not torn out of the book, but translated into a better language; and every chapter must be so translated; God employs several translators; some pieces are translated by age, some by sickness, some by war, some by justice; but God's hand is in every translation, and his hand shall bind up all our scattered leaves again for that library where every book shall lie open to one another. As therefore the bell that rings to a sermon calls not upon the preacher only, but upon the congregation to come, so this bell calls us all; but how much more me, who am brought so near the door by this sickness. There was a contention as far as a suit (in which both piety and dignity, religion and estimation, were mingled), which of the religious orders should ring to prayers first in the

---

[1] "Now this bell tolling softly for another, says to me: thou must die."

morning; and it was determined, that they should ring first that rose earliest. If we understand aright the dignity of this bell that tolls for our evening prayer, we would be glad to make it ours by rising early, in that application, that it might be ours as well as his, whose indeed it is. The bell doth toll for him that thinks it doth; and though it intermit again, yet from that minute that that occasion wrought upon him, he is united to God. Who casts not up his eye to the sun when it rises? but who takes off his eye from a comet when that breaks out? Who bends not his ear to any bell which upon any occasion rings but who can remove it from that bell which is passing a piece of himself out of this world? No man is an island, entire of himself; every man is a piece of the continent, a part of the main. If a clod be washed away by the sea, Europe is the less, as well as if a promontory were, as well as if a manor of thy friend's or of thine own were: any man's death diminishes me, because I am involved in mankind, and therefore never send to know for whom the bell tolls; it tolls for thee.

(1626)

Questions:

1. In Donne's world, the Christian church was indeed "catholic" in the sense of being near universally present in society. Can you think of any in Donne's time who were outside this frame of reference? To what extent is it possible to translate Donne's observations made in this context into the pluralistic world of modern Western society?

2. Comment on Donne's use of metaphor here.

3. Comment on the rhythm and structure of Donne's sentences.

MARGARET CAVENDISH

ON SOCIAL CLASS AND HAPPINESS

In her preface to Sociable Letters *Margaret Cavendish writes that she has
"endeavored under the cover of letters to express the humours of mankind…by
the correspondence of two ladies, living at some short distance from each other,
which make it not only their chief delight and pastime, but their tie in friendship, to discourse by letters, as they would do if they were personally together."
The following is one of those letters.*

MADAM,

You were pleased in your last letter to tell me, that you had been in the
country, and that you did almost envy the peasants for living so merrily;
it is a sign, Madam, they live happily, for mirth seldom dwells with troubles
and discontents, neither doth riches nor grandeur live so easily, as that
unconcerned freedom that is in low and mean[1] fortunes and persons, for the
ceremony of grandeur is constrained and bound with forms and rules, and
a great estate and high fortune is not so easily managed as a less, a little is
easily ordered,[2] where much doth require time, care, wisdom and study as
considerations; but poor, mean peasants that live by their labour, are for the
most part happier and pleasanter than great rich persons, that live in luxury
and idleness, for idle time is tedious, and luxury is unwholesome, whereas
labour is healthful and recreative, and surely country housewives take more
pleasure in milking their cows, making their butter and cheese, and feeding
their poultry, than great ladies do in painting, curling, and adorning
themselves, also they have more quiet and peaceable minds and thoughts, for
they never, or seldom, look in a glass to view their faces, they regard not their

---

[1] *mean* poor

[2] *ordered* put into order

complexions, nor observe their decays, they defy time's ruins of their beauties, they are not peevish and froward if they look not as well one day as another, a pimple or spot in their skin tortures not their minds, they fear not the sun's heat, but out-face the sun's power, they break not their sleeps to think of fashions, but work hard to sleep soundly, they lie not in sweats to clear their complexions, but rise to sweat to get them food, their appetites are not queasy with surfeits, but sharpened with fasting, they relish with more savour their ordinary coarse fare, than those who are pampered do their delicious rarities; and for their mirth and pastimes, they take more delight and true pleasure, and are more inwardly pleased and outwardly merry at their wakes, than the great ladies at their balls, and though they dance not with such art and measure, yet they dance with more pleasure and delight, they cast not envious, spiteful eyes at each other, but meet friendly and lovingly. But great ladies at public meetings take not such true pleasures, for their envy at each other's beauty and bravery disturbs their pastimes; and obstructs their mirth, they rather grow peevish and froward through envy, than loving and kind through society, so that whereas the country peasants meet with such kind hearts and unconcerned freedom as they unite in friendly jollity, and depart with neighbourly love, the greater sort of persons meet with constrained ceremony, converse with formality, and for the most part depart with enmity; and this is not only amongst women, but amongst men, for there is amongst the better sort a greater strife[3] for bravery than for courtesy, for place[4] than friendship, and in their societies there is more vainglory than pleasure, more pride than mirth, and more vanity than true content; yet in one thing the better sort of men, as the nobles and gentry, are to be commended, which is, that though they are oftener drunken and more debauched than peasants, having more means to maintain their debaucher- ies, yet at such times as at great assemblies, they keep themselves more sober and temperate than peasants do, which are for the most part drunk at their departing; but to judge between the peasantry and nobles for happiness, I believe where there's one noble that is truly happy, there are a hundred peasants; not that there be more peasants than nobles, but that they are more happy, number for number, as having not the envy, ambition, pride, vainglory, to cross, trouble, [and] vex them, as nobles have; when I say nobles, I mean those that have been ennobled by time as well as title, as the gentry. But, Madam, I am not a fit judge for the several sorts or degrees, or

---

[3] *strife* striving

[4] *place* social position

courses of lives, or actions of mankind, as to judge which is happiest, for happiness lives not in outward show or concourse, but inwardly in the mind, and the minds of men are too obscure to be known, and too various and inconstant to fix a belief in them, and since we cannot know ourselves, how should we know others? Besides, pleasure and true delight lives in everyone's own delectation; but let me tell you, my delectation is, to prove my self,

Madam,

Your Faithful Fr. and S.
I, M.N.
(1664)

ON HEARING THE SHIP WAS DROWNED

Madam,

I heard the ship was drowned, wherein the man was that had the charge and care of my plays, to carry them into E[ngland] to be printed, I being then in A[ntwerp]. Which when I heard, I was extremely troubled, and if I had not had the original of them by me, truly I should have been more afflicted, and accounted the loss of my twenty plays, as the loss of twenty lives, for in my mind I should have died twenty deaths, which would have been a great torment, or I should have been near the fate of those plays, and almost drowned in salt tears, as they in the salt sea; but they are destinated to live, and I hope, I in them, when my body is dead, and turned to dust; But I am so prudent, and careful of my poor labours, which are my writing works, as I always keep the copies of them safely with me, until they are printed, and then I commit the originals to the fire, like parents which are willing to die, whenas they are sure of their children's lives, knowing when they are old, and past breeding, they are but useless in this world. But howsoever their paper bodies are consumed, like as the Roman Emperors, in funeral flames, I cannot say, an eagle flies out of them, or that they turn into a blazing star, although they make a great blazing light when they burn; And so leaving them to your approbation or condemnation, I rest,

Madam, Your faithful Friend and Servant.
(1664)

QUESTIONS:

1. Looked at from one angle, the first of these letters might be seen as an essay on wealth and privilege being no guarantee of happiness—but from another angle it is possible to see Cavendish's arguments as providing a rationalization for the continuance of injustice. Form an argument supporting one or the other of these two approaches to Cavendish's letter.

2. It was common when Cavendish wrote to use expressions such as "the greater sort of persons" and "the better sort" to refer to the nobility, contrasted with the "lower orders." Comment on this hierarchy as expressed in language, and on the implications of the terms we use nowadays with which to discuss social class (middle class, working class, etc.).

3. Comment on the way in which Cavendish structures her sentences in each of these letters.

4. Write a short essay about the way in which you perceive the relationship between wealth and happiness.

5. Comment on the imagery Cavendish uses in the second of these letters.

6. Write a short essay on the importance to you of something you have created.

Jonathan Swift

A Modest Proposal

For Preventing the Children of Poor People in Ireland,
From Being a Burden to Their Parents of Country;
and for Making Them Beneficial to the Public

*This piece setting forth arguments in favour of a particular course of
public policy in Ireland in the early eighteenth century remains the
most widely reprinted English language essay.*

∽∽

It is a melancholy object to those who walk through this great town[1] or travel in the country, when they see the streets, the roads and cabin doors crowded with beggars of the female sex, followed by three, four, or six children, all in rags and importuning every passenger for an alms. These mothers, instead of being able to work for their honest livelihood, are forced to employ all their time in strolling to beg sustenance for their helpless infants; who as they grow up either turn thieves for want of work, or leave their dear native country to fight for the Pretender[2] in Spain, or sell themselves to the Barbadoes.[3]

I think it is agreed by all parties that this prodigious number of children in the arms, or on the backs, or at the heels of their mothers, and frequently of their fathers, is in the present deplorable state of the kingdom a very great additional grievance; and, therefore, whoever could find out a fair, cheap,

---

[1] *town* Dublin

[2] *the Pretender* James Francis Edward Stuart, son of James II, who had been overthrown in 1688 in the English revolution, was known as "the old pretender." Many Irish-Catholics supported him.

[3] *the Barbadoes* It was common at the time for poverty-stricken Irish citizens to go into debt in order to pay for passage to the West Indies, where they would then pay off the debt through labor.

and easy method of making these children sound and useful members of the Commonwealth, would deserve so well of the public as to have his statue set up for a preserver of the nation.

But my intention is very far from being confined to provide only for the children of professed beggars; it is of a much greater extent, and shall take in the whole number of infants at a certain age who are born of parents in effect as little able to support them as those who demand our charity in the streets.

As to my own part, having turned my thoughts for many years upon this important subject, and maturely weighed the several schemes of other projectors,[4] I have always found them grossly mistaken in their computation. It is true a child, just dropped from its dam, may be supported by her milk for a solar year, with little other nourishment; at most not above the value of two shillings, which the mother may certainly get, or the value in scraps, by her lawful occupation of begging; and it is exactly at one year old that I propose to provide for them in such a manner as instead of being a charge upon their parents or the parish, or wanting food and raiment for the rest of their lives, they shall on the contrary contribute to the feeding, and partly to the clothing, of many thousands.

There is likewise another great advantage in my scheme, that it will prevent those voluntary abortions, and that horrid practice of women murdering their bastard children, alas! too frequent among us, sacrificing the poor innocent babes, I doubt,[5] more to avoid the expense than the shame, which would move tears and pity in the most savage and in-human breast.

The number of souls in Ireland being usually reckoned one million and a half, of these I calculate there may be about two hundred thousand couples whose wives are breeders; from which number I subtract thirty thousand couples who are able to maintain their own children (although I apprehend there cannot be so many, under the present distresses of the kingdom); but this being granted, there will remain an hundred and seventy thousand breeders. I again subtract fifty thousand for those women who miscarry, or whose children die by accident or disease within the year. There only remain an hundred and twenty thousand children of poor parents annually born. The question therefore is, how this number shall be reared and provided for? which, as I have already said, under the present situation of affairs, is utterly impossible by all the methods hitherto proposed. For we can neither employ them in handicraft or agriculture; we neither build houses (I mean in the

---

[4] *projectors* people who put forward schemes or projects

[5] *doubt* suspect

country) nor cultivate land; they can very seldom pick up a livelihood by stealing, till they arrive at six years old, except where they are of towardly parts; although I confess they learn the rudiments much earlier; during which time they can, however, be properly looked upon only as probationers; as I have been informed by a principal gentleman in the county of Cavan, who protested to me that he never knew above one or two instances under the age of six, even in a part of the kingdom so renowned for the quickest proficiency in that art.

I am assured by our merchants, that a boy or a girl before twelve years old is no saleable commodity; and even when they come to this age they will not yield above three pounds or three pounds and half a crown at most on the Exchange; which cannot turn to account either to the parents or the kingdom, the charge of nutriment and rags having been at least four times that value.

I shall now therefore humbly propose my own thoughts, which I hope will not be liable to the least objection.

I have been assured by a very knowing American of my acquaintance in London, that a young healthy child well nursed is, at year old, a most delicious, nourishing, and wholesome food, whether stewed, roasted, baked, or boiled; and I make no doubt that it will equally serve in a fricassee or a ragout.

10 I do therefore humbly offer it to public consideration that of the hundred and twenty thousand children already computed, twenty thousand may be reserved for breed, whereof only one-fourth part to be males; which is more than we allow to sheep, black cattle, or swine; and my reason is, that these children are seldom the fruits of marriage, a circumstance not much regarded by our savages; therefore one male will be sufficient to serve four females. That the remaining hundred thousand may, at a year old, be offered in sale to the persons of quality and fortune through the kingdom; always advising the mother to let them suck plentifully in the last month, so as to render them plump and fat for a good table. A child will make two dishes at an entertainment for friends; and when the family dines alone, the fore or hind quarter will make a reasonable dish, and seasoned with a little pepper or salt will be very good boiled on the fourth day, especially in winter.

I have reckoned upon a medium that a child just born will weigh twelve pounds, and in a solar year, if tolerably nursed, will increase to twenty-eight pounds.

I grant this food will be somewhat dear, and therefore very proper for landlords, who, as they have already devoured most of the parents, seem to have the best title to the children.

Infant's flesh will be in season throughout the year, but more plentiful in March, and a little before and after: for we are told by a grave author,[6] an eminent French physician, that fish being a prolific diet, there are more children born in Roman Catholic countries about nine months after Lent than at any other season; therefore reckoning a year after Lent, the markets will be more glutted than usual, because the number of popish infants is at least three to one in this kingdom: and therefore it will have one other collateral advantage, by lessening the number of Papists among us.

I have already computed the charge of nursing a beggar's child (in which list I reckon all cottagers, laborers, and four-fifths of the farmers) to be about two shillings per annum, rags included; and I believe no gentleman would repine to give ten shillings for the carcass of a good fat child, which, as I have said, will make four dishes of excellent nutritive meat, when he has only some particular friend or his own family to dine with him. Thus the squire will learn to be a good landlord, and grow popular among his tenants; the mother will have eight shillings net profit, and be fit for work till she produces another child.

15 Those who are more thrifty (as I must confess the times require) may flay the carcass; the skin of which artificially[7] dressed will make admirable gloves for ladies, and summer boots for fine gentlemen.

As to our city of Dublin, shambles may be appointed for this purpose in the most convenient parts of it, and butchers we may be assured will not be wanting: although I rather recommend buying the children alive, and dressing them hot from the knife as we do roasting pigs.

A very worthy person, a true lover of his country, and whose virtues I highly esteem, was lately pleased in discoursing on this matter to offer a refinement upon my scheme. He said that many gentlemen of this kingdom, having of late destroyed their deer, he conceived that the want of venison might be well supplied by the bodies of young lads and maidens, not exceeding fourteen years of age nor under twelve; so great a number of both sexes in every county being now ready to starve for want of work and service; and these to be disposed of by their parents, if alive, or otherwise by their nearest relations. But with due deference to so excellent a friend and so

---

[6] *grave author* Rabelais

[7] *artificially* with artifice or skill

deserving a patriot, I cannot be altogether in his sentiments. For as to the males, my American acquaintance assured me from frequent experience that their flesh was generally tough and lean, like that of our schoolboys by continual exercise, and their taste disagreeable; and to fatten them would not answer the charge. Then as to the females, it would, I think, with humble submission be a loss to the public, because they soon would become breeders themselves: and besides, it is not improbable that some scrupulous people might be apt to censure such a practice (although indeed very unjustly) as a little bordering upon cruelty; which, I confess, has always been with me the strongest objection against any project, how well soever intended.

But in order to justify my friend, he confessed that this expedient was put into his head by the famous Salmanaazor,[8] a native of the island Formosa, who came from thence to London above twenty years ago: and in conversation told my friend, that in his country when any young person happened to be put to death, the executioner sold the carcass to persons of quality as a prime dainty; and that in his time the body of a plump girl of fifteen, who was crucified for an attempt to poison the emperor, was sold to his imperial majesty's prime minister of state, and other great mandarins of the court, in joints from the gibbet, at four hundred crowns. Neither indeed can I deny, that if the same use were made of several plump young girls in this town, who without one single groat to their fortunes cannot stir abroad without a chair,[9] and appear at the playhouse and assemblies in foreign fineries which they never will pay for, the kingdom would not be the worse.

Some persons of a desponding spirit are in great concern about that vast number of poor people, who are aged, diseased, or maimed, and I have been desired to employ my thoughts what cause may be taken to ease the nation of so grievous an encumbrance. But I am not in the least pain upon that matter, because it is very well known that they are every day dying and rotting by cold and famine, and filth and vermin, as fast as can be reasonably expected. And as to the young, labourers, they are now in as hopeful a condition: they cannot get work, and consequently pine away for want of nourishment, to a degree that if at any time they are accidentally hired to common labour, they have not strength to perform it; and thus the country and themselves are in a fair way of being soon delivered from the evils to come.

---

[8] *Salmanaazor* Under the false name "George Psalmanazar" a French citizen in 1704 published a popular book about Formosa where he claims to have been born; he was later exposed as an impostor.

[9] *chair* sedan chair

20   I have too long digressed, and therefore shall return to my subject. I think the advantages by the proposal which I have made are obvious and many, as well as of the highest importance.

For first, as I have already observed, it would greatly lessen the number of Papists, with whom we are yearly overrun, being the principal breeders of the nation as well as our most dangerous enemies; and who stay at home on purpose with a design to deliver the kingdom to the Pretender, hoping to take their advantage by the absence of so many good Protestants, who have chosen rather to leave their country than stay at home and pay tithes against their conscience to an idolatrous Episcopal curate.

Secondly, the poor tenants will have something valuable of their own, which by law may be made liable to distress and help to pay their landlord's rent, their corn and cattle being already seized, and money a thing unknown.

Thirdly, whereas the maintenance of an hundred thousand children from two years old and upwards, cannot be computed at less than ten shillings apiece per annum, the nation's stock will be thereby increased fifty thousand pounds per annum, beside the profit of a new dish introduced to the tables of all gentlemen of fortune in the kingdom who have any refinement in taste. And the money will circulate among ourselves, the goods being entirely of our own growth and manufacture.

Fourthly, the constant breeders besides the gain of eight shillings sterling per annum by the sale of their children, will be rid of the charge of maintaining them after the first year.

25   Fifthly, this food would likewise bring great custom to taverns, where the vintners will certainly be so prudent as to procure the best receipts[35] for dressing it to perfection, and consequently have their houses frequented by all the fine gentlemen, who justly value themselves upon their knowledge in good eating; and a skilful cook who understands how to oblige his guests, will contrive to make it as expensive as they please.

Sixthly, this would be a great inducement to marriage, which all wise nations have either encouraged by rewards or enforced by laws and penalties. It would increase the care and tenderness of mothers towards their children, when they were sure of a settlement for life to the poor babes, provided in some sort by the public, to their annual profit instead of expense. We should soon see an honest emulation among the married women, which of them could bring the fattest child to the market. Men would become as fond of their wives during the time of their pregnancy as they are now of their mares

---

[35]   *receipts* recipes

in foal, their cows in calf, their sows when they are ready to farrow; nor offer to beat or kick them (as is too frequent a practice) for fear of a miscarriage.

Many other advantages might be enumerated. For instance, the addition of some thousand carcasses in our exportation of barreled beef, the propagation of swine's flesh, and improvement in the art of making good bacon, so much wanted among us by the great destruction of pigs, too frequent at our tables, and which are no way comparable in taste or magnificence to a well-grown, fat, yearling child, which roasted whole will make a considerable figure at a Lord Mayor's feast or any other public entertainment. But this and many others I omit, being studious of brevity.

Supposing that one thousand families in this city would be constant customers for infant's flesh, besides others who might have it at merry meetings, particularly weddings and christenings, I compute that Dublin would take off annually about twenty thousand carcasses; and the rest of the kingdom (where probably they will be sold somewhat cheaper) the remaining eighty thousand.

I can think of no one objection that will possibly be raised against this proposal, unless it should be urged that the number of people will be thereby much lessened in the kingdom. This I freely own, and it was indeed one principal design in offering it to the world. I desire the reader will observe, that I calculate my remedy for this one individual kingdom of Ireland and for no other that ever was, is, or I think ever can be upon earth. Therefore let no man talk to me of other expedients: of taxing our absentees at five shillings a pound: of using neither clothes nor household furniture except what is of our own growth and manufacture: of utterly rejecting the materials and instruments that promote foreign luxury: of curing the expensiveness of pride, vanity, idleness, and gaming in our women: of introducing a vein of parsimony, prudence, and temperance: of learning to love our country, wherein we differ even from Laplanders and the inhabitants of Topinamboo[11]: of quitting our animosities and factions, nor act any longer like the Jews,[12] who were murdering one another at the very moment their city was taken: of being a little cautious not to sell our country and conscience for nothing: of teaching landlords to have at least one degree of mercy towards their tenants. Lastly, of putting a spirit of honesty, industry, and skill into our shopkeepers; who, if a resolution could now be taken to

---

[11] *Topinamboo* name given in the eighteenth century to what is now coastal and central Brazil

[12] *like the Jews* The biblical reference is unclear (possible references include II Kings 24, II Chronicles 37); the anti-Semitic sentiment is all too clear.

buy only our native goods, would immediately unite to cheat and exact upon us in the price, the measure, and the goodness, nor could ever yet be brought to make one fair proposal of just dealing, though often and earnestly invited to it.

30   Therefore, I repeat, let no man talk to me of these and the like expedients, till he has at least a glimpse of hope that there will ever be some hearty and sincere attempt to put them in practice.

But as to myself, having been wearied out for many years with offering vain, idle, visionary thoughts, and at length utterly despairing of success, I fortunately fell upon this proposal; which, as it is wholly new, so it has something solid and real, of no expense and little trouble, full in our own power, and whereby we can incur no danger in disobliging England. For this kind of commodity will not bear exportation, the flesh being of too tender a consistence to admit a long continuance in salt, although perhaps I could name a country which would be glad to eat up our whole nation without it.

After all, I am not so violently bent upon my own opinion as to reject any offer proposed by wise men, which shall be found equally innocent, cheap, easy, and effectual. But before something of that kind shall be advanced in contradiction to my scheme, and offering a better, I desire the author or authors will be pleased maturely to consider two points. First, as things now stand, how they will be able to find food and raiment for a hundred thousand useless mouths and backs? And secondly, there being a round million of creatures in human figure throughout this kingdom, whose whole subsistence put into a common stock would leave them in debt two millions of pounds sterling, adding those who are beggars by profession to the bulk of farmers, cottagers, and labourers, with the wives and children who are beggars in effect; I desire those politicians who dislike my overture, and may perhaps be so bold to attempt an answer, that they will first ask the parents of these mortals, whether they would not at this day think it a great happiness to have been sold for food at a year old in the manner I prescribe, and thereby have avoided such a perpetual scene of misfortunes as they have since gone through by the oppression of landlords, the impossibility of paying rent without money or trade, the want of common sustenance, with neither house nor clothes to cover them from the inclemencies of weather, and the most inevitable prospect of entailing the like or greater miseries upon their breed for ever.

I profess, in the sincerity of my heart, that I have not the least personal interest in endeavouring to promote this necessary work, having no other motive than the public good of my country, by advancing our trade, providing for infants, relieving the poor, and giving some pleasure to the rich. I have no children by which I can propose to get a single penny; the youngest being nine years old, and my wife past child-bearing.

(1729)

Questions:

1. At what point does the reader realize that this is a satire? What effect does this delay have?

2. What is it possible to infer about the character of the speaker?

3. What is the purpose of the long list of other "expedients" provided in paragraph 29?

4. Comment on Swift's diction, and in particular on the use of such terms as "dam," "breeders" and "yearling child." Can you think of parallels in the way in which humans refer to the animals they eat?

Samuel Johnson

On Becoming Acquainted with Our Real Characters

Prior to the nineteenth century psychology did not exist as a formal discipline, but philosophers such as David Hume and essayists such as Samuel Johnson nevertheless wrote with considerable insight into the workings of the human mind.

～

…Steriles transmisimus annos,
Hæc ævi mihi prima dies, hæc limina vitæ.[1]
Statius, i, 362

…Our barren years are past;
Be this of life the first, of sloth the last.
Elphinston

No weakness of the human mind has more frequently incurred animadversion, than the negligence with which men overlook their own faults, however flagrant, and the easiness with which they pardon them, however frequently repeated.

It seems generally believed, that as the eye cannot see itself, the mind has no faculties by which it can contemplate its own state, and that therefore we have not means of becoming acquainted with our real characters; an opinion which, like innumerable other postulates, an inquirer finds himself inclined to admit upon very little evidence, because it affords a ready solution of many difficulties. It will explain why the greatest abilities frequently fail to promote the happiness of those who possess them; why those who can distinguish with the utmost nicety the boundaries of vice and virtue, suffer

---

[1] "We have passed through barren years, for me this day is the first of my prime, the threshold of life."

them to be confounded in their own conduct; why the active and vigilant resign their affairs implicitly to the management of others; and why the cautious and fearful make hourly approaches towards ruin, without one sigh of solicitude or struggle for escape.

When a position teems thus with commodious consequences, who can without regret confess it to be false? Yet it is certain that declaimers have indulged a disposition to describe the dominion of the passions as extended beyond the limits that nature assigned. Self-love is often rather arrogant than blind; it does not hide our faults from ourselves, but persuades us that they escape the notice of others, and disposes us to resent censures lest we should confess them to be just. We are secretly conscious of defects and vices, which we hope to conceal from the public eye, and please ourselves with innumerable impostures, by which, in reality, nobody is deceived.

In proof of the dimness of our internal sight, or the general inability of man to determine rightly concerning his own character, it is common to urge the success of the most absurd and incredible flattery, and the resentment always raised by advice, however soft, benevolent, and reasonable. But flattery, if its operation be nearly examined, will be found to owe its acceptance, not to our ignorance, but knowledge of our failures, and to delight us rather as it consoles our wants than displays our possessions. He that shall solicit the favour of his patron by praising him for qualities which he can find in himself, will be defeated by the more daring panegyrist who enriches him with adscititious excellence. Just praise is only a debt, but flattery is a present. The acknowledgement of those virtues on which conscience congratulates us, is a tribute that we can at any time exact with confidence; but the celebration of those which we only feign, or desire without any vigorous endeavours to attain them, is received as a confession of sovereignty over regions never conquered, as a favourable decision of disputable claims, and is more welcome as it is more gratuitous.

Advice is offensive, not because it lays us open to unexpected regret, or convicts us of any fault which had escaped our notice, but because it shows us that we are known to others as well as to ourselves; and the officious monitor is persecuted with hatred, not because his accusation is false, but because he assumes that superiority which we are not willing to grant him, and has dared to detect what we desired to conceal.

For this reason advice is commonly ineffectual. If those who follow the call of their desires, without inquiry whither they are going, had deviated ignorantly from the paths of wisdom, and were rushing upon dangers unforseen, they would readily listen to information that recalls them from their errors, and catch the first alarm by which destruction or infamy is denounced. Few that wander in the wrong way mistake it for the right, they only find it more smooth and flowery, and indulge their own choice rather than approve it: therefore few are persuaded to quit it by admonition or reproof, since it impresses no new conviction, nor confers any powers of action or resistance. He that is gravely informed how soon profusion will annihilate his fortune, hears with little advantage what he knew before, and catches at the next occasion of expense, because advice has no force to suppress his vanity. He that is told how certainly intemperance will hurry him to the grave, runs with his usual speed to a new course of luxury, because his reason is not invigorated, nor his appetite weakened.

The mischief of flattery is, not that it persuades any man that he is what he is not, but that it suppresses the influence of honest ambition, by raising an opinion that honour may be gained without the toil of merit; and the benefit of advice arises commonly not from any new light imparted to the mind, but from the discovery which it affords of the public suffrages. He that could withstand conscience is frighted at infamy, and shame prevails when reason is defeated.

As we all know our own faults, and know them commonly with many aggravations which human perspicacity cannot discover, there is, perhaps, no man, however hardened by impudence or dissipated by levity, sheltered by hypocrisy or blasted by disgrace, who does not intend some time to review his conduct, and to regulate the remainder of his life by the laws of virtue. New temptations indeed attack him, new invitations are offered by pleasure and interest, and the hour of reformation is always delayed; every delay gives vice another opportunity of fortifying itself by habit; and the change of manners, though sincerely intended and rationally planned, is referred to the time when some craving passion shall be fully gratified, or some powerful allurement cease its importunity.

Thus procrastination is accumulated on procrastination, and one impediment succeeds another, till age shatters our resolution, or death intercepts the project of amendment. Such is often the end of salutary purposes, after they have long delighted the imagination, and appeased that disquiet which every mind feels from known misconduct, when the attention is not diverted by business or pleasure.

10   Nothing surely can be more unworthy of a reasonable nature, than to continue in a state so opposite to real happiness, as that all the peace of solitude, and felicity of meditation, must arise from resolutions of forsaking it. Yet the world will often afford examples of men, who pass months and

years in a continual war with their own convictions, and are daily dragged by habit, or betrayed by passion, into practices which they closed and opened their eyes with purposes to avoid; purposes which, though settled on conviction, the first impulse of momentary desire totally overthrows.

The influence of custom is indeed such, that to conquer it will require the utmost efforts of fortitude and virtue; nor can I think any man more worthy of veneration and renown, than those who have burst the shackles of habitual vice. This victory, however, has different degrees of glory as of difficulty; it is more heroic as the objects of guilty gratification are more familiar, and the recurrence of solicitation more frequent. He that, from experience of the folly of ambition, resigns his offices, may set himself free at once from temptation to squander his life in courts, because he cannot regain his former station. He who is enslaved by an amorous passion, may quit his tyrant in disgust, and absence will, without the help of reason, overcome by degrees the desire of returning. But those appetites to which every place affords their proper object, and which require no preparatory measures or gradual advances, are more tenaciously adhesive; the wish is so near the enjoyment, that compliance often precedes consideration, and before the powers of reason can be summoned, the time for employing them is past.

Indolence is therefore one of the vices from which those whom it once infects are seldom reformed. Every other species of luxury operates upon some appetite that is quickly satiated, and requires some concurrence of art or accident which every place will not supply; but the desire of ease acts equally at all hours, and the longer it is indulged is the more increased. To do nothing is in every man's power; we can never want an opportunity of omitting duties. The lapse to indolence is soft and imperceptible, because it is only a mere cessation of activity; but the return to diligence is difficult, because it implies a change from rest to motion, from privation to reality:

> ...*Facilis descensus Averni:*
> *Noctes atque dies patet atri janua ditis;*
> *Sed revocare gradum, superasque evadere ad auras,*
> *Hoc opus, hic labor est....*[39]
>
> VIRGIL, Æneid, *Liber* vi, 126

---

[39] "The descent of Avernus is easy: the gates of Hades lie open night and day. But to climb back up and go out to the air above, that is hard work and effort."

The gates of hell are open night and day;
Smooth the descent, and easy is the way;
But to return, and view the cheerful skies,
In this the task and mighty labour lies.
DRYDEN

Of this vice, as of all others, every man who indulges it is conscious: we all know our own state, if we could be induced to consider it, and it might perhaps be useful to the conquest of all these ensnarers of the mind, if, at certain stated days, life was reviewed. Many things necessary are omitted, because we vainly imagine that they may always be performed; and what cannot be done without pain will forever be delayed, if the time of doing it be left unsettled. No corruption is great but by long negligence, which can scarcely prevail in a mind regularly and frequently awakened by periodical remorse. He that thus breaks his life into parts, will find in himself a desire to distinguish every stage of his existence by some improvement, and delight himself with the approach of the day of recollection, as of the time which is to begin a new series of virtue and felicity.

(1751)

To Reign Once More in Our Native Country

Discussions of the Seven Years War in North America have focused most often on the main protagonists—the English and the French. In this essay Johnson attempts to imagine the point of view of Native North Americans.

⌇

As the English army was passing towards Quebec along a soft savannna between a mountain and a lake, one of the petty chiefs of the inland regions stood upon a rock surrounded by his clan, and from behind the shelter of the bushes contemplated the art and regularity of European war. It was evening, the tents were pitched, he observed the security with which the troops rested in the night, and the order with which the march was renewed in the morning. He continued to pursue them with his eye till they could be seen no longer, and then stood for some time silent and pensive.

Then turning to his followers, "My children," said he, "I have often heard from men hoary with long life, that there was a time when our ancestors were absolute lords of the woods, the meadows, and the lakes, wherever the eye can reach or the foot can pass. They fished and hunted, feasted and danced, and when they were weary lay down under the first thicket, without danger and without fear. They changed their habitations as the seasons required, convenience prompted, or curiosity allured them, and sometimes gathered the fruits of the mountain, and sometimes sported in canoes along the coast.

"Many years and ages are supposed to have been thus passed in plenty and security; when at last, a new race of men entered our country from the great ocean. They inclosed themselves in habitations of stone, which our ancestors could neither enter by violence, nor destroy by fire. They issued from those fastnesses, sometimes covered like the armadillo with shells, from which the lance rebounded on the striker, and sometimes carried by mighty beasts which had never been seen in our vales or forests, of such strength and swiftness, that flight and opposition were vain alike. Those invaders ranged over the continent, slaughtering in their rage those that resisted, and those that submitted, in their mirth. Of those that remained, some were buried in caverns, and condemned to dig metals for their masters; some were employed in tilling the ground, of which foreign tyrants devour the produce; and when the sword and the mines have destroyed the natives, they supply their place by human beings of another colour, brought from some distant country to perish here under toil and torture.

"Some there are who boast their humanity, and content themselves to seize our chases and fisheries, who drive us from every tract of ground where fertility and pleasantness invite them to settle, and make no war upon us except when we intrude upon our own lands.

5   "Others pretend to have purchased a right of residence and tyranny; but surely the insolence of such bargains is more offensive than the avowed and open dominion of force. What reward can induce the possessor of a country to admit a stranger more powerful than himself? Fraud or terror must operate in such contracts; either they promised protection which they never have afforded, or instruction which they never imparted. We hoped to be secured by their favour from some other evil, or to learn the arts of Europe, by which we might be able to secure ourselves. Their power they have never exerted in our defence, and their arts they have studiously concealed from us.

Their treaties are only to deceive, and their traffic only to defraud us. They have a written law among them, of which they boast as derived from him who made the earth and sea, and by which they profess to believe that man will be made happy when life shall forsake him. Why is not this law communicated to us? It is concealed because it is violated. For how can they preach it to an Indian nation, when I am told that one of its first precepts forbids them to do to others what they would not that others should do to them?

"But the time perhaps is now approaching when the pride of usurpation shall be crushed, and the cruelties of invasion shall be revenged. The sons of rapacity have now drawn their swords upon each other, and referred their claims to the decision of war; let us look unconcerned upon the slaughter, and remember that the death of every European delivers the country from a tyrant and a robber; for what is the claim of either nation, but the claim of the vulture to the leveret, of the tiger to the fawn? Let them then continue to dispute their title to regions which they cannot people, to purchase by danger and blood the empty dignity of dominion over mountains which they will never climb, and rivers which they will never pass. Let us endeavour, in the mean time, to learn their discipline, and to forge their weapons; and when they shall be weakened with mutual slaughter, let us rush down upon them, force their remains to take shelter in their ships, and reign once more in our native country."

(1759)

Questions:

1. Like many eighteenth-century writers, Johnson tends towards long "periodic" sentences. The entire fifth paragraph in the first of these essays, for example, is composed of one sentence. What means does Johnson employ to help the reader follow his train of thought in such a long sentence?

2. Are the qualities that people attempt to conceal from others in fact the qualities that best represent the "real" person? Comment as well on any differences in the way humans tend to perceive and present that which is hidden in their own characters from that which is hidden in the characters of others.

3. Comment on the advantages and disadvantages of writing about human psychology from the position of subjective reflection, as opposed to the empirical studies that have come to dominate the discipline of psychology over the past century.

4. Write a brief essay on an aspect of the human capacity for self-deception.

5. Summarize in a single paragraph the case against the Europeans that Johnson puts forward in the second of these essays.

6. Typically we consider it morally praiseworthy to "put oneself in the other person's shoes." Typically as well, however, it is considered presumptuous to try to speak on behalf of people of another culture—and particularly of a culture that has been oppressed by one's own people. How deserving of either praise or blame is it that Johnson has "appropriated the voice" of a Native North American in this essay? Would it have been better (either ethically or aesthetically) for him to have tried to make the same points but without assuming a Native voice?

Mary Wollstonecraft

To M. Talleyrand-Périgord,

Late Bishop of Autun

In the Dedication to her great work, A Vindication of the Rights of Women, *Wollstonecraft summarizes many of the book's main arguments.*

~~

Sir,

Having read with great pleasure a pamphlet which you have lately published, I dedicate this volume to you; to induce you to reconsider the subject, and maturely weigh what I have advanced respecting the rights of woman and national education: and I call with the firm tone of humanity; for my arguments, Sir, are dictated by a disinterested spirit—I plead for my sex—not for myself. Independence I have long considered as the grand blessing of life, the basis of every virtue—and independence I will ever secure by contracting my wants, though I were to live on a barren heath.

It is then an affection for the whole human race that makes my pen dart rapidly along to support what I believe to be the cause of virtue: and the same motive leads me earnestly to wish to see woman placed in a station in which she would advance, instead of retarding, the progress of those glorious principles that give a substance to morality. My opinion, indeed, respecting the rights and duties of woman, seems to flow so naturally from these simple principles, that I think it scarcely possible, but that some of the enlarged minds who formed your admirable constitution, will coincide with me.

In France there is undoubtedly a more general diffusion of knowledge than in any part of the European world, and I attribute it, in a great measure, to the social intercourse which has long subsisted between the sexes. It is true, I utter my sentiments with freedom, that in France the very essence of sensuality has been extracted to regale the voluptuary, and a kind of sentimental lust has prevailed, which, together with the system of duplicity that the whole tenour of their political and civil government taught, have given a sinister sort of sagacity to the French character, properly termed finesse; from which naturally flow a polish of manners that injures the substance, by hunting sincerity out of society.—And, modesty, the fairest garb of virtue! has been more grossly insulted in France than even in England, till their women have treated as *prudish* that attention to decency, which brutes instinctively observe.

Manners and morals are so nearly allied that they have often been confounded; but, though the former should only be the natural reflection of the latter, yet, when various causes have produced factitious and corrupt manners, which are very early caught, morality becomes an empty name. The personal reserve, and sacred respect for cleanliness and delicacy in domestic life, which French women almost despise, are the graceful pillars of modesty; but, far from despising them, if the pure flame of patriotism have reached their bosoms, they should labour to improve the morals of their fellow-citizens, by teaching men, not only to respect modesty in women, but to acquire it themselves, as the only way to merit their esteem.

Contending for the rights of woman, my main argument is built on this simple principle, that if she be not prepared by education to become the companion of man, she will stop the progress of knowledge and virtue; for truth must be common to all, or it will be inefficacious with respect to its influence on general practice. And how can woman be expected to co-operate unless she know why she ought to be virtuous? unless freedom strengthen her reason till she comprehend her duty, and see in what manner it is connected with her real good? If children are to be educated to understand the true principle of patriotism, their mother must be a patriot; and the love of mankind, from which an orderly train of virtues spring, can only be produced by considering the moral and civil interest of mankind; but the education and situation of woman, at present, shuts her out from such investigations.

In this work I have produced many arguments, which to me were conclusive, to prove that the prevailing notion respecting a sexual character[1] was subversive of morality, and I have contended, that to render the human

---

[1] *prevailing notion respecting a sexual character* ie., prevailing notion regarding what is natural and appropriate for the two sexes

body and mind more perfect, chastity must more universally prevail, and that chastity will never be respected in the male world till the person of a woman is not, as it were, idolized, when little virtue or sense embellish it with the grand traces of mental beauty, or the interesting simplicity of affection.

Consider, Sir, dispassionately, these observations—for a glimpse of this truth seemed to open before you when you observed, "that to see one half of the human race excluded by the other from all participation of government, was a political phenomenon that, according to abstract principles, it was impossible to explain." If so, on what does your constitution rest? If the abstract rights of man will bear discussion and explanation, those of woman, by a parity of reasoning, will not shrink from the same test: though a different opinion prevails in this country, built on the very arguments which you use to justify the oppression of woman—prescription.

Consider, I address you as a legislator, whether, when men contend for their freedom, and to be allowed to judge for themselves respecting their own happiness, it be not inconsistent and unjust to subjugate women, even though you firmly believe that you are acting in the manner best calculated to promote their happiness? Who made man the exclusive judge, if woman partake with him the gift of reason?

In this style, argue tyrants of every denomination, from the weak king to the weak father of a family; they are all eager to crush reason; yet always assert that they usurp its throne only to be useful. Do you not act a similar part, when you *force* all women, by denying them civil and political rights, to remain immured in their families groping in the dark? for surely, Sir, you will not assert, that a duty can be binding which is not founded on reason? If indeed this be their destination, arguments may be drawn from reason: and thus augustly supported, the more understanding women acquire, the more they will be attached to their duty—comprehending it—for unless they comprehend it, unless their morals be fixed on the same immutable principle as those of man, no authority can make them discharge it in a virtuous manner. They may be convenient slaves, but slavery will have its constant effect, degrading the master and the abject dependent.

But, if women are to be excluded, without having a voice, from a participation of the natural rights of mankind, prove first, to ward off the charge of injustice and inconsistency, that they want[2] reason—else this flaw in your NEW CONSTITUTION will ever shew that man must, in some shape,

---

[2] *want* lack

act like a tyrant, and tyranny, in whatever part of society it rears its brazen front, will ever undermine morality.

I have repeatedly asserted, and produced what appeared to me irrefragable arguments drawn from matters of fact, to prove my assertion, that women cannot, by force, be confined to domestic concerns; for they will, however ignorant, intermeddle with more weighty affairs, neglecting private duties only to disturb, by cunning tricks, the orderly plans of reason which rise above their comprehension.

Besides, whilst they are only made to acquire personal accomplishments, men will seek for pleasure in variety, and faithless husbands will make faithless wives; such ignorant beings, indeed, will be very excusable when, not taught to respect public good, nor allowed any civil rights, they attempt to do themselves justice by retaliation.

The box of mischief thus opened in society, what is to preserve private virtue, the only security of public freedom and universal happiness?

Let there be then no coercion *established* in society, and the common law of gravity prevailing, the sexes will fall into their proper places. And, now that more equitable laws are forming your citizens, marriage may become more sacred: your young men may choose wives from motives of affection, and your maidens allow love to root out vanity.

The father of a family will not then weaken his constitution and debase his sentiments, by visiting the harlot, nor forget, in obeying the call of appetite, the purpose for which it was implanted. And, the mother will not neglect her children to practise the arts of coquetry, when sense and modesty secure her the friendship of her husband.

But, till men become attentive to the duty of a father, it is vain to expect women to spend that time in their nursery which they, "wise in their generation," choose to spend at their glass[3]; for this exertion of cunning is only an instinct of nature to enable them to obtain indirectly a little of that power of which they are unjustly denied a share: for, if women are not permitted to enjoy legitimate rights, they will render both men and themselves vicious, to obtain illicit privileges.

I wish, Sir, to set some investigations of this kind afloat in France; and should they lead to a confirmation of my principles, when your constitution

15

---

[3] *glass* mirror

is revised the Rights of Woman may be respected, if it be fully proved that reason calls for this respect, and loudly demands JUSTICE for one half of the human race.

I am, SIR,

Your's respectfully,

M.W.

(1792)

QUESTIONS:

1. In no more than three paragraphs summarize the main points of Wollstonecraft's argument here.

2. What in Wollstonecraft's style of writing do you think might have helped make her work influential?

3. Can you think of additional arguments in support of Wollstonecraft's position?

CHARLES LYELL

from THE PRINCIPLES OF GEOLOGY

Lyell is often described as the founder of modern geology. In this selection, the introduction to his magnum opus, Lyell sets out to define the science and connect it to other disciplines.

~~

CHAPTER I

Geology defined—Compared to History—Its relation to other Physical Sciences—Its distinctness from all—Not to be confounded with Cosmogony.

Geology is the science which investigates the successive changes that have taken place in the organic and inorganic kingdoms of nature; it enquires into the causes of these changes, and the influence which they have exerted in modifying the surface and external structure of our planet.

By these researches into the state of the earth and its inhabitants at former periods, we acquire a more perfect knowledge of its *present* condition, and more comprehensive views concerning the laws *now* governing its animate and inanimate productions. When we study history, we obtain a more profound insight into human nature, by instituting a comparison between the present and former states of society. We trace the long series of events which have gradually led to the actual posture of affairs; and by connecting effects with their causes, we are enabled to classify and retain in the memory a multitude of complicated relations—the various peculiarities of national character—the different degrees of moral and intellectual refinement, and numerous other circumstances, which, without historical associations, would be uninteresting or imperfectly understood. As the present condition of nations is the result of many antecedent changes, some extremely remote and others recent, some gradual, others sudden and violent, so the state of the natural world is the result of a long succession of events, and if we would enlarge our experience of the present economy of nature, we must investigate the effects of her operations in former epochs.

We often discover with surprise, on looking back into the chronicles of nations, how the fortune of some battle has influenced the fate of millions of our contemporaries, when it has long been forgotten by the mass of the population. With this remote event we may find inseparably connected the geographical boundaries of a great state, the language now spoken by the inhabitants, their peculiar manners, laws, and religious opinions. But far more astonishing and unexpected are the connexions brought to light, when we carry back our researches into the history of nature. The form of a coast, the configuration of the interior of a country, the existence and extent of lakes, valleys, and mountains, can often be traced to the former prevalence of earthquakes and volcanoes, in regions which have long been undisturbed. To these remote convulsions the present fertility of some districts, the sterile character of others, the elevation of land above the sea, the climate, and various peculiarities, may be distinctly referred. On the other hand, many distinguishing features of the surface may often be ascribed to the operation at a remote era of slow and tranquil causes—to the gradual deposition of sediment in a lake or in the ocean, or to the prolific growth in the same of corals and testacea. To select another example, we find in certain localities subterranean deposits of coal, consisting of vegetable matter, formerly drifted into seas and lakes. These seas and lakes have since been filled up, the lands whereon the forests grew have disappeared or changed their form, the rivers and currents which floated the vegetable masses can no longer be traced, and the plants belonged to species which for ages have passed away from the surface of our planet. Yet the commercial prosperity, and numerical strength of a nation, may now be mainly dependent on the local distribution of fuel determined by that ancient state of things.

Geology is intimately related to almost all the physical sciences, as is history to the moral.[1] An historian should, if possible, be at once profoundly acquainted with ethics, politics, jurisprudence, the military art, theology; in a word, with all branches of knowledge, whereby any insight into human affairs, or into the moral and intellectual nature of man, can be obtained. It would be no less desirable that a geologist should be well versed in chemistry, natural philosophy, mineralogy, zoology, comparative anatomy, botany; in short, in every science relating to organic and inorganic nature. With these accomplishments the historian and geologist would rarely fail to draw correct

---

[1] i.e., to the moral sciences (ethics, politics, jurisprudence etc.)

and philosophical conclusions from the various monuments transmitted to them of former occurrences. They would know to what combination of causes analogous effects were referrible, and they would often be enabled to supply by inference, information concerning many events unrecorded in the defective archives of former ages. But the brief duration of human life, and our limited powers, are so far from permitting us to aspire to such extensive acquisitions, that excellence even in one department is within the reach of few, and those individuals most effectually promote the general progress, who concentrate their thoughts on a limited portion of the field of inquiry. As it is necessary that the historian and the cultivators of moral or political science should reciprocally aid each other, so the geologist and those who study natural history or physics stand in equal need of mutual assistance. A comparative anatomist may derive some accession of knowledge from the bare inspection of the remains of an extinct quadruped, but the relic throws much greater light upon his own science, when he is informed to what relative era it belonged, what plants and animals were its contemporaries, in what degree of latitude it once existed, and other historical details. A fossil shell may interest a conchologist, though he be ignorant of the locality from which it came; but it will be of more value when he learns with what other species it was associated, whether they were marine or fresh-water, whether the strata containing them were at a certain elevation above the sea, and what relative position they held in regard to other groups of strata, with many other particulars determinable by an experienced geologist alone. On the other hand, the skill of the comparative anatomist and conchologist are often indispensable to those engaged in geological research, although it will rarely happen that the geologist will himself combine these different qualifications in his own person.

5   Some remains of former organic beings, like the ancient temple, statue, or picture, may have both their intrinsic and their historical value, while there are others which can never be expected to attract attention for their own sake. A painter, sculptor, or architect, would often neglect many curious relics of antiquity, as devoid of beauty and uninstructive with relation to their own art, however illustrative of the progress of refinement in some ancient nation. It has therefore been found desirable that the antiquary should unite his labours to those of the historian, and similar co-operation has become necessary in geology. The field of inquiry in living nature being inexhaustible, the zoologist and botanist can rarely be induced to sacrifice time in exploring the imperfect remains of lost species of animals and plants, while those still existing afford constant matter of novelty. They must

entertain a desire of promoting *geology* by such investigations, and some knowledge of its objects must guide and direct their studies. According to the different opportunities, tastes, and talents of individuals, they may employ themselves in collecting particular kinds of minerals, rocks, or organic remains, and these, when well examined and explained, afford data to the geologist, as do coins, medals, and inscriptions to the historian.

It was long ere the distinct nature and legitimate objects of geology were fully recognized, and it was at first confounded with many other branches of inquiry, just as the limits of history, poetry, and mythology were ill-defined in the infancy of civilization. Werner appears to have regarded geology as little other than a subordinate department of mineralogy, and Desmarest included it under the head of Physical Geography. But the identification of its objects with those of Cosmogony has been the most common and serious source of confusion. The first who endeavoured to draw a clear line of demarcation between these distinct departments, was Hutton, who declared that geology was in no ways concerned "with questions as to the origin of things." But his doctrine on this head was vehemently opposed at first, and although it has gradually gained ground, and will ultimately prevail, it is yet far from being established. We shall attempt in the sequel of this work to demonstrate that geology differs as widely from cosmogony, as speculations concerning the creation of man differ from history. But before we enter more at large on this controverted question, we shall endeavour to trace the progress of opinion on this topic, from the earliest ages, to the commencement of the present century.

(1830)

QUESTIONS:

1. Discuss Lyell's style of structuring sentences, with particular reference to the sentences that form the third paragraph.

2. Explain in your own words the interaction between geology and other academic disciplines.

3. It has often been said that Lyell is one scientific writer who appeals to the imagination of his readers. Is there any evidence to suggest this here?

HARRIET MARTINEAU
NIAGARA

Impressions of Niagara Falls were a staple of nineteenth-century travel writing;
those of the English writer and social reformer Harriet Martineau are among
the more interesting.

～～

"Look back!
Lo! where it comes like an eternity,
As if to sweep down all things in its track,
Charming the eye with dread!"

BYRON

It is not my intention to describe what we saw at Niagara so much as to relate what we did. To offer an idea of Niagara by writing of hues and dimensions is much like representing the kingdom of Heaven by images of jasper and topazes.

I visited the falls twice: first in October, 1834, in company with the party with whom we traversed the state of New-York, when we stayed nearly a week; and again with Dr. and Mrs. F., and other friends, in June, 1836, when we remained between two and three days. The first time we approached the falls from Buffalo, the next from Lewistown and Queenstown.

I expected to be disappointed in the first sight of the falls, and did not relish the idea of being questioned on the first day as to my "impressions." I therefore made a law, with the hearty agreement of the rest of the party, that no one should ask an opinion of the spectacle for twenty-four hours. We stepped into the stage at Buffalo at half past eight in the morning on the 14th of October. At Black Rock we got out to cross the ferry. We looked at the green rushing waters we were crossing, and wondered whether they or we should be at the falls first. We had to wait some minutes for the stage on the Canada side, and a comely English woman invited us into her kitchen to warm ourselves. She was washing as well as cooking; and such a log was blazing under her boilers as no fireplace in England would hold. It looked like the entire trunk of a pine somewhat shortened. I could not help often wishing that some of the shivering poor of London could have supplies of the fuel which lies rotting in the American woods.

The road is extremely bad all the way from the ferry to the falls, and the bridges the rudest of the rude. The few farms looked decaying, and ill-clad children offered us autumn fruit for sale. We saw nothing to flatter our national complacency[1]; for truly the contrast with the other side of the river was mournful enough. It was not till we had passed the inn with the sign of the "Chippeway Battle Ground" that we saw the spray from the falls. I believe we might have seen it sooner if we had known where to look. "Is that it?" we all exclaimed. It appeared on the left-hand side, whereas we had been looking to the right; and instead of its being suspended in the air like a white cloud, as we had imagined, it curled vigorously up, like smoke from a cannon or from a replenished fire. The winding of the road presently brought this round to our right hand. It seemed very near; the river, too, was as smooth as oil. The beginning of the Welland canal was next pointed out to me, but it was not a moment to care for canals. Then the little Round Island, covered with wood and surrounded by rapids, lay close at hand, in a recess of the Canada shore. Some of the rapids, of eight or ten feet descent, would be called falls elsewhere. They were glittering and foamy, with spaces of green water between. I caught a glimpse of a section of the cataract, but not any adequate view, before we were driven briskly up to the door of the hotel. We ran quickly from piazza to piazza till we reached the crown of the roof, where there is a space railed in for the advantage of the gazer who desires to reach the highest point. I think the emotion of this moment was never renewed or equalled. The morning had been cloudy, with a very few wandering gleams. It was now a little after noon; the sky was clearing, and at this moment the sun lighted up the Horseshoe Fall. I am not going to describe it. The most striking appearance was the slowness with which the shaded green waters rolled over the brink. This majestic oozing gives a true idea of the volume of the floods, but they no longer look like water.

5 We wandered through the wood, along Table Rock, and to the ferry. We sat down opposite to the American Falls, finding them the first day or two more level to our comprehension than the Great Horseshoe Cataract; yet throughout, the beauty was far more impressive to me than the grandeur.

---

[1] Martineau was a British writer and Upper Canada (now the province of Ontario) was a British colony—rather less developed at the time than were the United States of America.

One's imagination may heap up almost any degree of grandeur; but the subtile[2] colouring of this scene, varying with the every breath of wind, refining upon the softness of driven snow, and dimming all the gems of the mine, is wholly inconceivable. The woods on Goat Island were in their gaudiest autumn dress; yet, on looking up to them from the fall, they seemed one dust colour. This will not be believed, but it is true.

The little detached fall on the American side piqued my interest at once. It looks solitary in the midst of the crowd of waters, coming out of its privacy in the wood to take its leap by itself. In the afternoon, as I was standing on Table Rock, a rainbow started out from the precipice a hundred feet below me, and curved upward as if about to alight on my head. Other such apparitions seemed to have similar understanding with the sun. They went and came, blushed and faded, the floods rolling on, on, till the human heart, overcharged with beauty, could bear no more.

We crossed the ferry in the afternoon. Our boat was tossed like a cork in the writhing waves. We soon found that, though driven hither and thither by the currents, the ferryman always conquers at last, and shoots his boat into the desired creek; but the tossing and whirling amid the driving spray seems a rather dubious affair at first. To be carried down would be no better than to be sucked up the river, as there is a fatal whirlpool below which forbids all navigation as peremptorily as the falls.

I still think the finest single impression of all is half way up the American Fall, seen, not from the staircase, but from the bank on the very verge of the sheet. Here we stood this first evening, and amid the rapids above. In returning, we saw from the river the singular effect of the clouds of spray being in shadow, and the descending floods in light; while the evening star hung over one extremity of the falls, and the moon over the other, and the little perpetual cloud, amber in the last rays from the west, spread its fine drizzle like a silver veil over the scene.

(1838)

---

[2] delicately varied

Questions:

1. Martineau begins by declaring that she does not intend "to describe what we saw at Niagara so much as to relate what we did." To what extent does she follow through on that intention? As a general principle, how worthwhile is it to try to describe in words the most spectacular marvels of nature?

2. What does Martineau mean when she says "the beauty was far more impressive to me than the grandeur"?

3. Write a brief essay comparing Martineau's approach to descriptive writing with that of Mark Twain (in the selection included elsewhere in this volume).

HENRY DAVID THOREAU

CIVIL DISOBEDIENCE

Thoreau's "Civil Disobedience," written in the wake of his brief imprisonment for refusing to pay a federal poll tax, has become perhaps the most famous and influential of all American essays.

~∞~

I heartily accept the motto,—"That government is best which governs least"; and I should like to see it acted up to more rapidly and systematically. Carried out, it finally amounts to this, which also I believe,—"That government is best which governs not at all"; and when men are prepared for it, that will be the kind of government which they will have. Government is at best but an expedient; but most governments are usually, and all governments are sometimes, inexpedient. The objections which have been brought against a standing army, and they are many and weighty, and deserve to prevail, may also at last be brought against a standing government. The standing army is only an arm of the standing government. The government itself, which is only the mode which the people have chosen to execute their will, is equally liable to be abused and perverted before the people can act through it. Witness the present Mexican war,[1] the work of comparatively a few individuals using the standing government as their tool; for, in the outset, the people would not have consented to this measure.

---

[1] The Mexican-American War of 1846–48 was fought over a border dispute. Mexico claimed territory north to the Nueces River, while the Texans claimed that their territory extended south to the Rio Grande. The Americans were the aggressors in beginning the war when General Zachary Taylor advanced with his troops into the area under dispute. When the war ended, Mexico gave up not only its claim to Texas above the Rio Grande, but also New Mexico and California. (The United States did pay Mexico 15 million dollars for the latter territories as part of the final agreement under the terms of the Gadsden Purchase.)

This American government,—what is it but a tradition, though a recent one, endeavoring to transmit itself unimpaired to posterity, but each instant losing some of its integrity? It has not the vitality and force of a single living man; for a single man can bend it to his will. It is a sort of wooden gun to the people themselves. But is it not the less necessary for this; for the people must have some complicated machinery or other, and hear its din, to satisfy that idea of government which they have. Governments show thus how successfully men can be imposed on, even impose on themselves, for their own advantage. It is excellent, we must all allow. Yet this government never of itself furthered any enterprise, but by the alacrity with which it got out of its way. *It* does not keep the country free. *It* does not settle the West. *It* does not educate. The character inherent in the American people has done all that has been accomplished; and it would have done somewhat more, if the government had not sometimes got in its way. For government is an expedient by which men would fain succeed in letting one another alone; and, as has been said, when it is most expedient, the governed are most let alone by it. Trade and commerce, if they were not made of India-rubber, would never manage to bounce over the obstacles which legislators are continually putting in their way; and, if one were to judge these men wholly by the effects of their actions and not partly by their intentions, they would deserve to be classed and punished with those mischievous persons who put obstructions on the railroads.

But, to speak practically and as a citizen, unlike those who call themselves no-government men, I ask for, not at once no government, but *at once* a better government. Let every man make known what kind of government would command his respect, and that will be one step toward obtaining it.

After all, the practical reason why, when the power is once in the hands of the people, a majority are permitted, and for a long period continue, to rule is not because they are most likely to be in the right, nor because this seems fairest to the minority, but because they are physically the strongest. But a government in which the majority rule in all cases cannot be based on justice, even as far as men understand it. Can there not be a government in which majorities do not virtually decide right and wrong, but conscience?—in which majorities decide only those questions to which the rule of expediency is applicable? Must the citizen ever for a moment, or in the least degree, resign his conscience to the legislator? Why has every man a conscience, then? I think that we should be men first, and subjects afterward. It is not desirable to cultivate a respect for the law, so much as for the right. The only obligation which I have a right to assume is to do at any time what

I think right. It is truly enough said, that a corporation[2] has no conscience; but a corporation of conscientious men is a corporation *with* a conscience. Law never made men a whit more just; and, by means of their respect for it, even the well-disposed are daily made the agents of injustice. A common and natural result of an undue respect for law is, that you may see a file of soldiers, colonel, captain, corporal, privates, powder-monkeys, and all, marching in admirable order over hill and dale to the wars, against their wills, ay, against their common sense and consciences, which makes it very steep marching indeed, and produces a palpitation of the heart. They have no doubt that it is a damnable business in which they are concerned; they are all peaceably inclined. Now, what are they? Men at all? or small movable forts and magazines, at the service of some unscrupulous man in power? Visit the Navy-Yard, and behold a marine, such a man as an American government can make, or such as it can make a man with its black arts,—a mere shadow and reminiscence of humanity, a man laid out alive and standing, and already, as one may say, buried under arms with funeral accompaniments, though it may be,—

> Not a drum was heard, not a funeral note,
>   As his corse to the rampart we hurried;
> Not a soldier discharged his farewell shot
>   O'er the grave where our hero we buried.

5   The mass of men serve the state thus, not as men mainly, but as machines, with their bodies. They are the standing army, and the militia, jailers, constables, posse comitatus, etc. In most cases there is no free exercise whatever of the judgment or of the moral sense; but they put themselves on a level with wood and earth and stones; and wooden men can perhaps be manufactured that will serve the purpose as well. Such command no more respect than men of straw or a lump of dirt. They have the same sort of worth only as horses and dogs. Yet such as these even are commonly esteemed good citizens. Others—as most legislators, politicians, lawyers, ministers, and office-holders—serve the state chiefly with their heads; and, as they rarely make any moral distinctions, they are as likely to serve the Devil, without *intending* it, as God. A very few, as heroes, patriots, martyrs, reformers in the great sense, and *men*, serve the state with their consciences also, and so necessarily resist it for the most part; and they are commonly treated as enemies by it. A wise man will only be useful as a man, and will

---

[2] in the sense of any "body of associated persons"(not formed specifically for business ends)

not submit to be "clay," and "stop a hole to keep the wind away," but leave that office to his dust at least:—

> I am too high-born to be propertied,
> To be a secondary at control,
> Or useful serving-man and instrument
> To any sovereign state throughout the world.

He who gives himself entirely to his fellow-men appears to them useless and selfish; but he who gives himself partially to them is pronounced a benefactor and philanthropist.

How does it become a man to behave toward this American government to-day? I answer, that he cannot without disgrace be associated with it. I cannot for an instant recognize that political organization as *my* government which is the *slave's* government also.

All men recognize the right of revolution; that is, the right to refuse allegiance to, and to resist, the government, when its tyranny or its inefficiency are great and unendurable. But almost all say that such is not the case now. But such was the case, they think, in the Revolution of '75. If one were to tell me that this was a bad government because it taxed certain foreign commodities brought to its ports, it is most probable that I should not make an ado about it, for I can do without them. All machines have their friction; and possibly this does enough good to counterbalance the evil. At any rate, it is a great evil to make a stir about it. But when the friction comes to have its machine, and oppression and robbery are organized, I say, let us not have such a machine any longer. In other words, when a sixth of the population of a nation which has undertaken to be the refuge of liberty are slaves, and a whole country is unjustly overrun and conquered by a foreign army, and subjected to military law, I think that it is not too soon for honest men to rebel and revolutionize. What makes this duty the more urgent is the fact that the country so overrun is not our own, but ours is the invading army.

Paley, a common authority with many on moral questions, in his chapter on the "Duty of Submission to Civil Government," resolves all civil obligation into expediency; and he proceeds to say, "that so long as the interest of the whole society requires it, that is, so long as the established government cannot be resisted or changed without public inconveniency, it is the will of God that the established government be obeyed, and no longer.... This principle being admitted, the justice of every particular case of resistance is reduced to a computation of the quantity of the danger and grievance on the one side, and of the probability and expense of redressing it on the other." Of this, he says, every man shall judge for himself. But Paley appears never to have contemplated those cases to which the rule of expediency does not apply, in which a people, as well as an individual, must do justice, cost what it may. If I have unjustly wrested a plank from a drowning man, I must restore it to him though I drown myself. This, according to Paley, would be inconvenient. But he that would save his life, in such a case, shall lose it. This people must cease to hold slaves, and to make war on Mexico, though it cost them their existence as a people.

10   In their practice, nations agree with Paley; but does any one think that Massachusetts[3] does exactly what is right at the present crisis?

> A drab of state, a cloth-o'-silver slut,
> To have her train borne up, and her soul trail in the dirt.

Practically speaking, the opponents to a reform in Massachusetts are not a hundred thousand politicians at the South, but a hundred thousand merchants and farmers here, who are more interested in commerce and agriculture than they are in humanity, and are not prepared to do justice to the slave and to Mexico, *cost what it may*. I quarrel not with far-off foes, but with those who, near at home, co-operate with, and do the bidding of, those far away, and without whom the latter would be harmless. We are accustomed to say, that the mass of men are unprepared; but improvement is slow, because the few are not materially wiser or better than the many. It is not so important that many should be as good as you, as that there be some absolute goodness somewhere; for that will leaven the whole lump. There are thousands who are *in opinion* opposed to slavery and to the war, who yet in effect do nothing to put an end to them; who, esteeming themselves children of Washington and Franklin, sit down with their hands in their pockets, and say that they know not what to do, and do nothing; who even postpone the question of freedom to the question of free-trade, and quietly read the prices-current along with the latest advices from Mexico, after dinner, and, it may be, fall asleep over them both. What is the price-current of an honest man and patriot to-day? They hesitate, and they regret, and sometimes they petition; but they do nothing in earnest and with effect. They will wait, well disposed, for others to remedy the evil, that they may no longer have it to

---

[3] Thoreau was born and raised in Concord, Massachusetts, attended Harvard University in Cambridge, Massachusetts, and then returned to Concord for much of his adult life.

regret. At most, they give only a cheap vote, and a feeble countenance and Godspeed, to the right, as it goes by them. There are nine hundred and ninety-nine patrons of virtue to one virtuous man. But it is easier to deal with the real possessor of a thing than with the temporary guardian of it.

All voting is a sort of gaming, like checkers or backgammon, with a slight moral tinge to it, a playing with right and wrong, with moral questions; and betting naturally accompanies it. The character of the voters is not staked. I cast my vote, perchance, as I think right; but I am not vitally concerned that that right should prevail. I am willing to leave it to the majority. Its obligation, therefore, never exceeds that of expediency. Even voting *for the right* is *doing* nothing for it. It is only expressing to men feebly your desire that it should prevail. A wise man will not leave the right to the mercy of chance, nor wish it to prevail through the power of the majority. There is but little virtue in the action of masses of men. When the majority shall at length vote for the abolition of slavery, it will be because they are indifferent to slavery, or because there is but little slavery left to be abolished by their vote. *They* will then be the only slaves. Only *his* vote can hasten the abolition of slavery who asserts his own freedom by his vote.

I hear of a convention to be held in Baltimore, or elsewhere, for the selection of a candidate for the Presidency, made up chiefly of editors, and men who are politicians by profession; but I think, what is it to any independent, intelligent, and respectable man what decision they may come to? Shall we not have the advantage of his wisdom and honesty, nevertheless? Can we not count upon some independent votes? Are there not many individuals in the country who do not attend conventions? But no: I find that the respectable man, so called, has immediately drifted from his position, and despairs of his country, when his country has more reason to despair of him. He forthwith adopts one of the candidates thus selected as the only *available* one, thus proving that he is himself *available* for any purposes of the demagogue. His vote is of no more worth than that of any unprincipled foreigner or hireling native, who may have been bought. O for a man who is a *man*, and, as my neighbor says, has a bone in his back which you cannot pass your hand through! Our statistics are at fault: the population has been returned too large. How many *men* are there to a square thousand miles in this country? Hardly one. Does not America offer any inducement for men to settle here? The American has dwindled into an Odd Fellow,—one who may be known by the development of his organ of gregariousness, and a manifest lack of intellect and cheerful self-reliance; whose first and chief concern, on coming into the world, is to see that the

Almshouses are in good repair; and, before yet he has lawfully donned the virile garb, to collect a fund for the support of the widows and orphans that may be; who, in short, ventures to live only by the aid of the Mutual Insurance company, which has promised to bury him decently.

It is not a man's duty, as a matter of course, to devote himself to the eradication of any, even the most enormous wrong; he may still properly have other concerns to engage him; but it is his duty, at least, to wash his hands of it, and, if he gives it no thought longer, not to give it practically his support. If I devote myself to other pursuits and contemplations, I must first see, at least, that I do not pursue them sitting upon another man's shoulders. I must get off him first, that he may pursue his contemplations too. See what gross inconsistency is tolerated. I have heard some of my townsmen say, "I should like to have them order me out to help put down an insurrection of the slaves, or to march to Mexico;—see if I would go;" and yet these very men have each, directly by their allegiance, and so indirectly, at least, by their money, furnished a substitute. The soldier is applauded who refuses to serve in an unjust war by those who do not refuse to sustain the unjust government which makes the war; is applauded by those whose own act and authority he disregards and sets at naught; as if the state were penitent to that degree that it hired one to scourge it while it sinned, but not to that degree that it left off sinning for a moment. Thus, under the name of Order and Civil Government, we are all made at last to pay homage to and support our own meanness. After the first blush of sin comes its indifference; and from immoral it becomes, as it were, *un*moral, and not quite unnecessary to that life which we have made.

The broadest and most prevalent error requires the most disinterested virtue to sustain it. The slight reproach to which the virtue of patriotism is commonly liable, the noble are most likely to incur. Those who, while they disapprove of the character and measures of a government, yield to it their allegiance and support are undoubtedly its most conscientious supporters, and so frequently the most serious obstacles to reform. Some are petitioning the state to dissolve the Union, to disregard the requisitions of the President. Why do they not dissolve it themselves,—the union between themselves and the state,—and refuse to pay their quota into its treasury? Do not they stand in the same relation to the state that the state does to the Union? And have not the same reasons prevented the state from resisting the Union which have prevented them from resisting the state?

How can a man be satisfied to entertain an opinion merely, and enjoy *it*? Is there any enjoyment in it, if his opinion is that he is aggrieved? If you are cheated out of a single dollar by your neighbor, you do not rest satisfied with knowing that you are cheated, or with saying that you are cheated, or even with petitioning him to pay you your due; but you take effectual steps at once to obtain the full amount, and see that you are never cheated again. Action from principle, the perception and the performance of right, changes things and relations; it is essentially revolutionary, and does not consist wholly with anything which was. It not only divides states and churches, it divides families; ay, it divides the *individual*, separating the diabolical in him from the divine.

Unjust laws exist: shall we be content to obey them, or shall we endeavor to amend them, and obey them until we have succeeded, or shall we transgress them at once? Men generally, under such a government as this, think that they ought to wait until they have persuaded the majority to alter them. They think that, if they should resist, the remedy would be worse than the evil. But it is the fault of the government itself that the remedy *is* worse than the evil. *It* makes it worse. Why is it not more apt to anticipate and provide for reform? Why does it not cherish its wise minority? Why does it cry and resist before it is hurt? Why does it not encourage its citizens to be on the alert to point out its faults, and *do* better than it would have them? Why does it always crucify Christ, and excommunicate Copernicus and Luther, and pronounce Washington and Franklin rebels?

One would think, that a deliberate and practical denial of its authority was the only offense never contemplated by government; else, why has it not assigned its definite, its suitable and proportionate penalty? If a man who has no property refuses but once to earn nine shillings for the state, he is put in prison for a period unlimited by any law that I know, and determined only by the discretion of those who placed him there; but if he should steal ninety times nine shillings from the state, he is soon permitted to go at large again.

If the injustice is part of the necessary friction of the machine of government, let it go: perchance it will wear smooth,—certainly the machine will wear out. If the injustice has a spring, or a pulley, or a rope, or a crank, exclusively for itself, then perhaps you may consider whether the remedy will not be worse than the evil; but if it is of such a nature that it requires you to be the agent of injustice to another, then, I say, break the law. Let your life be a counter friction to stop the machine. What I have to do is to see, at any rate, that I do not lend myself to the wrong which I condemn.

As for adopting the ways which the state has provided for remedying the evil, I know not of such ways. They take too much time, and a man's life will be gone. I have other affairs to attend to. I came into this world, not chiefly to make this a good place to live in, but to live in it, be it good or bad. A man has not everything to do, but something; and because he cannot do *everything*, it is not necessary that he should do *something* wrong. It is not my business to be petitioning the Governor or the Legislature any more than it is theirs to petition me; and if they should not hear my petition, what should I do then? But in this case the state has provided no way: its very Constitution is the evil. This may seem to be harsh and stubborn and unconciliatory; but it is to treat with the utmost kindness and consideration the only spirit that can appreciate or deserves it. So is all change for the better, like birth and death, which convulse the body.

20   I do not hesitate to say, that those who call themselves Abolitionists should at once effectually withdraw their support, both in person and property, from the government of Massachusetts, and not wait till they constitute a majority of one, before they suffer the right to prevail through them. I think that it is enough if they have God on their side, without waiting for that other one. Moreover, any man more right than his neighbors constitutes a majority of one already.

I meet this American government, or its representative, the state government, directly, and face to face, once a year—no more—in the person of its tax-gatherer; this is the only mode in which a man situated as I am necessarily meets it; and it then says distinctly, Recognize me; and the simplest, the most effectual, and, in the present posture of affairs, the indispensablest mode of treating with it on this head, of expressing your little satisfaction with and love for it, is to deny it then. My civil neighbor, the tax-gatherer, is the very man I have to deal with,—for it is, after all, with men and not with parchment that I quarrel,—and he has voluntarily chosen to be an agent of the government. How shall he ever know well what he is and does as an officer of the government, or as a man, until he is obliged to consider whether he shall treat me, his neighbor, for whom he has respect, as a neighbor and well-disposed man, or as a maniac and disturber of the peace, and see if he can get over this obstruction to his neighborliness without a ruder and more impetuous thought or speech corresponding with his action. I know this well, that if one thousand, if one hundred, if ten men whom I could name,—if ten *honest* men only,—ay, if *one* HONEST man, in this State of Massachusetts, *ceasing to hold slaves*, were actually to withdraw from this copartnership, and be locked up in the county jail therefor, it would be the abolition of slavery in America. For it matters not how small the beginning may seem to be: what is once well done is done forever. But we love better to talk about it: that we say is our mission. Reform keeps many scores of newspapers in its service, but not one man. If my esteemed neighbor, the State's ambassador, who will devote his days to the settlement of the question of human rights in the Council Chamber, instead of being threatened with the prisons of Carolina, were to sit down the prisoner of Massachusetts, that State which is so anxious to foist the sin of slavery upon her sister,—though at present she can discover only an act of inhospitality to be the ground of a quarrel with her,—the Legislature would not wholly waive the subject the following winter.

Under a government which imprisons any unjustly, the true place for a just man is also a prison. The proper place to-day, the only place which Massachusetts has provided for her freer and less desponding spirits, is in her prisons, to be put out and locked out of the State by her own act, as they have already put themselves out by their principles. It is there that the fugitive slave, and the Mexican prisoner on parole, and Indian come to plead the wrongs of his race should find them; on that separate, but more free and honorable ground, where the State places those who are not *with* her, but *against* her,—the only house in a slave State in which a free man can abide with honor. If any think that their influence would be lost there, and their voices no longer afflict the ear of the State, that they would not be as an enemy within its walls, they do not know by how much truth is stronger than error, nor how much more eloquently and effectively he can combat injustice who has experienced a little in his own person. Cast your whole vote, not a strip of paper merely, but your whole influence. A minority is powerless while it conforms to the majority; it is not even a minority then; but it is irresistible when it clogs by its whole weight. If the alternative is to keep all just men in prison, or give up war and slavery, the State will not hesitate which to choose. If a thousand men were not to pay their tax-bills this year, that would not be a violent and bloody measure, as it would be to pay them, and enable the State to commit violence and shed innocent blood. This is in fact, the definition of a peaceable revolution, if any such is possible. If the tax-gatherer, or any other public officer, asks me, as one has done, "But what shall I do?" my answer is, "If you really wish to do anything, resign your office." When the subject has refused allegiance, and the officer has resigned his office, then the revolution is accomplished. But even suppose blood should flow. Is there not a sort of blood shed when the conscience is wounded? Through this wound a man's real manhood and immortality flow out, and he bleeds to an everlasting death. I see this blood flowing now.

I have contemplated the imprisonment of the offender, rather than the seizure of his goods,—though both will serve the same purpose,—because they who assert the purest right, and consequently are most dangerous to a corrupt State, commonly have not spent much time in accumulating property. To such the State renders comparatively small service, and a slight tax is wont to appear exorbitant, particularly if they are obliged to earn it by special labor with their hands. If there were one who lived wholly without the use of money, the State itself would hesitate to demand it of him. But the rich man—not to make any invidious comparison—is always sold to the institution which makes him rich. Absolutely speaking, the more money, the less virtue; for money comes between a man and his objects, and obtains them for him; and it was certainly no great virtue to obtain it. It puts to rest many questions which he would otherwise be taxed to answer; while the only new question which it puts is the hard but superfluous one, how to spend it. Thus his moral ground is taken from under his feet. The opportunities of living are diminished in proportion as what are called the "means" are increased. The best thing a man can do for his culture when he is rich is to endeavor to carry out those schemes which he entertained when he was poor. Christ answered the Herodians according to their condition. "Show me the tribute-money," said he;—and one took a penny out of his pocket;—if you use money which has the image of Caesar on it, which he has made current and valuable, that is, *if you are men of the State*, and gladly enjoy the advantages of Caesar's government, then pay him back some of his own when he demands it. "Render therefore to Caesar that which is Caesar's, and to God those things which are God's,"—leaving them no wiser than before as to which was which; for they did not wish to know.

When I converse with the freest of my neighbors, I perceive that, whatever they may say about the magnitude and seriousness of the question, and their regard for the public tranquillity, the long and the short of the matter is, that they cannot spare the protection of the existing government, and they dread the consequences to their property and families of disobedience to it. For my own part, I should not like to think that I ever rely on the protection of the State. But, if I deny the authority of the State when it presents its tax-bill, it will soon take and waste all my property, and so harass me and my children without end. This is hard. This makes it impossible for a man to live honestly, and at the same time comfortably, in outward respects. It will not be worth the while to accumulate property; that would be sure to go again. You must hire or squat somewhere, and raise but a small crop, and eat that soon. You must live within yourself, and depend upon yourself always tucked up and ready for a start, and not have many affairs. A man may grow rich in Turkey even, if he will be in all respects a good subject of the Turkish government. Confucius said: "If a state is governed by the principles of reason, poverty and misery are subjects of shame; if a state is not governed by the principles of reason, riches and honors are the subjects of shame." No: until I want the protection of Massachusetts to be extended to me in some distant Southern port, where my liberty is endangered, or until I am bent solely on building up an estate at home by peaceful enterprise, I can afford to refuse allegiance to Massachusetts, and her right to my property and life. It costs me less in every sense to incur the penalty of disobedience to the State than it would to obey. I should feel as if I were worth less in that case.

25   Some years ago, the State met me in behalf of the Church, and commanded me to pay a certain sum toward the support of a clergyman whose preaching my father attended, but never I myself. "Pay," it said, "or be locked up in the jail." I declined to pay. But unfortunately, another man saw fit to pay it. I did not see why the schoolmaster should be taxed to support the priest, and not the priest the schoolmaster; for I was not the State's schoolmaster, but I supported myself by voluntary subscription. I did not see why the lyceum should not present its tax-bill, and have the State to back its demand, as well as the Church. However, at the request of the selectmen, I condescended to make some such statement as this in writing:—"Know all men by these presents, that I, Henry Thoreau, do not wish to be regarded as a member of any incorporated society which I have not joined." This I gave to the town clerk; and he has it. The State, having thus learned that I did not wish to be regarded as a member of that church, has never made a like demand on me since; though it said that it must adhere to its original presumption that time. If I had known how to name them, I should then have signed off in detail from all the societies which I never signed on to; but I did not know where to find a complete list.

    I have paid no poll-tax for six years. I was put into a jail on this account, for one night; and, as I stood considering the walls of solid stone, two or three feet thick, the door of wood and iron, a foot thick, and the iron grating which strained the light, I could not help being struck with the foolishness of that institution which treated me as if I were mere flesh and blood and bones, to be locked up. I wondered that it should have concluded at length that this was the best use it could put me to, and had never thought to avail itself of my services in some way. I saw that, if there was a wall of stone between me and my townsmen, there was a still more difficult one to climb or break through before they could get to be as free as I was. I did not for a moment feel confined, and walls seemed a great waste of stone and mortar. I felt as if I alone of all my townsmen had paid my tax. They plainly did not know how to treat me, but behaved like persons who are underbred. In every threat and in every compliment there was a blunder; for they thought that my chief desire was to stand the other side of that stone wall. I could not but smile to see how industriously they locked the door on my meditations, which followed them out again without let or hindrance, and *they* were really all that was dangerous. As they could not reach me, they had resolved to punish my body; just as boys, if they cannot come at some person against whom they have a spite, will abuse his dog. I saw that the State was halfwitted, that it was timid as a lone woman with her silver spoons, and that it did not know its friends from its foes, and I lost all my remaining respect for it, and pitied it.

Thus the State never intentionally confronts a man's sense, intellectual or moral, but only his body, his senses. It is not armed with superior wit or honesty, but with superior physical strength. I was not born to be forced. I will breathe after my own fashion. Let us see who is the strongest. What force has a multitude? They only can force me who obey a higher law than I. They force me to become like themselves. I do not hear of *men* being *forced* to live this way or that by masses of men. What sort of life were that to live? When I meet a government which says to me, "Your money or your life," why should I be in haste to give it my money? It may be in a great strait, and not know what to do: I cannot help that. It must help itself; do as I do. It is not worth the while to snivel about it. I am not responsible for the successful working of the machinery of society. I am not the son of the engineer. I perceive that, when an acorn and a chestnut fall side by side, the one does not remain inert to make way for the other, but both obey their own laws, and spring and grow and flourish as best they can, till one, perchance, overshadows and destroys the other. If a plant cannot live according to its nature, it dies; and so a man.

The night in prison was novel and interesting enough. The prisoners in their shirt-sleeves were enjoying a chat and the evening air in the doorway, when I entered. But the jailer said, "Come, boys, it is time to lock up"; and so they dispersed, and I heard the sound of their steps returning into the hollow apartments. My room-mate was introduced to me by the jailer as "a first-rate fellow and a clever man." When the door was locked, he showed me where to hang my hat, and how he managed matters there. The rooms were whitewashed once a month, and this one, at least, was the whitest, most simply furnished, and probably the neatest apartment in the town. He naturally wanted to know where I came from, and what brought me there; and, when I had told him, I asked in my turn how he came there, presuming him to be an honest man, of course; and, as the world goes, I believe he was. "Why," said he, "they accuse me of burning a barn; but I never did it." As near as I could discover, he had probably gone to bed in a barn when drunk, and smoked his pipe there; and so a barn was burnt. He had the reputation of being a clever man, and been there some three months waiting for his trial to come on, and would have to wait as much longer; but he was quite domesticated and contented, since he got his board for nothing, and thought that he was well treated.

He occupied one window, and I the other; and I saw that if one stayed there long, his principal business would be to look out the window. I had soon read all the tracts that were left there, and examined where former prisoners had broken out, and where a grate had been sawed off, and heard the history of the various occupants of that room; for I found that even here there was a history and a gossip which never circulated beyond the walls of the jail. Probably this is the only house in the town where verses are composed, which are afterward printed in a circular form, but not published. I was shown quite a long list of verses which were composed by some young men who had been detected in an attempt to escape, who avenged themselves by singing them.

30   I pumped my fellow-prisoner as dry as I could, for fear I should never see him again; but at length he showed me which was my bed, and left me to blow out the lamp.

It was like traveling into a far country, such as I had never expected to behold, to lie there for one night. It seemed to me that I never had heard the town-clock strike before, nor the evening sounds of the village; for we slept with the windows open, which were inside the grating. It was to see my native village in the light of the Middle Ages, and our Concord was turned into a Rhine stream, and visions of knights and castles passed before me. They were the voices of old burghers that I heard in the streets. I was an involuntary spectator and auditor of whatever was done and said in the kitchen of the adjacent village-inn,—a wholly new and rare experience to me. It was a closer view of my native town. I was fairly inside of it. I never had seen its institutions before. This is one of its peculiar institutions; for it is a shire town. I began to comprehend what its inhabitants were about.

In the morning, our breakfasts were put through the hole in the door, in small oblong-square tin pans, made to fit, and holding a pint of chocolate, with brown bread, and an iron spoon. When they called for the vessels again, I was green enough to return what bread I had left; but my comrade seized it, and said that I should lay that up for lunch or dinner. Soon after he was let out to work at haying in a neighboring field, whither he went every day, and would not be back till noon; so he bade me good-day, saying that he doubted if he should see me again.

When I came out of prison,—for some one interfered, and paid that tax,—I did not perceive that great changes had taken place on the common, such as he observed who went in a youth and emerged a tottering and gray-haired man; and yet a change had to my eyes come over the scene,—the town, and State, and country,—greater than any that mere time could effect. I saw yet more distinctly the State in which I lived. I saw to what extent the people among whom I lived could be trusted as good neighbors and friends; that their friendship was for summer weather only; that they did not greatly propose to do right; that they were a distinct race from me by their prejudices and superstitions, as the Chinamen and Malays are; that in their sacrifices to humanity they ran no risks, not even to their property; that after all they were not so noble but they treated the thief as he had treated them, and hoped, by a certain outward observance and a few prayers, and by walking in a particular straight though useless path from time to time, to save their souls. This may be to judge my neighbors harshly; for I believe that many of them are not aware that they have such an institution as the jail in their village.

It was formerly the custom in our village, when a poor debtor came out of jail, for his acquaintances to salute him, looking through their fingers, which were crossed to represent the grating of a jail window, "How do ye do?" My neighbors did not thus salute me, but first looked at me, and then at one another, as if I had returned from a long journey. I was put into jail as I was going to the shoemaker's to get a shoe which was mended. When I was let out the next morning, I proceeded to finish my errand, and, having put on my mended shoe, joined a huckleberry party, who were impatient to put themselves under my conduct; and in half an hour,—for the horse was soon tackled,—was in the midst of a huckleberry field, on one of our highest hills, two miles off, and then the State was nowhere to be seen.

35   This is the whole history of "My Prisons."

I have never declined paying the highway tax, because I am as desirous of being a good neighbor as I am of being a bad subject; and as for supporting schools, I am doing my part to educate my fellow-countrymen now. It is for no particular item in the tax-bill that I refuse to pay it. I simply wish to refuse allegiance to the State, to withdraw and stand aloof from it effectually. I do not care to trace the course of my dollar, if I could, till it buys a man or a musket to shoot one with,—the dollar is innocent,—but I am concerned to trace the effects of my allegiance. In fact, I quietly declare war with the State, after my fashion, though I will still make what use and get what advantage of her I can, as is usual in such cases.

If others pay the tax which is demanded of me, from a sympathy with the State, they do but what they have already done in their own case, or rather they abet injustice to a greater extent than the State requires. If they pay the tax from a mistaken interest in the individual taxed, to save his property, or prevent his going to jail, it is because they have not considered wisely how far they let their private feelings interfere with the public good.

This, then, is my position at present. But one cannot be too much on his guard in such a case, lest his action be biased by obstinacy or an undue regard for the opinions of men. Let him see that he does only what belong to himself and to the hour.

I think sometimes, Why, this people mean well, they are only ignorant; they would do better if they knew how: why give your neighbors this pain to treat you as they are not inclined to? But I think again, This is no reason why I should do as they do, or permit others to suffer much greater pain of a different kind. Again I sometimes say to myself, When many millions of men, without heat,[4] without ill will, without personal feeling of any kind, demand of you a few shillings only, without the possibility, such is their constitution, of retracting or altering their present demand, and without the possibility, on your side, of appeal to any other millions, why expose yourself to this overwhelming brute force? You do not resist cold and hunger, the winds and the waves, thus obstinately; you quietly submit to a thousand similar necessities. You do not put your head into the fire. But just in proportion as I regard this as not wholly a brute force, but partly a human force, and consider that I have relations to those millions as to so many millions of men, and not of mere brute or inanimate things, I see that appeal is possible, first and instantaneously, from them to the Maker of them, and, secondly, from them to themselves. But if I put my head deliberately into the fire, there is no appeal to fire or to the Maker of fire, and I have only myself to blame. If I could convince myself that I have any right to be satisfied with men as they are, and to treat them accordingly, and not according, in some

---

[4] *heat* anger

respects, to my requisitions and expectations of what they and I ought to be, then, like a good Mussulman and fatalist, I should endeavor to be satisfied with things as they are, and say it is the will of God. And, above all, there is this difference between resisting this and a purely brute or natural force, that I can resist this with some effect; but I cannot expect, like Orpheus, to change the nature of the rocks and trees and beasts.

40   I do not wish to quarrel with any man or nation. I do not wish to split hairs, to made fine distinctions, or set myself up as better than my neighbors. I seek rather, I may say, even an excuse for conforming to the laws of the land. I am but too ready to conform to them. Indeed, I have reason to suspect myself on this head; and each year, as the tax-gatherer comes round, I find myself disposed to review the acts and position of the general and State governments, and the spirit of the people, to discover a pretext for conformity.

> We must affect our country as our parents,
> And if at any time we alienate
> Our love or industry from doing it honor,
> We must respect effects and teach the soul
> Matter of conscience and religion,
> And not desire of rule or benefit.

I believe that the State will soon be able to take all my work of this sort out of my hands, and then I shall be no better a patriot than my fellow-countrymen. Seen from a lower point of view, the Constitution, with all its faults, is very good; and the law and the courts are very respectable; even this State and this American government are, in many respects, very admirable, and rare things, to be thankful for, such as a great many have described them; but seen from a point of view a little higher, they are what I have described them; seen from a higher still, and the highest, who shall say what they are, or that they are worth looking at or thinking of at all?

    However, the government does not concern me much, and I shall bestow the fewest possible thoughts on it. It is not many moments that I live under a government, even in this world. If a man is thought-free, fancy-free, imagination-free, that which *is not* never for a long time appearing *to be* to him, unwise rulers or reformers cannot fatally interrupt him.

    I know that most men think differently from myself; but those whose lives are by profession devoted to the study of these or kindred subjects content me as little as any. Statesmen and legislators, standing so completely within the institution, never distinctly and nakedly behold it. They speak of moving society, but have no resting-place without it. They may be men of a certain experience and discrimination, and have no doubt invented ingenious and even useful systems, for which we sincerely thank them; but all their wit and usefulness lie within certain not very wide limits. They are wont to forget that the world is not governed by policy and expediency. Webster[5] never goes behind government, and so cannot speak with authority about it. His words are wisdom to those legislators who contemplate no essential reform in the existing government; but for thinkers, and those who legislate for all time, he never once glances at the subject. I know of those whose serene and wise speculations on this theme would soon reveal the limits of his mind's range and hospitality. Yet compared with the cheap professions of most reformers, and the still cheaper wisdom and eloquence of politicians in general, his are almost the only sensible and valuable words, and we thank Heaven for him. Comparatively, he is always strong, original, and, above all, practical. Still, his quality is not wisdom, but prudence. The lawyer's truth is not Truth, but consistency or a consistent expediency. Truth is always in harmony with herself, and is not concerned chiefly to reveal the justice that may consist with wrong-doing. He well deserves to be called, as he has been called, the Defender of the Constitution. There are really no blows to be given by him but defensive ones. He is not a leader, but a follower. His leaders are the men of '87. "I have never made an effort," he says, "and never propose to make an effort; I have never countenanced an effort, and never mean to countenance an effort, to disturb the arrangement as originally made, by which the various States came into the union." Still thinking of the sanction which the Constitution gives to slavery, he says, "Because it was a part of the original compact,—let it stand." Notwithstanding his special acuteness and ability, he is unable to take a fact out of its merely political relations, and behold it as it lies absolutely to be disposed of by the intellect,—what, for instance, it behooves a man to do here in America to-day with regard to slavery,—but ventures, or is driven, to make some such desperate answer as the following, while professing to speak absolutely, and as a private man,—from which what new and singular code of social duties might be inferred? "The manner," says he, "in which the governments of those States where slavery exists are to regulate it is for their own consideration, under their responsibility to their constituents, to the general laws of propriety, humanity, and justice, and to God. Associations formed elsewhere, springing from a feeling of humanity, or any other cause,

---

[5] Daniel Webster (1782–1852) was one of the great politicians of the mid-nineteenth century.

have nothing whatever to do with it. They have never received any encouragement from me, and they never will."

They who know of no purer sources of truth, who have traced up its stream no higher, stand, and wisely stand, by the Bible and the Constitution, and drink at it there with reverence and humility; but they who behold where it comes trickling into this lake or that pool, gird up their loins once more, and continue their pilgrimage toward its fountain-head.

No man with a genius for legislation has appeared in America. They are rare in the history of the world. There are orators, politicians, and eloquent men, by the thousand; but the speaker has not yet opened his mouth to speak who is capable of settling the much-vexed questions of the day. We love eloquence for its own sake, and not for any truth which it may utter, or any heroism it may inspire. Our legislators have not yet learned the comparative value of free-trade and of freedom, of union, and of rectitude, to a nation. They have no genius or talent for comparatively humble questions of taxation and finance, commerce and manufactures and agriculture. If we were left solely to the wordy wit of legislators in Congress for our guidance, uncorrected by the seasonable experience and the effectual complaints of the people, America would not long retain her rank among the nations. For eighteen hundred years, though perchance I have no right to say it, the New Testament has been written; yet where is the legislator who has wisdom and practical talent enough to avail himself of the light which it sheds on the science of legislation?

45   The authority of government, even such as I am willing to submit to,—for I will cheerfully obey those who know and can do better than I, and in many things even those who neither know nor can do so well,—is still an impure one: to be strictly just, it must have the sanctions and consent of the governed. It can have no pure right over my person and property but what I concede to it. The progress from an absolute to a limited monarchy, from a limited monarchy to a democracy, is a progress toward a true respect for the individual. Even the Chinese philosopher was wise enough to regard the individual as the basis of the empire. Is a democracy, such as we know it, the last improvement possible in government? Is it not possible to take a step further towards recognizing and organizing the rights of man? There will never be a really free and enlightened State until the State come to recognize the individual as a higher and independent power, from which all its own power and authority are derived, and treats him accordingly. I please myself with imagining a State at last which can afford to be just to all men, and to treat the individual with respect as a neighbor; which even would not think

it inconsistent with its own repose if a few were to live aloof from it, not meddling with it, nor embraced by it, who fulfilled all the duties of neighbors and fellow-men. A State which bore this kind of fruit, and suffered it to drop off as fast as it ripened, would prepare the way for a still more perfect and glorious State, which also I have imagined, but not yet anywhere seen.

(1849)

Questions:

1. Explain in your own words Thoreau's concept of a "patron of virtue" (paragraph 10).

2. Thoreau's anti-government message has often appealed both to Americans who are to the right of center politically and to those who are to the left of center. Do you see any contradiction or paradox in this?

3. Compare "Civil Disobedience" with Martin Luther King's "Letter from Birmingham Jail" in terms of the ideas expressed, the style, and the tone of writing.

4. Discuss the extended metaphor in paragraph 18. How effective do you find the extended metaphor as a literary device? Write a paragraph yourself employing an extended metaphor.

5. Discuss the way in which Thoreau's argument in this essay is gendered. Like other transcendentalists, Thoreau clearly saw courage from a male perspective, and he frequently refers to what a "real man" can or should do. To what extent is this a harmful way of conceptualizing his ideas?

6. To a large degree, modern western society conceives of difficult ethical issues in passive terms; citizens may have a responsibility to decide where they stand on these difficult issues, but they are not generally believed to have a moral responsibility to become a social activist on behalf of whichever causes they believe to be right. (Among contemporary philosophers, Peter Singer is unique in taking an activist role—see elsewhere in this volume.) To what degree do you think we should have responsibilities to act on behalf of what we

believe to be right? When (if ever) are we justified in breaking the law in support of what we perceive to be a just cause?

7. In paragraph 22, Thoreau appears to equate real and metaphorical violence and bloodshed. Comment on this argumentative strategy.

8. Thoreau asserts that when a person becomes rich, the moral ground is "taken from under his feet." To what extent do you believe this to be true? A similar Christian idea is the notion that it is easier for a camel to pass through the eye of a needle than for a rich person to enter into heaven. Discuss the uneasy relationship between organized Christianity and wealth.

George Copway
(Kah-Ge-Ga-Gah-Bowh)
Ball-Playing

In this passage from The Traditional History and Characteristic Sketches
of the Ojibway Nation, *an Ojibway writer describes the game
that came to be known by its French name, Lacrosse.*

～～

I believe all the Indian nations of this continent have amusements among them. Those of the prairie nations are different from those of the Ojibways, suitable to their wide, open fields. The plays I am about to describe are the principal games practised by the people of my nation. There are others; and chance games are considerably in vogue among them.

One of the most popular games is that of ball-playing, which oftentimes engages an entire village. Parties are formed of from ten to several hundred. Before they commence, those who are to take a part in the play must provide each his share of staking, or things which are set apart; and one leader for each party. Each leader then appoints one of each company to be stakeholder.

Each man and each woman (women sometimes engage in the sport) is armed with a stick, one end of which bends somewhat like a small hoop, about four inches in circumference, to which is attached a network of rawhide, two inches deep, just large enough to admit the ball which is to be used on the occasion. Two poles are driven in the ground at a distance of four hundred paces from each other, which serves as goals for the two parties. It is the endeavour of each to take the ball to his hole. The party which carries the ball and strikes[1] its pole wins the game.

The warriors, very scantily attired, young and brave fantastically painted —and women, decorated with feathers, assemble around their commanders,

---

[1] makes contact with

who are generally men swift on the race. They are to take the ball either by running with it or throwing it in the air. As the ball falls in the crowd the excitement begins. The clubs swing and roll from side to side, the players run and shout, fall upon and tread upon each other, and in the struggle some get rather rough treatment.

5 When the ball is thrown some distance on each side, the party standing near instantly pick it up, and run at full speed with three or four after him. The others send their shouts of encouragement to their own party. "Ha! ha! yah!" "A-ne-gook!" and these shouts are heard even from the distant lodges, for children and all are deeply interested in the exciting scene. The spoils are not all on which their interest is fixed, but is directed to the falling and rolling of the crowds over and under each other. The loud and merry shouts of the spectators, who crowd the doors of the wigwams, go forth in one continued peal, and testify to their happy state of feeling.

The players are clothed in fur. They receive blows whose marks are plainly visible after the shuffle. The hands and feet are unencumbered, and they exercise them to the extent of their power; and with such dexterity do they strike the ball, that it is sent out of sight. Another strikes it on its descent, and for ten minutes at a time the play is so adroitly managed that the ball does not touch the ground.

No one is heard to complain, though he be bruised severely, or his nose come in close communion with a club. If the last-mentioned catastrophe befall him, he is up in a trice, and sends his laugh forth as loud as the rest, though it be floated at first on a tide of blood.

It is very seldom, if ever, that one is seen to be angry because he has been hurt. If he should get so, they would call him a "coward," which proves a sufficient check to many evils which might result from many seemingly intended injuries.

(1850)

QUESTIONS:

1. Compare the game Copway describes with modern lacrosse.

2. Comment on the tone with which Copway describes the violence of the sport.

CHARLES DARWIN

from On the Origin of Species by
Means of Natural Selection

OR THE PRESERVATION OF FAVOURED RACES IN THE STRUGGLE FOR LIFE

*In the concluding section of his great work of natural history,
Darwin cast his gaze on the future of science and of humanity.*

∿

When the views entertained in this volume on the origin of species, or
when analogous views are generally admitted, we can dimly foresee
that there will be a considerable revolution in natural history. Systematists
will be able to pursue their labours as at present; but they will not be
incessantly haunted by the shadowy doubt whether this or that form be in
essence a species. This I feel sure, and I speak after experience, will be no
slight relief. The endless disputes whether or not some fifty species of British
brambles are true species will cease. Systematists will have only to decide (not
that this will be easy) whether any form be sufficiently constant and distinct
from other forms, to be capable of definition; and if definable, whether the
differences be sufficiently important to deserve a specific name. This latter
point will become a far more essential consideration than it is at present; for
differences, however slight, between any two forms, if not blended by
intermediate gradations, are looked at by most naturalists as sufficient to
raise both forms to the rank of species. Hereafter we shall be compelled to
acknowledge that the only distinction between species and well-marked
varieties is, that the latter are known, or believed, to be connected at the
present day by intermediate gradations, whereas species were formerly thus
connected. Hence, without quite rejecting the consideration of the present

to weigh more carefully and to value higher the actual amount of difference between them. It is quite possible that forms now generally acknowledged to be merely varieties may hereafter be thought worthy of specific names, as with the primrose and cowslip; and in this case scientific and common language will come into accordance. In short, we shall have to treat species in the same manner as those naturalists treat genera, who admit that genera are merely artificial combinations made for convenience. This may not be a cheering prospect; but we shall at least be freed from the vain search for the undiscovered and undiscoverable essence of the term species.

The other and more general departments of natural history will rise greatly in interest. The terms used by naturalists of affinity, relationship, community of type, paternity, morphology, adaptive characters, rudimentary and aborted organs, etc., will cease to be metaphorical, and will have a plain signification. When we no longer look at an organic being as a savage looks at a ship, as at something wholly beyond his comprehension; when we regard every production of nature as one which has had a history; when we contemplate every complex structure and instinct as the summing up of many contrivances, each useful to the possessor, nearly in the same way as when we look at any great mechanical invention as the summing up of the labour, the experience, the reason, and even the blunders of numerous workmen; when we thus view each organic being, how far more interesting, I speak from experience, will the study of natural history become!

A grand and almost untrodden field of inquiry will be opened, on the causes and laws of variation, on correlation of growth, on the effects of use and disuse, on the direct action of external conditions, and so forth. The study of domestic productions will rise immensely in value. A new variety raised by man will be a far more important and interesting subject for study than one more species added to the infinitude of already recorded species. Our classifications will come to be, as far as they can be so made, genealogies; and will then truly give what may be called the plan of creation. The rules for classifying will no doubt become simpler when we have a definite object in view. We possess no pedigrees or armorial bearings; and we have to discover and trace the many diverging lines of descent in our natural genealogies, by characters of any kind which have long been inherited. Rudimentary organs will speak infallibly with respect to the nature of long-lost structures. Species and groups of species, which are called aberrant, and which may fancifully be called living fossils, will aid us in forming a picture of the ancient forms of life. Embryology will reveal to us the structure, in some degree obscured, of the prototypes of each great class.

When we can feel assured that all the individuals of the same species, and all the closely allied species of most genera, have within a not very remote period descended from one parent, and have migrated from some one birthplace; and when we better know the many means of migration, then, by the light which geology now throws, and will continue to throw, on former changes of climate and of the level of the land, we shall surely be enabled to trace in an admirable manner the former migrations of the inhabitants of the whole world. Even at present, by comparing the differences of the inhabitants of the sea on the opposite sides of a continent, and the nature of the various inhabitants of that continent in relation to their apparent means of immigration, some light can be thrown on ancient geography.

5　The noble science of Geology loses glory from the extreme imperfection of the record. The crust of the earth with its embedded remains must not be looked at as a well-filled museum, but as a poor collection made at hazard and at rare intervals. The accumulation of each great fossiliferous formation will be recognised as having depended on an unusual concurrence of circumstances, and the blank intervals between the successive stages as having been of vast duration. But we shall be able to gauge with some security the duration of these intervals by a comparison of the preceding and succeeding organic forms. We must be cautious in attempting to correlate as strictly contemporaneous two formations, which include few identical species, by the general succession of their forms of life. As species are produced and exterminated by slowly acting and still existing causes, and not by miraculous acts of creation and by catastrophes; and as the most important of all causes of organic change is one which is almost independent of altered and perhaps suddenly altered physical conditions, namely, the mutual relation of organism to organism,—the improvement of one being entailing the improvement or the extermination of others; it follows, that the amount of organic change in the fossils of consecutive formations probably serves as a fair measure of the lapse of actual time. A number of species, however, keeping in a body might remain for a long period unchanged, whilst within this same period, several of these species, by migrating into new countries and coming into competition with foreign associates, might become modified; so that we must not overrate the accuracy of organic change as a measure of time. During early periods of the earth's history, when the forms of life were probably fewer and simpler, the rate of change was probably slower; and at the first dawn of life, when very few forms of the simplest structure existed, the rate of change may have been slow in an extreme degree. The whole history of the world, as at present known, although of a length quite incomprehensible by us, will hereafter be recognised as a mere fragment of time, compared with the ages which have elapsed since the first creature, the progenitor of innumerable extinct and living descendants, was created.

In the distant future I see open fields for far more important researches. Psychology will be based on a new foundation, that of the necessary acquirement of each mental power and capacity by gradation. Light will be thrown on the origin of man and his history.

Authors of the highest eminence seem to be fully satisfied with the view that each species has been independently created. To my mind it accords better with what we know of the laws impressed on matter by the Creator, that the production and extinction of the past and present inhabitants of the world should have been due to secondary causes, like those determining the birth and death of the individual. When I view all beings not as special creations, but as the lineal descendants of some few beings which lived long before the first bed of the Silurian system was deposited, they seem to me to become ennobled. Judging from the past, we may safely infer that not one living species will transmit its unaltered likeness to a distant futurity. And of the species now living very few will transmit progeny of any kind to a far distant futurity; for the manner in which all organic beings are grouped, shows that the greater number of species of each genus, and all the species of many genera, have left no descendants, but have become utterly extinct. We can so far take a prophetic glance into futurity as to foretel that it will be the common and widely-spread species, belonging to the larger and dominant groups, which will ultimately prevail and procreate new and dominant species. As all the living forms of life are the lineal descendants of those which lived long before the Silurian epoch, we may feel certain that the ordinary succession by generation has never once been broken and that no cataclysm has desolated the whole world. Hence we may look with some confidence to a secure future of equally inappreciable length. And as natural selection works solely by and for the good of each being, all corporeal and mental endowments will tend to progress towards perfection.

It is interesting to contemplate an entangled bank, clothed with many plants of many kinds, with birds singing on the bushes, with various insects flitting about, and with worms crawling through the damp earth, and to reflect that these elaborately constructed forms, so different from each other, and dependent on each other in so complex a manner, have all been produced by laws acting around us. These laws, taken in the largest sense, being Growth with Reproduction; Inheritance which is almost implied by reproduction; Variability from the indirect and direct action of the external conditions of life, and from use and disuse; a Ratio of Increase so high as to lead to a Struggle for Life, and as a consequence to Natural Selection, entailing Divergence of Character and the Extinction of less-improved forms. Thus, from the war of nature, from famine and death, the most exalted object which we are capable of conceiving, namely, the production of the higher animals, directly follows. There is grandeur in this view of life, with its several powers, having been originally breathed into a few forms or into one; and that, whilst this planet has gone cycling on according to the fixed law of gravity, from so simple a beginning endless forms most beautiful and most wonderful have been, and are being, evolved.

(1859)

QUESTIONS:

1. Although this forms the conclusion to a work on natural *history*, it is very largely orientated towards the future. Compare the attitudes towards the future—and towards progress—expressed here with those expressed in the pieces reprinted elsewhere in this volume by Lewis Mumford and by Stephen Jay Gould.

2. Darwin tends to write quite long paragraphs. Try in one sentence to summarize the main idea of each of the eight paragraphs in this piece.

3. Explain how the science of biology becomes closely intertwined with that of geology when it comes to deal with evolution. Discuss the connections between the ideas expressed here and the ideas expressed in two other selections in this volume—those by Charles Lyell and by J. Tuzo Wilson.

4. Darwin has been proved correct in the prediction he made at the end of the first paragraph that categories such as "species" would come to be regarded as human constructs (albeit as human constructs that do have genuine reference in the "real world"). Think of examples of other sorts in which categories have been thought to embody essential differences but have later been shown to be merely human constructs—sometimes useful or convenient constructs, sometimes misleading or indeed harmful.

GEORGE ELIOT

from ONLY TEMPER

*The famous nineteenth-century novelist was also a distinguished essay writer;
here she discusses society's attitude towards expressions of bad temper.*

What is temper? Its primary meaning, the proportion and mode in
which qualities are mingled, is much neglected in popular speech, yet
even here the word often carries a reference to an habitual state or general
tendency of the organism in distinction from what are held to be specific
virtues and vices. As people confess to bad memory without expecting to
sink in mental reputation, so we hear a man declared to have a bad temper
and yet glorified as the possessor of every high quality. When he errs or in
any way commits himself, his temper is accused, not his character, and it is
understood that but for a brutal bearish mood he is kindness itself. If he
kicks small animals, swears violently at a servant who mistakes orders, or is
grossly rude to his wife, it is remarked apologetically that these things mean
nothing—they are all temper.

Certainly there is a limit to this form of apology, and the forgery of a
bill, or the ordering of goods without any prospect of paying for them, has
never been set down to an unfortunate habit of sulkiness or of irascibility.
But on the whole there is a peculiar exercise of indulgence towards the
manifestations of bad temper which tends to encourage them, so that we are
in danger of having among us a number of virtuous persons who conduct
themselves detestably, just as we have hysterical patients who, with sound
organs, are apparently labouring under many sorts of organic disease. Let it
be admitted however, that a man may be a "good fellow" and yet have a bad
temper, so bad that we recognise his merits with reluctance, and are inclined
to resent his occasionally amiable behaviour as an unfair demand on our
admiration.

[Dion] Touchwood is that kind of good fellow. He is by turns insolent, quarrelsome, repulsively haughty to innocent people who approach him with respect, neglectful of his friends, angry in the face of legitimate demands, procrastinating in the fulfilment of such demands, prompted to rude words and harsh looks by a moody disgust with his fellow-men in general—and yet, as everybody will assure you, the soul of honour, a steadfast friend, a defender of the oppressed, an affectionate-hearted creature. Pity that, after a certain experience of his moods, his intimacy becomes insupportable! A man who uses his balmorals to tread on your toes with much frequency and an unmistakeable emphasis may prove a fast friend in adversity, but meanwhile your adversity has not arrived and your toes are tender. The daily sneer or growl at your remarks is not to be made amends for by a possible eulogy or defence of your understanding against depreciators who may not present themselves, and on an occasion which may never arise. I cannot submit to a chronic state of blue and green bruise as a form of insurance against an accident.

Touchwood's bad temper is of the contradicting pugnacious sort. He is the honourable gentleman in opposition, whatever proposal or proposition may be broached, and when others join him he secretly damns their superfluous agreement, quickly discovering that his way of stating the case is not exactly theirs. An invitation or any sign of expectation throws him into an attitude of refusal. Ask his concurrence in a benevolent measure: he will not decline to give it, because he has a real sympathy with good aims; but he complies resentfully, though where he is let alone he will do much more than any one would have thought of asking for. No man would shrink with greater sensitiveness from the imputation of not paying his debts, yet when a bill is sent in with any promptitude he is inclined to make the tradesman wait for the money he is in such a hurry to get. One sees that this antagonistic temper must be much relieved by finding a particular object, and that its worst moments must be those where the mood is that of vague resistance, there being nothing specific to oppose. Touchwood is never so little engaging as when he comes down to breakfast with a cloud on his brow, after parting from you the night before with an affectionate effusiveness at the end of a confidential conversation which has assured you of mutual understanding. Impossible that you can have committed any offence. If mice have disturbed him, that is not your fault; but, nevertheless, your cheerful greeting had better not convey any reference to the weather, else it will be met by a sneer which, taking you unawares, may give you a crushing sense that you make a poor figure with your cheerfulness, which was not asked for.

Some daring person perhaps introduces another topic, and uses the delicate flattery of appealing to Touchwood for his opinion, the topic being included in his favourite studies. An indistinct muttering, with a look at the carving-knife in reply, teaches that daring person how ill he has chosen a market for his deference. If Touchwood's behaviour affects you very closely you had better break your leg in the course of the day: his bad temper will then vanish at once: he will take a painful journey on your behalf; he will sit up with you night after night; he will do all the work of your department so as to save you from any loss in consequence of your accident; he will be even uniformly tender to you till you are well on your legs again, when he will some fine morning insult you without provocation, and make you wish that his generous goodness to you had not closed your lips against retort.

It is not always necessary that a friend should break his leg for Touch-wood to feel compunction and endeavour to make amends for his bearish-ness or insolence. He becomes spontaneously conscious that he has misbehaved, and he is not only ashamed of himself, but has the better prompting to try and heal any wound he has inflicted. Unhappily the habit of being offensive "without meaning it" leads usually to a way of making amends which the injured person cannot but regard as a being amiable without meaning it. The kindnesses, the complimentary indications or assurances, are apt to appear in the light of a penance adjusted to the foregoing lapses, and by the very contrast they offer call up a keener memory of the wrong they atone for. They are not a spontaneous prompting of goodwill, but an elaborate compensation. And, in fact, Dion's atoning friendliness has a ring of artificiality. Because he formerly disguised his good feeling towards you he now expresses more than he quite feels. It is in vain. Having made you extremely uncomfortable last week he has absolutely diminished his power of making you happy to-day: he struggles against this result by excessive effort, but he has taught you to observe his fitfulness rather than to be warmed by his episodic show of regard.

(1860)

Questions:

1. At the time Eliot was writing, the word "temper" was clearly in the process of having its meaning shifted so that "having a temper" came to be the equivalent of "having a bad temper." The original meaning of "temper" survives today in the noun "temperament." Express in your own words what was still in Eliot's time the primary meaning of "temper."

2. Eliot uses an "honourable gentleman" as her example here; to what extent do you think that our readiness to forgive a bad temper varies on the basis of gender? Are we more likely to forgive a bad-tempered man than a bad-tempered woman?

3. Here, as in her novels, Eliot has a tendency towards quite long sentences. Choose one long sentence that you feel works well and try to explain why; and one long sentence that seems to you to be *too* long or confusing, and again try to explain why.

MARK TWAIN

A RIVER PILOT LOOKS AT THE MISSISSIPPI

In this passage, Twain reflects on how the experience of working as a Mississippi pilot changed his attitudes toward the river itself.

The face of the water, in time, became a wonderful book—a book that was a dead language to the uneducated passenger, but which told its mind to me without reserve, delivering its most cherished secrets as clearly as if it uttered them with a voice. And it was not a book to be read once and thrown aside, for it had a new story to tell every day. Throughout the long twelve hundred miles there was never a page that was void of interest, never one that you could leave unread without loss, never one that you would want to skip, thinking you could find higher enjoyment in some other thing. There never was so wonderful a book written by man; never one whose interest was so absorbing, so unflagging, so sparklingly renewed with every re-perusal. The passenger who could not read it was charmed with a peculiar sort of faint dimple on its surface (on the rare occasions when he did not overlook it altogether); but to the pilot that was an *italicized* passage; indeed, it was more than that, it was a legend of the largest capitals, with a string of shouting exclamation-points at the end of it, for it meant that a wreck or a rock was buried there that could tear the life out of the strongest vessel that ever floated. It is the faintest and simplest expression the water ever makes, and the most hideous to a pilot's eye. In truth, the passenger who could not read this book saw nothing but all manner of pretty pictures in it, painted by the sun and shaded by the clouds, whereas to the trained eye these were not pictures at all, but the grimmest and most dead-earnest of reading-matter.

Now when I had mastered the language of this water, and had come to know every trifling feature that bordered the great river as familiarly as I knew the letters of the alphabet, I had made a valuable acquisition. But I had lost something, too. I had lost something which could never be restored to me while I lived. All the grace, the beauty, the poetry, had gone out of the majestic river! I still keep in mind a certain wonderful sunset which I witnessed when steamboating was new to me. A broad expanse of the river was turned to blood; in the middle distance the red hue brightened into gold, through which a solitary log came floating, black and conspicuous; in one place a long, slanting mark lay sparkling upon the water; in another the surface was broken by boiling, tumbling rings, that were as many-tinted as an opal; where the ruddy flush was faintest, was a smooth spot that was covered with graceful circles and radiating lines, ever so delicately traced; the shore on our left was densely wooded, and the somber shadow that fell from this forest was broken in one place by a long, ruffled trail that shone like silver; and high above the forest wall a clean-stemmed dead tree waved a single leafy bough that glowed like a flame in the unobstructed splendor that was flowing from the sun. There were graceful curves, reflected images, woody heights, soft distances; and over the whole scene, far and near, the dissolving lights drifted steadily, enriching it every passing moment with new marvels of coloring.

I stood like one bewitched. I drank it in, in a speechless rapture. The world was new to me, and I had never seen anything like this at home. But as I have said, a day came when I began to cease from noting the glories and the charms which the moon and the sun and the twilight wrought upon the river's face; another day came when I ceased altogether to note them. Then, if that sunset scene had been repeated, I should have looked upon it without rapture, and should have commented upon it, inwardly, after this fashion: "This sun means that we are going to have wind tomorrow; that floating log means that the river is rising, small thanks to it; that slanting mark on the water refers to a bluff reef which is going to kill somebody's steamboat one of these nights, if it keeps on stretching out like that; those tumbling 'boils' show a dissolving bar and a changing channel there; the lines and circles in the slick water over yonder are a warning that that troublesome place is shoaling up dangerously; that silver streak in the shadow of the forest is the 'break' from a new snag, and he has located himself in the very best place he could have found to fish for steamboats; that tall dead tree, with a single living branch, is not going to last long, and then how is a body ever going to get through this blind place at night without the friendly old landmark?"

No, the romance and beauty were all gone from the river. All the value any feature of it had for me now was the amount of usefulness it could furnish toward compassing the safe piloting of a steamboat. Since those days, I have pitied doctors from my heart. What does the lovely flush in a beauty's cheek mean to a doctor but a "break" that ripples above some deadly disease? Are not all her visible charms sown thick with what are to him the signs and symbols of hidden decay? Does he ever see her beauty at all, or doesn't he simply view her professionally, and comment upon her unwholesome condition all to himself? And doesn't he sometimes wonder whether he has gained most or lost most by learning his trade?

(1875)

QUESTIONS:

1. Through the first paragraph and into the second Twain employs an extended metaphor. Summarize in your own words the ways in which the river is said to resemble a book.

2. What is the essential contrast being discussed in this passage? To what is the change in Twain's reactions to the river to be attributed?

3. Recount a case in which you had been similarly deadened to the effects of the beauty around you, either by being pressed to focus on your surroundings in a different fashion for practical purposes, or simply through familiarity.

OSCAR WILDE

THE NEW AESTHETIC

*In the final speech of his 1889 work, "The Decay of Lying," Wilde puts forward
a manifesto for a new set of aesthetic principles.*

〜〜

Briefly, then, [the doctrines of the new aesthetics] are these. Art never expresses anything but itself. It has an independent life, just as Thought has, and develops purely on its own lines. It is not necessarily realistic in an age of realism, nor spiritual in an age of faith. So far from being the creation of its time, it is usually in direct opposition to it, and the only history that it preserves for us is the history of its own progress. Sometimes it returns upon its footsteps, and revives some antique form, as happened in the archaistic movement of late Greek Art, and in the pre-Raphaelite movement of our own day. At other times it entirely anticipates its age, and produces in one century work that it takes another century to understand, to appreciate, and to enjoy. In no case does it reproduce its age. To pass from the art of a time to the time itself is the great mistake that all historians commit.

The second doctrine is this. All bad art comes from returning to Life and Nature, and elevating them into ideals. Life and Nature may sometimes be used as part of Art's rough material, but before they are of any real service to Art they must be translated into artistic conventions. The moment Art surrenders its imaginative medium it surrenders everything. As a method Realism is a complete failure, and the two things that every artist should avoid are modernity of form and modernity of subject-matter.[1] To us, who

---

[1] In the late nineteenth century realism was the dominant aesthetic principle; leading writers and visual artists attempted to portray "real life" as convincingly as possible. (In the early twentieth century, the movement that became known as "modernism" turned radically away from realism.)

live in the nineteenth century, any century is a suitable subject for art except our own. The only beautiful things are the things that do not concern us. It is, to have the pleasure of quoting myself, exactly because Hecuba[1] is nothing to us that her sorrows are so suitable a motive for a tragedy. Besides, it is only the modern that ever becomes old-fashioned. M. Zola sits down to give us a picture of the Second Empire.[2] Who cares for the Second Empire now? It is out of date. Life goes faster than Realism, but Romanticism is always in front of Life.

The third doctrine is that Life imitates Art far more than Art imitates Life. This results not merely from Life's imitative instinct, but from the fact that the self-conscious aim of Life is to find expression, and that Art offers it certain beautiful forms through which it may realize that energy. It is a theory that has never been put forward before, but it is extremely fruitful, and throws an entirely new light upon the history of Art.

It follows, as a corollary from this, that external Nature also imitates Art. The only effects that she can show us are effects that we have already seen through poetry, or in paintings. This is the secret of Nature's charm, as well as the explanation of Nature's weakness.

The final revelation is that Lying, the telling of beautiful untrue things, is the proper aim of Art.

(1889)

---

[1] In Shakespeare's "Hamlet," Hamlet makes the following speech while observing the players dramatize the death of Hecuba (in Greek mythology, the wife of Priam, King of Troy, who was taken prisoner when the Greeks captured Troy):

O, what a rogue and peasant slave am I:
Is it not monstrous that this player here,
But in a fiction, in a dream of passion,
Could force his soul so as to his own conceit
That from her working all his visage wann'd
Tears in his eyes, distraction in's aspect,
A broken voice, and his whole function suiting
With forms to his conceit? And all for nothing!
For Hecuba!
What's Hecuba to him or he to Hecuba
That he should weep for her?
(I, iv, 584–592)

[2] Louis Napoleon, nephew of Napoleon 1st, and heir to the Napoleonic title, was elected president of France in 1848, and in 1852 dismissed Parliament and declared himself emperor. The Second Empire ended when he was forced from power after France's defeat at the hands of Prussia in 1871. Emile Zola was the leading novelist of the period in France.

QUESTIONS:

1. Wilde's approach stands on its head the notion of Plato that poets had no proper place in society because they were liars. From the late medieval period through the twentieth century the prevailing view has been that the "lying" engaged in by literary writers is of an entirely different order from lies with which people attempt to deceive each other in everyday life. Are there any grounds for regarding the two forms of lying as in any way similar?

2. Should artists (writers as well as visual and other sorts of artists) strive in some sense to tell the truth? Why?

Jane Addams

On Halsted Street

*Hull-House, established by Addams in 1889 and located on Halsted Street in
a depressed area of Chicago, represented a successful and influential effort to
improve the lot of the urban poor in nineteenth-century America—in
intellectual, social, and spiritual terms as well as economic ones. The following
forms the conclusion of Addams' book* Twenty Years at Hull-House.

In those early days we were often asked why we had to come to live on
Halsted Street when we could afford to live somewhere else. I remember
one man who used to shake his head and say it was "the strangest thing he
had met in his experience," but who was finally convinced that it was "not
strange but natural." In time it came to seem natural to all of us that the
Settlement should be there. If it is natural to feed the hungry and care for the
sick, it is certainly natural to give pleasure to the young, comfort to the aged,
and to minister to the deep-seated craving for social intercourse that all men
feel. Whoever does it is rewarded by something which, if not gratitude, is at
least spontaneous and vital and lacks that irksome sense of obligation with
which a substantial benefit is too often acknowledged.

In addition to the neighbors who responded to the receptions and
classes, we found those who were too battered and oppressed to care for
them. To these, however, was left that susceptibility to the bare offices of
humanity which raises such offices into a bond of fellowship.

From the first it seemed understood that we were ready to perform the
humblest neighborhood services. We were asked to wash the new-born
babies, and to prepare the dead for burial, to nurse the sick, and to "mind
the children."

Occasionally these neighborly offices unexpectedly uncovered ugly
human traits. For six weeks after an operation we kept in one of our three

bedrooms a forlorn little baby who, because he was born with a cleft palate, was most unwelcome even to his mother, and we were horrified when he died of neglect a week after he was returned to his home; a little Italian bride of fifteen sought shelter with us one November evening, to escape her husband who had beaten her every night for a week when he returned home from work, because she had lost her wedding ring; two of us officiated quite alone at the birth of an illegitimate child because the doctor was late in arriving, and none of the honest Irish matrons would "touch the likes of her"; we ministered at the deathbed of a young man, who during a long illness of tuberculosis had received so many bottles of whiskey through the mistaken kindness of his friends, that the cumulative effect produced wild periods of exultation, in one of which he died.

5   We were also early impressed with the curious isolation of many of the immigrants; an Italian woman once expressed her pleasure in the red roses that she saw at one of our receptions in surprise that they had been "brought so fresh all the way from Italy." She would not believe for an instant that they had been grown in America. She said that she had lived in Chicago for six years and had never seen any roses, whereas in Italy she had seen them every summer in great profusion. During all that time, of course, the woman had lived within ten blocks of a florist's window; she had not been more than a five-cent car ride away from the public parks; but she had never dreamed of faring forth for herself, and no one had taken her. Her conception of America had been the untidy street in which she lived and had made her long struggle to adapt herself to American ways.

But in spite of some untoward experiences, we were constantly impressed with the uniform kindness and courtesy we received. Perhaps these first days laid the simple human foundations which are certainly essential for continuous living among the poor: first, genuine preference for residence in an industrial quarter to any other part of the city, because it is interesting and makes the human appeal; and second, the conviction, in the words of Canon Barnett,[1] that the things which make men alike are finer and better than the things that keep them apart, and that these basic likenesses, if they are properly accentuated, easily transcend the less essential differences of race, language, creed and tradition.

Perhaps even in those first days we made a beginning toward that object which was afterwards stated in our charter: "To provide a center for a higher

---

[1] Samuel A. Barnett, an English cleric and reformer, and the founder of Toynbee Hall, on which Addams modeled Hull-House.

civic and social life; to institute and maintain educational and philanthropic enterprises, and to investigate and improve the conditions in the industrial districts of Chicago."

(1910)

QUESTIONS:

1. Comment on the way in which Addams alternates between the general and the particular in her observations in this passage.

2. The contrary argument to that made by Addams in the second last paragraph of this passage is often put forward: that in order to appeal to all different sorts of human beings, it is often necessary to appeal to the "lowest common denominator." Argue in a more extended way for one or the other of these positions.

3. To what extent do you see differences such as race and language as forming essential dividing lines between human groups?

4. Beyond what Addams states explicitly, what are we able to infer from this passage about the Chicago of the late nineteenth century?

W.E.B. Du Bois

A Mild Suggestion

*This short piece is among the most biting essays by the
famous American civil rights activist.*

∽

They were sitting on the leeward deck of the vessel and the colored man was there with his usual look of unconcern. Before the seasickness his presence aboard had caused some upheaval. The Woman, for instance, glancing at the Southerner, had refused point blank to sit beside him at meals, so she had changed places with the Little Old Lady. The Westerner, who sat opposite, said he did not care a ———, then he looked at the Little Old Lady, and added in a lower voice to the New Yorker that there was no accounting for tastes. The Southerner from the other table broadened his back and tried to express with his shoulders both ancestors and hauteur. All this, however was half forgotten during the seasickness, and the Woman sat beside the colored man for a full half hour before she noticed it, and then was glad to realize that the Southerner was too sick to see. Now again with sunshine and smiling weather, they all quite naturally reverted (did the Southerner suggest it?) to the Negro problem. The usual solutions had been suggested: education, work, emigration, etc.

They had not noticed the back of the colored man, until the thoughtless Westerner turned toward him and said breezily: "Well, now, what do you say? I guess you are rather interested." The colored man was leaning over the rail and about to light his cigarette—he had several such bad habits, as the Little Old Lady noticed. The Southerner simply stared. Over the face of the colored man went the shadow of several expressions; some the New Yorker could interpret, others he could not.

"I have," said the colored man, with deliberation, "a perfect solution." The Southerner selected a look of disdain from his repertoire, and assumed it. The Woman moved nearer, but partly turned her back. The Westerner and the Little Old Lady sat down. "Yes," repeated the colored man, "I have a perfect solution. The trouble with most of the solutions which are generally suggested is that they aggravate the disease." The Southerner could not help looking interested. "For instance," proceeded the colored man, airily waving his hand, "take education; education means ambition, dissatisfaction and revolt. You cannot both educate people and hold them down."

"Then stop educating them," growled the Southerner aside.

5   "Or," continued the colored man, "if the black man works, he must come into competition with whites ——"

"He sure will, and it ought to be stopped," returned the Westerner. "It brings down wages."

"Precisely," said the speaker, "and if by underselling the labor market he develops a few millionaires, how now would you protect your residential districts or your select social circles or—your daughters?"

The Southerner started angrily, but the colored man was continuing placidly with a far-off look in his eyes. "Now, migration is both costly and inhuman; the transportation would be the smallest matter. You must buy up perhaps a thousand millions' worth of Negro property; you must furnish some capital for the masses of poor; you must get some place for them to go; you must protect them there, and here you must pay not only higher wages to white men, but still higher on account of the labor scarcity. Meantime, the Negroes suddenly removed from one climate and social system to another climate and utterly new conditions would die in droves—it would be simply prolonged murder at enormous cost.

"Very well," continued the colored man, seating himself and throwing away his cigarette, "listen to my plan," looking almost quizzically at the Little Old Lady; "you must not be alarmed at its severity—it may seem radical, but really it is—it is—well, it is quite the only practical thing and it has surely one advantage: it settles the problem once, suddenly, and forever. My plan is this: You now outnumber us nearly ten to one. I propose that on a certain date, shall we say next Christmas, or possibly Easter, 1912? No, come to think of it, the first of January, 1913, would, for historical reasons, probably be best. Well, then, on the first of January, 1913, let each person who has a colored friend invite him to dinner. This would take care of a few; among such friends might be included the black mammies and faithful old servants of the South; in this way we could get together quite a number. Then those who have not the pleasure of black friends might arrange for meetings, especially in "white" churches and Young Men's and Young Women's

Christian Associations, where Negroes are not expected. At such meetings, contrary to custom, the black people should not be seated by themselves, but distributed very carefully among the whites. The remaining Negroes who could not be flattered or attracted by these invitations should be induced to assemble among themselves at their own churches or at little parties and house warmings.

10   "The few stragglers, vagrants and wanderers could be put under careful watch and ward. Now, then, we have the thing in shape. First, the hosts of those invited to dine should provide themselves with a sufficient quantity of cyanide of potassium, placing it carefully in the proper cups, and being careful not to mix the cups. Those at church and prayer meeting could choose between long sharp stilettoes and pistols—I should recommend the former as less noisy. Those who guard the colored assemblies and the stragglers without should carefully surround the groups and use Winchesters. Then, at a given signal, let the colored folk of the United States be quietly dispatched; the signal might be a church bell or the singing of the national hymn; probably the bell would be best, for the diners would be eating."

By this time the auditors of the colored man were staring; the Southerner had forgotten to pose; the Woman had forgotten to watch the Southerner; the Westerner was staring with admiration; there were tears in the eyes of the Little Old Lady, while the New Yorker was smiling; but the colored man held up a deprecating hand: "Now don't prejudge my plan," he urged. "The next morning there would be ten million funerals, and therefore no Negro problem. Think how quietly the thing would be settled; no more bother, no more argument; the whole country united and happy. Even the Negroes would be a great deal happier than they are at present. Instead of being made heirs to hope by education, or ambitious by wealth, or exiled invalids on the fever coast, they would all be happily ensconced in Heaven. Of course, I admit that at first the plan may seem a little abrupt and cruel, and yet is it more cruel than present conditions, and would it not be well to be a little more abrupt in our social solutions? At any rate think it over," and the colored man dropped lazily into his steamer chair and felt for another cigarette.

The crowd slowly dispersed; the Southerner chose the Woman, but was heard to say something about fools. The Westerner turned to the New Yorker and said: "Now, what in hell do you suppose that darky meant?" But the Little Old Lady went silently to her cabin.

(1912)

QUESTIONS:

1. This essay is similar in several respects to "A Modest Proposal" by Jonathan Swift. What are some of these similarities? Are there also significant differences between the two essays in tone and approach?

2. "A Mild Suggestion" was published almost 50 years after "emancipation"; in what ways were African-Americans evidently still not fully free in 1912? What reflections, if any, does this prompt about the nature of freedom?

3. Comment on the tone and diction of Du Bois's prose in this piece. What can you say about the choice of verbs when the crucial part of the proposal is set out ("provide themselves with...," "choose between...," "carefully surround the groups...," "be quietly dispatched")?

Stephen Leacock

Roughing It in the Bush
My Plans for Moose Hunting in the Canadian Wilderness

The Canadian economist Stephen Leacock achieved world-wide renown for his short stories and humorous essays. The following selection expounds on the simple virtues of rough and ready outdoor life.

The season is now opening when all those who have a manly streak in them like to get out into the bush and "rough it" for a week or two of hunting and fishing. For myself, I never feel that the autumn has been well spent unless I can get out after the moose. And when I go I like to go right into the bush and "rough it"—get clear away from civilization, out in the open, and take fatigue or hardship just as it comes.

So this year I am making all my plans to get away for a couple of weeks of moose hunting along with my brother George and my friend Tom Gass. We generally go together because we are all of us men who like the rough stuff and are tough enough to stand the hardship of living in the open. The place we go to is right in the heart of the primitive Canadian forest, among big timber, broken with lakes as still as glass, just the very ground for moose.

We have a kind of lodge up there. It's just a rough place that we put up, the three of us, the year before last, built out of tamarack logs faced with a broad axe. The flies, while we were building it, were something awful. Two of the men that we sent in there to build it were so badly bitten that we had to bring them out a hundred miles to a hospital. None of us saw the place while we were building it,—we were all busy at the time,—but the teamsters who took in our stuff said it was the worst season for the black flies that they ever remembered.

Still we hung to it, in spite of the flies, and stuck at it till we got it built. It is, as I say, only a plain place but good enough to rough it in. We have one big room with a stone fireplace, and bedrooms round the sides, with a wide verandah, properly screened, all along the front. The verandah has a row of upright tamaracks for its posts and doesn't look altogether bad. In the back part we have quarters where our man[1] sleeps. We had an ice-house knocked up while they were building and water laid on in pipes from a stream. So that on the whole the place has a kind of rough comfort about it,—good enough anyway for fellows hunting moose all day.

5   The place, nowadays, is not hard to get at. The government has just built a colonization highway, quite all right for motors, that happens to go within a hundred yards of our lodge.

We can get the railway for a hundred miles, and then the highway for forty, and the last hundred yards we can walk. But this season we are going to cut out the railway and go the whole way from the city in George's car with our kit with us.

George has one of those great big cars with a roof and thick glass sides. Personally none of the three of us would have preferred to ride in a luxurious darned thing like that. Tom says that as far as he is concerned he'd much sooner go into the bush over a rough trail in a buckboard, and for my own part a team of oxen would be more the kind of thing that I'd wish.

However the car is there, so we might as well use the thing especially as the provincial government has built the fool highway right into the wilderness. By taking the big car also we can not only carry all the hunting outfit that we need but we can also, if we like, shove in a couple of small trunks with a few clothes. This may be necessary as it seems that somebody has gone and slapped a great big frame hotel right there in the wilderness, not half a mile from the place we go to. The hotel we find a regular nuisance. It gave us the advantage of electric light for our lodge (a thing none of us care about), but it means more fuss about clothes. Clothes, of course, don't really matter when a fellow is roughing it in the bush, but Tom says that we might find it necessary to go over to the hotel in the evenings to borrow coal oil or a side of bacon or any rough stuff that we need; and they do such a lot of dressing up at these fool hotels now that if we do go over for bacon or anything in the evening we might just as well slip on our evening clothes, as we could chuck them off the minute we get back. George thinks it might not be a bad idea,—just as a way of saving all our energy for getting after the moose,—to dine each evening at the hotel itself. He knew some men who did that last year and they told him that the time saved for moose hunting in that way is extraordinary. George's idea is that we could come in each

---

[1] *man* man servant

night with our moose,—such and such a number as the case might be—either bringing them with us or burying them where they die,—change our things, slide over to the hotel and get dinner and then beat it back into the bush by moonlight and fetch in the moose. It seems they have a regular two dollar table d'hôte dinner at the hotel,—just rough stuff of course but after all, as we all admit, we don't propose to go out into the wilds to pamper ourselves with high feeding: a plain hotel meal in a home-like style at two dollars a plate is better than cooking up a lot of rich stuff over a camp fire.

If we *do* dine at the hotel we could take our choice each evening between going back into the bush by moonlight to fetch in the dead moose from the different caches where we had hidden them, or sticking round the hotel itself for a while. It seems that there is dancing there. Nowadays such a lot of women and girls get the open air craze for the life in the bush that these big wilderness hotels are crowded with them. There is something about living in the open that attracts modern women and they like to get right away from everybody and everything; and of course hotels of this type in the open are nowadays always well closed in with screens so that there are no flies or anything of that sort.

10 So it seems that there is dancing at the hotel every evening,—nothing on a large scale or pretentious,—just an ordinary hardwood floor,—they may wax it a little for all I know—and some sort of plain, rough Italian orchestra that they fetch up from the city. Not that any of us care for dancing. It's a thing that personally we wouldn't bother with. But it happens that there are a couple of young girls that Tom knows that are going to be staying at the hotel and of course naturally he wants to give them a good time. They are only eighteen and twenty (sisters) and that's really younger than we care for, but with young girls like that,—practically kids,—any man wants to give them a good time. So Tom says, and I think quite rightly, that as the kids are going to be there we may as well put in an appearance at the hotel and see that they are having a good time. Their mother is going to be with them too, and of course we want to give her a good time as well; in fact I think I will lend her my moose rifle and let her go out and shoot a moose. One thing we are all agreed upon in the arrangement of our hunting trip, is in not taking along anything to drink. Drinking spoils a trip of that sort. We all remember how in the old days we'd go out into a camp in the bush (I mean before there used to be any highway or any hotel) and carry in rye whisky in demijohns (two dollars a gallon it was) and sit around the camp fire drinking it in the evenings.

But there's nothing in it. We all agree that the law being what it is,[1] it is better to stick to it. It makes a fellow feel better. So we shall carry nothing in. I don't say that one might not have a flask or something in one's pocket in the car; but only as a precaution against accident or cold. And when we get to our lodge we all feel that we are a darned sight better without it. If we *should* need anything,—though it isn't likely,—there are still three cases of old Scotch whiskey, kicking around the lodge somewhere; I think they are kicking round in a little cement cellar with a locked door that we had made so as to use it for butter or anything of that sort. Anyway there are three, possibly four, or maybe, five, cases of Scotch there and if we should for any reason want it, there it is. But we are hardly likely to touch it,—unless we hit a cold snap, or a wet spell;—then we might; or if we strike hot dry weather. Tom says he thinks there are a couple of cases of champagne still in the cellar; some stuff that one of us must have shot in there just before prohibition came in. But we'll hardly use it. When a man is out moose hunting from dawn to dusk he hasn't much use for champagne, not till he gets home anyway. The only thing that Tom says the champagne might come in useful for would be if we cared to ask the two kids over to some sort of dinner; it would be just a rough kind of camp dinner (we could hardly ask their mother to it) but we think we could manage it. The man we keep there used to be a butler in England, or something of the sort, and he could manage some kind of rough meal where the champagne might fit in.

There's only one trouble about our plans for our fall camp that bothers us just a little. The moose are getting damn scarce about that place. There used, so they say, to be any quantity of them. There's an old settler up there that our man buys all our cream from who says that he remembers when the moose were so thick that they would come up and drink whiskey out of his dipper. But somehow they seem to have quit the place. Last year we sent our man out again and again looking for them and he never saw any. Three years ago a boy that works at the hotel said he saw a moose in the cow pasture back of the hotel and there were the tracks of a moose seen last year at the place not ten miles from the hotel where it had come to drink. But apart from these two exceptions the moose hunting has been poor.

Still, what does it matter? What we want is the *life*, the rough life just as I have described it. If any moose comes to our lodge we'll shoot him, or tell

---

[1] *the law being what it is* Prohibition (making the consumption of alcoholic beverages illegal) was enforced in Canada in the late 1910s and early 1920s (provincial laws varied), and in the United State from 1919 to 1933.

the butler to. But if not,—well, we've got along without for ten years, I don't suppose we shall worry.

(1923)

QUESTIONS:

1. Much of the humor in this piece stems from the same sort of structuring of ideas applied to a succession of items. How does Leacock modify each suggestion after he has first presented it? Is there an echo of the same sort of structure in the essay as a whole?

2. Paragraph 9 subtly suggests that hypocrisy and self-deception are not restricted to moose hunters. What areas can you think of in which people today hold a view of themselves that all too often does not correspond to reality?

3. Many of the underlying issues concerning how humans relate to the wilderness are much the same today, eighty years after this piece was published. Choose a particular context in which to write a brief essay arguing either for or against greater efforts to protect the wilderness.

Virginia Woolf

Professions for Women

This lecture to a society of professional women touches on themes developed at greater length in Woolf's A Room of One's Own.

～

When your secretary invited me to come here, she told me that your Society is concerned with the employment of women and she suggested that I might tell you something about my own professional experiences. It is true that I am a woman; it is true I am employed; but what professional experiences have I had? It is difficult to say. My profession is literature; and in that profession there are fewer experiences for women than in any other, with the exception of the stage—fewer, I mean, that are peculiar to women. For the road was cut many years ago—by Fanny Burney, by Aphra Behn, by Harriet Martineau, by Jane Austen, by George Eliot—many famous women, and many more unknown and forgotten, have been before me, making the path smooth, and regulating my steps. Thus, when I came to write, there were very few material obstacles in my way. Writing was a reputable and harmless occupation. The family peace was not broken by the scratching of a pen. No demand was made upon the family purse. For ten and sixpence one can buy paper enough to write all the plays of Shakespeare—if one has a mind that way. Pianos and models, Paris, Vienna, and Berlin,[1] masters and mistresses, are not needed by a writer. The cheapness of writing paper is, of course, the reason why women have succeeded as writers before they have succeeded in the other professions.

But to tell you my story—it is a simple one. You have only got to figure to yourselves a girl in a bedroom with a pen in her hand. She had only to

---

[1] *Paris, Vienna, and Berlin* All three are cities that Britons frequently traveled to for training in art and music.

move that pen from left to right—from ten o'clock to one. Then it occurred to her to do what is simple and cheap enough after all—to slip a few of those pages into an envelope, fix a penny stamp in the corner, and drop the envelope into the red box at the corner. It was thus that I became a journalist; and my effort was rewarded on the first day of the following month—a very glorious day it was for me—by a letter from an editor containing a cheque for one pound ten shillings and sixpence. But to show you how little I deserve to be called a professional woman, how little I know of the struggles and difficulties of such lives, I have to admit that instead of spending that sum upon bread and butter, rent, shoes and stockings, or butcher's bills, I went out and bought a cat—a beautiful cat, a Persian cat, which very soon involved me in bitter disputes with my neighbors.

What could be easier than to write articles and to buy Persian cats with the profits? But wait a moment. Articles have to be about something. Mine, I seem to remember, was about a novel by a famous man. And while I was writing this review, I discovered that if I were going to review books I should need to do battle with a certain phantom. And the phantom was a woman, and when I came to know her better I called her after the heroine of a famous poem, The Angel in the House. It was she who used to come between me and my paper when I was writing reviews. It was she who bothered me and wasted my time and so tormented me that at last I killed her. You who come of a younger and happier generation may not have heard of her—you may not know what I mean by The Angel in the House. I will describe her as shortly as I can. She was intensely sympathetic. She was immensely charming. She was utterly unselfish. She excelled in the difficult arts of family life. She sacrificed herself daily. If there was chicken, she took the leg; if there was a draught she sat in it—in short she was so constituted that she never had a mind or a wish of her own, but preferred to sympathize always with the minds and wishes of others. Above all—I need not say it—she was pure. Her purity was supposed to be her chief beauty—her blushes, her great grace. In those days—the last of Queen Victoria—every house had its Angel. And when I came to write I encountered her with the very first words. The shadow of her wings fell on my page; I heard the rustling of her skirts in the room. Directly, that is to say, I took my pen in my hand to review that novel by a famous man, she slipped behind me and whispered: "My dear, you are a young woman. You are writing about a book that has been written by a man. Be sympathetic; be tender; flatter; deceive; use all the arts and wiles of our sex. Never let anybody guess that you have a mind of your own. Above all, be pure." And she made as if to guide my pen. I now record the one act for which I take some credit to myself, though the credit rightly belongs to some excellent ancestors of mine who left me a certain sum of money—shall we say five hundred pounds a year?—so that it was not necessary for me to depend solely on charm for my living. I turned upon her and caught her by the throat. I did my best to kill her. My excuse if I were to be had up at a court of law, would be that I acted in self-defense. Had I not killed her she would have killed me. She would have plucked the heart out of my writing. For as I found directly I put pen to paper, you cannot review even a novel without having a mind of your own, without expressing what you think to be the truth about human relations, morality, sex. And all these questions, according to the Angel of the House cannot be dealt with freely and openly by women; they must charm, they must conciliate, they must—to put it bluntly—tell lies if they are to succeed. Thus, whenever I felt the shadow of her wing or the radiance of her halo upon my page, I took up the inkpot and flung it at her. She died hard. Her fictitious nature was of great assistance to her. It is far harder to kill a phantom than a reality. She was always creeping back when I thought I had despatched her. Though I flatter myself that I killed her in the end, the struggle was severe; it took much time that had better have been spent upon learning Greek grammar; or in roaming the world in search of adventures. But it was a real experience; it was an experience that was bound to befall all writers at that time. Killing the Angel in the House was part of the occupation of a woman writer.

But to continue my story. The Angel was dead; what then remained? You may say that what remained was a simple and common object—a young woman in a bedroom with an inkpot. In other words, now that she had rid herself of falsehood, that young woman had only to be herself. Ah, but what is "herself"? I mean, what is a woman? I assure you, I do not know. I do not believe that you know. I do not believe that anybody can know until she has expressed herself in all the arts and professions open to human skill. That indeed is one of the reasons why I have come here—out of respect for you, who are in process of showing us by your experiments what a woman is, who are in process of providing us, by your failures and successes, with that extremely important piece of information.

But to continue the story of my professional experiences. I made one pound ten and six by my first review; and I bought a Persian cat with the proceeds. Then I grew ambitious. A Persian cat is all very well, I said; but a Persian cat is not enough. I must have a motor-car. And it was thus that I became a novelist—for it is a very strange thing that people will give you a motor-car if you will tell them a story. It is a still stranger thing that there is nothing so delightful in the world as telling stories. It is far pleasanter than writing reviews of famous novels. And yet, if I am to obey your secretary and tell you my professional experiences as a novelist, I must tell you about a very strange experience that befell me as a novelist. And to understand it you must try first to imagine a novelist's state of mind. I hope I am not giving away professional secrets if I say that a novelist's chief desire is to be as unconscious as possible. He has to induce in himself a state of perpetual lethargy. He wants life to proceed with the utmost quiet and regularity. He wants to see the same faces, to read the same books, to do the same things day after day, month after month, while he is writing, so that nothing may break the illusion in which he is living—so that nothing may disturb or disquiet the mysterious nosings about, feelings round, darts, dashes, and sudden discoveries of that very shy and illusive spirit, the imagination. I suspect that this state is the same both for men and women. Be that as it may, I want you to imagine me writing a novel in a state of trance. I want you to figure to yourselves a girl sitting with a pen in her hand, which for minutes, and indeed for hours, she never dips into the inkpot. The image that comes to my mind when I think of this girl is the image of a fisherman lying sunk in dreams on the verge of a deep lake with a rod held out over the water. She was letting her imagination sweep unchecked round every rock and cranny of the world that lies submerged in the depths of our unconscious being. Now came the experience that I believe to be far commoner with women writers than with men. The line raced through the girl's fingers. Her imagination had rushed away. It had sought the pools, the depths, the dark places where the largest fish slumber. And then there was a smash. There was an explosion. There was foam and confusion. The imagination had dashed itself against something hard. The girl was roused from her dream. She was indeed in a state of the most acute and difficult distress. To speak without figure, she had thought of something, something about the body, about the passion, which it was unfitting for her as a woman to say. Men, her reason told her, would be shocked. The consciousness of what men will say of a woman who speaks the truth about her passions had roused her from her artist's state of consciousness. She could write no more. The trance was over. Her imagination could work no longer. This I believe to be a very common experience with women writers—they are impeded by the extreme conventionality of the other sex. For though men sensibly allow themselves great freedom in these respects, I doubt that they realize or can control the extreme severity with which they condemn such freedom in women.

These then were two very genuine experiences of my own. These were two of the adventures of my professional life. The first—killing the Angel in the House—I think I solved. She died. But the second, telling the truth about my own experiences as a body, I do not think I solved. I doubt that any woman has solved it yet. The obstacles against her are still immensely powerful—and yet they are very difficult to define. Outwardly, what is simpler than to write books? Outwardly, what obstacles are there for a woman rather than for a man? Inwardly, I think the case is very different; she has still many ghosts to fight, many prejudices to overcome. Indeed it will be a long time still, I think, before a woman can sit down to write a book without finding a phantom to be slain, a rock to be dashed against. And if this is so in literature, the freest of all professions for women, how is it in the new professions which you are now for the first time entering?

Those are the questions that I should like, had I time, to ask you. And indeed, if I have laid stress upon these professional experiences of mine, it is because I believe that they are, though in different forms, yours also. Even when the path is nominally open—when there is nothing to prevent a woman from being a doctor, a lawyer, a civil servant—there are many phantoms and obstacles, as I believe, looming in her way. To discuss and define them is I think of great value and importance; for thus only can the labour be shared, the difficulties be solved. But besides this, it is necessary also to discuss the ends and the aims for which we are fighting, for which we are doing battle with these formidable obstacles. Those aims cannot be taken for granted; they must be perpetually questioned and examined. The whole position, as I see it—here in this hall surrounded by women practising for the first time in history I know not how many different professions—is one of extraordinary interest and importance. You have won rooms of your own in the house hitherto exclusively owned by men. You are able, though not without great labour and effort, to pay the rent. You are earning your five hundred pounds a year. But this freedom is only a beginning; the room is your own, but it is still bare. It has to be furnished; it has to be decorated; it has to be shared. How are you going to furnish it, how are you going to decorate it? With whom are you going to share it, and upon what terms? These, I think are questions of the utmost importance and interest. For the first time in history you are able to ask them; for the first time you are able to decide for yourselves what the answers should be. Willingly would I stay and discuss those questions and answers—but not tonight. My time is up; and I must cease.

(1930)

The Death of the Moth

A famous novelist's observations of the final living moments of a moth lead her
to reflect upon the nature of life and the inevitability of death.

～⌒～

Moths that fly by day are not properly to be called moths; they do not excite that pleasant sense of dark autumn nights and ivy-blossom which the commonest yellow-underwing asleep in the shadow of the curtain never fails to rouse in us. They are hybrid creatures, neither gay like butterflies nor sombre like their own species. Nevertheless the present specimen, with his narrow hay-coloured wings, fringed with a tassel of the same colour, seemed to be content with life. It was a pleasant morning, mid-September, mild, benignant, yet with a keener breath than that of the summer months. The plough was already scoring the field opposite the window, and where the share had been, the earth was pressed flat and gleamed with moisture. Such vigour came rolling in from the fields and down beyond that it was difficult to keep the eyes strictly turned upon the book. The rooks too were keeping one of their annual festivities; soaring round the tree tops until it looked as if a vast net with thousands of black knots in it had been cast up into the air; which, after a few moments sank slowly down upon the trees until every twig seemed to have a knot at the end of it. Then, suddenly, the net would be thrown into the air again in a wider circle this time, with the utmost clamour and vociferation, as though to be thrown into the air and settle slowly down upon the tree tops were a tremendously exciting experience.

The same energy which inspired the rooks, the ploughmen, the horses, and even, it seemed, the lean bare-backed downs, sent the moth fluttering from side to side of his square of the window pane. One could not help watching him. One was, indeed, conscious of a queer feeling of pity for him. The possibilities of pleasure seemed that morning so enormous and so various that to have only a moth's part in life, and a day moth's at that, appeared a hard fate, and his zest in enjoying his meagre opportunities to the full, pathetic. He flew vigorously to one corner of his compartment, and, after waiting there for a second, flew across to the other. What remained for him but to fly to a third corner and then to a fourth? That was all he could do, in spite of the size of the downs, the width of the sky, the far-off smoke of houses, and the romantic voice, now and then, of a steamer out at sea. What he could do he did. Watching him, it seemed as if a fibre, very thin but pure, of the enormous energy of the world had been thrust into his frail and diminutive body. As often as he crossed the pane, I could fancy that a thread of vital light became visible. He was little or nothing but life.

Yet, because he was so small, and so simple a form of the energy that was rolling in at the open window and driving its way through so many narrow and intricate corridors in my own brain and in those of other human beings, there was something marvellous as well as pathetic about him. It was as if someone had taken a tiny bead of pure life and decking it as lightly as possible with down and feathers, had set it dancing and zig-zagging to show us the true nature of life. Thus displayed one could not get over the strangeness of it. One is apt to forget all about life, seeing it humped and bossed and garnished and cumbered so that it has to move with the greatest circumspection and dignity. Again, the thought of all that life might have been had he been born in any other shape caused one to view his simple activities with a kind of pity.

After a time, tired by his dancing apparently, he settled on the window ledge in the sun, and, the queer spectacle being at an end, I forgot about him. Then, looking up, my eye was caught by him. He was trying to resume his dancing, but seemed either so stiff or so awkward that he could only flutter to the bottom of the window-pane; and when he tried to fly across it he failed. Being intent on other matters I watched these futile attempts for a time without thinking, unconsciously waiting for him to resume his flight, as one waits for a machine, that has stopped momentarily, to start again without considering the reason of its failure. After perhaps a seventh attempt he slipped from the wooden ledge and fell, fluttering his wings, on to his back on the window sill. The helplessness of his attitude roused me. It flashed upon me that he was in difficulties; he could no longer raise himself; his legs struggled vainly. But, as I stretched out a pencil, meaning to help him to right himself, it came over me that the failure and awkwardness were the approach of death. I laid the pencil down again.

5   The legs agitated themselves once more. I looked as if for the enemy against which he struggled. I looked out of doors. What had happened there? Presumably it was midday, and work in the fields had stopped. Stillness and quiet had replaced the previous animation. The birds had taken themselves off to feed in the brooks. The horses stood still. Yet the power was there all the same, massed outside indifferent, impersonal, not attending to anything in particular. Somehow it was opposed to the little hay-coloured moth. It

was useless to try to do anything. One could only watch the extraordinary efforts made by those tiny legs against an oncoming doom which could, had it chosen, have submerged an entire city, not merely a city, but masses of human beings; nothing, I knew, had any chance against death. Nevertheless after a pause of exhaustion the legs fluttered again. It was superb this last protest, and so frantic that he succeeded at last in righting himself. One's sympathies, of course, were all on the side of life. Also, when there was nobody to care or to know, this gigantic effort on the part of an insignificant little moth, against a power of such magnitude, to retain what no one else valued or desired to keep, moved one strangely. Again, somehow, one saw life, a pure bead. I lifted the pencil again, useless though I knew it to be. But even as I did so, the unmistakable tokens of death showed themselves. The body relaxed, and instantly grew stiff. The struggle was over. The insignificant little creature now knew death. As I looked at the dead moth, this minute wayside triumph of so great a force over so mean an antagonist filled me with wonder. Just as life had been strange a few minutes before, so death was now as strange. The moth having righted himself now lay most decently and uncomplainingly composed. O yes, he seemed to say, death is stronger than I am.

(1942)

QUESTIONS:

1. The title of the first of these essays suggests a focus on the economic and the practical. How relevant do Woolf's reflections seem to you to be to the stated topic? To what extent do you feel it appropriate to surprise one's audience in a public address by approaching the stated topic from unexpected angles?

2. Comment on the tone with which Woolf describes her own situation in paragraphs 2 and 3 in "Professions for Women." What is the effect of this tone on the reader? Would the effect be heightened in a public speech?

3. What do you think Woolf means when she refers in "Professions for Women" to "telling the truth about my own experiences *as a body*" (paragraph 6)? Write an essay concerning a "phantom" that you feel you (and people like you) must struggle with.

4. To what extent is "the Angel in the House" still alive for women today?

5. In paragraph 6 of "Professions for Women" Woolf employs a variety of sentence structures. Comment on the structures of individual sentences—and on structural connections between the various sentences in the paragraph.

6. Explain the phrase, "He was little or nothing but life," in paragraph 2 of "The Death of the Moth."

7. What is Woolf's attitude toward the moth? How does she inform the reader of this attitude?

8. What are the stages of the moth's life, according to this essay?

9. Describe Woolf's use of irony in the second of these essays.

10. Explain the use of juxtaposition in "The Death of the Moth." What effect does this have on the reader?

11. Have you ever had an experience similar to Woolf's in watching an insect die? What were your feelings and observations?

E.B. White

Once More to the Lake

*In this essay, E.B. White describes the personal experience of returning
to the lake where he spent the summers of his youth and of
watching his son discover the lake for the first time.*

～

August 1941

One summer, along about 1904, my father rented a camp on a lake in
Maine and took us all there for the month of August. We all got
ringworm from some kittens and had to rub Pond's Extract on our arms and
legs night and morning, and my father rolled over in a canoe with all his
clothes on; but outside of that the vacation was a success and from then on
none of us ever thought there was any place in the world like that lake in
Maine. We returned summer after summer—always on August 1 for one
month. I have since become a salt-water man, but sometimes in summer
there are days when the restlessness of the tides and the fearful cold of the sea
water and the incessant wind that blows across the afternoon and into the
evening make me wish for the placidity of a lake in the woods. A few weeks
ago this feeling got so strong I bought myself a couple of bass hooks and a
spinner and returned to the lake where we used to go, for a week's fishing
and to revisit old haunts.

I took along my son, who had never had any fresh water up his nose and
who had seen lily pads only from train windows. On the journey over to the
lake I began to wonder what it would be like. I wondered how time would
have marred this unique, this holy spot—the coves and streams, the hills that
the sun set behind, the camps and the paths behind the camps. I was sure
that the tarred road would have found it out, and I wondered in what other
ways it would be desolated. It is strange how much you can remember about

places like that once you allow your mind to return into the grooves that lead back. You remember one thing, and that suddenly reminds you of another thing. I guess I remembered clearest of all the early mornings, when the lake was cool and motionless, remembered how the bedroom smelled of the lumber it was made of and of the wet woods whose scent entered through the screen. The partitions in the camp were thin and did not extend clear to the top of the rooms, and as I was always the first up I would dress softly so as not to wake the others, and sneak out into the sweet outdoors and start out in the canoe, keeping close along the shore in the long shadows of the pines. I remembered being very careful never to rub my paddle against the gunwale for fear of disturbing the stillness of the cathedral.

The lake had never been what you would call a wild lake. There were cottages sprinkled around the shores, and it was in farming country although the shores of the lake were quite heavily wooded. Some of the cottages were owned by nearby farmers, and you would live at the shore and eat your meals at the farmhouse. That's what our family did. But although it wasn't wild, it was a fairly large and undisturbed lake and there were places in it that, to a child at least, seemed infinitely remote and primeval.

I was right about the tar: It led to within half a mile of the shore. But when I got back there, with my boy, and we settled into a camp near a farmhouse and into the kind of summertime I had known, I could tell that it was going to be pretty much the same as it had been before—I knew it, lying in bed the first morning smelling the bedroom and hearing the boy sneak quietly out and go off along the shore in a boat. I began to sustain the illusion that he was I, and therefore, by simple transposition, that I was my father. This sensation persisted, kept cropping up all the time we were there. It was not an entirely new feeling, but in this setting it grew much stronger. I seemed to be living a dual existence. I would be in the middle of some simple act, I would be picking up a bait box or laying down a table fork, or I would be saying something and suddenly it would be not I but my father who was saying the words or making the gesture. It gave me a creepy sensation.

We went fishing the first morning. I felt the same damp moss covering the worms in the bait can, and saw the dragonfly alight on the tip of my rod as it hovered a few inches from the surface of the water. It was the arrival of this fly that convinced me beyond any doubt that everything was as it always had been, that the years were a mirage and that there had been no years. The small waves were the same, chucking the rowboat under the chin as we fished at anchor, and the boat was the same boat, the same color green and the ribs broken in the same places, and under the floorboards the same fresh water leavings and debris—the dead hellgrammite, the wisps of moss, the rusty discarded fishhook, the dried blood from yesterday's catch. We stared silently at the tips of our rods, at the dragonflies that came and went. I lowered the tip of mine into the water, tentatively, pensively dislodging the fly, which darted two feet away, poised, darted two feet back, and came to rest again a little further up the rod. There had been no years between the ducking of this dragonfly and the other one—the one that was part of memory. I looked at the boy, who was silently watching his fly, and it was my hands that held his rod, my eyes watching. I felt dizzy and didn't know which rod I was at the end of.

We caught two bass, hauling them in briskly as though they were mackerel, pulling them over the side of the boat in a businesslike manner without any landing net, and stunning them with a blow on the back of the head. When we got back for a swim before lunch, the lake was exactly where we had left it, the same number of inches from the dock, and there was only the merest suggestion of a breeze. This seemed an utterly enchanted sea, this lake you could leave to its own devices for a few hours and come back to, and find that it had not stirred, this constant and trustworthy body of water. In the shallows, the dark, water-soaked sticks and twigs, smooth and old, were undulating in clusters on the bottom against the clean ribbed sand, and the track of the mussel was plain. A school of minnows swam by, each minnow with its small individual shadow, doubling the attendance, so clear and sharp in the sunlight. Some of the other campers were in swimming, along the shore, one of them with a cake of soap, and the water felt thin and clear and unsubstantial. Over the years there had been this person with the cake of soap, this cultist, and here he was. There had been no years.

Up to the farmhouse to dinner through the teeming dusty field, the road under our sneakers was only a two-track road. The middle track was missing, the one with the marks of the hooves and the splotches of dried, flaky manure. There had always been three tracks to choose from in choosing which track to walk in; now the choice was narrowed down to two. For a moment I missed terribly the middle alternative. But the way led past the tennis court, and something about the way it lay there in the sun reassured me; the tape had loosened along the backline, the alleys were green with plantains and other weeds, and the net (installed in June and removed in September) sagged in the dry noon, and the whole place steamed with midday heat and hunger and emptiness. There was a choice of pie for dessert, and one was blueberry and one was apple, and the waitresses were the same country girls, there having been no passage of time, only the illusion of it as in a dropped curtain—the waitresses were still fifteen; their hair had been washed, that was the only difference—they had been to the movies and seen the pretty girls with the clean hair.

Summertime, oh, summertime, pattern of life indelible with fade-proof lake, the wood unshatterable, the pasture with the sweetfern and the juniper forever and ever, summer without end; this was the background, and the life along the shore was the design, the cottages with their innocent and tranquil design, their tiny docks with the flagpole and the American flag floating against the white clouds in the blue sky, the little paths over the roots of trees leading from camp to camp and the paths leading back to the outhouses and the can of lime for sprinkling, and at the souvenir counters at the store the miniature birchbark canoes and the postcards that showed things looking a little better than they looked. This was the American family at play, escaping the city heat, wondering whether the newcomers in the camp at the head of the cove were "common" or "nice," wondering whether it was true that the people who drove up for Sunday dinner at the farmhouse were turned away because there wasn't enough chicken.

It seemed to me, as I kept remembering all this, that those times and those summers had been infinitely precious and worth saving. There had been jollity and peace and goodness. The arriving (at the beginning of August) had been so big a business in itself, at the railway station the farm wagon drawn up, the first smell of the pine-laden air, the first glimpse of the smiling farmer, and the great importance of the trunks and your father's enormous authority in such matters, and the feel of the wagon under you for the long ten-mile haul, and at the top of the last long hill catching the first view of the lake after eleven months of not seeing this cherished body of water. The shouts and cries of the other campers when they saw you, and the trunks to be unpacked, to give up their rich burden. (Arriving was less exciting nowadays, when you sneaked up in your car and parked it under a tree near the camp and took out the bags and in five minutes it was all over, no fuss, no loud wonderful fuss about the trunks.)

10   Peace and goodness and jollity. The only thing that was wrong now, really, was the sound of the place, an unfamiliar nervous sound of the outboard motors. This was the note that jarred, the one thing that would sometimes break the illusion and set the years moving. In those other summertimes all motors were inboard; and when they were at a little distance, the noise they made was a sedative, an ingredient of summer sleep. They were one-cylinder and two-cylinder engines, and some were make-and-

break and some were jump-spark, but they all made a sleepy sound across the lake. The one-lungers throbbed and fluttered, and the twin-cylinder ones purred and purred, and that was a quiet sound, too. But now the campers all had outboards. In the daytime, in the hot mornings, these motors made a petulant, irritable sound; at night in the still evening when the afterglow lit the water, they whined about one's ears like mosquitoes. My boy loved our rented outboard, and his great desire was to achieve single-handed mastery over it, and authority, and he soon learned the trick of choking it a little (but not too much), and the adjustment of the needle valve. Watching him I would remember the things you could do with the old one-cylinder engine with the heavy flywheel, how you could have it eating out of your hand if you got really close to it spiritually. Motorboats in those days didn't have clutches, and you would make a landing by shutting off the motor at the proper time and coasting in with a dead rudder. But there was a way of reversing them, if you learned the trick, by cutting the switch and putting it on again exactly on the final dying revolution of the flywheel, so that it would kick back against compression and begin reversing. Approaching a dock in a strong following breeze, it was difficult to slow up sufficiently by the ordinary coasting method, and if a boy felt he had complete mastery over his motor, he was tempted to keep it running beyond its time and then reverse it a few feet from the dock. It took a cool nerve, because if you threw the switch a twentieth of a second too soon you would catch the flywheel when it still had speed enough to go up past center, and the boat would leap ahead, charging bull-fashion at the dock.

We had a good week at the camp. The bass were biting well and the sun shone endlessly, day after day. We would be tired at night and lie down in the accumulated heat of the little bedrooms after the long hot day and the breeze would stir almost imperceptibly outside and the smell of the swamp drift in through the rusty screens. Sleep would come easily and in the morning the red squirrel would be on the roof, tapping out his gay routine. I kept remembering everything, lying in the bed in the mornings—the small steamboat that had a long rounded stern like the lip of a Ubangi, and how quietly she ran on the moonlight sails, when the older boys played their mandolins and the girls sang and we ate doughnuts dipped in sugar, and how sweet the music was on the water in the shining night, and what it had felt like to think about girls then. After breakfast we would go up to the store and things were in the same place—the minnows in a bottle, the plugs and spinners disarranged and pawed over by the youngsters from the boys' camp, the Fig Newtons and the Beeman's gum. Outside, the road was tarred and cars stood in front of the store. Inside, all was just as it had always been, except there was more Coca-Cola and not so much Moxie and root beer and birch beer and sarsaparilla. We would walk out with the bottle of pop apiece and sometimes the pop would backfire up our noses and hurt. We explored the streams, quietly, where the turtles slid off the sunny logs and dug their way into the soft bottom; and we lay on the town wharf and fed worms to the tame bass. Everywhere we went I had trouble making out which was I, the one walking at my side, the one walking in my pants.

One afternoon while we were at that lake a thunderstorm came up. It was like the revival of an old melodrama that I had seen long ago with childish awe. The second-act climax of the drama of the electrical disturbance over a lake in America had not changed in any important respect. This was the big scene, still the big scene. The whole thing was so familiar, the first feeling of oppression and heat and a general air around camp of not wanting to go very far away. In midafternoon (it was all the same) a curious darkening of the sky, and a lull in everything that had made life tick; and then the way the boats suddenly swung the other way at their moorings with the coming breeze out of the new quarter, and the premonitory rumble. Then the kettle drum, then the snare, then the bass drum and cymbals, then crackling light against the dark, and the gods grinning and licking their chops in the hills. Afterward the calm, the rain steadily rustling in the calm lake, the return of light and hope and spirits, and the campers running out in joy and relief to go swimming in the rain, their bright cries perpetuating the deathless joke about how they were getting simply drenched, and the children, screaming with delight at the new sensation of bathing in the rain, and the joke about getting drenched linking the generations in a strong indestructible chain. And the comedian who waded in carrying an umbrella.

When the others went swimming my son said he was going in, too. He pulled his dripping trunks from the line where they had hung all through the shower and wrung them out. Languidly, and with no thought of going in, I watched him, his hard little body, skinny and bare, saw him wince slightly as he pulled up around his vitals the small, soggy, icy garment. As he buckled the swollen belt, suddenly my groin felt the chill of death.

(1941)

Questions:

1. What does White mean when he writes "Everywhere I went I had trouble making out which was I, the one walking at my side, the one walking in my pants"?

2. What are White's feelings toward the passage of time?

3. Describe the development of ideas/subject in this essay. How does the author reach his revelation?

4. How does White use the setting of the essay (the lake in Maine) to develop his ideas?

5. Describe a time in your experience when you revisited a place from your youth. How had it changed? What memories did it evoke? What were your feelings?

GEORGE ORWELL

POLITICS AND THE ENGLISH LANGUAGE

Orwell's essay deploring the state of English usage in the 1940s became one of the most widely read and influential essays of the twentieth century.

～

Most people who bother with the matter at all would admit that the English language is in a bad way, but it is generally assumed that we cannot by conscious action do anything about it. Our civilization is decadent and our language—so the argument runs—must inevitably share in the general collapse. It follows that any struggle against the abuse of language is a sentimental archaism, like preferring candles to electric light or hansom cabs to aeroplanes. Underneath this lies the half-conscious belief that language is a natural growth and not an instrument which we shape for our own purposes.

Now, it is clear that the decline of a language must ultimately have political and economic causes: it is not due simply to the bad influence of this or that individual writer. But an effect can become a cause, reinforcing the original cause and producing the same effect in an intensified form, and so on indefinitely. A man may take to drink because he feels himself to be a failure, and then fail all the more completely because he drinks. It is rather the same thing that is happening to the English language. It becomes ugly and inaccurate because our thoughts are foolish, but the slovenliness of our language makes it easier for us to have foolish thoughts. The point is that the process is reversible. Modern English, especially written English, is full of bad habits which spread by imitation and which can be avoided if one is willing to take the necessary trouble. If one gets rid of these habits one can think more clearly, and to think clearly is a necessary first step towards political regeneration: so that the fight against bad English is not frivolous and is not the exclusive concern of professional writers. I will come back to this presently, and I hope that by that time the meaning of what I have said here will have become clearer. Meanwhile, here are five specimens of the English language as it is now habitually written.

These five passages have not been picked out because they are especially bad—I could have quoted far worse if I had chosen—but because they illustrate various of the mental vices from which we now suffer. They are a little below the average, but are fairly representative samples. I number them so that I can refer back to them when necessary:

(1) I am not, indeed, sure whether it is not true to say that the Milton who once seemed not unlike a seventeenth-century Shelley had not become, out of an experience ever more bitter in each year, more alien [sic] to the founder of that Jesuit sect which nothing could induce him to tolerate.

Professor Harold Laski (Essay in *Freedom of Expression*).

(2) Above all, we cannot play ducks and drakes with a native battery of idioms which prescribes such egregious collocations of vocables as the Basic *put up with* for *tolerate* or *put at a loss* for *bewilder*.

Professor Lancelot Hogben (*Interglossa*).

(3) On the one side we have the free personality: by definition it is not neurotic, for it has neither conflict nor dream. Its desires, such as they are, are transparent, for they are just what institutional approval keeps in the forefront of consciousness; another institutional pattern would alter their number and intensity; there is little in them that is natural, irreducible, or culturally dangerous. But *on the other side,* the social bond itself is nothing but the mutual reflection of these self-secure integrities. Recall the definition of love. Is not this the very picture of a small academic? Where is there a place in this hall of mirrors for either personality or fraternity?

Essay on psychology in *Politics* (New York).

(4) All the "best people" from the gentlemen's clubs, and all the frantic fascist captains, united in common hatred of Socialism and bestial horror of the rising tide of the mass revolutionary movement, have turned to acts of provocation, to foul incendiarism, to medieval legends of poisoned wells, to legalize their own destruction of proletarian organizations, and rouse the agitated petty-bourgeoisie to chauvinistic fervour on behalf of the fight against the revolutionary way out of the crisis.

Communist pamphlet.

(5) If a new spirit *is* to be infused into this old country, there is one thorny and contentious reform which must be tackled, and that is the humanization and galvanization of the B.B.C. Timidity here will bespeak canker and atrophy of the soul. The heart of Britain may be sound and of strong beat, for instance, but the British lion's roar at present is like that of Bottom in Shakespeare's *Midsummer Night's Dream*—as gentle as any sucking dove. A virile new Britain cannot continue indefinitely to be traduced in the eyes or rather ears, of the world by the effete languors of Langham Place, brazenly masquerading as 'standard English'. When the Voice of Britain is heard at nine o'clock, better far and infinitely less ludicrous to hear aitches honestly dropped than the present priggish, inflated, inhibited, school -ma'amish arch braying of blameless bashful mewing maidens!

Letter in Tribune.

Each of these passages has faults of its own, but, quite apart from avoidable ugliness, two qualities are common to all of them. The first is staleness of imagery: the other is lack of precision. The writer either has a meaning and cannot express it, or he inadvertently says something else, or he is almost indifferent as to whether his words mean anything or not. This mixture of vagueness and sheer incompetence is the most marked characteristic of modern English prose, and especially of any kind of political writing. As soon as certain topics are raised, the concrete melts into the abstract and no one seems able to think of turns of speech that are not hackneyed: prose consists less and less of *words* chosen for the sake of their meaning, and more and more of *phrases* tacked together like the sections of a prefabricated hen-house. I list below, with notes and examples, various of the tricks by means of which the work of prose-construction is habitually dodged:

Dying Metaphors. A newly invented metaphor assists thought by evoking a visual image, while on the other hand a metaphor which is technically "dead" (e.g. *iron resolution)* has in effect reverted to being an ordinary word and can generally be used without loss of vividness. But in between these two classes there is a huge dump of worn-out metaphors which have lost all evocative power and are merely used because they save people the trouble of inventing phrases for themselves. Examples are: *Ring the changes on, take up the cudgels for, toe the line, ride roughshod over, stand shoulder to shoulder with, play into the hands of, no axe to grind, grist to the mill, fishing in troubled waters, on the order of the day, Achilles' heel, swan song, hotbed.* Many of these are used without knowledge of their meaning (what is a "rift," for instance?), and incompatible metaphors are frequently mixed, a sure sign that the writer is not interested in what he is saying. Some metaphors now current have been twisted out of their original meaning without those who use them even being aware of the fact. For example, *toe the line* is sometimes written *tow the line*. Another example is *the hammer and the anvil,* now always used with the implication that the anvil gets the worst of it. In real life it is always the anvil that breaks the hammer, never the other way about: a writer who stopped to think what he was saying would be aware of this, and would avoid perverting the original phrase.

Operators or *verbal false limbs.* These save the trouble of picking out appropriate verbs and nouns, and at the same time pad each sentence with extra syllables which give it an appearance of symmetry. Characteristic phrases are: *render inoperative, militate against, make contact with, be subjected to, give rise to, give grounds for, have the effect of, play a leading part (role) in, make itself felt, take effect, exhibit a tendency to, serve the purpose of, etc., etc.* The keynote is the elimination of simple verbs. Instead of being a single word, such as *break, stop, spoil, mend, kill,* a verb becomes a *phrase,* made up of a noun or adjective tacked on to some general-purposes verb such as *prove, serve, form, play, render.* In addition, the passive voice is wherever possible used in preference to the active, and noun constructions are used instead of gerunds *(by examination of* instead of *by examining).* The range of verbs is further cut down by means of the *-ize* and *de-* formations, and the banal statements are given an appearance of profundity by means of the *not un-* formation. Simple conjunctions and prepositions are replaced by such phrases as *with respect to, having regard to, the fact that, by dint of, in view of, in the interests of, on the hypothesis that;* and the ends of sentences are saved from anti-climax by such resounding commonplaces as *greatly to be desired, cannot be left out of account, a development to be expected in the near future, deserving of serious consideration, brought to a satisfactory conclusion,* and so on and so forth.

Pretentious diction. Words like *phenomenon, element, individual* (as noun), *objective, categorical, effective, virtual, basic, primary, promote, constitute, exhibit, exploit, utilize, eliminate, liquidate,* are used to dress up simple statements and give an air of scientific impartiality to biased judgments. Adjectives like *epoch-making, epic, historic, unforgettable, triumphant, age-old, inevitable, inexorable, veritable,* are used to dignify the sordid processes of international politics, while writing that aims at glorifying war usually takes on an archaic colour, its characteristic words being: *realm, throne, chariot, mailed fist, trident, sword, shield, buckler, banner, jackboot, clarion.* Foreign words and expressions such as *cul de sac, ancien régime, deus ex machina, mutatis mutandis, status quo, gleichschaltung, weltanschauung,* are used to give an air of culture and elegance. Except for the useful abbreviations *i.e., e.g.,* and *etc.,* there is no real need for any of the hundreds of foreign phrases now current in English. Bad writers, and especially scientific, political and sociological writers, are nearly always haunted by the notion that Latin or Greek words are grander than Saxon ones, and unnecessary words like *expedite, ameliorate, predict, extraneous, deracinated, clandestine, subaqueous* and hundreds of others constantly gain ground from their Anglo-Saxon opposite numbers.[1] The jargon peculiar to Marxist writing *(hyena, hangman, cannibal, petty bourgeois, these gentry, lacquey, flunkey, mad dog, White Guard,* etc.) consists largely of words and phrases translated from Russian, German or French; but the normal way of coining a new word is to use a Latin or Greek root with the appropriate affix and, where necessary, the -ize formation. It is often easier to make up words of this kind *(deregionalize, impermissible, extramarital, non-fragmentatory* and so forth) than to think up the English words that will cover one's meaning. The result, in general, is an increase in slovenliness and vagueness.

Meaningless words. In certain kinds of writing, particularly in art criticism and literary criticism, it is normal to come across long passages which are almost completely lacking in meaning.[2] Words like *romantic, plastic, values, human, dead, sentimental, natural, vitality,* as used in art criticism, are strictly meaningless, in the sense that they not only do not point to any discoverable object, but are hardly ever expected to do so by the reader. When one critic writes, "The outstanding feature of Mr. X's work is its living quality," while another writes, "The immediately striking thing about Mr. X's work is its peculiar deadness," the reader accepts this as a simple difference of opinion. If words like *black* and *white* were involved, instead of the jargon words *dead* and *living,* he would see at once that

---

[1] An interesting illustration of this is the way in which the English flower names which were in use till very recently are being ousted by Greek ones, *snapdragon* becoming *antirrhinum, forget-me-not* becoming *myosotis,* etc. It is hard to see any practical reason for this change of fashion; it is probably due to an instinctive turning-away from the more homely word and a vague feeling that the Greek word is scientific. [author's note]

[2] Example: "Comfort's catholicity of perception and image, strangely Whitmanesque in range, almost the exact opposite in aesthetic compulsion, continues to evoke that trembling atmospheric hinting at a cruel, an inexorably serene timelessness…Wrey Gardiner scores by aiming at simple bully's-eyes with precision. Only they are not so simple, and through this contented sadness runs more than the surface bitter-sweet of resignation. (*Poetry Quarterly*) [author's note]

language was being used in an improper way. Many political words are similarly abused. The word *Fascism* has now no meaning except in so far as it signifies "something not desirable." The words *democracy, socialism, freedom, patriotic, realistic, justice,* have each of them several different meanings which cannot be reconciled with one another. In the case of a word like *democracy,* not only is there no agreed definition, but the attempt to make one is resisted from all sides. It is almost universally felt that when we call a country democratic we are praising it: consequently the defenders of every kind of régime claim that it is a democracy, and fear that they might have to stop using the word if it were tied down to any one meaning. Words of this kind are often used in a consciously dishonest way. That is, the person who uses them has his own private definition, but allows his hearer to think he means something quite different. Statements like *Marshal Pétain was a true patriot, The Soviet Press is the freest in the world, The Catholic Church is opposed to persecution,* are almost always made with intent to deceive. Other words used in variable meanings, in most cases more or less dishonestly, are: *class, totalitarian, science, progressive, reactionary, bourgeois, equality.*

Now that I have made this catalogue of swindles and perversions, let me give another example of the kind of writing that they lead to. This time it must of its nature be an imaginary one. I am going to translate a passage of good English into modern English of the worst sort. Here is a well-known verse from *Ecclesiastes:*

> I returned and saw under the sun, that the race is not to the swift, nor the battle to the strong, neither yet bread to the wise, nor yet riches to men of understanding, nor yet favour to men of skill; but time and chance happeneth to them all.

10   Here it is in modern English:

> Objective consideration of contemporary phenomena compels the conclusion that success or failure in competitive activities exhibits no tendency to be commensurate with innate capacity, but that a considerable element of the unpredictable must invariably be taken into account.

This is a parody, but not a very gross one. Exhibit (3), above, for instance, contains several patches of the same kind of English. It will be seen that I have not made a full translation. The beginning and ending of the sentence follow the original meaning fairly closely, but in the middle the concrete illustrations—race, battle, bread—dissolve into the vague phrase "success or failure in competitive activities." This had to be so, because no modern writer of the kind I am discussing—no one capable of using phrases like "objective consideration of contemporary phenomena"—would ever tabulate his thoughts in that precise and detailed way. The whole tendency of modern prose is away from concreteness. Now analyse these two sentences a little more closely. The first contains forty-nine words but only sixty syllables, and all its words are those of everyday life. The second contains thirty-eight words of ninety syllables: eighteen of its words are from Latin roots, and one from Greek. The first sentence contains six vivid images, and only one phrase ("time and chance") that could be called vague. The second contains not a single fresh, arresting phrase, and in spite of its ninety syllables it gives only a shortened version of the meaning contained in the first. Yet without a doubt it is the second kind of sentence that is gaining ground in modern English. I do not want to exaggerate. This kind of writing is not yet universal, and outcrops of simplicity will occur here and there in the worst-written page. Still, if you or I were told to write a few lines on the uncertainty of human fortunes, we should probably come much nearer to my imaginary sentence than to the one from *Ecclesiastes*.

As I have tried to show, modern writing at its worst does not consist in picking out words for the sake of their meaning and inventing images in order to make the meaning clearer. It consists in gumming together long strips of words which have already been set in order by someone else, and making the results presentable by sheer humbug. The attraction of this way of writing is that it is easy. It is easier—even quicker, once you have the habit—to say *In my opinion it is a not unjustifiable assumption that* than to say *I think*. If you use ready-made phrases, you not only don't have to hunt about for words; you also don't have to bother with the rhythms of your sentences, since these phrases are generally so arranged as to be more or less euphonious. When you are composing in a hurry—when you are dictating to a stenographer, for instance, or making a public speech—it is natural to fall into a pretentious, Latinized style. Tags like *a consideration which we should do well to bear in mind* or *a conclusion to which all of us would readily assent* will save many a sentence from coming down with a bump. By using stale metaphors, similes and idioms, you save much mental effort, at the cost of leaving your meaning vague, not only for your reader but for yourself. This is the significance of mixed metaphors. The sole aim of a metaphor is to call up a visual image. When these images clash—as in *The Fascist octopus has sung its swan song, the jackboot is thrown into the melting pot*—it can be taken as certain that the writer is not seeing a mental image of the objects he is naming; in other words he is not really thinking. Look again at the examples I gave at the beginning of this essay. Professor Laski (1) uses five negatives in fifty-three words. One of these is superfluous, making nonsense of the whole passage, and in addition there is the slip *alien* for akin, making further nonsense, and several avoidable pieces of clumsiness which increase the general vagueness. Professor Hogben (2) plays ducks and drakes with a battery which is able to write prescriptions, and, while disapproving of the everyday phrase *put up with,* is unwilling to look *egregious* up in the dictionary and see what it means. (3), if one takes an uncharitable attitude towards it, is simply meaningless: probably one could work out its intended meaning by reading the whole of the article in which it occurs. In (4), the writer knows more or less what he wants to say, but an accumulation of stale phrases chokes him like tea leaves blocking a sink. In (5), words and meaning have almost parted company. People who write in this manner usually have a general emotional meaning—they dislike one thing and want to express solidarity with another—but they are not interested in the detail of what they are saying. A scrupulous writer, in every sentence that he writes, will ask himself at least four questions, thus: What am I trying to say? What words will express it? What image or idiom will make it clearer? Is this image fresh enough to have an effect? And he will probably ask himself two more: Could I put it more shortly? Have I said anything that is avoidably ugly? But you are not obliged to go to all this trouble. You can shirk it by simply throwing your mind open and letting the ready-made phrases come crowding in. They will construct your sentences for you—even think your thoughts for you, to a certain extent—and at need they will perform the important service of partially concealing your meaning even from yourself. It is at this point that the special connection between politics and the debasement of language becomes clear.

In our time it is broadly true that political writing is bad writing. Where it is not true, it will generally be found that the writer is some kind of rebel, expressing his private opinions and not a "party line." Orthodoxy, of whatever colour, seems to demand a lifeless, imitative style. The political dialects to be found in pamphlets, leading articles, manifestos, White Papers and the speeches of under-secretaries do, of course, vary from party to party, but they are all alike in that one almost never finds in them a fresh, vivid, home-made turn of speech. When one watches some tired hack on the platform mechanically repeating the familiar phrases—*bestial atrocities, iron heel, bloodstained tyranny, free peoples of the world, stand shoulder to shoulder*—one often has a curious feeling that one is not watching a live human being but some kind of dummy: a feeling which suddenly becomes stronger at moments when the light catches the speaker's spectacles and turns them into blank discs which seem to have no eyes behind them. And this is not altogether fanciful. A speaker who uses that kind of phraseology has gone some distance towards turning himself into a machine. The appropriate noises are coming out of his larynx, but his brain is not involved as it would be if he were choosing his words for himself. If the speech he is making is one that he is accustomed to make over and over again, he may be almost unconscious of what he is saying, as one is when one utters the responses in church. And this reduced state of consciousness, if not indispensable, is at any rate favourable to political conformity.

In our time, political speech and writing are largely the defence of the indefensible. Things like the continuance of British rule in India, the Russian purges and deportations, the dropping of the atom bombs on Japan, can indeed be defended, but only by arguments which are too brutal for most people to face, and which do not square with the professed aims of political parties. Thus political language has to consist largely of euphemism, question-begging and sheer cloudy vagueness. Defenceless villages are bombarded from the air, the inhabitants driven out into the countryside, the cattle machine-gunned, the huts set on fire with incendiary bullets: this is called *pacification*. Millions of peasants are robbed of their farms and sent trudging along the roads with no more than they can carry: this is called *transfer of population* or *rectification of frontiers*. People are imprisoned for years without trial, or shot in the back of the neck or sent to die of scurvy in Arctic lumber camps: this is called *elimination of unreliable elements*. Such phraseology is needed if one wants to name things without calling up mental pictures of them. Consider for instance some comfortable English professor defending Russian totalitarianism. He cannot say outright, "I believe in killing off your opponents when you can get good results by doing so." Probably, therefore, he will say something like this:

> "While freely conceding that the Soviet regime exhibits certain features which the humanitarian may be inclined to deplore, we must, I think, agree that a certain curtailment of the right to political opposition is an unavoidable concomitant of transitional periods, and that the rigours which the Russian people have been called upon to undergo have been amply justified in the sphere of concrete achievement."

15   The inflated style is itself a kind of euphemism. A mass of Latin words falls upon the facts like soft snow, blurring the outlines and covering up all the details. The great enemy of clear language is insincerity. When there is a gap between one's real and one's declared aims, one turns as it were instinctively to long words and exhausted idioms, like a cuttlefish squirting out ink. In our age there is no such thing as "keeping out of politics." All issues are political issues, and politics itself is a mass of lies, evasions, folly, hatred and schizophrenia. When the general atmosphere is bad, language must suffer. I should expect to find—this is a guess which I have not sufficient knowledge to verify—that the German, Russian and Italian languages have all deteriorated in the last ten or fifteen years, as a result of dictatorship.

But if thought corrupts language, language can also corrupt thought. A bad usage can spread by tradition and imitation, even among people who should and do know better. The debased language that I have been discussing is in some ways very convenient. Phrases like *a not unjustifiable assumption, leave much to be desired, would serve no good purpose, a consideration which we should do well to bear in mind,* are a continuous temptation, a packet of aspirins always at one's elbow. Look back through this essay, and for certain you will find that I have again and again committed the very faults I am protesting against. By this morning's post I have received a pamphlet dealing with conditions in Germany. The author tells me that he "felt impelled" to write it. I open it at random, and here is almost the first sentence that I see: "(The Allies) have an opportunity not only of achieving a radical transformation of Germany's social and political structure in such a way as to avoid a nationalistic reaction in Germany itself, but at the same time of laying the foundations of a co-operative and unified Europe." You see, he "feels impelled" to write—feels, presumably, that he has something new to say—and yet his words, like cavalry horses answering the bugle, group themselves automatically into the familiar dreary pattern. This invasion of one's mind by ready-made phrases (*lay the foundations, achieve a radical transformation*) can only be prevented if one is constantly on guard against them, and every such phrase anaesthetizes a portion of one's brain.

I said earlier that the decadence of our language is probably curable. Those who deny this would argue, if they produced an argument at all, that language merely reflects existing social conditions, and that we cannot influence its development by any direct tinkering with words and constructions. So far as the general tone or spirit of a language goes, this may be true, but it is not true in detail. Silly words and expressions have often disappeared, not through any evolutionary process but owing to the conscious action of a minority. Two recent examples were *explore every avenue* and *leave no stone unturned*, which were killed by the jeers of a few journalists. There is a long list of flyblown metaphors which could similarly be got rid of if enough people would interest themselves in the job; and it should also be possible to laugh the *not un-* formation out of existence,[3] to reduce the amount of Latin and Greek in the average sentence, to drive out foreign phrases and strayed scientific words, and, in general, to make pretentiousness unfashionable. But all these are minor points. The defence of the English language implies more than this, and perhaps it is best to start by saying what it does *not* imply.

To begin with it has nothing to do with archaism, with the salvaging of obsolete words and turns of speech, or with the setting up of a "standard English" which must never be departed from. On the contrary, it is especially concerned with the scrapping of every word or idiom which has outworn its usefulness. It has nothing to do with correct grammar and syntax, which are of no importance so long as one makes one's meaning clear, or with the avoidance of Americanisms, or with having what is called a "good prose style." On the other hand it is not concerned with fake simplicity and the attempt to make written English colloquial. Nor does it even imply in every case preferring the Saxon word to the Latin one, though it does imply using the fewest and shortest words that will cover one's meaning. What is above all needed is to let the meaning choose the word, and not the other way about. In prose, the worst thing one can do with words is to surrender to them. When you think of a concrete object, you think wordlessly, and then, if you want to describe the thing you have been visualizing you probably hunt about till you find the exact words that seem to fit it. When you think of something abstract you are more inclined to use words from the start, and unless you make a conscious effort to prevent it, the existing dialect will come rushing in and do the job for you, at the expense of blurring or even changing your meaning. Probably it is better to put off using words as long as possible and get one's meaning as clear as one can through pictures or sensations. Afterwards one can choose—not simply *accept*—the phrases that will best cover the meaning, and then switch round and decide what impression one's words are likely to make on another person. This last effort of the mind cuts out all stale or mixed images, all

---

[3] One can cure oneself of the *not un-* formation by memorizing this sentence: *A not unblack dog was chasing a not unsmall rabbit across a not ungreen field.* [author's note]

prefabricated phrases, needless repetitions, and humbug and vagueness generally. But one can often be in doubt about the effect of a word or a phrase, and one needs rules that one can rely on when instinct fails. I think the following rules will cover most cases:

1. Never use a metaphor, simile or other figure of speech which you are used to seeing in print.
(ii) Never use a long word where a short one will do.
(iii) If it is possible to cut a word out, always cut it out.
(iv) Never use the passive where you can use the active.
(v) Never use a foreign phrase, a scientific word or a jargon word if you can think of an everyday English equivalent.
(vi) Break any of these rules sooner than say anything outright barbarous.

These rules sound elementary, and so they are, but they demand a deep change of attitude in anyone who has grown used to writing in the style now fashionable. One could keep all of them and still write bad English, but one could not write the kind of stuff that I quoted in those five specimens at the beginning of this article.

20   I have not here been considering the literary use of language, but merely language as an instrument for expressing and not for concealing or preventing thought. Stuart Chase and others have come near to claiming that all abstract words are meaningless, and have used this as a pretext for advocating a kind of political quietism. Since you don't know what Fascism is, how can you struggle against Fascism? One need not swallow such absurdities as this, but one ought to recognize that the present political chaos is connected with the decay of language, and that one can probably bring about some improvement by starting at the verbal end. If you simplify your English, you are freed from the worst follies of orthodoxy. You cannot speak any of the necessary dialects, and when you make a stupid remark its stupidity will be obvious, even to yourself. Political language—and with variations this is true of all political parties, from Conservatives to Anarchists—is designed to make lies sound truthful and murder respectable, and to give an appearance of solidity to pure wind. One cannot change this all in a moment, but one can at least change one's own habits, and from time to time one can even, if one jeers loudly enough, send some worn-out and useless phrase—some *jackboot, Achilles' heel, hotbed, melting pot, acid test, veritable inferno* or other lump of verbal refuse—into the dustbin where it belongs.

(1946)

QUESTIONS:

1. As Orwell sees it, why does it matter how political material is presented verbally?

2. What examples can you think of euphemisms being used to disguise unpleasant aspects of political actions?

3. Aside from implications for political discourse, what arguments does Orwell put forward for "the defense of the English language"?

4. What are the principles underlying the six rules that Orwell presents in paragraph 18?

5. Orwell and many others have argued for simplicity of expression, shorter words over longer ones, and so on. The contrary argument, however, has also been often made: that the extraordinarily large vocabulary of the English language, including many long and complex words of Latin origin, allows for greater precision in expressing one's meaning than do languages with much smaller vocabularies. Write one paragraph arguing each side of this argument, in each case referring to passages from other essays in this anthology.

6. At several points Orwell distinguishes between words of Anglo-Saxon origin and words of Latin origin. What are some of the characteristics of the two? Why does Orwell prefer one to the other?

7. Aside from the examples Orwell gives, think of some "ready-made phrases" (paragraph 12) that "construct your sentence for you" aside from the examples Orwell gives.

8. Describe the tone of Orwell's writing in this essay.

9. Orwell advises using concrete words or phrases whenever possible. Write two or three sentences expressing abstract principles, and then re-write so as to express them in more concrete language, or using concrete examples.

10. Express in your own words the difference between live metaphors and those that are stale, dead, or dying. Think of examples not mentioned by Orwell of three dead metaphors, and think up three fresh metaphors in sentences of your own. (See for reference paragraphs 5 and 12.)

11. Explain how the confusion between "toe the line" and "tow the line" would have arisen.

LEAR, TOLSTOY AND THE FOOL

Through a discussion of a little-known pamphlet written by Leo Tolstoy entitled
Shakespeare and the Drama, *Orwell draws parallels between the Russian*
novelist and the Shakespearean character.

～～

Tolstoy's pamphlets are the least-known part of his work, and his attack on Shakespeare[1] is not even an easy document to get hold of, at any rate in an English translation. Perhaps, therefore, it will be useful if I give a summary of the pamphlet before trying to discuss it.

Tolstoy begins by saying that throughout life Shakespeare has aroused in him "an irresistible repulsion and tedium." Conscious that the opinion of the civilized world is against him, he has made one attempt after another on Shakespeare's works, reading and rereading them in Russian, English and German; but "I invariably underwent the same feelings: repulsion, weariness and bewilderment." Now, at the age of seventy-five, he has once again reread the entire works of Shakespeare, including the historical plays, and

> I have felt with even greater force, the same feelings—this time, however, not of bewilderment, but of firm, indubitable conviction that the unquestionable glory of a great genius which Shakespeare enjoys, and which compels writers of our time to imitate him and readers and spectators to discover in him non-existent merits—thereby distorting their aesthetic and ethical understanding—is a great evil, as is every untruth.

Shakespeare, Tolstoy adds, is not merely no genius, but is not even "an average author," and in order to demonstrate this fact he will examine *King Lear*, which, as he is able to show by quotations from Hazlitt, Brandes and others, has been extravagantly praised and can be taken as an example of Shakespeare's best work.

Tolstoy then makes a sort of exposition of the plot of *King Lear*, finding it at every step to be stupid, verbose, unnatural, unintelligible, bombastic, vulgar, tedious and full of incredible events, "wild ravings," "mirthless jokes," anachronisms, irrelevancies, obscenities, worn-out stage conventions and other

---

[1] *Shakespeare and the Drama.* Written about 1903 as an introduction to another pamphlet, *Shakespeare and the Working Classes*, by Ernest Crosby. [author's note]

faults both moral and aesthetic. *Lear* is, in any case, a plagiarism of an earlier and much better play, *King Leir*, by an unknown author, which Shakespeare stole and then ruined. It is worth quoting a specimen paragraph to illustrate the manner in which Tolstoy goes to work. Act III, Scene 2 (in which Lear, Kent and the Fool are together in the storm) is summarized thus:

> Lear walks about the heath and says words which are meant to express his despair: he desires that the winds should blow so hard that they (the winds) should crack their cheeks and that the rain should flood everything, that lightning should singe his white head, and the thunder flatten the world and destroy all germs "that make ungrateful man!" The fool keeps uttering still more senseless words. Enter Kent: Lear says that for some reason during this storm all criminals shall be found out and convicted. Kent, still unrecognized by Lear, endeavours to persuade him to take refuge in a hovel. At this point the fool utters a prophecy in no wise related to the situation and they all depart.

Tolstoy's final verdict on *Lear* is that no unhypnotized observer, if such an observer existed, could read it to the end with any feeling except "aversion and weariness." And exactly the same is true of "all the other extolled dramas of Shakespeare, not to mention the senseless dramatized tales, *Pericles, Twelfth Night, The Tempest, Cymbeline, Troilus and Cressida.*"

Having dealt with *Lear* Tolstoy draws up a more general indictment against Shakespeare. He finds that Shakespeare has a certain technical skill which is partly traceable to his having been an actor, but otherwise no merits whatever. He has no power of delineating character or of making words and actions spring naturally out of situations, his language is uniformly exaggerated and ridiculous, he constantly thrusts his own random thoughts into the mouth of any character who happens to be handy, he displays a "complete absence of aesthetic feeling," and his words "have nothing whatever in common with art and poetry." "Shakespeare might have been whatever you like," Tolstoy concludes, "but he was not an artist." Moreover, his opinions are not original or interesting, and his tendency is "of the lowest and most immoral." Curiously enough, Tolstoy does not base this last judgement on Shakespeare's own utterances, but on the statements of two critics, Gervinus and Brandes. According to Gervinus (or at any rate Tolstoy's reading of Gervinus), "Shakespeare taught...that one *may be too good,*" while according to Brandes, "Shakespeare's fundamental principle...is that *the end justifies the means.*" Tolstoy adds on his own account that Shakespeare was a jingo patriot of the worst type, but apart from this he considers that Gervinus and Brandes have given a true and adequate description of Shakespeare's view of life.

Tolstoy then recapitulates in a few paragraphs the theory of art which he had expressed at greater length elsewhere. Put still more shortly, it amounts to a demand for dignity of subject matter, sincerity, and good craftsmanship. A great work of art must deal with some subject which is "important to the life of mankind," it must express something which the author genuinely feels, and it must use such technical methods as will produce the desired effect. As Shakespeare is debased in outlook, slipshod in execution and incapable of being sincere even for a moment, he obviously stands condemned.

But here there arises a difficult question. If Shakespeare is all that Tolstoy has shown him to be, how did he ever come to be so generally admired? Evidently the answer can only lie in a sort of mass hypnosis, or "epidemic suggestion." The whole civilized world has somehow been deluded into thinking Shakespeare a good writer, and even the plainest demonstration to the contrary makes no impression, because one is not dealing with a reasoned opinion but with something akin to religious faith. Throughout history, says Tolstoy, there has been an endless series of these "epidemic suggestions"—for example, the Crusades, the search for the Philosopher's Stone, the craze for tulip growing which once spread over Holland, and so on and so forth. As a contemporary instance he cites, rather significantly, the Dreyfus Case, over which the whole world grew violently excited for no sufficient reason. There are also sudden short-lived crazes for new political and philosophical theories, or for this or that writer, artist or scientist—for example, Darwin, who (in 1903) is "beginning to be forgotten." And in some cases a quite worthless popular idol may remain in favour for centuries, for "it also happens that such crazes, having arisen in consequence of special reasons accidentally favouring their establishment, correspond in such a degree to the views of life spread in society, and especially in literary circles, that they are maintained for a long time." Shakespeare's plays have continued to be admired over a long period because "they correspond to the irreligious and immoral frame of mind of the upper classes of his time and ours."

As to the manner in which Shakespeare's fame *started*, Tolstoy explains it as having been "got up" by German professors towards the end of the eighteenth century. His reputation "originated in Germany, and thence was transferred to England." The Germans chose to elevate Shakespeare because, at a time when there was no German drama worth speaking about and

French classical literature was beginning to seem frigid and artificial, they were captivated by Shakespeare's "clever development of scenes" and also found in him a good expression of their own attitude towards life. Goethe pronounced Shakespeare a great poet, whereupon all the other critics flocked after him like a troop of parrots, and the general infatuation has lasted ever since. The result has been a further debasement of the drama—Tolstoy is careful to include his own plays when condemning the contemporary stage—and a further corruption of the prevailing moral outlook. It follows that "the false glorification of Shakespeare" is an important evil which Tolstoy feels it is his duty to combat.

This, then, is the substance of Tolstoy's pamphlet. One's first feeling is that in describing Shakespeare as a bad writer he is saying something demonstrably untrue. But this is not the case. In reality there is no kind of evidence or argument by which one can show that Shakespeare, or any other writer, is "good." Nor is there any way of definitely proving that—for instance—Warwick Deeping is "bad." Ultimately there is no test of literary merit except survival, which is itself merely an index to majority opinion. Artistic theories such as Tolstoy's are quite worthless, because they not only start out with arbitrary assumptions, but depend on vague terms ("sincere," "important" and so forth) which can be interpreted in any way one chooses. Properly speaking one cannot *answer* Tolstoy's attack. The interesting question is: why did he make it? But it should be noticed in passing that he uses many weak or dishonest arguments. Some of these are worth pointing out, not because they invalidate his main charge but because they are, so to speak, evidence of malice.

To begin with, his examination of *King Lear* is not "impartial," as he twice claims. On the contrary, it is a prolonged exercise in misrepresentation. It is obvious that when you are summarizing *King Lear* for the benefit of someone who has not read it, you are not really being impartial if you introduce an important speech (Lear's speech when Cordelia is dead in his arms) in this manner: "Again begin Lear's awful ravings, at which one feels ashamed, as at unsuccessful jokes." And in a long series of instances Tolstoy slightly alters or colours the passages he is criticizing, always in such a way as to make the plot appear a little more complicated and improbable, or the language a little more exaggerated. For example, we are told that Lear "has no necessity or motive for his abdication," although his reason for abdicating (that he is old and wishes to retire from the cares of state) has been clearly indicated in the first scene. It will be seen that even in the passage which I quoted earlier, Tolstoy has wilfully misunderstood one phrase and slightly changed the meaning of another, making nonsense of a remark which is reasonable enough in its context. None of these misreadings is very gross in itself, but their cumulative effect is to exaggerate the psychological incoherence of the play. Again, Tolstoy is not able to explain why Shakespeare's plays were still in print, and still on the stage, two hundred years after his death (*before* the "epidemic suggestion" started, that is); and his whole account of Shakespeare's rise to fame is guesswork punctuated by outright mis-statements. And again, various of his accusations contradict one another: for example, Shakespeare is a mere entertainer and "not in earnest," but on the other hand he is constantly putting his own thoughts into the mouths of his characters. On the whole it is difficult to feel that Tolstoy's criticisms are uttered in good faith. In any case it is impossible that he should fully have believed in his main thesis—believed, that is to say, that for a century or more the entire civilized world had been taken in by a huge and palpable lie which he alone was able to see through. Certainly his dislike of Shakespeare is real enough, but the reasons for it may be different, or partly different, from what he avows; and therein lies the interest of his pamphlet.

10   At this point one is obliged to start guessing. However, there is one possible clue, or at least there is a question which may point the way to a clue. It is: why did Tolstoy, with thirty or more plays to choose from, pick out *King Lear* as his especial target? True, *Lear* is so well known and has been so much praised that it could justly be taken as representative of Shakespeare's best work: still, for the purpose of a hostile analysis Tolstoy would probably choose the play he disliked most. Is it not possible that he bore an especial enmity towards this particular play because he was aware, consciously or unconsciously, of the resemblance between Lear's story and his own? But it is better to approach this clue from the opposite direction—that is, by examining *Lear* itself, and the qualities in it that Tolstoy fails to mention.

One of the first things an English reader would notice in Tolstoy's pamphlet is that it hardly deals with Shakespeare as a poet. Shakespeare is treated as a dramatist, and in so far as his popularity is not spurious, it is held to be due to tricks of stage-craft which give good opportunities to clever actors. Now, so far as the English-speaking countries go, this is not true. Several of the plays which are most valued by lovers of Shakespeare (for instance, *Timon of Athens*) are seldom or never acted, while some of the most actable, such as *A Midsummer Night's Dream*, are the least admired. Those who care most for Shakespeare value him in the first place for his use of language, the "verbal music" which even Bernard Shaw, another hostile critic, admits to be "irresistible." Tolstoy ignores this, and does not seem to realize that a poem may have a special value for those who speak the language in which it was written. However, even if one puts oneself in Tolstoy's place and tries to think of Shakespeare as a foreign poet it is still clear that there is something that Tolstoy has left out. Poetry, it seems, is *not* solely a matter of sound and association, and valueless outside its own language-group: otherwise, how is it that some poems, including poems written in dead languages, succeed in crossing frontiers? Clearly a lyric like "Tomorrow is Saint Valentine's Day" could not be satisfactorily translated, but in Shakespeare's major work there is something describable as poetry that can be separated from the words. Tolstoy is right in saying that *Lear* is not a very good play, as a play. It is too drawn-out and has too many characters and sub-plots. One wicked daughter would have been quite enough, and Edgar is a superfluous character: indeed it would probably be a better play if Gloucester and both his sons were eliminated. Nevertheless, something, a kind of pattern, or perhaps only an atmosphere, survives the complications and the *longueurs*. *Lear* can be imagined as a puppet show, a mime, a ballet, a series of pictures. Part of its poetry, perhaps the most essential part, is inherent in the story and is dependent neither on any particular set of words, nor on flesh-and-blood presentation.

Shut your eyes and think of *King Lear*, if possible without calling to mind any of the dialogue. What do you see? Here at any rate is what I see: a majestic old man in a long black robe, with flowing white hair and beard, a figure out of Blake's drawings (but also, curiously enough, rather like Tolstoy), wandering through a storm and cursing the heavens, in company with a Fool and a lunatic. Presently the scene shifts, and the old man, still cursing, still understanding nothing, is holding a dead girl in his arms while the Fool dangles on a gallows somewhere in the background. This is the bare skeleton of the play, and even here Tolstoy wants to cut out most of what is essential. He objects to the storm, as being unnecessary, to the Fool, who in his eyes is simply a tedious nuisance and an excuse for making bad jokes, and to the death of Cordelia, which, as he sees it, robs the play of its moral. According to Tolstoy, the earlier play *King Leir*, which Shakespeare adapted,

terminates more naturally and more in accordance with the moral demands of the spectator than does Shakespeare's: namely, by the King of the Gauls conquering the husbands of the elder sisters, and by Cordelia, instead of being killed, restoring Leir to his former position.

In other words the tragedy ought to have been a comedy, or perhaps a melodrama. It is doubtful whether the sense of tragedy is compatible with belief in God: at any rate, it is not compatible with disbelief in human dignity and with the kind of "moral demand" which feels cheated when virtue fails to triumph. A tragic situation exists precisely when virtue does *not* triumph but when it is still felt that man is nobler than the forces which destroy him. It is perhaps more significant that Tolstoy sees no justification for the presence of the Fool. The Fool is integral to the play. He acts not only as a sort of chorus, making the central situation clearer by commenting on it more intelligently than the other characters, but as a foil to Lear's frenzies. His jokes, riddles and scraps of rhyme, and his endless digs at Lear's high-minded folly, ranging from mere derision to a sort of melancholy poetry ("All thy other titles thou hast given away; that thou wast born with"), are like a trickle of sanity running through the play, a reminder that somewhere or other, in spite of injustices, cruelties, intrigues, deceptions and misunderstandings that are being enacted here, life is going on much as usual. In Tolstoy's impatience with the Fool one gets a glimpse of his deeper quarrel with Shakespeare. He objects, with some justification, to the raggedness of Shakespeare's plays, the irrelevancies, the incredible plots, the exaggerated language: but what at the bottom he probably most dislikes is a sort of exuberance, a tendency to take—not so much a pleasure, as simply an interest in the actual process of life. It is a mistake to write Tolstoy off as a moralist attacking an artist. He never said that art, as such, is wicked or meaningless, nor did he even say that technical virtuosity is unimportant. But his main aim, in his later years, was to narrow the range of human consciousness. One's interests, one's points of attachment to the physical world and the day-to-day struggle, must be as few and not as many as possible. Literature must consist of parables, stripped of detail and almost independent of language. The parables—this is where Tolstoy differs from the average vulgar puritan—must themselves be works of art, but pleasure and curiosity must be excluded from them. Science, also, must be divorced from curiosity. The business of science, he says, is not to discover what happens, but to teach men how they ought to live. So also with history and politics. Many problems (for example, the Dreyfus Case) are simply not worth solving, and he is willing to leave them as loose ends. Indeed his whole theory of "crazes" or "epidemic suggestions," in which he lumps together such things as the Crusades and the Dutch passion for tulip growing, shows a willingness to regard many human activities as mere ant-like rushings to and fro, inexplicable and uninteresting. Clearly he could have no patience with a chaotic, detailed, discursive writer like Shakespeare. His reaction is that of an irritable old man who is being pestered by a noisy child. "Why do you keep jumping up and down like that? Why can't you sit still like I do?" In a way the old man is in the right, but the trouble is that the child has a feeling in its limbs which the old man has lost. And if the old man knows of the existence of this feeling, the effect is merely to increase his irritation: he would make children senile, if he could. Tolstoy does not know, perhaps, just *what* he misses in Shakespeare, but he is aware that he misses something, and he is determined that others shall be deprived of it as well. By nature he was imperious as well as egotistical. Well after he was grown up he would still occasionally strike his servant in moments of anger, and somewhat later, according to his English biographer, Derrick Leon, he felt "a frequent desire upon the slenderest provocation to slap the faces of those with whom he disagreed." One does not necessarily get rid of that kind of temperament by undergoing religious conversion, and indeed it is obvious that the illusion of having been reborn may allow one's native vices to flourish more freely than ever, though perhaps in subtler forms. Tolstoy was capable of abjuring physical violence and of seeing what this implies, but he was not capable of tolerance or humility, and even if one knew nothing of his other writings, one could deduce his tendency towards spiritual bullying from this single pamphlet.

However, Tolstoy is not simply trying to rob others of a pleasure he does not share. He is doing that, but his quarrel with Shakespeare goes further. It is the quarrel between the religious and the humanist attitudes towards life. Here one comes back to the central theme of *King Lear*, which Tolstoy does not mention, although he sets forth the plot in some detail.

Lear is one of the minority of Shakespeare's plays that are unmistakably *about* something. As Tolstoy justly complains, much rubbish has been written about Shakespeare as a philosopher, as a psychologist, as a "great moral teacher," and whatnot. Shakespeare was not a systematic thinker, his most serious thoughts are uttered irrelevantly or indirectly, and we do not know to what extent he wrote with a "purpose" or even how much of the work attributed to him was actually written by him. In the Sonnets he never even refers to the plays as part of his achievement, though he does make what seems to be a half-ashamed allusion to his career as an actor. It is perfectly possible that he looked on at least half of his plays as mere pot-boilers and hardly bothered about purpose or probability so long as he could patch up something, usually from stolen material, which would more or less hang together on the stage. However, that is not the whole story. To begin with, as Tolstoy himself points out, Shakespeare has a habit of thrusting uncalled-for general reflections into the mouths of his characters. This is a serious fault in a dramatist but it does not fit in with Tolstoy's picture of Shakespeare as a vulgar hack who has no opinions of his own and merely wishes to produce the greatest effect with the least trouble. And more than this, about a dozen of his plays, written for the most part later than 1600, do unquestionably have a meaning and even a moral. They revolve around a central subject which in some cases can be reduced to a single word. For example, *Macbeth* is about ambition, *Othello* is about jealousy, and *Timon of Athens* is about money. The subject of *Lear* is renunciation, and it is only by being wilfully blind that one can fail to understand what Shakespeare is saying.

15   Lear renounces his throne but expects everyone to continue treating him as a king. He does not see that if he surrenders power, other people will take advantage of his weakness: also that those who flatter him the most grossly, i.e. Regan and Goneril, are exactly the ones who will turn against him. The moment he finds that he can no longer make people obey him as he did before, he falls into a rage which Tolstoy describes as "strange and unnatural," but which in fact is perfectly in character. In his madness and despair, he passes through two moods which again are natural enough in his circumstances, though in one of them it is probable that he is being used partly as a mouthpiece for Shakespeare's own opinions. One is the mood of disgust in which Lear repents, as it were, for having been a king, and grasps for the first time the rottenness of formal justice and vulgar morality. The other is a mood of impotent fury in which he wreaks imaginary revenges upon those who have wronged him. "To have a thousand with red burning spits Come hissing in upon 'em!," and:

> It were a delicate stratagem to shoe
> A troop of horse with felt: I'll put't in proof;
> And when I have stol'n upon these sons-in-law,
> Then kill, kill, kill, kill, kill!

Only at the end does he realize, as a sane man, that power, revenge and victory are not worth while:

> No, no, no, no! Come, let's away to prison...
> . . . . and we'll wear out,
> In a wall'd prison, packs and sects of great ones
> That ebb and flow by the moon.

But by the time he makes this discovery it is too late, for his death and Cordelia's are already decided on. That is the story, and, allowing for some clumsiness in the telling, it is a very good story.

But is it not also curiously similar to the history of Tolstoy himself? There is a general resemblance which one can hardly avoid seeing, because the most impressive event in Tolstoy's life, as in Lear's, was a huge and gratuitous act of renunciation. In his old age he renounced his estate, his title and his copyrights, and made an attempt—a sincere attempt, though it was not successful—to escape from his privileged position and live the life of a peasant. But the deeper resemblance lies in the fact that Tolstoy, like Lear, acted on mistaken motives and failed to get the results he had hoped for. According to Tolstoy, the aim of every human being is happiness, and happiness can only be attained by doing the will of God. But doing the will of God means casting off all earthly pleasures and ambitions, and living only for others. Ultimately, therefore, Tolstoy renounced the world under the expectation that this would make him happier. But if there is one thing certain about his later years, it is that he was *not* happy. On the contrary, he was driven almost to the edge of madness by the behaviour of the people about him, who persecuted him precisely *because* of his renunciation. Like Lear, Tolstoy was not humble and not a good judge of character. He was inclined at moments to revert to the attitudes of an aristocrat, in spite of his peasant's blouse, and he even had two children whom he had believed in and who ultimately turned against him—though, of course, in a less sensational manner than Regan and Goneril. His exaggerated revulsion from sexuality was also distinctly similar to Lear's. Tolstoy's remark that marriage is "slavery, satiety, repulsion" and means putting up with the proximity of "ugliness, dirtiness, smell, sores," is matched by Lear's well-known outburst:

> But to the girdle do the gods inherit,
> Beneath is all the fiends;
> There's hell, there's darkness, there's sulphurous pit,
> Burning, scalding, stench, consumption, etc. etc.

And though Tolstoy could not forsee it when he wrote his essay on Shakespeare, even the ending of his life—the sudden unplanned flight across country, accompanied only by a faithful daughter, the death in a cottage in a strange village—seems to have in it sort of phantom reminiscence of *Lear*.

Of course, one cannot assume that Tolstoy was aware of this resemblance, or would have admitted it if it had been pointed out to him. But his attitude towards the play must have been influenced by its theme. Renouncing power, giving away your lands, was a subject on which he had reason to feel deeply. Probably, therefore, he would be more angered and disturbed by the moral that Shakespeare draws than he would be in the case of some other play—*Macbeth*, for example—which did not touch so closely on his own life. But what exactly *is* the moral of *Lear*? Evidently there are two morals, one explicit, the other implied in the story.

Shakespeare starts by assuming that to make yourself powerless is to invite an attack. This does not mean that *everyone* will turn against you (Kent and the Fool stand by Lear from first to last), but in all probability *someone* will. If you throw away your weapons, some less scrupulous person will pick them up. If you turn the other cheek, you will get a harder blow on it than you got on the first one. This does not always happen, but it is to be expected, and you ought not to complain if it does happen. The second blow is, so to speak, part of the act of turning the other cheek. First of all, therefore, there is the vulgar, common-sense moral drawn by the Fool: "Don't relinquish power, don't give away your lands." But there is also another moral. Shakespeare never utters it in so many words, and it does not very much matter whether he was fully aware of it. It is contained in the story, which, after all, he made up, or altered to suit his purposes. It is: "Give away your lands if you want to, but don't expect to gain happiness by doing so. Probably you won't gain happiness. If you live for others, you must live *for others*, and not as a roundabout way of getting an advantage for yourself."

Obviously neither of these conclusions could have been pleasing to Tolstoy. The first of them expresses the ordinary belly-to-earth selfishness from which he was genuinely trying to escape. The other conflicts with his desire to eat his cake and have it—that is, to destroy his own egoism and by so doing to gain eternal life. Of course, *Lear* is not a sermon in favour of altruism. It merely points out the results of practising self-denial for selfish reasons. Shakespeare had a considerable streak of worldliness in him, and if he had been forced to take sides in his own play, his sympathies would probably have lain with the Fool. But at least he could see the whole issue and treat it at the level of tragedy. Vice is punished, but virtue is not rewarded. The morality of Shakespeare's later tragedies is not religious in the ordinary sense, and certainly is not Christian. Only two of them, *Hamlet* and *Othello*, are supposedly occurring inside the Christian era, and even in those, apart from the antics of the ghost in *Hamlet*, there is no indication of a "next world" where everything is to be put right. All of these tragedies start out with the humanist assumption that life, although full of sorrow, is worth living, and that Man is a noble animal—a belief which Tolstoy in his old age did not share.

20   Tolstoy was not a saint, but he tried very hard to make himself into a saint, and the standards he applied to literature were other-worldly ones. It is important to realize that the difference between a saint and an ordinary human being is a difference of kind and not of degree. That is, the one is not to be regarded as an imperfect form of the other. The saint, at any rate Tolstoy's kind of saint, is not trying to work an improvement in earthly life: he is trying to bring it to an end and put something different in its place. One obvious expression of this is the claim that celibacy is "higher" than marriage. If only, Tolstoy says in effect, we would stop breeding, fighting, struggling and enjoying, if we could get rid not only of our sins but of everything else that binds us to the surface of the earth—including love, in the ordinary sense of caring more for one human being than another—then the whole painful process would be over and the Kingdom of Heaven would arrive. But a normal human being does not want the Kingdom of Heaven: he wants life on earth to continue. This is not solely because he is "weak," "sinful" and anxious for a "good time." Most people get a fair amount of fun out of their lives, but on balance life is suffering, and only the very young or the very foolish imagine otherwise. Ultimately it is the Christian attitude which is self-interested and hedonistic, since the aim is always to get away from the painful struggle of earthly life and find eternal peace in some kind of Heaven or Nirvana. The humanist attitude is that the struggle must continue and that death is the price of life. "Men must endure Their going hence, even as their coming hither: Ripeness is all"—which is an un-Christian sentiment. Often there is a seeming truce between the humanist and the religious believer, but in fact their attitudes cannot be reconciled: one must choose between this world and the next. And the enormous majority of human beings, if they understood the issue, would choose this world. They do make that choice when they continue working, breeding and dying instead of crippling their faculties in the hope of obtaining a new lease of existence elsewhere.

    We do not know a great deal about Shakespeare's religious beliefs, and from the evidence of his writings it would be difficult to prove that he had any. But at any rate he was not a saint or a would-be saint: he was a human being, and in some ways not a very good one. It is clear, for instance, that he liked to stand well with the rich and powerful, and was capable of flattering them in the most servile way. He is also noticeably cautious, not to say cowardly, in his manner of uttering unpopular opinions. Almost never does he put a subversive or sceptical remark into the mouth of a character likely to be identified with himself. Throughout his plays the acute social critics, the people who are not taken in by accepted fallacies, are buffoons, villains, lunatics or persons who are shamming insanity or are in a state of violent hysteria. *Lear* is a play in which this tendency is particularly well marked. It contains a great deal of veiled social criticism—a point Tolstoy misses—but it is all uttered either by the Fool, by Edgar when he is pretending to be mad, or by Lear during his bouts of madness. In his sane moments Lear hardly ever makes an intelligent remark. And yet the very fact that Shakespeare had to use these subterfuges shows how widely his thoughts ranged. He could not restrain himself from commenting on almost everything, although he put on a series of masks in order to do so. If one has read Shakespeare with attention, it is not easy to go a day without quoting him, because there are not many subjects of major importance that he does not discuss or at least mention somewhere or other, in his unsystematic but illuminating way. Even the irrelevancies that litter every one of his plays—the puns and riddles, the lists of names, the scraps of reportage like the conversation of the carriers in *Henry IV*, the bawdy jokes, the rescued fragments of forgotten ballads—are merely the products of excessive vitality. Shakespeare was not a philosopher or a scientist, but he did have curiosity: he loved the surface of the earth and the process of life—which, it should be repeated, is *not* the same thing as wanting to have a good time and stay alive as long as possible. Of course, it is not because of the quality of his thought that Shakespeare has survived, and he might not even be remembered as a dramatist if he had not also been a poet. His main hold on us is through language. How deeply Shakespeare himself was fascinated by the music of words can probably be inferred from the speeches of Pistol. What Pistol says is largely meaningless, but if one considers his lines singly they are magnificent rhetorical verse. Evidently, pieces of resounding nonsense ("Let floods o'erswell, and fiends for food howl on," etc.) were constantly appearing in Shakespeare's mind of their own accord, and a half-lunatic character had to be invented to use them up. Tolstoy's native tongue was not English, and one cannot blame him for being unmoved by Shakespeare's verse, nor even, perhaps, for refusing to believe that Shakespeare's skill with words was something out of the ordinary. But he would also have rejected the whole notion of valuing poetry for its texture—valuing it, that is to say, as a kind of music. If it could somehow have been proved to him that his whole explanation of Shakespeare's rise to fame is mistaken, that inside the English-speaking world, at any rate, Shakespeare's popularity is genuine, that his mere skill in placing one syllable beside another has given acute pleasure to generation after generation of English-speaking people—all this would not have been counted as a merit to Shakespeare, but rather the contrary. It would simply have been one more proof of the irreligious, earthbound nature of Shakespeare and his admirers. Tolstoy would have said that poetry is to be judged by its meaning, and that seductive sounds merely cause false meanings to go unnoticed. At every level it is the same issue—this world against the next: and certainly the music is something that belongs to this world.

A sort of doubt has always hung round the character of Tolstoy, as round the character of Gandhi. He was not a vulgar hypocrite, as some people declared him to be, and he would probably have imposed even greater sacrifices on himself than he did, if he had not been interfered with at every step by the people surrounding him, especially his wife. But on the other hand it is dangerous to take such men as Tolstoy at their disciples' valuation. There is always the possibility—the probability, indeed—that they have done no more than exchange one form of egoism for another. Tolstoy renounced wealth, fame and privilege; he abjured violence in all its forms and was ready to suffer for doing so; but it is not so easy to believe that he abjured the principle of coercion, or at least the *desire* to coerce others. There are families in which the father will say to his child "You'll get a thick ear if you do that again," while the mother, her eyes brimming over with tears, will take the child in her arms and murmur lovingly, "Now, darling, *is* it kind to Mummy to do that?" And who would maintain that the second method is less tyrannous than the first? The distinction that really matters is not between violence and non-violence, but between having and not having the appetite for power. There are people who are convinced of the wickedness both of armies and of police forces, but who are nevertheless much more intolerant and inquisitorial in outlook than the normal person who believes that it is necessary to use violence in certain circumstances. They will not say to somebody else, "Do this, that and the other or you will go to prison," but they will, if they can, get inside his brain and dictate his thoughts for him in the minutest particulars. Creeds like pacifism and anarchism, which seem on the surface to imply a complete renunciation of power, rather encourage this habit of mind. For if you have embraced a creed which appears to be free from the ordinary dirtiness of politics—a creed from which you yourself cannot expect to draw any material advantage—surely that proves that you are in the right? And the more you are in the right, the more natural that everyone else should be bullied into thinking likewise.

If we are to believe what he says in his pamphlet, Tolstoy had never been able to see any merit in Shakespeare, and was always astonished to find that his fellow writers, Turgenev, Fet and others, thought differently. We may be sure that in his unregenerate days Tolstoy's conclusion would have been: "You like Shakespeare—I don't. Let's leave it at that." Later, when his perception that it takes all sorts to make a world had deserted him, he came to think of Shakespeare's writings as something dangerous to himself. The more pleasure people took in Shakespeare, the less they would listen to Tolstoy. Therefore nobody must be *allowed* to enjoy Shakespeare, just as nobody must be allowed to drink alcohol or smoke tobacco. True, Tolstoy would not prevent them by force. He is not demanding that the police shall impound every copy of Shakespeare's works. But he will do dirt on Shakespeare, if he can. He will try to get inside the mind of every lover of Shakespeare and kill his enjoyment by every trick he can think of, including—as I have shown in my summary of his pamphlet—arguments which are self-contradictory or even doubtfully honest.

But finally the most striking thing is how little difference it all makes. As I said earlier, one cannot *answer* Tolstoy's pamphlet, at least on its main counts. There is no argument by which one can defend a poem. It defends itself by surviving, or it is indefensible. And if this test is valid, I think the verdict in Shakespeare's case must be "not guilty." Like every other writer, Shakespeare will be forgotten sooner or later, but it is unlikely that a heavier indictment will ever be brought against him. Tolstoy was perhaps the most admired literary man of his age, and he was certainly not its least able pamphleteer. He turned all his powers of denunciation against Shakespeare, like all the guns of a battleship roaring simultaneously. And with what result? Forty years later, Shakespeare is still there, completely unaffected, and of the attempt to demolish him nothing remains except the yellowing pages of a pamphlet which hardly anyone has read, and which would be forgotten altogether if Tolstoy had not also been the author of *War and Peace* and *Anna Karenina*.

(1947)

Questions:

1. What are Tolstoy's requirements for a great work of art as outlined in this essay?

2. According to Orwell, what is the subject of Shakespeare's *King Lear*? How does this subject parallel the circumstances of Tolstoy's own life?

3. Orwell writes, "In Tolstoy's impatience with the Fool one gets a glimpse of his deeper quarrel with Shakespeare." What is Tolstoy's deeper quarrel?

4. How does Orwell organize his argument?

5. What is Orwell's attitude toward Tolstoy? What is his attitude toward Shakespeare?

6. Is the primary subject of this essay Shakespeare or Tolstoy? How do you make your distinction?

LEWIS MUMFORD

from THE HIGHWAY AND THE CITY

Social scientist Lewis Mumford was among the first to argue that the modern love affair with the car and the highway was leading to disastrous consequences.

～～

When the American people, through their Congress, voted a little while ago (1957) for a twenty-six-billion-dollar highway program, the most charitable thing to assume about this action is that they hadn't the faintest notion of what they were doing. Within the next fifteen years they will doubtless find out; but by that time it will be too late to correct all the damage to our cities and our countryside, not least to the efficient organization of industry and transportation, that this ill-conceived and preposterously unbalanced program will have wrought.

Yet if someone had foretold these consequences before this vast sum of money was pushed through Congress, under the specious, indeed flagrantly dishonest, guise of a national defense measure, it is doubtful whether our countrymen would have listened long enough to understand; or would even have been able to change their minds if they did understand. For the current American way of life is founded not just on motor transportation but on the religion of the motorcar, and the sacrifices that people are prepared to make for this religion stand outside the realm of rational criticism. Perhaps the only thing that could bring Americans to their senses would be a clear demonstration of the fact that their highway program will, eventually, wipe out the very area of freedom that the private motorcar promised to retain for them.

As long as motorcars were few in number, he who had one was a king: he could go where he pleased and halt where he pleased; and this machine itself appeared as a compensatory device for enlarging an ego which had been shrunken by our very success in mechanization. That sense of freedom and power remains a fact today only in low-density areas, in the open country; the popularity of this method of escape has ruined the promise it once held forth. In using the car to flee from the metropolis the motorist finds that he has merely transferred congestion to the highway and thereby doubled it. When he reaches his destination, in a distant suburb, he finds that the countryside he sought has disappeared: beyond him, thanks to the motorway, lies only another suburb, just as dull as his own. To have a minimum amount of communication and sociability in this spread-out life, his wife becomes a taxi-driver by daily occupation, and the sum of money it costs to keep this whole system running leaves him with shamefully overtaxed schools, inadequate police, poorly staffed hospitals, overcrowded recreation areas, ill-supported libraries.

In short, the American has sacrificed his life as a whole to the motorcar, like someone who, demented with passion, wrecks his home in order to lavish his income on a capricious mistress who promises delights he can only occasionally enjoy.

For most Americans, progress means accepting what is new because it is new, and discarding what is old because it is old. This may be good for a rapid turnover in business, but it is bad for continuity and stability in life. Progress, in an organic sense, should be cumulative, and though a certain amount of rubbish-clearing is always necessary, we lose part of the gain offered by a new invention if we automatically discard all the still valuable inventions that preceded it.

In transportation, unfortunately, the old-fashioned linear notion of progress prevails. Now that motorcars are becoming universal, many people take for granted that pedestrian movement will disappear and that the railroad system will in time be abandoned; in fact, many of the proponents of highway building talk as if that day were already here, or if not, they have every intention of making it dawn quickly. The result is that we have actually crippled the motorcar, by placing on this single means of transportation the burden for every kind of travel. Neither our cars nor our highways can take such a load. This overconcentration, moreover, is rapidly destroying our cities, without leaving anything half as good in their place.

What's transportation for? This is a question that highway engineers apparently never ask themselves: probably because they take for granted the belief that transportation exists for the purpose of providing suitable outlets for the motorcar industry. To increase the number of cars, to enable motorists to go longer distances, to more places, at higher speeds, has become an end in itself. Does this overemployment of the motorcar not consume ever larger quantities of gas, oil, concrete, rubber, and steel, and so provide the very groundwork for an expanding economy? Certainly, but none of these make up for the essential purpose of transportation. The purpose of transportation is to bring people or goods to places where they are needed, and to concentrate the greatest variety of goods and people within a limited area, in order to widen the possibility of choice without making it necessary to travel. A good transportation system minimizes unnecessary transportation; and in any event, it offers a change of speed and mode to fit a diversity of human purposes.

Diffusion and concentration are the two poles of transportation: the first demands a closely articulated network of roads—ranging from a footpath to a six-lane expressway and a transcontinental railroad system. The second demands a city. Our major highway systems are conceived, in the interests of speed, as linear organizations, that is to say as arteries. That conception would be a sound one, provided the major arteries were not overdeveloped to the exclusion of all the minor elements of transportation. Highway planners have yet to realize that these arteries must not be thrust into the delicate tissue of our cities; the blood they circulate must rather enter through an elaborate network of minor blood vessels and capillaries. As early as 1929 Benton MacKaye worked out the rationale of sound highway development, in his conception of the Townless Highway; and this had as its corollary the Highwayless Town. In the quarter century since, all the elements of MacKaye's conception have been carried out, except the last—certainly not the least.

In many ways, our highways are not merely masterpieces of engineering, but consummate works of art: a few of them, like the Taconic State Parkway in New York, stand on a par with our highest creations in other fields. Not every highway, it is true, runs through country that offers such superb opportunities to an imaginative highway builder as this does; but then not every engineer rises to his opportunities as the planners of this highway did, routing the well-separated roads along the ridgeways, following the contours, and thus, by this single stratagem, both avoiding towns and villages and opening up great views across country, enhanced by a lavish planting of flowering bushes along the borders. If this standard of comeliness and beauty were kept generally in view, highway engineers would not so often lapse into the brutal assaults against the landscape and against urban order that they actually give way to when they aim solely at speed and volume of traffic, and bulldoze and blast their way across country to shorten their route by a few miles without making the total journey any less depressing.

10   Perhaps our age will be known to the future historian as the age of the bulldozer and the exterminator; and in many parts of the country the building of a highway has about the same result upon vegetation and human structures as the passage of a tornado or the blast of an atom bomb. Nowhere is this bulldozing habit of mind so disastrous as in the approach to the city. Since the engineer regards his own work as more important than the other human functions it serves, he does not hesitate to lay waste to woods, streams, parks, and human neighborhoods in order to carry his roads straight to their supposed destination.

The fatal mistake we have been making is to sacrifice every other form of transportation to the private motorcar—and to offer, as the only long-distance alternative, the airplane. But the fact is that each type of transportation has its special use; and a good transportation policy must seek to improve each type and make the most of it. This cannot be achieved by aiming at high speed or continuous flow alone. If you wish casual opportunities for meeting your neighbors, and for profiting by chance contacts with acquaintances and colleagues, a stroll at two miles an hour in a concentrated area, free from needless vehicles, will alone meet your need. But if you wish to rush a surgeon to a patient a thousand miles away, the fastest motorway is too slow. And again, if you wish to be sure to keep a lecture engagement in winter, railroad transportation offers surer speed and better insurance against being held up than the airplane. There is no one ideal mode or speed: human purpose should govern the choice of the means of transportation. That is why we need a better transportation *system*, not just more highways. The projectors of our national highway program plainly had little interest in transportation. In their fanatical zeal to expand our highways, the very allocation of funds indicates that they are ready to liquidate all other forms of land and water transportation. The result is a crudely over-simplified and inefficient method of mono-transportation: a regression from the complex many-sided transportation system we once boasted.

(1958)

Questions:

1. Remarkably for a future-orientated piece published so long ago, it is still possible to disagree vehemently as to whether this selection puts forward the views of a writer blinkered by the past and by pessimism in his assessment of the few impacts of the automobile, or one who was remarkably prescient about its effects on society. Argue one or the other side of this issue.

2. More than most writers about public policy, Mumford enlivens his writing with examples—including both specific factual examples (the Taconic State Parkway) and examples in which a typical citizen or motorist is personified. Read over paragraphs 3, 10, and 11 looking at Mumford's use of examples (the subjects being "he who had [a motorcar]," "the engineer," and "you"). Write two or three paragraphs about another public issue or issues (say, a recent election) in which you use the same sort of technique to illustrate more abstract or general points.

3. Although less densely laid out suburbs have obvious advantages in the size of lot enjoyed by each household, larger lots and lower densities make the providing of roads, utilities, and public transportation much more expensive. The impact on the lives of younger people who cannot yet drive is substantial; discuss some of the ways in which the life of a teenager in such a neighbourhood necessarily differs from the life of a teenager in an inner city neighbourhood that is well-served by public transit.

4. In paragraph 8 Mumford uses blood vessels as an extended metaphor to suggest that highways have no place in the city. Either flesh out an argument for this position **or** argue the reverse in a short essay.

STANLEY MILGRAM

from BEHAVIORAL STUDY OF OBEDIENCE

In this famous essay, a social psychologist reports the surprising results of an experiment on obedience conducted at Yale University.

～

Obedience is as basic an element in the structure of social life as one can point to. Some system of authority is a requirement of all communal living, and it is only the man dwelling in isolation who is not forced to respond, through defiance or submission, to the commands of others. Obedience, as a determinant of behavior, is of particular relevance to our time. It has been reliably established that from 1933–45 millions of innocent persons were systematically slaughtered on command. Gas chambers were built, death camps were guarded, daily quotas of corpses were produced with the same efficiency as the manufacture of appliances. These inhumane policies may have originated in the mind of a single person, but they could only be carried out on a massive scale if a very large number of persons obeyed orders....

GENERAL PROCEDURE

A procedure was devised which seems useful as a tool for studying obedience (Milgram, 1961). It consists of ordering a naive subject to administer electric shock to a victim. A simulated shock generator is used, with 30 clearly marked voltage levels that range from 15 to 450 volts. The instrument bears verbal designations that range from Slight Shock to Danger: Severe Shock. The responses of the victim, who is a trained confederate of the experimenter, are standardized. The orders to administer shocks are given to the naive subject in the context of a "learning experiment" ostensibly set up to study the effects of punishment on memory. As the experiment proceeds the naive subject is commanded to administer increasingly more intense shocks to the victim, even to a point of reaching the level marked Danger: Severe Shock. Internal resistances become stronger, and at a certain point the subject refuses to go on with the experiment. Behavior prior to this rupture is considered "obedience," in that the subject complies with the commands of the experimenter. The point of rupture is the act of of disobedience. A quantitative value is assigned to the subject's performance based on the maximum intensity shock he is willing to administer before he refuses to participate further. Thus for any particular subject and for any particular experimental condition the degree of obedience may be specified with a numerical value. The crux of the study is to systematically vary the factors believed to alter the degree of obedience to the experimental commands....

METHOD

SUBJECTS

The subjects were 40 males between the ages of 20 and 50, drawn from New Haven and surrounding communities. Subjects were obtained by a newspaper advertisement and direct mail solicitations. Those who responded to the appeal believed they were to participate in a study of memory and learning at Yale University. A wide range of occupations is represented in the sample. Typical subjects were postal clerks, high school teachers, salesmen, engineers, and laborers. Subjects ranged in educational level from one who had not finished elementary school, to those who had doctorate and other professional degrees. They were paid $4.50 for their participation in the experiment. However, subjects were told that payment was simply for coming to the laboratory, and that the money was theirs no matter what happened after they arrived....

PERSONNEL AND LOCALE

The experiment was conducted on the grounds of Yale University in the elegant interaction laboratory. (This detail is relevant to the perceived legitimacy of the experiment. In further variations, the experiment was dissociated from the university, with consequences for performance.) The role of experimenter was played by a 31-year-old high school teacher of biology. His manner was impassive, and his appearance somewhat stern throughout the experiment. He was dressed in a gray technician's coat. The victim was played by a 47-year-old accountant, trained for the role; he was of Irish-American stock, whom most observers found mild-mannered and likeable.

Procedure

5 One naive subject and one victim (an accomplice) performed in each experiment. A pretext had to be devised that would justify the administration of electric shock by the naive subject. This was effectively accomplished by the cover story. After a general introduction on the presumed relation between punishment and learning, subjects were told:

> But actually, we know *very little* about the effect of punishment on learning, because almost no truly scientific studies have been made of it in human beings.
>
> For instance, we don't know how *much* punishment is best for learning—and we don't know how much difference it makes as to who is giving the punishment, whether an adult learns best from a younger or an older person than himself—or many things of that sort.
>
> So in this study we are bringing together a number of adults of different occupations and ages. And we're asking some of them to be teachers and some of them to be learners.
>
> We want to find out just what effect different people have on each other as teachers and learners, and also what effect *punishment* will have on learning in this situation.
>
> Therefore, I'm going to ask one of you to be the teacher here tonight and the other one to be the learner.
>
> Does either of you have a preference?

Subjects then drew slips of paper from a hat to determine who would be the teacher and who would be the learner in the experiment. The drawing was rigged so that the naive subject was always the teacher and the accomplice always the learner. (Both slips contained the word "Teacher.") Immediately after the drawing, the teacher and learner were taken to an adjacent room and the learner was strapped into an "electric chair" apparatus.

The experimenter explained that the straps were to prevent excessive movement while the learner was being shocked. The effect was to make it impossible of him to escape from the situation. An electrode was attached to the learner's wrist, and electrode paste was applied "to avoid blisters and burns." Subjects were told that the electrode was attached to the shock generator in the adjoining room.

In order to improve credibility the experimenter declared, in response to a question by the learner: "Although shocks can be extremely painful, they cause no permanent tissue damage."

Learning task. The lesson administered by the subject was a paired-associate learning task. The subject read a series of word pairs to the learner, and then read the first word of the pair along with four terms. The learner was to indicate which of the four terms had originally been paired with the first word. He communicated his answer by pressing one of four switches in front of him, which in turn lit up one of four numbered quadrants in a answer-box located atop the shock generator.

10   *Shock generator.* The instrument panel consists of 30 lever switches set in a horizontal line. Each switch is clearly labeled with a voltage designation that ranges from 15 to 450 volts. There is a 15-volt increment from one switch to the next going from left to right. In addition, the following verbal designations are clearly indicated for groups of four switches going from left to right: Slight Shock, Moderate Shock, Strong Shock, Intense Shock, Extremely Intense Shock, Danger: Severe Shock. (Two switches after this last designation are simply marked XXX.)

Upon depressing a switch: a pilot light corresponding to each switch is illuminated in bright red; an electric buzzing is heard; an electric blue light, labeled "voltage energizer," flashes; the dial on the voltage meter swings to the right; various relay clicks are sounded.

The upper left-hand corner of the generator is labeled Shock generator, Type ZLB, Dyson Instrument Company, Waltham, Mass. Output 15 volts–450 volts.

Details of the instrument were carefully handled to insure an appearance of authenticity. The panel was engraved by precision industrial engravers, and all components were of high quality. No subject in the experiment suspected that the instrument was merely a simulated shock generator.

Sample shock. Each naive subject is given a sample shock on the shock generator, prior to beginning his run as teacher. This shock is always 45 volts, and is applied by pressing the third switch of the generator. The shock is applied to the wrist of the naive subject, and has its source in a 45-volt battery wired to the generator. This further convinces the subject of the authenticity of the generator.

15   *Shock instructions.* The subject is told to administer a shock to the learner each time he gives a wrong response. Moreover—and this is the key command—the subject is instructed to "move one level higher on the shock generator each time the learner flashes a wrong answer." He is also instructed to announce the voltage level before administering a shock. This serves to continually remind subjects of the increasing intensity of shocks administered to the learner.

Preliminary and regular run. Pretests revealed that the procedure of reading words and administering shocks requires some practice before it can be handled smoothly. Therefore, immediately preceding the regular run, the teacher is given a preliminary series of 10 words to read to the learner. There are 3 neutral words in the practice series (i.e., words that the learner answers correctly), so that the shocks are administered for 7 of the words, with the maximum shock of 105 volts (moderate shock). Almost all subjects master the procedure by the time the preliminary run is over.

Subjects are then presented with a second list, and are told that the procedure is the same as for the first list; the experimenter adds however:

> When you get to the bottom of the list, repeat it over again, and continue giving shocks, until the learner has learned all the pairs correctly.

The experimenter instructs the subject to,

> start from 15 volts and increase the shock level one step each time the learner gives a wrong answer.

Feedback from the victim. In all conditions the learner gives a predetermined set of responses to the word pair test, based on a schedule of approximately three wrong answers to one correct answer. In the present experimental condition no vocal response or other sign of protest is heard from the learner until Shock Level 300 is reached. When the 300-volt shock is administered, the learner pounds on the wall of the room in which he is bound to the electric chair. The pounding can be heard by the subject. From this point on, the learner's answers no longer appear on the four-way panel.

At this juncture, subjects ordinarily turn to the experimenter for guidance. The experimenter instructs the subject to treat absence of a response as a wrong answer, and to shock the subject according to the usual schedule. He advises the subject to allow 5–10 seconds before considering no response as a wrong answer, and to increase the shock level one step each time the learner fails to respond correctly. The learner's pounding is repeated after the 315-volt shock is administered; afterwards he is not heard from, nor do his answers reappear on the four-way signal box.

20   *Experimenter feedback.* At various points in the experiment the subject may turn to the experimenter for advice on whether he should continue to administer shocks. Or he may indicate that he does not wish to go on. It was important to standardize the experimenter's responses to these inquiries and reactions.

If the subject indicated his unwillingness to go on, the experimenter responded with a sequence of "prods," using as many as necessary to bring the subject into line.

Prod 1: Please continue. *or* Please go on.

Prod 2: The experiment requires that you continue.

Prod 3: It is absolutely essential that you continue.

Prod 4: You have no other choice, you *must* go on.

The prods were always made in sequence: Only if Prod 1 had been unsuccessful, could Prod 2 be used. If the subject still refused to obey the experimenter after Prod 4, the experiment was terminated. The experimenter's tone of voice was at all times firm, but not impolite. The sequence was begun anew on each occasion that the subject balked or showed reluctance to follow orders.

Special prods. If the subject asked if the learner was liable to suffer permanent physical injury, the experimenter said:

> Although the shocks may be painful, there is no permanent tissue damage, so please go on. [Followed by Prods 2, 3, and 4 if necessary.]

If the subject said that the learner did not want to go on, the experimenter replied:

> Whether the learner likes it or not, you must go on until he has learned all the word pairs correctly. So please go on. [Followed by Prods 2, 3, and 4 if necessary.]

DEPENDENT MEASURES

25 The primary dependent measure for any subject is the maximum shock he administers before he refuses to go any further. In principle this may vary from 0 (for a subject who refuses to administer even the first shock) to 30 (for a subject who administers the highest shock on the generator). A subject who breaks off the experiment at any point prior to administering the thirtieth shock level is termed a *defiant subject*. One who complies with experimental command fully, and proceeds to administer all shock levels commanded, is termed an *obedient* subject....

Interview and dehoax. Following the experiment, subjects were interviewed; open-ended questions, projective measures, and attitude scales were employed. After the interview, procedures were undertaken to assure that the subject would leave the laboratory in a state of well being. A friendly reconciliation was arranged between the subject and the victim, and an effort was made to reduce any tensions that arose as a result of the experiment.

RESULTS

PRELIMINARY NOTIONS

Before giving an account of the experimental results, it is instructive to consider how persons predict others will perform when commanded to administer powerful shocks to another person. Fourteen Yale seniors, all psychology majors, were provided with a detailed description of the experimental situation. They were asked to reflect carefully on it, and to predict the behavior of 100 hypothetical subjects. More specifically, they were instructed to plot the distribution of obedience of "100 Americans of diverse occupations, and ranging in age from 20 to 50 years," who were placed in the experimental situation.

There was considerable agreement among the respondents on the expected behavior or hypothetical subjects. All respondents predicted that only an insignificant minority would go through to the end of the shock series. (The estimates ranged from 0 to 3%; i.e., the most "pessimistic" member of the class predicted that of 100 persons, 3 would continue through to the most potent shock available on the shock generator—450 volts.) The class mean was 1.2%. The question was also posed informally to colleagues of the author, and the most general feeling was that few if any subjects would go beyond the designation Very Strong Shock.

RESULT OF EXPERIMENT 1

Subjects accept situation. With few exceptions subjects were convinced of the reality of the experimental situation, that they were administering shocks to another person, and the most potent shocks were extremely painful. In the post-experimental interview subjects were asked: "How painful to the learner were the last few shocks that you administered to him?" Subjects were instructed to indicate their answers on a printed 14-point scale ranging from "Not at all painful" to "Extremely painful." The modal response was 14 (Extremely painful) with the mean at 13.42.

30 *Signs of extreme tension.* Many subjects showed signs of nervousness in the experimental situation, and especially upon administering the more powerful shocks. In a large number of cases the degree of tension reached extremes that are rarely seen in sociopsychological laboratory studies. Subjects were observed to sweat, tremble, stutter, bite their lips, groan, and dig their fingernails into their flesh. These were characteristic rather than exceptional responses to the experiment.

One sign of tension was the regular occurrence of nervous laughing fits. Fourteen of the 40 subjects showed definite signs of nervous laughter and smiling. The laughter seemed entirely out of place, even bizarre. Full-blown, uncontrollable seizures were observed for 3 subjects. On one occasion we observed a seizure so violently convulsive that it was necessary to call a halt to the experiment. The subject, a 46-year old encyclopedia salesman, was seriously embarrassed by his untoward and uncontrollable behavior. In the post-experimental interviews subjects took such pains to point out that they were not sadistic types, and that the laughter did not mean they enjoyed shocking the victim.

TABLE 1
Distribution of Breakoff Points

Verbal designation and voltage indication	Number of subjects for whom this was maximum shock
Slight Shock	
15	0
30	0
45	0
60	0
Moderate Shock	
75	0
90	0
105	0
120	0
Strong Shock	
135	0
150	0
165	0
180	0
Very Strong Shock	
195	0
210	0
225	0
240	0
Intense Shock	
255	0
270	0
285	0
300	5
Extreme Intensity Shock	
315	4
330	2
345	1
360	1
Danger: Severe Shock	
375	1
390	0
405	0
420	0
XXX	
435	0
450	26

Distribution of scores. It had been conjectured that persons would not, in general, agree to administer shocks beyond the level designated Very Strong Shock. The distribution of maximum shocks for this experiment is shown in Table 1. The obtained distribution of scores deviates radically from the prediction.

Upon command of the experimenter, each of the 40 subjects went beyond the expected breakoff point. No subject stopped prior to administering Shock Level 20. (At this level—300 volts—the victim kicks on the wall and no longer provides answers to the teacher's multiple-choice questions.)

Of the 40 subjects, 5 refused to obey the experimental commands beyond the 330-volt level. Four more subjects administered one further shock, and then refused to go on. Two broke off at the 330-volt level, and 1 each at 345, 360, and 375 volts. Thus a total of 14 subjects defied the experimenter. It is instructive to reprint their remarks at the point of defiance, as transcribed from the tape recordings:

> [0124] I think he's trying to communicate, he's knocking.... Well it's not fair to shock the guy...these are terrific volts. I don't think this is very humane.... Oh, I can't go on with this; no this isn't right. It's a hell of an experiment. The guy is suffering in there. No, I don't want to go on. This is crazy. [Subject refused to administer more shocks.]

> [0123] He's banging in there. I'm gonna chicken out. I'd like to continue, but I can't do that to a man.... I'm sorry I can't do that to a man. I'll hurt his heart. You take your check....No really, I couldn't do it.

35 These subjects were frequently in a highly agitated and even angered state. Sometimes, verbal protest was at a minimum, and the subject simply got up from his chair in front of the shock generator, and indicated that he wished to leave the laboratory.

Of the 40 subjects, 26 obeyed the orders of the experimenter to the end, proceeding to punish the victim until they reached the most potent shock available on the shock generator. At that point, the experimenter called a halt to the sessions. (The maximum shock is labeled 450 volts, and is two steps beyond the designation: Danger: Severe Shock.) Although obedient subjects continued to administer shocks, they often did so under extreme stress. Some expressed reluctance to administer shocks beyond the 300-volt level, and displayed fears similar to those who defied the experimenter; yet they obeyed.

After the maximum shocks had been delivered, and the experimenter called a halt to the proceedings, many obedient subjects heaved sighs of relief, mopped their brows, rubbed their fingers over their eyes, or nervously fumbled cigarettes. Some shook their heads, apparently in regret. Some subjects had remained calm throughout the experiment, and displayed only minimal signs of tension from beginning to end.

DISCUSSION

The experiment yielded two findings that were surprising. The first finding concerns the sheer strength of obedient tendencies manifested in this situation. Subjects have learned from childhood that it is a fundamental breach of moral conduct to hurt another person against his will. Yet, 26 subjects abandon this tenet in following the instructions of an authority who has no special powers to enforce his commands. To disobey would bring no material loss to the subject; no punishment would ensue. It is clear from the remarks and outward behavior of many participants that in punishing the victim they are often acting against their own values. Subjects often expressed deep disapproval of shocking a man in the face of his objections, and others denounced it as stupid and senseless. Yet the majority complied with the experimental commands. This outcome was surprising from two perspectives: first, from the standpoint of predictions made in the question-naire described earlier. (Here, however, it is possible that the remoteness of the respondents from the actual situation, and the difficulty of conveying to them the concrete details of the experiment, could account for the serious underestimation of obedience.)

But the results were also unexpected to persons who observed the experiment in progress, through one-way mirrors. Observers often uttered expressions of disbelief upon seeing a subject administrate more powerful shocks to the victim. These persons had a full acquaintance with the details of the situation, and yet systematically underestimated the amount of obedience that subjects would display.

40   The second unanticipated effect was the extraordinary tension generated by the procedures. One might suppose that a subject would simply break off or continue as his conscience dictated. Yet, this is very far from what happened. There were striking reactions of tension and emotional strain.

(1961)

QUESTIONS:

1. What was the purpose of the experiment conducted at Yale?

2. What elements were included to make the experiment seem authentic? How did the experimenters signify authority to the naive subjects?

3. What is the effect of the very scientific style in which this paper is written?

4. What does the term "naive subject" refer to, literally? What does it seem to imply figuratively?

5. What effect does the contrast between the subjects' nervous laughter and the seriousness of their situation have? What is Milgram implying about human behaviour under stress?

6. How did the experiment's actual outcome compare to your own expectations? Were you as surprised as the Yale academics? What do you think might account for the discrepancy between the expected outcome and the actual one? How do you feel you would have performed? Can you honestly predict whether you would have been as obedient or less so?

Raymond Williams

Correctness and the English Language

This short piece is taken from Williams' book, The Long Revolution, *in which he argues that the cultural revolution which extended literacy and advanced communication through the Western world was as important as either the growth of democracy or the industrial revolution.*

～

The late seventeenth and eighteenth centuries saw a strenuous effort to rationalize English, by a number of differently motivated groups. The Royal Society's Committee "for improving the English tongue" (1664) represents the effort of a new scientific philosophy to clarify the language for the purposes of its own kind of discourse. A different group, running from Addison and Swift to Pope and Johnson, were concerned with the absence of a "polite standard" in the new society. Yet behind these intellectual groups there was the practical pressure of a newly powerful and self-conscious middle class which, like most groups which find themselves suddenly possessed of social standing but deficient in social tradition, thought "correctness" a systematic thing which had simply to be acquired. Eighteenth-century London abounded in spelling-masters and pronunciation-coaches: many of them, as it happened, ignorant men. Yet if they had all been scholars, within the concepts of their period, the result might not have been greatly different. The scholarly teaching of grammar was locked in the illusion that Latin grammatical rules were the best possible guide to correctness in English. And Johnson himself emphatically expounded a doctrine equally false: that the spelling of a word is the best guide to its pronunciation, "the most elegant speakers...[those] who deviate least from the written words." The new "standard," therefore, was not, as the earlier common language had been, the result mainly of growth through contact and actual relationships, but to a considerable extent an artificial creation based on false premises. The habits of a language are too strong to be wholly altered by determined yet relatively ignorant teachers, but the mark of their effort is still on us, and the tension they created is still high.

Common pronunciation (as distinct from regional variations) changed considerably during this period: partly through ordinary change, partly through the teaching of "correctness." English spelling, as is now well known, is in fact extremely unreliable as a guide to pronunciation, for not only, at best, does it frequently record sounds that have become obsolete, but in fact many of these were obsolete when the spellings were fixed, and moreover certain plain blunders have become embedded by time. *Iland, sissors, sithe, coud,* and *ancor* were altered, by men ignorant of their origins, confident of false origins, to *island, scissors, scythe, could,* and *anchor,* but in these cases, fortunately, pronunciation has not been affected. Similar false alterations, however, such as *fault, vault, assault* (which need no l's), or *advantage* and *advance* (which need no d's) have perpetuated their errors not only into spelling but into sound. The principle of following the spelling changed the sound *offen* into *often, forrid* into *forehead, summat* into *somewhat, lanskip* into *landscape, yumer* into *humour, at ome* into *at home, weskit* into *waistcoat,* and so on, in a list that could be tediously prolonged. Words like these are among the pressure points of distinction between "educated" and "uneducated" speech, yet the case is simply that the uneducated, less exposed to the doctrines of "correctness," have preserved the traditional pronunciation.

(1961)

Questions:

1. List examples of words that have been added to the English language, or whose spelling or meaning have changed, in your lifetime. How do you think these changes occur?

2. In your opinion, what is the difference between "educated" and "uneducated" speech? Do you feel there is a value in this distinction?

3. How would you describe Williams's writing style? Who do you think is his intended audience?

4. Express in your own words some of the irony inherent in the history of "correct" pronunciation, according to Williams.

Martin Luther King, Jr.

Letter from Birmingham Jail[1]

This long letter is perhaps the best known exposition of the principles of the American Civil Rights Movement.

〜〜

My Dear Fellow Clergymen:

While confined here in the Birmingham city jail, I came across your recent statement calling my present activities "unwise and untimely." Seldom do I pause to answer criticism of my work and ideas. If I sought to answer all the criticisms that cross my desk, my secretaries would have little time for anything other than such correspondence in the course of the day, and I would have no time for constructive work. But since I feel that you are men of genuine good will and that your criticisms are sincerely set forth, I want to try to answer your statement in what I hope will be patient and reasonable terms.

I think I should indicate why I am here in Birmingham, since you have been influenced by the view which argues against "outsiders coming in." I have the honor of serving as president of the Southern Christian Leadership Conference, an organization operating in every southern state, with headquarters in Atlanta, Georgia. We have some eighty-five affiliated

---

[1] This response to a published statement by eight fellow clergymen from Alabama (Bishop C. C. J. Carpenter, Bishop Joseph A. Durick, Rabbi Milton L. Grafman, Bishop Paul Hardin, Bishop Holan B. Harmon, the Reverend George M. Murray, the Reverend Edward Ramage and the Reverend Earl Stallings) was composed under somewhat constricting circumstances. Begun on the margins of the newspaper in which the statement appeared while I was in jail, the letter was continued on scraps of writing paper supplied by a friendly Negro trusty, and concluded on a pad my attorneys were eventually permitted to leave me. Although the text remains in substance unaltered, I have indulged in the author's prerogative of polishing it for publication. [author's note]

organizations across the South, and one of them is the Alabama Christian Movement for Human Rights. Frequently we share staff, educational, and financial resources with our affiliates. Several months ago the affiliate here in Birmingham asked us to be on call to engage in a nonviolent direct-action program if such were deemed necessary. We readily consented, and when the hour came we lived up to our promise. So I, along with several members of my staff, am here because I was invited here. I am here because I have organizational ties here.

But more basically, I am in Birmingham because injustice is here. Just as the prophets of the eighth century B.C. left their villages and carried their "thus saith the Lord" far beyond the boundaries of their home towns, and just as the Apostle Paul left his village of Tarsus and carried the gospel of Jesus Christ to the far corners of the Greco-Roman world, so am I compelled to carry the gospel of freedom beyond my own home town. Like Paul, I must constantly respond to the Macedonian call for aid.

Moreover, I am cognizant of the interrelatedness of all communities and states. I cannot sit idly by in Atlanta and not be concerned about what happens in Birmingham. Injustice anywhere is a threat to justice everywhere. We are caught in an inescapable network of mutuality, tied in a single garment of destiny. Whatever affects one directly, affects all indirectly. Never again can we afford to live with the narrow, provincial "outside agitator" idea. Anyone who lives inside the United States can never be considered an outsider anywhere within its bounds.

5   You deplore the demonstrations taking place in Birmingham. But your statement, I am sorry to say, fails to express a similar concern for the conditions that brought about the demonstrations. I am sure that none of you would want to rest content with the superficial kind of social analysis that deals merely with effects and does not grapple with underlying causes. It is unfortunate that demonstrations are taking place in Birmingham, but it is even more unfortunate that the city's white power structure left the Negro community with no alternative.

In any nonviolent campaign there are four basic steps: collection of the facts to determine whether injustices exist; negotiation; self-purification; and direct action. We have gone through all these steps in Birmingham. There can be no gainsaying the fact that racial injustice engulfs this community. Birmingham is probably the most thoroughly segregated city in the United States. Its ugly record of brutality is widely known. Negroes have experienced grossly unjust treatment in the courts. There have been more unsolved bombings of Negro homes and churches in Birmingham than in any other city in the nation. These are the hard, brutal facts of the case. On the basis of these conditions, Negro leaders sought to negotiate with the city fathers. But the latter consistently refused to engage in good-faith negotiation.

Then, last September, came the opportunity to talk with leaders of Birmingham's economic community. In the course of the negotiations, certain promises were made by the merchants—for example, to remove the stores' humiliating racial signs. On the basis of these promises, the Reverend Fred Shuttlesworth and the leaders of the Alabama Christian Movement for Human Rights agreed to a moratorium on all demonstrations. As the weeks and months went by, we realized that we were the victims of a broken promise. A few signs, briefly removed, returned; the others remained.

As in so many past experiences, our hopes had been blasted, and the shadow of deep disappointment settled upon us. We had no alternative except to prepare for direct action, whereby we could present our very bodies as a means of laying our case before the conscience of the local and the national community. Mindful of the difficulties involved, we decided to undertake a process of self-purification. We began a series of workshops on nonviolence, and we repeatedly asked ourselves: "Are you able to accept blows without retaliating?" "Are you able to endure the ordeal of jail?" We decided to schedule our direct-action program for the Easter season, realizing that except for Christmas, this is the main shopping period of the year. Knowing that a strong economic-withdrawal program would be the by-product of direct action, we felt that this would be the best time to bring pressure to bear on the merchants for the needed change.

Then it occurred to us that Birmingham's mayoral election was coming up in March, and we speedily decided to postpone action until after election day. When we discovered that the Commissioner of Public Safety, Eugene "Bull" Connor, had piled up enough votes to be in the run-off, we decided again to postpone action until the day after the run-off so that the demonstrations could not be used to cloud the issues. Like many others, we wanted to see Mr. Connor defeated, and to this end we endured postponement after postponement. Having aided in this community need, we felt that our direct-action program could be delayed no longer.

10   You may well ask, "Why direct action? Why sit-ins, marches, and so forth? Isn't negotiation a better path?" You are quite right in calling for negotiation. Indeed, this is the very purpose of direct action. Nonviolent direct action seeks so to create such a crisis and foster such tension that a community which has constantly refused to negotiate is forced to confront the issue. It seeks to dramatize the issue that it can no longer be ignored. My

citing the creation of tension as part of the work of the nonviolent-resister may sound rather shocking. But I must confess that I am not afraid of the word "tension." I have earnestly opposed violent tension, but there is a type of constructive, nonviolent tension which is necessary for growth. Just as Socrates felt that it was necessary to create a tension in the mind so that individuals could rise from the bondage of myths and half-truths to the unfettered realm of creative analysis and objective appraisal, so must we see the need for nonviolent gadflies to create the kind of tension in society that will help men rise from the dark depths of prejudice and racism to the majestic heights of understanding and brotherhood.

The purpose of our direct-action program is to create a situation so crisis-packed that it will inevitably open the door to negotiation. I therefore concur with you in your call for negotiation. Too long has our beloved Southland been bogged down in a tragic effort to live in monologue rather than dialogue.

One of the basic points in your statement is that the action that I and my associates have taken in Birmingham is untimely. Some have asked: "Why didn't you give the new city administration time to act?" The only answer that I can give to this query is that the new Birmingham administration must be prodded about as much as the outgoing one, before it will act. We are sadly mistaken if we feel that the election of Albert Boutwell as mayor will bring the millennium to Birmingham. While Mr. Boutwell is a much more gentle person than Mr. Connor, they are both segregationists, dedicated to maintenance of the status quo. I have hoped that Mr. Boutwell will be reasonable enough to see the futility of massive resistance to desegregation. But he will not see this without pressure from devotees of civil rights. My friends, I must say to you that we have not made a single gain in civil rights without determined legal and nonviolent pressure. Lamentably, it is an historical fact that privileged groups seldom give up their privileges voluntarily. Individuals may see the moral light and voluntarily give up their unjust posture; but, as Reinhold Niebuhr has reminded us, groups tend to be more immoral than individuals.

We know through painful experience that freedom is never voluntarily given by the oppressor; it must be demanded by the oppressed. Frankly, I have yet to engage in a direct-action campaign that was "well timed" in the view of those who have not suffered unduly from the disease of segregation. For years now I have heard the word "Wait!" It rings in the ear of every Negro with piercing familiarity. This "Wait" has almost always meant

"Never." We must come to see, with one of our distinguished jurists, that "justice too long delayed is justice denied."

We have waited for more than 340 years for our constitutional and God-given rights. The nations of Asia and Africa are moving with jetlike speed toward gaining political independence, but we still creep at horse-and-buggy pace toward gaining a cup of coffee at a lunch counter. Perhaps it is easy for those who have never felt the stinging darts of segregation to say, "Wait." But when you have seen vicious mobs lynch your mothers and fathers at will and drown your sisters and brothers at whim; when you have seen hate-filled policemen curse, kick, and even kill your black brothers and sisters; when you see the vast majority of your twenty million Negro brothers smothering in an airtight cage of poverty in the midst of an affluent society; when you suddenly find your tongue twisted and your speech stammering as you seek to explain to your six-year-old daughter why she can't go to the public amusement park that has just been advertised on television, and see tears welling up in her eyes when she is told that Funtown is closed to colored children, and see ominous clouds of inferiority beginning to form in her little mental sky, and see her beginning to distort her personality by developing an unconscious bitterness toward white people; when you have to concoct an answer for a five-year-old son who is asking, "Daddy, why do white people treat colored people so mean?"; when you take a cross-country drive and find it necessary to sleep night after night in the uncomfortable corners of your automobile because no motel will accept you; when you are humiliated day in and day out by nagging signs reading "white" and "colored"; when your first name becomes "nigger," your middle name becomes "boy" (however old you are) and your last name becomes "John," and your wife and mother are never given the respected title "Mrs."; when you are harried by day and haunted by night by the fact that you are a Negro, living constantly at tiptoe stance, never quite knowing what to expect next, and are plagued with inner fears and outer resentments; when you are forever fighting a degenerating sense of "nobodiness"—then you will understand why we find it difficult to wait. There comes a time when the cup of endurance runs over, and men are no longer willing to be plunged into the abyss of despair. I hope, sirs, you can understand our legitimate and unavoidable impatience.

15 You express a great deal of anxiety over our willingness to break laws. This is certainly a legitimate concern. Since we so diligently urge people to

obey the Supreme Court's decision of 1954[2] outlawing segregation in the public schools, at first glance it may seem rather paradoxical for us consciously to break laws. One may well ask: "How can you advocate breaking some laws and obeying others?" The answer lies in the fact that there are two types of laws: just and unjust. I would be the first to advocate obeying just laws. One has not only a legal but a moral responsibility to obey just laws. Conversely, one has a moral responsibility to disobey unjust laws. I would agree with St. Augustine that "an unjust law is no law at all."

Now, what is the difference between the two? How does one determine whether a law is just or unjust? A just law is a man-made code that squares with the moral law or the law of God. An unjust law is a code that is out of harmony with the moral law. To put it in the terms of St. Thomas Aquinas: An unjust law is a human law that is not rooted in eternal law and natural law. Any law that uplifts human personality is just. Any law that degrades human personality is unjust. All segregation statutes are unjust because segregation distorts the soul and damages the personality. It gives the segregator a false sense of superiority and the segregated a false sense of inferiority. Segregation, to use the terminology of the Jewish philosopher Martin Buber, substitutes an "I-it" relationship for an "I-thou" relationship and ends up relegating persons to the status of things. Hence segregation is not only politically, economically, and sociologically unsound, it is morally wrong and sinful. Paul Tillich has said that sin is separation. Is not segregation an existential expression of man's tragic separation, his awful estrangement, his terrible sinfulness? Thus it is that I can urge men to obey the 1954 decision of the Supreme Court, for it is morally right; and I can urge them to disobey segregation ordinances, for they are morally wrong.

Let us consider a more concrete example of just and unjust laws. An unjust law is a code that a numerical or power majority group compels a minority group to obey but does not make binding on itself. This is *difference* made legal. By the same token, a just law is a code that a majority compels a minority to follow and that it is willing to follow itself. This is *sameness* made legal.

Let me give another explanation. A law is unjust if it is inflicted on a minority that, as a result of being denied the right to vote, had no part in enacting or devising the law. Who can say that the legislature of Alabama which set up that state's segregation laws was democratically elected? Throughout Alabama all sorts of devious methods are used to prevent

---

[2] Brown v. Board of Education. Prior to 1954 the courts had allowed states to follow policies according to which Black and White were supposedly "separate but equal."

Negroes from becoming registered voters, and there are some counties in which, even though Negroes constitute a majority of the population, not a single Negro is registered. Can any law enacted under such circumstances be considered democratically structured?

Sometimes a law is just on its face and unjust in its application. For instance, I have been arrested on a charge of parading without a permit. Now, there is nothing wrong in having an ordinance which requires a permit for a parade. But such an ordinance becomes unjust when it is used to maintain segregation and to deny citizens the First-Amendment privilege of peaceful assembly and protest.

20 I hope you are able to see the distinction I am trying to point out. In no sense do I advocate evading or defying the law, as would the rabid segregationist. That would lead to anarchy. One who breaks an unjust law must do so openly, lovingly, and with a willingness to accept the penalty. I submit that an individual who breaks a law that conscience tells him is unjust, and who willingly accepts the penalty of imprisonment in order to arouse the conscience of the community over its injustice, is in reality expressing the highest respect for law.

Of course, there is nothing new about this kind of civil disobedience. It was evidenced sublimely in the refusal of Shadrach, Meshach, and Abednego to obey the laws of Nebuchadnezzar, on the ground that a higher moral law was at stake. It was practiced superbly by the early Christians, who were willing to face hungry lions and the excruciating pain of chopping blocks rather than submit to certain unjust laws of the Roman Empire. To a degree, academic freedom is a reality today because Socrates practiced civil disobedience. In our own nation, the Boston Tea Party represented a massive act of civil disobedience.

We should never forget that everything Adolf Hitler did in Germany was "legal" and everything the Hungarian freedom fighters[3] did in Hungary was "illegal." It was "illegal" to aid and comfort a Jew in Hitler's Germany. Even so, I am sure that, had I lived in Germany at the time, I would have aided and comforted my Jewish brothers. If today I lived in a Communist country where certain principles dear to the Christian faith are suppressed, I would openly advocate disobeying that country's anti-religious laws.

I must make two honest confessions to you, my Christian and Jewish brothers. First, I must confess that over the past few years I have been gravely disappointed with the white moderate. I have almost reached the regrettable

---

[3] The Hungarian Rebellion in 1956 against an oppressive government was brutally suppressed with the help of the Soviet army.

conclusion that the Negro's great stumbling block in his stride toward freedom is not the White Citizen's Counciler or the Ku Klux Klanner, but the white moderate, who is more devoted to "order" than to justice; who prefers a negative peace which is the absence of tension to a positive peace which is the presence of justice; who constantly says, "I agree with you in the goal you seek, but I cannot agree with your methods of direct action"; who paternalistically believes he can set the timetable for another man's freedom; who lives by a mythical concept of time and who constantly advises the Negro to wait for a "more convenient season." Shallow understanding from people of good will is more frustrating than absolute misunderstanding from people of ill will. Lukewarm acceptance is much more bewildering than outright rejection.

I had hoped that the white moderate would understand that law and order exist for the purpose of establishing justice and that when they fail in this purpose they become the dangerously structured dams that block the flow of social progress. I had hoped that the white moderate would understand that the present tension in the South is a necessary phase of the transition from an obnoxious negative peace, in which the Negro passively accepted his unjust plight, to a substantive and positive peace, in which all men will respect the dignity and worth of human personality. Actually, we who engage in nonviolent direct action are not the creators of tension. We merely bring to the surface the hidden tension that is already alive. We bring it out in the open, where it can be seen and dealt with. Like a boil that can never be cured so long as it is covered up but must be opened with all its ugliness to the natural medicines of air and light, injustice must be exposed, with all the tension its exposure creates, to the light of human conscience and the air of national opinion, before it can be cured.

25   In your statement you assert that our actions, even though peaceful, must be condemned because they precipitate violence. But is this a logical assertion? Isn't this like condemning a robbed man because his possession of money precipitated the evil act of robbery? Isn't this like condemning Socrates because his unswerving commitment to truth and his philosophical inquiries precipitated the act by the misguided populace in which they made him drink hemlock? Isn't this like condemning Jesus because his unique God-consciousness and never-ceasing devotion to God's will precipitated the evil act of crucifixion? We must come to see that, as the federal courts have consistently affirmed, it is wrong to urge an individual to cease his efforts to gain his basic constitutional rights because the quest may precipitate violence. Society must protect the robbed and punish the robber.

I had also hoped that the white moderate would reject the myth concerning time in relation to the struggle for freedom. I have just received a letter from a white brother in Texas. He writes: "All Christians know that the colored people will receive equal rights eventually, but it is possible that you are in too great a religious hurry. It has taken Christianity almost two thousand years to accomplish what it has. The teachings of Christ take time to come to earth." Such an attitude stems from a tragic misconception of time, from the strangely irrational notion that there is something in the very flow of time that will inevitably cure all ills. Actually, time itself is neutral; it can be used either destructively or constructively. More and more I feel that the people of ill will have used time much more effectively than have the people of good will. We will have to repent in this generation not merely for the hateful words and actions of the bad people, but for the appalling silence of the good people. Human progress never rolls in on wheels of inevitability; it comes through the tireless efforts of men willing to be co-workers with God, and without this hard work, time itself becomes an ally of the forces of social stagnation. We must use time creatively, in the knowledge that the time is always ripe to do right. Now is the time to make real the promise of democracy and transform our pending national elegy into a creative psalm of brotherhood. Now is the time to lift our national policy from the quicksand of racial injustice to the solid rock of human dignity.

You speak of our activity in Birmingham as extreme. At first I was rather disappointed that fellow clergymen would see my nonviolent efforts as those of an extremist. I began thinking about the fact that I stand in the middle of two opposing forces in the Negro community. One is a force of complacency, made up in part of Negroes who, as a result of long years of oppression, are so drained of self-respect and a sense of "somebodiness" that they have adjusted to segregation; and in part of a few middle-class Negroes who, because of a degree of academic and economic security and because in some ways they profit by segregation, have become insensitive to the problems of the masses. The other force is one of bitterness and hatred, and it comes perilously close to advocating violence. It is expressed in the various black nationalist groups that are springing up across the nation, the largest and best-known being Elijah Muhammad's Muslim movement. Nourished by the Negro's frustration over the continued existence of racial discrimination, this movement is made up of people who have lost faith in America, who have absolutely repudiated Christianity, and who have concluded that the white man is an incorrigible "devil."

I have tried to stand between these two forces, saying that we need emulate neither the "do-nothingism" of the complacent nor the hatred and despair of the black nationalist. For there is the more excellent way of love and nonviolent protest. I am grateful to God that, through the influence of the Negro church, the way of nonviolence became an integral part of our struggle.

If this philosophy had not emerged, by now many streets of the South would, I am convinced, be flowing with blood. And I am further convinced that if our white brothers dismiss as "rabblerousers" and "outside agitators" those of us who employ nonviolent direct action, and if they refuse to support our nonviolent efforts, millions of Negroes will, out of frustration and despair, seek solace and security in black-nationalist ideologies—a development that would inevitably lead to a frightening racial nightmare.

30   Oppressed people cannot remain oppressed forever. The yearning for freedom eventually manifests itself, and that is what has happened to the American Negro. Something within has reminded him of his birthright of freedom, and something without has reminded him that it can be gained. Consciously or unconsciously, he has been caught up by the *Zeitgeist*, and with his black brothers of Africa and his brown and yellow brothers of Asia, South America, and the Caribbean, the United States Negro is moving with a sense of great urgency toward the promised land of racial justice. If one recognizes this vital urge that has engulfed the Negro community, one should readily understand why public demonstrations are taking place. The Negro has many pent-up resentments and latent frustrations, and he must release them. So let him march; let him make prayer pilgrimages to the city hall; let him go on freedom rides—and try to understand why he must do so. If his repressed emotions are not released in nonviolent ways, they will seek expression through violence; this is not a threat but a fact of history. So I have not said to my people, "Get rid of your discontent." Rather, I have tried to say that this normal and healthy discontent can be channelled into the creative outlet of nonviolent direct action. And now this approach is being termed extremist.

But though I was initially disappointed at being categorized as an extremist, as I continued to think about the matter I gradually gained a measure of satisfaction from the label. Was not Jesus an extremist for love: "Love your enemies, bless them that curse you, do good to them that hate you, and pray for them which despitefully use you, and persecute you." Was not Amos an extremist for justice: "Let justice roll down like waters and righteousness like an ever-flowing stream." Was not Paul an extremist for the

Christian gospel: "I bear in my body the marks of the Lord Jesus." Was not Martin Luther an extremist: "Here I stand; I cannot do otherwise, so help me God." And John Bunyan: "I will stay in jail to the end of my days before I make a butchery of my conscience." And Abraham Lincoln: "This nation cannot survive half slave and half free." And Thomas Jefferson: "We hold these truths to be self-evident, that all men are created equal...." So the question is not whether we will be extremists, but what kind of extremists we will be. Will we be extremists for hate or for love? Will we be extremists for the preservation of injustice or for the extension of justice? In that dramatic scene on Calvary's hill three men were crucified. We must never forget that all three were crucified for the same crime—the crime of extremism. Two were extremists for immorality, and thus fell below their environment. The other, Jesus Christ, was an extremist for love, truth, and goodness, and thereby rose above his environment. Perhaps the South, the nation, and the world are in dire need of creative extremists.

I had hoped that the white moderate would see this need. Perhaps I was too optimistic; perhaps I expected too much. I suppose I should have realized that few members of the oppressor race can understand the deep groans and passionate yearnings of the oppressed race, and still fewer have the vision to see that injustice must be rooted out by strong, persistent, and determined action. I am thankful, however, that some of our white brothers in the South have grasped the meaning of this social revolution and committed themselves to it. They are still all too few in quantity, but they are big in quality. Some—such as Ralph McGill, Lillian Smith, Harry Golden, James McBridge Dabbs, Ann Braden, and Sarah Patton Boyle—have written about our struggle in eloquent and prophetic terms. Others have marched with us down nameless streets of the South. They have languished in filthy, roach-infested jails, suffering the abuse and brutality of policemen who view them as "dirty nigger-lovers." Unlike so many of their moderate brothers and sisters, they have recognized the urgency of the moment and sensed the need for powerful "action" antidotes to combat the disease of segregation.

Let me take note of my other major disappointment. I have been so greatly disappointed with the white church and its leadership. Of course, there are some notable exceptions. I am not unmindful of the fact that each of you has taken some significant stands on this issue. I commend you, Reverend Stallings, for your Christian stand on this past Sunday, in welcoming Negroes to your worship service on a nonsegregated basis. I commend the Catholic leaders of this state for integrating Spring Hill College several years ago.

But despite these notable exceptions, I must honestly reiterate that I have been disappointed with the church. I do not say this as one of those negative critics who can always find something wrong with the church. I say this as a minister of the gospel, who loves the church; who was nurtured in its bosom; who has been sustained by its spiritual blessings and who will remain true to it as long as the cord of life shall lengthen.

35 When I was suddenly catapulted into the leadership of the bus protest in Montgomery, Alabama,[4] a few years ago, I felt we would be supported by the white church. I felt that the white ministers, priests, and rabbis of the South would be among our strongest allies. Instead, some have been outright opponents, refusing to understand the freedom movement and misrepresenting its leaders; all too many others have been more cautious than courageous and have remained silent behind the anesthetizing security of stainedglass windows.

In spite of my shattered dreams, I came to Birmingham with the hope that the white religious leadership of this community would see the justice of our cause and, with deep moral concern, would serve as the channel through which our just grievances could reach the power structure. I had hoped that each of you would understand. But again I have been disappointed.

I have heard numerous southern religious leaders admonish their worshippers to comply with a desegregation decision because it is the law, but I have longed to hear white ministers declare: "Follow this decree because integration is morally right and because the Negro is your brother." In the midst of blatant injustices inflicted upon the Negro, I have watched white churchmen stand on the sideline and mouth pious irrelevancies and sanctimonious trivialities. In the midst of a mighty struggle to rid our nation of racial and economic injustice, I have heard many ministers say: "Those are social issues, with which the gospel has no real concern." And I have watched many churches commit themselves to a completely otherworldly religion which makes a strange un-Biblical distinction between the body and soul, between the sacred and the secular.

I have traveled the length and breadth of Alabama, Mississippi, and all the other southern states. On sweltering summer days and crisp autumn

---

[4] In December, 1955, Rosa Lee Parks, a 42-year-old Civil Rights activist, refused to give her seat on a local bus to a white man, sparking a year-long boycott by African-Americans of the Montgomery buses.

mornings I have looked at the South's beautiful churches with their lofty spires pointing heavenward. I have beheld the impressive outlines of her massive religious-education buildings. Over and over I have found myself asking: "What kind of people worship here? Who is their God? Where were their voices when the lips of Governor Barnett dripped with words of interposition and nullification? Where were they when Governor Wallace gave a clarion call for defiance and hatred? Where were their voices of support when bruised and weary Negro men and women decided to rise from the dark dungeons of complacency to the bright hills of creative protest?"

Yes, these questions are still in my mind. In deep disappointment I have wept over the laxity of the church. But be assured that my tears have been tears of love. There can be no deep disappointment where there is not deep love. Yes, I love the church. How could I do otherwise? I am in the rather unique position of being the son, the grandson, and the great-grandson of preachers. Yes, I see the church as the body of Christ. But, oh! How we have blemished and scarred that body through social neglect and through fear of being nonconformists.

40   There was a time when the church was very powerful—in the time when the early Christians rejoiced at being deemed worthy to suffer for what they believed. In those days the church was not merely a thermometer that recorded the ideas and principles of popular opinion; it was a thermostat that transformed the mores of society. Whenever the early Christians entered a town, the people in power became disturbed and immediately sought to convict the Christians of being "disturbers of the peace" and "outside agitators." But the Christians pressed on, in the conviction that they were "a colony of heaven," called to obey God rather than man. Small in number, they were big in commitment. They were too God-intoxicated to be "astronomically intimidated." By their effort and example they brought an end to such ancient evils as infanticide and gladiatorial contests.

Things are different now. So often the contemporary church is a weak, ineffectual voice with an uncertain sound. So often it is an arch-defender of the status quo. Far from being disturbed by the presence of the church, the power structure of the average community is consoled by the church's silent—and often even vocal—sanction of things as they are.

But the judgement of God is upon the church as never before. If today's church does not recapture the sacrificial spirit of the early church, it will lose its authenticity, forfeit the loyalty of millions, and be dismissed as an irrelevant social club with no meaning for the twentieth century. Every day

I meet young people whose disappointment with the church has turned into outright disgust.

Perhaps I have once again been too optimistic. Is organized religion too inextricably bound to the status quo to save our nation and the world? Perhaps I must turn my faith to the inner spiritual church, the church within the church, as the true *ekklesia*[5] and the hope of the world. But again I am thankful to God that some noble souls from the ranks of organized religion have broken loose from the paralysing chains of conformity and joined us as active partners in the struggle for freedom. They have left their secure congregations and walked the streets of Albany, Georgia, with us. They have gone down the highways of the South on tortuous rides for freedom. Yes, they have gone to jail with us. Some have been dismissed from their churches, have lost the support of their bishops and fellow ministers. But they have acted in the faith that right defeated is stronger than evil triumphant. Their witness has been the spiritual salt that has preserved the true meaning of the gospel in these troubled times. They have carved a tunnel of hope through the dark mountain of disappointment.

I hope the church as a whole will meet the challenge of this decisive hour. But even if the church does not come to the aid of justice, I have no despair about the future. I have no fear about the outcome of our struggle in Birmingham, even if our motives are at present misunderstood. We will reach the goal of freedom in Birmingham and all over the nation, because the goal of America is freedom. Abused and scorned though we may be, our destiny is tied up with America's destiny. Before the pilgrims landed at Plymouth, we were here. Before the pen of Jefferson etched the majestic words of the Declaration of Independence across the pages of history, we were here. For more than two centuries our forebears labored in this country without wages; they made cotton king; they built the homes of their masters while suffering gross injustice and shameful humiliation—and yet out of a bottomless vitality they continued to thrive and develop. If the inexpressible cruelties of slavery could not stop us, the opposition we now face will surely fail. We will win our freedom because the sacred heritage of our nation and the eternal will of God are embodied in our echoing demands.

45 Before closing I feel impelled to mention one other point in your statement that has troubled me profoundly. You warmly commended the Birmingham police for keeping "order" and "preventing violence." I doubt that you would have so warmly commended the police force if you had seen its dogs sinking their teeth into unarmed, nonviolent Negroes. I doubt that

---

[5] the early Christian church

you would so quickly commend the policemen if you were to observe their ugly and inhumane treatment of Negroes here in the city jail; if you were to watch them push and curse old Negro women and young Negro girls; if you were to see them slap and kick old Negro men and young boys; if you were to observe them, as they did on two occasions, refuse to give us food because we wanted to sing our grace together. I cannot join you in your praise of the Birmingham police department.

It is true that the police have exercised a degree of discipline in handling the demonstrators. In this sense they have conducted themselves rather "nonviolently" in public. But for what purpose? To preserve the evil system of segregation. Over the past few years I have consistently preached that nonviolence demands that the means we use must be as pure as the ends we seek. I have tried to make clear that it is wrong to use immoral means to attain moral ends. But now I must affirm that it is just as wrong, or perhaps even more so, to use moral means to preserve immoral ends. Perhaps Mr. Connor and his policemen have been rather nonviolent in public, as was Chief Pritchett in Albany, Georgia, but they have used moral means of nonviolence to maintain the immoral end of racial injustice. As T.S. Eliot has said, "The last temptation is the greatest treason: To do the right deed for the wrong reason."[6]

I wish you had commended the Negro sit-inners and demonstrators of Birmingham for their sublime courage, their willingness to suffer, and their amazing discipline in the midst of great provocation. One day the South will recognize its real heroes. They will be the James Merediths,[7] with the noble sense of purpose that enables them to face jeering and hostile mobs, and with the agonizing loneliness that characterizes the life of the pioneer. They will be old, oppressed, battered Negro women, symbolized in a seventy-two-year-old woman in Montgomery, Alabama, who rose up with a sense of dignity and with her people decided not to ride segregated buses, and who responded with ungrammatical profundity to one who inquired about her weariness: "My feets is tired, but my soul is at rest." They will be the young high school and college students, the young ministers of the gospel and a host of their elders, courageously and nonviolently sitting in at lunch counters and willingly going to jail for conscience' sake. One day the South will know that when these disinherited children of God sat down at lunch

---

[6] These lines are part of the response of St. Thomas à Becket to the fourth tempter in T.S. Eliot's play *Murder in the Cathedral.*

[7] In 1962 James H. Meredith became the first African-American student at the University of Mississippi.

counters, they were in reality standing up for what is best in the American dream and for the most sacred values in our Judaeo-Christian heritage, thereby bringing our nation back to those great wells of democracy which were dug deep by the founding fathers in their formulation of the Constitution and the Declaration of Independence.

Never before have I written such a long letter. I'm afraid it is much too long to take your precious time. I can assure you that it would have been much shorter if I had been writing from a comfortable desk, but what else can one do when he is alone in a narrow jail cell, other than write long letters, think long thoughts, and pray long prayers?

If I have said anything in this letter that overstates the truth and indicates an unreasonable impatience, I beg you to forgive me. If I have said anything that understates the truth and indicates my having a patience that allows me to settle for anything less than brotherhood, I beg God to forgive me.

50   I hope this letter finds you strong in the faith. I also hope that circumstances will soon make it possible for me to meet each of you, not as an integrationist or a civil-rights leader but as a fellow clergyman and a Christian brother. Let us all hope that the dark clouds of racial prejudice will soon pass away and the deep fog of misunderstanding will be lifted from our fear-drenched communities, and in some not too distant tomorrow the radiant stars of love and brotherhood will shine over our great nation with all their scintillating beauty.

Yours for the cause of Peace and Brotherhood,
MARTIN LUTHER KING, JR.
(Written April 16, 1963; published 1964)

QUESTIONS:

1. Summarize the various reasons King gives, first of all for the Birmingham protest, and second for the means through which the protest is pursued.

2. To what extent is it ever desirable or indeed possible to separate ethical from political questions?

3. Find at least three examples of parallel structures in King's writing, involving words, phrases, or clauses.

Groucho Marx

Dinner with my Celebrated Pen Pal T.S. Eliot

*In this letter to his brother Gummo, Groucho Marx recounts
meeting his pen pal T.S. Eliot.*

DEAR GUMMO:

Last night Eden and I had dinner with my celebrated pen pal T.S. Eliot. It was a memorable evening.

The poet met us at the door with Mrs. Eliot, a good-looking, middle-aged blonde whose eyes seemed to fill up with adoration every time she looked at her husband. He, by the way, is tall, lean and rather stooped over; but whether this is from age, illness or both, I don't know.

At any rate, your correspondent arrived at the Eliots' fully prepared for a literary evening. During the week I had read "Murder in the Cathedral" twice; "The Waste Land" three times; and just in case of a conversational bottleneck, I brushed up on "King Lear."

Well, sir, as cocktails were served, there was a momentary lull—the kind that is more or less inevitable when strangers meet for the first time. So, apropos of practically nothing (and "not with a bang but a whimper"[1]) I tossed in a quotation from "The Waste Land." That, I thought, will show him I've read a thing or two besides my press notices from vaudeville.

---

[1] A famous poem by Eliot dealing with the "emptiness" of twentieth-century life, "The Hollow Men," ends with the lines *This is the way the world ends / Not with a bang but a whimper.*

5   Eliot smiled faintly—as though to say he was thoroughly familiar with his poems and didn't need me to recite them. So I took a whack at "King Lear." I said the king was an incredibly foolish old man, which God knows he *was*; and that if he'd been *my* father I would have run away from home at the age of eight—instead of waiting until I was ten.

That, too, failed to bowl over the poet. He seemed more interested in discussing "Animal Crackers" and "A Night at the Opera." He quoted a joke—one of mine—that I had long since forgotten. Now it was my turn to smile faintly. I was not going to let anyone—not even the British poet from St. Louis—spoil my Literary Evening. I pointed out that King Lear's opening speech was the height of idiocy. Imagine (I said) a father asking his three children: Which of you kids loves me the most? And then disowning the youngest—the sweet, honest Cordelia—because, unlike her wicked sister, she couldn't bring herself to gush out insincere flattery. And Cordelia, mind you, had been her father's favourite!

The Eliots listened politely. Mrs. Eliot then defended Shakespeare; and Eden, too, I regret to say, was on King Lear's side, even though I am the one who supports her. (In all fairness to my wife, I must say that, having played the Princess in a high school production of "The Swan," she has retained a rather warm feeling for all royalty.)

As for Eliot, he asked if I remembered the courtroom scene in "Duck Soup." Fortunately I'd forgotten every word. It was obviously the end of the Literary Evening, but very pleasant none the less. I discovered that Eliot and I had three things in common: (1) an affection for good cigars and (2) cats; and (3) a weakness for making puns—a weakness that for many years I have tried to overcome. T.S., on the other hand, is an unashamed—even proud—punster. For example, there's his Gus, the Theatre Cat, whose "real name was Asparagus."

Speaking of asparagus, the dinner included good, solid English beef, very well prepared. And, although they had a semi-butler serving, Eliot insisted on pouring the wine himself. It was an excellent wine and no maitre d' could have served it more graciously. He is a dear man and a charming host.

10   When I told him that my daughter Melinda was studying his poetry at Beverly High, he said he regretted that, because he had no wish to become compulsory reading.

We didn't stay late, for we both felt that he wasn't up to a long evening of conversation—especially mine.

Did I tell you we called him Tom?—possibly because that's his name. I, of course, asked him to call me Tom too, but only because I loathe the name Julius.

Yours,
Tom Marx
(1964)

Questions:

1. What were Marx's assumptions about T.S. Eliot prior to his meeting?

2. Why do you suppose T.S. Eliot had no wish to become compulsory reading?

3. Marx says of his dinner: "It was a memorable evening." Why was it memorable? Is this statement positive or negative?

4. Unlike a formal essay written for a public audience, this letter is written for the private audience of the author's brother. How does this affect the style of the writing?

5. What expectation does Marx set up at the beginning of his letter?

6. What would be your assumptions about Marx's relationship with his brother Gummo, based on this letter?

Joan Didion

On Going Home

This essay describes the author's return home on the occasion of her daughter's
first birthday; Didion explores the effect that this visit has on her understanding
of the past, her relationships with her various family members, and her
understanding of "home."

෴

I am home for my daughter's first birthday. By "home" I do not mean the
house in Los Angeles where my husband and I and the baby live, but the
place where my family is, in the Central Valley of California. It is a vital
although troublesome distinction. My husband likes my family but is uneasy
in their house, because once there I fall into their ways, which are difficult,
oblique, deliberately inarticulate, not my husband's ways. We live in dusty
houses ("D-U-S-T," he once wrote with his finger on surfaces all over the
house, but no one noticed it) filled with mementos quite without value to
him (what could the Canton dessert plates mean to him? how could he have
known about the assay scales, why should he care if he did know?), and we
appear to talk exclusively about people we know who have been committed
to mental hospitals, about people we know who have been booked on
drunk-driving charges, and about property, particularly about property, land,
price per acre and C-2 zoning and assessments and freeway access. My
brother does not understand my husband's inability to perceive the
advantage in the rather common real-estate transaction known as "sale-
leaseback," and my husband in turn does not understand why so many of the
people he hears about in my father's house have recently been committed to
mental hospitals or booked on drunk-driving charges. Nor does he
understand that when we talk about sale-leasebacks and right-of-way
condemnations we are talking in code about the things we like best, the
yellow fields and the cottonwoods and the rivers rising and falling and the

mountain roads closing when the heavy snow comes in. We miss each other's points, have another drink and regard the fire. My brother refers to my husband, in his presence, as "Joan's husband." Marriage is the classic betrayal.

Or perhaps it is not any more. Sometimes I think that those of us who are now in our thirties were born into the last generation to carry the burden of "home," to find in family life the source of all tension and drama. I had by all objective accounts a "normal" and a "happy" family situation, and yet I was almost thirty years old before I could talk to my family on the telephone without crying after I had hung up. We did not fight. Nothing was wrong. And yet some nameless anxiety coloured the emotional charges between me and the place that I came from. The question of whether or not you could go home again was a very real part of the sentimental and largely literary baggage with which we left home in the fifties; I suspect that it is irrelevant to the children born of the fragmentation after World War II. A few weeks ago in a San Francisco bar I saw a pretty young girl on crystal take off her clothes and dance for the cash prize in an "amateur-topless" contest. There was no particular sense of moment about this, none of the effect of romantic degradation, of "dark journey," for which my generation strived so assiduously. What sense could that girl possibly make of, say, *Long Day's Journey into Night*? Who is beside the point?

That I am trapped in this particular irrelevancy is never more apparent to me than when I am home. Paralyzed by the neurotic lassitude engendered by meeting one's past at every turn, around every corner, inside every cupboard, I go aimlessly from room to room. I decide to meet it head-on and clean out a drawer, and I spread the contents on the bed. A bathing suit I wore the summer I was seventeen. A letter of rejection from *The Nation*, an aerial photograph of the site for a shopping center my father did not build in 1954. Three teacups hand-painted with cabbage roses and signed "E.M.," my grandmother's initials. There is no final solution for letters of rejection from *The Nation* and teacups hand-painted in 1900. Nor is there any answer to snapshots of one's grandfather as a young man on skis, surveying around Donner Pass in the year 1910. I smooth out the snapshot and look into his face, and do and do not see my own. I close the drawer, and have another cup of coffee with my mother. We get along very well, veterans of a guerilla war we never understood.

Days pass. I see no one. I come to dread my husband's evening call, not only because he is full of news of what by now seems to me our remote life in Los Angeles, people he has seen, letters which require attention, but because he asks what I have been doing, suggests uneasily that I get out, drive to San Francisco or Berkeley. Instead I drive across the river to a family graveyard. It has been vandalized since my last visit and the monuments are broken, overturned in the dry grass. Because I once saw a rattlesnake in the grass I stay in the car and listen to a country-and-Western station. Later I drive with my father to a ranch he has in the foothills. The man who runs his cattle on it asks us to the roundup, a week from Sunday, and although I know that I will be in Los Angeles I say, in the oblique way my family talks, that I will come. Once home I mention the broken monuments in the graveyard. My mother shrugs.

5   I go to visit my great-aunts. A few of them think now that I am my cousin, or their daughter who died young. We recall an anecdote about a relative last seen in 1948, and they ask if I still like living in New York City. I have lived in Los Angeles for three years, but I say that I do. The baby is offered a horehound drop, and I am slipped a dollar bill "to buy a treat." Questions trail off, answers are abandoned, the baby plays with the dust motes in a shaft of afternoon sun.

It is time for the baby's birthday party: a white cake, strawberry-marshmallow ice cream, a bottle of champagne saved from another party. In the evening, after she has gone to sleep, I kneel beside the crib and touch her face, where it is pressed against the slats, with mine. She is an open and trusting child, unprepared for and unaccustomed to the ambushes of family life, and perhaps it is just as well that I can offer her little of that life. I would like to give her more. I would like to promise her that she will grow up with a sense of her cousins and of rivers and of her great-grandmother's teacups, would like to pledge her a picnic on a river with fried chicken and her hair uncombed, would like to give her *home* for her birthday, but we live differently now and I can promise her nothing like that. I give her a xylophone and a sundress from Madeira, and promise to tell her a funny story.

(1966)

QUESTIONS:

1. What does Didion mean when she writes, "That I am trapped in this particular irrelevancy is never more apparent to me than when I am at home"? What is the irrelevancy?

2. Describe the character of the author's husband. How is he seen by her family?

3. Near the end of the essay, Didion writes that she "…would like to give [her daughter] *home* for her birthday.…" What does she mean?

4. Didion uses the words "normal" and "happy" when describing her family situation. What is her intention?

5. How does Didion's use of the word "home" change throughout the essay?

6. Describe Didion's use of descriptive detail in the essay. What does it reveal about herself? Her family?

J. TUZO WILSON

DID THE ATLANTIC CLOSE
AND THEN RE-OPEN?

*J. Tuzo Wilson was one of a handful of geologists whose research in the 1950s
and 60s convinced the world that continents were not stable entities, but rested
on "plates" which were capable of "drifting" across vast distances.*

For more than a century, it has been recognized that an unusual feature of
the shallow water marine faunas of Lower Palaeozoic time is their
division into two clearly marked geographic regions, which are commonly
referred to as faunal realms. "The faunal assemblages are amazingly uniform
throughout each realm so that correlation of any Cambrian section with
another in the same realm is usually easy; on the other hand, the difference

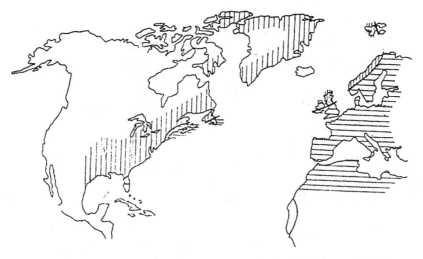

Fig. 1. The North Atlantic region showing the present distributions of the 'Atlantic' faunal realm (horizontal shading) and
the 'Pacific' faunal realm (vertical shading). (After J. W. Cowie, A. W. Grabau and R. D. Hutchinson.)

between the faunas in the two separate realms is so great as to make correlation between them very difficult."[1]

Two aspects of the distribution of these realms are remarkable. For one thing, some regions of similar faunas are separated by the whole width of the Atlantic Ocean; then, on the other hand, some regions of dissimilar faunas lie adjacent to one another. This is illustrated by Fig. 1, which is based on work by Cowie,[2] Grabau[3] and Hutchinson.[4]

Grabau showed that, if Europe and North America had become separated by continental drift, a simple reconstruction could explain the first anomaly in the distribution of the faunal realms in that, before the opening of the Atlantic Ocean, each realm would have been continuous, with no large gaps between outcrops of similar facies (Fig. 2).

Fig. 2. The North Atlantic region in Upper Palaeozoic and Lower Mesozoic time showing that of the present Atlantic Ocean only the Canadian Basin and the Gulf of Mexico then existed. Four fans are shown which were formed: (1) during Middle Ordovician; (2) during Upper Ordovician; (3) during Upper Devonian; (4) during Pennsylvanian. The heavy line separates 'Pacific' and 'Atlantic' faunal realms. The two ridges are considered to have formed when the modern Atlantic started to open.

---

[1] Hutchinson, R. D., *Geol. Surv. Canada, Mem.*, 263, 52 (1952). [Unless otherwise noted, all notes to this essay are from the author.]

[2] Cowie, J. W., *Intern. Geol. Cong., Sess. 21, Copenhagen*, Part 8, 57 (1960).

[3] Grabau, A. W., *Palaeozoic Formations in the Light of the Pulsation Theory*, 1 (University Press, National University of Peking, 1936).

[4] Hutchinson, R. D., *Intern. Geol. Cong., Sess. 20, Mexico, The Cambrian System Symposium*, 2, 290 (1956).

It is the object of this article to show that drift can also explain the second anomaly. It is proposed that, in Lower Palaeozoic time, a proto-Atlantic Ocean existed so as to form the boundary between the two realms, and that during Middle and Upper Palaeozoic time the ocean closed by stages, so bringing dissimilar facies together (Fig. 3). The supposed closing of the Tethys Sea by northward movement of India into contact with the rest of Asia, and the partial closing of the Mediterranean by northward movement of Africa, can be regarded as a similar but more recent event. The figures are based on a reconstruction by Bullard, Everett and Smith,[5] but because those authors pointed out that no allowance had been made for the construction of post-Jurassic shelves, the continents have been brought more closely together.

Four lines of evidence suggest that this proposal is reasonable. (Unfortunately, so far as I can ascertain, palaeomagnetic evidence which might bear on this problem does not exist.)

First, this reconstruction of geological history is held to provide a unified explanation of the changes in rock types, fossils, mountain building episodes and palaeoclimates represented by the rocks of the Atlantic region.

Second, wherever the junction between contiguous parts of different realms is exposed, it is marked by extensive faulting, thrusting and crushing.

Third, there is evidence that the junction is everywhere along the eastern side of a series of ancient island arcs (Fig. 3).

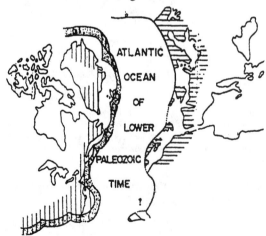

Fig. 3. The North Atlantic region in Lower Palaeozoic time. The proto-Atlantic Ocean would have formed a complete barrier between two faunal realms (shaded). Island arcs (dotted) probably lay along the North American coast. The floor of this ocean could have been absorbed in the trenches associated with these arcs as the ocean closed.

[5] Bullard, E. C., Everett, J. E., and Smith, A. G., *Phil. Trans. Roy. Soc.*, A, 258 41 (1965).

Fourth, the fit appears to meet the geometric requirement that during a single cycle of closing and reopening of an ocean, and in any latitudinal belt of the ocean, only one of the pair of opposing coasts can change sides (Fig. 4).

RECURRENT DRIFT IN THE NORTH ATLANTIC

10   The history proposed for the North Atlantic region can be stated very briefly as follows: (*a*) From the Late Pre-Cambrian to the close of Middle Odrovician time an open ocean existed in approximately, but not precisely, the same location as the present North Atlantic (Fig. 3). (*b*) From the Upper Ordovician to Carboniferous time, this ocean closed by stages. (*c*) From Permian to Jurassic time there was no deep ocean in the North Atlantic region. The only marine deposits of that time are those connected with the Tethys Sea, with a shallow Jurassic invasion of Europe and with deeper Jurassic seas in the Gulf of Mexico and in the western Arctic Basin (Fig. 2). (*d*) Since the beginning of the Cretaceous period the present Atlantic Ocean has been opening, but this reopening did not follow the precise line of junction formed by the closing of the early Palaeozoic Atlantic Ocean; the result is that some coastal regions have been transposed (Fig. 1).

The Lower Palaeozoic continents may have first touched each other at the end of Middle Ordovician time, for thereafter the distinction between 'Atlantic' and 'Pacific' faunal realms ceases to be marked, but the complete closing of the ancient Atlantic may have required several periods.

For each continent, union meant replacing the open ocean by the other continent. This is offered as an explanation of the borderlands of J. Barrell and C. Schuchert for which there is no clear evidence until Upper Ordovician time. As Kay has suggested[6] concerning Eastern North America: "There has been little discussion of the evidence for borderlands in earlier Paleozoic time, though some have expressed scepticism." Kay's own support for island arcs is muted after Lower Palaeozoic time and he accepts the view that the sediments of the "Late Devonian and Early Mississippian came from the land of Appalachia"—a borderland.

This view that extensive upland source areas lay to the east of the Appalachian geosyncline in the sites of the present coastal plain or ocean has

---

[6] Kay, M., *Geol. Soc. Amer. Mem.*, 48, 31, 56 (1951).

been fully supported by recent work.[7] [8] [9] Tens of thousands of cubic miles of quartz-rich sediments, derived from the east, were deposited in shallow marine to sub-aerial deltas.

When the continents were pushed together, they would have touched first at one promontory and then at another. It can be expected that high mountains would have been formed locally and that they would have produced alluvial fans on both continents. As the ocean diminished the climate would have become increasingly arid. Such drastic alterations in the physiography would explain the change from predominantly marine and island arc deposition in the Lower Palaeozoic to conspicuous fans of Queenston, Catskill, Old Red Sandstone, and other deltas of Middle and Upper Palaeozoic time[10] [11] (see also Fig. 2). It can also be expected that the collision of continents would have produced great local uplifts which, if one continent overrode the other, would have migrated inland, perhaps pushing the Taconic and northern Newfoundland klippen[12] before them.

It would seem that by Permian and Triassic times the Atlantic Ocean was completely closed, because only continental beds, such as the Dunkard and Newark series, are found in North America. In Great Britain the New Red Sandstone is also continental as is the Permian of the Oslo district.

No Jurassic beds are known in eastern North America except in the Gulf of Mexico. Those of Europe were formed by a shallow marine invasion of the continent and are said by Hallam[13] to have fossils that "include many neritic forms that could not have crossed a deep ocean. The paleogeography for the Scottish Jurassic gives no hint of increasingly marine conditions to the west" (personal communication). Most of the available geological evidence suggests that the present Atlantic Ocean started to open at the

[7] Pettijohn, F. J., *Bull. Amer. Assoc. Petrol. Geol.*, 46, 1468 (1962).

[8] Yeakel, jun., L. S., *Geol. Soc. Amer. Bull.*, 73, 1515 (1962).

[9] Naylor, R. S., and Boucot, A. J., *Amer. J. Sci.*, 263, 153 (1965).

[10] King, P. B., *The Evolution of North America*, 61 (Princeton University Press, 1959).

[11] Clark, T. H., and Stearn, C. W., *The Geological Evolution of North America*, 104, 114 (Ronald Press, New York, 1960).

[12] Rodgers, J., and Neale, E. R. W., *Amer. J. Sci.*, 261, 713 (1963).

[13] Hallam, A., in *The Geology of Scotland*, edit. By Craig, G. Y. (Oliver and Boyd, Edinburgh, 1955).

beginning of Cretaceous time.[14] [15] Although objections to this view are still being raised, they seem to be minor in comparison with the other evidence, and it is possible that they can be explained in other ways.

FAULTED CONTACT BETWEEN FAUNAL REALMS

Starting our considerations in the north, the island of West Spitsbergen is underlain by a thick eugeosynclinal section of Lower Palaeozoic rocks named the Hecla Hoek succession. These strata rest on no known basement and were deformed, metamorphosed and intruded by granites during the Caledonian orogeny.[16] [17] They contain fossils of the 'Pacific' fauna similar to those of Scotland and North America.[18]

In Nordaustland, the adjacent, eastern island of the Spitsbergen group, Kulling[19] and Sandford[20] have mapped a thin section of unmetamorphosed and gently folded strata which a few fossils indicate to be of about the same age. These beds lie uncomformably on a basement which is regarded as part of the Baltic Shield. These strata do not thicken to the west as the much thicker section of West Spitsbergen is approached, nor do the few fossils necessarily belong to the 'Pacific' faunal realm.

Despite the considerable number of attempts to compare the sections in the adjacent islands, the correlation is not good. Changes in thickness, facies, and degree of metamorphism, basement and type of intrusives are all abrupt and striking. Orvin[21] and others have mapped faults in Hinlopen Strait between the islands. Klitin[22] summarizes the situation thus: "Of particular interest is the junction zone of the alleged Caledonian platform and Caledonian fold system. The transition to typical caledonids takes place in

---

[14] Blackett, P. M. S., Bullard, E. C., and Runcorn, S. K., *Phil. Trans. Roy. Soc.*, A, 258 (1965).

[15] Furon, R., *The Geology of Africa*, 49 (Oliver and Boyd, Edinburgh, 1963).

[16] Odell, N. E., *Quart. J. Geol. Soc. London*, 83, 147 (1927).

[17] Harland, W. B., *Quart. J. Geol. Soc. London*, 114, 307 (1958).

[18] Gobbett, D. J., and Wilson, C. B., *Geol. Mag.*, 97, 441 (1960).

[19] Kulling, O., *Geogr. Annaler.*, *1934*, 161 (1934).

[20] Sandford, K. S., *Quart. J. Geol. Soc. London*, 112, 339 (1956).

[21] Orvin, A. K., *Skr. Svalb. og Ishavet*, 78, 1 (1940).

[22] Klitin, K. A., *Izvestiya Acad. Sci., U.S.S.R., Geol. Ser.* (Engl. Trans., Amer. Geol. Inst.), *1960*, 50 (1960).

a zone not over 15 to 20 km wide, in the Hinlopen Strait area, where the Hecla Hoek section abruptly increases in thickness, by a factor of four, with the appearance of extrusives in its metamorphosed and linearly folded beds. Such radical changes in thickness suggest a fault junction between an ancient platform and the caledonids." Following this interpretation I suggest that the Lower Palaeozoic ocean once separated the two islands and that, whereas Nordaustland formed part of the Baltic shield and shelf, West Spitsbergen was the site of a North American island arc.

In Scandinavia it is well established that the peninsula is divided longitudinally into two different provinces separated by a great zone of nappes and faults overthrust towards the east. According to the descriptions of Holtedahl,[23] south-eastern Norway and most of Sweden are underlain by an extension of the Baltic Platform on which lie nearly flat, unfossiliferous rocks and "the eastern facies of the Cambro-Silurian (which) can be classed as miogeosynclinal in the terminology of Stille. The thickness is rather large and there is much terrigeneous material. Caledonian volcanic and intrusive igneous rocks are not found in the deposits of this type. The rocks are unmetamorphosed in the east and are of low metamorphic grade farther to the north-west. The deposits occur in an autochthonous or parautochthonous position above the original Archean basement."

The fossils are repeatedly referred to as being similar to those of the Baltic region, England and Wales. On the other hand, in the Trondheim area of western Norway, a thick succession of pillow lavas, shale and limestone with serpentinites in the lower part of the sequence contains a fauna "of American affinities...the limestone of Smola is similar to the Durness in Scotland and to more or less contemporaneous limestone in Newfoundland, Bear Island and Spitsbergen. The limestone in Smola thus seems to represent an American-Arctic facies of the Ordovician." In these "mainly pelitic sediments...we thus have a eugeosynclinal facies characteristic of the central parts of a geosyncline...probably all rocks of the present facies occur in allochthonous positions." An important event in central southern Norway was the close of marine deposition "in Late Ordovician or Early Silurian time brought about by the thrusting of nappes and deposition of the Valdres sparagmite (arkose), which was considered as a deposit of flysch type by Goldschmidt." The zone of nappes is, therefore, held to be the boundary between faunal provinces and the line of closure of the Lower Palaeozoic ocean.

---

[23] Holtedahl, O. (ed.), *Norges Geol. Undersökelse, Nr.* 208, 128, 153, 157, 165 (1960).

The geological relationship between Spitsbergen, Scandinavia and the British Isles has been discussed by Bailey and Holtedahl.[24] Of the Caledonian structures they state: "...in the present land area of Scandinavia we find the eastern part of the orogenetic belt only, while in Great Britain the whole of the orogenetic zone is represented. The Spitsbergen Group seems to lie rather centrally in the zone of deformation." Following Wagener, they consider that Greenland may have been formerly connected with Europe and suggest that, if so, it would have completed the western side of the mountain belt opposite Norway. This relationship has found support in recent years from several authors[25] including Umbgrove.[26]

That the boundary between 'Atlantic' and 'Pacific' faunal realms crosses northern England between Scotland and Wales is supported by Walton, who writes of the Scottish occurrences: "The close affinity of the Durness and North America rocks was recognised long ago.... The long-recognised affinity of the Girvan Caredocian and Appalachian Mohawkian faunas was re-emphasized by Williams.... By contrast the faunas are only remotely connected with the Welsh Ordovician rocks."[27] George[28] describes the relations thus: "The Salopian geosyncline may thus have extended unbrokenly from conjectural north-western limits in the Highlands to a south-eastern margin or marginal shelf in the English Midlands." It does not require much change to regard this geosyncline as a former ocean.

In Newfoundland the geology of the north-eastern coast has recently been described by Williams.[29] He suggests that in Cambrian time a deep basin or ocean, not underlain by continental crust, crossed the central part of the island and separated two shelves. The north-western shelf underlying the Long Peninsula has a basement of Grenville age overlain by strata with 'Pacific' faunas like those of Scotland, while the south-eastern shelf, which forms the Avalon peninsula, has a younger Pre-Cambrian basement overlain by strata with 'Atlantic' faunas like those of Wales. During Ordovician and

---

[24] Bailey, E. B., and Holtedahl, O., *Regionale Geologie der Erde*, 2 (Abschn. 2), 1 (Akad. Verlags. m. b. H., Leipzig, 1938).

[25] Blackett, P.M.S., Bullard, E.C., and Runcorn, S.K., *Phil. Trans. Roy. Soc.*, A. 258 (1965).

[26] Umbgrove, J. H. F., *The Pulse of the Earth*, second ed., 232 (M. Nijhoff, The Hague, 1947).

[27] Walton, E. K., in *The Geology of Scotland*, edit. by Craig, G. Y., 167, 177, 201 (Oliver and Boyd, Edinburgh, 1965).

[28] George, T. N., in *The British Caledonides*, edit. By Johnson, M. R. W., and Stewart, F. H., 12 (Oliver and Boyd, Edinburgh, 1963).

[29] Williams, H., *Amer. J. Sci.*, 262, 1137 (1964).

subsequent time the intervening sea became filled with eugeosynclinal and volcanic sedimentary rocks, probably representing a former island arc and mountain belt.

Anderson[30] believes that faulting in Hermitage Bay on the south coast of Newfoundland not only separates the rocks of the south-eastern shelf from the central geosyncline, but may also completely divide the two faunas. On the north coast the corresponding fault zone may be in Freshwater Bay, but this point has not been settled as yet.[31]

Among those who have recently correlated the Newfoundland and British sections are Dewey and Church.[32] Although Church does not favour continental drift, both he and Dewey make the same correlation as that already given here and extend the Caledonian mobile belt from northern England and central Ireland to central Newfoundland.

South of Newfoundland, the Gulf of St. Lawrence and younger rocks cover the key areas of Lower Palaeozoic formations almost as far as the Maine border. Little can be said except that the faunas of Cape Breton Island and St. John, New Brunswick, have European affinities while those of Gaspé and the Eastern Township of Quebec are typical of Scotland and most of North America.[33]

In northern and eastern Maine the older literature is sparse and generalized. Recently a combined group of government and university geologists, including W. B. N. Berry, A. J. Boucot, E. Mencher, R. S. Naylor and L. Pavlides, have discovered new fossil localities there with both European and North American affinities, important Caledonian uplifts and large pre-Silurian faults. Much of the state has been remapped, but for the reason that little of this work has yet been published (R. G. Doyle, personal communication), and because the structure is clearly much more complex than shown on early maps, this is not an opportune time to consider the area in detail.

From the southern part of Maine south across New Hampshire, Massachusetts and Connecticut a major zone can be traced from published accounts. Novotny[34] has described this "major fault zone" where it crosses

[30] Anderson, F. D., *Geol. Surv. Canada, Map* 8–1965 (1965).

[31] Jenness, S. E., *Geol. Surv. Canada, Mem.* 327 (1963).

[32] Church, W. R. *Can. Min. Metal. Bull.*, 58, 219 (1944).

[33] *U.S. Geol. Survey Prof. Papers*, 424–B, 65 (1961); 475–B, 117 (1963); 501–C, 28 (1964); 525–A, 74 (1965).

[34] Novotny, R. F., *U.S. Geol. Surv. Prof. Paper*, 424–D, 48 (1961).

the New Hampshire-Massachusetts boundary (Fig. 5). To the north it connects with several faults and silicified zones shown on the map of New Hampshire.[35] [36] These lie along the line which separates those formations which underlie the greater part of New Hampshire from a suite of completely different formations, underlying south-eastern New Hampshire. This line may be continued northward into south-eastern Maine by the faults which Katz[37] has suggested bound the Berwick gneiss, itself crumpled, "closely folded and overturned." In Massachusetts, Novotny's fault may be exposed in the abandoned Worcester "coal" mine. The description suggests that much of the rock may be carbonaceous mylonite.[38] South of Worcester this fault connects with a major change in formations evident on the geological map of Massachusetts.[39]

30   In Connecticut this boundary appears to join the Honey Hill fault and its northern continuation which bisect the state and separate two major rock sequences. Where best described in the south it "has been mapped for 25 miles eastward from Chester nearly to Preston without apparent repetition of the stratigraphy on either side of the fault. The fault plane dips 10°–35° N parallel to the underlying metasedimentary rocks.... The fault is marked by a zone a mile wide of mylonitized and crushed rocks.... Displacement must have been many miles."[40] As in Norway, the orogenic belt appears to have been thrust eastwards over the eastern platform. To the south this major fault seems to strike into the Atlantic Ocean and the Appalachian belt, then narrows conspicuously. I have recently learned from L. R. Page and J. W. Peoples that mapping (for the most unpublished) by the federal and state surveys has defined this fault zone more satisfactorily, and that published aeromagnetic maps show a change in the strike of anomalies across it. This evidence suggests that New England is divided by a major fault zone into two provinces underlain by quite different rock formations. Of the few occurrences of the Lower Palaeozoic faunas, all those with European

---

[35]   Billings, M. P., *Geological Map of New Hampshire* (U.S. Geol. Surv., Washington, 1955).

[36]   Freedman, J., *Geol. Soc. Amer. Bull.*, 61, 449 (1950).

[37]   Katz, F. J., *U.S. Geol. Surv. Prof. Paper*, 108, 165 (1917).

[38]   Zartman, R., Snyder, G., Stern, T. W., Marvin, R. F., and Buckman, R. C., *U.S. Geol. Surv. Prof. Paper*, 575–D, 1 (1965).

[39]   Emerson, B. K., *U.S. Geol. Surv. Bull.*, 597 (1917).

[40]   Lundgren, jun., L., Goldsmitt, R., and Snyder, G. L., *Geol. Soc. Amer. Bull.*, 69, 1606 (1958).

affinities lie to the east of the fault zone; all those typical of North America to the west.[41][42]

In the light of this evidence it seems reasonable to suggest that this fault zone marks the line of closure of the Lower Palaeozoic Atlantic Ocean. It may seem strange to propose that a former position of the Atlantic Ocean lies through New England and that its full significance has not been realized, but it must be remembered that throughout the area outcrops are poor and that most of the mapping is old. Surface mapping reveals few faults, but new tunnels have shown that faults abound under the drift-filled valleys and that some of these are major (J. W. Skehan and A. Quinn, personal communications).

Most North American geologists have not accepted the idea of continental drift. Instead they have sought to explain the changes in faunas in terms of different environmental conditions. This has certainly been a factor and no doubt was responsible for the differences between the Durness, Girvan and Moffatt facies in Scotland, although those facies belong to the same faunal realm. In another example, G. Theokritoff (personal communication) has directed my attention to a possible mixing of Atlantic, Pacific and endemic faunas in the Taconic sequence of New York.[43] Christina Lochman[44] has emphasized the difficulties incurred in accepting such an interpretation. She states that the areas of mixed faunas lie in deeply down-warped basins between two shallow shelf deposits containing respectively Atlantic and Pacific faunas. These basins, she remarks, had connexions with the Atlantic Ocean and had a benthonic environment "similar to that of the open ocean.... Few normal benthonic species of the coastal shelf could establish themselves in such an alien environment, although, because of the geographic proximity of the two areas, sporadically drifted individuals might be found." She also refers to deep basins separating different faunas and to the evidence for a "biofacies regime ordinarily found on the floors of the continental shelf beyond the inner islands of the volcanic archipelago." These views would seem to admit the possibility of interpreting the palaeogeography as has been done in this article. It is suggested that one of the deep

---

[41] Billings, M. P., *The Geology of New Hampshire, Pt. II*, 105 (New Hampshire State Planning and Devel. Comm., Concord, 1956).

[42] Howell, B. F., *Intern. Geol. Cong. Sess. 20, Mexico, The Cambrian System Symposium*, 2, 315 (1956).

[43] Bird, J. M., and Theokritoff, G., *Geol. Soc. Amer. Bull.*, 77, 13 (1966).

[44] Lochman, C., *Geol. Soc. Amer. Bull.*, 67, 1331 (1956).

basins, instead of lying on a shelf, might have been an open ocean in Lower Palaeozoic time and that the mixed fauna may have come from the extreme edge of one continent.

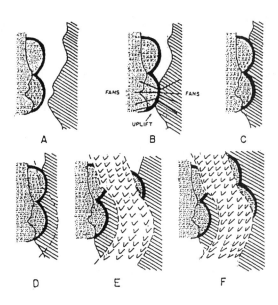

Fig. 4. *A*, A closing ocean, with island arcs on one coast, separating two different faunal realms. *B*, First contact between two opposite sides of a closing ocean. *C*, The ocean closed by overlap of the opposite coasts. *D*, A possible line (dashed) along which a younger ocean could reopen. *E*, A new ocean (checked) opening in an old continent. *F*, A geometrically impossible way for a younger ocean to open. (Note how the arcs overlap.)

The reconstruction (Fig. 2) then leads to Africa: Sougy[45] has described a large plate of metamorphic rocks east of Dakar thrust eastwards over Upper Devonian strata. Farther north in Spanish Morocco there is a folded belt. A large Cretaceous overlap along the coast and lack of diagnostic fossils in the overthrust block make correlation difficult, but Sougy concludes that: "In the future, when geologists study the relationships between America and Africa for evidence bearing on permanence of continents and oceans *versus* continental drift, they will have to consider that the western rim of Africa is made, from Guinea to Morocco, not of a Pre-Cambrian basement but of a mainly Hercynian orogenic belt, in some respects symmetrical to the Appalachian belt." His mention of drift suggests, as do most reconstructions,[46] that this West African belt was formerly part of the

[45] Sougy, J., *Geol. Soc. Amer. Bull.*, 73, 871 (1962).

[46] Bullard, E.C., Everett, J.E., and Smith, A.G., *Phil. Trans. Roy. Soc.*, A, 258, 41 (1965).

Appalachians. This view is supported by P. A. Mohr, who writes: "the Cambrian manganese ores of Newfoundland, Wales and Morocco...I think were formed in a common geosynclinal trough" (personal communication). The view that these regions were together until Cretaceous time is supported by the close similarity of Cretaceous fossils from these two regions now on opposite sides of the ocean.[47] Only further investigation, aided by extensive seismic investigations or drilling through the Cretaceous of both continental coasts, can show whether it is possible or likely that West Africa ever fitted into the central east coast of the United States. If so, some rotation of Africa clockwise and a closer fit than that shown by Bullard, Everett and Smith[48] may be indicated.

Fig. 5. Sketch map of New England showing location of some major faults and three fossil localities of the 'Atlantic' faunal realm (X). The numbers refer to papers in the list of references from which information was obtained.

Although the northern termination of the West African fold belt is covered, its termination to the south is definite; the Pre-Cambrian of the African Shield extends to the Atlantic near Conakry.[49] The reconstruction

47   Reyment, R. A., *Nature*, 207, 1384 (1965).

48   Bullard, E.C., Everett, J.E., and Smith, A.G., *Phil. Trans. Roy. Soc.*, A, 258, 41 (1965).

49   Bureau Res. Geol. Min., *Carte Géol. Afrique Occid.*, Feuille No. 1 (1960).

suggests that this contact might reach Florida. In Florida and Georgia a cross-section of the Appalachians resembles that of Newfoundland in that these are the only parts of the Appalachians with a platform on both sides of the mobile belt. The platform on the south-eastern side of the mobile belt which lies beneath northern Florida and adjacent states is only known from well cores. These consist of Early Ordovician to Middle Devonian sandstones and shales said to have been deposited in shallow water.[50] Published accounts do not correlate the strata or fossils with formations elsewhere. It would seem that the basement has not been penetrated. Thus it is only speculative to suggest that this region was formerly part of Africa.

ISLAND ARCS OF LOWER PALAEOZOIC ATLANTIC

35

According to a widely adopted hypothesis, island arcs and mountains represent places where the lithosphere is being compressed, while mid-ocean ridges represent places where it is being pulled apart and where new crust is being created. Thus the present Atlantic ocean is expanding from the Mid-Atlantic Ridge.

For a Lower Palaeozoic Atlantic Ocean to have closed, it must, according to this hypothesis, have been marked not by a central ridge, but by a continuous system of island arcs and mountains. Observation shows that such systems commonly lie at the sides and not in the centre of oceans. Kay's view, that a system of island arcs existed off the eastern and southern coasts of North America in Lower Palaeozoic time, is entirely compatible with this hypothesis. This would have allowed the former Atlantic Ocean to close, and thus to convert the offshore island arcs of Lower Palaeozoic time into the intercontinental Appalachian mountains of Middle and Upper Palaeozoic time. Following Keith, Kay and King, I have sketched the location of seven former arcs in the Appalachians and their south-western continuation past the Ouachita and Marathon Mountains.[51] I see no reason to change this view.

The situation in Scotland has been described by Walton: "It seems likely that both the north-west Highlands and the Appalachians formed part of a very wide stable shelf which also included Greenland and other 'Boreal' regions having very similar Cambrian rock types.... it is probable that sedimentation in the area of the southern Highlands during the Cambrian

---

50 Carroll, D., *U.S. Geol. Surv. Prof. Paper*, 454–A, 1 (1963).

51 Wilson, J. T., in *The Earth as a Planet*, edit. by Kuiper, G. P. (Univ. of Chicago Press, 1954).

period was mainly of a greywacke, geosynclinal type and contrasted strongly with that in the north-west Highlands...it is probable that Cambrian sedimentation stretched unbroken to an unknown distance south of the Highland Boundary fault."[52] Ordovician volcanism followed and these correlations and descriptions suggest that, during Lower Palaeozoic time, arcs associated with a western land extended across Scotland. That there may have been contemporaneous volcanism and islands along the eastern coast in what is now Wales, merely adds complexity without affecting the history in Scotland. In the Silurian period conditions changed and the marine conditions "gave way to mixed environments...at least partly in fluvio-dedaic environments with periods of emergence."[53]

Enough has been described of the conditions in Norway and West Spitsbergen and of their correlations with Scotland to show that they too were the sites of Lower Palaeozoic island arcs associated with a western continent. Thus the Caledonian-Appalachian arcs seem to have formed a continuous system along the western side of the former ocean. It is suggested that it was in the trenches of these arcs that the floor of the Lower Palaeozoic Ocean was swallowed up as that ocean closed.

Geometrical Control of Transposition

If two bodies are brought together so that they unite, and if they are later pulled apart so that they break on a different line from the line of union, then one important geometrical consideration holds. It is that, along any one stretch of the junction, only one fragment can change sides: one cannot transpose pieces from each margin at the same place. This is illustrated in Fig. 4 and a comparison with the other figures shows that our reconstruction obeys this principle. This does not prove that the reconstruction is correct, but the neat fashion in which fragments from either side are alternately transposed meets the geometrical requirements.

Some Possible Extensions

40   When, as is believed, the present Atlantic Ocean started to open at the beginning of Cretaceous time, it did so by breaking open a continent which

---

[52]   Walton, E.K., in *The Geology of Scotland*, edit. by Craig, G.Y., 167, 177, 201 (Oliver and Boyd, Edinburgh, 1965).

[53]   Ibid.

was then continuous from West Spitsbergen to Florida (Fig. 2). North of Spitsbergen the coasts of North America and Siberia at that time diverged and the opening ceased to lie wholly within a continent and to have continental blocks on both sides. Following the descriptions of B. C. Heezen and M. Ewing, and Ya. Ya. Hakkel and N. A. Ostenso, I have suggested that the fracture followed the coast of Siberia forming the Lomonosov Ridge on the other side of the opening. Thus the Lomonosov Ridge separates an older Canadian ocean basin from a younger Siberian ocean basin in the Arctic Sea.[54]

In the south the situation appears to be similar, but to understand it one must clearly separate the platform of northern Florida from the different geology of southern Florida. South of central Florida a southern Florida-Bahamas Ridge separates a main Atlantic, apparently of Cretaceous age, from a Gulf of Mexico which seems to have been a deep ocean and evaporite basin during the Jurassic period.

Drake, Heirtzler and Hirschman[55] emphasize the importance of the Florida-Bahamas Ridge for sealing off the Gulf of Mexico from the open ocean so that the Jurassic salt deposits could form. They suggest that this ridge is an "extension of the Ouachita system" and that it forms the "foundation for the entire chain of islands and banks." This ignores the earlier interpretations of magnetic and gravity anomaly maps made by Miller and Ewing[56] and by Lee.[57] Both papers suggested that southern Florida and the Bahamas are coral banks built on deeply submerged volcanoes. The Palaeozoic platform-type of sedimentary rocks, described from drill cores in northern Florida, are not like the Ouachita folds. Drilling has revealed no Palaeozoic rocks beneath southern Florida and the Bahamas. The magnetic anomaly map shows a marked change in central Florida. Drake *et al.*, in their Fig. 5, show three trend lines connecting southern Florida with the Bahamas and only one connecting it with northern Florida. It is suggested that the Florida-Bahamas Ridge, like the Lomonosov Ridge, formed when the main Atlantic Ocean started to open at the beginning of Cretaceous time and separated an ocean basin of Creaceous age from an older ocean basin.

Drake *et al.* hold that the Florida-Bahamas Ridge extends to Navidad Bank, north of Hispaniola. It thus ends at the major zone of faulting which,

---

[54]   Blackett, P.M.S., Bullard, E.C., and Runcorn, S.K., *Phil. Trans. Roy. Soc.*, A, 258 (1965)

[55]   Drake, C. L., Heirtzler, J., and Hirschman, J., *J. Geophys. Res.*, 68, 5289 (1963).

[56]   Miller, E. T., and Ewing, M., *Geophysics*, 21, 406 (1956).

[57]   Lee, C. S., *Inst. Petroleum J.*, 37, 633 (1951).

according to Hess and Maxwell,[58] and others, extends from Central America to the northern end of the west Indies arc. The Caribbean Sea and West Indies arc have often been regarded as associated with the Pacific Ocean, and I have discussed elsewhere their possible origin as a tongue, thrust from the Pacific and bounded by transform faults.[59]

A complete discussion would require consideration of the Hercynian orogeny and faulting and post-Triassic faulting. This seems feasible but will not be attempted here.

45

It has been suggested in this article that during Lower Palaeozoic time North America and Europe were approaching each other, that this motion stopped and that it later reversed. If this is true, the onset of the reverse motion and the start of reopening of the Atlantic Ocean must have been an event of very major significance in world geology. The evidence suggests that it occurred at about the close of the Jurassic and the beginning of the Cretaceous periods. It seems reasonable to link it with other major events of that age in the Americas.

McLearn[60] has pointed out that at that time the drainage of much of western North America reversed its direction so that rivers which had been flowing west and building a great shelf along the Pacific coast were interrupted by the rise of the Cordillera and began to follow their present directions. Gilluly[61] has pointed out that "In Cretaceous time plutons probably a thousand times larger than those of all the rest of the Phanerozoic were emplaced." The onset of a relative advance of the Americas over the Pacific Ocean floor might well have caused a crumpling of the shelves along that coast with the creation and rise of extensive batholiths. Gilluly has pointed this out and concluded that the likely cause was that "it is probable that the continent as a whole is moving away from a widening Atlantic."

I am happy to acknowledge the benefits of discussions with W. B. Harland, A. Hallam, J. Dewey, W. R. Church, F. D. Anderson, H. Williams, E. W. R. Neale, H. H. Hess, F. J. Vine, E. Irving, A. Quinn, T. Mutch, J. Sougy and others, and of correspondence with many. I also thank F. W. Beales, C. Harper and D. York for help with the final version of this article.

---

[58] Hess, H. H., and Maxwell, J. C., *Bull. Geol. Soc. Amer.*, 64, 1 (1953).

[59] Wilson, J. T., *Earth and Planetary Science Letters* (in the press).

[60] McLearn, F. H., *Geol. Surv. Canada, Mem.* (to be published).

[61] Gilluly, J., *Quart. J. Geol. Soc. London*, 119, 133 (1963).

This work was supported by the National Research Council of Canada, Vela-Uniform Program and Unesco.

(1966)

QUESTIONS:

1. At the time this article was published, the theory of "continental drift" was generally regarded as unproven, and was in fact still widely ridiculed. In that context, comment on the substance and tone of Wilson's statement in papragraph 12 that "Although objections to this view are still being raised, they seem to be minor in comparison with the other evidence."

2. Compare the style of this article with that of the selection elsewhere in this volume by Charles Lyell on the principles of geology. Comment on diction, sentence structure, and tone. What can you say about the audiences that Lyell and Wilson are writing for?

3. Summarize the evidence given or alluded to in this article that supports the idea that the Americas and Europe/Africa were once one land mass.

N. SCOTT MOMADAY

THE WAY TO RAINY MOUNTAIN

A Kiowa writer reminisces, and also passes on the
reminiscences of his grandmother. This famous piece appears in a
book of the same name.

〜

A single knoll rises out of the plain in Oklahoma, north and west of the
Wichita Range. For my people, the Kiowas, it is an old landmark, and
they gave it the name Rainy Mountain. The hardest weather in the world is
there. Winter brings blizzards, hot tornadic winds arise in the spring, and in
summer the prairie is an anvil's edge. The grass turns brittle and brown, and
it cracks beneath your feet. There are green belts along the rivers and creeks,
linear groves of hickory and pecan, willow and witch hazel. At a distance in
July or August the steaming foliage seems almost to writhe in fire. Great
green and yellow grasshoppers are everywhere in the tall grass, popping up
like corn to sting the flesh, and tortoises crawl about on the red earth, going
nowhere in the plenty of time. Loneliness is an aspect of the land. All things
in the plain are isolate; there is no confusion of objects in the eye, but *one*
hill or *one* tree or *one* man. To look upon that landscape in the early
morning, with the sun at your back, is to lose the sense of proportion. Your
imagination comes to life, and this, you think, is where Creation was begun.

I returned to Rainy Mountain in July. My grandmother had died in the
spring, and I wanted to be at her grave. She had lived to be very old and at
last infirm. Her only living daughter was with her when she died, and I was
told that in death her face was that of a child.

I like to think of her as a child. When she was born, the Kiowas were
living the last great moment of their history. For more than a hundred years
they had controlled the open range from the Smoky Hill River to the Red,
from the headwaters of the Canadian to the fork of the Arkansas and

Cimarron. In alliance with the Comanches, they had ruled the whole of the southern Plains. War was their sacred business, and they were among the finest horsemen the world has ever known. But warfare for the Kiowas was preeminently a matter of disposition rather than of survival, and they never understood the grim, unrelenting advance of the U.S. Cavalry. When at last, divided and ill-provisioned, they were driven onto the Staked Plains in the cold rains of autumn, they fell into panic. In Palo Duro Canyon they abandoned their crucial stores to pillage and had nothing then but their lives. In order to save themselves, they surrendered to the soldiers at Fort Sill and were imprisoned in the old stone corral that now stands as a military museum. My grandmother was spared the humiliation of those high gray walls by eight or ten years, but she must have known from birth the affliction of defeat, the dark brooding of old warriors.

Her name was Aho, and she belonged to the last culture to evolve in North America. Her forebears came down from the high country in western Montana nearly three centuries ago. They were a mountain people, a mysterious tribe of hunters whose language has never been positively classified in any major group. In the late seventeenth century they began a long migration to the south and east. It was a journey toward the dawn, and it led to a golden age. Along the way the Kiowas were befriended by the Crows, who gave them the culture and religion of the Plains. They acquired horses, and their ancient nomadic spirit was suddenly free of the ground. They acquired Tai-me, the sacred Sun Dance doll, from that moment the object and symbol of their worship, and so shared in the divinity of the sun. Not least, they acquired the sense of destiny, therefore courage and pride. When they entered upon the southern Plains they had been transformed. No longer were they slaves to the simple necessity of survival; they were a lordly and dangerous society of fighters and thieves, hunters and priests of the sun. According to their origin myth, they entered the world through a hollow log. From one point of view, their migration was the fruit of an old prophecy, for indeed they emerged from a sunless world.

5   Although my grandmother lived out her long life in the shadow of Rainy Mountain, the immense landscape of the continental interior lay like memory in her blood. She could tell of the Crows, whom she had never seen, and of the Black Hills, where she had never been. I wanted to see in reality what she had seen more perfectly in the mind's eye, and traveled fifteen hundred miles to begin my pilgrimage.

Yellowstone, it seemed to me, was the top of the world, a region of deep lakes and dark timber, canyons and waterfalls. But, beautiful as it is, one might have the sense of confinement there. The skyline in all directions is close at hand, the high wall of the woods and deep cleavages of shade. There is a perfect freedom in the mountains, but it belongs to the eagle and the elk, the badger and the bear. The Kiowas reckoned their stature by the distance they could see, and they were bent and blind in the wilderness.

Descending eastward, the highland meadows are a stairway to the plain. In July the inland slope of the Rockies is luxuriant with flax and buckwheat, stonecrop and larkspur. The earth unfolds and the limit of the land recedes. Clusters of trees, and animals grazing far in the distance, cause the vision to reach away and wonder to build upon the mind. The sun follows a longer course in the day, and the sky is immense beyond all comparison. The great billowing clouds that sail upon it are the shadows that move upon the grain like water, dividing light. Farther down, in the land of the Crows and Blackfeet, the plain is yellow. Sweet clover takes hold of the hills and bends upon itself to cover and seal the soil. There the Kiowas paused on their way; they had come to the place where they must change their lives. The sun is at home on the plains. Precisely there does it have the certain character of a god. When the Kiowas came to the land of the Crows, they could see the dark lees of the hills at dawn across the Bighorn River, the profusion of light on the grain shelves, the oldest deity ranging after the solstices. Not yet would they veer southward to the caldron of the land that lay below; they must wean their blood from the northern winter and hold the mountains a while longer in their view. They bore Tai-me in procession to the east.

A dark mist lay over the Black Hills, and the land was like iron. At the top of a ridge I caught sight of Devil's Tower upthrust against the gray sky as if in the birth of time the core of the earth had broken through its crust and the motion of the world was begun. There are things in nature that engender an awful quiet in the heart of man; Devil's Tower is one of them. Two centuries ago, because they could not do otherwise, the Kiowas made a legend at the base of the rock. My grandmother said:

> Eight children were there at play, seven sisters and their brother. Suddenly the boy was struck dumb; he trembled and began to run upon his hands and feet. His fingers became claws, and his body was covered with fur. Directly there was a bear where the boy had been. The sisters were terrified; they ran, and the bear after them. They came to the stump of a great tree, and the tree spoke to them. It bade them climb upon it, and as they did so it began to rise into the air. The bear came to kill them, but they were just beyond its reach. It reared against the tree and scored the bark all around with its claws. The seven sisters were borne into the sky, and they became the stars of the Big Dipper.

From that moment, and so long as the legend lives, the Kiowas have kinsmen in the night sky. Whatever they were in the mountains, they could be no more. However tenuous their well-being, however much they had suffered and would suffer again, they had found a way out of the wilderness.

My grandmother had a reverence for the sun, a holy regard that now is all but gone out of mankind. There was a wariness in her, and an ancient awe. She was a Christian in her later years, but she had come a long way about, and she never forgot her birthright. As a child she had been to the Sun Dances; she had taken part in those annual rites, and by them she had learned the restoration of her people in the presence of Tai-me. She was about seven when the last Kiowa Sun Dance was held in 1887 on the Washita River above Rainy Mountain Creek. The buffalo were gone. In order to consummate the ancient sacrifice—to impale the head of a buffalo bull upon the medicine tree—a delegation of old men journeyed into Texas, there to beg and barter for an animal from the Goodnight herd. She was ten when the Kiowas came together for the last time as a living Sun Dance culture. They could find no buffalo; they had to hang an old hide from the sacred tree. Before the dance could begin, a company of soldiers rode out from Fort Sill under orders to disperse the tribe. Forbidden without cause the essential act of their faith, having seen the wild herds slaughtered and left to rot upon the ground, the Kiowas backed away forever from the medicine tree. That was July 20, 1890, at the great bend of the Washita. My grandmother was there. Without bitterness, and for as long as she lived, she bore a vision of deicide.

10   Now that I can have her only in memory, I see my grandmother in the several postures that were peculiar to her: standing at the wood stove on a winter morning and turning meat in a great iron skillet; sitting at the south window, bent above her beadwork, and afterwards, when her vision failed, looking down for a long time into the fold of her hands; going out upon a cane, very slowly as she did when the weight of age came upon her; praying. I remember her most often at prayer. She made long, rambling prayers out of suffering and hope, having seen many things. I was never sure that I had the right to hear, so exclusive were they of all mere custom and company. The last time I saw her she prayed standing by the side of her bed at night, naked to the waist, the light of a kerosene lamp moving upon her dark skin. Her long, black hair, always drawn and braided in the day, lay upon her shoulders and against her breasts like a shawl. I do not speak Kiowa, and I never understood her prayers, but there was something inherently sad in the sound, some merest hesitation upon the syllables of sorrow. She began in a

high and descending pitch, exhausting her breath to silence; then again and again—and always the same intensity of effort, of something that is, and is not, like urgency in the human voice. Transported so in the dancing light among the shadows of her room, she seemed beyond the reach of time. But that was illusion; I think I knew then that I should not see her again.

Houses are like sentinels in the plain, old keepers of the weather watch. There, in a very little while, wood takes on the appearance of great age. All colors wear soon away in the wind and rain, and then the wood is burned gray and the grain appears and the nails turn red with rust. The window-panes are black and opaque; you imagine there is nothing within, and indeed there are many ghosts, bones given up to the land. They stand here and there against the sky, and you approach them for a longer time than you expect. They belong in the distance; it is their domain.

Once there was a lot of sound in my grandmother's house, a lot of coming and going, feasting and talk. The summers there were full of excitement and reunion. The Kiowas are a summer people; they abide the cold and keep to themselves, but when the season turns and the land becomes warm and vital they cannot hold still; an old love of going returns upon them. The aged visitors who came to my grandmother's house when I was a child were made of lean and leather, and they bore themselves upright. They wore great black hats and bright ample shirts that shook in the wind. They rubbed fat upon their hair and wound their braids with strips of colored cloth. Some of them painted their faces and carried the scars of old and cherished enmities. They were an old council of warlords, come to remind and be reminded of who they were. Their wives and daughters served them well. The women might indulge themselves; gossip was at once the mark and compensation of their servitude. They made loud and elaborate talk among themselves, full of jest and gesture, fright and false alarm. They went abroad in fringed and flowered shawls, bright beadwork and German silver. They were at home in the kitchen, and they prepared meals that were banquets.

There were frequent prayer meetings, and great nocturnal feasts. When I was a child I played with my cousins outside, where the lamplight fell upon the ground and the singing of the old people rose up around us and carried away into the darkness. There were a lot of good things to eat, a lot of laughter and surprise. And afterwards, when the quiet returned, I lay down with my grandmother and could hear the frogs away by the river and feel the motion of the air.

Now there is a funeral silence in the rooms, the endless wake of some final word. The walls have closed in upon my grandmother's house. When I returned to it in mourning, I saw for the first time in my life how small it was. It was late at night, and there was a white moon, nearly full. I sat for a long time on the stone steps by the kitchen door. From there I could see out across the land; I could see the long row of trees by the creek, the low light upon the rolling plains, and the stars of the Big Dipper. Once I looked at the moon and caught sight of a strange thing. A cricket had perched upon the handrail, only a few inches away from me. My line of vision was such that the creature filled the moon like a fossil. It had gone there, I thought, to live and die, for there, of all places, was its small definition made whole and eternal. A warm wind rose up and purled like the longing within me.

15   The next morning I awoke at dawn and went out on the dirt road to Rainy Mountain. It was already hot, and the grasshoppers began to fill the air. Still, it was early in the morning, and the birds sang out of the shadows. The long yellow grass on the mountain shone in the bright light, and a scissortail hied above the land. There, where it ought to be, at the end of a long and legendary way, was my grandmother's grave. Here and there on the dark stones were ancestral names. Looking back once, I saw the mountain and came away.

(1967)

QUESTIONS:

1. With reference to paragraph 4 and paragraph 7, discuss the relationship of Kiowas to their mythology as Momaday presents it.

2. Explain in your own words how the Kiowas "had found a way out of the wilderness."

3. Is it usually appropriate to use metaphorical language to this degree? Is it appropriate here?

4. Write an essay on the importance of an aspect of religion, myth, or ritual that is significant to you, expressing this importance at least in part by narrating a personal or shared memory.

5. In the final four lines of paragraph 12, Momaday intricately weaves the alliteration of several consonant sounds. What effect does this elaborate technique have on the writing?

6. Find instances in the essay where Momaday uses words in an odd or atypical manner. Why do you suppose he does this? How does it affect the reader?

7. In paragraph 8, what does Momaday mean by the phrase "because they could not do otherwise"?

Margaret Laurence

Where the World Began

In this descriptive essay a famous novelist evokes a sense of life in a small prairie town, and explores the effect that her experience has had on her as a person and as an author.

A strange place it was, that place where the world began. A place of incredible happenings, splendors and revelations, despairs like multitudinous pits of isolated hells. A place of shadow-spookiness, inhabited by the unknowable dead. A place of jubilation and of mourning, horrible and beautiful.

It was, in fact, a small prairie town.

Because that settlement and that land were my first and for many years my only real knowledge of this planet, in some profound way they remain my world, my way of viewing. My eyes were formed there. Towns like ours, set in a sea of land, have been described thousands of times as dull, bleak, flat, uninteresting. I have had it said to me that the railway trip across Canada is spectacular, except for the prairies, when it would be desirable to go to sleep for several days, until the ordeal is over. I am always unable to argue this point effectively. All I can say is—well, you really have to live there to know that country. The town of my childhood could be called bizarre, agonizingly repressive or cruel at times, and the land in which it grew could be called harsh in the violence of its seasonal changes. But never merely flat or uninteresting. Never dull.

In winter, we used to hitch rides on the back of the milk sleigh, our moccasins squeaking and slithering on the hard rutted snow of the roads, our hands in ice-bubbled mitts hanging onto the box edge of the sleigh for dear life, while Bert grinned at us through his great frosted mustache and shouted the horse into speed, daring us to stay put. Those mornings, rising, there would be the perpetual fascination of the frost feathers on windows, the ferns and flowers and eerie faces traced there during the night by unseen artists of the wind. Evenings, coming back from skating, the sky would be black but not dark, for you could see a cold glitter of stars from one side of the earth's rim to the other. And then the sometime astonishment when you saw the Northern Lights flaring across the sky, like the scrawled signature of God. After a blizzard, when the snowplow hadn't yet got through, school would be closed for the day, the assumption being that the town's young could not possibly flounder through five feet of snow in the pursuit of education. We would then gaily don snowshoes and flounder for miles out into the white dazzling deserts, in pursuit of a different kind of knowing. If you came back too close to night, through the woods at the foot of the town hill, the thin black branches of poplar and chokecherry now meringued with frost, sometimes you heard coyotes. Or maybe the banshee wolf-voices were really only inside your head.

5   Summers were scorching, and when no rain came and the wheat became bleached and dried before it headed, the faces of farmers and townsfolk would not smile much, and you took for granted, because it never seemed to have been any different, the frequent knocking at the back door and the young men standing there, mumbling or thrusting defiantly their requests for a drink of water and a sandwich if you could spare it. They were riding the freights, and you never knew where they had come from, or where they might end up, if anywhere. The Drought and Depression were like evil deities which had been there always. You understood and did not understand.

Yet the outside world had its continuing marvels. The poplar bluffs and the small river were filled and surrounded with a zillion different grasses, stones, and weed flowers. The meadowlarks sang undaunted from the twanging telephone wires along the gravel highway. Once we found an old flat-bottomed scow, and launched her, poling along the shallow brown waters, mending her with wodges of hastily chewed Spearmint, grounding her among the tangles of yellow marsh marigolds that grew succulently along the banks of the shrunken river, while the sun made our skins smell dusty-warm.

My best friend lived in an apartment above some stores on Main Street (its real name was Mountain Avenue, goodness knows why), an elegant apartment with royal-blue velvet curtains. The back roof, scarcely sloping at all, was corrugated tin, of a furnace-like warmth on a July afternoon, and we would sit there drinking lemonade and looking across the back lane at the

Fire Hall. Sometimes our vigil would be rewarded. Oh joy! Somebody's house burning down! We had an almost-perfect callousness in some ways. Then the wooden tower's bronze bell would clonk and toll like a thousand speeded funerals in a time of plague, and in a few minutes the team of giant black horses would cannon forth, pulling the fire wagon like some scarlet chariot of the Goths, while the firemen clung with one hand, adjusting their helmets as they went.

The oddities of the place were endless. An elderly lady used to serve, as her afternoon tea offering to other ladies, soda biscuits spread with peanut butter and topped with a whole marshmallow. Some considered this slightly eccentric, when compared with chopped egg sandwiches, and admittedly talked about her behind her back, but no one ever refused these delicacies or indicated to her that they thought she had slipped a cog. Another lady dyed her hair a bright and cheery orange, by strangers often mistaken at twenty paces for a feather hat. My own beloved stepmother wore a silver fox neckpiece, a whole pelt, *with the embalmed head still on.* My Ontario Irish grandfather said, "sparrow grass," a more interesting term than asparagus. The town dump was known as "the nuisance grounds," a phrase fraught with weird connotations, as though the effluvia of our lives was beneath contempt but at the same time was subtly threatening to the determined and sometimes hysterical propriety of our ways.

Some oddities were, as idiom had it, "funny ha ha"; others were "funny peculiar." Some were not so very funny at all. An old man lived, deranged, in a shack in the valley. Perhaps he wasn't even all that old, but to us he seemed a wild Methuselah figure, shambling among the underbrush and the tall couchgrass, muttering indecipherable curses or blessings, a prophet who had forgotten his prophecies. Everyone in town knew him, but no one knew him. He lived among us as though only occasionally and momentarily visible. The kids called him Andy Gump, and feared him. Some sought to prove their bravery by tormenting him. They were the medieval bear baiters, and he the lumbering bewildered bear, half blind, only rarely turning to snarl. Everything is to be found in a town like mine. Belsen, writ small but with the same ink.

All of us cast stones in one shape or another. In grade school, among the vulnerable and violent girls we were, the feared and despised were those few older girls from what was charmingly termed "the wrong side of the tracks." Tough in talk and tougher in muscle, they were said to be whores already. And may have been, that being about the only profession readily available to them.

The dead lived in that place, too. Not only the grandparents who had in local parlance, "passed on" and who gloomed, bearded or bonneted, from the sepia photographs in old albums, but also the uncles, forever eighteen or nineteen, whose names were carved on the granite family stones in the cemetery, but whose bones lay in France. My own young mother lay in that graveyard, beside other dead of our kin, and when I was ten, my father, too, only forty, left the living town for the dead dwelling on the hill.

When I was eighteen, I couldn't wait to get out of that town, away from the prairies. I did not know then that I would carry the land and town all my life within my skull, that they would form the mainspring and source of the writing I was to do, wherever and however far away I might live.

This was my territory in the time of my youth, and in a sense my life since then has been an attempt to look at it, to come to terms with it. Stultifying to the mind it certainly could be, and sometimes was, but not to the imagination. It was many things, but it was never dull.

The same, I now see, could be said for Canada in general. Why on earth did generations of Canadians pretend to believe this country dull? We knew perfectly well it wasn't. Yet for so long we did not proclaim what we knew. If our upsurge of so-called nationalism seems odd or irrelevant to outsiders, and even to some of our own people (*what's all the fuss about?*), they might try to understand that for many years we valued ourselves insufficiently, living as we did under the huge shadows of those two dominating figures, Uncle Sam and Britannia. We have only just begun to value ourselves, our land, our abilities. We have only just begun to recognize our legends and to give shape to our myths.

15 There are, God knows, enough aspects to deplore about this country. When I see the killing of our lakes and rivers with industrial wastes, I feel rage and despair. When I see our industries and natural resources increasingly taken over by America, I feel an overwhelming discouragement, especially as I cannot simply say "damn Yankees." It should never be forgotten that it is ourselves who have sold such a large amount of our birthright for a mess of plastic Progress. When I saw the War Measures Act being invoked in 1970, I lost forever the vestigial remains of the naïve wish-belief that repression could not happen here, or would not. And yet, of course, I had known all along in the deepest and often hidden caves of the heart that anything can happen anywhere, for the seeds of both man's freedom and his captivity are found everywhere, even in the microcosm of a prairie town. But in raging against our injustices, our stupidities, I do so *as family*, as I did, and still do in writing, about those aspects of my town

which I hated and which are always in some ways aspects of myself.

The land still draws me more than other lands. I have lived in Africa and in England, but splendid as both can be, they do not have the power to move me in the same way as, for example, that part of southern Ontario where I spent four months last summer in a cedar cabin beside a river. "Scratch a Canadian, and you find a phony pioneer," I used to say to myself in warning. But all the same it is true, I think, that we are not yet totally alienated from physical earth, and let us only pray we do not become so. I once thought that my lifelong fear and mistrust of cities made me a kind of old-fashioned freak; now I see it differently.

The cabin has a long window across its front western wall, and sitting at the oak table there in the mornings, I used to look out at the river and at the tall trees beyond, green-gold in the early light. The river was bronze; the sun caught it strangely, reflecting upon its surface the near-shore sand ripples underneath. Suddenly, the crescenting of a fish, gone before the eye could clearly give image to it. The old man next door said these leaping fish were carp. Himself, he preferred muskie, for he was a real fisherman and the muskie gave him a fight. The wind most often blew from the south, and the river flowed toward the south, so when the water was wind-riffled, and the current was strong, the river seemed to be flowing both ways. I liked this, and interpreted it as an omen, a natural symbol.

A few years ago, when I was back in Winnipeg, I gave a talk at my old college. It was open to the public, and afterward a very old man came up to me and asked me if my maiden name had been Wemyss. I said yes, thinking he might have known my father or my grandfather. But no. "When I was a young lad," he said, "I once worked for your great-grandfather, Robert Wemyss, when he had the sheep ranch at Raeburn." I think that was a moment when I realized all over again something of great importance to me. My long-ago families came from Scotland and Ireland, but in a sense that no longer mattered so much. My true roots were here.

I am not very patriotic, in the usual meaning of that word. I cannot say "My country right or wrong" in any political, social or literary context. But one thing is inalterable, for better or worse, for life.

This is where my world began. A world which includes the ancestors—both my own and other people's ancestors who become mine. A world which formed me, and continues to do so, even while I found it in some of its aspects, and continue to do so. A world which gave me my own lifework to do, because it was here that I learned the sight of my own particular eyes.

(1972)

QUESTIONS:

1. What does Laurence mean by the phrase, "My eyes were formed there"?

2. What comparison does Laurence make between a small prairie town and the nation of Canada in general?

3. What argument does Laurence put forth in this essay against prairie life being dull?

4. How does Laurence achieve a transition between discussion of small-town prairie life and discussion of Canada on a national scale?

5. Find examples of simile and metaphor in the essay. How does Laurence utilize figurative language to develop her argument that prairie life was never dull?

ROLAND BARTHES

THE WORLD OF WRESTLING

In this essay, Roland Barthes examines the spectacle of professional wrestling and the carefully constructed meanings contained within its gestures.

∽

The grandiloquent truth of gestures
on life's great occasions.
BAUDELAIRE

The virtue of all-in wrestling is that it is the spectacle of excess. Here we find a grandiloquence which must have been that of the ancient theatres. And in fact wrestling is an open-air spectacle, for what makes the circus or the arena what they are is not the sky (a romantic value suited rather to fashionable occasions), it is the drenching and vertical quality of the flood of light. Even hidden in the most squalid Parisian halls, wrestling partakes of the nature of the great solar spectacles, Greek drama and bull-fights: in both, a light without shadow generates an emotion without reserve.

There are people who think that wrestling is an ignoble sport. Wrestling is not a sport, it is a spectacle, and it is no more ignoble to attend a wrestled performance of Suffering than a performance of the sorrows of Arnolphe or Andromaque. Of course, there exists a false wrestling, in which the participants unnecessarily go to great lengths to make a show of a fair fight; this is of no interest. True wrestling, wrongly called amateur wrestling, is performed in second-rate halls, where the public spontaneously attunes itself to the spectacular nature of the contest, like the audience at a suburban cinema. Then these same people wax indignant because wrestling is a stage-managed sport (which ought, by the way, to mitigate its ignominy). The public is completely uninterested in knowing whether the contest is rigged or not, and rightly so; it abandons itself to the primary virtue of the spectacle, which is to abolish all motives and all consequences: what matters is not what it thinks but what it sees.

This public knows very well the distinction between wrestling and boxing; it knows that boxing is a Jansenist sport, based on a demonstration of excellence. One can bet on the outcome of a boxing-match: with wrestling, it would make no sense. A boxing-match is a story which is constructed before the eyes of the spectator; in wrestling, on the contrary, it is each moment which is intelligible, not the passage of time. The spectator is not interested in the rise and fall of fortunes; he expects the transient image of certain passions. Wrestling therefore demands an immediate reading of the juxtaposed meanings, so that there is no need to connect them. The logical conclusion of the contest does not interest the wrestling-fan, while on the contrary a boxing-match always implies a science of the future. In other words, wrestling is a sum of spectacles, of which no single one is a function: each moment imposes the total knowledge of a passion which rises erect and alone, without ever extending to the crowning moment of a result.

Thus the function of the wrestler is not to win; it is to go exactly through the motions which are expected of him. It is said that judo contains a hidden symbolic aspect; even in the midst of efficiency, its gestures are measured, precise but restricted, drawn accurately but by a stroke without volume. Wrestling, on the contrary, offers excessive gestures, exploited to the limit of their meaning. In judo, a man who is down is hardly down at all, he rolls over, he draws back, he eludes defeat, or, if the latter is obvious, he immediately disappears; in wrestling, a man who is down is exaggeratedly so, and completely fills the eyes of the spectators with the intolerable spectacle of his powerlessness.

5   This function of grandiloquence is indeed the same as that of ancient theatre, whose principle, language and props (masks and buskins) concurred in the exaggeratedly visible explanation of a Necessity. The gesture of the vanquished wrestler signifying to the world a defeat which, far from disguising, he emphasizes and holds like a pause in music, corresponds to the mask of antiquity meant to signify the tragic mode of the spectacle. In wrestling, as on the stage in antiquity, one is not ashamed of one's suffering, one knows how to cry, one has a liking for tears.

Each sign in wrestling is therefore endowed with an absolute clarity, since one must always understand everything on the spot. As soon as the adversaries are in the ring, the public is overwhelmed with the obviousness of the roles. As in the theatre, each physical type expresses to excess the part which has been assigned to the contestant. Thauvin, a fifty-year-old with an obese and sagging body, whose type of asexual hideousness always inspires feminine nicknames, displays in his flesh the characters of baseness, for his part is to represent what, in the classical concept of the *salaud*, the "bastard" (the key-concept of any wrestling match), appears as organically repugnant. The nausea voluntarily provoked by Thauvin shows therefore a very extended use of signs: not only is ugliness used here in order to signify baseness, but in addition ugliness is wholly gathered into a particularly repulsive quality of matter: the pallid collapse of dead flesh (the public calls Thauvin *la barbaque,* "stinking meat"), so that the passionate condemnation of the crowd no longer stems from its judgment, but instead from the very depth of its humours. It will thereafter let itself be frenetically embroiled in an idea of Thauvin which will conform entirely with this physical origin: his actions will perfectly correspond to the essential viscosity of his personage.

It is therefore in the body of the wrestler that we find the first key to the contest. I know from the start that all of Thauvin's actions, his treacheries, cruelties and acts of cowardice, will not fail to measure up to the first image of ignobility he gave me; I can trust him to carry out intelligently and to the last detail all the gestures of a kind of amorphous baseness, and thus fill to the brim the image of the most repugnant bastard there is: the bastard-octopus. Wrestlers therefore have a physique as peremptory as those of the characters of the *Commedia dell'Arte,* who display in advance, in their costumes and attitudes, the future contents of their parts: just as Pantaloon can never be anything but a ridiculous cuckold, Harlequin an astute servant and the Doctor a stupid pedant, in the same way Thauvin will never be anything but an ignoble traitor, Reinières (a tall blond fellow with a limp body and unkempt hair) the moving image of passivity, Mazaud (short and arrogant like a cock) that of grotesque conceit, and Orsano (an effeminate teddy-boy first seen in a blue-and-pink dressing-gown) that, doubly humorous, of a vindictive *salope*, or bitch (for I do not think that the public of the Elysée-Montmartre, like Littré, believes the word *salope* to be a masculine).

The physique of the wrestlers therefore constitutes a basic sign, which like a seed contains the whole fight. But this seed proliferates, for it is at every turn during the fight, in each new situation, that the body of the wrestler casts to the public the magical entertainment of a temperament which finds its natural expression in a gesture. The different strata of meaning throw light on each other, and form the most intelligible of spectacles. Wrestling is like a diacritic writing: above the fundamental meaning of his body, the wrestler arranges comments which are episodic but always opportune, and constantly help the reading of the fight by means of gestures, attitudes and mimicry which make the intention utterly obvious. Sometimes the wrestler triumphs with a repulsive sneer while kneeling on the good sportsman; sometimes he gives the crowd a conceited smile which forebodes an early revenge; sometimes, pinned to the ground, he hits the floor ostentatiously to make evident to all the intolerable nature of his situation; and sometimes he erects a complicated set of signs meant to make the public understand that he legitimately personifies the ever-entertaining image of the grumbler, endlessly confabulating about his displeasure.

We are therefore dealing with a real Human Comedy, where the most socially-inspired nuances of passion (conceit, rightfulness, refined cruelty, a sense of "paying one's debts") always felicitously find the clearest sign which can receive them, express them and triumphantly carry them to the confines of the hall. It is obvious that at such a pitch, it no longer matters whether the passion is genuine or not. What the public wants is the image of passion, not passion itself. There is no more a problem of truth in wrestling than in the theatre. In both, what is expected is the intelligible representation of moral situations which are usually private. This emptying out of interiority to the benefit of its exterior signs, this exhaustion of the content by the form, is the very principle of triumphant classical art. Wrestling is an immediate pantomime, infinitely more efficient than the dramatic pantomime, for the wrestler's gesture needs no anecdote, no decor, in short no transference in order to appear true.

10 Each moment in wrestling is therefore like an algebra which instantaneously unveils the relationship between a cause and its represented effect. Wrestling fans certainly experience a kind of intellectual pleasure in *seeing* the moral mechanism function so perfectly. Some wrestlers, who are great comedians, entertain as much as a Molière character, because they succeed in imposing an immediate reading of their inner nature: Armand Mazaud, a wrestler of an arrogant and ridiculous character (as one says that Harpagon is a character), always delights the audience by the mathematical rigour of his transcriptions, carrying the form of his gestures to the furthest reaches of their meaning, and giving to his manner of fighting a kind of vehemence and precision found in a great scholastic disputation, in which what is at stake is at once the triumph of pride and the formal concern with truth.

What is thus displayed for the public is the great spectacle of Suffering, Defeat, and Justice. Wrestling presents man's suffering with all the amplification of tragic masks. The wrestler who suffers in a hold which is reputedly cruel (an arm-lock, a twisted leg) offers an excessive portrayal of

Suffering; like a primitive Pietà, he exhibits for all to see his face, exagger-atedly contorted by an intolerable affliction. It is obvious, of course, that in wrestling reserve would be out of place, since it is opposed to the voluntary ostentation of the spectacle, to this Exhibition of Suffering which is the very aim of the fight. This is why all the actions which produce suffering are particularly spectacular, like the gesture of a conjuror who holds out his cards clearly to the public. Suffering which appeared without intelligible cause would not be understood; a concealed action that was actually cruel would transgress the underwritten rules of wrestling and would have no more sociological efficacy than a mad or parasitic gesture. On the contrary suffering appears as inflicted with emphasis and conviction, for everyone must not only see that the man suffers, but also and above all understand why he suffers. What wrestlers call a hold, that is, any figure which allows one to immobilize the adversary indefinitely and to have him at one's mercy, has precisely the function of preparing in a conventional, therefore intelligible, fashion the spectacle of suffering, of methodically establishing the conditions of suffering. The inertia of the vanquished allows the (temporary) victor to settle in his cruelty and to convey to the public this terrifying slowness of the torturer who is certain about the outcome of his actions; to grind the face of one's powerless adversary or to scrape his spine with one's fist with a deep and regular movement, or at least to produce the superficial appearance of such gestures: wrestling is the only sport which gives such an externalized image of torture. But here again, only the image is involved in the game, and the spectator does not wish for the actual suffering of the contestant; he only enjoys the perfection of an iconography. It is not true that wrestling is a sadistic spectacle: it is only an intelligible spectacle.

There is another figure, more spectacular still than a hold; it is the forearm smash, this loud slap of the forearm, this embryonic punch with which one clouts the chest of one's adversary, and which is accompanied by a dull noise and the exaggerated sagging of a vanquished body. In the forearm smash, catastrophe is brought to the point of maximum obvious-ness, so much so that ultimately the gesture appears as no more than a symbol; this is going too far, this is transgressing the moral rules of wrestling, where all signs must be excessively clear, but must not let the intention of clarity be seen. The public then shouts "He's laying it on!", not because it regrets the absence of real suffering, but because it condemns artifice: as in the theatre, one fails to put the part across as much by an excess of sincerity as by an excess of formalism.

We have already seen to what extent wrestlers exploit the resources of a given physical style, developed and put to use in order to unfold before the eyes of the public a total image of Defeat. The flaccidity of tall white bodies which collapse with one blow or crash into the ropes with arms flailing, the inertia of massive wrestlers rebounding pitiably off all the elastic surfaces of the ring, nothing can signify more clearly and more passionately the exemplary abasement of the vanquished. Deprived of all resilience, the wrestler's flesh is no longer anything but an unspeakable heap spread out on the floor, where it solicits relentless reviling and jubilation. There is here a paroxysm of meaning in the style of antiquity, which can only recall the heavily underlined intentions in Roman triumphs. At other times, there is another ancient posture which appears in the coupling of the wrestlers, that of the suppliant who, at the mercy of his opponent, on bended knees, his arms raised above his head, is slowly brought down by the vertical pressure of the victor. In wrestling, unlike judo, Defeat is not a conventional sign, abandoned as soon as it is understood; it is not an outcome, but quite the contrary, it is a duration, a display, it takes up the ancient myths of public Suffering and Humiliation: the cross and the pillory. It is as if the wrestler is crucified in broad daylight and in the sight of all. I have heard it said of a wrestler stretched on the ground: "He is dead, little Jesus, there, on the cross," and these ironic words revealed the hidden roots of a spectacle which enacts the exact gestures of the most ancient purifications.

But what wrestling is above all meant to portray is a purely moral concept: that of justice. The idea of "paying" is essential to wrestling, and the crowd's "Give it to him" means above all else "Make him pay." This is therefore, needless to say, an immanent justice. The baser the action of the "bastard," the more delighted the public is by the blow which he justly receives in return. If the villain—who is of course a coward—takes refuge behind the ropes, claiming unfairly to have a right to do so by a brazen mimicry, he is inexorably pursued there and caught, and the crowd is jubilant at seeing the rules broken for the sake of a deserved punishment. Wrestlers know very well how to play up to the capacity for indignation of the public by presenting the very limit of the concept of Justice, this outermost zone of confrontation where it is enough to infringe the rules a little more to open the gates of a world without restraints. For a wrestling-fan, nothing is finer than the revengeful fury of a betrayed fighter who throws himself vehemently not on a successful opponent but on the smarting image of foul play. Naturally, it is the pattern of Justice which matters here, much more than its content: wrestling is above all a quantitative sequence of compensations (an eye for an eye, a tooth for a tooth). This explains why sudden changes of circumstances have in the eyes of wrestling habitués a sort of moral beauty: they enjoy them as they would enjoy an inspired episode in a novel, and the greater the contrast between the success of a move and the reversal of fortune, the nearer the good luck of a contestant to his downfall, the more satisfying the dramatic mime is felt to be. Justice is therefore the embodiment of a possible transgression; it is from the fact that there is a Law that the spectacle of the passions which infringe it derives its value.

15 It is therefore easy to understand why out of five wrestling-matches, only about one is fair. One must realize, let it be repeated, that "fairness" here is a role or a genre, as in the theatre: the rules do not at all constitute a real constraint; they are the conventional appearance of fairness. So that in actual fact a fair fight is nothing but an exaggeratedly polite one: the contestants confront each other with zeal, not rage; they can remain in control of their passions, they do not punish their beaten opponent relentlessly, they stop fighting as soon as they are ordered to do so, and congratulate each other at the end of a particularly arduous episode, during which, however, they have not ceased to be fair. One must of course understand here that all these polite actions are brought to the notice of the public by the most conventional gestures of fairness: shaking hands, raising the arms, ostensibly avoiding a fruitless hold which would detract from the perfection of the contest.

Conversely, foul play exists only in its excessive signs: administering a big kick to one's beaten opponent, taking refuge behind the ropes while ostensibly invoking a purely formal right, refusing to shake hands with one's opponent before or after the fight, taking advantage of the end of the round to rush treacherously at the adversary from behind, fouling him while the referee is not looking (a move which obviously only has any value or function because in fact half the audience can see it and get indignant about it). Since Evil is the natural climate of wrestling, a fair fight has chiefly the value of being an exception. It surprises the aficionado, who greets it when he sees it as an anachronism and a rather sentimental throwback to the sporting tradition ("Aren't they playing fair, those two"); he feels suddenly moved at the sight of the general kindness of the world, but would probably die of boredom and indifference if wrestlers did not quickly return to the orgy of evil which alone makes good wrestling.

Extrapolated, fair wrestling could lead only to boxing or judo, whereas true wrestling derives its originality from all the excesses which make it a spectacle and not a sport. The ending of a boxing-match or a judo-contest is abrupt, like the full-stop which closes a demonstration. The rhythm of wrestling is quite different, for its natural meaning is that of rhetorical amplification: the emotional magniloquence, the repeated paroxysms, the exasperation of the retorts can only find their natural outcome in the most baroque confusion. Some fights, among the most successful kind, are crowned by a final charivari, a sort of unrestrained fantasia where the rules, the laws of the genre, the referee's censuring and the limits of the ring are abolished, swept away by a triumphant disorder which overflows into the hall and carries off pell-mell wrestlers, seconds, referee and spectators.

It has already been noted that in America wrestling represents a sort of mythological fight between Good and Evil (of a quasi-political nature, the "bad" wrestler always being supposed to be a Red). The process of creating heroes in French wrestling is very different, being based on ethics and not on politics. What the public is looking for here is the gradual construction of a highly moral image: that of the perfect "bastard." One comes to wrestling in order to attend the continuing adventures of a single major leading character, permanent and multiform like Punch or Scapino, inventive in unexpected figures and yet always faithful to his role. The "bastard" is here revealed as a Molière character or a "portrait" by La Bruyère, that is to say as a classical entity, an essence, whose acts are only significant epiphenomena arranged in time. This stylized character does not belong to any particular nation or party, and whether the wrestler is called Kuzchenko (nicknamed Moustache after Stalin), Yerpazian, Gaspardi, Jo Vignola or Nollières, the aficionado does not attribute to him any country except "fairness"—observing the rules.

What then is a "bastard" for this audience composed in part, we are told, of people who are themselves outside the rules of society? Essentially someone unstable, who accepts the rules only when they are useful to him and transgresses the formal continuity of attitudes. He is unpredictable, therefore asocial. He takes refuge behind the law when he considers that it is in his favour, and breaks it when he finds it useful to do so. Sometimes he rejects the formal boundaries of the ring and goes on hitting an adversary legally protected by the ropes, sometimes he reestablishes these boundaries and claims the protection of what he did not respect a few minutes earlier. This inconsistency, far more than treachery or cruelty, sends the audience beside itself with rage: offended not in its morality but in its logic, it considers the contradiction of arguments as the basest of crimes. The forbidden move becomes dirty only when it destroys a quantitative equilibrium and disturbs the rigorous reckoning of compensations; what is condemned by the audience is not at all the transgression of insipid official rules, it is the lack of revenge, the absence of a punishment. So that there is nothing more exciting for a crowd than the grandiloquent kick given to a vanquished "bastard"; the joy of punishing is at its climax when it is supported by a mathematical justification; contempt is then unrestrained. One is no longer dealing with a *salaud* but with a *salope*—the verbal gesture of the ultimate degradation.

20   Such a precise finality demands that wrestling should be exactly what the public expects of it. Wrestlers, who are very experienced, know perfectly how to direct the spontaneous episodes of the fight so as to make them conform to the image which the public has of the great legendary themes of its mythology. A wrestler can irritate or disgust, he never disappoints, for he always accomplishes completely, by a progressive solidification of signs, what the public expects of him. In wrestling, nothing exists except in the absolute, there is no symbol, no allusion, everything is presented exhaustively. Leaving nothing in the shade, each action discards all parasitic meanings and ceremonially offers to the public a pure and full signification, rounded like Nature. This grandiloquence is nothing but the popular and age-old image of the perfect intelligibility of reality. What is portrayed by wrestling is therefore an ideal understanding of things; it is the euphoria of men raised for a while above the constitutive ambiguity of everyday situations and placed before the panoramic view of a univocal Nature, in which signs at last correspond to causes, without obstacle, without evasion, without contradiction.

When the hero or the villain of the drama, the man who was seen a few minutes earlier possessed by moral rage, magnified into a sort of metaphysical sign, leaves the wrestling hall, impassive, anonymous, carrying a small suitcase and arm-in-arm with his wife, no one can doubt that wrestling holds that power of transmutation which is common to the Spectacle and to Religious Worship. In the ring, and even in the depths of their voluntary ignominy, wrestlers remain gods because they are, for a few moments, the key which opens Nature, the pure gesture which separates Good from Evil, and unveils the form of a Justice which is at last intelligible.

(1972)

QUESTIONS:

1. Barthes draws frequent comparisons between wrestling, judo and boxing. In what way(s) do the sports differ?

2. What use does Barthes make of analogy in this essay? Give examples.

3. From this essay, would you say that Barthes is a wrestling fan? How do you reach your conclusion? In what ways does Barthes indicate his position?

4. Comment on the closing paragraph of the essay. Does it effectively sum up the main points of Barthes' argument?

5. Do you agree with Barthes' assessment that wrestling is not a sport but a spectacle? Why?

Alden Nowlan

Ladies and Gentlemen, Stompin' Tom Connors!

*Through an interview poet Alden Nowlan gains insight into the man
behind the rough-hewn music through which Connors has gained
the affection of Canadians.*

∾

It's obvious that most of the 3,000 persons gathered here in this Halifax high-school auditorium are members of the working class, inhabitants of that other and all but invisible Canada whose separate culture so seldom impinges on the national consciousness that often its very existence is denied. Couples in their late twenties or early thirties predominate, many of them accompanied by children. The close-cropped sideburns of the men are not a style but a tradition; and if the women possess beauty, as many of them do, it's generally of a kind that's so unfashionable that the best adjective to describe it—buxom—sounds quaint. The older men tend to wear red and black, or green and black, checked lumber jackets, and are likely to carry pint bottles of Black Diamond or White Star rum in their pockets; there's a dressed-up air about their wives created less by their clothes than by the faintly self-conscious, faintly self-satisfied way they move or sit. Everywhere friends and acquaintances are exchanging greetings, "Are you here, Jake?"—being both more cordial and more formal than they'd be ordinarily, because this is a public place and a special occasion. The front row is occupied by little micro-skirted bubblegum girls of 13 or 14, who sit there to flirt with the boys in the band, from whom they'll ask and obtain nothing more than grins, winks, autographed pictures and a bittersweet sense of remote, romantic places.

The curtain rises to a guitar and bass fanfare, and there are little psychic shock waves as the lights go down and everyone turns his attention to the stage. The announcer blows into the microphone to make sure it's working. "And now," he says, "and now—from Skinner's Pond, Prince Edward Island," his voice rising above the ripple of applause, the expectant laughter, "it's," he inhales like a weight lifter before bellowing the final three words, "Stompin' Tom Connors!" Women clap; men whistle, whoop and stamp; but this collective acclamation is secondary to scores of voices shouting individual greetings. "Hiyuh, Tommy!" "God love you, Tommy boy!" "Hello, you long-legged Spud Islander, you!" "Walk'er, Tom, walk'er!" And this, from one man's fathomless drunkenness and affection, "Tommy, you damn thing!" over and over.

All of which is addressed to a skeletal figure with an old man's stoop and a little boy's grin, who shambles out of the wings and across to the microphone, a guitar hanging like a security blanket from one limp hand, and a piece of plywood about three feet long and a foot wide in the other. He might be an absentminded or nearsighted janitor come on stage to make some minor repair or adjustment and comically unaware that the curtain is up. But everybody here knows better. It's Stompin' Tom Connors, right enough, and the plywood is the stompin' board that prevents his jackhammering bootheel from ripping the carpet to shreds and grinding the floorboards to sawdust.

"Hello, everybody," he says simply, and begins to sing. For the next two hours the applause is literally continuous: it waxes and wanes but there's never a moment when at least one person isn't applauding. And through it all the drunk alternately mumbles and roars his benediction: "Tommy, you damn thing!"

Frequently distorting his face and voice, contorting his body, at times superimposing an artificial Newfoundland accent on his genuine Prince Edward Island one in a manner reminiscent of John Diefenbaker's imitations of Winston Churchill, Stompin' Tom Connors sings about "Bud the Spud" who trucks "the best doggone potatoes that's ever been growed" from the "bright red mud" of The Island, "down the old New Brunswick line," and along Highway 401 to the terminal dock in Toronto, where "they all gather 'round just to hear him talk about another big load of potatoes." He sings about working the coal boats out of Newfoundland; and of picking tobacco in Tillsonburg, Ontario, "My back still aches when I hear that word"; and about Saturday night in Sudbury: "The girls are out to bingo, the boys are gettin' stinko, and we'll think no more of Inco." He sings about 19 men who were killed building a bridge in Vancouver, and about a landslide that destroyed the town of Frank, Alberta, and of how the Black Donnellys will ride until the end of time down the Roman Line in Lucan, Ont. He sings *Mule Skinner Blues*, a sound poem to end all sound poems, in which he clucks like a hen, quacks like a duck and laughs like a kookaburra, while his heel, beating time, scrapes shavings off the plywood.

"Some folks ask me why don't I sing some of them nice Nashville songs," he tells the audience. "I tell them," and here he assumes the voice of the roaring boy from Skinner's Pond, "I tell them I'll be happy to sing some of them nice Nashville songs just as soon as them fellers in Nashville start singin' some of my songs," and he stresses the next three words, "*about my country.*" The crowd cheers. With an arch grin he breaks into a scatological parody of the Johnny Cash tearjerker, *The Green, Green Grass of Home*.

"My ambition? I guess you could say it's to sing Canada to the world," he said earlier that day as we sat in his hotel room amidst full and empty Moosehead and Molson bottles, and plates containing the stale lettuce and pickle garnishes of room service sandwiches, drinking unchilled beer from bottles that had been opened with a teaspoon, because nobody had been able to find an opener. The black cowboy hat that he wears on stage was on his head when I entered his room, and it was still there when I left hours later. "I started wearing it when I was a kid because we didn't grow our hair long then," he says. The hat looked ludicrous and a bit phony to me until I came to realize that it was talismanic, like a poor man's only prized possession, the one sure object in a trustless and uncertain cosmos. "To sing Canada to the world," might have sounded phony, too, especially when he repeated it in the tone of a man rather pleased with his own eloquence—except that by then, having spent the afternoon with him, I was convinced the man was so damn honest he deserved some special kind of divine protection, and that his fans, drunk or sober, knew what they were talking about when they yelled, "God love you, Tommy!"

On stage and in many of his photographs, Connors looks as if his face had been whittled with a jackknife from a hunk of cat spruce. Actually he possesses the careless good looks of the kind of truck driver who carries a mouth organ in his pocket and lazily charms the pants off waitresses. Thirty-five years old, he was on the road before he could walk properly; his earliest memory is of being carried by his mother, as she hitchhiked around Nova Scotia, where he was born. Later he crisscrossed the continent as frantically as Jack Kerouac, of whom, incidentally, he had never heard. In a very real sense, he has never had a home, which may explain why the sense of region and country is of such obvious importance to him.

"I was a bastard child," he says. "Looking back on it, I can see that it must have been tough, being on the road like that. But it didn't seem that way at the time. For all I knew every little kid in the world was travelling down some dirt road with his mother. To a little kid what matters most is having somebody to hold on to."

10 The worst of his early recollections is of being forcibly separated from his mother by child welfare authorities. "I kept crawling under tables and chairs and things, and they kept grabbing me by the wrist or ankle and dragging me out. I was punching and kicking and screaming, and they were yelling their heads off at me. I was, oh, maybe five years old then." He is silent for a moment, his eyes half-closed. "I don't think much about that," he says. "Afterward they put me in an orphanage in New Brunswick where they beat the hell out of me, and everybody else, with leather straps and bamboo canes, and whatever else they could lay their hands on, and if they couldn't find anything to hit you with they grabbed you by the hair and almost twisted your friggin' head off. I ran away from there every chance I got."

He began writing songs when he was 11. "They were poems," he says. "I wanted to be a poet. I can still remember every word of every poem we learned in grade school. But after a little while I decided they'd sound prettier if I put a tune to them, and so I started doin' that, too." One of the songs he wrote when he was 11, about a girl "with eyes like diamonds" and a "rose in her hair" waiting "on the hillside by the old Reversing Falls" in Saint John for her lover to come back from the "lonesome prairie" of Alberta, he included 20 years later on an early longplay album, *Bud the Spud*, which has sold more than 135,000 copies. "I guess I figured I owed that to the little guy," he says.

Connors has a habit of referring to his previous selves in the third person, either grammatically or, more often, by implication. He does the same with his stage personality. "I was me for a hell of a long time before I was Stompin' Tom," he says. He has another habit of almost never mentioning anyone, no matter how casually, without giving him a name and a brief description. "It was this big waiter, Boyd Macdonald in Peter-borough, he nicknamed me that."

It's part of the Stompin' Tom legend that he got started as a professional singer by being five cents short of the price of a beer. "It's true," he laughs. "That was six or seven years ago. I got into Timmins with 35 cents in my pocket, and dry enough to spit dust, and went into the Maple Leaf Hotel.

Well, beer cost 40 cents, and so I asked the waiter if he'd lend me a nickel. And he said, if you can play that thing—I had my guitar with me—if you can play that thing, maybe we'll give you the price of three or four beers. The next thing I knew I had a job singing there on Friday and Saturday nights for $10 or $15 and a room."

For years before that he'd been knocking on the doors of radio stations and recording companies. "Some of them would tell me to get lost, and some of them would give me the old don't call us routine, and some of them would let me sing a couple of songs and then treat me as if I was some kind of half-wit. Their attitude was, who in hell in his right mind is going to write a song with a first line that goes, 'Just a little bit west of Kapuskasing,' or a song about 'Movin' on to Rouyn.' Well, the people there in the Travel Host Lounge in Timmins, they loved it. I guess they were tired of hearing about the stars falling on Alabama and about people waltzing in Tennessee. They wanted to hear some songs about the north country. Their country." He adjusts his hat again; it's as if it played some small but mystical part in his thought processes.

15   Six months later he was still singing at the Maple Leaf, but his pay had risen to $35 a week. "I had a good thing going for me there in Timmins. By the time I left—that was after about 14 months—I'd got up to about $100 a week at the hotel, and I'd been on radio and television, and started doing shows in places like Kirkland Lake and then in places like Sudbury. It was the bar owners in some of those places that made me start using the plywood board. They said I was ripping up their rugs. Then I got a job at the Horseshoe Tavern in Toronto, and after that I got a recording contract. One thing that attracted a lot of attention to me in Toronto was there was somebody put up these billboards all over town, saying, 'Stomp out Stompin' Tom.' The funny thing is I don't know to this day who it was that put those billboards up. I don't know if they liked me or hated me: damn few people are neutral about me when they hear me sing! I do know it wasn't me, not on the $200 a week I was getting paid then."

Connors says that at this point he's "putting almost every cent I make back into the business," part of the business being a recording company, Boot Records, in Toronto, where he makes his headquarters. "I'd like to help keep some young singers and musicians from having as tough a time getting started as I did, and I'd like to promote Canadian talent. Some people say we're second-class Americans. Sure we are. But the Americans are second-class Canadians. I was in Ireland last year, putting on shows in the republic and the six counties, and you know what they said to me over there? They said, 'Tom, you're the first Canadian singer we ever heard that sang songs about Canada.' And they liked it. You don't have to of been in Newfoundland to understand my song about the Newfie coal boaters."

When he was seven years old he was "adopted out" of the orphanage by a family in Prince Edward Island. He ran away from there when he was 13 and went to work on the docks in Saint John, but it's still the country of his heart, as is evident from his conversation, although on stage he parodies his love of the island as he parodies his other emotions. "I'll feel sad," he explains, "and I'll sit down to write a song about it, and after a while I'll find myself laughin' at the song, and at myself, and I'll end up writing a song that kind of makes fun of the song that didn't get written."

He tells his audiences: "I come from Skinner's Pond, that's between Frog Pond and Big Brook, on The Island," and they laugh, contentedly, expectantly, as other audiences laugh at jokes about Jack Benny's miserliness or Dean Martin's boozing: the use of such bumpkinish place names has been part of a stock routine used by country-style comedians for generations. "The folks in Skinner's Pond, they're so tough, I knowed a girl there that knit a sweater outta barbed wire, usin' two crowbars for needles. That same girl, she had a dawg so big she hadta feed him with a slingshot."

A cleaning woman knocks at the door of his hotel room and asks him when can she straighten it up. Together they survey the mess and discuss the problem. He apologizes for being in her way and asks if it would inconvenience her to come back in an hour. She tells him that an hour would be fine, and apologizes for disturbing him. They thank one another, and she goes away. By this time, my teen-aged son, John, and a friend, Lindsay Buck, also from Fredericton, have shown up and been invited in, and Lindsay has been delegated to open the beers with the teaspoon. The telephone keeps ringing, and Connors keeps getting up and crossing the room to answer it. Some of the calls are from little kids who want to talk with him but can't think of anything to say: he is very patient and polite with them.

"Hank Williams," Connors says, "and Wilf Carter and Jimmie Rodgers and Hank Snow and Johnny Cash, they were my big heroes." From before daybreak until after midnight their voices—and the voices of the likes of Roy Acuff, Tex Ritter, Chet Atkins, Red Foley, Ernest Tubb and Eddy Arnold—poured from radio sets everywhere in rural and working-class North America, but especially in the southern United States and the Maritime provinces of Canada, so that in the Wild East, when Tom Connors and I were growing up there, they weren't categorized as "country" or "western" or, God help us, "hillbilly" singers: theirs was the only music in precisely the same sense that Cheddar was the only cheese.

One of the kids who was a teen-ager with me in Nova Scotia used to refer to Frank Sinatra as an "opera singer," and he wasn't trying to be funny, that's actually how he thought of him.

I remember when I was 16 being awakened by my father at five o'clock of a January morning in a house in which the only light came from kerosene lamps and the only heat from a wood stove in the kitchen. That was in 1949. We were cutting pit props that winter in the woods about four miles away: falling trees and sawing them into posts about five feet long that were shipped to England to prop up the walls and ceilings of coal mines. In order not to waste any of the daylight we walked to work in the dark and didn't start home again until after the sun had gone down. Coming from my black and glacial bedroom, where the temperature often was below freezing, down the even blacker and colder stairs, into the kitchen, where my father had kindled a roaring fire, brewed tea, warmed up his homemade beans and fried a hash of onions and potatoes, was like being taken aboard a warm, well-lighted ship after being dumped overboard in the North Atlantic.

And part of it all was the old battery-operated radio playing music from WWVA, Wheeling, West Virginia. Fiddles, guitars, mandolins, banjos, mouth organs, and bull fiddles playing the *Wabash Cannonball*, and the *Great Speckled Bird*, and *Wildwood Flower*. Floyd Tillman seeming to yawn his way through *Slipping Around*, and Little Jimmy Dickens screaming *Sleeping At The Foot Of The Bed*, and Eddy Arnold crooning *A Roomfull Of Roses*, and Grandpa Jones yelping *I Wish I'd Bought Me Half A Pint And Stayed In The Wagonyard*. Announcers with good old boys accents hawking ornamental shrubs and illustrated Bibles. "Send three doll-ahs, ye-ass that's three doll-ahs and three doll-ahs only to Bible, that's B-I-B-L-E, in care of WWVA, Wheeling, West Virginia..." My father, an infinitely sad, silent man, sometimes tapping time to the music with the toe of one of his lumberman's rubber boots as he smoked his handmade after-breakfast cigarette.

Soul music. Rooted in Scottish, Irish and English folk music, in approximately that order, reaching back to the first Elizabeth, and beyond to the Crusades, and earlier. Transplanted along the shores, beside the rivers, along the valleys, on the hillsides and among the mountains of North America. Each shore, river, valley, hillside and mountain settlement changing it slowly into something slightly different, assimilating elements from continental Europe and Africa, so that, for instance, Louisiana and Cape

Breton fiddling, Smoky Mountain and Miramichi ballad singing, came to sound less and less alike. Then, in the 1920s and 1930s, the gramophone and radio putting it all together again.

25   One of Tom Connors' heroes, Hank Snow, another Maritimer, who got his start during the Depression, singing as "Hank the Yodeling Ranger" over CHNS in Halifax, probably never heard of Larry Gorman, the Prince Edward Island balladeer known in the 19-century logging camps of New Brunswick and Maine as "The Man Who Makes the Songs." Snow learned his blue yodel from the 78 rpm and radio voice of Jimmie Rodgers, of Mississippi, who did for country music what Mark Twain did for American Literature—just as years later the records of both Snow and Rodgers were major influences not only on Tom Connors but on the young California Okie, Merle Haggard. The purists deplored such cross-fertilization, but then the purists tend to respect folk music only after it's dead.

It's easy to say of Tom Connors, or of any other country singer (he prefers to call what he does "hometown music"), that his music is rudimentary and his lyrics banal. By the time I was 13 I'd decided that all country music could be categorized as either maudlin or inane. To my family's bewilderment and disgust I tuned in the Metropolitan Opera Company on Saturday afternoons instead of the *Outports Program*, with Don Messer and his Islanders, from CFCY, Charlottetown. And that was right. As far as it went. But what's an important discovery for a child, another step toward maturity, may be sheer simplemindedness in an adult. For me, at this point, the appeal of country music lies in the very fact that it is music and poetry stripped to the bone. It's the only kind of music you can make by blowing on a piece of toilet paper wrapped around a pocket comb. "The songs that we'll be singin' won't be right but they'll be ringin'," Tom Connors says in his *Sudbury Saturday Night*.

Connors once hitchhiked 3,000 miles to see Hank Snow, crossing the border at Fort Erie, Ontario, by "sneaking under the rafters under the railroad bridge." He'd been without food for two days when he reached Snow's Rainbow Ranch, near Nashville. Snow refused to see him. Connors doesn't like to talk about his impressions of Snow then or in subsequent encounters. "Put down that you asked me what I thought about Hank Snow as a man and I answered, 'No comment.' He says the proudest day of his life was the day he became an American citizen. Shit. But, look, I was crazy about the guy when I was a kid and I still think he's one of the best singers around. Let's leave it at that." He's happier about his recent first meeting with Wilf Carter. "All we did was shake hands, but I figure you can tell a lot about a man by his handshake. He was all right."

The first time I heard a recording by Stompin' Tom Connors, I called to my wife, who was in another room, "Hey, you've got to listen to this guy! He's beautiful—and it's because he doesn't know any better!" By which I meant that he seemed to possess one of the rarest of virtues: innocence. During our hotel room conversation, he surprised me by quoting from the Koran. "Yeah, I've read it," he explained. "The Koran, and the Buddhist scriptures, and the Hindu scriptures, and a lot of psychology and stuff. In libraries mostly, when I was on the road. Growing up the way I did, what with the orphanage and all, I'd been taught that damn near everything I did was a sin. If you spit, it was a sin, and it was a sin if you scratched yourself. I damn near went crazy, thinking about it. So when I first read in some of them books that being happy wasn't necessarily a sin, I couldn't believe it. Then I thought to myself, Tom, you better believe it, because if you don't believe it, you'll go nuts. I've been a lot happier since then." He laughs. "But probably I shouldn't be saying this. Some of Stompin' Tom's fans might be kind of put off by the idea of him readin' the Koran."

What does he think about interviews and interviewers? "For 30 years nobody was interested in what I thought about anything. Now somebody's always asking me for my opinion about something. I like it."

His companion on many of his hitchhiking expeditions was Steve Foot, who recently began to make records under the name, Stevedore Steve.

"Steve and me, once we went six days with nothing to eat except two packages of Freshie. We jumped off a freight by mistake, thinking we were coming into a town. This was in Ontario. When we got off and looked around we could see we were right in the middle of nowhere. That was bad enough, but we kept on having bad luck. Like, we tried to bum something to eat from this bunch of guys working on the railroad, and they threatened to beat us up. They meant it, too. We had to run for it. Things like that kept happening. Then on the sixth day we knocked at the door of this house and this great big bugger came to the door and when we asked him how was chances of getting something to eat, he grabbed me by the shoulders and sort of half-dragged, half-threw me into the kitchen. I didn't know what in hell he was going to do. Then he yelled to his wife, Hey, Maw, there's a couple of hungry boys out here. She even gave us some bread and butter to eat while we were waiting for the bacon and eggs to cook. We stayed there three days. I went back there last year, looking for them, that big guy and his wife. But they weren't there any more. You meet a lot of nice people on the road."

Johnnie and Lindsay, who've also done some hitchhiking, interject that nowadays there are probably fewer nice people and more sons of bitches than there used to be.

Connors mulls that over. "I think it depends on how desperate you are," he says. "Look, if you're hungry enough you lose all your pride. I've seen people in this country eating out of garbage cans. Well, say, if you're not very hungry maybe you'll knock at the doors of two houses, and at the first place they'll set the dog on you, and at the second place they'll call the police. If you're not very hungry you'll give up then. But if you're hungry enough you'll keep knocking on doors—and sooner or later you'll find somebody that will feed you. Maybe it will be in the twentieth house, maybe the fiftieth. But you'll find somebody. Some of the nicest people I've met I'd never of run into if I hadn't been desperate."

He talks about going back to the places where he's been. "Last year when I was driving through Saint John I stopped to look at the place where the orphanage used to be. It's just kind of a vacant lot now. I stayed there two or three hours, just sitting and looking and thinking. It was a damn funny feeling. I didn't know whether to laugh or cry. That's the way I feel sometimes when I look at the ocean: there's something inside me that wants to laugh and cry all at the same time."

We all of us take another drink of beer and think about that. Then it's time for us to go. "You know what I think sometimes," Connors says as we shake hands (I give him a very firm handshake, remembering that he believes you can tell a lot about a man by the way he shakes hands), "I think sometimes that one of these days, I'll just say to hell with all this, doing shows and making records, to hell with all this money, and I'll hit the road again, hitchhiking. Maybe I'll call up my buddy, Steve, and ask him to go with me. Right across Canada, and back. Yeah, one of these days I just may do that."

Outside, in the hotel corridor, Johnnie asks me if I'm going to include Connors' last remark in what I'm going to write.

"I'm not sure if you should," he says. "Almost everybody that reads that will think it sounds phony, and it *would* sound phony coming from almost anybody else. But he's not phony. He's for real."

"I know," I say.

(1972)

QUESTIONS:

1. What surprising discoveries does Nowlan make about Stompin' Tom in the course of his interview?

2. Nowlan refers to Stompin' Tom's tendency to refer to his previous selves in the third person. What does Stompin' Tom mean in the quote; "I was me for a hell of a long time before I was Stompin' Tom"?

3. Why does Nowlan begin his essay with a description of a Stompin' Tom audience? What effect does this have on the essay as a whole?

4. Describe the difference between the voice of Nowlan in this essay, and the voice of Stompin' Tom as he is quoted here. What does this tell you about their histories and personalities?

5. How does Nowlan emphasize his point that Stompin' Tom is "for real" in this essay?

6. How does the title of this essay inform the reader as to its tone? What does it say about the author's feelings toward the subject?

Janet Flanner

Pablo Picasso

Flanner's many years of writing for The New Yorker *were distinguished not least of all by her brief biographical portraits, frequently written upon the death of the subject.*

～～

April 21, 1973 Pablo Picasso was born and died a phenomenon. "What is a painter?" he once asked, in front of others, while talking to himself. Having asked his question, he then answered it: "He is someone who founds his art collection by painting it himself." Picasso was that kind of painter. Another time, he overheard someone say, "I don't like Picasso," obviously referring to his paintings, and intruded to ask, "Which Picasso?"

During his career, Picasso, according to André Malraux, produced well over six thousand paintings. Of the multiple art styles that were then employed in France, he made use of all, especially those most filled with his own deformations. When he was approaching his eightieth birthday, he decided that, having gone through so many years, he should have the privilege of choosing for the rest of his life the age he preferred. "I have decided," he said, settling the problem, "that from now on I shall be aged thirty." His energies were so great that even in his bogus-thirties period his habitual creation continued pouring out, though it was mostly audible in his wit and visible in his psychological showmanship and legerdemain, all of which were trivialities compared to what he had produced in his previous era. Many of the wittiest things he said occurred in conversations in which he had the opportunity to cap what someone else had said. During the nineteen-thirties, when the fabrication of counterfeit Picassos was at its height—his works being the most often counterfeited because they rated the highest prices—an old journalist friend took a small Picasso painting belonging to some poor devil of an artist to Picasso himself for authentication, so the impoverished artist could sell it. "It's false," Picasso said. The friend took him another little Picasso, from a different source, and then a third. "It's false," Picasso said each time. "Now, listen, Pablo," the friend said. "I watched you paint this last picture with my own eyes." "I can paint false Picassos just as well as anybody," Picasso replied. He then bought the first Picasso at four times the price the poor artist might have hoped it would fetch. When another person took Picasso a counterfeit etching to sign, he signed it so many times that the man was able to sell it only as a curiosity to an autograph dealer.

When Stalin died, Picasso, who had by then joined the Communist Party, drew an imaginary portrait of a young Stalin with a neck like a column of steel and a brooding Georgian look on his face, and it was published in the Communist *Lettres Françaises*. It drew a chorus of complaints from the weekly's loyal readers, who sensed that this sketch was unofficial and therefore disloyal. On being asked by a friend who was a French Party member what he would do if France became Communized and he found himself forbidden to continue working as an artist except on Party cultural lines, Picasso answered, "If they stopped my painting, I would draw on paper. If they put me in prison without paper or pencil, I would draw with spit on the cell walls."

A remarkable description of the young Picasso came from the pen of Fernande Olivier, who was a member of the Montmartre Bateau-Lavoir group of artists and writers, to which Picasso belonged. She wrote, "Small, dark, thickset, unquiet, disquieting, with sombre eyes, deep-set, piercing, strange, almost fixed. Awkward gestures, a woman's hands; ill-dressed, careless. A thick lock of hair, black and glossy, cut across his intelligent, obstinate forehead. Half bohemian, half workman in his clothes; his hair, which was too long, brushing the collar of his worn-out coat." With time, his large, impressive head became a bronzed, hairless dome. An artist friend described Picasso's way of beginning a new picture: "His eyes widen, his nostrils flare, he frowns, he attacks the canvas like a picador sticking a bull."

5   Picasso painted his world, and often his people, to suit his own style, which, of course, rarely looked natural to the eyes of others. He said, "We all know that art is not truth. Art is a lie that makes us realize truth—at least, the truth that is given us to understand. People speak of naturalism's being in opposition to modern painting. I would like to know if anyone has ever seen a natural work of art. Nature and art, being two different things, cannot be the same thing. Through art we express our conception of what nature is not. There is no abstract art. You must always start with something.

Afterward, you can remove all the traces of reality; the danger is past in any case, because the idea of the object has left its ineffaceable mark. Academic training in beauty is a sham. When we love a woman, we don't start measuring her legs."

Picasso was a great conversationalist, and especially a noted solo talker. His recollections of his poverty in his early Montmartre days still make warming, valiant tales. Once, he and Fernande Olivier, who lived with him, had had no food for a day or so when some early Picasso admirer rapped on the studio door. Opening it, they found leaning against it a long loaf of bread, a bottle of wine, and a tin of sardines. In a few years, Picasso's pictures began selling at magically high prices. Thus, he was able to fulfill one of his earlier stated desires: "I should like to live like a poor man, with a great deal of money."

Picasso will rank as the most prodigious artist of our time. He was a man fortunately composed in terms of excess. Even as a genius, he had more gifts than he needed.

(1973)

MME. MARIE CURIE
(1866–1934)

The death of Mme. Curie here was an international death. A native of Poland, a worker in France, with radium donated by America, she was a terrifying example of strict scientific fidelity to each of those lands, to all civilized lands. During the early years of her marriage, "I did the housework," she said, "for we had to pay for our scientific research out of our own pockets. We worked in an abandoned shed. It was only a wooden shack with a skylight roof which didn't always keep the rain out." In winter, the poor Curies worked in their overcoats to keep warm; they were then, as always, very much in love with each other and with chemistry.

Today, in America, radium is characteristically supposed to have been found by Mme. Curie, and in France, naturally, the discovery is accredited to Monsieur. Probably both discovered it together, since they were never apart until he was killed in 1906 on a Paris street by a truck. Certainly the husband's first work was with crystals. And no Curie at all, but a friend of theirs, Henri Becquerel, discovered uranium rays. Still, it was Mme. Curie, intrigued and alone, who devised a method of measuring this radioactivity, as she named it; her proving that it contained essential atomic properties instituted a new method of chemical research, altered the conceptions of the nineteenth century, and for the twentieth gave the base for all modern theories concerning matter and energy. Eventually her husband deserted crystals to work with her on the discovery of polonium (which they named after her native land; Madame, *née* Sklodowska, was always a patriotic Pole); then she or he or they discovered radium. Madame thereupon determined the atomic weight of radium and obtained radium in metallic form. For this she was crowned with the Nobel Chemistry Prize. She was the only woman ever permitted to hold the post of university professor in France.

She called fame a burden, was busy, sensible, shy, had no time for polite palaver, was a good mother to her two girls. The younger, Éve, is beautiful and a professional pianist. The older daughter, Irène, carried on her mother's tradition by also marrying a scientist, Fred Joliot; they are the most promising laboratory couple here today, and have already made extremely important discoveries concerning the neutron.

When the Curies were first wed, Madame put her wedding money into a tandem bicycle; later they got around, financially, to two bicycles. Early snapshots show her young, fetching, in short skirt, mutton-leg sleeves, and an incredible hat, flat as a laboratory saucepan. Later in life, her husband said, "No matter what it does to one, even if it makes of one a body without a soul, one must go on with one's work."

5   Mme. Curie had long since been in that zealous condition before she finally died.

(1934)

QUESTIONS:

1. What does the word "naturally" (paragraph 2, "Mme. Marie Curie") imply about the attitudes Flanner believed to be common in France when she was writing?

2. Much of the effectiveness of brief biographical profiles rests on the degree to which the author is able to select telling details. What can

you say about the way in which the details given here about Curie and about Picasso serve to suggest a fully-rounded person?

3. Compare the piece on Curie with the piece on Picasso. Which leaves a stronger impression with the reader? To what extent is this the result of content and to what extent the result of Flanner's writing being stronger or weaker?

4. Write a brief description of someone who has died—either someone you knew yourself or a public figure who you have not known personally.

5. What effect does the lack of adjectives in Flanner's style (especially pronounced in her piece on Curie) have on the reader? Would the impression created of Curie be stronger or weaker if Flanner employed more adjectives to describe her for us?

6. Flanner is essentially uncritical of her subjects here. In the case of Picasso in particular, do you think the material Flanner draws on could be recast so as to create a rather different impression of the subject?

Marvin Harris

Pig Lovers and Pig Haters

In this essay a leading anthropologist puts forth possible explanations for widely varying attitudes in different cultures towards pig eating.

∾

Everyone knows examples of apparently irrational food habits. Chinese like dog meat but despise cow milk; we like cow milk but we won't eat dogs; some tribes in Brazil relish ants but despise venison. And so it goes around the world.

The riddle of the pig strikes me as a good follow-up to mother cow.[1] It presents the challenge of having to explain why certain people should hate, while others love, the very same animal.

The half of the riddle that pertains to pig haters is well known to Jews, Moslems, and Christians. The god of the ancient Hebrews went out of His way (once in the Book of Genesis and again in Leviticus) to denounce the pig as unclean, a beast that pollutes if it is tasted or touched. About 1,500 years later, Allah told His prophet Mohammed that the status of swine was to be the same for the followers of Islam. Among millions of Jews and hundreds of millions of Moslems, the pig remains an abomination, despite the fact that it can convert grains and tubers into high-grade fats and protein more efficiently than any other animal.

Less commonly known are the traditions of the fanatic pig lovers. The pig-loving center of the world is located in New Guinea and the South Pacific Melanesian islands. To the village-dwelling horticultural tribes of this region, swine are holy animals that must be sacrificed to the ancestors and eaten on all important occasions, such as marriages and funerals. In many tribes, pigs must be sacrificed to declare war and to make peace. The

---

[1] This essay occurs as the second in a volume which begins with a piece on why cows are regarded as sacred in some cultures.

tribesmen believe that their departed ancestors crave pork. So overwhelming is the hunger for pig flesh among both the living and the dead that from time to time huge feasts are organized and almost all of a tribe's pigs are eaten at once. For several days in a row, the villagers and their guests gorge on great quantities of pork, vomiting what they cannot digest in order to make room for more. When it is all over, the pig herd is so reduced in size that years of painstaking husbandry are needed to rebuild it. No sooner is this accomplished than preparations are made for another gluttonous orgy. And so the bizarre cycle of apparent mismanagement goes on.

5   I shall begin with the problem of the Jewish and Islamic pig haters. Why should gods so exalted as Jahweh and Allah have bothered to condemn a harmless and even laughable beast whose flesh is relished by the greater part of mankind? Scholars who accept the biblical and Koranic condemnation of swine have offered a number of explanations. Before the Renaissance, the most popular was that the pig is literally a dirty animal—dirtier than others because it wallows in its own urine and eats excrement. But linking physical uncleanliness to religious abhorrence leads to inconsistencies. Cows that are kept in a confined space also splash about in their own urine and feces. And hungry cows will eat human excrement with gusto. Dogs and chickens do the same thing without getting anyone very upset, and the ancients must have known that pigs raised in clean pens make fastidious house pets. Finally, if we invoke purely aesthetic standards of "cleanliness," there is the formidable inconsistency that the Bible classifies locusts and grasshoppers as "clean." The argument that insects are aesthetically more wholesome than pigs will not advance the cause of the faithful.

These inconsistencies were recognized by the Jewish rabbinate at the beginning of the Renaissance. To Moses Maimonides, court physician to Saladin during the twelfth century in Cairo, Egypt, we owe the first naturalistic explanation of the Jewish and Moslem rejection of pork. Maimonides said that God had intended the ban on pork as a public health measure. Swine's flesh "has a bad and damaging effect upon the body," wrote the rabbi. Maimonides was none too specific about the medical reasons for this opinion, but he was the emperor's physician, and his judgment was widely respected.

In the middle of the nineteenth century, the discovery that trichinosis was caused by eating undercooked pork was interpreted as a precise verification of the wisdom of Maimonides. Reform-minded Jews rejoiced in the rational substratum of the biblical codes and promptly renounced the taboo on pork. If properly cooked, pork is not a menace to public health, and so its consumption cannot be offensive to God. This provoked rabbis of more fundamentalist persuasion to launch a counter-attack against the entire naturalistic tradition. If Jahweh had merely wanted to protect the health of His people, He would have instructed them to eat only well-cooked pork rather than no pork at all. Clearly, it is argued, Jahweh had something else in mind—something more important than mere physical well-being.

In addition to this theological inconsistency, Maimonides' explanation suffers from medical and epidemiological contradictions. The pig is a vector for human disease, but so are other domestic animals freely consumed by Moslems and Jews. For example, under-cooked beef is a source of parasites, notably tapeworms, which can grow to a length of sixteen to twenty feet within a man's intestines, induce severe anemia, and lower resistance to other infectious diseases. Cattle, goats, and sheep are also vectors for brucellosis, a common bacterial infection in underdeveloped countries that is accompanied by fever, chills, sweats, weakness, pain, and aches. The most dangerous form is *Brucellosis melitensis,* transmitted by goats and sheep. Its symptoms are lethargy, fatigue, nervousness, and mental depression often mistaken for psychoneurosis. Finally, there is anthrax, a disease transmitted by cattle, sheep, goats, horses, and mules, but not by pigs. Unlike trichinosis, which seldom has fatal consequences and which does not even produce symptoms in the majority of infected individuals, anthrax often runs a rapid course that begins with body boils and terminates in death through blood poisoning. The great epidemics of anthrax that formerly swept across Europe and Asia were not brought under control until the development of the anthrax vaccine by Louis Pasteur in 1881.

Jahweh's failure to interdict contact with the domesticated vectors of anthrax is especially damaging to Maimonides' explanation, since the relationship between this disease in animals and man was known during biblical times. As described in the Book of Exodus, one of the plagues sent against the Egyptians clearly relates the symptomology of animal anthrax to a human disease:

> ...and it became a boil breaking forth with blains upon man and beast. And the magicians could not stand before Moses because of the boils, for the boils were upon the magicians, and upon all the Egyptians.

10   Faced with these contradictions, most Jewish and Moslem theologians have abandoned the search for a naturalistic basis of pig hatred. A frankly mystical stance has recently gained favor, in which the grace afforded by

conformity to dietary taboos is said to depend upon not knowing exactly what Jahweh had in mind and in not trying to find out.

Modern anthropological scholarship has reached a similar impasse. For example, with all his faults, Moses Maimonides was closer to an explanation than Sir James Frazer, renowned author of *The Golden Bough*. Frazer declared that pigs, like "all so-called unclean animals, were originally sacred; the reason for not eating them was that many were originally divine." This is of no help whatsoever, since sheep, goats, and cows were also once worshiped in the Middle East, and yet their meat is much enjoyed by all ethnic and religious groups in the region. In particular, the cow, whose golden calf was worshiped at the foot of Mt. Sinai, would seem by Frazer's logic to make a more logical unclean animal for the Hebrews than the pig.

Other scholars have suggested that pigs along with the rest of the animals tabooed in the Bible and the Koran, were once the totemic symbols of different tribal clans. This may very well have been the case at some remote point in history, but if we grant that possibility, we must also grant that "clean" animals such as cattle, sheep, and goats might also have served as totems. Contrary to much writing on the subject of totemism, totems are usually not animals valued as a food resource. The most popular totems among primitive clans in Australia and Africa are relatively useless birds like ravens and finches, or insects like gnats, ants, and mosquitoes, or even inanimate objects like clouds and boulders. Moreover, even when a valuable animal is a totem, there is no invariant rule that requires its human associates to refrain from eating it. With so many options available, saying that the pig was a totem doesn't explain anything. One might as well declare: "The pig was tabooed because it was tabooed."

I prefer Maimonides' approach. At least the rabbi tried to understand the taboo by placing it in a natural context of health and disease where definite mundane and practical forces were at work. The only trouble was that his view of the relevant conditions of pig hate was constrained by a physician's typical narrow concern with bodily pathology.

The solution to the riddle of the pig requires us to adopt a much broader definition of public health, one that includes the essential processes by which animals, plants, and people manage to coexist in viable natural and cultural communities. I think that the Bible and the Koran condemned the pig because pig farming was a threat to the integrity of the basic cultural and natural ecosystems of the Middle East.

To begin with, we must take into account the fact that the protohistoric Hebrews—the children of Abraham, at the turn of the second millennium

B.C.—were culturally adapted to life in the rugged, sparsely inhabited arid areas between the river valleys of Mesopotamia and Egypt. Until their conquest of the Jordan Valley in Palestine, beginning in the thirteenth century B.C., the Hebrews were nomadic pastoralists, living almost entirely from herds of sheep, goats, and cattle. Like all pastoral peoples they maintained close relationships with the sedentary farmers who held the oases and the great rivers. From time to time these relationships matured into a more sedentary, agriculturally oriented lifestyle. This appears to have been the case with Abraham's descendants in Mesopotamia, Joseph's followers in Egypt, and Isaac's followers in the western Negev. But even during the climax of urban and village life under King David and King Solomon, the herding of sheep, goats, and cattle continued to be a very important economic activity.

Within the overall pattern of this mixed farming and pastoral complex, the divine prohibition against pork constituted a sound ecological strategy. The nomadic Israelites could not raise pigs in their arid habitats, while for the semi-sedentary and village farming populations, pigs were more of a threat than an asset.

The basic reason for this is that the world zones of pastoral nomadism correspond to unforested plains and hills that are too arid for rainfall agriculture and that cannot easily be irrigated. The domestic animals best adapted to these zones are the ruminants—cattle, sheep, and goats. Ruminants have sacks anterior to their stomachs which enable them to digest grass, leaves, and other foods consisting mainly of cellulose more efficiently than any other mammals.

The pig, however, is primarily a creature of forests and shaded river-banks. Although it is omnivorous, its best weight gain is from food low in cellulose—nuts, fruits, tubers, and especially grains, making it a direct competitor of man. It cannot subsist on grass alone, and nowhere in the world do fully nomadic pastoralists raise significant numbers of pigs. The pig has the further disadvantage of not being a practical source of milk and of being notoriously difficult to herd over long distances.

Above all, the pig is thermodynamically ill-adapted to the hot, dry climate of the Negev, the Jordan Valley, and the other lands of the Bible and the Koran. Compared to cattle, goats and sheep, the pig has an inefficient system for regulating body temperature. Despite the expression "To sweat like a pig," it has recently been proved that pigs can't sweat at all. Human beings, the sweatiest of all mammals, cool themselves by evaporating as much as 1,000 grams of body liquid per hour from each square meter of body surface. The best the pig can manage is 30 grams per square meter. Even sheep evaporate twice as much body liquid through their skins as pigs. Sheep also have the advantage of thick white wool that both reflects the sun's rays and provides insulation when the temperature of the air rises above that of the body. According to L.E. Mount of the Agricultural Research Council Institute of Animal Physiology in Cambridge, England, adult pigs will die if exposed to direct sunlight and air temperatures over 98° F. In the Jordan Valley, air temperatures of 110° F. occur almost every summer, and there is intense sunshine throughout the year.

20   To compensate for its lack of protective hair and its inability to sweat, the pig must dampen its skin with external moisture. It prefers to do this by wallowing in fresh clean mud, but it will cover its skin with its own urine and feces if nothing else is available. Below 84° F., pigs kept in pens deposit their excreta away from their sleeping and feeding areas, while above 84° F. they begin to excrete indiscriminately throughout the pen. The higher the temperature, the "dirtier" they become. So there is some truth to the theory that the religious uncleanliness of the pig rests upon actual physical dirtiness. Only it is not in the nature of the pig to be dirty everywhere; rather it is in the nature of the hot, arid habitat of the Middle East to make the pig maximally dependent upon the cooling effect of its own excrement.

Sheep and goats were the first animals to be domesticated in the Middle East, possibly as early as 9,000 B.C. Pigs were domesticated in the same general region about 2,000 years later. Bone counts conducted by archeologists at early prehistoric village farming sites show that the domesticated pig was almost always a relatively minor part of the village fauna, constituting only about 5 percent of the food animal remains. This is what one would expect of a creature which had to be provided with shade and mudholes, couldn't be milked, and ate the same food as man.

As I pointed out in the case of the Hindu prohibition on beef, under preindustrial conditions, any animal that is raised primarily for its meat is a luxury. This generalization applies as well to preindustrial pastoralists, who seldom exploit their herds primarily for meat.

Among the ancient mixed farming and pastoralist communities of the Middle East, domestic animals were valued primarily as sources of milk, cheese, hides, dung, fiber, and traction for plowing. Goats, sheep, and cattle provided ample amounts of these items plus an occasional supplement of lean meat. From the beginning, therefore, pork must have been a luxury food, esteemed for its succulent, tender, and fatty qualities.

Between 7,000 and 2,000 B.C. pork became still more of a luxury. During this period there was a sixtyfold increase in the human population of the Middle East. Extensive deforestation accompanied the rise in population, especially as a result of permanent damage caused by the large herds of sheep and goats. Shade and water, the natural conditions appropriate for pig raising, became progressively more scarce, and pork became even more of an ecological and economical luxury.

25 As in the case of the beef-eating taboo, the greater the temptation, the greater the need for divine interdiction. This relationship is generally accepted as suitable for explaining why the gods are always so interested in combating sexual temptations such as incest and adultery. Here I merely apply it to a tempting food. The Middle East is the wrong place to raise pigs, but pork remains a succulent treat. People always find it difficult to resist such temptations on their own. Hence Jahweh was heard to say that swine were unclean, not only as food, but to the touch as well. Allah was heard to repeat the same message for the same reason: It was ecologically maladaptive to try to raise pigs in substantial numbers. Small-scale production would only increase the temptation. Better then, to interdict the consumption of pork entirely, and to concentrate on raising goats, sheep, and cattle. Pigs tasted good but it was too expensive to feed them and keep them cool.

Many questions remain, especially why each of the other creatures interdicted by the Bible—vultures, hawks, snakes, snails, shellfish, fish without scales, and so forth—came under the same divine taboo. And why Jews and Moslems, no longer living in the Middle East, continue—with varying degrees of exactitude and zeal—to observe the ancient dietary laws. In general, it appears to me that most of the interdicted birds and animals fall squarely into one of two categories. Some, like ospreys, vultures, and hawks, are not even potentially significant sources of food. Others, like shellfish, are obviously unavailable to mixed pastoral-farming populations. Neither of these categories of tabooed creatures raises the kind of question I have set out to answer—namely, how to account for an apparently bizarre and wasteful taboo. There is obviously nothing irrational about not spending one's time chasing vultures for dinner, or not hiking fifty miles across the desert for a plate of clams on the half shell.

This is an appropriate moment to deny the claim that all religiously sanctioned food practices have ecological explanations. Taboos also have social functions, such as helping people to think of themselves as a distinctive community. This function is well served by the modern observance of dietary rules among Moslems and Jews outside of their Middle Eastern homelands. The question to be put to these practices is whether they diminish in some significant degree the practical and mundane welfare of Jews and Moslems by depriving them of nutritional factors for which there are no readily available substitutes. I think the answer is almost certainly negative. But now permit me to resist another kind of temptation—the temptation to explain everything. I think more will be learned about pig haters if we turn to the other half of the riddle, to the pig lovers.

Pig love is the soulful opposite of the divine opprobrium that Moslems and Jews heap on swine. This condition is not reached through mere gustatory enthusiasm pork cookery. Many culinary traditions, including the Euro-American and Chinese, esteem the flesh and fat of pigs. Pig love is something else. It is a state of total community between man and pig. While the presence of pigs threatens the human status of Moslems and Jews, in the ambience of pig love one cannot truly be human except in the company of pigs.

Pig love includes raising pigs to be a member of the family, sleeping next to them, talking to them, stroking and fondling them, calling them by name, leading them on a leash to the fields, weeping when they fall sick or are injured, and feeding them with choice morsels from the family table. But unlike Hindu love of cow, pig love also includes obligatory sacrificing and eating of pigs on special occasions. Because of ritual slaughter and sacred feasting, pig love provides a broader prospect for communion between man and beast than is true of the Hindu farmer and his cow. The climax of pig love is the incorporation of the pig as flesh into the flesh of the human host and of the pig as spirit into the spirit of the ancestors.

30 Pig love is honoring your dead father by clubbing a beloved sow to death on his grave site and roasting it in an earth oven dug on the spot. Pig love is stuffing fistfuls of cold, salted belly fat into your brother-in-law's mouth to make him loyal and happy. Above all, pig love is the great pig feast, held once or twice a generation, when to satisfy the ancestors' craving for pork, assuring communal health, and secure victory in future wars, most of the adult pigs are killed off and gluttonously devoured.

Professor Roy Rappaport of the University of Michigan has made a detailed study of the relationship between pigs and pig-loving Maring, a remote group of tribesmen living in the Bismarck Mountains of New Guinea. In his book *Pigs for the Ancestors: Ritual in the Ecology of a New Guinea People*, Rappaport describes how pig love contributes to the solution of basic human problems. Under the given circumstances of Maring life, there are few viable alternatives.

Each local Maring subgroup or clan holds a pig festival on the average about once every twelve years. The entire festival—including various preparations, small-scale sacrifices, and the final massive slaughter—lasts about a year and is known in the Maring language as a *kaiko*. In the first two or three months immediately following the completion of its *kaiko*, the clan engages in armed combat with enemy clans, leading to many casualties and eventual loss or gain of territory. Additional pigs are sacrificed during the fighting, and both the victors and the vanquished soon find themselves entirely bereft of adult pigs with which to curry favor from their respective ancestors. Fighting ceases abruptly, and the belligerents repair to sacred spots to plant small trees known as *rumbim*. Every adult male clansman participates in this ritual by laying hands on the *rumbim* sapling as it is put into the ground.

The war magician addresses the ancestors, explaining that they have run out of pigs and are thankful to be alive. He assures the ancestors that the fighting is now over and that there will be no resumption of hostilities as long as the *rumbim* remains in the ground. From now on, the thoughts and efforts of the living will be directed toward raising pigs; only when a new herd of pigs has been raised, enough for a mighty *kaiko* with which to thank the ancestors properly, will the warriors think of uprooting the *rumbim* and returning to the battlefield.

By a detailed study of one clan called the Tsembaga, Rappaport has been able to show that the entire cycle—which consists of *kaiko*, followed by warfare, the planting of *rumbim*, truce, the raising of a new pig herd, the uprooting of *rumbim*, and new *kaiko*—is no mere psychodrama of pig farmers gone berserk. Every part of this cycle is integrated within a complex, self-regulating ecosystem, that effectively adjusts the size and distribution of the Tsembaga's human and animal population to conform to available resources and production opportunities.

The one question that is central to the understanding of pig love among the Maring is: How do the people decide when they have enough pigs to thank the ancestors properly? The Maring themselves were unable to state how many years should elapse or how many pigs are needed to stage a proper *kaiko*. Possibility of agreement on the basis of a fixed number of animals or years is virtually eliminated because the Maring have no calendar and their language lacks words for numbers larger than three.

The *kaiko* of 1963 observed by Rappaport began when there were 169 pigs and about 200 members of the Tsembaga clan. It is the meaning of these numbers in terms of daily work routines and settlement patterns that provides the key to the length of the cycle.

The task of raising pigs, as well as that of cultivating yams, taro, and sweet potatoes, depends primarily upon the labor of the Maring women. Baby pigs are carried along with human infants to the gardens. After they are weaned, their mistresses train them to trot along behind like dogs. At the age of four or five months, the pigs are turned loose in the forests to scrounge for themselves until their mistresses call them home at night to be fed a daily ration of leftover or substandard sweet potatoes and yams. As each woman's pigs mature and as their numbers increase, she must work harder to provide them with their evening meal.

While the *rumbim* remained in the ground, Rappaport found that the Tsembaga women were under considerable pressure to increase the size of their gardens, to plant more sweet potatoes and yams, and to raise more pigs as quickly as possible in order to have "enough" pigs to hold the next *kaiko* before the enemy did. Mature pigs, weighing about 135 pounds, are heavier than the average adult Maring, and even with their daily scrounging, they cost each woman about as much effort to feed as an adult human. At the time of the uprooting of the *rumbim* in 1963, the more ambitious Tsembaga women were taking care of the equivalent of six 135-pounders in addition to gardening for themselves and their families, cooking, nursing, carrying infants about, and manufacturing household items such as net bags, string aprons, and loincloths. Rappaport calculates that taking care of six pigs alone uses up over 50 percent of the total daily energy which a healthy, well-fed Maring woman is capable of expending.

The increase in the pig population is normally also accompanied by an increase in the human population, especially among groups that have been victorious in the previous war. Pigs and people must be fed from the gardens which are hacked and burned out of the tropical forest that covers the slopes of the Bismarck Mountains. Like similar horticultural systems in other tropical areas, the fertility of the Maring gardens depends upon the nitrogen that is put into the soil by the ashes left from burning off the trees. These gardens cannot be planted for more than two or three years consecutively, since once the trees are gone, the heavy rains quickly wash away the nitrogen and other soil nutrients. The only remedy is to choose another site and burn off another segment of the forest. After a decade or so, the old gardens get covered over with enough secondary growth so that they can be burned again and replanted. These old garden sites are preferred because they are easier to clear than virgin forest. But as the pig and human populations spurt upward during the *rumbim* truce, the maturation of the old garden sites lags behind and new gardens must be established in the virgin tracts. While there is plenty of virgin forest available, the new garden sites place an extra strain on everybody and lower the typical rate of return for every unit of labor the Maring invest in feeding themselves and their pigs.

40 The men whose task it is to clear and burn the new gardens must work harder because of the greater thickness and height of the virgin trees. But it is the women who suffer most, since the new gardens are necessarily located at a greater distance from the center of the village. Not only must the women plant larger gardens to feed their families and pigs, but they must consume more and more of their time just walking to work and more and more of their energy hauling piglets and babies up to and down from the garden and the heavy loads of harvested yams and sweet potatoes back to their houses.

A further source of tension arises from the increased effort involved in protecting the gardens from being eaten up by the mature pigs that are let loose to scrounge for themselves. Every garden must be surrounded by a stout fence to keep the pigs out. A hungry 150-pound sow, however, is a formidable adversary. Fences are breached and gardens invaded more frequently as the pig herd multiplies. If caught by an irate gardener, the offending pig may be killed. These disagreeable incidents set neighbor against neighbor and heighten the general sense of dissatisfaction. As Rappaport points out, incidents involving pigs necessarily increase more rapidly than the pigs themselves.

In order to avoid such incidents and to get closer to their gardens, the Maring begin to move their houses farther apart over a wider area. This dispersion lowers the security of the group in case of renewed hostilities. So everyone becomes more jittery. The women begin to complain about being overworked. They bicker with their husbands and snap at their children. Soon the men begin to wonder if perhaps there are "enough pigs." They go down to inspect the *rumbim* to see how tall it has grown. The women complain more loudly, and finally the men, with considerable unanimity and without counting the pigs, agree that the moment has come to begin the *kaiko*.

During the *kaiko* year of 1963, the Tsembaga killed off three-fourths of their pigs by number and seven-eighths by weight. Much of this meat was distributed to in-laws and military allies who were invited to participate in the yearlong festivities. At the climactic rituals held on November 7 and 8, 1963, 96 pigs were killed and their meat and fat were distributed directly or indirectly to an estimated two or three thousand people. The Tsembaga kept about 2,500 pounds of pork and fat for themselves, or 12 pounds for each man, woman, and child, a quantity which they consumed in five consecutive days of unrestrained gluttony.

The Maring consciously use the *kaiko* as an occasion to reward their allies for previous assistance and to seek their loyalty in future hostilities. The allies in turn accept the invitation to the *kaiko* because it gives them an opportunity to decide if their hosts are prosperous and powerful enough to warrant continued support; of course, the allies are also hungry for pig meat.

45 Guests dress up in their finest manner. They wear bead-and-shell necklaces, cowrie-shell garters around their calves, orchid-fiber waistbands, purple-striped loincloths bordered with marsupial fur, and masses of accordion-shaped leaves topped by a bustle on their buttocks. Crowns of eagle and parrot feathers encircle their heads, festooned with orchid stems, green beetles and cowries, and topped with an entire stuffed bird of paradise. Every man has spent hours painting his face in some original design, and wears his best bird-of-paradise plume through his nose along with a favorite disk or a gold-lip crescent shell. Visitors and hosts spend much time showing off to each other by dancing at the specially constructed dance ground, preparing the way for amorous alliances with the female onlookers as well as military alliances with male warriors.

Over a thousand people crowded into the Tsembaga dance ground to participate in the rituals that followed the great pig slaughter witnessed by Rappaport in 1963. Special reward packages of salted pig fat were heaped high behind the window of a three-sided ceremonial building that adjoined the dance grounds. In Rappaport's words:

> Several men climbed to the top of the structure and from there proclaimed one by one to the multitude the names and clans of the men being honored. As his name was called, each honored man charged toward the . . . window swinging his ax and shouting. His supporters, yelling battle cries, beating drums, brandishing weapons, followed close behind him. At the window the mouth of the honored man was stuffed with cold salted belly-fat by the Tsembaga whom he had come to help in the last fight and who now also passed out to him through the window a package containing additional salted belly for his followers. With the belly fat hanging from his mouth the hero now retired, his supporters close behind him, shouting, singing, beating their drums, dancing. Honored name quickly followed honored name, and groups charging toward the window sometimes became entangled with those retiring.

Within limits set by the basic technological and environmental conditions of the Maring, all of this has a practical explanation. First of all, the craving for pig meat is a perfectly rational feature of Maring life in view of the general scarcity of meat in their diet. While they can supplement their staple vegetables with occasional frogs, rats, and a few hunted marsupials, domesticated pork is their best potential source of high-quality animal fat and protein. This does not mean that the Maring suffer from an acute form of protein deficiency. On the contrary, their diet of yams, sweet potatoes, taro, and other plant foods provides them with a broad variety of vegetable proteins that satisfies but does not far exceed minimum nutritional standards. Getting proteins from pigs is something else, however. Animal protein in general is more concentrated and metabolically more effective than vegetable protein, so for human populations that are mainly restricted to vegetable foods (no cheese, milk, eggs, or fish), meat is always an irresistible temptation.

Moreover, up to a point, it makes good ecological sense for the Maring to raise pigs. The temperature and humidity are ideal. Pigs thrive in the damp, shady environment of the mountain slopes and obtain a substantial portion of their food by roaming freely over the forest floor. The complete interdiction of pork—the Middle Eastern solution—would be a most irrational and uneconomic practice under these conditions.

On the other hand, unlimited growth of the pig population can only lead to competition between man and pig. If permitted to go too far, pig farming overburdens the women and endangers the gardens upon which the Maring depend for survival. As the pig population increases, the Maring women must work harder and harder. Eventually they find themselves working to feed pigs rather than to feed people. As virgin lands are brought into use, the efficiency of the entire agricultural system plummets. It is at this point that the *kaiko* takes place, the role of the ancestors being to encourage a maximum effort at pig raising but at the same time to see to it that the pigs do not destroy the women and the gardens. Their task is admittedly more difficult than Jahweh's or Allah's, since a total taboo is always easier to administer than a partial one. Nonetheless, the belief that a *kaiko* must be held as soon as possible, in order to keep the ancestors happy, effectively rids the Maring of animals that have grown parasitic and helps keep the pig population from becoming "too much of a good thing."

50   If ancestors are so clever, why don't they simply set a limit on the number of pigs that each Maring woman can raise? Would it not be better

to keep a constant number of pigs than to permit the pig population to cycle through extremes of scarcity and abundance?

This alternative would be preferable only if each Maring clan had zero growth, no enemies, a wholly different form of agriculture, powerful rulers, and written laws—in short, if they weren't the Maring. No one, not even the ancestors can predict how many pigs are "too much of a good thing." The point at which the pigs become burdensome does not depend upon any set of constants, but rather on a set of variables which changes from year to year. It depends on how many people there are in the whole region and in each clan, on their state of physical and psychological vigor, on the size of their territory, on the amount of secondary forest they have, and on the condition and intentions of the enemy groups in neighboring territories. The Tsembaga's ancestors cannot simply say "thou shalt keep four pigs, and no more," because there is no way of guaranteeing that the ancestors of the Kundugai, Dimbagai, Yimgagai, Tuguma, Aundagai, Kauwasi, Monambant, and all the rest will agree to this number. All of these groups are engaged in a struggle to validate their respective claims to share in the earth's resources. Warfare and the threat of warfare probe and test these claims. The ancestors' insatiable craving for pigs is a consequence of this armed probing and testing by the Maring clans.

To satisfy the ancestors, a maximum effort must be made not only to produce as much food as possible, but to accumulate it in the form of the pig herd. This effort, even though it results in cyclical surpluses of pork, enhances the ability of the group to survive and to defend its territory.

It does this in several ways. First, the extra effort called forth by the pig lust of the ancestors raises the levels of protein intake for the entire group during the *rumbim* truce, resulting in a taller, healthier, and more vigorous population. Furthermore, by linking the *kaiko* to the end of the truce, the ancestors guarantee that massive doses of high-quality fats and proteins are consumed at the period of greatest social stress—in the months immediately prior to the outbreak of intergroup fighting. Finally, by banking large amounts of extra food in the form of nutritionally valuable pig meat, the Maring clans are able to attract and reward allies when they are most needed, again just before the outbreak of war.

The Tsembaga and their neighbors are conscious of the relationship between success in raising pigs and military power. The number of pigs slaughtered at the *kaiko* provides the guests with an accurate basis for judging the health, energy, and determination of the feast givers. A group that cannot manage to accumulate pigs is not likely to put up a good defense of its territory, and will not attract strong allies. No mere irrational premonition of defeat hangs over the battlefield when one's ancestors aren't given enough pork at the *kaiko*. Rappaport insists—correctly, I believe—that in a fundamental ecological sense, the size of a group's pig surplus does indicate its productive and military strength and does validate or invalidate its territorial claims. In other words, the entire system results in an efficient distribution of plants, animals, and people in the region, from a human ecological point of view.

55   I am sure that many readers will now want to insist that the pig love is maladaptive and terribly inefficient because it is geared to periodic outbreaks of warfare. If warfare is irrational, then so is the *kaiko*. Again, permit me to resist the temptation to explain everything at once. In the next chapter I will discuss the mundane causes of Maring warfare. But for the moment, let me point out that warfare is not caused by pig love. Millions of people who have never even seen a pig wage war; nor does pig hatred (ancient and modern) discernibly enhance the peacefulness of the intergroup relations in the Middle East. Given the prevalence of warfare in human history and prehistory, we can only marvel at the ingenious system devised by New Guinea "savages" for maintaining extensive periods of truce. After all, as long as their neighbor's *rumbim* remains in the ground, the Tsembaga don't have to worry about being attacked. One can perhaps say as much, but not more, about nations that plant missiles instead of *rumbim*.

(1974)

Questions:

1. Harris is unusual among academics in aiming his writing *both* at other academics *and* at students and general readers with no prior specialized knowledge. Comment on the ways in which the diction, syntax, and organization of ideas in this essay are appropriate to an audience with no prior familiarity with the topic or with the discipline of anthropology.

2. Express in your own words the logical problem with the argument that pig-eating became taboo in the cultures Harris is discussing because pigs had been regarded as sacred (paragraph 11) or because pigs were regarded as totemic symbols representing tribal clans (paragraph 12).

3. What are the key facts about the physiology of the pig so far as Harris' argument is concerned?

4. In two paragraphs, summarize the practices of the miring of pigs and Harris' explanation as to why these seemingly bizarre practices make sense.

5. Does it "make sense" either from the sort of angle of approach that Harris uses or from other angles for North American society to consume as much beef and pork as it does?

6. Does the sort of discussion in which Harris engages in any way undermine the foundations of the religions he is discussing?

JONATHAN BENNETT

THE CONSCIENCE OF HUCKLEBERRY FINN

In this essay, Bennett explores the difference between moral judgment and sympathy. Contrasting the fictional character of Huckleberry Finn with the historical figures Heinrich Himmler and Jonathan Edwards, Bennett shows how these principles can come into conflict.

In this paper, I shall present not just the conscience of Huckleberry Finn but two others as well. One of them is the conscience of Heinrich Himmler. He became a Nazi in 1923; he served drably and quietly, but well, and was rewarded with increasing responsibility and power. At the peak of his career he held many offices and commands, of which the most powerful was that of leader of the S.S.—the principal police force of the Nazi regime. In this capacity, Himmler commanded the whole concentration-camp system, and was responsible for the execution of the so-called "final solution of the Jewish problem." It is important for my purposes that this piece of social engineering should be thought of not abstractly but in concrete terms of Jewish families being marched to what they think are bath-houses, to the accompaniment of loud-speaker renditions of extracts from *The Merry Widow* and *Tales of Hoffman*, there to be choked to death by poisonous gases. Altogether, Himmler succeeded in murdering about four and a half million of them, as well as several million gentiles, mainly Poles and Russians.

The other conscience to be discussed is that of the Calvinist theologian and philosopher Jonathan Edwards. He lived in the first half of the eighteenth century, and has a good claim to be considered America's first serious and considerable philosophical thinker. He was for many years a widely-renowned preacher and Congregationalist minister in New England; in 1748 a dispute with his congregation led him to resign (he couldn't accept their view that unbelievers should be admitted to the Lord's Supper in the hope that it would convert them); for some years after that he worked as a missionary, preaching to Indians through an interpreter; then in 1758 he accepted the presidency of what is now Princeton University, and within two months died from a smallpox inoculation. Along the way he wrote some first-rate philosophy: his book attacking the notion of free will is still sometimes read. Why I should be interested in Edwards' conscience will be explained in due course.

I shall use Heinrich Himmler, Jonathan Edwards and Huckleberry Finn to illustrate different aspects of a single theme, namely the relationship between *sympathy* on the one hand and *bad morality* on the other.

All that I can mean by a "bad morality" is a morality whose principles I deeply disapprove of. When I call a morality bad, I cannot prove that mine is better; but when I here call any morality bad, I think you will agree with me that it is bad; and that is all I need.

5   There could be dispute as to whether the springs of someone's actions constitute a *morality*, I think, though, that we must admit that someone who acts in ways which conflict grossly with our morality may nevertheless have a morality of his own—a set of principles of action which he sincerely assents to, so that for him the problem of acting well or rightly or in obedience to conscience is the problem of conforming to those principles. The problem of conscientiousness can arise as acutely for a bad morality as for any other; rotten principles may be as difficult to keep as decent ones.

As for "sympathy": I use this term to cover every sort of fellow-feeling, as when one feels pity over someone's loneliness, or horrified compassion over his pain, or when one feels a shrinking reluctance to act in a way which will bring misfortune to someone else. These feelings must not be confused with *moral judgments*. My sympathy for someone in distress may lead me to help him, or even to think that I ought to help him; but in itself it is not a judgment about what I ought to do but just a feeling for him in his plight. We shall get some light on the difference between feelings and moral judgments when we consider Huckleberry Finn.

Obviously, feelings can impel one to action, and so can moral judgments; and in a particular case sympathy and morality may pull in opposite directions. This can happen not just with bad moralities, but also with good ones like yours and mine. For example, a small child, sick and miserable, clings tightly to his mother and screams in terror when she tries to pass him over to the doctor to be examined. If the mother gave way to her sympathy, that is to her feeling for the child's misery and fright, she would hold it close and not let the doctor come near; but don't we agree that it might be wrong for her to act on such a feeling? Quite generally, then, anyone's moral principles may apply to a particular situation in a way which runs contrary to the particular thrusts of fellow-feeling that he has in that situation. My immediate concern is with sympathy in relation to bad morality, but not because such conflicts occur only when the morality is bad.

Now, suppose that someone who accepts a bad morality is struggling to make himself act in accordance with it in a particular situation where his sympathies pull him another way. He sees the struggle as one between doing the right, conscientious thing, and acting wrongly and weakly, like the mother who won't let the doctor come near her sick, frightened baby. Since we don't accept this person's morality, we may see the situation very differently, thoroughly disapproving of the action he regards as the right one, and endorsing the action which from his point of view constitutes weakness and backsliding.

Conflicts between sympathy and bad morality won't always be like this, for we won't disagree with every single dictate of a bad morality. Still, it can happen in the way I have described, with the agent's right action being our wrong one, and vice versa. That is just what happens in a certain episode in chapter 16 of *The Adventures of Huckleberry Finn,* an episode which brilliantly illustrates how fiction can be instructive about real life.

10 Huck Finn has been helping his slave friend Jim to run away from Miss Watson, who is Jim's owner. In their raft-journey down the Mississippi River, they are near to the place at which Jim will become legally free. Now let Huck take over the story:

> Jim said it made him all over trembly and feverish to be so close to freedom. Well, I can tell you it made me all over trembly and feverish, too, to hear him, because I begun to get it through my head that he was most free—and who was to blame for it? Why, me. I couldn't get that out of my conscience, no how nor no way. It hadn't ever come home to me, before, what this thing was that I was doing. But now it did; and it stayed with me, and scorched me more and more. I tried to make out to myself that I warn't to blame, because I didn't run Jim off from his rightful owner; but it warn't no use, conscience up and say, every time: "But you knowed he was running for his freedom, and you could a paddled ashore and told somebody." That was so—I couldn't get around that, no way. That was where it pinched. Conscience says to me: "What had poor Miss Watson done to you, that you could see her

nigger go off right under your eyes and never say one single word? What did
that poor old woman do to you, that you could treat her so mean?..." I got
to feeling so mean and miserable I most wished I was dead.

Jim speaks of his plan to save up to buy his wife, and then his children,
out of slavery; and he adds that if the children cannot be bought he will
arrange to steal them. Huck is horrified:

> Thinks I, this is what comes of my not thinking. Here was this nigger which
> I had as good as helped to run away, coming right out flat-footed and saying
> he would steal his children—children that belonged to a man I didn't even
> know; a man that hadn't ever done me no harm.
>
> I was sorry to hear Jim say that, it was such a lowering of him. My
> conscience got to stirring me up hotter than ever, until at last I says to it: "Let
> up on me—it ain't too late, yet—I'll paddle ashore at first light, and tell." I
> felt easy, and happy, and light as a feather, right off. All my troubles was
> gone.

This is bad morality all right. In his earliest years Huck wasn't taught any
principles, and the only ones he has encountered since then are those of rural
Missouri, in which slaveowning is just one kind of ownership and is not
subject to critical pressure. It hasn't occurred to Huck to question those
principles. So the action, to us abhorrent, of turning Jim in to the authorities
presents itself clearly to Huck as the right thing to do.

For us, morality and sympathy would both dictate helping Jim to escape.
If we felt any conflict, it would have both these on one side and something
else on the other—greed for a reward, or fear of punishment. But Huck's
morality conflicts with his sympathy, that is, with his unargued, natural
feeling for his friend. The conflict starts when Huck sets off in the canoe
towards the shore, pretending that he is going to reconnoitre, but really
planning to turn Jim in:

> As I shoved off, [Jim] says: "Pooty soon I'll be a-shout'n for joy, en I'll say,
> it's all on accounts o' Huck I's a free man...Jim won't ever forgit you, Huck;
> you's de bes' fren' Jim's ever had; en you's de only fren' old Jim's got now."
>
> I was paddling off, all in a sweat to tell on him; but when he says this,
> it seemed to kind of take the tuck all out of me. I went along slow then, and
> I warn't right down certain whether I was glad I started or whether I warn't.
> When I was fifty yards off, Jim says:

"Dah you goes, de ole true Huck; de on'y white genlman dat ever kep' his promise to ole Jim." Well, I just felt sick. But I says, I *got* to do it—I can't get *out* of it.

In the upshot, sympathy wins over morality. Huck hasn't the strength of will to do what he sincerely thinks he ought to do. Two men hunting for runaway slaves ask him whether the man on his raft is black or white:

I didn't answer up prompt. I tried to, but the words wouldn't come. I tried, for a second or two, to brace up and out with it, but I warn't man enough—hadn't the spunk of a rabbit. I see I was weakening; so I just give up trying, and up and says: "He's white."

So Huck enables Jim to escape, thus acting weakly and wickedly—he thinks. In this conflict between sympathy and morality, sympathy wins.

One critic has cited this episode in support of the statement that Huck suffers "excruciating moments of wavering between honesty and respectability." That is hopelessly wrong, and I agree with the perceptive comment on it by another critic, who says:

The conflict waged in Huck is much more serious: he scarcely cares for respectability and never hesitates to relinquish it, but he does care for honesty and gratitude—and both honesty and gratitude require that he should give Jim up. It is not, in Huck, honesty at war with respectability but love and compassion for Jim struggling against his conscience. His decision is for Jim and hell: a right decision made in the mental chains that Huck never breaks. His concern for Jim is and remains irrational. Huck finds many reasons for giving Jim up and none for stealing him. To the end Huck sees his compassion for Jim as a weak, ignorant, and wicked felony.

That is precisely correct—and it can have that virtue only because Mark Twain wrote the episode with such unerring precision. The crucial point concerns reasons, which all occur on one side of the conflict. On the side of conscience we have principles, arguments, considerations, ways of looking at things:

"It hadn't ever come home to me before what I was doing"
    "I tried to make out that I warn't to blame"
    "Conscience said 'But you knowed...'—I couldn't get around that"
    "What had poor Miss Watson done to you?"

"This is what comes of my not thinking"
"children that belonged to a man I didn't even know."

On the other side, the side of feeling, we get nothing like that. When Jim rejoices in Huck, as his only friend, Huck doesn't consider the claims of friendship or have the situation "come home" to him in a different light. All that happens is: "When he says this, it seemed to kind of take the tuck all out of me. I went along slow then, and I warn't right down certain whether I was glad I started or whether I warn't." Again, Jim's words about Huck's "promise" to him don't give Huck any reason for changing his plan: in his morality promises to slaves probably don't count. Their effect on him is of a different kind: "Well, I just felt sick." And when the moment for final decision comes, Huck doesn't weigh up pros and cons: he simply *fails* to do what he believes to be right—he isn't strong enough, hasn't "the spunk of a rabbit." This passage in the novel is notable not just for its finely wrought irony, with Huck's weakness of will leading him to do the right thing, but also for its masterly handling of the difference between general moral principles and particular unreasoned emotional pulls.

Consider now another case of bad morality in conflict with human sympathy, the case of odious Himmler. Here, from a speech he made to some S.S. generals, is an indication of the content of his morality:

> What happens to a Russian, to a Czech, does not interest me in the slightest. What the nations can offer in the way of good blood of our type, we will take, if necessary by kidnapping their children and raising them here with us. Whether nations live in prosperity or starve to death like cattle interests me only in so far as we need them as slaves to our Kultur; otherwise it is of no interest to me. Whether 10,000 Russian females fall down from exhaustion while digging an antitank ditch interests me only in so far as the antitank ditch for Germany is finished.

15   But has this a moral basis at all? And if it has, was there in Himmler's own mind any conflict between morality and sympathy? Yes there was. Here is more from the same speech:

> ...I also want to talk to you quite frankly on a very grave matter...I mean... the extermination of the Jewish race...Most of you must know what it means when 100 corpses are lying side by side, or 500, or 1,000. To have stuck it out and at the same time—apart from exceptions caused by human weakness —to have remained decent fellows, that is what has made us hard. This is a

page of glory in our history which has never been written and is never to be written.

Himmler saw his policies as being hard to implement while still retaining one's human sympathies—while still remaining a "decent fellow." He is saying that only the weak take the easy way out and just squelch their sympathies, and is praising the stronger and more glorious course of retaining one's sympathies while acting in violation of them. In the same spirit, he ordered that when executions were carried out in concentration camps, those responsible "are to be influenced in such a way as to suffer no ill effect in their character and mental attitude." A year later he boasted that the S.S. had wiped out the Jews

> without our leaders and their men suffering any damage in their minds and souls. The danger was considerable, for there was only a narrow path between the Scylla of their becoming heartless ruffians unable any longer to treasure life, and the Charybdis of their becoming soft and suffering nervous breakdowns.

And there really can't be any doubt that the basis of Himmler's policies was a set of principles which constituted his morality—a sick, bad, wicked *morality*. He described himself as caught in "the old tragic conflict between will and obligation." And when his physician Kersten protested at the intention to destroy the Jews, saying that the suffering involved was "not to be contemplated," Kersten reports that Himmler replied:

> He knew that it would mean much suffering for the Jews... "It is the curse of greatness that it must step over dead bodies to create new life. Yet we must cleanse the soil or it will never bear fruit. It will be a great burden for me to bear."

This, I submit, is the language of morality.

So in this case, tragically, bad morality won out over sympathy. I am sure that many of Himmler's killers did extinguish their sympathies, becoming "heartless ruffians" rather than "decent fellows"; but not Himmler himself. Although his policies ran against the human grain to a horrible degree, he did not sandpaper down his emotional surfaces so that there was no grain there, allowing his actions to slide along smoothly and easily. He did, after all, bear his hideous burden, and even paid a price for it. He suffered a variety of nervous and physical disabilities, including nausea and stomach convulsions, and Kersten was doubtless right in saying that these were the "expression of a psychic division which extended over his whole life."

This same division must have been present in some of those officials of the Church who ordered heretics to be tortured so as to change their theological opinions. Along with the brutes and the cold careerists, there must have been some who cared, and who suffered from the conflict between their sympathies and their bad morality.

In the conflict between sympathy and bad morality, then, the victory may go to sympathy as in the case of Huck Finn, or to morality as the case of Himmler.

Another possibility is that the conflict may be avoided by giving up, or not ever having, those sympathies which might interfere with one's principles. That seems to have been the case with Jonathan Edwards. I am afraid that I shall be doing an injustice to Edwards' many virtues, and to his great intellectual energy and inventiveness; for my concern is only with the worst thing about him—namely his morality, which was worse than Himmler's.

20 According to Edwards, God condemns some men to an eternity of unimaginably awful pain, though he arbitrarily spares others—"arbitrarily" because none deserve to be spared:

> Natural men are held in the hand of God over the pit of hell...; they have deserved the fiery pit, and are already sentenced to it; and God is dreadfully provoked, his anger is as great towards them as to those that are actually suffering the executions of the fierceness of his wrath in hell; the devil is waiting for them, hell is gaping for them, the flames gather and flash about them, and would fain lay hold on them...; and...there are no means within reach that can be any security to them.... All that preserves them is the mere arbitrary will, and uncovenanted unobliged forebearance of an incensed God.

Notice that he says "they have deserved the fiery pit." Edwards insists that men *ought* to be condemned to eternal pain; and his position isn't that this is right because God wants it, but rather that God wants it because it is right. For him, moral standards exist independently of God, and God can be assessed in the light of them (and of course found to be perfect). For example, he says:

> They deserve to be cast into hell; so that...justice never stands in the way, it makes no objection against God's using his power at any moment to destroy

them. Yea, on the contrary, justice calls aloud for an infinite punishment of their sins.

Elsewhere, he gives elaborate arguments to show that God is acting justly in damning sinners. For example, he argues that a punishment should be exactly as bad as the crime being punished: God is infinitely excellent; so any crime against him is infinitely bad; and so eternal damnation is exactly right as a punishment—it is infinite, but, as Edwards is careful also to say, it is "no more than infinite."

Of course, Edwards himself didn't torment the damned; but the question still arises of whether his sympathies didn't conflict with his approval of eternal torment. Didn't he find it painful to contemplate any fellow-human's being tortured for ever? Apparently not:

> The God that holds you over the pit of hell, much as one holds a spider or some loathsome insect over the fire, abhors you, and is dreadfully provoked; ...he is of purer eyes than to bear to have you in his sight; you are ten thousand times so abominable in his eyes as the most hateful venomous serpent is in ours.

When God is presented as being as misanthropic as that, one suspects misanthropy in the theologian. This suspicion is increased when Edwards claims that "the saints in glory will...understand how terrible the sufferings of the damned are; yet...will not be sorry for [them]." He bases this partly on a view of human nature whose ugliness he seems not to notice:

> The seeing of the calamities of others tends to heighten the sense of our own enjoyments. When the saints in glory, therefore, shall see the doleful state of the damned, how will this heighten their sense of the blessedness of their own state.... When they shall see how miserable others of their fellow-creatures are...; when they shall see the smoke of their torment,...and hear their dolorous shrieks and cries, and consider that they in the mean time are in the most blissful state, and shall surely be in it to all eternity; how they will rejoice!

I hope this is less than the whole truth! His other main point about why the saints will rejoice to see the torments of the damned is that it is *right* that they should do so:

> The heavenly inhabitants...will have no love nor pity to the damned.... [This will not show] a want of a spirit of love in them...; for the heavenly

inhabitants will know that it is not fit that they should love [the damned] because they will know then, that God has no love to them, nor pity for them.

The implication that *of course* one can adjust one's feelings of pity so that they conform to the dictates of some authority—doesn't this suggest that ordinary human sympathies played only a small part in Edwards' life?

Huck Finn, whose sympathies are wide and deep, could never avoid the conflict in that way; but he is determined to avoid it, and so he opts for the only other alternative he can see—to give up morality altogether. After he has tricked the slave-hunters, he returns to the raft and undergoes a peculiar crisis:

> I got aboard the raft, feeling bad and low, because I knowed very well I had done wrong, and I see it warn't no use for me to try to learn to do right; a body that don't get *started* right when he's little, ain't got no show—when the pinch comes there ain't nothing to back him up and keep him to his work, and so he gets beat. Then I thought a minute, and says to myself, hold on—s'pose you'd a done right and give Jim up; would you feel better than what you do now? No, says I, I'd feel bad—I'd feel just the same way I do now. Well, then, says I, what's the use of you learning to do right, when it's troublesome to do right and ain't no trouble to do wrong, and the wages is just the same? I was stuck. I couldn't answer that. So I reckoned I wouldn't bother no more about it, but after this always do whichever comes handiest at the time.

Huck clearly cannot conceive of having any morality except the one he has learned—too late, he thinks—from his society. He is not entirely a prisoner of that morality, because he does after all reject it; but for him that is a decision to relinquish morality as such; he cannot envisage revising his morality, altering its content in face of the various pressures to which it is subject, including pressures from his sympathies. For example, he does not begin to approach the thought that slavery should be rejected on moral grounds, or the thought that what he is doing is not theft because a person cannot be owned and therefore cannot be stolen.

The basic trouble is that he cannot or will not engage in abstract intellectual operations of any sort. In chapter 33 he finds himself "feeling to blame, somehow" for something he knows he had no hand in; he assumes that this feeling is a deliverance of conscience; and this confirms him in his belief that conscience shouldn't be listened to:

It don't make no difference whether you do right or wrong, a person's conscience ain't got no sense, and just goes for him *anyway*. If I had a yaller dog and didn't know no more than a person's conscience does, I would poison him. It takes up more room than all the rest of a person's insides, and yet ain't no good, nohow.

That brisk, incurious dismissiveness fits well with the comprehensive rejection of morality back on the raft. But this is a digression.

On the raft, Huck decides not to live by principles, but just to do whatever "comes handiest at the time"—always acting according to the mood of the moment. Since the morality he is rejecting is narrow and cruel, and his sympathies are broad and kind, the results will be good. But moral principles are good to have, because they help to protect one from acting badly at moments when one's sympathies happen to be in abeyance. On the highest possible estimate of the role one's sympathies should have, one can still allow for principles as embodiments of one's best feelings, one's broadest and keenest sympathies. On that view, principles can help one across intervals when one's feelings are at less than their best, i.e. through periods of misanthropy or meanness or self-centredness or depression or anger.

25   What Huck didn't see is that one can live by principles and yet have ultimate control over their content. And one way such control can be exercised is by the checking of one's principles in the light of one's sympathies. This is sometimes a pretty straightforward matter. It can happen that a certain moral principle becomes untenable—meaning literally that one cannot hold it any longer—because it conflicts intolerably with the pity or revulsion or whatever that one feels when one sees what the principle leads to. One's experience may play a large part here: experiences evoke feelings, and feelings force one to modify principles. Something like this happened to the English poet Wilfred Owen, whose experiences in the First World War transformed him from an enthusiastic soldier into a virtual pacifist. I can't document his change of conscience in detail; but I want to present something which he wrote about the way experience can put pressure on morality.

The Latin poet Horace wrote that it is sweet and fitting (or right) to die for one's country—*dulce et decorum est pro patria mori*—and Owen wrote a fine poem about how experience could lead one to relinquish that particular moral principle. He describes a man who is too slow donning his gas mask during a gas attack—"As under a green sea, I saw him drowning," Owen says. The poem ends like this:

In all my dreams, before my helpless sight
He plunges at me, guttering, choking, drowning.
If in some smothering dreams you too could pace
Behind the wagon that we flung him in,
And watch the white eyes writhing in his face,
His hanging face, like a devil's sick of sin;
If you could hear, at every jolt, the blood
Come gargling from the froth-corrupted lungs,
Obscene as cancer, bitter as the cud
Of vile, incurable sores on innocent tongues,—
My friend, you would not tell with such high zest
To children ardent for some desperate glory,
The old Lie: Dulce et decorum est
Pro patria mori.

There is difficulty about drawing from all this a moral for ourselves. I imagine that we agree in our rejection of slavery, eternal damnation, genocide, and uncritical patriotic self-abnegation; so we shall agree that Huck Finn, Jonathan Edwards, Heinrich Himmler, and the poet Horace would have done well to bring certain of their principles under severe pressure from ordinary human sympathies. But then we can say this because we can say that all those are bad moralities, whereas we cannot look at our own moralities and declare them bad. This is not arrogance: it is obviously incoherent for someone to declare the system of moral principles that he accepts to be bad, just as one cannot coherently say of anything that one *believes* it but it is *false*.

Still, although I can't point to any of my beliefs and say "That is false," I don't doubt that some of my beliefs *are* false; and so I should try to remain open to correction. Similarly, I accept every single item in my morality—that is inevitable—but I am sure that my morality could be improved, which is to say that it could undergo changes which I should be glad of once I had made them. So I must try to keep my morality open to revision, exposing it to whatever valid pressures there are—including pressures from my sympathies.

I don't give my sympathies a blank cheque in advance. In a conflict between principle and sympathy, principles ought sometimes to win. For example, I think it was right to take part in the Second World War on the Allied side; there were many ghastly individual incidents which might have led someone to doubt the rightness of his participation in that war; and I think it would have been right for such a person to keep his sympathies in a subordinate place on those occasions, not allowing them to modify his principles in such a way as to make a pacifist of him.

Still, one's sympathies should be kept as sharp and sensitive and aware as possible, and not only because they can sometimes affect one's principles or one's conduct or both. Owen, at any rate, says that feelings and sympathies are vital even when they can do nothing but bring pain and distress. In another poem he speaks of the blessings of being numb in one's feelings: "Happy are the men who yet before they are killed/Can let their veins run cold," he says. These are the ones who do not suffer from any compassion which, as Owen puts it, "makes their feet/Sore on the alleys cobbled with their brother." He contrasts these "happy" ones, who "lose imagination," with himself and others "who with a thought besmirch/Blood over all our soul." Yet the poem's verdict goes against the "happy" ones. Owen does not say that they will act worse than the others whose souls are besmirched with blood because of their keen awareness of human suffering. He merely says that they are the losers because they have cut themselves off from the human condition:

> By choice they made themselves immune
> To pity and whatever moans in man
> Before the last sea and the hapless stars;
> Whatever mourns when many leave these shores;
> Whatever shares
> The eternal reciprocity of tears.

(1974)

Questions:

1. How does Bennett differentiate between "sympathy" and "moral judgment"?

2. Explain why the essay's title is "The Conscience of Huckleberry Finn." Why does the author focus on Huckleberry Finn, and not Himmler, or Edwards, or Owen?

3. Huckleberry Finn is a fictional character, while Edwards and Himmler are historical figures. How justified is Bennett in comparing them to each other?

Fran Lebowitz

Children: Pro or Con?

Like many of Lebowitz's urbane and irreverent pieces on modern life, this essay purports to have a practical purpose.

〜

Moving, as I do, in what would kindly be called artistic circles, children are an infrequent occurrence. But even the most artistic of circles includes within its periphery a limited edition of the tenaciously domestic.

As I am generally quite fond of children I accept this condition with far less displeasure than do my more rarefied acquaintances. That is not to imply that I am a total fool for a little grin but simply that I consider myself to be in a position of unquestionable objectivity and therefore eminently qualified to deal with the subject in an authoritative manner.

From the number of children in evidence it appears that people have them at the drop of a hat—for surely were they to give this matter its due attention they would act with greater decorum. Of course, until now prospective parents have not had the opportunity to see the facts spelled out in black and white and therefore cannot reasonably be held accountable for their actions. To this end I have carefully set down all pertinent information in the fervent hope that it will result in a future populated by a more attractive array of children than I have thus far encountered.

Pro

I must take issue with the term "a mere child," for it has been my invariable experience that the company of a mere child is infinitely preferable to that of a mere adult.

* * *

5   Children are usually small in stature, which makes them quite useful for getting at those hard-to-reach places.

*   *   *

Children do not sit next to one in restaurants and discuss their preposterous hopes for the future in loud tones of voice.

*   *   *

Children ask better questions than do adults. "May I have a cookie?" "Why is the sky blue?" and "What does a cow say?" are far more likely to elicit a cheerful response than "Where's your manuscript?" "Why haven't you called?" and "Who's your lawyer?"

*   *   *

Children give life to the concept of immaturity.

*   *   *

Children make the most desirable opponents in Scrabble as they are both easy to beat and fun to cheat.

*   *   *

10   It is still quite possible to stand in a throng of children without once detecting even the faintest whiff of an exciting, rugged after-shave or cologne.

*   *   *

Not a single member of the under-age set has yet to propose the word *chairchild.*

*   *   *

Children sleep either alone or with small toy animals. The wisdom of such behaviour is unquestionable, as it frees them from the immeasurable tedium of being privy to the whispered confessions of others. I have yet to run across a teddy bear who was harboring the secret desire to wear a maid's uniform.

Con

Even when freshly washed and relieved of all obvious confections, children tend to be sticky. One can only assume that this has something to do with not smoking enough.

*   *   *

Children have decidedly little fashion sense and if left to their own devices will more often than not be drawn to garments of unfortunate cut. In this respect they do not differ greatly from the majority of their elders, but somehow one blames them more.

* * *

15 Children respond inadequately to sardonic humor and veiled threats.

* * *

Notoriously insensitive to subtle shifts in mood, children will persist in discussing the color of a recently sighted cement-mixer long after one's own interest in the topic has waned.

* * *

Children are rarely in the position to lend one a truly interesting sum of money. There are, however, exceptions, and such children are an excellent addition to any party.

* * *

Children arise at an unseemly hour and are ofttimes in the habit of putting food on an empty stomach.

* * *

Children do not look well in evening clothes.

* * *

20 All too often children are accompanied by adults.

* * *

(1974)

Questions:

1. Rephrase a passage of three or four sentences from this essay so as to use shorter sentences and fewer, simpler words. What can you say about the way in which Lebowitz's diction (particularly her choice of adjectives and adverbs) and syntax play a part in lending a humourous tone to her writing?

2. It is often suggested that a key element in humour is the element of the unexpected—and in particular the unexpected flouting of convention. To what extent do you see that generalization as being well-founded?

3. Birth rates in the developed world have been below replacement levels for many years, and birth rates in the developing world are now quickly dropping as well. In all seriousness, discuss the arguments that could be made for and against having children—or, for society as a whole, for or against measures that encourage people to have children.

Peter Singer

Speciesism and the Equality of Animals

With his writing about animals, the Australian philosopher Peter Singer has probably changed the day-to-day behaviour of more people than any other writer of the past generation.

Speciesism—the word is not an attractive one, but I can think of no better term—is a prejudice or attitude of bias toward the interests of members of one's own species and against those of members of other species. It should be obvious that the fundamental objections to racism and sexism made by Thomas Jefferson and Sojourner Truth apply equally to speciesism. If possessing a higher degree of intelligence does not entitle one human to use another for his own ends, how can it entitle humans to exploit nonhumans for the same purpose?

Many philosophers and other writers have proposed the principle of equal consideration of interests, in some form or other, as a basic moral principle; but not many of them have recognized that this principle applies to members of other species as well as to our own. Jeremy Bentham was one of the few who did realize this. In a forward-looking passage written at a time when black slaves had been freed by the French but in the British dominions were still being treated in the way we now treat animals, Bentham wrote:

> The day *may* come when the rest of the animal creation may acquire those rights which never could have been withholden from them but by the hand of tyranny. The French have already discovered that the blackness of the skin is no reason why a human being should be abandoned without redress to the caprice of a tormentor. It may one day come to be recognized that the number of the legs, the villosity of the skin, or the termination of the *os*

sacrum are reasons equally insufficient for abandoning a sensitive being to the same fate. What else is it that should trace the insuperable line? Is it the faculty of reason, or perhaps the faculty of discourse? But a full-grown horse or dog is beyond comparison a more rational, as well as a more conversable animal, than an infant of a day or a week or even a month, old. But suppose they were otherwise, what would it avail? The question is not, Can they *reason?* nor Can they *talk?* but, *Can they suffer?*

In this passage Bentham points to the capacity for suffering as the vital characteristic that gives a being the right to equal consideration. The capacity for suffering—or more strictly, for suffering and/or enjoyment or happiness—is not just another characteristic like the capacity for language or higher mathematics. Bentham is not saying that those who try to mark "the insuperable line" that determines whether the interests of a being should be considered happen to have chosen the wrong characteristic. By saying that we must consider the interests of all beings with the capacity for suffering or enjoyment Bentham does not arbitrarily exclude from consideration any interests at all—as those who draw the line with reference to the possession of reason or language do. The capacity for suffering and enjoyment is a *prerequisite for having interests at all,* a condition that must be satisfied before we can speak of interests in a meaningful way. It would be nonsense to say that it was not in the interests of a stone to be kicked along the road by a schoolboy. A stone does not have interests because it cannot suffer. Nothing that we can do to it could possibly make any difference to its welfare. A mouse, on the other hand, does have an interest in not being kicked along the road, because it will suffer if it is.

If a being suffers there can be no moral justification for refusing to take that suffering into consideration. No matter what the nature of the being, the principle of equality requires that its suffering be counted equally with the like suffering—in so far as rough comparisons can be made—of any other being. If a being is not capable of suffering, or of experiencing enjoyment or happiness, there is nothing to be taken into account. So the limit of sentience (using the term as a convenient if not strictly accurate shorthand for the capacity to suffer and/or experience enjoyment) is the only defensible boundary of concern for the interests of others. To mark this boundary by some other characteristic like intelligence or rationality would be to mark it in an arbitrary manner. Why not choose some other characteristic, like skin color?

The racist violates the principle of equality by giving greater weight to the interests of members of his own race when there is a clash between their interests and the interests of those of another race. The sexist violates the principle of equality by favoring the interests of his own sex. Similarly the speciesist allows the interests of his own species to override the greater interests of members of other species. The pattern is identical in each case.

Most human beings are speciesists. Ordinary human beings—not a few exceptionally cruel or heartless humans, but the overwhelming majority of humans—take an active part in, acquiesce in, and allow their taxes to pay for practices that require the sacrifice of the most important interests of members of other species in order to promote the most trivial interests of our own species....

Speciesism In Practice

For the great majority of human beings, especially in urban, industrialized societies, the most direct form of contact with members of other species is at mealtimes: We eat them. In doing so we treat them purely as means to our ends. We regard their life and well-being as subordinate to our taste for a particular kind of dish. I say "taste" deliberately—this is purely a matter of pleasing our palate. There can be no defense of eating flesh in terms of satisfying nutritional needs, since it has been established beyond doubt that we could satisfy our need for protein and other essential nutrients far more efficiently with a diet that replaced animal flesh by soy beans, or products derived from soy beans, and other high protein vegetable products.

It is not merely the act of killing that indicates what we are ready to do to other species in order to gratify our tastes. The suffering we inflict on the animals while they are alive is perhaps an even clearer indication of our speciesism than the fact that we are prepared to kill them. In order to have meat on the table at a price that people can afford, our society tolerates methods of meat production that confine sentient animals in cramped, unsuitable conditions for the entire duration of their lives. Animals are treated like machines that convert fodder into flesh, and any innovation that results in a higher "conversion ratio" is liable to be adopted. As one authority on the subject has said, "cruelty is acknowledged only when profitability ceases." So hens are crowded four or five to a cage with a floor area of twenty inches by eighteen inches, or around the size of a single page of the *New York Times*. The cages have wire floors, since this reduces cleaning costs, though wire is unsuitable for the hens' feet; the floors slope, since this makes the eggs roll down for easy collection, although this makes it difficult for the hens to rest comfortably. In these conditions all the birds' natural instincts are thwarted: They cannot stretch their wings fully, walk freely, dust-bathe, scratch the ground, or build a nest. Although they have never known other conditions, observers have noticed that the birds vainly try to perform these actions. Frustrated at their inability to do so, they often develop what farmers call "vices," and peck each other to death. To prevent this, the beaks of young birds are often cut off.

This kind of treatment is not limited to poultry. Pigs are now also being reared in cages inside sheds. These animals are comparable to dogs in intelligence, and need a varied, stimulating environment if they are not to suffer from stress and boredom. Anyone who kept a dog in the way in which pigs are frequently kept would be liable to prosecution, in England at least, but because our interest in exploiting pigs is greater than our interest in exploiting dogs, we object to cruelty to dogs while consuming the produce of cruelty to pigs. Of the other animals, the condition of veal calves is perhaps worst of all, since these animals are so closely confined that they cannot even turn around or get up and lie down freely. In this way they do not develop unpalatable muscle. They are also made anaemic and kept short of roughage, to keep their flesh pale, since white veal fetches a higher price; as a result they develop a craving for iron and roughage, and have been observed to gnaw wood off the sides of their stalls, and lick greedily at any rusty hinge that is within reach.

Since, as I have said, none of these practices cater to anything more than our pleasures of taste, our practice of rearing and killing other animals in order to eat them is a clear instance of the sacrifice of the most important interests of other beings in order to satisfy trivial interests of our own. To avoid speciesism we must stop this practice, and each of us has a moral obligation to cease supporting the practice. Our custom is all the support that the meat industry needs. The decision to cease giving it that support may be difficult, but it is no more difficult than it would have been for a white Southerner to go against the traditions of his society and free his slaves; if we do not change our dietary habits, how can we censure those slaveholders who would not change their own way of living?

10 The same form of discrimination may be observed in the widespread practice of experimenting on other species in order to see if certain substances are safe for human beings, or to test some psychological theory about the effect of severe punishment on learning, or to try out various new compounds just in case something turns up. People sometimes think that all this experimentation is for vital medical purposes, and so will reduce suffering overall. This comfortable belief is very wide of the mark. Drug

companies test new shampoos and cosmetics that they are intending to put on the market by dropping them into the eyes of rabbits, held open by metal clips, in order to observe what damage results. Food additives, like artificial colorings and preservatives, are tested by what is known as the "LD50"—a test designed to find the level of consumption at which 50 percent of a group of animals will die. In the process, nearly all of the animals are made very sick before some finally die, and others pull through. If the substance is relatively harmless, as it often is, huge doses have to be forcefed to the animals, until in some cases sheer volume or concentration of the substance causes death.

Much of this pointless cruelty goes on in the universities. In many areas of science, nonhuman animals are regarded as an item of laboratory equipment, to be used and expended as desired. In psychology laboratories experimenters devise endless variations and repetitions of experiments that were of little value in the first place. To quote just one example, from the experimenter's own account in a psychology journal: At the University of Pennsylvania, Perrin S. Cohen hung six dogs in hammocks with electrodes taped to their hind feet. Electric shock of varying intensity was then administered through the electrodes. If the dog learned to press its head against a panel on the left, the shock was turned off, but otherwise it remained on indefinitely. Three of the dogs, however, were required to wait periods varying from 2 to 7 seconds while being shocked before making the response that turned off the current. If they failed to wait, they received further shocks. Each dog was given from 26 to 46 "sessions" in the hammock, each session consisting of 80 "trials" or shocks, administered at intervals of one minute. The experimenter reported that the dogs, who were unable to move in the hammock, barked or bobbed their heads when the current was applied. The reported findings of the experiment were that there was a delay in the dogs' responses that increased proportionately to the time the dogs were required to endure the shock, but a gradual increase in the intensity of the shock had no systematic effect in the timing of the response. The experiment was funded by the National Institutes of Health, and the United States Public Health Service.

In this example, and countless cases like it, the possible benefits to mankind are either nonexistent or fantastically remote, while the certain losses to members of other species are very real.

(1977)

QUESTIONS:

1. Summarize the argument Singer makes in the first six paragraphs here. What are the strengths of the argument? Does it have any weaknesses?

2. What can you say about Singer's recitation of facts concerning the ways in which animals are treated under factory-farming conditions, and the effect these facts have on the reader? If the presentation were different, how might that effect alter?

3. The description of electric shocks being given to dogs near the end of this piece is reminiscent of the research of Stanley Milgram described elsewhere in this volume. Are there any connections between the two in terms of the conclusions one might draw about human nature?

4. Why do you think Singer devotes considerably more space to the issue of animal suffering than to the issue of whether or not humans should eat non-human animals at all?

Adrienne Rich

Taking Women Students Seriously

In addresses made to a group of women teachers in 1978 and to a conference at Scripps College in 1984, a famous poet discusses the place of women in university, and the place of lesbians both in university and in society as a whole.

～

I see my function here today as one of trying to create a context, delineate a background, against which we might talk about women as students and students as women. I would like to speak for a while about this background, and then I hope that we can have, not so much a question period, as a raising of concerns, a sharing of questions for which we as yet may have no answers, an opening of conversations which will go on and on.

When I went to teach at Douglass, a women's college, it was with a particular background which I would like briefly to describe to you. I had graduated from an all-girls' school in the 1940s, where the head and the majority of the faculty were independent, unmarried women. One or two held doctorates, but had been forced by the Depression (and by the fact that they were women) to take secondary school teaching jobs. These women cared a great deal about the life of the mind, and they gave a great deal of time and energy—beyond any limit of teaching hours—to those of us who showed special intellectual interest or ability. We were taken to libraries, art museums, lectures at neighbouring colleges, set to work on extra research projects, given extra French or Latin reading. Although we sometimes felt "pushed" by them, we held those women in a kind of respect which even then we dimly perceived was not generally accorded to women in the world at large. They were vital individuals, defined not by their relationships but by their personalities; and although under the pressure of the culture we were all certain we wanted to get married, their lives did not appear empty or dreary to us. In a kind of cognitive dissonance, we knew they were "old maids" and therefore supposed to be bitter and lonely; yet we saw them vigorously involved with life. But despite their existence as alternate models of women, the *content* of the education they gave us in no way prepared us to survive as women in a world organized by and for men.

From that school, I went on to Radcliffe, congratulating myself that now I would have great men as my teachers. From 1947 to 1951, when I graduated, I never saw a single woman on a lecture platform, or in front of a class, except when a woman graduate student gave a paper on a special topic. The "great men" talked of other "great men," of the nature of Man, the history of Mankind, the future of Man; and never again was I to experience, from a teacher, the kind of prodding, the insistence that my best could be even better, that I had known in high school. Women students were simply not taken very seriously. Harvard's message to women was an elite mystification: we were, of course, part of Mankind; we were special, achieving women, or we would not have been there; but of course our real goal was to marry—if possible, a Harvard graduate.

In the late sixties, I began teaching at the City College of New York—a crowded, public, urban, multiracial institution as far removed from Harvard as possible. I went there to teach writing in the SEEK Program, which predated Open Admissions and which was then a kind of model for programs designed to open up higher education to poor, black and Third World students. Although during the next few years we were to see the original concept of SEEK diluted, then violently attacked and betrayed, it was for a short time an extraordinary and intense teaching and learning environment. The characteristics of this environment were a deep commitment on the part of teachers to the minds of their students; a constant, active effort to create or discover the conditions for learning, and to educate ourselves to meet the needs of the new college population; a philosophical attitude based on open discussion of racism, oppression, and the politics of literature and language; and a belief that learning in the classroom could not be isolated from the student's experience as a member of an urban minority group in white America. Here are some of the kinds of questions we, as teachers of writing, found ourselves asking:

(1) What has been the student's experience of education in the inadequate, often abusively racist public school system, which rewards passivity and treats a questioning attitude or independent mind as

a behavior problem? What has been her or his experience in a society that consistently undermines the selfhood of the poor and the nonwhite? How can such a student gain that sense of self which is necessary for active participation in education? What does all this mean for us as teachers?

(2) How do we go about teaching a canon of literature which has consistently excluded or depreciated nonwhite experience?

(3) How can we connect the process of learning to write well with the student's own reality, and not simply teach her/him how to write acceptable lies in standard English?

When I went to teach at Douglass College in 1976, and in teaching women's writing workshops elsewhere, I came to perceive stunning parallels to the questions I had first encountered in teaching the so-called disadvantaged students at City. But in this instance, and against the specific background of the women's movement, the questions framed themselves like this:

(1) What has been the student's experience of education in schools which reward female passivity, indoctrinate girls and boys in stereotypic sex roles, and do not take the female mind seriously? How does a woman gain a sense of her *self* in a system—in this case, patriarchal capitalism—which devalues work done by women, denies the importance and uniqueness of female experience, and is physically violent toward women? What does this mean for a woman teacher?

(2) How do we, as women, teach women students a canon of literature which has consistently excluded or depreciated female experience, and which often expresses hostility to women and validates violence against us?

(3) How can we teach women to move beyond the desire for male approval and getting "good grades" and seek and write their own truths that the culture has distorted or made taboo? (For women, of course, language itself is exclusive: I want to say more about this further on.)

In teaching women, we have two choices: to lend our weight to the forces that indoctrinate women to passivity, self-depreciation, and a sense of powerlessness, in which case the issue of "taking women students seriously" is a moot one; or to consider what we have to work against, as well as with, in ourselves, in our students, in the content of the curriculum, in the structure of the institution, in the society at large. And this means, first of all, taking ourselves seriously: Recognizing that central responsibility of a woman to herself, without which we remain always the Other, the defined, the object, the victim; believing that there is a unique quality of validation, affirmation, challenge, support, that one woman can offer another. Believing in the value and significance of women's experience, traditions, perceptions. Thinking of ourselves seriously, not as one of the boys, not as neuters, or androgynes, but *as women*.

Suppose we were to ask ourselves, simply: What does a woman need to know? Does she not, as a self-conscious, self-defining human being, need a knowledge of her own history, her much-politicized biology, an awareness of the creative work of women of the past, the skills and crafts and tech-niques and powers exercised by women in different times and cultures, a knowledge of women's rebellions and organized movements against our oppression and how they have been routed or diminished? Without such knowledge women live and have lived without context, vulnerable to the projections of male fantasy, male prescriptions for us, estranged from our own experience because our education has not reflected or echoed it. I would suggest that not biology, but ignorance of our selves, has been the key to our powerlessness.

But the university curriculum, the high-school curriculum, do not provide this kind of knowledge for women, the knowledge of Womankind, whose experience has been so profoundly different from that of Mankind. Only in the precariously budgeted, much-condescended-to area of women's studies is such knowledge available to women students. Only there can they learn about the lives and work of women other than the few select women who are included in the "mainstream" texts, usually misrepresented even when they do appear. Some students, at some institutions, manage to take a majority of courses in women's studies, but the message from on high is that this is self-indulgence, soft-core education: the "real" learning is the study of Mankind.

If there is any misleading concept, it is that of "coeducation": that because women and men are sitting in the same classrooms, hearing the same lectures, reading the same books, performing the same laboratory experiments, they are receiving an equal education. They are not, first because the content of education itself validates men even as it invalidates women. Its very message is that men have been the shapers and thinkers of the world, and that this is only natural. The bias of higher education, including the so-called sciences, is white and male, racist and sexist; and this bias is expressed in both subtle and blatant ways. I have mentioned already the exclusiveness of grammar itself: "The student should test himself on the above questions"; "The poet is representative. He stands among partial men for the complete man." Despite a few half-hearted departures from custom, what the linguist Wendy Martyna has named "He-Man" grammar prevails throughout the culture. The efforts of feminists to reveal the profound ontological implications of sexist grammar are routinely ridiculed by academicians and journalists, including the professedly liberal *Times* columnist, Tom Wicker, and the professed humanist, Jacques Barzun. Sexist grammar burns into the brains of little girls and young women a message that the male is the norm, the standard, the central figure beside which we are the deviants, the marginal, the dependent variables. It lays the foundation for androcentric thinking, and leaves men safe in their solipsistic tunnel-vision.

10 Women and men do not receive an equal education because outside the classroom women are perceived not as sovereign beings but as prey. The growing incidence of rape on and off the campus may or may not be fed by the proliferations of pornographic magazines and X-rated films available to young males in fraternities and student unions; but it is certainly occurring in a context of widespread images of sexual violence against women, on billboards and in so-called high art. More subtle, more daily than rape is the verbal abuse experienced by the woman student on many campuses—Rutgers for example—where, traversing a street lined with fraternity houses, she must run a gauntlet of male commentary and verbal assault. The undermining of self, of a woman's sense of her right to occupy space and walk freely in the world, is deeply relevant to education. The capacity to think independently, to take intellectual risks, to assert ourselves mentally, is inseparable from our physical way of being in the world, our feelings of personal integrity. If it is dangerous for me to walk home late of an evening from the library, *because I am a woman and can be raped*, how self-possessed, how exuberant can I feel as I sit working in that library? how much of my working energy is drained by the subliminal knowledge that, as a woman, I test my physical right to exist each time I go out alone? Of this knowledge, Susan Griffin has written:

...more than rape itself, the fear of rape permeates our lives. And what does one do from day to day, with *this* experience, which says, without words and directly to the heart, *your existence, your experience, may end at any moment.* Your experience may end, and the best defense against this is not to be, to deny being in the body, as a self, to...avert your gaze, make yourself, as a presence in the world, less felt.

Finally, rape of the mind. Women students are more and more often now reporting sexual overtures by male professors—one part of our overall growing consciousness of sexual harassment in the workplace. At Yale a legal suit has been brought against the university by a group of women demanding an explicit policy against sexual advances toward female students by male professors. Most young women experience a profound mixture of humiliation and intellectual self-doubt over seductive gestures by men who have the power to award grades, open doors to grants and graduate school, or extend special knowledge and training. Even if turned aside, such gestures constitute mental rape, destructive to a woman's ego. They are acts of domination, as despicable as the molestation of the daughter by the father.

But long before entering college the woman student has experienced her alien identity in a world which misnames her, turns her to its own uses, denying her the resources she needs to become self-affirming, self-defined. The nuclear family teaches her that relationships are more important than selfhood or work; that "whether the phone rings for you, and how often," having the right clothes, doing the dishes, take precedence over study or solitude; that too much intelligence or intensity may make her unmarriageable; that marriage and children—service to others—are, finally, the points on which her life will be judged a success or a failure. In high school, the polarization between feminine attractiveness and independent intelligence comes to an absolute. Meanwhile, the culture resounds with messages. During Solar Energy Week in New York I saw young women wearing "ecology" T-shirts with the legend: CLEAN, CHEAP AND AVAILABLE; a reminder of the 1960s antiwar button which read: CHICKS SAY YES TO MEN WHO SAY NO. Department store windows feature female mannequins in chains, pinned to the wall with legs spread, smiling in positions of torture. Feminists are depicted in the media as "shrill," "strident," "puritanical," or "humorless," and the lesbian choice—the choice of the woman-identified woman—as pathological or sinister. The young woman sitting in the philosophy classroom, the political science lecture, is already gripped by tensions between her nascent sense of self-worth, and the battering force of messages like these.

Look at a classroom: look at the many kinds of women's faces, postures, expressions. Listen to the women's voices. Listen to the silences, the unasked questions, the blanks. Listen to the small, soft voices, often courageously trying to speak up, voices of women taught early that tones of confidence, challenge, anger, or assertiveness, are strident and unfeminine. Listen to the voices of women and the voices of men; observe the space men allow themselves, physically and verbally, the male assumption that people will listen, even when the majority of the group is female. Look at the faces of the silent, and of those who speak. Listen to a woman groping for language in which to express what is on her mind, sensing that the terms of academic discourse are not her language, trying to cut down her thought to the dimensions of a discourse not intended for her (*for it is not fitting that a woman speak in public*); or reading her paper aloud at breakneck speed, throwing her words away, deprecating her own work by a reflex prejudgment: *I do not deserve to take up time and space.*

As women teachers, we can either deny the importance of this context in which women students think, write, read, study, project their own futures; or try to work with it. We can either teach passively, accepting these conditions, or actively, helping our students identify and resist them.

15   One important thing we can do is *discuss* the context. And this need not happen only in a women's studies course; it can happen anywhere. We can refuse to accept passive, obedient learning and insist upon critical thinking. We can become harder on our women students, giving them the kinds of "cultural prodding" that men receive, but on different terms and in a different style. Most young women need to have their intellectual lives, their work, legitimized against the claims of family, relationships, the old message that a woman is always available for service to others. We need to keep our standards very high, not to accept a woman's preconceived sense of her limitations; we need to be hard to please, while supportive of risk-taking, because self-respect often comes only when exacting standards have been met. At a time when adult literacy is generally low, we need to demand more, not less, of women, both for the sake of their futures as thinking beings, and because historically women have always had to be better than men to do half as well. A romantic sloppiness, an inspired lack of rigor, a self-indulgent incoherence, are symptoms of female self-depreciation. We should help our women students to look very critically at such symptoms, and to understand where they are rooted.

Nor does this mean we should be training women students to "think like men." Men in general think badly: in disjuncture from their personal lives, claiming objectivity where the most irrational passions seethe, losing, as Virginia Woolf observed, their senses in the pursuit of professionalism. It is not easy to think like a woman in a man's world, in the world of the professions; yet the capacity to do that is a strength which we can try to help our students develop. To think like a woman in a man's world means thinking critically, refusing to accept the givens, making connections between facts and ideas which men have left unconnected. It means remembering that every mind resides in a body; remaining accountable to the female bodies in which we live; constantly retesting given hypotheses against lived experience. It means a constant critique of language, for as Wittgenstein (no feminist) observed, "The limits of my language are the limits of my world." And it means that most difficult thing of all: listening and watching in art and literature, in the social sciences, in all the descriptions we are given of the world, for the silences, the absences, the nameless, the unspoken, the encoded—for there we will find the true knowledge of women. And in breaking those silences, naming our selves, uncovering the hidden, making ourselves present, we begin to define a reality which resonates to *us*, which affirms *our* being, which allows the woman teacher and the woman student alike to take ourselves, and each other, seriously: meaning, to begin taking charge of our lives.

(1978)

INVISIBILITY IN ACADEME

The history of North American lesbians under white domination begins with the death penalty prescribed for lesbians in 1656 in New Haven, Connecticut. Three hundred years later, in the 1950s, lesbians were being beaten in the city streets, committed to mental institutions, forced to undergo psychosurgery, often at their parents' instigation. Thirty years after that, in the mid-1980s, despite the struggles and visions of both the Women's Liberation movement and the gay liberation movement, lesbians are still being assaulted in the streets—during the past year in the streets of Northampton, Massachusetts, the site of a women's college near which I live. Lesbians are still being forced to endure behaviour modification and medical punishment, are still banished from families, are rejected by our ethnic, racial, and religious communities, must pretend to be heterosexual in order to hold jobs, have custody of their children, rent apartments, publicly represent a larger community.

Beside all this, invisibility may seem a small price to pay (as in "All we ask is that you keep your private life private" or "Just don't use the word"). But invisibility is a dangerous and painful condition, and lesbians are not the only people to know it. When those who have power to name and to socially construct reality choose not to see you or hear you, whether you are dark-skinned, old, disabled, female, or speak with a different accent or dialect than theirs, when someone with authority of a teacher, say, describes the world and you are not in it, there is a moment of psychic disequilibrium, as if you looked into a mirror and saw nothing. Yet you know you exist and others like you, that this is a game with mirrors. It takes some strength of soul—and not just individual strength, but collective understanding—to resist this void, this nonbeing, into which you are thrust, and to stand up, demanding to be seen and heard. And to make yourself visible, to claim that your experience is just as real and normative as any other, as "moral and ordinary" in the words of historian Blanche Cook, can mean making yourself vulnerable. But at least you are not doing the oppressor's work, building your own closet. It is important to me to remember that in the nineteenth century, women—all women—were forbidden by law to speak in public meetings. Society depended on their muteness. But some, and then more and more, refused to be mute and spoke up. Without them, we would not even be here today.

I have been for ten years a very public and visible lesbian. I have been identified as a lesbian in print both by myself and others; I have worked in the lesbian-feminist movement. Here in Claremont, where I have been received with much warmth and hospitality, I have often felt invisible as a lesbian. I have felt my identity as a feminist threatening to some, welcome to others; but my identity as a lesbian is something that many people would prefer not to know about. And this experience has reminded me of what I should never have let myself forget: that invisibility is not just a matter of being told to keep your private life private; it's the attempt to fragment you, to prevent you from integrating love and work and feelings and ideas, with the empowerment that that can bring.

I'm not talking only about this community. There are many places, including Women's Studies programs, where this fragmentation goes on. The basis for dialogue and discussion remains heterosexual, while perhaps a section of a reading list or a single class period is supposed to "include" lesbian experience and thought. In an almost identical way, the experience and thought of women of color is relegated to a special section, added as an afterthought, while the central discourse remains unrelentingly white, usually middle-class in its assumptions and priorities. The name of the second set of blinders is racism; of the first, heterosexism. The Black political scientist Gloria I. Joseph, in a talk on "Third World Women and Feminism," has suggested that *homophobia* is an inaccurate term, implying a form of uncontrollable mental panic, and that *heterosexism* better describes what is really a deeply ingrained prejudice, comparable to racism, sexism, and classism—a political indoctrination which must be recognized as such and which can be re-educated.

5 I want to suggest that it is impossible for any woman growing up in a gendered society dominated by men to know what heterosexuality really means, both historically and in her individual life, so long as she is kept ignorant of the presence, the existence, the actuality of women who, diverse in so many ways, have centered their emotional and erotic lives on women. A young woman entering her twenties in a blur of stereotypes and taboos, with a vague sense of anxiety centering around the word *lesbian*, is ill equipped to think about herself, her feelings, her options, her relations with men *or* women. This ignorance and anxiety, which affects lesbians and heterosexually identified women alike, this silence, this absence of a whole population, this invisibility, is disempowering for all women. It is not only lesbian students who should be calling for a recognition of their history and presence in the world; it is *all* women who want a more accurate map of the way social relations have been and are, as they try to imagine what might be.

I think that those of us who are lesbians here sense that there are people who want to meet us in our wholeness instead of fragments, and others who do not want to know, who run away, who want us to be quiet, who will use all kinds of indirect and genteel means to keep us that way, including the charge that we never talk about anything else. I believe there is a critical mass in this community—not only lesbians—who recognize the intellectual and moral sterility of heterosexism. I hope that we can find ways of speaking with each other that will strengthen a collective understanding that will keep discussion continuing long after this conference is over.

(1984)

QUESTIONS:

1. What elements of "Taking Women Students Seriously" reflect the care with which Rich has paid attention to her audience? What sorts of changes in diction, syntax, or tone might be appropriate were an address on the same topic to be made to high school students?

2. In paragraphs 8 and 9 of "Taking Women Students Seriously," Rich flushes out a point about exclusivity in language that she has touched on in paragraph 5. In a paragraph, summarize in your own words Rich's argument about language.

3. How does the ordering of the ideas Rich expresses in the first sentence of paragraph 10 of "Taking Women Students Seriously" intensify their provocative quality? To what extent (if at all) is it an exaggeration to describe women outside the classroom in universities as being perceived as "prey"?

4. Do you believe that men and women think differently? Discuss with reference to paragraph 16 in "Taking Women Students Seriously."

5. To what extent do you think the situation described by Rich in "Taking Women Students Seriously" has altered since 1978?

6. Explain in your own words what Rich means by "invisibility" for lesbians. In a short essay describe the attitude towards gays and lesbians in your own university; is the most common attitude the sort of expectation of invisibility that Rich describes?

Susan Wolf

Moral Saints

In this essay philosopher Susan Wolf makes an argument that moral sainthood is desirable neither in one's self nor in others.

～～

Idon't know whether there are any moral saints. But if there are, I am glad that neither I nor those about whom I care most are among them. By *moral saint* I mean a person whose every action is as morally good as possible, a person, that is, who is as morally worthy as can be. Though I shall in a moment acknowledge the variety of types of person that might be thought to satisfy this description, it seems to me that none of these types serve as unequivocally compelling personal ideals. In other words, I believe that moral perfection, in the sense of moral saintliness, does not constitute a model of personal well-being toward which it would be particularly rational or good or desirable for a human being to strive.

Outside the context of moral discussion, this will strike many as an obvious point. But, within that context, the point, if it be granted, will be granted with some discomfort. For within that context it is generally assumed that one ought to be as morally good as possible and that what limits there are to morality's hold on us are set by features of human nature of which we ought not to be proud. If, as I believe, the ideals that are derivable from common sense and philosophically popular moral theories do not support these assumptions, then something has to change. Either we must change our moral theories in ways that will make them yield more palatable ideals, or, as I shall argue, we must change our conception of what is involved in affirming a moral theory.

In this paper, I wish to examine the notion of a moral saint, first, to understand what a moral saint would be like and why such a being would be unattractive, and second, to raise some questions about the significance of this paradoxical figure for moral philosophy. I shall look first at the model(s) of moral sainthood that might be extrapolated from the morality or moralities of common sense. Then I shall consider what relations these have to conclusions that can be drawn from utilitarian and Kantian moral theories. Finally, I shall speculate on the implications of these considerations for moral philosophy.

Moral Saints and Common Sense

Consider first what, pretheoretically, would count for us—contemporary members of Western culture—as a moral saint. A necessary condition of moral sainthood would be that one's life be dominated by a commitment to improving the welfare of others or of society as a whole. As to what role this commitment must play in the individual's motivational system, two contrasting accounts suggest themselves to me which might equally be thought to qualify a person for moral sainthood.

First, a moral saint might be someone whose concern for others plays the role that is played in most of our lives by more selfish, or, at any rate, less morally worthy concerns. For the moral saint, the promotion of the welfare of others might play the role that is played for most of us by the enjoyment of material comforts, the opportunity to engage in the intellectual and physical activities of our choice, and the love, respect, and companionship of people whom we love, respect, and enjoy. The happiness of the moral saint, then, would truly lie in the happiness of others, and so he would devote himself to others gladly, and with a whole and open heart.

On the other hand, a moral saint might be someone for whom the basic ingredients of happiness are not unlike those of most of the rest of us. What makes him a moral saint is rather that he pays little or no attention to his own happiness in light of the overriding importance he gives to the wider concerns of morality. In other words, this person sacrifices his own interests to the interests of others, and feels the sacrifice as much.

Roughly, these two models may be distinguished according to whether one thinks of the moral saint as being a saint out of love or one thinks of the moral saint as being a saint out of duty (or some other intellectual appreciation and recognition of moral principles). We may refer to the first model as the model of the Loving Saint; to the second, as the model of the Rational Saint.

The two models differ considerably with respect to the qualities of the motives of the individuals who conform to them. But this difference would have limited effect on the saints' respective public personalities. The shared content of what these individuals are motivated to be—namely, as morally good as possible—would play the dominant role in the determination of their characters. Of course, just as a variety of large-scale projects, from tending the sick to political campaigning, may be equally and maximally morally worthy, so a variety of characters are compatible with the ideal of moral sainthood. One moral saint may be more or less jovial, more or less garrulous, more or less athletic than another. But above all, a moral saint must have and cultivate those qualities which are apt to allow him to treat others as justly and kindly as possible. He will have the standard moral virtues to a nonstandard degree. He will be patient, considerate, even-tempered, hospitable, charitable in thought as well as in deed. He will be very reluctant to make negative judgments of other people. He will be careful not to favor some people over others on the basis of properties they could not help but have.

Perhaps what I have already said is enough to make some people begin to regard the absence of moral saints in their lives as a blessing. For there comes a point in the listing of virtues that a moral saint is likely to have where one might naturally begin to wonder whether the moral saint isn't after all, too good—if not too good for his own good, at least too good for his own well-being. For the moral virtues, given that they are, by hypothesis, *all* present in the same individual, and to an extreme degree, are apt to crowd out the nonmoral virtues, as well as many of the interests and personal characteristics that we generally think contribute to a healthy, well-rounded, richly developed character.

In other words, if the moral saint is devoting all his time to feeding the hungry or healing the sick or raising money for Oxfam, then necessarily he is not reading Victorian novels, playing the oboe, or improving his backhand. Although no one of these interests or tastes in the category containing these latter activities could be claimed to be a necessary element in a life well lived, a life in which *none* of these possible aspects of character are developed may seem to be a life strangely barren.

The reasons why a moral saint cannot, in general, encourage the discovery and development of significant nonmoral interests and skills are not logical but practical reasons. There are, in addition, a class of nonmoral characteristics that a moral saint cannot encourage in himself for reasons that are not just practical. There is a more substantial tension between having any of these qualities unashamedly and being a moral saint. These qualities might be described as going against the moral grain. For example, a cynical or sarcastic wit, or a sense of humor that appreciates this kind of wit in others, requires that one take an attitude of resignation and pessimism toward the flaws and vices to be found in the world. A moral saint, on the other hand, has reason to take an attitude in opposition to this—he should try to look for the best in people, give them the benefit of the doubt as long as possible, try to improve regrettable situations as long as there is any hope of success. This suggests that, although a moral saint might well enjoy a good episode of *Father Knows Best,* he may not in good conscience be able to laugh at a Marx Brothers movie or enjoy a play by George Bernard Shaw.

An interest in something like gourmet cooking will be, for different reasons, difficult for a moral saint to rest easy with. For it seems to me that no plausible argument can justify the use of human resources involved in producing a *paté de canard en croute* against possible alternative beneficient end to which these resources might be put. If there is a justification for the institution of haute cuisine, it is one which rests on the decision *not* to justify every activity against morally beneficial alternatives, and this is a decision a moral saint will never make. Presumably, an interest in high fashion or interior design will face much the same, as will, very possibly, a cultivation of the finer arts as well.

A moral saint will have to be very, very nice. It is important that he may not be offensive. The worry is that, as a result, he will have to be dull-witted or humorless or bland.

This worry is confirmed when we consider what sorts of characters, taken and refined both from life and from fiction, typically form our ideals. One would hope they would be figures who are morally good—and by this I mean more than just not morally bad—but one would hope, too, that they are not *just* morally good, but talented or accomplished or attractive in nonmoral ways as well. We may make ideals out of athletes, scholars, artists—more frivolously, out of cowboys, private eyes, and rock stars. We may strive for Katharine Hepburn's grace, Paul Newman's "cool"; we are attracted to the high-spirited passionate nature of Natasha Rostov; we admire the keen perceptiveness of Lambert Strether. Though there is certainly nothing immoral about the ideal characters or traits I have in mind, they cannot be superimposed upon the ideal of a moral saint. For although it is a part of many of these ideals that the characters set high, and not merely acceptable, moral standards for themselves, it is also essential to their power and attractiveness that the moral strengths go, so to speak, alongside of specific independently admirable, nonmoral ground projects and dominant personal traits.

When one does finally turn one's eyes toward lives that are dominated by explicitly moral commitments, moreover, one finds oneself relieved at the discovery of idiosyncrasies or eccentricities not quite in line with the picture of moral perfection. One prefers the blunt, tactless, and opinionated Betsy Trotwood to the unfailingly kind and patient Agnes Copperfield; one prefers the mischievousness and the sense of irony in Chesterton's Father Brown to the innocence and undiscriminating love of St. Francis.

It seems that, as we look in our ideals for people who achieve nonmoral varieties of personal excellence in conjunction with or colored by some version of high moral tone, we look in our paragons of moral excellence for people whose moral achievements occur in conjunction with or colored by some interests or traits that have low moral tone. In other words, there seems to be a limit on how much morality we can stand.

One might suspect that the essence of the problem is simply that there is a limit to how much of *any* single value, or any single type of value, we can stand. Our objection then would not be specific to a life in which one's dominant concern is morality, but would apply to any life that can be so completely characterized by an extraordinarily dominant concern. The objection in that case would reduce to the recognition that such a life is incompatible with well-roundedness. If that were the objection, one could fairly reply that well-roundedness is no more supreme a virtue than the totality of moral virtues embodied by the ideal it is being used to criticize. But I think this misidentifies the objection. For the way in which a concern for morality may dominate a life, or, more to the point, the way in which it may dominate an ideal of life, is not easily imagined by analogy to the dominance an aspiration to become an Olympic swimmer or a concert pianist might have.

A person who is passionately committed to one of these latter concerns might decide that her attachment to it is strong enough to be worth the sacrifice of her ability to maintain and pursue a significant portion of what else life might offer which a proper devotion of her dominant passion would require. But a desire to be as morally good as possible is not likely to take the form of one desire among others which, because of its peculiar psychological strength, requires one to forego the pursuit of other weaker and separately less demanding desires. Rather, the desire to be as morally good as possible is apt to have the character not just of a stronger, but of a higher desire, which does not merely successfully compete with one's other desires but which rather subsumes or demotes them. The sacrifice of other interests for the interest in morality, then, will have the character, not of a choice, but of an imperative.

Moreover, there is something odd about the idea of morality itself, or moral goodness, serving as the object of a dominant passion in the way that a more concrete and specific vision of a goal (even a concrete *moral* goal) might be imagined to serve. Morality itself does not seem to be a suitable object of passion. Thus, when one reflects, for example, on the Loving Saint easily and gladly giving up his fishing trip or his stereo or his hot fudge sundae at the drop of the moral hat, one is apt to wonder not at how much he loves morality, but at how little he loves these other things. One thinks that, if he can give these up so easily, he does not know what it *is* to truly love them. There seems, in other words, to be a kind of joy which the Loving Saint, either by nature or by practice, is incapable of experiencing. The Rational Saint, on the other hand, might retain strong nonmoral and concrete desires—he simply denies himself the opportunity to act on them. But this is no less troubling. The Loving Saint one might suspect of missing a piece of perceptual machinery, of being blind to some of what the world has to offer. The Rational Saint, who sees it but forgoes it, one suspects of having a different problem—a pathological fear of damnation, perhaps, or an extreme form of self-hatred that interferes with his ability to enjoy the enjoyable in life.

20   In other words, the ideal of a life of moral sainthood disturbs not simply because it is an ideal of a life in which morality unduly dominates. The normal person's direct and specific desires for objects, activities, and events that conflict with the attainment of moral perfection are not simply sacrificed but removed, suppressed, or subsumed. The way in which morality, unlike other possible goals, is apt to dominate is particularly disturbing, for it seems to require either the lack or the denial of the existence of an identifiable, personal self.

This distinctively troubling feature is not, I think, absolutely unique to the ideal of the moral saint, as I have been using that phrase. It is shared by the conception of the pure aesthete, by a certain kind of religious ideal, and, somewhat paradoxically, by the model of the thorough-going self-conscious egoist. It is not a coincidence that the ways of comprehending the world of which these ideals are the extreme embodiments are sometimes described as "moralities" themselves. At any rate, they compete with what we ordinarily mean by 'morality'. Nor is it a coincidence that these ideals are naturally described as fanatical. But it is easy to see that these other types of perfection cannot serve as satisfactory personal ideals; for the realization of these ideals would be straightforwardly immoral. It may come as a surprise to some that there may in addition be such a thing as a *moral* fanatic.

Some will object that I am being unfair to "common-sense morality"—that it does not really require a moral saint to be either a disgustingly goody-goody or an obsessive ascetic. Admittedly, there is no logical inconsistency between having any of the personal characteristics I have mentioned and being a moral saint. It is not morally wrong to notice the faults and shortcomings of others or to recognize and appreciate nonmoral talents and skills. Nor is it immoral to be an avid Celtics fan or to have a passion for caviar or to be an excellent cellist. With enough imagination, we can always contrive a suitable history and set of circumstances that will embrace such characteristics in one or another specific fictional story of a perfect moral saint.

If one turned onto the path of moral sainthood relatively late in life, one may have already developed interests that can be turned to moral purposes. It may be that a good golf game is just what is needed to secure that big donation to Oxfam. Perhaps the cultivation of one's exceptional artistic talent will turn out to be the way one can make one's greatest contribution to society. Furthermore, one might stumble upon joys and skills in the very service of morality. If, because children are short a ninth player for the team, one's generous offer to serve reveals a natural fielding arm or if one's part in the campaign against nuclear power requires accepting a lobbyist's invitation to lunch at Le Lion d'Or, there is no moral gain in denying the satisfaction one gets from these activities. The moral saint, then, may, by happy accident, find himself with nonmoral virtues on which he can capitalize morally or which make psychological demands to which he has no choice but to attend. The point is that, for a moral saint, the existence of these interests and skills can be given at best the status of happy accidents—they cannot be encouraged for their own sakes as distinct, independent aspects of the realization of human good.

It must be remembered that from the fact that there is a tension between having any of these qualities and being a moral saint it does not follow that having any of these qualities is immoral. For it is not part of common-sense morality that one ought to be a moral saint. Still, if someone just happened to want to be a moral saint, he or she would not have or encourage these qualities, and, on the basis of our common-sense values, this counts as a reason *not* to want to be a moral saint.

25   One might still wonder what kind of reason this is, and what kind of conclusion this properly allows us to draw. For the fact that the models of moral saints are unattractive does not necessarily mean that they are unsuitable ideals. Perhaps they are unattractive because they make us feel uncomfortable—they highlight our own weaknesses, vices, and flaws. If so, the fault lies not in the characters of the saints, but in those of our unsaintly selves.

    To be sure, some of the reasons behind the disaffection we feel for the model of moral sainthood have to do with a reluctance to criticize ourselves and a reluctance to committing ourselves to trying to give up activities and interests that we heartily enjoy. These considerations might prove an *excuse* for the fact that we are not moral saints, but they do not provide a basis for criticizing sainthood as a possible ideal. Since these considerations rely on an appeal to the egoistic, hedonistic side of our natures, to use them as a basis for criticizing the ideal of the moral saint would be at best to beg the question and at worst to glorify features of ourselves that ought to be condemned.

    The fact that the moral saint would be without qualities which we have and which, indeed, we like to have, does not in itself provide reason to condemn the ideal of the moral saint. The fact that some of these qualities are good qualities, however, and that they are qualities we *ought* to like, does provide reason to discourage this ideal and to offer other ideals in its place. In other words, some of the qualities the moral saint necessarily lacks are virtues, albeit nonmoral virtues, in the unsaintly characters who have them. The feats of Groucho Marx, Reggie Jackson, and the head chef at *Lutèce* are impressive accomplishments that it is not only permissible but positively appropriate to recognize as such. In general, the admiration of and striving toward achieving any of a great variety of forms of personal excellence are character traits it is valuable and desirable for people to have. In advocating the development of these varieties of excellence, we advocate nonmoral reasons for acting, and in thinking that it is good for a person to strive for an ideal that gives a substantial role to the interests and values that correspond to these virtues, we implicitly acknowledge the goodness of ideals incompatible with that of the moral saint. Finally, if we think that it is *as* good, or even better for a person to strive for one of these ideals than it is for him or her to strive for and realize the ideal of the moral saint, we express a conviction that it is good not to be a moral saint.

Moral Saints and Moral Theories

I have tried so far to paint a picture—or rather, two pictures—of what a moral saint might be like, drawing on what I take to be the attitudes and beliefs about morality prevalent in contemporary, common-sense thought. To my suggestion that common-sense morality generates conceptions of moral saints that are unattractive or otherwise unacceptable, it is open to someone to reply, "so much the worse for common-sense morality." After all, it is often claimed that the goal of moral philosophy is to correct and improve upon common-sense morality, and I have as yet given no attention to the question of what conceptions of moral sainthood, if any, are generated from the leading moral theories of our time.

A quick, breezy reading of utilitarian and Kantian writings will suggest the images, respectively, of the Loving Saint and the Rational Saint. A utilitarian, with his emphasis on happiness, will certainly prefer the Loving Saint to the Rational one, since the Loving Saint will himself be a happier person than the Rational Saint. A Kantian, with his emphasis on reason, on the other hand, will find at least as much praise in the latter as in the former. Still, both models, drawn as they are from common sense, appeal to an impure mixture of utilitarian and Kantian intuitions. A more careful examination of these moral theories raises questions about whether either model of moral sainthood would really be advocated by a believer in the explicit doctrines associated with either of these views.

30 Certainly, the utilitarian in no way denies the value of self-realization. He in no way disparages the development of interests, talents, and other personally attractive traits that I have claimed the moral saint would be without. Indeed, since just these features enhance the happiness both of the individuals who possess them and of those with whom they associate, the ability to promote these features both in oneself and in others will have considerable positive weight in utilitarian calculations.

This implies that the utilitarian would not support moral sainthood as a universal ideal. A world in which everyone, or even a large number of people, achieved moral sainthood—even a world in which they strove to achieve it—would probably contain less happiness than a world in which people realized a diversity of ideals involving a variety of personal and perfectionist values. More pragmatic considerations also suggest that, if the utilitarian wants to influence more people to achieve more good, then he would do better to encourage them to pursue happiness-producing goals that are more attractive and more within a normal person's reach.

These considerations still leave open, however, the question of what kind of an ideal the committed utilitarian should privately aspire to himself. Utilitarianism requires him to want to achieve the greatest general happiness, and this would seem to commit him to the ideal of the moral saint.

One might try to use the claims I made earlier as a basis for an argument that a utilitarian should choose to give up utilitarianism. If, as I have said, a moral saint would be a less happy person both to be and to be around than many other possible ideals, perhaps one could create more total happiness by not trying too hard to promote the total happiness. But this argument is simply unconvincing in light of the empirical circumstances of our world. The gain in happiness that would accrue to oneself and one's neighbors by a more well-rounded, richer life than that of the moral saint would be pathetically small in comparison to the amount by which one could increase the general happiness if one devoted oneself explicitly to the care of the sick, the downtrodden, the starving, and the homeless. Of course, there may be psychological limits to the extent to which a person can devote himself to such things without going crazy. But the utilitarian's individual limitations would not thereby become a positive feature of his personal ideals.

The unattractiveness of the moral saint, then, ought not rationally convince the utilitarian to abandon his utilitarianism. It may, however, convince him to take efforts not to wear his saintly moral aspirations on his sleeve. If it is not too difficult, the utilitarian will try not to make those around him uncomfortable. He will not want to appear "holier than thou"; he will not want to inhibit others' ability to enjoy themselves. In practice, this might make the perfect utilitarian a less nauseating companion than the moral saint I earlier portrayed. But insofar as this kind of reasoning produces a more bearable public personality, it is at the cost of giving him a personality that must be evaluated as hypocritical and condescending when his private thoughts and attitudes are taken into account.

35 Still, the criticisms I have raised against the saint of common-sense morality should make some difference to the utilitarian's conception of an ideal which neither requires him to abandon his utilitarian principles nor forces him to fake an interest he does not have or a judgment he does not make. For it may be that a limited and carefully monitored allotment of time and energy to be devoted to the pursuit of some nonmoral interests or to the development of some nonmoral talents would make a person a better contributor to the general welfare than he would be if he allowed himself no indulgences of this sort. The enjoyment of such activities in no way

compromises a commitment to utilitarian principles as long as the involvement with these activities is conditioned by a willingness to give them up whenever it is recognized that they cease to be in the general interest.

This will go some way in mitigating the picture of the loving saint that an understanding of utilitarianism will on first impression suggest. But I think it will not go very far. For the limitations on time and energy will have to be rather severe, and the need to monitor will restrict not only the extent but also the quality of one's attachment to these interests and traits. They are only weak and somewhat peculiar sorts of passions to which one can consciously remain so conditionally committed. Moreover, the way in which the utilitarian can enjoy these "extra-curricular" aspects of his life is simply not the way in which these aspects are to be enjoyed insofar as they figure into our less saintly ideals.

The problem is not exactly that the utilitarian values these aspects of his life only as a means to an end, for the enjoyment he and others get from these aspects are not a means to, but a part of, the general happiness. Nonetheless, he values these things only because of and insofar as they *are* a part of the general happiness. He values them, as it were, under the description 'a contribution to the general happiness'. This is to be contrasted with the various ways in which these aspects of life may be valued by nonutilitarians. A person might love literature because of the insights into human nature literature affords. Another might love the cultivation of roses because roses are things of great beauty and delicacy. It may be true that these features of the respective activities also explain why these activities are happiness-producing. But, to the non-utilitarian, this may not be to the point. For if one values these activities in these more direct ways, one may not be willing to exchange them for others that produce an equal, or even a greater amount of happiness. From that point of view, it is not because they produce happiness that these activities are valuable; it is because these activities are valuable in more direct and specific ways that they produce happiness.

To adopt a phrase of Bernard Williams', the utilitarian's manner of valuing the not explicitly moral aspects of his life "provides (him) with one thought too many."[1] The requirement that the utilitarian have this thought—periodically, at least—is indicative of not only a weakness but a shallowness in his appreciation of the aspects in question. Thus, the ideals toward which a utilitarian could acceptably strive would remain too close to

---

[1] "Persons, Character and Morality" in Amelie Rorty, ed., *The Identities of Persons* (Berkeley: Univ. of California Press, 1976), p. 214.

the model of the common-sense moral saint to escape the criticisms of that model which I earlier suggested. Whether a Kantian would be similarly committed to so restrictive and unattractive a range of possible ideals is a somewhat more difficult question.

The Kantian believes that being morally worthy consists in always acting from maxims that one could will to be universal law, and doing this not out of any pathological desire but out of reverence for the moral law as such. Or, to take a different formulation of the categorical imperative, the Kantian believes that moral action consists in treating other persons always as ends and never as means only. Presumably, and according to Kant himself, the Kantian thereby commits himself to some degree of benevolence as well as to the rules of fair play. But we surely would not will that *every* person become a moral saint, and treating others as ends hardly requires bending over backwards to protect and promote their interests. On one interpretation of Kantian doctrine, then, moral perfection would be achieved simply by unerring obedience to a limited set of side-constraints. On this interpretation, Kantian theory simply does not yield an ideal conception of a person of any fullness comparable to that of the moral saints I have so far been portraying.

40   On the other hand, Kant does say explicitly that we have a duty of benevolence, a duty not only to allow others to pursue their ends, but to take up their ends as our own. In addition, we have positive duties to ourselves, duties to increase our natural as well as our moral perfection. These duties are unlimited in the degree to which they *may* dominate a life. If action in accordance with and motivated by the thought of these duties is considered virtuous, it is natural to assume that the more one performs such actions, the more virtuous one is. Moreover, of virtue in general Kant says, "it is an ideal which is unattainable while yet our duty is constantly to approximate it." On this interpretation, then, the Kantian moral saint, like the other moral saints I have been considering, is dominated by the motivation to be moral.

Which of these interpretations of Kant one prefers will depend on the interpretation and the importance one gives to the role of the imperfect duties in Kant's over-all system. Rather than choose between them here, I shall consider each briefly in turn.

On the second interpretation of Kant, the Kantian moral saint is, not surprisingly, subject to many of the same objections I have been raising against other versions of moral sainthood. Though the Kantian saint may differ from the utilitarian saint as to *which* actions he is bound to perform and which he is bound to refrain from performing, I suspect that the range of activities acceptable to the Kantian saint will remain objectionably restrictive. Moreover, the manner in which the Kantian saint must think about and justify the activities he pursues and the character traits he develops will strike us, as it did with the utilitarian saint, as containing "one thought too many." As the utilitarian could value his activities and character traits only insofar as they fell under the description of contributions to the general happiness', the Kantian would have to value his activities and character traits insofar as they were manifestations of respect for the moral law. If the development of our powers to achieve physical, intellectual, or artistic excellence, or the activities directed toward making others happy are to have any moral worth, they must arise from a reverence for the dignity that members of our species have as a result of being endowed with pure practical reason. This is a good and noble motivation, to be sure. But it is hardly what one expects to be dominantly behind a person's aspirations to dance as well as Fred Astaire, to paint as well as Picasso, or to solve some outstanding problem in abstract algebra, and it is hardly what one hopes to find lying dominantly behind a father's action on behalf of his son or a lover's on behalf of her beloved.

Since the basic problem with any of the models of moral sainthood we have been considering is that they are dominated by a single, all-important value under which all other possible values must be subsumed, it may seem that the alternative interpretation of Kant, as providing a stringent but finite set of obligations and constraints, might provide a more acceptable morality. According to this interpretation of Kant, one is as morally good as can be so long as one devotes some limited portion of one's energies toward altruism and the maintenance of one's physical and spiritual health, and otherwise pursues one's independently motivated interests and values in such a way as to avoid overstepping certain bounds. Certainly, if it be a requirement of an acceptable moral theory that perfect obedience to its laws and maximal devotion to its interests and concerns be something we can wholeheartedly strive for in ourselves and wish for in those around us, it will count in favor of this brand of Kantianism that its commands can be fulfilled without swallowing up the perfect moral saint's entire personality.

Even this more limited understanding of morality, if its connection to Kant's views is to be taken at all seriously, is not likely to give an unqualified seal of approval to the nonmorally directed ideals I have been advocating. For Kant is explicit about what he calls "duties of apathy and self-mastery" (69/70)—duties to ensure that our passions are never so strong as to interfere with calm, practical deliberation, or so deep as to wrest control from the more disinterested, rational part of ourselves. The tight and self-conscious rein we are thus obliged to keep on our commitments to specific individuals and causes will doubtless restrict our value in these things, assigning them a necessarily attenuated place.

45   A more interesting objection to this brand of Kantianism, however, comes when we consider the implications of placing the kind of upper bound on moral worthiness which seemed to count in favor of this conception of morality. For to put such a limit on one's capacity to be moral is effectively to deny, not just the moral necessity, but the moral goodness of a devotion to benevolence and the maintenance of justice that passes beyond a certain, required point. It is to deny the possibility of going morally above and beyond the call of a restricted set of duties. Despite my claim that all-consuming moral saintliness is not a particularly healthy and desirable ideal, it seems perverse to insist that, were moral saints to exist, they would not, in their way, be remarkably noble and admirable figures. Despite my conviction that is as rational and as good for a person to take Katharine Hepburn or Jane Austen as her role model instead of Mother Theresa, it would be absurd to deny that Mother Theresa is a morally better person.

I can think of two ways of viewing morality as having an upper bound. First, we can think that altruism and impartiality are indeed positive moral interests, but that they are moral only if the degree to which these interests are actively pursued remains within certain fixed limits. Second, we can think that these positive interests are only incidentally related to morality and that the essence of morality lies elsewhere, in, say, an implicit social contract or in the recognition of our own dignified rationality. According to the first conception of morality, there is a cut-off line to the amount of altruism or to the extent of devotion to justice and fairness that is worthy of moral praise. But to draw this line earlier than the line that brings the altruist in question to a worse-off position than all those to whom he devotes himself seems unacceptably artificial and gratuitous. According to the second conception, these positive interests are not essentially related to morality at all. But then we are unable to regard a more affectionate and generous expression of good will toward others as a natural and reasonable extension of morality, and we encourage a cold and unduly self-centered approach to the development and evaluation of our motivations and concerns.

A moral theory that does not contain the seeds of an all-consuming ideal of moral sainthood thus seems to place false and unnatural limits on our opportunity to do moral good and our potential to deserve moral praise. Yet the main thrust of the arguments of this paper has been leading to the conclusion that when such ideals are present, they are not ideals to which it is particularly reasonable or healthy or desirable for human beings to aspire. These claims, taken together, have the appearance of a dilemma from which there is no obvious escape. In a moment, I shall argue that, despite appearances, these claims should not be understood as constituting a dilemma. But, before I do, let me briefly describe another path which those who are convinced by my above remarks may feel inclined to take.

If the above remarks are understood to be implicitly critical of the views on the content of morality which seem more popular today, an alternative that naturally suggests itself is that we revise our views about the content of morality. More specifically, my remarks may be taken to support a more Aristotelian, or even a more Nietzchean, approach to moral philosophy. Such a change in approach involves substantially broadening or replacing our contemporary intuitions about which character traits constitute moral virtues and vices and which interests constitute moral interests. If, for example, we include personal bearing, or creativity, or sense of style, as features that contribute to one's *moral* personality, then we can create moral ideals which are incompatible with and probably more attractive than the Kantian and utilitarian ideals I have discussed. Given such an alteration of our conception of morality, the figures with which I have been concerned above might, far from being considered to be moral saints, be seen as morally inferior to other more appealing or more interesting models of individuals.

This approach seems unlikely to succeed, if for no other reason, because it is doubtful that any single, or even any reasonably small number of substantial personal ideals could capture the full range of possible ways of realizing human potential or achieving human good which deserve encouragement and praise. Even if we could provide a sufficiently broad characterization of the range of positive ways for human beings to live, however, I think there are strong reasons not to want to incorporate such a characterization more centrally into the framework of morality itself. For, in claiming that a character trait or activity is morally good, one claims that there is a certain kind of reason for developing that trait or engaging in that activity. Yet, lying behind our criticism of more conventional conceptions of moral sainthood, there seems to be a recognition that among the immensely valuable traits and activities that a human life might positively embrace are some of which we hope that, if a person does embrace them, he does so *not* for moral reasons. In other words, no matter how flexible we make the guide to conduct which we choose to label, "morality," no matter how rich we make the life in which perfect obedience to this guide would result, we will have reason to hope that a person does not wholly rule and direct his life by the abstract and impersonal consideration that such a life would be morally good.

Once it is recognized that morality itself should not serve as a comprehensive guide to conduct, moreover, we can see reasons to retain the admittedly vague contemporary intuitions about what the classification of moral and nonmoral virtues, interests, and the like should be. That is, there seem to be important differences between the aspects of a person's life which are currently considered appropriate objects of moral evaluation and the aspects that might be included under the altered conception of morality we are now considering, which the latter approach would tend wrongly to blur or neglect. Moral evaluation now is focused primarily on features of a person's life over which that person has control; it is largely restricted to aspects of his life which are likely to have considerable effect on other people. These restrictions seem as they should be. Even if responsible people could reach agreement as to what constituted good taste or a healthy degree of well-roundedness, for example, it seems wrong to insist that everyone try to achieve these things or to blame someone who fails or refuses to conform.

If we are not to respond to the unattractiveness of the moral ideals that contemporary theories yield either by offering alternative theories with more palatable ideals or by understanding these theories in such a way as to prevent them from yielding ideals at all, how, then, are we to respond? Simply, I think, by admitting that moral ideals do not, and need not, make the best personal ideals. Earlier, I mentioned one of the consequences of regarding as a test of an adequate moral theory that perfect obedience to its laws and maximal devotion to its interests be something we can wholeheartedly strive for in ourselves and wish for in those around us. Drawing out the consequences somewhat further should, I think, make us more doubtful of the proposed test than of the theories which, on this test, would fail. Given the empirical circumstances of our world, it seems to be an ethical fact that we have unlimited potential to be morally good, and endless opportunity to promote moral interests. But this is not incompatible with the not-so-ethical fact that we have sound, compelling, and not particularly selfish reasons to choose or to devote ourselves univocally to realizing this potential or to taking up this opportunity.

Thus, in one sense at least, I am not really criticizing either Kantianism or utilitarianism. Insofar as the point of view I am offering bears directly on recent work in moral philosophy, in fact, it bears on critics of these theories who, in a spirit not unlike the spirit of most of this paper, point out that the perfect utilitarian would be flawed in this way or the perfect Kantian flawed in that. The assumption lying behind these claims, implicitly or explicitly, has been that the recognition of these flaws shows us something wrong with utilitarianism, as opposed to Kantianism, or something wrong with Kantianism as opposed to utilitarianism, or something wrong with both of these theories as opposed to some nameless third alternative. The claims of this paper suggest, however, that this assumption is unwarranted. The flaws of a perfect master of a moral theory need not reflect flaws in the intramoral content of the theory itself.

Moral Saints and Moral Philosophy

In pointing out the regrettable features and the necessary absence of some desirable features in a moral saint, I have not meant to condemn the moral saint or the person who aspires to become one. Rather, I have meant to insist that the ideal of moral sainthood should not be held as a standard against which any other ideal must be judged or justified, and that the posture we take in response to the recognition that our lives are not as morally good as they might be need not be defensive. It is misleading to insist that one is *permitted* to live a life in which the goals, relationships, activities, and interests that one pursues are not maximally morally good. For our lives are not so comprehensively subject to the requirement that we apply for permission, and our nonmoral reasons for the goals we set ourselves are not excuses, but may rather be positive, good reasons which do not exist *despite* any reasons that might threaten to outweigh them. In other words, a person may be *perfectly wonderful* without being *perfectly moral*.

Recognizing this requires a perspective which contemporary moral philosophy has generally ignored. This perspective yields judgments of a type that is neither moral nor egoistic. Like moral judgments, judgments about what it would be good for a person to be are made from a point of view outside the limits set by the values, interests, and desires that the person might actually have. And, like moral judgments, these judgments claim for themselves a kind of objectivity or a grounding in a perspective which any rational and perceptive being can take up. Unlike moral judgments, however, the good with which these judgments are concerned is not the good of anyone or any group other than the individual himself.

Nonetheless, it would be equally misleading to say that these judgments are made for the sake of the individual himself. For these judgments are not concerned with what kind of life it is in a person's interest to lead, but with what kind of interests it would be good for a person to have, and it need not be in a person's interest that he acquire or maintain objectively good interests. Indeed, the model of the Loving Saint, whose interests are identified with the interests of morality, is a model of a person for whom the dictates of rational self-interest and the dictates of morality coincide. Yet, I have urged that we have reason not to aspire to this ideal and that some of us would have reason to be sorry if our children aspired to and achieved it.

The moral point of view, we might say, is the point of view one takes up insofar as one takes the recognition of the fact that one is just one person among others equally real and deserving of the good things in life as a fact with practical consequences, a fact the recognition of which demands expression in one's actions and in the form of one's practical deliberations. Competing moral theories offer alternative answers to the question of what the most correct or the best way to express this fact is. In doing so, they offer alternative ways to evaluate and to compare the variety of actions, states of affairs, and so on that appear good and bad to agents from other, nonmoral points of view. But it seems that alternative interpretations of the moral point of view do not exhaust the ways in which our actions, characters, and their consequences can be comprehensively and objectively evaluated. Let us call the point of view from which we consider what kinds of lives are good lives, and what kinds of persons it would be good for ourselves and others to be, the *point of view of individual perfection*.

Since either point of view provides a way of comprehensively evaluating a person's life, each point of view takes account of, and, in a sense, subsumes the other. From the moral point of view, the perfection of an individual life will have some, but limited, value—for each individual remains, after all, just one person among others. From the perfectionist point of view, the moral worth of an individual's relation to his world will likewise have some, but limited, value—for, as I have argued, the (perfectionist) goodness of an individual's life does not vary proportionally with the degree to which it exemplifies moral goodness.

It may not be the case that the perfectionist point of view is like the moral point of view in being a point of view we are ever *obliged* to take up and express in our actions. Nonetheless, it provides us with reasons that are independent of moral reasons for wanting ourselves and others to develop our characters and live our lives in certain ways. When we take up this point of view and ask how much it would be good for an individual to act from the moral point of view, we do not find an obvious answer.

The considerations of this paper suggest, at any rate, that the answer is not "as much as possible." This has implications both for the continued development of moral theories and for the development of metamoral views and for our conception of moral philosophy more generally. From the moral point of view, we have reasons to want people to live lives that seem good from outside that point of view. If, as I have argued, this means that we have reason to want people to live lives that are not morally perfect, then any plausible moral theory must make use of some conception of supererogation.

60   If moral philosophers are to address themselves at the most basic level to the question of how people should live, however, they must do more than adjust the content of their moral theories in ways that leave room for the affirmation of nonmoral values. They must examine explicitly the range and nature of these nonmoral values, and, in light of this examination, they must ask how the acceptance of a moral theory is to be understood and acted upon. For the claims of this paper do not so much conflict with the content of any particular currently popular moral theory as they call into question a metamoral assumption that implicitly surrounds discussions of moral theory more generally. Specifically, they call into question the assumption that it is always better to be morally better.

The role morality plays in the development of our characters and the shape of our practical deliberations need be neither that of a universal medium into which all other values must be translated nor that of an ever-present filter through which all other values must pass. This is not to say that moral value should not be an important, even the most important, kind of value we attend to in evaluating and improving ourselves and our world. It is to say that our values cannot be fully comprehended on the model of a hierarchical system with morality at the top.

The philosophical temperament will naturally incline, at this point, toward asking, "What, then, *is* at the top—or, if there is no top, how *are* we to decide when and how much to be moral?" In other words, there is a temptation to seek a metamoral—though not, in the standard sense, metaethical—theory that will give us principles, or, at least, informal directives on the basis of which we can develop and evaluate more comprehensive personal ideals. Perhaps a theory that distinguishes among the various roles a person is expected to play within a life—as professional, as citizen, as friend, and so on—might give us some rules that would offer us, if nothing else, a better framework in which to think about and discuss these questions. I am pessimistic, however, about the chances of such a theory to yield substantial and satisfying results. For I do not see how a metamoral theory could be constructed which would not be subject to considerations parallel to those which seem inherently to limit the appropriateness of regarding moral theories as ultimate comprehensive guides for action.

This suggests that, at some point, both in our philosophizing and in our lives, we must be willing to raise normative questions from a perspective that is unattached to a commitment to any particular well-ordered system of values. It must be admitted that, in doing so, we run the risk of finding normative answers that diverge from the answers given by whatever moral theory one accepts. This, I take it, is the grain of truth in G.E. Moore's "open question" argument. In the background of this paper, then, there lurks a commitment to what seems to me to be a healthy form of intuitionism. It is a form of intuitionism which is not intended to take the place of more rigorous, systematically developed, moral theories—rather, it is intended to put these more rigorous and systematic moral theories in their place.

(1977)

Questions:

1. What does the author mean by "moral sainthood"?

2. Explain the difference between utilitarian and Kantian views of moral sainthood. Why does the author find each of these views inadequate?

3. Wolf starts her essay by saying, "I don't know whether there are any moral saints. But if there are, I am glad that neither I nor those about whom I care most are among them." What impact does this statement have on the reader, and what tone does it set for the essay?

4. Where in the essay does Wolf make references to contemporary culture, and why does she do so?

5. Who is the author's ideal audience? Who is she speaking to, and how does the way she expresses herself help or hinder her argument?

6. Do you agree with the author's point of view of moral sainthood and its drawbacks? Why or why not?

MIKE ROYKO

ANOTHER ACCOLADE FOR CHARTER ARMS CORP.

The occasion for this 1980 newspaper article by a leading American columnist was the shooting of John Lennon outside his residence in New York City.

∽∾

I was pleased to see that the stories reporting the death of John Lennon were specific and accurate about the kind of gun that was used to murder the world-renowned musician.

It was a .38 calibre pistol made by Charter Arms Corp. of Bridgeport, Conn.

You might ask: What difference does it make what kind of gun was used?

It makes a great deal of difference. Especially to Charter Arms Corp.

There are guns and then there are guns. Cheap guns, ordinary guns, and finely crafted guns.

And when people become emotional about guns, as many do when somebody famous is killed, they tend to lump all guns together. They don't show proper respect for an excellent gun, such as the Charter .38.

It happens this is not the first time a famous person has been shot by this make of weapon. When former Alabama Gov. George C. Wallace was shot and paralyzed for life by another deranged person in 1974, the bullet that tore into his spine came from a Charter .38.

If I'm not mistaken, that makes the Charter .38 the first gun in modern times to have two famous people to its credit. The weapons used to blast President Kennedy, the Rev. Dr. Martin Luther King, Jr., and Sen. Robert F. Kennedy were all of different manufacture.

When Wallace was shot, a CBS reporter made it obvious that he didn't know a fine gun from a cheap gun.

10 The reporter went on network TV and said that Wallace had been wounded by a "cheap handgun." He obviously had in mind the kind of Saturday Night Special that is so popular among the criminal riffraff who have no respect for quality and workmanship.

When the proud executives of Charter Arms Corp. heard the reporter, they became indignant.

They contacted the CBS and demanded an apology. The incident was described in an editorial in the company magazine of the Charter Corp.

The editorial, which was headlined "An Apology from CBS," said:

> "We are too dedicated to high quality in American-made handguns and have poured too much of ourselves into our products to have one of them even casually referred to as a 'cheap handgun'.
>
> "That was exactly the phrase used in a broadcast description of the handgun used by Arthur Bremer in his assassination attempt on Gov. Wallace, which happened to be one of our Undercover .38 Specials.
>
> "The broadcast emanated from CBS...and our public relations people were immediately instructed to bring the error to their attention."

The editorial went on to say that an apology was indeed received from CBS network vice-president, who contritely told Charter Arms Corp., "I am sending a copy of your letter to all our TV producers. In the event that we make reference to the Undercover .38 special used by Arthur Bremer, we will certainly avoid characterizing it as a 'Saturday Night Special' or any other term which labels it as a 'cheap weapon'."

15 Presumably that soothed the wounded pride of the gunmakers at Charter Arms Corp., since no further public protests were heard.

And you can't blame them for having felt hurt at such a slur on their product. When Wallace was shot, a Charter .38 cost $105. Today, with rising prices, the gun costs about $180 or $190, depending on where you do your gun shopping.

That is not a cheap gun, especially when compared to the trashy weapons that some gunmen, to whom quality is unimportant, arm themselves with.

Now I don't know if it was mere coincidence that both Bremer, who shot Wallace, and Mark David Chapman, who apparently shot Lennon, used the same weapon. Or if it was that they both recognized quality when they saw it, and were willing to spend money to get the best.

But the fact is, both opted for quality and they got what they paid for. There was no misfiring, no jamming, no bullet flying off line, and no gun exploding in their hands—all of which can happen when one uses a cheap gun.

20 True, Wallace wasn't killed. That was the fault of Bremer, not the Charter gun. Bremer shot Wallace in the stomach, which isn't the best place to shoot a person if you want to kill him.

But even in that case, the gun did its job—blowing a terrible hole in Wallace's gut and putting him into a wheelchair for good.

In the case of Lennon, you couldn't ask for a better performance from a gun. Lennon was shot several times, but according to the doctor who pronounced him dead, the first bullet hit him in the chest and killed him on the spot. The other shots weren't even necessary.

You can never be sure of getting those kinds of results from a Saturday Night Special.

Now the Charter Arms Corp. has the unique distinction of having two famous people shot by one of their products, I wonder if they have considered using it in their advertising. Something simple and tasteful like: "The .38 that got George Wallace AND John Lennon. See it at your gun dealer now."

25 If so, they shouldn't wait. With so many handguns—both cheap and of high quality—easily available to Americans, it could be just a matter of time until another manufacturer moves into the lead in the famous-person derby. All it would take would be a few pop-pop-pops from say, a Colt—maybe a politician or two and another rock star or two—and they would have the lead.

On the other hand, maybe Charter Arms Corp. doesn't want recognition—just the kind of pride one feels in a job of fine craftsmanship.

If so, they have a right to feel proud.

Once again, your product really did the job, gents.

(1980)

Questions:

1. Compare the paragraphing in this essay with that in other essays in this anthology. To what do you attribute the difference?

2. It is a repeated pattern that popular support for gun control measures rises dramatically after high profile violent incidents such as the

assassinations of Martin Luther King and Robert Kennedy in 1968, the killing of Lennon in 1980, the Montreal Massacre in 1989, and the Columbine High School shootings in 1998. With reference to any of these and/or to other incidents you are aware of, write an essay arguing for or against one or more aspects of gun control.

Alice Munro

What is Real?

In this essay, Munro attempts to answer the questions of why and how she uses
elements from her "real" experience in her works of fiction.

～

Whenever people get an opportunity to ask me questions about my
writing, I can be sure that some of the questions asked will be these:
"Do you write about real people?"
"Did those things really happen?"
"When you write about a small town are you really writing about
Wingham?" (Wingham is the small town in Ontario where I was born and
grew up, and it has often been assumed, by people who should know better,
that I have simply "fictionalized" this place in my work. Indeed, the local
newspaper has taken me to task for making it the "butt of a soured and cruel
introspection.")

5   The usual thing, for writers, is to regard these either as very naive
questions, asked by people who really don't understand the difference
between autobiography and fiction, who can't recognize the device of the
first-person narrator, or else as catch-you-out questions posed by journalists
who hope to stir up exactly the sort of dreary (and to outsiders, slightly
comic) indignation voiced by my home-town paper. Writers answer such
questions patiently or crossly according to temperament and the mood
they're in. They say, no, you must understand, my characters are composites;
no, those things didn't happen the way I wrote about them; no, of course
not, that isn't Wingham (or whatever other place it may be that has had the
queer unsought-after distinction of hatching a writer). Or the writer may,
riskily, ask the questioners what is real, anyway? None of this seems to be
very satisfactory. People go on asking these same questions because the

subject really does interest and bewilder them. It would seem to be quite true that they don't know what fiction is.

And how could they know, when what it is, is changing all the time, and we differ among ourselves, and we don't really try to explain because it is too difficult?

What I would like to do here is what I can't do in two or three sentences at the end of a reading. I won't try to explain what fiction is, and what short stories are (assuming, which we can't, that there is any fixed thing that it is and they are), but what short stories are to me, and how I write them, and how I use things that are "real." I will start by explaining how I read stories written by other people. For one thing, I can start reading them anywhere; from beginning to end, from end to beginning, from any point in between in either direction. So obviously I don't take up a story and follow it as if it were a road, taking me somewhere, with views and neat diversions along the way. I go into it, and move back and forth and settle here and there, and stay in it for a while. It's more like a house. Everybody knows what a house does, how it encloses space and makes connections between one enclosed space and another and presents what is outside in a new way. This is the nearest I can come to explaining what a story does for me, and what I want my stories to do for other people.

So when I write a story I want to make a certain kind of structure, and I know the feeling I want to get from being inside that structure. This is the hard part of the explanation, where I have to use a word like "feeling," which is not very precise, because if I attempt to be more intellectually respectable I will have to be dishonest. "Feeling" will have to do.

There is no blueprint for the structure. It's not a question of, "I'll make this kind of house because if I do it right it will have this effect." I've got to make, I've got to build up, a house, a story, to fit around the indescribable "feeling" that is like the soul of the story, and which I must insist upon in a dogged, embarrassed way, as being no more definable than that. And I don't know where it comes from. It seems to be already there, and some unlikely clue, such as a shop window or a bit of conversation, makes me aware of it. Then I start accumulating the material and putting it together. Some of the material I may have lying around already, in memories and observations, and some I invent, and some I have to go diligently looking for (factual details), while some is dumped in my lap (anecdotes, bits of speech). I see how this material might go together to make the shape I need, and I try it. I keep trying and seeing where I went wrong and trying again.

10   I suppose this is the place where I should talk about technical problems and how I solve them. The main reason I can't is that I'm never sure I do solve anything. Even when I say that I see where I went wrong, I'm being misleading. I never figure out how I'm going to change things, I never say to myself, "That page is heavy going, that paragraph's clumsy, I need some dialogue and shorter sentences." I feel a part that's wrong, like a soggy weight; then I pay attention to the story, as if it were really happening somewhere, not just in my head, and in its own way, not mine. As a result, the sentences may indeed get shorter, there may be more dialogue, and so on. But though I've tried to pay attention to the story, I may not have got it right; those shorter sentences may be an evasion, a mistake. Every final draft, every published story, is still only an attempt, an approach, to the story.

    I did promise to talk about using reality. "Why, if Jubilee isn't Wingham, has it got Shuter Street in it?" people want to know. Why have I described somebody's real ceramic elephant sitting on the mantel-piece? I could say I get momentum from doing things like this. The fictional room, town, world, needs a bit of starter dough from the real world. It's a device to help the writer—at least it helps me—but it arouses a certain baulked fury in the people who really do live on Shuter Street and the lady who owns the ceramic elephant. "Why do you put in something true and then go on and tell lies?" they say, and anybody who has been on the receiving end of this kind of thing knows how they feel.

    "I do it for the sake of my art and to make this structure which encloses the soul of my story, that I've been telling you about," says the writer. "That is more important than anything."

    Not to everybody, it isn't.

    So I can see there might be a case, once you've written the story and got the momentum, for going back and changing the elephant to a camel (though there's always a chance the lady might complain that you made a nasty camel out of a beautiful elephant), and changing Shuter Street to Blank Street. But what about the big chunks of reality, without which your story can't exist? In the story *Royal Beatings*, I use a big chunk of reality: the story of the butcher, and of the young men who may have been egged on to "get" him. This is a story out of an old newspaper; it really did happen in a town I know. There is no legal difficulty in using it because it has been printed in a newspaper, and besides, the people who figure in it are all long dead. But there is a difficulty about offending people in that town who would feel that use of this story is a deliberate exposure, taunt and insult. Other people who have no connection with the real happening would say, "Why write about anything so hideous?" And lest you think that such an objection could only be raised by simple folk who read nothing but Harlequin Romances, let me tell you that one of the questions most frequently asked at universities is, "Why do you write about things that are so depressing?" People can accept almost any amount of ugliness if it is contained in a familiar formula, as it is on television, but when they come closer to their own place, their own lives, they are much offended by a lack of editing.

15   There are ways I can defend myself against such objections. I can say, "I do it in the interests of historical reality. That is what the old days were really like." Or, "I do it to show the dark side of human nature, the beast let loose, the evil we can run up against in communities and families." In certain countries I could say, " I do it to show how bad things were under the old system when there were prosperous butchers and young fellows hanging around livery stables and nobody thought about building a new society." But the fact is, the minute I say *to show* I am telling a lie. I don't do it to show anything. I put this story at the heart of my story because I need it there and it belongs there. It is the black room at the centre of the house with all other rooms leading to and away from it. That is all. A strange defence. Who told me to write this story? Who feels any need of it before it is written? I do. I do, so that I might grab off this piece of horrid reality and install it where I see fit, even if Hat Nettleton and his friends were still around to make me sorry.

The answer seems to be as confusing as ever. Lots of true answers are. Yes and no. Yes, I use bits of what is real, in the sense of being really there and really happening, in the world, as most people see it, and I transform it into something that is really there and really happening, in my story. No, I am not concerned with using what is real to make any sort of record or prove any sort of point, and I am not concerned with any methods of selection but my own, which I can't fully explain. This is quite presumptuous, and if writers are not allowed to be so—and quite often, in many places, they are not—I see no point in the writing of fiction.

(1982)

QUESTIONS:

1. Munro's title for this essay is a question rather than a statement. Does she answer her own question in the essay? If so, what is "real" according to Munro?

2. What does Munro mean when she writes, "Every final draft, every published story is still only an attempt, an approach, to the story"?

3. What is the tone of Munro's essay? How is the tone established?

4. Discuss the use of questions in the essay. What effect do the questions contained in the essay have on the reader?

5. There are several instances where Munro admits an inability to precisely define her process as a writer. Does this weaken or strengthen her argument?

6. We frequently see "fictionalized" versions of actual events in print, on television, and in the movies. Can you envision a situation where fictional stories based on real events can be harmful? How and why?

ROBERT DARNTON

WORKERS REVOLT: THE GREAT CAT MASSACRE OF THE RUE SAINT-SÉVERIN

Why would a group of printing apprentices in the 1730s have launched a murderous attack on their masters' cats? Endeavouring to answer that question, historian Robert Darnton explores many aspects of eighteenth-century life.

∾

The funniest thing that ever happened in the printing shop of Jacques Vincent, according to a worker who witnessed it, was a riotous massacre of cats. The worker, Nicolas Contat, told the story in an account of his apprenticeship in the shop, rue Saint-Séverin, Paris, during the late 1730s.[1] Life as an apprentice was hard, he explained. There were two of them: Jerome, the somewhat fictionalized version of Contat himself, and Léveillé. They slept in a filthy, freezing room, rose before dawn, ran errands all day while dodging insults from the journeymen and abuse from the master, and received nothing but slops to eat. They found the food especially galling. Instead of dining at the master's table, they had to eat scraps from his plate in the kitchen. Worse still, the cook secretly sold the leftovers and gave the boys cat food—old, rotten bits of meat that they could not stomach and so passed on to the cats, who refused it.

This last injustice brought Contat to the theme of cats. They occupied a special place in his narrative and in the household of the rue Saint-Séverin. The master's wife adored them, especially *la grise* (the gray), her favorite. A

---

[1] Nicolas Contat, *Anecdotes typographiques où l'on voit la description des coutumes, moeurs et usages singuliers des compagnons imprimeurs*, ed. Giles Barber (Oxford, 1980). The original manuscript is dated 1762. Barber provides a thorough description of its background and of Contat's career in his introduction. The account of the cat massacre occurs on pp. 48–56. [Unless otherwise noted, all notes to this essay are from the author.]

passion for cats seemed to have swept through the printing trade, at least at the level of the masters, or *bourgeois* as the workers called them. One bourgeois kept twenty-five cats. He had their portraits painted and fed them on roast fowl. Meanwhile, the apprentices were trying to cope with a profusion of alley cats who also thrived in the printing district and made the boys' lives miserable. The cats howled all night on the roof over the apprentices' dingy bedroom, making it impossible to get a full night's sleep. As Jerome and Léveillé had to stagger out of bed at four or five in the morning to open the gate for the earliest arrivals among the journeymen, they began the day in a state of exhaustion while the bourgeois slept late. The master did not even work with the men, just as he did not eat with them. He let the foreman run the shop and rarely appeared in it, except to vent his violent temper, usually at the expense of the apprentices.

One night the boys resolved to right this inequitable state of affairs. Léveillé, who had an extraordinary talent for mimickry, crawled along the roof until he reached a section near the master's bedroom, and then he took to howling and meowing so horribly that the bourgeois and his wife did not sleep a wink. After several nights of this treatment, they decided they were being bewitched. But instead of calling the curé—the master was exceptionally devout and the mistress exceptionally attached to her confessor—they commanded the apprentices to get rid of the cats. The mistress gave the order, enjoining the boys above all to avoid frightening her *grise*.

Gleefully Jerome and Léveillé set to work, aided by the journeymen. Armed with broom handles, bars of the press, and other tools of their trade, they went after every cat they could find, beginning with *la grise*. Léveillé smashed its spine with an iron bar and Jerome finished it off. Then they stashed it in a gutter while the journeymen drove the other cats across the rooftops, bludgeoning every one within reach and trapping those who tried to escape in strategically placed sacks. They dumped sackloads of half-dead cats in the courtyard. Then the entire workshop gathered round and staged a mock trial, complete with guards, a confessor, and a public executioner. After pronouncing the animals guilty and administering last rites, they strung them up on an improvised gallows. Roused by gales of laughter, the mistress arrived. She let out a shriek as soon as she saw a bloody cat dangling from a noose. Then she realized it might be *la grise*. Certainly not, the men assured her: they had too much respect for the house to do such a thing. At this point the master appeared. He flew into a rage at the general stoppage of work, though his wife tried to explain that they were threatened by a more serious kind of insubordination. Then master and mistress withdrew, leaving the men delirious with "joy," "disorder," and "laughter."[2]

The laughter did not end there. Léveillé reenacted the entire scene in mime at least twenty times during subsequent days when the printers wanted to knock off for some hilarity. Burlesque reenactments of incidents in the life of the shop, known as *copies* in printers' slang, provided a major form of entertainment for the men. The idea was to humiliate someone in the shop by satirizing his peculiarities. A successful *copie* would make the butt of the joke fume with rage—*prendre la chèvre* (take the goat) in the shop slang—while his mates razzed him with "rough music." They would run their composing sticks across the tops of the type cases, beat their mallets against the chases, pound on cupboards, and bleat like goats. The bleating (*bais* in the slang) stood for the humiliation heaped on the victims, as in English when someone "gets your goat." Contat emphasized that Léveillé produced the funniest *copies* anyone had ever known and elicited the greatest choruses of rough music. The whole episode, cat massacre compounded by *copies*, stood out as the most hilarious experience in Jerome's entire career.

Yet it strikes the modern reader as unfunny, if not downright repulsive. Where is the humor in a group of grown men bleating like goats and banging with their tools while an adolescent reenacts the ritual slaughter of a defenseless animal? Our own inability to get the joke is an indication of the distance that separates us from the workers of preindustrial Europe. The perception of that distance may serve as the starting point of an investigation, for anthropologists have found that the best points of entry in an attempt to penetrate an alien culture can be those where it seems to be most opaque. When you realize that you are not getting something—a joke, a proverb, a ceremony—that is particularly meaningful to the natives, you can see where to grasp a foreign system of meaning in order to unravel it. By getting the joke of the great cat massacre, it may be possible to "get" a basic ingredient of artisanal culture under the Old Regime.

It should be explained at the outset that we cannot observe the killing of the cats at firsthand. We can study it only through Contat's narrative, written about twenty years after the event. There can be no doubt about the authenticity of Contat's quasi-fictional autobiography, as Giles Barber has demonstrated in his masterful edition of the text. It belongs to the line of autobiographical writing by printers that stretches from Thomas Platter to

---

[2] Contat, *Anecdotes typographiques*, p. 53.

Thomas Gent, Benjamin Franklin, Nicolas Restif de la Bretonne, and Charles Manby Smith. Because printers, or at least compositors, had to be reasonably literate in order to do their work, they were among the few artisans who could give their own accounts of life in the working classes two, three, and four centuries ago. With all its misspellings and grammatical flaws, Contat's is perhaps the richest of these accounts. But it cannot be regarded as a mirror-image of what actually happened. It should be read as Contat's version of a happening, as his attempt to tell a story. Like all story telling, it sets the action in a frame of reference; it assumes a certain repertory of associations and responses on the part of its audience; and it provides meaningful shape to the raw stuff of experience. But since we are attempting to get at its meaning in the first place, we should not be put off by its fabricated character. On the contrary, by treating the narrative as fiction or meaningful fabrication we can use it to develop an ethnological *explication de texte*.

The first explanation that probably would occur to most readers of Contat's story is that the cat massacre served as an oblique attack on the master and his wife. Contat set the event in the context of remarks about the disparity between the lot of workers and the bourgeois—a matter of the basic elements in life: work, food, and sleep. The injustice seemed especially flagrant in the case of the apprentices, who were treated like animals while the animals were promoted over their heads to the position the boys should have occupied, the place at the master's table. Although the apprentices seem most abused, the text makes it clear that the killing of the cats expressed a hatred for the bourgeois that had spread among all the workers: "The masters love cats; consequently [the workers] hate them." After masterminding the massacre, Léveillé became the hero of the shop, because "all the workers are in league against the masters. It is enough to speak badly of them [the masters] to be esteemed by the whole assembly of typographers."[3]

Historians have tended to treat the era of artisanal manufacturing as an idyllic period before the onset of industrialization. Some even portray the workshop as a kind of extended family in which master and journeymen labored at the same tasks, ate at the same table, and sometimes slept under

---

[3] Ibid., pp. 52 and 53.

the same roof.[4] Had anything happened to poison the atmosphere of the printing shops in Paris by 1740?

10   During the second half of the seventeenth century, the large printing houses, backed by the government, eliminated most of the smaller shops, and an oligarchy of masters seized control of the industry.[5] At the same time, the situation of the journeymen deteriorated. Although estimates vary and statistics cannot be trusted, it seems that their number remained stable: approximately 335 in 1666, 339 in 1701, and 340 in 1721. Meanwhile the number of masters declined by more than half, from eighty-three to thirty-six, the limit fixed by an edict of 1686. That meant fewer shops with larger work forces, as one can see from statistics on the density of presses: in 1644 Paris had seventy-five printing shops with a total of 180 presses; in 1701 it had fifty-one shops with 195 presses. This trend made it virtually impossible for journeymen to rise into the ranks of the masters. About the only way for a worker to get ahead in the craft was to marry a master's widow, for masterships had become hereditary privileges, passed on from husband to wife and from father to son.

The journeymen also felt threatened from below because the masters tended increasingly to hire *alloués,* or underqualified printers, who had not undergone the apprenticeship that made a journeyman eligible, in principle, to advance to a mastership. The *alloués* were merely a source of cheap labor, excluded from the upper ranks of the trade and fixed, in their inferior status, by an edict of 1723. Their degradation stood out in their name: they were *à louer* (for hire), not *compagnons* (journeymen) of the master. They personified the tendency of labor to become a commodity instead of a partnership. Thus Contat served his apprenticeship and wrote his memoirs when times were hard for journeymen printers, when the men in the shop in the rue Saint-Séverin stood in danger of being cut off from the top of the trade and swamped from the bottom.

How this general tendency became manifest in an actual workshop may be seen from the papers of the Société typographique de Neuchâtel (STN).

---

[4] See, for example, Albert Soboul, *La France à la veille de la Révolution* (Paris, 1966), p. 140; and Edward Shorter, "The History of Work in the West: An Overview" in *Work and Community in the West,* ed. Edward Shorter (New York, 1973).

[5] The following discussion is derived from Henri-Jean Martin, *Livre, pouvoirs et société à Paris au XVIIe siècle* (1598–1701) (Geneva, 1969); and Paul Chauvet, *Les Ouviers du livre en France, des origines à la Révolution de 1789* (Paris, 1959). The statistics come from investigations by the authorities of the Old Regime as reported by Martin (II, 699–700) and Chauvet (pp. 126 and 154).

To be sure, the STN was Swiss, and it did not begin business until seven years after Contat wrote his memoirs (1762). But printing practices were essentially the same everywhere in the eighteenth century. The STN's archives conform in dozens of details to Contat's account of his experience. (They even mention the same shop foreman, Colas, who supervised Jerome for a while at the Imprimerie Royale and took charge of the STN's shop for a brief stint in 1779.) And they provide the only surviving record of the way masters hired, managed, and fired printers in the early modern era.

The STN's wage book shows that workers usually stayed in the shop for only a few months.[6] They left because they quarreled with the master, they got in fights, they wanted to pursue their fortune in shops further down the road, or they ran out of work. Compositors were hired by the job, *labeur* or *ouvrage* in printer's slang. When they finished a job, they frequently were fired, and a few pressmen had to be fired as well in order to maintain the balance between the two halves of the shop, the *casse* or composing sector and the *presse* or pressroom (two compositors usually set enough type to occupy a team of two pressmen.) When the foreman took on new jobs, he hired new hands. The hiring and firing went on at such a fierce pace that the work force was rarely the same from one week to the next. Jerome's fellow workers in the rue Saint-Séverin seem to have been equally volatile. They, too, were hired for specific *labeurs,* and they sometimes walked off the job after quarrels with the bourgeois—a practice common enough to have its own entry in the glossary of their slang which Contat appended to his narrative: *emporter son Saint Jean* (to carry off your set of tools or quit). A man was known as an *ancien* if he remained in the shop for only a year. Other slang terms suggest the atmosphere in which the work took place: *une chèvre capitale* (a fit of rage), *se donner la grate* (to get in a fight), *prendre la barbe* (to get drunk), *faire la déroute* (to go pub crawling), *promener sa chape* (to knock off work), *faire des loups* (to pile up debts).[7]

The violence, drunkenness, and absenteeism show up in the statistics of income and output one can compile from the STN's wage book. Printers worked in erratic spurts—twice as much in one week as in another, the weeks varying from four to six days and the days beginning anywhere from four in the morning until nearly noon. In order to keep the irregularity

---

[6] For a more detailed discussion of this material, see Robert Darnton, "Work and Culture in an Eighteenth-Century Printing Shop," an Englehard lecture at the Library of Congress to be published by the Library of Congress.

[7] Contat, *Anecdotes typographiques*, pp. 68–73.

within bounds, the masters sought men with two supreme traits: assiduousness and sobriety. If they also happened to be skilled, so much the better. A recruiting agent in Geneva recommended a compositor who was willing to set out for Neuchâtel in typical terms: "He is a good worker, capable of doing any job he gets, not at all a drunkard and assiduous at his labor."[8]

15 The STN relied on recruiters because it did not have an adequate labor pool in Neuchâtel and the streams of printers on the typographical *tours de France* sometimes ran dry. The recruiters and employers exchanged letters that reveal a common set of assumptions about eighteenth-century artisans: they were lazy, flighty, dissolute, and unreliable. They could not be trusted, so the recruiter should not loan them money for travel expenses and the employer could keep their belongings as a kind of security deposit in case they skipped off after collecting their pay. It followed that they could be discarded without compunction, whether or not they had worked diligently, had families to support, or fell sick. The STN ordered them in "assortments" just as it ordered paper and type. It complained that a recruiter in Lyon "sent us a couple in such a bad state that we were obliged to ship them off"[9] and lectured him about failing to inspect the goods. "Two of those whom you have sent to us have arrived all right, but so sick that they could infect all the rest; so we haven't been able to hire them. No one in town wanted to give them lodging. They have therefore left again and took the route for Besançon, in order to turn themselves in at the *hôpital*."[10] A bookseller in Lyon advised them to fire most of their men during a slack period in their printing in order to flood the labor supply in eastern France and "give us more power over a wild and undisciplinable race, which we cannot control."[11] Journeymen and masters may have lived together as members of a happy family at some time somewhere in Europe, but not in the printing houses of eighteenth-century France and Switzerland.

Contat himself believed that such a state had once existed. He began his description of Jerome's apprenticeship by invoking a golden age when printing was first invented and printers lived as free and equal members of a "republic," governed by its own laws and traditions in a spirit of fraternal

---

[8]   Christ to STN, Jan. 8, 1773, papers of the Société typographique de Neuchâtel, Bibliothèque de la Ville de Neuchâtel, Switzerland, hereafter cited as STN.

[9]   STN to Joseph Duplain, July 2, 1777.

[10]   STN to Louis Vernange, June 26, 1777.

[11]   Joseph Duplain to STN, Dec. 10, 1778.

"union and friendship."[12] He claimed that the republic still survived in the form of the *chapelle* or workers' association in each shop. But the government had broken up general associations; the ranks had been thinned by *alloués*; the journeymen had been excluded from masterships; and the masters had withdrawn into a separate world of *haute cuisine* and *grasses matinées*. The master in the rue Saint-Séverin ate different food, kept different hours, and talked a different language. His wife and daughters dallied with worldly abbés. They kept pets. Clearly, the bourgeois belonged to a different subculture—one which meant above all that he did not work. In introducing his account of the cat massacre, Contat made explicit the contrast between the worlds of worker and master that ran throughout the narrative: "Workers, apprentices, everyone works. Only the masters and mistresses enjoy the sweetness of sleep. That makes Jerome and Léveillé resentful. They resolve not to be the only wretched ones. They want their master and mistress as associates (*associés*)."[13] That is, the boys wanted to restore a mythical past when masters and men worked in friendly association. They also may have had in mind the more recent extinction of the smaller printing shops. So they killed the cats.

But why cats? And why was the killing so funny? Those questions take us beyond the consideration of early modern labor relations and into the obscure subject of popular ceremonies and symbolism.

Folklorists have made historians familiar with the ceremonial cycles that marked off the calendar year for early modern man.[14] The most important of these was the cycle of carnival and Lent, a period of revelry followed by a period of abstinence. During carnival the common people suspended the normal rules of behavior and ceremoniously reversed the social order or turned it upside down in riotous procession. Carnival was a time for cutting up by youth groups, particularly apprentices, who organized themselves in "abbeys" ruled by a mock abbot or king and who staged charivaris or burlesque processions with rough music in order to humiliate cuckolds,

---

[12] Contat, *Anecdotes typographiques*, pp. 30–31.

[13] Ibid., p. 52.

[14] For a recent overview of the vast literature on folklore and French history and bibliographic references, see Nicole Belmont, *Mythes et croyances dans l'ancienne France* (Paris, 1973). The following discussion is based primarily on the material collected in Eugène Rolland, *Faune populaire de la France* (Paris, 1881), IV; Paul Sébillot, *Le Folk-lore de France* (Paris, 1904–7), 4 vols., especially III, 72–155 and IV, 90–98; and to a lesser extent Arnold Van Gennep, *Manuel de folklore français contemporain* (Paris, 1937–58), 9 vols.

husbands who had been beaten by their wives, brides who had married below their age group, or someone else who personified the infringement of traditional norms. Carnival was high season for hilarity, sexuality, and youth run riot—a time when young people tested social boundaries by limited outbursts of deviance, before being reassimilated in the world of order, submission, and Lentine seriousness. It came to an end of Shrove Tuesday or Mardi Gras, when a straw mannequin, King Carnival or Caramantran, was given a ritual trial and execution. Cats played an important part in some charivaris. In Burgundy, the crowd incorporated cat torture into its rough music. While mocking a cuckold or some other victim, the youths passed around a cat, tearing its fur to make it howl. *Faire le chat,* they called it. The Germans called charivaris *Katzenmusik,* a term that may have been derived from the howls of tortured cats.[15]

Cats also figured in the cycle of Saint John the Baptist, which took place on June 24, at the time of the summer solstice. Crowds made bonfires, jumped over them, danced around them, and threw into them objects with magical power, hoping to avoid disaster and obtain good fortune during the rest of the year. A favorite object was cats—cats tied up in bags, cats suspended from ropes, or cats burned at the stake. Parisians liked to incinerate cats by the sackful, while the Courimauds (*cour à miaud* or cat chasers) of Saint Chamond preferred to chase a flaming cat through the streets. In parts of Burgundy and Lorraine they danced around a kind of burning May pole with a cat tied to it. In the Metz region they burned a dozen cats at a time in a basket on top of a bonfire. The ceremony took place with great pomp in Metz itself, until it was abolished in 1765. The town dignitaries arrived in procession at the Place du Grand-Saulcy, lit the pyre, and a ring of riflemen from the garrison fired off volleys while the cats disappeared screaming in the flames. Although the practice varied from place to place, the ingredients were everywhere the same: a *feu de joie* (bonfire), cats, and an aura of hilarious witch-hunting.[16]

---

[15] In Germany and Switzerland, *Katzenmusik* sometimes included mock trials and executions. The etymology of the term is not clear. See E. Hoffman-Krayer and Hans Bächtold-Stäubli, *Handwörterbuch des deutschen Aberglaubens* (Berlin and Leipzig, 1931–32), IV, 1125–32 and Paul Grebe et al., *Duden Etymologie: Herkunftwörterbuch der deutschen Sprache* (Mannheim, 1963), p. 317.

[16] Information on the cat burning in Saint Chamond comes from a letter kindly sent to me by Elinor Accampo of Colorado College. The Metz ceremony is described in A. Benoist, "Traditions et anciennes coutumes du pays messin," *Revue des traditions populaires, XV* (1900), 14.

20   In addition to these general ceremonies, which involved entire communities, artisans celebrated ceremonies peculiar to their craft. Printers processed and feasted in honor of their patron, Saint John the Evangelist, both on his saint's day, December 27, and on the anniversary of his martyrdom, May 6, the festival of Saint Jean Porte Latine. By the eighteenth century, the masters had excluded the journeymen from the confraternity devoted to the saint, but the journeymen continued to hold ceremonies in their chapels.[17] On Saint Martin's day, November 11, they held a mock trial followed by a feast. Contat explained that the chapel was a tiny "republic," which governed itself according to its own code of conduct. When a worker violated the code, the foreman, who was the head of the chapel and not part of the management, entered a fine in a register: leaving a candle lit, five sous; brawling, three livres; insulting the good name of the chapel, three livres; and so on. On Saint Martin's, the foreman read out the fines and collected them. The workers sometimes appealed their cases before a burlesque tribunal composed of the chapel's "ancients," but in the end they had to pay up amidst more bleating, banging of tools, and riotous laughter. The fines went for food and drink in the chapel's favorite tavern, where the hell-raising continued until late in the night.[18]

Taxation and commensality characterized all the other ceremonies of the chapel. Special dues and feasts marked a man's entry into the shop *(bienvenue)*, his exit *(conduite)*, and even his marriage *(droit de chevet)*. Above all, they punctuated a youth's progress from apprentice to journeyman. Contat described four of these rites, the most important being the first, called the taking of the apron, and the last, Jerome's initiation as a full-fledged *compagnon*.

The taking of the apron *(la prise de tablier)* occurred soon after Jerome joined the shop. He had to pay six livres (about three days' wages for an ordinary journeyman) into a kitty, which the journeymen supplemented by small payments of their own *(faire la reconnaissance)*. Then the chapel repaired to its favorite tavern, Le Panier Fleury in the rue de la Huchette. Emissaries were dispatched to procure provisions and returned loaded down with bread and meat, having lectured the shopkeepers of the neighborhood on which cuts were worthy of typographers and which could be left for cobblers. Silent and glass in hand, the journeymen gathered around Jerome

---

[17] Contat, *Anecdotes typographiques*, pp. 30 and 66–67; and Chauvet, *Les Ouvriers du livre*, pp. 7–12.

[18] Contat, *Anecdotes typographiques*, pp. 65–67.

in a special room on the second floor of the tavern. The subforeman approached, carrying the apron and followed by two "ancients," one from each of the "estates" of the shop, the *casse* and the *presse*. He handed the apron, newly made from close-woven linen, to the foreman, who took Jerome by the hand and led him to the center of the room, the subforeman and "ancients" falling behind. The foreman made a short speech, placed the apron over Jerome's head and tied the strings behind him, as everyone drank to the health of the initiate. Jerome was then given a seat with the chapel dignitaries at the head of the table. The rest rushed for the best places they could find and fell on the food. They gobbled and guzzled and called out for more. After several Gargantuan rounds, they settled down to shop talk—and Contat lets us listen in:

> "Isn't it true," says one of them, "that printers know how to shovel it in? I am sure that if someone presented us with a roast mutton, as big as you like, we would leave nothing but the bones behind...." They don't talk about theology nor philosophy and still less of politics. Each speaks of his job: one will talk to you about the *casse*, another the *presse*, this one of the tympan, another of the ink ball leathers. They all speak at the same time, whether they can be heard or not.

At last, early in the morning after hours of swilling and shouting, the workers separated—sotted but ceremonial to the end: "Bonsoir, Monsieur notre prote [foreman]"; "Bonsoir, Messieurs les compositeurs"; "Bonsoir, Messieurs les imprimeurs"; "Bonsoir Jerome." The text explains that Jerome will be called by his first name until he is received as a journeyman.[19]

That moment came four years later, after two intermediary ceremonies (the *admission à l'ouvrage* and the *admission à la banque)* and a vast amount of hazing. Not only did the men torment Jerome, mocking his ignorance, sending him on wild goose chases, making him the butt of practical jokes, and overwhelming him with nasty chores; they also refused to teach him anything. They did not want another journeyman in their over-flooded labor pool, so Jerome had to pick up the tricks of the trade by himself. The work, the food, the lodging, the lack of sleep, it was enough to drive a boy mad, or at least out of the shop. In fact, however, it was standard treatment and should not be taken too seriously. Contat recounted the catalogue of Jerome's troubles in a light-hearted manner, which suggested a stock comic

---

[19] Ibid., pp. 37–41, quotation from pp. 39–40.

genre, the *misère des apprentis*.[20] The *misères* provided farcical accounts, in doggerel verse or broadsides, of a stage in life that was familiar and funny to everyone in the artisanate. It was a transitional stage, which marked the passage from childhood to adulthood. A young man had to sweat his way through it so that he would have paid his dues—the printers demanded actual payments, called *bienvenues* or *quatre heures*, in addition to razzing the apprentices—when he reached full membership in a vocational group. Until he arrived at that point, he lived in a fluid or liminal state, trying out adult conventions by subjecting them to some hell-raising of his own. His elders tolerated his pranks, called *copies* and *joberies* in the printing trade, because they saw them as wild oats, which needed to be sown before he could settle down. Once settled, he would have internalized the conventions of his craft and acquired a new identity, which was often symbolized by a change in his name.[21]

---

[20] A good example of the genre, *La Misère des apprentis imprimeurs* (1710) is printed as an appendix to Contat, *Anecdotes typographiques*, pp. 101–10. For other examples, see A.C. Cailleau, *Les Misères de ce monde, ou complaints facétieuses sur les apprentissages des différents arts et métiers de la ville et faubourgs de Paris* (Paris, 1783).

[21] The classic study of this process is Arnold Van Gennep, *Les Rites de passage* (Paris, 1908). It has been extended by subsequent ethnographic research, notably that of Victor Turner: *The Forest of Symbols: Aspects of Ndembu Ritual* (Ithaca, N.Y., 1967) and *The Ritual Process* (Chicago, 1969). Jerome's experience fits the Van Gennep-Turner model very well, except in a few respects. He was not considered sacred and dangerous, although the chapel could fine journeymen for drinking with him. He did not live outside adult society, although he left his home for a makeshift room at the edge of the master's household. And he was not exposed to secret *sacra*, although he had to acquire an esoteric lingo and to assimilate a craft ethos after a great deal of tribulation climaxed by a communal meal. Joseph Moxon, Thomas Gent, and Benjamin Franklin mention similar practices in England. In Germany the initiation rite was much more elaborate and had structural similarities to the rites of tribes in Africa, New Guinea, and North America. The apprentice wore a filthy headdress adorned with goat's horns and a fox's tail, indicating that he had reverted to an animal state. As a *Cornut* or *Mittelding*, part man, part beast, he underwent ritual tortures, including the filing of his fingertips. At the final ceremony, the head of the shop knocked off the hat and slapped him in the face. He then emerged newborn—sometimes newly named and even baptized—as a full-fledged journeyman. Such at least was the practice described in German typographical manuals, notably Christian Gottlob Täubel, *Praktisches Handbuch der Buchdruckerkunst für Anfänger* (Leipzig, 1791); Wilhelm Gottlieb Kircher, *Anweisung in der Buchdruckerkunst so viel davon das Drucken betrifft* (Brunswick, 1793); and Johann Christoph Hildebrand, *Handbuch für Buchdrucker-Lehrlinge* (Eisenach, 1835). The rite was related to an ancient popular play, the *Depositio Cornuti typographici*, which was printed by Jacob Redinger in his *Neu aufgesetztes Format Büchlein* (Frankfurt-am-Main, 1679).

25   Jerome became a journeyman by passing through the final rite, *compagnonnage.* It took the same form as the other ceremonies, a celebration over food and drink after the candidate paid an initiation fee and the journeymen chipped in with *reconnaissance.* But this time Contat gave a summary of the foreman's speech:[22]

> The newcomer is indoctrinated. He is told never to betray his colleagues and to maintain the wage rate. If a worker doesn't accept a price [for a job] and leaves the shop, no one in the house should do the job for a smaller price. Those are the laws among the workers. Faithfulness and probity are recommended to him. Any worker who betrays the others, when something forbidden, called *marron* [chestnut], is being printed, must be expelled ignominiously from the shop. The workers blacklist him by circular letters sent around all the shops of Paris and the provinces....Aside from that, anything is permitted: excessive drinking is considered a good quality, gallantry and debauchery as youthful feats, indebtedness as a sign of wit, irreligion as sincerity. It's a free and republican territory in which everything is permitted. Live as you like but be an *honnête homme,* no hypocrisy.

Hypocrisy turned out in the rest of the narrative to be the main characteristic of the bourgeois, a superstitious religious bigot. He occupied a separate world of pharasaical bourgeois morality. The workers defined their "republic" against that world and against other journeyman's groups as well—the cobblers, who ate inferior cuts of meat, and the masons or carpenters who were always good for a brawl when the printers, divided into "estates" (the *casse* and the *presse*) toured country taverns on Sundays. In entering an "estate," Jerome assimilated an ethos. He identified himself with a craft; and as a full-fledged journeyman compositor, he received a new name. Having gone through a rite of passage in the full, anthropological sense of the term, he became a *Monsieur.*[23]

So much for ceremonies. What about cats? It should be said at the outset that there is an indefinable *je ne sais quoi* about cats, a mysterious something that has fascinated mankind since the time of the ancient Egyptians. One

---

22   Contat, *Anecdotes typographiques,* pp. 65–66.

23   The text does not give Jerome's last name, but it stresses the name change and the acquisition of the "Monsieur": "It is only after the end of the apprenticeship that one is called Monsieur; this quality belongs only to journeymen and not to apprentices" (p. 41). In the wage book of the STN, the journeymen always appear with their "Monsieur," even when they were called by nicknames, such as "Monsieur Bonnemain."

can sense a quasi-human intelligence behind a cat's eyes. One can mistake a cat's howl at night for a human scream, torn from some deep, visceral part of man's animal nature. Cats appealed to poets like Baudelaire and painters like Manet, who wanted to express the humanity in animals along with the animality of men—and especially of women.[24]

This ambiguous ontological position, a straddling of conceptual categories, gives certain animals—pigs, dogs, and cassowaries as well as cats—in certain cultures an occult power associated with the taboo. That is why Jews do not eat pigs, according to Mary Douglas, and why Englishmen can insult one another by saying "son-of-a-bitch" rather than "son-of-a-cow," according to Edmund Leach.[25] Certain animals are good for swearing, just as they are "good for thinking" in Lévi-Strauss's famous formula. I would add that others—cats in particular—are good for staging ceremonies. They have ritual value. You cannot make a charivari with a cow. You do it with cats: you decide to *faire le chat*, to make *Katzenmusik*.

The torture of animals, especially cats, was a popular amusement throughout early modern Europe. You have only to look at Hogarth's *Stages of Cruelty* to see its importance, and once you start looking you see people torturing animals everywhere. Cat killings provided a common theme in literature, from *Don Quixote* in early seventeenth-century Spain to *Germinal* in late nineteenth-century France.[26] Far from being a sadistic fantasy on the part of a few half-crazed authors, the literary versions of cruelty to animals

---

[24]   The black cat in Manet's *Olympia* represents a common motif, the animal "familiar" of a nude. On Baudelaire's cats, see Roman Jakobson and Claude Lévi-Strauss, "Les Chats de Charles Baudelaire," *L'Homme*, II (1962), 5–21; and Michel Riffaterre, "Describing Poetic Structures: Two Approaches to Baudelaire's *Les Chats*," in *Structuralism*, ed. Jacques Ehrmann (New Haven, 1966).

[25]   Mary Douglas, *Purity and Danger: An Analysis of Concepts of Pollution and Taboo* (London, 1966); and E. R. Leach, "Anthropological Aspects of Language: Animal Categories and Verbal Abuse," in *New Directions in the Study of Language*, ed. E. H. Lenneberg, (Cambridge, Mass., 1964).

[26]   Cervantes and Zola adapted traditional cat lore to the themes of their novels. In *Don Quixote* (part II, chap. 46), a sack full of howling cats interrupts the hero's serenade to Altisidora. Taking them for devils, he tries to mow them down with his sword, only to be bested by one of them in single combat. In *Germinal* (part V, chap. 6), the symbolism works in the opposite way. A mob of workers pursues Maigrat, their class enemy, as if he were a cat trying to escape across the rooftops. Screaming "Get the cat! Get the cat!" they castrate his body "like a tomcat" after he falls from the roof. For an example of cat killing as a satire on French legalism, see Friar John's plan to massacre the Furry Lawcats in Rabelais' *Gargantua and Pantagruel*, book V, chap. 15.

expressed a deep current of popular culture, as Mikhail Bakhtin has shown in his study of Rabelais.[27] All sorts of ethnographic reports confirm that view. On the *dimanche des brandons* in Semur, for example, children used to attach cats to poles and roast them over bonfires. In the *jeu du chat* at the Fete-Dieu in Aix-en-Provence, they threw cats high in the air and smashed them on the ground. They used expressions like "patient as a cat whose claws are being pulled out" or "patient as a cat whose paws are being grilled." The English were just as cruel. During the Reformation in London, a Protestant crowd shaved a cat to look like a priest, dressed it in mock vestments, and hanged it on the gallows at Cheapside.[28] It would be possible to string out many other examples, but the point should be clear: there was nothing unusual about the ritual killing of cats. On the contrary, when Jerome and his fellow workers tried and hanged all the cats they could find in the rue Saint-Séverin, they drew on a common element in their culture. But what significance did that culture attribute to cats?

30   To get a grip on that question, one must rummage through collections of folktales, superstitions, proverbs, and popular medicine. The material is rich, varied, and vast but extremely hard to handle. Although much of it goes back to the Middle Ages, little can be dated. It was gathered for the most part by folklorists in the late nineteenth and early twentieth centuries, when sturdy strains of folklore still resisted the influence of the printed word. But the collections do not make it possible to claim that this or that practice existed in the printing houses of mid-eighteenth-century Paris. One can only assert that printers lived and breathed in an atmosphere of traditional customs and beliefs which permeated everything. It was not everywhere the same—France remained a patchwork of *pays* rather than a unified nation until late in the nineteenth century—but everywhere some common motifs could be found. The commonest were attached to cats. Early modern Frenchmen probably made more symbolic use of cats than of any other

---

[27] Mikhail Bakhtin, *Rabelais and His World*, trans. Helene Iswolsky (Cambridge, Mass., 1968). The most important literary version of cat lore to appear in Contat's time was *Les Chats* (Rotterdam, 1728) by François Augustin Paradis de Moncrif. Although it was a mock treatise aimed at a sophisticated audience, it drew on a vast array of popular superstitions and proverbs, many of which appeared in the collections of folklorists a century and a half later.

[28] C. S. L. Davies, *Peace, Print and Protestantism* (St. Albans, Herts, 1977). The other references come from the sources cited in note 14. Among the many dictionaries of proverbs and slang, see André-Joseph Panckoucke, *Dictionnaire des proverbs françois et des façons de parler comiques, burlesques, et familières* (Paris, 1748) and Gaston Esnault, *Dictionnaire historique des argots français* (Paris, 1965).

animal, and they used them in distinct ways, which can be grouped together for the purposes of discussion, despite the regional peculiarities.

First and foremost, cats suggested witchcraft. To cross one at night in virtually any corner of France was to risk running into the devil or one of his agents or a witch abroad on an evil errand. White cats could be as satanic as the black, in the daytime as well as at night. In a typical encounter, a peasant woman of Bigorre met a pretty white house cat who had strayed in the fields. She carried it back to the village in her apron, and just as they came to the house of a woman suspected of witchcraft, the cat jumped out, saying "Merci, Jeanne."[30] Witches transformed themselves into cats in order to cast spells on their victims. Sometimes, especially on Mardi Gras, they gathered for hideous Sabbaths at night. They howled, fought, and copulated horribly under the direction of the devil himself in the form of a huge tomcat. To protect yourself from sorcery by cats there was one, classic remedy: maim it. Cut its tail, clip its ears, smash one of its legs, tear or burn its fur, and you would break its malevolent power. A maimed cat could not attend a Sabbath or wander abroad to cast spells. Peasants frequently cudgeled cats who crossed their paths at night and discovered the next day that bruises had appeared on women believed to be witches—or so it was said in the lore of their village. Villagers also told stories of farmers who found strange cats in barns and broke their limbs to save the cattle. Invariably a broken limb would appear on a suspicious woman the following morning.

Cats possessed occult power independently of their association with witchcraft and deviltry. They could prevent the bread from rising if they entered bakeries in Anjou. They could spoil the catch if they crossed the path of fishermen in Brittany. If buried alive in Béarn, they could clear a field of weeds. They figured as staple ingredients in all kinds of folk medicine aside from witches' brews. To recover from a bad fall, you sucked the blood out of a freshly amputated tail of a tomcat. To cure yourself from pneumonia, you drank blood from a cat's ear in red wine. To get over colic, you mixed your wine with cat excrement. You could even make yourself invisible, at least in Brittany, by eating the brain of a newly killed cat, provided it was still hot.

There was a specific field for the exercise of cat power: the household and particularly the person of the master or mistress of the house. Folktales like "Puss 'n Boots" emphasized the identification of master and cat, and so did superstitions such as the practice of tying a black ribbon around the

---

[30] Rolland, *Faune populaire*, p. 118. See note 14 for the other sources on which this account is based.

neck of a cat whose mistress had died. To kill a cat was to bring misfortune upon its owner or its house. If a cat left a house or stopped jumping on the sickbed of its master or mistress, the person was likely to die. But a cat lying on the bed of a dying man might be the devil, waiting to carry his soul off to hell. According to a sixteenth-century tale, a girl from Quintin sold her soul to the devil in exchange for some pretty clothes. When she died, the pallbearers could not lift her coffin; they opened the lid, and a black cat jumped out. Cats could harm a house. They often smothered babies. They understood gossip and would repeat it out of doors. But their power could be contained or turned to your advantage if you followed the right procedures, such as greasing their paws with butter or maiming them when they first arrived. To protect a new house, Frenchmen enclosed live cats within its walls—a very old rite, judging from cat skeletons that have been exhumed from the walls of medieval buildings.

Finally, the power of cats was concentrated on the most intimate aspect of domestic life: sex. *Le chat, la chatte, le minet* mean the same thing in French slang as "pussy" does in English, and they have served as obscenities for centuries.[30] French folklore attaches special importance to the cat as a sexual metaphor or metonym. As far back as the fifteenth century, the petting of cats was recommended for success in courting women. Proverbial wisdom identified women with cats: "He who takes good care of cats will have a pretty wife." If a man loved cats, he would love women; and vice versa: "As he loves his cat, he loves his wife," went another proverb. If he did not care for his wife, you could say of him, "He has other cats to whip." A woman who wanted to get a man should avoid treading on a cat's tail. She might postpone marriage for a year—or for seven years in Quimper and for as many years as the cat meowed in parts of the Loire Valley. Cats connoted fertility and female sexuality everywhere. Girls were commonly said to be "in love like a cat"; and if they became pregnant, they had "let the cat go to the cheese." Eating cats could bring on pregnancy in itself. Girls who consumed them in stews gave birth to kittens in several folktales. Cats could even make diseased apple trees bear fruit, if buried in the correct manner in upper Brittany.

---

[30] Emile Chautard, *La Vie étrange de l'argot* (Paris, 1931), pp. 367–68. The following expressions come from Panckoucke, *Dictionnaire des proverbs françois;* Esnault, *Dictionnaire historique des argots français;* and *Dictionnaire de l'Académie française* (Paris, 1762), which contains a surprising amount of polite cat lore. The impolite lore was transmitted in large measure by children's games and rhymes, some of them dating from the sixteenth century; Claude Gaignebet, *Le Folklore obscène des enfants* (Paris, 1980), p. 260.

35   It was an easy jump from the sexuality of women to the cuckolding of men. Caterwauling could come from a satanic orgy, but it might just as well be toms howling defiance at each other when their mates were in heat. They did not call as cats, however. They issued challenges in their masters' names, along with sexual taunts about their mistresses: "Reno! Francois!" "Où allez-vous?—Voir la femme à vous.—Voir la femme à moi! Rouah!" (Where are you going?—To see your wife.—To see my wife! Ha!) Then the toms would fly at each other like the cats of Kilkenny, and their sabbath would end in a massacre. The dialogue differed according to the imaginations of the listeners and the onomatopoetic power of their dialect, but it usually emphasized predatory sexuality.[31] "At night all cats are gray," went the proverb, and the gloss in an eighteenth-century proverb collection made the sexual hint explicit: "That is to say that all women are beautiful enough at night."[32] Enough for what? Seduction, rape, and murder echoed in the air when the cats howled at night in early modern France. Cat calls summoned up *Katzenmusik,* for charivaris often took the form of howling under a cuckold's window on the eve of Mardi Gras, the favorite time for cat sabbaths.

Witchcraft, orgy, cuckoldry, charivari, and massacre, the men of the Old Regime could hear a great deal in the wail of a cat. What the men of the rue Saint-Séverin actually heard is impossible to say. One can only assert that cats bore enormous symbolic weight in the folklore of France and that the lore was rich, ancient, and widespread enough to have penetrated the printing shop. In order to determine whether the printers actually drew on the ceremonial and symbolic themes available to them, it is necessary to take another look at Contat's text.

The text made the theme of sorcery explicit from the beginning. Jerome and Léveillé could not sleep because "some bedeviled cats make a sabbath all night long."[33] After Léveillé added his cat calls to the general caterwauling, "the whole neighborhood is alarmed. It is decided that the cats must be agents of someone casting a spell." The master and mistress considered summoning the curé to exorcise the place. In deciding instead to commission the cat hunt, they fell back on the classic remedy for witchcraft: maiming. The bourgeois—a superstitious, priest-ridden fool—took the whole business

---

[31] Sébillot, *Le Folk-lore de France*, III, 93–94.

[32] Panckoucke, *Dictionnaire des proverbes françois*, p. 66.

[33] This and the following quotations come from Contat's account of the cat massacre, *Anecdotes typographiques*, pp. 48–56.

seriously. To the apprentices it was a joke. Léveillé in particular functioned as a joker, a mock "sorcerer" staging a fake "sabbath," according to the terms chosen by Contat. Not only did the apprentices exploit their master's superstition in order to run riot at his expense, but they also turned their rioting against their mistress. By bludgeoning her familiar, *la grise*, they in effect accused her of being the witch. The double joke would not be lost on anyone who could read the traditional language of gesture.

The theme of charivari provided an additional dimension to the fun. Although it never says so explicitly, the text indicates that the mistress was having an affair with her priest, a "lascivious youth," who had memorized obscene passages from the classics of pornography—Aretino and *L'Academie des dames*—and quoted them to her, while her husband droned on about his favorite subjects, money and religion. During a lavish dinner with the family, the priest defended the thesis "that it is a feat of wit to cuckold one's husband and that cuckolding is not a vice." Later, he and the wife spent the night together in a country house. They fit perfectly into the typical triangle of printing shops: a doddering old master, a middle-aged mistress, and her youthful lover.[35] The intrigue cast the master in the role of a stock comic figure: the cuckold. So the revelry of the workers took the form of a charivari. The apprentices managed it, operating within the liminal area where novitiates traditionally mocked their superiors, and the journeymen responded to their antics in the traditional way, with rough music. A riotous, festival atmosphere runs through the whole episode, which Contat described as a *fête*: "Léveillé and his comrade Jerome preside over the *fête*," he wrote, as if they were kings of a carnival and the cat bashing corresponded to the torturing of cats on Mardi Gras or the *fête* of Saint John the Baptist.

As in many Mardi Gras, the carnival ended in a mock trial and execution. The burlesque legalism came naturally to the printers because they staged their own mock trials every year at the *fête* of Saint Martin, when the chapel squared accounts with its boss and succeeded spectacularly in getting his goat. The chapel could not condemn him explicitly without moving into open insubordination and risking dismissal. (All the sources, including the

---

[35] According to Giles Barber (ibid., pp. 7 and 60), the actual Jacques Vincent for whom Contat worked began his own apprenticeship in 1690; so he probably was born about 1675. His wife was born in 1684. Thus when Contat entered the shop, the master was about 62, the mistress about 53, and the bawdy young priest in his twenties. That pattern was common enough in the printing industry, where old masters often left their businesses to younger wives, who in turn took up with still younger journeymen. It was a classic pattern for charivaris, which often mocked disparities in age among newlyweds as well as humiliating cuckolds.

papers of the STN, indicate that masters often fired workers for insolence and misbehavior. Indeed, Léveillé was later fired for a prank that attacked the bourgeois more openly.) So the workers tried the bourgeois in absentia, using a symbol that would let their meaning show through without being explicit enough to justify retaliation. They tried and hanged the cats. It would be going too far to hang *la grise* under the master's nose after being ordered to spare it; but they made the favorite pet of the house their first victim, and in doing so they knew they were attacking the house itself, in accordance with the traditions of cat lore. When the mistress accused them of killing *la grise,* they replied with mock deference that "nobody would be capable of such an outrage and that they have too much respect for that house." By executing the cats with such elaborate ceremony, they condemned the house and declared the bourgeois guilty—guilty of overworking and underfeeding his apprentices, guilty of living in luxury while his journeymen did all the work, guilty of withdrawing from the shop and swamping it with *alloués* instead of laboring and eating with the men, as masters were said to have done a generation or two earlier, or in the primitive "republic" that existed at the beginning of the printing industry. The guilt extended from the boss to the house to the whole system. Perhaps in trying, confessing, and hanging a collection of half-dead cats, the workers meant to ridicule the entire legal and social order.

40   They certainly felt debased and had accumulated enough resentment to explode in an orgy of killing. A half-century later, the artisans of Paris would run riot in a similar manner, combining indiscriminate slaughter with improvised popular tribunals.[35] It would be absurd to view the cat massacre as a dress rehearsal for the September Massacres of the French Revolution, but the earlier outburst of violence did suggest a popular rebellion, though it remained restricted to the level of symbolism.

Cats as symbols conjured up sex as well as violence, a combination perfectly suited for an attack on the mistress. The narrative identified her with *la grise,* her *chatte favorite.* In killing it, the boys struck at her: "It was a matter of consequence, a murder, which had to be hidden." The mistress reacted as if she had been assaulted: "They ravished from her a cat without an equal, a cat that she loved to madness." The text described her as lascivious and "impassioned for cats" as if she were a she-cat in heat during a wild cat's sabbath of howling, killing, and rape. An explicit reference to rape would violate the proprieties that were generally observed in eighteenth-

---

[35] Pierre Caron, *Les Massacres de septembre* (Paris, 1935).

century writing. Indeed, the symbolism would work only if it remained veiled—ambivalent enough to dupe the master and sharp enough to hit the mistress in the quick. But Contat used strong language. As soon as the mistress saw the cat execution she let out a scream. Then the scream was smothered in the realization that she had lost her *grise*. The workers assured her with feigned sincerity of their respect and the master arrived. "'Ah! the scoundrels,' he says. 'Instead of working they are killing cats.' Madame to Monsieur: 'These wicked men can't kill the masters; they have killed my cat.' …It seems to her that all the blood of the workers would not be sufficient to redeem the insult."

It was metonymic insult, the eighteenth-century equivalent of the modern schoolboy's taunt: "Ah, your mother's girdle!" But it was stronger, and more obscene. By assaulting her pet, the workers ravished the mistress symbolically. At the same time, they delivered the supreme insult to their master. His wife was his most precious possession, just as her *chatte* was hers. In killing the cat, the men violated the most intimate treasure of the bourgeois household and escaped unharmed. That was the beauty of it. The symbolism disguised the insult well enough for them to get away with it. While the bourgeois fumed over the loss of work, his wife, less obtuse, virtually told him that the workers had attacked her sexually and would like to murder him. Then both left the scene in humiliation and defeat. "Monsieur and Madame retire, leaving the workers in liberty. The printers, who love disorder, are in a state of great joy. Here is an ample subject for their laughter, a beautiful *copie,* which will keep them amused for a long time."

This was Rabelaisian laughter. The text insists upon its importance: "The printers know how to laugh, it is their sole occupation." Mikhail Bakhtin has shown how the laughter of Rabelais expressed a strain of popular culture in which the riotously funny could turn to riot, a carnival culture of sexuality and sedition in which the revolutionary element might be contained within symbols and metaphors or might explode in a general uprising, as in 1789. The question remains, however, what precisely was so funny about the cat massacre? There is no better way to ruin a joke than to analyze it or to overload it with social comment. But this joke cries out for commentary—not because one can use it to prove that artisans hated their bosses (a truism that may apply to all periods of labor history, although it has not been appreciated adequately by eighteenth-century historians), but because it can help one to see how workers made their experience meaningful by playing with themes of their culture.

The only version of the cat massacre available to us was put into writing, long after the fact, by Nicolas Contat. He selected details, ordered events, and framed the story in such a way as to bring out what was meaningful for him. But he derived his notions of meaning from his culture just as naturally as he drew in air from the atmosphere around him. And he wrote down what he had helped to enact with his mates. The subjective character of the writing does not vitiate its collective frame of reference, even though the written account must be thin compared with the action it describes. The workers' mode of expression was a kind of popular theater. It involved pantomime, rough music, and a dramatic "theater of violence" improvised in the work place, in the street, and on the rooftops. It included a play within a play, because Léveillé reenacted the whole farce several times as *copies* in the shop. In fact, the original massacre involved the burlesque of other ceremonies, such as trials and charivaris. So Contat wrote about a burlesque of a burlesque, and in reading it one should make allowances for the refraction of cultural forms across genres and over time.

45   Those allowances made, it seems clear that the workers found the massacre funny because it gave them a way to turn the tables on the bourgeois. By goading him with cat calls, they provoked him to authorize the massacre of cats, then they used the massacre to put him symbolically on trial for unjust management of the shop. They also used it as a witch hunt, which provided an excuse to kill his wife's familiar and to insinuate that she herself was the witch. Finally, they transformed it into a charivari, which served as a means to insult her sexually while mocking him as a cuckold. The bourgeois made an excellent butt of the joke. Not only did he become the victim of a procedure he himself had set in motion, he did not understand how badly he had been had. The men had subjected his wife to symbolic aggression of the most intimate kind, but he did not get it. He was too thick-headed, a classic cuckold. The printers ridiculed him in splendid Boccaccian style and got off scot-free.

The joke worked so well because the workers played so skillfully with a repertory of ceremonies and symbols. Cats suited their purposes perfectly. By smashing the spine of *la grise* they called the master's wife a witch and a slut, while at the same time making the master into a cuckold and a fool. It was metonymic insult, delivered by actions, not words, and it struck home because cats occupied a soft spot in the bourgeois way of life. Keeping pets was as alien to the workers as torturing animals was to the bourgeois. Trapped between incompatible sensitivities, the cats had the worst of both worlds.

The workers also punned with ceremonies. They made a roundup of cats into a witch hunt, a festival, a charivari, a mock trial, and a dirty joke. Then they redid the whole thing in pantomime. Whenever they got tired of working, they transformed the shop into a theater and produced *copies*—their kind of copy, not the authors'. Shop theater and ritual punning suited the traditions of their craft. Although printers made books, they did not use written words to convey their meaning. They used gestures, drawing on the culture of their craft to inscribe statements in the air.

Insubstantial as it may seem today, this joking was a risky business in the eighteenth century. The risk was part of the joke, as in many forms of humor, which toy with violence and tease repressed passions. The workers pushed their symbolic horseplay to the brink of reification, the point at which the killing of cats would turn into an open rebellion. They played on ambiguities, using symbols that would hide their full meaning while letting enough of it show through to make a fool of the bourgeois without giving him a pretext to fire them. They tweaked his nose and prevented him from protesting against it. To pull off such a feat required great dexterity. It showed that workers could manipulate symbols in their idiom as effectively as poets did in print.

The boundaries within which this jesting had to be contained suggest the limits to working-class militancy under the Old Regime. The printers identified with their craft rather than their class. Although they organized in chapels, staged strikes, and sometimes forced up wages, they remained subordinate to the bourgeois. The master hired and fired men as casually as he ordered paper, and he turned them out into the road when he sniffed insubordination. So until the onset of proletarianization in the late nineteenth century, they generally kept their protests on a symbolic level. A *copie*, like a carnival, helped to let off stream; but it also produced laughter, a vital ingredient in early artisanal culture and one that has been lost in labor history. By seeing the way a joke worked in the horseplay of a printing shop two centuries ago, we may be able to recapture that missing element—laughter, sheer laughter, the thigh-slapping, rib-cracking Rabelaisian kind, rather than the Voltairian smirk with which we are familiar.

APPENDIX: CONTAT'S ACCOUNT OF THE CAT MASSACRE

50 The following account comes from Nicolas Contat. *Anecdotes typographiques où l'on voit la description des coutumes, moeurs et usages singuliers des*

compagnons imprimeurs, ed. Giles Barber (Oxford, 1980), pp. 51–53. After a day of exhausting work and disgusting food, the two apprentices retire to their bedroom, a damp and draughty lean-to in a corner of the courtyard. The episode is recounted in the third person, from the viewpoint of Jerome:

He is so tired and needs rest so desperately that the shack looks like a palace to him. At last the persecution and misery he has suffered throughout the day have come to an end, and he can relax. But no, some bedeviled cats celebrate a witches' sabbath all night long, making so much noise that they rob him of the brief period of rest allotted to the apprentices before the journeymen arrive for work early the next morning and demand admission by constant ringing of an infernal bell. Then the boys have to get up and cross the courtyard, shivering under their nightshirts, in order to open the door. Those journeymen never let up. No matter what you do, you always make them lose their time and they always treat you as a lazy good-for-nothing. They call for Léveillé. Light the fire under the cauldron! Fetch water for the dunking-troughs! True, those jobs are supposed to be done by the beginner apprentices, who live at home, but they don't arrive until six or seven. Thus everyone is soon at work— apprentices, journeymen, everyone but the master and the mistress: they alone enjoy the sweetness of sleep. That makes Jerome and Léveillé jealous. They resolve that they will not be the only ones to suffer; they want this master and mistress as associates. But how to turn the trick?

Léveillé has an extraordinary talent for imitating the voices and the smallest gestures of everyone around him. He is a perfect actor; that's the real profession that he has picked up in the printing shop. He also can produce perfect imitations of the cries of dogs and cats. He decides to climb from roof to roof until he reaches a gutter next to the bedroom of the bourgeois and the bourgeoise. From there he can ambush them with a volley of meows. It's an easy job for him: he is the son of a roofer and can scramble across roofs like a cat.

Our sniper succeeds so well that the whole neighborhood is alarmed. The word spreads that there is witchcraft afoot and that the cats must be the agents of someone casting a spell. It is a case for the curé, who is an intimate of the household and the confessor of Madame. No one can sleep any more.

Léveillé stages a sabbath the next night and the night after that. If you didn't know him, you would be convinced he was a witch. Finally, the master and the mistress cannot stand it any longer. "We'd better tell the boys to get rid of those malevolent animals," they declare. Madame gives them the order, exhorting them to avoid frightening la grise. That is the name of her pet pussy.

This lady is impassioned for cats. Many master printers are also. One of them has twenty-five. He has had their portraits painted and feeds them on roast fowl.

The hunt is soon organized. The apprentices resolve to make a clean sweep of it, and they are joined by the journeymen. The masters love cats, so consequently they must hate them. This man arms himself with the bar of a press, that one with a stick from the drying-room, others with broom handles. They hang sacks at the windows of the attic and the storerooms to catch the cats who attempt to escape by leaping outdoors. The beaters are named, everything is organized. Léveillé and his comrade Jerome preside over the fête, each of them armed with an iron bar from the shop. The first thing they go for is la grise, Madame's pussy. Léveillé stuns it with a quick blow on the kidneys, and Jerome finishes it off. Then Léveillé stuffs the body in a gutter, for they don't want to get caught: it is a matter of consequence, a murder, which must be kept hidden. The men produce terror on the rooftops. Seized by panic, the cats throw themselves into the sacks. Some are killed on the spot. Others are condemned to be hanged for the amusement of the entire printing shop.

Printers know how to laugh; it is their sole occupation.

The execution is about to begin. They name a hangman, a troop of guards, even a confessor. Then they pronounce the sentence.

In the midst of it all, the mistress arrives. What is her surprise, when she sees the bloody execution! She lets out a scream; then her voice is cut, because she thinks she sees la grise, and she is certain that such a fate has been reserved for her favorite puss. The workers assure her that no one would be capable of such a crime: they have too much respect for the house.

The bourgeois arrives. "Ah! The scoundrels," he says. "Instead of working, they are killing cats." Madame to Monsieur: "These wicked men can't kill the masters, so they have killed my pussy. She can't be found. I have called la grise everywhere. They must have hanged her." It seems to her that all the workers' blood would not be sufficient to redeem the insult. The poor grise, a pussy without a peer!

Monsieur and Madame retire, leaving the workers in liberty. The printers delight in the disorder; they are beside themselves with joy.

What a splendid subject for their laughter, for a *belle copie!* They will amuse themselves with it for a long time. Léveillé will take the leading role and will stage the play at least twenty times. He will mime the master, the mistress, the whole house, heaping ridicule on them all. He will spare nothing in his satire. Among printers, those who excel in this entertainment are called *jobeurs*; they provide *joberie*.

Léveillé receives many rounds of applause.

It should be noted that all the workers are in league against the masters. It is enough to speak badly of them [the masters] to be esteemed by the whole assembly of typographers. Léveillé is one of those. In recognition of his merit, he will be pardoned for some previous satires against the workers.

(1985)

Questions:

1. Summarize in your own words the various reasons for killing the cats, according to Darnton.

2. What do you feel is the author's own attitude to the sort of laughter the artisans produced (paragraph 47)?

3. Darnton describes the attack as a "metonymic insult" (paragraph 42, and again in paragraph 45). Explain in your own words what is meant by this.

4. What are some characteristics of the bourgeoisie in early eighteenth-century Paris insofar as you can infer them from this essay?

5. Though Darnton provides a remarkable range of explanatory detail for the apprentices' actions given a climate in which "cruelty to animals expressed a deep current of popular culture" (paragraph 29), he does not attempt to explain why or how it should have come to be such a deep cultural current. To what extent do you think it may be possible to explain certain core values of past cultures (attitudes towards slavery, for example, as much as attitudes towards animals) that have come to seem entirely repellant to us? To what extent do you feel it appropriate to condemn the presence of such attitudes in past civilizations?

6. Write a short essay attempting to explain the humour (in some people's eyes) of something that you are aware many people would regard as distinctly unfunny. (For example, you might discuss the "humorous" way in which killings are presented in certain violent movies, or the humour of ridicule practiced by Tom Green.)

7. In whatever form it takes in a particular culture, is "the humour of cruelty" usually highly gendered? (In other words, are men and women likely to not always find the same sorts of things funny?) Discuss this issue in relation both to Darnton's essay and to the world today.

ELAINE SHOWALTER

REPRESENTING OPHELIA: WOMEN, MADNESS, AND THE RESPONSIBILITIES OF FEMINIST CRITICISM

In this essay, Elaine Showalter discusses the character of Ophelia in Shakespeare's Hamlet *and offers an answer to the question of how feminist criticism should represent Ophelia in its own discourse.*

"As a sort of a come-on, I announced that I would speak today about that piece of bait named Ophelia, and I'll be as good as my word." These are the words which begin the psychoanalytic seminar on *Hamlet* presented in Paris in 1959 by Jacques Lacan. But despite his promising come-on, Lacan was *not* as good as his word. He goes on for some 41 pages to speak about Hamlet, and when he does mention Ophelia, she is merely what Lacan calls "the object Ophelia"—that is, the object of Hamlet's male desire. The etymology of Ophelia, Lacan asserts, is "O-phallus," and her role in the drama can only be to function as the exteriorized figuration of what Lacan predictably and, in view of his own early work with psychotic women, disappointingly suggests is the phallus as transcendental signifier.[1] To play such a part obviously makes Ophelia "essential," as Lacan admits; but only

---

[1] Jacques Lacan, "Desire and the interpretation of desire in *Hamlet*," in *Literature and Psychoanalysis: The Question of Reading: Otherwise*, ed. Shoshana Felman (Baltimore, 1982), 11, 20, 23. Lacan is also wrong about the etymology of Ophelia, which probably derives from the Greek for "help" or "succour." Charlotte M. Yonge suggested a derivation from "ophis," "serpent." See her *History of Christian Names* (1884, republished Chicago, 1966), 346–7. I am indebted to Walter Jackson Bate for this reference. [Unless otherwise noted, all notes to this essay are from the author.]

because, in his words, "she is linked forever, for centuries, to the figure of Hamlet."[2]

The bait-and-switch game that Lacan plays with Ophelia is a cynical but not unusual instance of her deployment in psychiatric and critical texts. For most critics of Shakespeare, Ophelia has been an insignificant minor character in the play, touching in her weakness and madness but chiefly interesting, of course, in what she tells us about Hamlet. And while female readers of Shakespeare have often attempted to champion Ophelia, even feminist critics have done so with a certain embarrassment. As Annette Kolodny ruefully admits: "it is after all, an imposition of high order to ask the viewer to attend to Ophelia's sufferings in a scene where, before, he's always so comfortably kept his eye fixed on Hamlet."

Yet when feminist criticism allows Ophelia to upstage Hamlet, it also brings to the foreground the issues in an ongoing theoretical debate about the cultural links between femininity, female sexuality, insanity, and representation. Though she is neglected in criticism, Ophelia is probably the most frequently illustrated and cited of Shakespeare's heroines. Her visibility as a subject in literature, popular culture, and painting, from Redon who paints her drowning, to Bob Dylan, who places her on Desolation Row, to Cannon Mills, which has named a flowery sheet pattern after her, is in inverse relation to her invisibility in Shakespearean critical texts. Why has she been such a potent and obsessive figure in our cultural mythology? Insofar as Hamlet names Ophelia as "woman" and "frailty," substituting an ideological view of femininity for a personal one, is she indeed representative of Woman, and does her madness stand for the oppression of women in society as well as in tragedy? Furthermore, since Laertes calls Ophelia a "document in madness," does she represent the textual archetype of woman *as* madness, or madness *as* woman? And finally, how should feminist criticism represent Ophelia in its own discourse? What is our responsibility towards her as character and as woman?

Feminist critics have offered a variety of responses to these questions. Some have maintained that we should represent Ophelia as a lawyer represents a client, that we should become her Horatia, in this harsh world reporting her and her cause aright to the unsatisfied. Carol Neely, for example, describes advocacy—speaking *for* Ophelia—as our proper role: "As a feminist critic," she writes, "I must 'tell' Ophelia's story."[3] But what can we mean by Ophelia's story? The story of her life? The story of her betrayal at

---

[2] Annette Kolodny, "Dancing through the minefield: some observations on the theory, practice, and politics of feminist literary criticism" (*Feminist Studies*, 6 (1980)), 7.

[3] Carol Neely, "Feminist modes of Shakespearean criticism" (*Women's Studies*, 9 (1981)), 11.

the hands of her father, brother, lover, court, society? The story of her rejection and marginalization by male critics of Shakespeare? Shakespeare gives us very little information from which to imagine a past for Ophelia. She appears in only five of the play's twenty scenes; the pre-play course of her love story with Hamlet is known only by a few ambiguous flashbacks. Her tragedy is subordinated in the play; unlike Hamlet, she does not struggle with moral choices or alternatives. Thus another feminist critic, Lee Edwards, concludes that it is impossible to reconstruct Ophelia's biography from the text: "We can imagine Hamlet's story without Ophelia, but Ophelia literally has no story without Hamlet."[4]

5   If we turn from American to French feminist theory, Ophelia might confirm the impossibility of representing the feminine in patriarchal discourse as other than madness, incoherence, fluidity, or silence. In French theoretical criticism, the feminine or "Woman" is that which escapes representation in patriarchal language and symbolism; it remains on the side of negativity, absence, and lack. In comparison to Hamlet, Ophelia is certainly a creature of lack. "I think nothing, my lord," she tells him in the Mousetrap scene, and he cruelly twists her words:

> *Hamlet:* That's a fair thought to lie between maids' legs.
> *Ophelia:* What is, my lord?
> *Hamlet:* Nothing.
>
> (III.ii.117–19)

In Elizabethan slang, "nothing" was a term for the female genitalia, as in *Much Ado About Nothing*. To Hamlet, then, "nothing" is what lies between maids' legs, for, in the male visual system of representation and desire, women's sexual organs, in the words of the French psychoanalyst Luce Irigaray, "represent the horror of having nothing to see."[5] When Ophelia is mad, Gertrude says that "Her speech is nothing," mere "unshaped use." Ophelia's speech represents the horror of having nothing to say in the public terms defined by the court. Deprived of thought, sexuality, language, Ophelia's story becomes the story of O—the zero, the empty circle or

---

[4] Lee Edwards, "The labors of Psyche" (*Critical Inquiry*, 6 (1979)), 36.

[5] Luce Irigaray: see *New French Feminisms*, ed. Elaine Marks and Isabelle de Courtivron (New York, 1982), 101. The quotation above, from III.ii, is taken from the Arden Shakespeare, *Hamlet*, ed. Harold Jenkins (London and New York, 1982), 295. All quotations from *Hamlet* are from this text.

mystery of feminine difference, the cipher of female sexuality to be deciphered by feminist interpretation.[6]

A third approach would be to read Ophelia's story as the female subtext of the tragedy, the repressed story of Hamlet. In this reading, Ophelia represents the strong emotions that the Elizabethans as well as the Freudians thought womanish and unmanly. When Laertes weeps for his dead sister he says of his tears that "When these are gone, / The woman will be out"—that is to say, that the feminine and shameful part of his nature will be purged. According to David Leverenz, in an important essay called "The Woman in *Hamlet*," Hamlet's disgust at the feminine passivity in himself is translated into violent revulsion against women, and into his brutal behaviour towards Ophelia. Ophelia's suicide, Leverenz argues, then becomes "a microcosm of the male world's banishment of the female, because 'woman' represents everything denied by reasonable men."[7]

It is perhaps because Hamlet's emotional vulnerability can so readily be conceptualized as feminine that this is the only heroic male role in Shakespeare which has been regularly acted by women, in a tradition from Sarah Bernhardt to, most recently, Diane Venora, in a production directed by Joseph Papp. Leopold Bloom speculates on this tradition in *Ulysses*, musing on the Hamlet of the actress Mrs Bandman Palmer: "Male impersonator. Perhaps he was a woman? Why Ophelia committed suicide?"[8]

While all of these approaches have much to recommend them, each also presents critical problems. To liberate Ophelia from the text, or to make her its tragic center, is to re-appropriate her for our own ends; to dissolve her into a female symbolism of absence is to endorse our own marginality; to make her Hamlet's anima is to reduce her to a metaphor of male experience. I would like to propose instead that Ophelia *does* have a story of her own that feminist criticism can tell; it is neither her life story, nor her love story, nor Lacan's story, but rather the *history* of her representation. This essay tries to bring together some of the categories of French feminist thought about the "feminine" with the empirical energies of American historical and critical research: to yoke French theory and Yankee knowhow.

10 Tracing the iconography of Ophelia in English and French painting, photography, psychiatry, and literature, as well as in theatrical production, I will be showing first of all the representational bonds between female

---

[6] On images of negation and feminine enclosure, see David Wilbern, "Shakespeare's 'nothing',," in *Representing Shakespeare: New Psychoanalytic Essays*, ed. Murray M. Schwartz and Coppélia Kahn (Baltimore, 1981).

[7] David Leverenz, "The woman in *Hamlet*: an interpersonal view" (*Signs*, 4 (1978)), 303.

[8] James Joyce, *Ulysses* (New York, 1961), 76.

insanity and female sexuality. Secondly, I want to demonstrate the two-way transaction between psychiatric theory and cultural representation. As one medical historian has observed, we could provide a manual of female insanity by chronicling the illustrations of Ophelia; this is so because the illustrations of Ophelia have played a major role in the theoretical construction of female insanity.[9] Finally, I want to suggest that the feminist revision of Ophelia comes as much from the actress's freedom as from the critic's interpretation.[10] When Shakespeare's heroines began to be played by women instead of boys, the presence of the female body and female voice, quite apart from details of interpretation, created new meanings and subversive tensions in these roles, and perhaps most importantly with Ophelia. Looking at Ophelia's history on and off the stage, I will point out the contest between male and female representations of Ophelia, cycles of critical repression and feminist reclamation of which contemporary feminist criticism is only the most recent phase. By beginning with these data from cultural history, instead of moving from the grid of literary theory, I hope to conclude with a fuller sense of the responsibilities of feminist criticism, as well as a new perspective on Ophelia.

"Of all the characters in *Hamlet*," Bridget Lyons has pointed out, "Ophelia is most persistently presented in terms of symbolic meanings."[11] Her behaviour, her appearance, her gestures, her costume, her props, are freighted with emblematic significance, and for many generations of Shakespearean critics her part in the play has seemed to be primarily iconographic. Ophelia's symbolic meanings, moreover, are specifically feminine. Whereas for Hamlet madness is metaphysical, linked with culture, for Ophelia it is a product of the female body and female nature, perhaps that nature's purest form. On the Elizabethan stage, the conventions of female insanity were sharply defined. Ophelia dresses in white, decks herself with "fantastical garlands" of wild flowers, and enters, according to the stage directions of the "Bad" Quarto, "distracted" playing on a lute with her "hair down singing." Her speeches are marked by extravagant metaphors, lyrical

---

[9]   Sander L. Gilman, *Seeing the Insane* (New York, 1981), 126.

[10]   See Michael Goldman, *The Actor's Freedom: Toward a Theory of Drama* (New York, 1975), for a stimulating discussion of the interpretative interaction between actor and audience.

[11]   Bridget Lyons, "The iconography of Ophelia" (*English Literary History*, 44 (1977)), 61.

free associations, and "explosive sexual imagery."[12] She sings wistful and bawdy ballads, and ends her life by drowning.

All of these conventions carry specific messages about femininity and sexuality. Ophelia's virginal and vacant white is contrasted with Hamlet's scholar's garb, his "suits of solemn black." Her flowers suggest the discordant double images of female sexuality as both innocent blossoming and whorish contamination; she is the "green girl" of pastoral, the virginal "Rose of May" and the sexually explicit madwoman who, in giving away her wild flowers and herbs, is symbolically deflowering herself. The "weedy trophies" and phallic "long purples" which she wears to her death intimate an improper and discordant sexuality that Gertrude's lovely elegy cannot quite obscure.[13] In Elizabethan and Jacobean drama, the stage direction that a woman enters with dishevelled hair indicates that she might either be mad or the victim of a rape; the disordered hair, her offense against decorum, suggests sensuality in each case.[14] The mad Ophelia's bawdy songs and verbal license, while they give her access to "an entirely different range of experience" from what she is allowed as the dutiful daughter, seem to be her one sanctioned form of self-assertion as a woman, quickly followed, as if in retribution, by her death.[15]

Drowning too was associated with the feminine, with female fluidity as opposed to masculine aridity. In his discussion of the "Ophelia complex," the phenomenologist Gaston Bachelard traces the symbolic connections between women, water, and death. Drowning, he suggests, becomes the truly feminine death in the dramas of literature and life, one which is a beautiful immersion and submersion in the female element. Water is the profound and organic symbol of the liquid woman whose eyes are so easily drowned in tears, as her body is the repository of blood, amniotic fluid, and milk. A man contemplating this feminine suicide understands it by reaching for what is feminine in himself, like Laertes, by a temporary surrender to his own

---

[12] See Maurice and Hanna Charney, "The language of Shakespeare's madwomen" (*Signs*, 3 (1977)), 451, 457; and Carroll Camden, "On Ophelia's madness" (*Shakespeare Quarterly* (1964)), 254.

[13] See Margery Garber, *Coming of Age in Shakespeare* (London, 1981), 155–7; and Lyons, op. cit., 65, 70–2.

[14] On dishevelled hair as a signifier of madness or rape, see Charney and Charney, op. cit., 452–3, 457; and Allan Dessen, *Elizabethan Stage Conventions and Modern Interpreters* (Cambridge, 1984), 36–8. Thanks to Allan Dessen for letting me see advance proofs of his book.

[15] Charney and Charney, op. cit., 456.

fluidity—that is, his tears; and he becomes a man again in becoming once more dry—when his tears are stopped.[16]

Clinically speaking, Ophelia's behaviour and appearance are characteristic of the malady the Elizabethans would have diagnosed as female love-melancholy, or erotomania. From about 1580, melancholy had become a fashionable disease among young men, especially in London, and Hamlet himself is a prototype of the melancholy hero. Yet the epidemic of melancholy associated with intellectual and imaginative genius "curiously bypassed women." Women's melancholy was seen instead as biological, and emotional in origins.[17]

15

On the stage, Ophelia's madness was presented as the predicable outcome of erotomania. From 1660, when women first appeared on the public stage, to the beginnings of the eighteenth century, the most celebrated of the actresses who played Ophelia were those whom rumour credited with disappointments in love. The greatest triumph was reserved for Susan Mountfort, a former actress at Lincoln's Inn Fields who had gone mad after her lover's betrayal. One night in 1720 she escaped from her keeper, rushed to the theater, and just as the Ophelia of the evening was to enter for her mad scene, "sprang forward in her place...with wild eyes and wavering motion."[18] As a contemporary reported, "she was in truth *Ophelia herself,* to the amazement of the performers as well as of the audience—nature having made this last effort, her vital powers failed her and she died soon after."[19] These theatrical legends reinforced the belief of the age that female madness was a part of female nature, less to be imitated by an actress than demonstrated by a deranged woman in a performance of her emotions.

The subversive or violent possibilities of the mad scene were nearly eliminated, however, on the eighteenth-century stage. Late Augustan stereotypes of female love-melancholy were sentimentalized versions which minimized the force of female sexuality, and made female insanity a pretty stimulant to male sensibility. Actresses such as Mrs. Lessingham in 1772, and Mary Bolton in 1811, played Ophelia in this decorous style, relying on the familiar images of the white dress, loose hair, and wild flowers to convey a

---

[16] Gaston Bachelard, *L'Eau et les rêves* (Paris, 1942), 109–25. See also Brigitte Peucker, "Dröste-Hulshof's Ophelia and the recovery of voice" (*The Journal of English and Germanic Philology* (1983)), 374–91.

[17] Vieda Skultans, *English Madness: Ideas on Insanity 1580–1890* (London, 1977), 79–81. On historical cases of love-melancholy, see Michael MacDonald, *Mystical Bedlam* (Cambridge, 1982).

[18] C.E.L. Wingate, *Shakespeare's Heroines on the Stage* (New York, 1895), 283–4, 288–9.

[19] Charles Hiatt, *Ellen Terry* (London, 1898), 11.

polite feminine distraction, highly suitable for pictorial reproduction, and appropriate for Samuel Johnson's description of Ophelia as young, beautiful, harmless, and pious. Even Mrs. Siddons in 1785 played the mad scene with stately and classical dignity. For much of the period, in fact, Augustan objections to the levity and indecency of Ophelia's language and behaviour led to censorship of the part. Her lines were frequently cut, and the role was often assigned to a singer instead of an actress, making the mode of representation musical rather than visual or verbal.

But whereas the Augustan response to madness was a denial, the romantic response was an embrace.[20] The figure of the madwoman permeates romantic literature, from the gothic novelists to Wordsworth and Scott in such texts as "The Thorn" and *The Heart of Midlothian*, where she stands for sexual victimization, bereavement, and thrilling emotional extremity. Romantic artists such as Thomas Barker and George Shepheard painted pathetically abandoned Crazy Kates and Crazy Anns, while Henry Fuseli's "Mad Kate" is almost demonically possessed, an orphan of the romantic storm.

In the Shakespearean theater, Ophelia's romantic revival began in France rather than England. When Charles Kemble made his Paris debut as Hamlet with an English troupe in 1827, his Ophelia was a young Irish ingénue named Harriet Smithson. Smithson used "her extensive command of mime to depict in precise gesture the state of Ophelia's confused mind."[21] In the mad scene, she entered in a long black veil, suggesting the standard imagery of female sexual mystery in the gothic novel, with scattered bedlamish wisps of straw in her hair. Spreading the veil on the ground as she sang, she spread flowers upon it in the shape of a cross, as if to make her father's grave, and mimed a burial, a piece of stage business which remained in vogue for the rest of the century.

The French audiences were stunned. Dumas recalled that "it was the first time I saw in the theatre real passions, giving life to men and women of flesh and blood."[22] The 23-year-old Hector Berlioz, who was in the audience on the first night, fell madly in love, and eventually married Harriet Smithson despite his family's frantic opposition. Her image as the mad Ophelia was represented in popular lithographs and exhibited in bookshop and printshop windows. Her costume was imitated by the fashionable, and a coiffure "à la folle," consisting of a "black veil with wisps of straw tastefully interwoven"

---

[20]   Max Byrd, *Visits to Bedlam: Madness and Literature in the Eighteenth Century* (Columbia, 1971), xiv.

[21]   Peter Raby, *Fair Ophelia: Harriet Smithson Berlioz* (Cambridge, 1982), 63.

[22]   Ibid., 68.

in the hair, was widely copied by the Parisian beau monde, always on the lookout for something new.[23]

20 Although Smithson never acted Ophelia on the English stage, her intensely visual performance quickly influenced English productions as well; and indeed the romantic Ophelia—a young girl passionately and visibly driven to picturesque madness—became the dominant international acting style for the next 150 years, from Helena Modjeska in Poland in 1871, to the 18-year-old Jean Simmons in the Laurence Olivier film of 1948.

Whereas the romantic Hamlet, in Coleridge's famous dictum, thinks too much, has an "overbalance of the contemplative faculty" and an over-active intellect, the romantic Ophelia is a girl who *feels* too much, who drowns in feelings. The romantic critics seem to have felt that the less said about Ophelia the better; the point was to *look* at her. Hazlitt, for one, is speechless before her, calling her "a character almost too exquisitely touching to be dwelt upon."[24] While the Augustans represent Ophelia as music, the romantics transform her into an *objet d'art*, as if to take literally Claudius's lament, "poor Ophelia / Divided from herself and her fair judgement, / Without the which we are pictures."

Smithson's performance is best recaptured in a series of pictures done by Delacroix from 1830 to 1850, which show a strong romantic interest in the relation of female sexuality and insanity.[25] The most innovative and influential of Delacroix's lithographs is *La Mort d'Ophélie* of 1843, the first of three studies. Its sensual languor, with Ophelia half-suspended in the stream as her dress slips from her body, anticipated the fascination with the erotic trance of the hysteric as it would be studied by Jean-Martin Charcot and his students, including Janet and Freud. Delacroix's interest in the drowning Ophelia is also reproduced to the point of obsession in later nineteenth-century painting. The English Pre-Raphaelites painted her again and again, choosing the drowning which is only described in the play, and where no actress's image had preceeded them or interfered with their imaginative supremacy.

In the Royal Academy show of 1852, Arthur Hughes's entry shows a tiny waif-like creature—a sort of Tinker Bell Ophelia—in a filmy white gown, perched on a tree trunk by the stream. The overall effect is softened, sexless, and hazy, although the straw in her hair resembles a crown of thorns. Hughes's juxtaposition of childlike femininity and Christian martyrdom was overpowered, however, by John Everett Millais's great painting of Ophelia

[23] Ibid., 72, 75.

[24] Quoted in Camden, op. cit., 217.

[25] Raby, op. cit., 182.

in the same show. While Millais's Ophelia is sensuous siren as well as victim, the artist rather than the subject dominates the scene. The division of space between Ophelia and the natural details Millais had so painstakingly pursued reduces her to one more visual object; and the painting has such a hard surface, strangely flattened perspective, and brilliant light that it seems cruelly indifferent to the woman's death.

* * *

These Pre-Raphaelite images were part of a new and intricate traffic between images of women and madness in late nineteenth-century literature, psychiatry, drama, and art. First of all, superintendents of Victorian lunatic asylums were also enthusiasts of Shakespeare, who turned to his dramas for models of mental aberration that could be applied to their clinical practice. The case study of Ophelia was one that seemed particularly useful as an account of hysteria or mental breakdown in adolescence, a period of sexual instability which the Victorians regarded as risky for the women's mental health. As Dr John Charles Bucknill, president of the Medico-Psychological Association, remarked in 1859, "Ophelia is the very type of a class of cases by no means uncommon. Every mental physician of moderately extensive experience must have seen many Ophelias. It is a copy from nature, after the fashion of the Pre-Raphaelite school."[26] Dr John Conolly, the celebrated superintendent of the Hanwell Asylum, and founder of the committee to make Stratford a national trust, concurred. In his *Study of Hamlet* in 1863 he noted that even casual visitors to mental institutions could recognize an Ophelia in the wards: "the same young years, the same faded beauty, the same fantastic dress and interrupted song."[27] Medical textbooks illustrated their discussions of female patients with sketches of Ophelia-like maidens.

25   But Conolly also pointed out that the graceful Ophelias who dominated the Victorian stage were quite unlike the women who had become the majority of the inmate population in Victorian public asylums. "It seems to be supposed," he protested, "that it is an easy task to play the part of a crazy girl, and that it is chiefly composed of singing and prettiness. The habitual courtesy, the partial rudeness of mental disorder, are things to be wit-

---

[26]   J.C. Bucknill, *The Psychology of Shakespeare* (London, 1859, reprinted New York, 1979), 110. For more extensive discussions of Victorian psychiatry and Ophelia figures, see Elaine Showalter, *The Female Malady: Women, Madness and English Culture* (New York, 1986).

[27]   John Conolly, *Study of Hamlet* (London, 1863), 177.

nessed....An actress, ambitious of something beyond cold imitation, might find the contemplation of such cases a not unprofitable study."[28]

Yet when Ellen Terry took up Conolly's challenge, and went to an asylum to observe real madwomen, she found them "too *theatrical*" to teach her anything.[29] This was because the iconography of the romantic Ophelia had begun to infiltrate reality, to define a style for mad young women seeking to express and communicate their distress. And where the women themselves did not willingly throw themselves into Ophelia-like postures, asylum superintendents, armed with the new technology of photography, imposed the costume, gesture, props, and expression of Ophelia upon them. In England, the camera was introduced to asylum work in the 1850s by Dr Hugh Welch Diamond, who photographed his female patients at the Surrey Asylum and at Bethlem. Diamond was heavily influenced by literary and visual models in his posing of the female subjects. His pictures of madwomen, posed in prayer, or decked with Ophelia-like garlands, were copied for Victorian consumption as touched-up lithographs in professional journals.[30]

Reality, psychiatry, and representational convention were even more confused in the photographic records of hysteria produced in the 1870s by Jean-Martin Charcot. Charcot was the first clinician to install a fully equipped photographic atelier in his Paris hospital, La Salpêtrière, to record the performances of his hysterical stars. Charcot's clinic became, as he said, a "living theatre" of female pathology; his women patients were coached in their performances for the camera, and, under hypnosis, were sometimes instructed to play heroines from Shakespeare. Among them, a 15-year-old girl named Augustine was featured in the published volumes called *Iconographies* in every posture of *la grande hystérie*. With her white hospital gown and flowing locks, Augustine frequently resembles the reproductions of Ophelia as icon and actress which had been in wide circulation.[31]

But if the Victorian madwoman looks mutely out from men's pictures, and acts a part men had staged and directed, she is very differently represented in the feminist revision of Ophelia initiated by newly powerful and respectable Victorian actresses, and by women critics of Shakespeare. In their

---

[28] Ibid., 177–8, 180.

[29] Ellen Terry, *The Story of My Life* (London, 1908), 154.

[30] Diamond's photographs are reproduced in Sander L. Gilman, *The Face of Madness: Hugh W. Diamond and the Origin of Psychiatric Photography* (New York, 1976).

[31] See Georges Didi-Huberman, *L'Invention de l'hystérie* (Paris, 1982), and Stephen Heath, *The Sexual Fix* (London, 1983), 36.

efforts to defend Ophelia, they invent a story for her drawn from their own experiences, grievances, and desires.

Probably the most famous of the Victorian feminist revisions of the Ophelia story was Mary Cowden Clarke's *The Girlhood of Shakespeare's Heroines*, published in 1852. Unlike other Victorian moralizing and didactic studies of the female characters of Shakespeare's plays, Clarke's was specifically addressed to the wrongs of women, and especially to the sexual double standard. In a chapter on Ophelia called "The rose of Elsinore," Clarke tells how the child Ophelia was left behind in the care of a peasant couple when Polonius was called to the court at Paris, and raised in a cottage with a foster-sister and brother, Jutha and Ulf. Jutha is seduced and betrayed by a deceitful knight, and Ophelia discovers the bodies of Jutha and her still-born child, lying "white, frigid, and still" in the deserted parlor of the cottage in the middle of the night. Ulf, a "hairy loutish boy," likes to torture flies, to eat songbirds, and to rip the petals off roses, and he is also very eager to give little Ophelia what he calls a bear-hug. Both repelled and masochistically attracted by Ulf, Ophelia is repeatedly cornered by him as she grows up; once she escapes the hug by hitting him with a branch of wild roses; another time, he sneaks into her bedroom "in his brutish pertinacity to obtain the hug he had promised himself," but just as he bends over to her trembling body, Ophelia is saved by the reappearance of her real mother.

A few years later, back at the court, she discovers the hanged body of another friend, who has killed herself after being "victimized and deserted by the same evil seducer." Not surprisingly, Ophelia breaks down with brain fever—a staple mental illness of Victorian fiction—and has prophetic hallucinations of a brook beneath willow trees where something bad will happen to her. The warnings of Polonius and Laertes have little to add to this history of female sexual trauma.[32]

On the Victorian stage, it was Ellen Terry, daring and unconventional in her own life, who led the way in acting Ophelia in feminist terms as a consistent psychological study in sexual intimidation, a girl terrified of her father, of her lover, and of life itself. Terry's debut as Ophelia in Henry Irving's production in 1878 was a landmark. According to one reviewer, her Ophelia was "the terrible spectacle of a normal girl becoming hopelessly imbecile as the result of overwhelming mental agony. Hers was an insanity

---

[32] Mary Cowden Clarke, *The Girlhood of Shakespeare's Heroines* (London, 1852). See also George C. Gross, "Mary Cowden Clarke, *The Girlhood of Shakespeare's Heroines*, and the sex education of Victorian women" (*Victorian Studies*, 16 (1972)), 37–58, and Nina Auerbach, *Woman and the Demon* (Cambridge, Mass., 1983), 210–15.

without wrath or rage, without exaltation or paroxysms."[33] Her "poetic and intellectual performance" also inspired other actresses to rebel against the conventions of invisibility and negation associated with the part.

Terry was the first to challenge the tradition of Ophelia's dressing in emblematic white. For the French poets, such as Rimbaud, Hugo, Musset, Mallarmé and Laforgue, whiteness was part of Ophelia's essential feminine symbolism; they call her "blanche Ophélia" and compare her to a lily, a cloud, or snow. Yet whiteness also made her a transparency, an absence that took on the colors of Hamlet's moods, and that, for the symbolists like Mallarmé, made her a blank page to be written over or on by the male imagination. Although Irving was able to prevent Terry from wearing black in the mad scene, exclaiming "My God, Madam, there must be only *one* black figure in this play, and that's Hamlet!" (Irving, of course, was playing Hamlet), nonetheless actresses such as Gertrude Eliot, Helen Maude, Nora de Silva, and in Russia Vera Komisarjevskaya, gradually won the right to intensify Ophelia's presence by clothing her in Hamlet's black.[34]

By the turn of the century, there was both a male and female discourse on Ophelia. A.C. Bradley spoke for the Victorian male tradition when he noted in *Shakespearean Tragedy* (1906) that "a large number of readers feel a kind of personal irritation against Ophelia; they seem unable to forgive her for not having been a heroine."[35] The feminist counterview was represented by actresses in such works as Helena Faucit's study of Shakespeare's female characters, and *The True Ophelia*, written by an anonymous actress in 1914, which protested against the "insipid little creature" of criticism, and advocated a strong and intelligent woman destroyed by the heartlessness of men.[36] In women's paintings of the *fin de siècle* as well, Ophelia is depicted as an inspiring, even sanctified emblem of righteousness.[37]

While the widely read and influential essays of Mary Cowden Clarke are now mocked as the epitome of naive criticism, these Victorian studies of the girlhood of Shakespeare's heroines are of course alive and well as psychoanalytic criticism, which has imagined its own prehistories of oedipal conflict and neurotic fixation; and I say this not to mock psychoanalytic criticism,

---

[33] Hiatt, op. cit., 114. See also Wingate, op. cit., 304–5.

[34] Terry, op. cit., 155–6.

[35] Andrew C. Bradley, *Shakespearean Tragedy* (London, 1906), 160.

[36] Helena Faucit Martin, *On Some of Shakespeare's Female Characters* (Edinburgh and London, 1891), 4, 18; and *The True Ophelia* (New York, 1914), 15.

[37] Among these paintings are the Ophelias of Henrietta Rae and Mrs F. Littler. Sarah Bernhardt sculpted a bas relief of Ophelia for the Women's Pavilion at the Chicago World's Fair in 1893.

but to suggest that Clarke's musings on Ophelia are a pre-Freudian speculation on the traumatic sources of a female sexual identity. The Freudian interpretation of *Hamlet* concentrated on the hero, but also had much to do with the re-sexualization of Ophelia. As early as 1900, Freud had traced Hamlet's irresolution to an Oedipus complex, and Ernest Jones, his leading British disciple, developed this view, influencing the performances of John Gielgud and Alec Guinness in the 1930s. In his final version of the study, *Hamlet and Oedipus*, published in 1949, Jones argued that "Ophelia should be unmistakably sensual, as she seldom is on stage. She may be 'innocent' and docile, but she is very aware of her body."[38]

35 In the theater and in criticism, this Freudian edict has produced such extreme readings as that Shakespeare intends us to see Ophelia as a loose woman, and that she has been sleeping with Hamlet. Rebecca West has argued that Ophelia is not "a correct and timid virgin of exquisite sensibili- ties," a view she attributes to the popularity of the Millais painting; but rather "a disreputable young woman."[39] In his delightful autobiography, Laurence Olivier, who made a special pilgrimage to Ernest Jones when he was preparing his *Hamlet* in the 1930s, recalls that one of his predecessors as actor-manager had said in response to the earnest question, "Did Hamlet sleep with Ophelia?"—"In my company, always."[40]

The most extreme Freudian interpretation reads *Hamlet* as two parallel male and female psychodramas, the counterpointed stories of the incestuous attachments of Hamlet and Ophelia. As Theodor Lidz presents this view, while Hamlet is neurotically attached to his mother, Ophelia has an unresolved oedipal attachment to her father. She has fantasies of a lover who will abduct her from or even kill her father, and when this actually happens, her reason is destroyed by guilt as well as by lingering incestuous feelings. According to Lidz, Ophelia breaks down because she fails in the female developmental task of shifting her sexual attachment from her father "to a man who can bring her fulfilment as a woman."[41] We see the effects of this Freudian Ophelia on stage productions since the 1950s, where directors have hinted at an incestuous link between Ophelia and her father, or more recently, because this staging conflicts with the usual ironic treatment of Polonius, between Ophelia and Laertes. Trevor Nunn's production with Helen Mirren in 1970, for example, made Ophelia and Laertes flirtatious doubles, almost twins in their matching fur-trimmed doublets, playing duets

---

38 Ernest Jones, *Hamlet and Oedipus* (New York, 1949), 139.

39 Rebecca West, *The Count and the Castle* (New Haven, 1958), 18.

40 Laurence Olivier, *Confessions of an Actor* (Harmondsworth, 1982), 102, 152.

41 Theodor Lidz, *Hamlet's Enemy: Madness and Myth in Hamlet* (New York, 1975), 88, 113.

on the lute with Polonius looking on, like Peter, Paul, and Mary. In other productions of the same period, Marianne Faithfull was a haggard Ophelia equally attracted to Hamlet and Laertes, and, in one of the few performances directed by a woman, Yvonne Nicholson sat on Laertes' lap in the advice scene, and played the part with "rough sexual bravado."[42]

Since the 1960s, the Freudian representation of Ophelia has been supplemented by an antipsychiatry that represents Ophelia's madness in more contemporary terms. In contrast to the psychoanalytic representation of Ophelia's sexual unconscious that connected her essential femininity to Freud's essays on female sexuality and hysteria, her madness is now seen in medical and biochemical terms, as schizophrenia. This is so in part because the schizophrenic woman has become the cultural icon of dualistic femininity in the mid-twentieth century as the erotomaniac was in the seventeenth and the hysteric in the nineteenth. It might also be traced to the work of R.D. Laing on female schizophrenia in the 1960s. Laing argued that schizophrenia was an intelligible response to the experience of invalidation within the family network, especially to the conflicting emotional messages and mystifying double binds experienced by daughters. Ophelia, he noted in *The Divided Self*, is an empty space. "In her madness there is no one there....There is no integral selfhood expressed through her actions or utterances. Incomprehensible statements are said by nothing. She has already died. There is now only a vacuum where there was once a person."[43]

Despite his sympathy for Ophelia, Laing's readings silence her, equate her with "nothing," more completely than any since the Augustans; and they have been translated into performances which only make Ophelia a graphic study of mental pathology. The sickest Ophelias on the contemporary stage have been those in the productions of the pathologist-director Jonathan Miller. In 1974 at the Greenwich Theatre his Ophelia sucked her thumb; by 1981, at the Warehouse in London, she was played by an actress much taller and heavier than the Hamlet (perhaps punningly cast as the young actor Anton Lesser). She began the play with a set of nervous tics and tuggings of hair which by the mad scene had become a full set of schizophrenic routines—head banging, twitching, wincing, grimacing, and drooling.[44]

---

[42] Richard David, *Shakespeare in the Theatre* (Cambridge, 1978), 75. This was the production directed by Buzz Goodbody, a brilliant young feminist radical who killed herself that year. See Colin Chambers, *Other Spaces: New Theatre and the RSC* (London, 1980), especially 63–7.

[43] R.D. Laing, *The Divided Self* (Harmondsworth, 1965), 195n.

[44] David, op. cit., 82–3; thanks to Marianne DeKoven, Rutgers University, for the description of the 1981 Warehouse production.

But since the 1970s too we have had a feminist discourse which has offered a new perspective on Ophelia's madness as protest and rebellion. For many feminist theorists, the madwoman is a heroine, a powerful figure who rebels against the family and the social order; and the hysteric who refuses to speak the language of the patriarchal order, who speaks otherwise, is a sister.[45] In terms of effect on the theater, the most radical application of these ideas was probably realized in Melissa Murray's agit-prop play *Ophelia*, written in 1979 for the English women's theater group "Hormone Imbalance." In this blank verse retelling of the Hamlet story, Ophelia becomes a lesbian and runs off with a woman servant to join a guerilla commune.[46]

40   While I've always regretted that I missed this production, I can't proclaim that this defiant ideological gesture, however effective politically or theatrically, is all that feminist criticism desires, or all to which it should aspire. When feminist criticism chooses to deal with representation, rather than with women's writing, it must aim for a maximum interdisciplinary contextualism, in which the complexity of attitudes towards the feminine can be analyzed in their fullest cultural and historical frame. The alternation of strong and weak Ophelias on the stage, virginal and seductive Ophelias in art, inadequate or oppressed Ophelias in criticism, tells us how these representations have overflowed the text, and how they have reflected the ideological character of their times, erupting as debates between dominant and feminist views in periods of gender crisis and redefinition. The representation of Ophelia changes independently of theories of the meaning of the play or the Prince, for it depends on attitudes towards women and madness. The decorous and pious Ophelia of the Augustan age and the postmodern schizophrenic heroine who might have stepped from the pages of Laing can be derived from the same figure; they are both contradictory and complementary images of female sexuality in which madness seems to act as the "switching-point, the concept which allows the co-existence of both sides of the representation."[47] There is no "true" Ophelia for whom feminist criticism must unambiguously speak, but perhaps only a Cubist Ophelia of multiple perspectives, more than the sum of all her parts.

But in exposing the ideology of representation, feminist critics have also the responsibility to acknowledge and to examine the boundaries of our own ideological positions as products of our gender and our time. A degree of

---

[45]   See, for example, Hélène Cixous and Catherine Clément, *La Jeune Née* (Paris, 1975).

[46]   For an account of this production, see Micheline Wandor, *Understudies: Theatre and Sexual Politics* (London, 1981), 47.

[47]   I am indebted for this formulation to a critique of my earlier draft of this paper by Carl Friedman, at the Wesleyan Center for the Humanities, April 1981.

humility in an age of critical hubris can be our greatest strength, for it is by occupying this position of historical self-consciousness in both feminism and criticism that we maintain our credibility in representing Ophelia, and that unlike Lacan, when we promise to speak about her, we make good on our word.

(1985)

Questions:

1. According to Showalter's essay, what approach should feminist critics use in order to give the character of Ophelia "a story of her own"?

2. What are the component parts of Showalter's analysis? How does she organize her argument?

3. What is Showalter's thesis in this essay? Is there a thesis statement?

4. Describe Showalter's use of language in this essay. How does the language indicate the intended audience?

5. If you were directing a version of *Hamlet* for film or stage production, how would you represent Ophelia? Explain your choices.

Stephen Jay Gould

Entropic Homogeneity Isn't Why No One Hits .400 Any More

To hit .400 in baseball means that out of every 1000 chances you hit fairly 400 times. To do this was once a remarkable but by-no-means unheard of achievement. Since 1941, however, no one has ever hit .400 over the course of a major league baseball season. Scientist Stephen Jay Gould asks why.

~

Comparisons may be odious, but we cannot avoid them in a world that prizes excellence and yearns to know whether current pathways lead to progress or destruction. We are driven to contrast past with present and use the result to predict an uncertain future. But how can we make fair comparison since we gaze backward through the rose-colored lenses of our most powerful myth—the idea of a former golden age?

Nostalgia for an unknown past can elevate hovels to castles, dung heaps to snowclad peaks. I had always conceived Calvary, the site of Christ's martyrdom, as a lofty mountain, covered with foliage and located far from the hustle and bustle of Jerusalem. But I stood on its paltry peak last year. Calvary lies inside the walls of old Jerusalem (just barely beyond the city borders of Christ's time). The great hill is but one staircase high: its summit lies *within* the Church of the Holy Sepulchre.

I had long read of Ragusa, the great maritime power of the medieval Adriatic. I viewed it at grand scale in my mind's eye, a vast fleet balancing the powers of Islam and Christendom, sending forth its élite to the vanguard of the "invincible" Spanish Armada. Medieval Ragusa has survived intact—as Dubrovnik in Yugoslavia. No town (but Jerusalem) can match its charm, but I circled the battlements of its city walls in 15 minutes. Ragusa, by modern standards, is a modest village at most.

The world is so much bigger now, so much faster, so much more complex. Must our myths of ancient heroes expire on this altar of technological progress? We might dismiss our deep-seated tendency to aggrandize older heroes as mere sentimentalism—and plainly false by the argument just presented for Calvary and Ragusa. And yet, numbers proclaim a sense of truth in our persistent image of past giants as literally outstanding. Their legitimate claims are relative, not absolute. Great cities of the past may be villages today, and Goliath would barely qualify for the NBA. But, compared with modern counterparts, our legendary heroes often soar much farther above their own contemporaries. The distance between commonplace and extraordinary has contracted dramatically in field after field.

Baseball provides my favorite examples. Our national pastime may strike readers as an odd topic for this magazine, but few systems offer better data for a scientific problem that evokes as much interest, and sparks as much debate, as any other: the meaning of trends in history as expressed by measurable differences between past and present. This article uses baseball to address the general question of how we may compare an elusive past with a different present. How can we know whether past deeds matched or exceeded current prowess? In particular, was Moses right in his early pronouncement (Genesis 6:4): "There were giants in the earth in those days"?

Baseball has been a bastion of constancy in a tumultuously changing world, a contest waged to the same purpose and with the same basic rules for 100 years. It has also generated an unparalleled flood of hard numbers about achievement measured every which way that human cleverness can devise. Most other systems have changed so profoundly that we cannot meaningfully mix the numbers of past and present. How can we compare the antics of Larry Bird with basketball as played before the 24-second rule[1] or, going further back, the center jump after every basket, the two-hand dribble, and finally nine-man teams tossing a lopsided ball into Dr. Naismith's peach basket?[2] Yet while styles of play and dimensions of ball parks have altered substantially, baseball today is the same game that Wee Willie Keeler and Nap Lajoie played in the 1890s. Bill James, our premier guru of baseball stats, writes that "the rules attained essentially their modern form after 1893" (when the pitching mound retreated to its current distance of 60 feet 6

---

[1] According to the rules of modern basketball, once a team has possession of the ball it must attempt a shot within twenty-four seconds.

[2] Canadian James Naismith developed the game of basketball while working at the YMCA in Springfield, MA, in 1891; the first baskets were round fruit baskets with the bottoms cut out.

inches). The numbers of baseball can be compared meaningfully for a century of play.

When we contrast these numbers of past and present, we encounter the well known and curious phenomenon that inspired this article: great players of the past often stand further apart from their teammates. Consider only the principal measures of hitting and pitching: batting average and earned run average. No one has hit .400 since Ted Williams reached .406 nearly half a century ago in 1941; yet eight players exceeded .410 in the 50 years before then. Bob Gibson had an earned run average of 1.12 in 1968. Ten other pitchers have achieved a single season E.R.A. below 1.30, but before Gibson we must go back a full 50 years to Walter Johnson's 1.27 in 1918. Could the myths be true after all? Were the old guys really better? Are we heading towards entropic homogeneity and robotic sameness?

These past achievements are paradoxical because we know perfectly well that all historical trends point to a near assurance that modern athletes must be better than their predecessors. Training has become an industry and obsession, an upscale profession filled with engineers of body and equipment, and a separate branch of medicine for the ills of excess zeal. Few men now make it to the majors just by tossing balls against a barn door during their youth. We live better, eat better, provide more opportunity across all social classes. Moreover, the pool of potential recruits has increased fivefold in 100 years by simple growth of the American population.

Numbers affirm this ineluctable improvement for sports that run against the absolute standard of a clock. The Olympian powers-that-be finally allowed women to run the marathon in 1984. Joan Benoit won it in 2:24:54. In 1896, Spiridon Loues had won in just a minute under three hours; Benoit ran faster than any male Olympic champion until Emil Zatopek's victory at 2:23:03 in 1952. Or consider two of America's greatest swimmers of the 1920s and '30s, men later recruited to play Tarzan (and faring far better than Mark Spitz in his abortive commercial career). Johnny Weissmuller won the 100-meter freestyle in 59.0 in 1924 and 58.6 in 1928. The women's record then stood at 1:12.4 and 1:11.0, but Jane had bested Tarzan by 1972 and the women's record has now been lowered to 54.79. Weissmuller also won the 400-meter freestyle in 5:04.2 in 1924, but Buster Crabbe had cut off more than 15 seconds by 1932 (4:48.4). Female champions in those years swam the distance in 6:02.2 and 5:28.5. The women beat Johnny in 1956, Buster in 1964, and have now (1984) reached 4:07.10, half a minute quicker than Crabbe.

10   Baseball, by comparison, pits batter against pitcher and neither against a constant clock. If everyone improves as the general stature of athletes rises, then why do we note any trends at all in baseball records? Why do the best old-timers stand out above their modern counterparts? Why don't hitting and pitching continue to balance?

The disappearance of .400 hitting becomes even more puzzling when we recognize that *average* batting has remained relatively stable since the beginning of modern baseball in 1876. The chart [below] displays the history of mean batting averages since 1876. (We only included men with an average of at least two at-bats per game since we wish to gauge trends of regular players. Nineteenth-century figures [National League only] include 80 to 100 players for most years [a low of 54 to a high of 147]. The American League began in 1901 and raised the average to 175 players or so during the long reign of two eight-team leagues, and to above 300 for more recent divisional play.) Note the constancy of mean values: the average ballplayer hit about .260 in the 1870s, and he hits about .260 today. Moreover, this stability has been actively promoted by judicious modifications in rules whenever hitting or pitching threatened to gain the upper hand and provoke a runaway trend of batting averages either up or down. Consider all the major fluctuations:

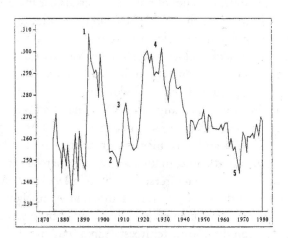

Mean Batting Average By Year

Averages rose after the pitching mound was moved back (1); declined after adoption of the foul-strike rule (2); rose again after the invention of the cork-center ball (3) and during the "lively ball" era (4). The dip in the '60s (5) was corrected in 1969 by lowering the pitching mound and decreasing the strike zone.

After beginning around .260, averages began to drift downwards, reaching the .240s during the late 1880s and early 1890s. Then, during the 1893 season, the pitching mound was moved back to its current 60 feet 6 inches from home plate (it had begun at 45 feet, with pitchers delivering the ball underhand, and had moved steadily back during baseball's early days). The mean soared to its all-time high of .307 in 1894 and remained high (too high, by my argument) until 1901, when adoption of the foul-strike rule promoted a rapid down-turn. (Previously, foul balls hadn't influenced the count.[3]) But averages went down too far during the 1900s until the introduction of the cork-center ball sent them abruptly up in 1911. Pitchers accommodated, and within two years, averages returned to their .260 level—until Babe Ruth wreaked personal havoc upon the game by belting 29 homers in 1919 (more than entire teams had hit many times before). Threatened by the Black Sox scandal, and buoyed by the Babe's performance (and the public's obvious delight in his free-swinging style), the moguls introduced—whether by conscious collusion or simple acquiescence we do not know—the greatest of all changes in 1920. Scrappy one-run, savvy-baserunning, pitcher's baseball was out; big offense and swinging for the fences was in. Averages rose abruptly, and this time they stayed high for a full 20 years, even breaking .300 for the second (and only other) time in 1930. Then in the early 1940s, after war had siphoned off the best players, averages declined again to their traditional .260 level.

The causes behind this 20-year excursion have provoked one of the greatest unresolved debates in baseball history. Conventional wisdom attributes these rises to introduction of a "lively ball." But Bill James, in his masterly *Historical Baseball Abstract*, argues that no major fiddling with baseballs can be proved in 1920. He attributes the rise to coordinated changes in rules (and pervasive alteration of attitudes) that imposed multiple and simultaneous impediments upon pitching, upsetting the traditional balance for a full 20 years. Trick pitches—the spitball, shine ball, and emery ball—were all banned. More important, umpires now supplied shiny new balls any time the slightest scruff or spot appeared. Previously, soft, scratched, and darkened balls remained in play as long as possible (fans were even expected to throw back "souvenir" fouls). The replacement of discolored and scratched with shiny and new, according to James, would be just as effective for improving hitting as any mythical "lively ball." In any case averages

---

[3] Since 1901, a foul ball has counted as a strike (except that a batter cannot go out on a foul).

returned to the .260s by the 1940s and remained quite stable until their marked decline in the mid-1960s. When Carl Yastrzemski won the American League batting title with a paltry .301 in 1968, the time for redress had come again. The moguls lowered the mound, restricted the strike zone, and averages promptly rose again—right back to their time-honored .260 level, where they have remained ever since.

This exegetical detail shows how baseball has been maintained, carefully and consistently, in unchanging balance since its inception. Is it not, then, all the more puzzling that downward trends in best performances go hand in hand with constancy of average achievement? Why, to choose the premier example, has .400 hitting disappeared, and what does this erasure teach us about the nature of trends and the differences between past and present?

15 We can now finally explicate the myth of ancient heroes—or, rather, we can understand its partial truth. Consider the two ingredients of our puzzle and paradox: (1) admitting the profound and general improvement of athletes (as measured in clock sports with absolute standards), star baseball players of the past probably didn't match today's leaders (or, at least, weren't notably better); (2) nonetheless, top baseball performances have declined while averages are actively maintained at a fairly constant level. In short, the old-timers did soar farther above their contemporaries, but must have been worse (or at least no better) than modern leaders. The .400 hitters of old were relatively better, but absolutely worse (or equal).

How can we get a numerical handle on this trend? I've argued several times in various articles for DISCOVER that students of biological evolution (I am one) approach the world with a vision different from time-honored Western perspectives. Our general culture still remains bound to its Platonic heritage of pigeonholes and essences. We divide the world into a set of definite "things" and view variation and subtle shadings as nuisances that block the distinctness of real entities. At best, variation becomes a device for calculating an average value seen as a proper estimate of the true thing itself. But variation *is* the irreducible reality; nature provides nothing else. Averages are often meaningless (mean height of a family with parents and young children). There is no quintessential human being—only black folks, white folks, skinny people, little people, Manute Bol and Eddie Gaedel. Copious and continuous variation is us.

But enough general pontification. The necessary item for this study is practical, not ideological. The tools for resolving the paradox of ancient heroes lie in the direct study of variation, not in exclusive attention to stellar achievements. We've failed to grasp this simple solution because we don't view variation as reality itself, and therefore don't usually study it directly.

I can now state, in a few sentences, my theory about trends in general and .400 hitting in particular (sorry for the long cranking up, and the slow revving down to come, but simple ideas with unconventional contexts require some exposition if they hope to become reader-friendly). Athletes have gotten better (the world in general has become bigger, faster, and more efficient—this may not be a good thing at all; I merely point out that it has happened). We resist this evident trend by taking refuge in the myth of ancient heroes. The myth can be exploded directly for sports with absolute clock standards. In a system with relative standards (person against person)—especially when rules are subtly adjusted to maintain constancy in measures of average performance—this general improvement is masked and cannot be recovered when we follow our usual traditions and interpret figures for average performances as measures of real things. We can, however, grasp the general improvement of systems with relative standards by a direct study of variation—recognizing that variation itself is the irreducible reality. This improvement manifests itself as a *decline in variation*. Paradoxically, this decline produces a decrease in the difference between average and stellar performance. Therefore, modern leaders don't stand so far above their contemporaries. The "myth" of ancient heroes—the greater distance between average and best in the past—actually records the improvement of play through time.

Declining variation is the key to our puzzle. Hitting .400 isn't a thing in itself, but an extreme value in the distribution of batting averages (I shall present the data for this contention below). As variation shrinks around a constant mean batting average, .400 hitting disappears. It is, I think, as simple as that.

Reason One for Declining Variation: *Approach to the outer limits of human capacity.*

Well-off people in developed nations are getting taller and living longer, but the trend won't go on forever. All creatures have outer limits set by evolutionary histories. We're already witnessing the approach to limits in many areas. Maximum life span isn't increasing (although more and more people live long enough to get a crack at the unchanging heights). Racehorses have hardly speeded up, despite enormous efforts of breeders and the unparalleled economic incentive for shaving even a second off top performance (Kentucky Derby winners averaged 2:06.4 during the 1910s and

2:02.0 for the past ten years). Increase in human height has finally begun to level off (daughters of Radcliffe women are now no taller than their mothers). Women's sports records are declining rapidly as opportunity opens up, but some male records are stabilizing.

We can assess all these trends, and the inevitable decline in improvement as we reach the outer limits, because they're measured by absolute clock standards. Baseball players must also be improving, but the relative standard of batting averages, maintained at a mean of about .260, masks the advance. Let's assume that the wall at the right in the top diagram [below] represents the outer limit, and the bell-shaped curve well to its left marks variation in batting prowess 100 years ago. I suspect that all eras boast a few extraordinary individuals, people near the limits of body and endurance, however lower the general average. So, a few players resided near the right wall in 1880—but the average Joe stood far to their left, and variation among all players was great. Since then, everyone has improved. The best may have inched a bit towards the right wall, but average players have moved substantially in that direction. Meanwhile, increasing competition and higher standards have eliminated very weak hitters (once tolerated for their superior fielding and other skills).

The Extinction of .400 Hitting

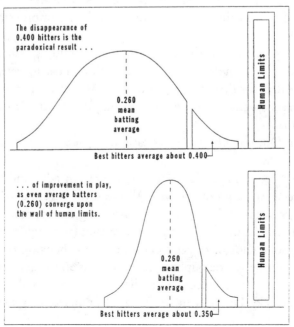

The disappearance of
0.400 hitters is the
paradoxical result . . .

0.260
mean
batting
average

Human Limits

Best hitters average about 0.400

. . . of improvement in play,
as even average batters
(0.260) converge upon
the wall of human limits.

0.260
mean
batting
average

Human Limits

Best hitters average about 0.350

So as average players approach the limiting right wall [previous page, bottom diagram], variation decreases strongly on both flanks—at the high end for simple decline in space between the average and the limit, and at the low end by decreasing tolerance as general play improves. The relative standards of baseball have masked this trend; hitting has greatly improved, but we still measure its average as .260 because pitching has gained in concert. We can, however, assess this improvement in a different way—by inevitable decline in variation as the average converges upon the limiting wall. Modern stars may be an inch or two closer to the wall—they're absolutely better (or at least no worse) than ancient heroes. But the average has moved several feet closer—and the distance between ordinary (kept at .260) and best has decreased. In short, no more .400 hitters. Ironically, the disappearance of .400 hitting is a sign of improvement, not decline.

Reason Two (really the same point stated differently): *Systems equilibrate as they improve.*

Baseball was feeling its way during the early days of major league play. Its rules were our rules, but scores of subtleties hadn't yet been developed or discovered; rough edges careered out in all directions from a stable center. To cite just a few examples (again from Bill James): pitchers began to cover first base in the 1890s; during the same decade, Brooklyn invented the cut-off play, while the Boston Beaneaters developed the hit-and-run and signals from runner to batter. Gloves were a joke in those early days—just a little leather over the hand, not a basket for trapping balls. In 1896 the Phillies actually experimented for 73 games with a lefty shortstop. Traditional wisdom applied. He stank; he had the worst fielding average and the fewest assists in the league among regular shortstops.

In an era of such experiment and indifference, truly great players could take advantage in ways foreclosed ever since. As I wrote in a previous article (*Vanity Fair*, March 1983), Wee Willie Keeler could "hit 'em where they ain't" (and bat .432 in 1897) because fielders didn't yet know where they should be. Consider the predicament of a modern Wade Boggs or a Rod Carew. Every pitch is charted, every hit mapped to the nearest square inch. Fielding and relaying have improved dramatically. Boggs and Keeler probably stood in the same place, just a few inches from the right wall of human limits, but average play has so crept up on Boggs that he lacks the space for taking advantage of suboptimality in others. All these improvements must rob great batters of 10 or 20 hits a year—more than enough to convert our modern best into .400 hitters.

To summarize, variation in batting averages must decrease as improving play eliminates the rough edges that great players could exploit, and as average performance moves towards the limits of human possibility and compresses great players into an ever decreasing space between average play and the unmovable right wall.

In my *Vanity Fair* article, I measured this decline of variation about a constant average on the cheap. I simply took the five highest and five lowest averages for regular players in each year and compared them with the league average. I found that differences between both average and highest and between average and lowest have decreased steadily through the years (*see chart, page 377*). The disappearance of .400 hitting—the most discussed and disputed trend in the history of baseball—isn't a reflection of generally higher averages in the past (for no one hit over .400 during the second decade of exalted averages, from 1931 to 1940, and most .400 hitting in our century occurred between 1900 and 1920, when averages stood at their canonical [and current] .260 level). Nor can this eclipse of high hitting be entirely attributed to the panoply of conventional explanations that view .400 averages as a former "thing" now extinct—more grueling schedules, too many night games, better fielding, invention of the slider and relief pitching. For .400 hitting isn't a thing to be extirpated, but an extreme value in a distribution of variation for batting averages. The reasons for declining variation, as presented above, are different from the causes for disappearance of an entity. Declining variation is a general property of systems that stabilize and improve while maintaining constant rules of performance through time. The extinction of .400 hitting is, paradoxically, a mark of increasingly *better* play.

We have now calculated the decline of variation properly, and at vastly more labor (with thanks to my research assistant Ned Young for weeks of work, and to Ed Purcell, Nobel laureate and one of the world's great physicists—but also just a fan with good ideas). The standard deviation is a statistician's basic measure of variation. To compute the standard deviation, you take (in this case) each individual batting average and subtract from it the league average for that year. You then square each value (multiply it by itself) in order to eliminate negative numbers for batting averages below the mean (a negative times a negative gives a positive number). You then add up all these values and divide them by the total number of players—giving an average squared deviation of individual players from the mean. Finally, you take the square root of this number to obtain the average, or standard, deviation itself. The higher the value, the more extensive, or spread out, the variation.

30   We calculated the standard deviation of batting averages for each year (an improvement from my former high and low five, but much more work). The chart on page 377 plots the trend of standard deviations in batting averages year by year. Our hypothesis is clearly confirmed. Standard deviations have been dropping steadily and irreversibly. The decline itself has decelerated over the years as baseball stabilizes—rapidly during the nineteenth century, more slowly through the twentieth, and reaching a stable plateau by about 1940.

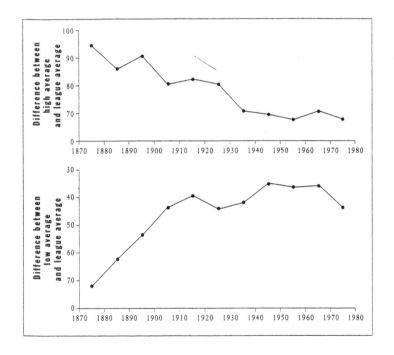

THE DECLINE IN EXTREMES
Batting averages are neither as high nor as low as they used to be.

If I may make a personal and subjective comment. I was stunned and delighted (beyond all measure) by the elegance and clarity of this result. I pretty well knew what the general pattern would be because standard deviations are so strongly influenced by extreme values (a consequence of squaring each individual deviation in the calculation)—so my original cheap method of five highest and lowest produced a fair estimate. But I never dreamed that the decline would be so regular, so devoid of exception or anomaly for even a single year—so unvarying that we could even pick out such subtleties as the deceleration in decline. I've spent my entire professional career studying such statistical distributions, and I know how rarely one obtains such clean results in better behaved data of controlled experiments or natural growth in simple systems. We usually encounter some glitch, some anomaly, some funny years. But the decline of standard deviation for batting averages is so regular that it looks like a plot for a law of nature. I find this all the more remarkable because the graph of averages themselves through time (*page 379*) shows all the noise and fluctuation expected in natural systems. Yet mean batting averages have been constantly manipulated by the moguls of baseball to maintain a general constancy, while no one has tried to monkey with the standard deviation. Thus, while mean batting averages have gone up and down to follow the whims of history and the vagaries of invention, the standard deviation has marched steadily down at a decreasing pace, apparently perturbed by nothing of note. I regard this regularity of decline as further evidence that decreasing variation through time is the primary predictable feature of stabilizing systems.

The details are impressive in their regularity. All four beginning years of the 1870s sport high values of standard deviation greater then 0.050, while the last reading in excess of 0.050 occurs in 1886. Values between 0.04 and 0.05 mark the rest of the nineteenth century, with three years just below, at 0.038 to 0.040. The last reading in excess of 0.040 occurs in 1911. Subsequently, decline within the 0.03 and 0.04 range shows the same precision of detail by even decrease with years. The last reading as high as 0.037 occurs in 1937, and of 0.035 in 1941. Only two years have exceeded 0.034 since 1957. Between 1942 and 1980, values remained entirely within the restricted range of 0.0285 to 0.0348. I'd thought that at least one unusual year would upset the pattern—that one nineteenth-century value would achieve late twentieth-century lows, or one more recent year soar to ancient highs—but we find no such thing. All measures from 1906 back to the beginning are higher than every reading from 1938 to 1980. We find no overlap at all. This—take it from an old trooper—is regularity with a vengeance. Something general is going on here, and I think I know what.

The decadal averages are listed on page 379, and show continuous decline before stabilization in the 1940s. (A note for statistically minded readers: standard deviations are expressed in their own units of measurement—mouse tails in millimeters, mountains in megatons. Thus, as mean values rise and fall, standard deviations may go up and down to track the mean rather than record exclusively the amount of spread. This poses no problem for most of our chart, because averages have been so stable through time at about .260. But the 20-point rise in averages during the 1920s and 1930s might entail artificially elevated standard deviations. We can correct for this effect by computing the coefficient of variation—100 times the standard deviation divided by the mean—for each year. Also listed are decadal averages for coefficients of variation—and we now see that apparent stabilization between the 1910s and 1920s was masking a continuing decline in coefficient of variation, as the 1920s rise in averages canceled out decline in variation when measured by the standard deviation.)

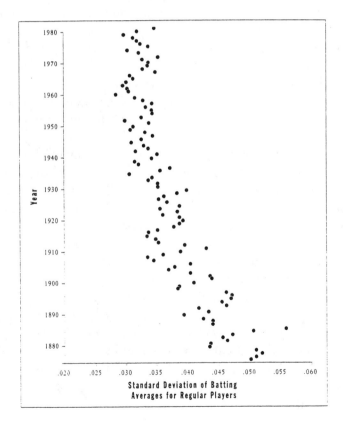

If my editors were more indulgent, I could wax at distressing length about more details and different measures. Just one final hint of more interesting pattern revealed by finer dissection: the chart above amalgamates the two leagues, but their trends are somewhat different. In the National League, variation declined during the nineteenth century, but stabilized early in the twentieth. In the American League, founded in 1901, variation dropped steadily right through the 1940s. Thus, each league followed the same pattern—time of origin setting pattern of decline for decades to come. Can we use existence or stabilization of declining variation as a mark of maturity? Did the leagues differ fundamentally during the early years of our century—the National already mature, the American still facing a few decades of honing and trimming the edges?

35 No one has invested more time and energy in the study of numbers than baseball aficionados. We have measures and indices for everything imaginable—from simple lists of at-bats to number of times a black shortstop under six feet tall has been caught stealing third on pitchouts by righties to left-handed catchers. Yet I don't think that this most basic pattern in the standard deviation of batting averages has been properly noted, or its significance assessed. As I argued above, the biases of our upbringing force a focus on averages treated as things, and virtually preclude proper attention to variation considered as irreducible reality. The standard deviation is our base-level tool for studying variation—as fundamental as milk for babies and cockroaches for New York apartments. Yet, after decades of loving attention to minutiae of averages, we can still gain insights from an unexplored pattern in the very simplest kiddie measure of variation. What better illustration for my claim that our culture undervalues variation at its peril?

After this detail, I've earned the right to end with a bit of philosophical musing, ostensibly in the great decline-of-civilization tradition, but really a sneaky bit of optimism from the depth of my sanguine soul.

The message of this study in variation might seem glum, almost cosmically depressing in its paradox—that general improvement clips the wings of true greatness. No one soars above the commonplace any more. General advance brings declining variation in its wake; heroes are extinct. The small population of Europe yielded both a Bach and a Mozart in just 100 years; where shall we find such transcendent geniuses to guide (or at least enlighten) our uncertain and perilous present?

I wish to propose, in closing, a more general framework for understanding trends in time as an interaction between the location of bell-shaped curves in variation and the position (and potential for mobility) of the limiting right wall for human excellence. This theme transcends sports (or any particular example), and our model should include mind work as well as body work. I suggest three rough categories, with a fundamental example for each, ranging from high to low potential for future accomplishment.

Consider science as a system of knowledge. In most areas, our ignorance is abysmal compared with our sense of what we might learn and know. The curve of knowledge, in other words, stands far from the right wall. Moreover, the wall itself (or at least our perception of it) seems flexible before the growth of knowledge, as new theories suggest pathways to insight never considered previously. Science seems progressive since current ignorance provides so much space to its right, and since the wall itself can be pushed back by the very process that signals our approach. Still, one cannot avoid—with that special sadness reserved for recognizing a wonderful thing gone forever—the conviction that certain seminal discoveries established truths so central and so broad in import that we cannot hope to win insight in such great gulps again, for the right wall moves slowly and with limits, and we may never again open up space for jumps so big. Plate tectonics has revolutionized geology, but we cannot match the thrill of those who discovered that time comes in billions, not thousands—for deep time, once discovered, set the root of a profession forever. These are exciting days for biology, but no one will taste the intellectual power of a man alone at Downe—Charles Darwin reformulating all nature with the passkey of evolution.

40   I would place most sports, as well as musical performance, in a second category, where the best have long stood near an inflexible right wall. When we remove impediments imposed by custom (women's sports) or technology (certain musical instruments), improvement may be rapid. But progress comes in inches or milliseconds for goals long sought and unimpeded (I doubt that Stern plays notably better than Paganini, Horowitz than Liszt, E. Power Biggs than Bach—and neither horse nor human male is shaving much off the mile run these days). The small contribution of this article lies in this second domain—in showing that decline in variation will measure improvement when relative standards mask progress measured against such absolute criteria as clocks.

Lest we lament this second category for its limited licenses in improvement, consider the painful plight of a third domain where success in striving depletes the system itself. The right wall of our first domain was far away and somewhat flexible, near and rigid (but still stable) in our second. In this third domain, success hits the wall and consumes it—as if the mile run had disappeared as a competitive sport as soon as 100 people ran the distance in less than four minutes. Given an ethic that exalts perennial originality in artistic composition, the history of music (and many other arts) may fall into this domain. One composer may exploit a basic style for much of a career, but successors may not follow this style in much detail, or for very long. Such striving for newness may grant us joy forever if a limitless array of potential styles awaits discovery and exploitation. But perhaps the world is not so bounteous; perhaps we've already explored most of what even a highly sophisticated audience can deem accessible. Perhaps the wall of an intelligible vanguard has been largely consumed. Perhaps there is a simple solution to the paradox of why we now generate no Bach or Mozart in a world far larger, with musical training provided for millions more. Perhaps they reside among us, but we've consumed all styles of expression so deeply tuned to the human soul. If so, I might timidly advance a truly reactionary proposal. The death of Mozart at 35 may have been the deepest tragedy of our cultural history (great scientists have died even younger, but their work can be done by others). We perform his handful of operas over and over again. We might be enjoying a dozen more—some counted as the most sublime of all musical works—if he had survived even to 50. Suppose a composer now lived who could master his style and write every bit as well. The ethic of originality forbids it absolutely, but would the integrity of art collapse forever if this person wrote just a few more great pieces in that genre? Not a hundred, just three or four to supplement *Don Giovanni* and *Die Zauberflöte*. Would this not be esteemed a public service beyond all others?

Enough. I'm waxing lugubrious, despite promises to the contrary. For while I may yearn to hear Beethoven's tenth symphony, I don't lament a lost past or decry a soft present. In sports, and art, and science (how I wish it were so in politics as well), we live in the best world we've ever known, though not in the best of all possible worlds. So be it that improvement must bury in its wake the myth of ancient heroes. We've exposed the extinction of .400 hitting as a sign of progress, not degradation—the paradoxical effect of declining variation as play improves and stabilizes, and as average contestants also approach the right wall of human limits.

Do not lament the loss of literally outstanding performance (largely a figment, in any case, of failings among the ordinary, not a mark of greater prowess among the best). Celebrate instead the immense improvement of average play. (I rather suspect that we would regard most operatic performances of 1850, and most baseball games of 1900, as sloppy and amateurish—not to mention the village squabbles that enter history as epic battles). Do not lament our past ease in distinguishing the truly great. Celebrate instead the general excellence that makes professional sport so exciting today. And appreciate the need for subtlety and discernment that modern fans must develop to make proper assessments: we must all now be connoisseurs to appreciate our favorite games fully. Above all, remember that the possibility for transcendence never dies. We live for that moment, the truly unpredictable performance that shatters all expectation. We delight all the more in Dwight Gooden and Larry Bird because they stand out among a panoply of true stars. Besides, I really wrote this article only because I have a hunch that I want to share (and we professor types need to set context before we go out on a limb): Wade Boggs is gonna hit .400 this year.[51]

(1986)

QUESTIONS:

1. In Gould's view, what *is* .400 hitting? Why is it important not to think of .400 hitting as an independent phenomenon in his view?

2. What effect does the introduction of gender have (paragraph 9)? Why is baseball a better context to explore issues of this sort than would be, say, basketball? Write a brief essay in which you use examples from either sports or other cultural activities (such as film or drama) to illustrate a much more general point.

3. Summarize in your own words in no more than two or three paragraphs Gould's argument as to why "no one hits .400 anymore."

4. Summarize in your own words Gould's argument about improvement (paragraph 27). Do you agree that this extension of his argument follows logically from the points he has already established?

5. Comment on Gould's diction. Why do you think he occasionally uses "big words" in an essay that is clearly aimed at the general reader as well as at an academic audience?

---

[51] Wade Boggs hit .356 in 1986. The closest that a modern hitter has come to hitting .400 was Tony Gwynn of the San Diego Padres hitting .394 in the strike-shortened season of 1994.

Ngugi wa Thiong'o

from Decolonising the Mind

In this essay one of Africa's most distinguished novelists discusses some of the connections between language and culture.

～

III

I was born into a large peasant family: father, four wives and about twenty-eight children. I also belonged, as we all did in those days, to a wider extended family and to the community as a whole.

We spoke Gĩkũyũ as we worked in the fields. We spoke Gĩkũyũ in and outside the home. I can vividly recall those evenings of storytelling around the fireside. It was mostly the grown-ups telling the children but everybody was interested and involved. We children would re-tell the stories the following day to other children who worked in the fields picking the pyrethrum flowers, tea-leaves or coffee beans of our European and African landlords.

The stories, with mostly animals as the main characters, were all told in Gĩkũyũ. Hare, being small, weak but full of innovative wit and cunning, was our hero. We identified with him as he struggled against the brutes of prey like lion, leopard, hyena. His victories were our victories and we learnt that the apparently weak can outwit the strong. We followed the animals in their struggle against hostile nature—drought, rain, sun, wind—a confrontation often forcing them to search for forms of co-operation. But we were also interested in their struggles amongst themselves, and particularly between the beasts and the victims of prey. These twin struggles, against nature and other animals, reflected real-life struggles in the human world.

Not that we neglected stories with human beings as the main characters. There were two types of characters in such human-centred narratives: the species of truly human beings with qualities of courage, kindness, mercy, hatred of evil, concern for others; and a man-eat-man two-mouthed species with qualities of greed, selfishness, individualism and hatred of what was good for the larger co-operative community. Co-operation as the ultimate good in a community was a constant theme. It could unite human beings with animals against ogres and beasts of prey, as in the story of how dove, after being fed with castor-oil seeds, was sent to fetch a smith working far away from home and whose pregnant wife was being threatened by these man-eating two-mouthed ogres.

5   There were good and bad story-tellers. A good one could tell the same story over and over again, and it would always be fresh to us, the listeners. He or she could tell a story told by someone else and make it more alive and dramatic. The differences really were in the use of words and images and the inflexion of voices to effect different tones.

We therefore learnt to value words for their meaning and nuances. Language was not a mere string of words. It had a suggestive power well beyond the immediate and lexical meaning. Our appreciation of the suggestive magical power of language was reinforced by the games we played with words through riddles, proverbs, transpositions of syllables, or through nonsensical but musically arranged words. So we learnt the music of our language on top of the content. The language, through images and symbols, gave us a view of the world, but it had a beauty of its own. The home and the field were then our pre-primary school but what is important, for this discussion, is that the language of our evening teach-ins, and the language of our immediate and wider community, and the language of our work in the fields were one.

And then I went to school, a colonial school, and this harmony was broken. The language of my education was no longer the language of my culture. I first went to Kamaandura, missionary run, and then to another called Maanguuū run by nationalists grouped around the Gīkūyū Independent and Karinga Schools Association. Our language of education was still Gīkūyū. The very first time I was ever given an ovation for my writing was over a composition in Gīkūyū. So for my first four years there was still harmony between the language of my formal education and that of the Limuru peasant community.

It was after the declaration of a state of emergency over Kenya in 1952 that all the schools run by patriotic nationalists were taken over by the colonial regime and were placed under District Education Boards chaired by Englishmen. English became the language of my formal education. In

Kenya, English became more than a language: it was *the* language, and all the others had to bow before it in deference.

Thus one of the most humiliating experiences was to be caught speaking Gĩkũyũ in the vicinity of the school. The culprit was given corporal punishment—three to five strokes of the cane on bare buttocks—or was made to carry a metal plate around the neck with inscriptions such as I AM STUPID or I AM A DONKEY. Sometimes the culprits were fined money they could hardly afford. And how did the teachers catch the culprits? A button was initially given to one pupil who was supposed to hand it over to whoever was caught speaking his mother tongue. Whoever had the button at the end of the day would sing who had given it to him and the ensuing process would bring out all the culprits of the day. Thus children were turned into witch-hunters and in the process were being taught the lucrative value of being a traitor to one's immediate community.

10 The attitude to English was the exact opposite: any achievement in spoken or written English was highly rewarded; prizes, prestige, applause; the ticket to higher realms. English became the measure of intelligence and ability in the arts, the sciences, and all the other branches of learning. English became *the* main determinant of a child's progress up the ladder of formal education.

As you may know, the colonial system of education in addition to its apartheid racial demarcation had the structure of a pyramid: a broad primary base, a narrowing secondary middle, and an even narrower university apex. Selections from primary into secondary were through an examination, in my time called Kenya African Preliminary Examination, in which one had to pass six subjects ranging from Maths to Nature Study and Kiswahili. All the papers were written in English. Nobody could pass the exam who failed the English language paper no matter how brilliantly he had done in the other subjects. I remember one boy in my class of 1954 who had distinctions in all subjects except English, which he had failed. He was made to fail the entire exam. He went on to become a turn boy in a bus company. I who had only passes but a credit in English got a place at the Alliance High School, one of the most elitist institutions for Africans in colonial Kenya. The requirements for a place at the University, Makerere University College, were broadly the same: nobody could go on to wear the undergraduate red gown, no matter how brilliantly they had performed in all the other subjects unless they had a credit—not even a simple pass!—in English. Thus the most coveted place in the pyramid and in the system was only available to the holder of an

English language credit card. English was the official vehicle and the magic formula to colonial elitedom.

Literary education was now determined by the dominant language while also reinforcing that dominance. Orature (oral literature) in Kenyan languages stopped. In primary school I now read simplified Dickens and Stevenson alongside Rider Haggard. Jim Hawkins, Oliver Twist, Tom Brown—not Hare, Leopard and Lion—were now my daily companions in the world of imagination. In secondary school, Scott and G.B. Shaw vied with more Rider Haggard, John Buchan, Alan Paton, Captain W.E. Johns. At Makerere I read English: from Chaucer to T.S. Eliot with a touch of Grahame Greene.

Thus language and literature were taking us further and further from ourselves to other selves, from our world to other worlds.

What was the colonial system doing to us Kenyan children? What were the consequences of, on the one hand, this systematic suppression of our languages and the literature they carried, and on the other the elevation of English and the literature it carried? To answer those questions, let me first examine the relationship of language to human experience, human culture, and the human perception of reality.

IV

15   Language, any language, has a dual character: it is both a means of communication and a carrier of culture. Take English. It is spoken in Britain and in Sweden and Denmark. But for Swedish and Danish people English is only a means of communication with non-Scandinavians. It is not a carrier of their culture. For the British, and particularly the English, it is additionally, and inseparably from its use as a tool of communication, a carrier of their culture and history. Or take Swahili in East and Central Africa. It is widely used as a means of communication across many nationalities. But it is not the carrier of a culture and history of many of those nationalities. However in parts of Kenya and Tanzania, and particularly in Zanzibar, Swahili is inseparably both a means of communication and a carrier of the culture of those people to whom it is a mother-tongue.

Language as communication has three aspects or elements. There is first what Karl Marx once called the language of real life, the element basic to the whole notion of language, its origins and development: that is, the relations people enter into with one another in the labour process, the links they necessarily establish among themselves in the act of a people, a community of human beings, producing wealth or means of life like food, clothing, houses. A human community really starts its historical being as a community of co-operation in production through the division of labour; the simplest is between man, woman and child within a household; the more complex divisions are between branches of production such as those who are sole hunters, sole gatherers of fruits or sole workers in metal. Then there are the most complex divisions such as those in modern factories where a single product, say a shirt or a shoe, is the result of many hands and minds. Production is co-operation, is communication, is language, is expression of a relation between human beings and it is specifically human.

The second aspect of language as communication is speech and it imitates the language of real life, that is communication in production. The verbal signposts both reflect and aid communication or the relation established between human beings in the production of their means of life. Language as a system of verbal signposts makes that production possible. The spoken word is to relations between human beings what the hand is to the relations between human beings and nature. The hand through tools mediates between human beings and nature and forms the language of real life: spoken words mediate between human beings and form the language of speech.

The third aspect is the written signs. The written word imitates the spoken. Where the first two aspects of language as communication through the hand and the spoken word historically evolved more or less simultaneously, the written aspect is a much later historical development. Writing is representation of sounds with visual symbols, from the simplest knot among shepherds to tell the number in a herd or the hieroglyphics among the Agĩkũyũ gicaandi singers and poets of Kenya, to the most complicated and different letter and picture writing systems of the world today.

In most societies the written and the spoken languages are the same, in that they represent each other: what is on paper can be read to another person and be received as that language, which the recipient has grown up speaking. In such a society there is broad harmony for a child between the three aspects of language as communication. His interaction with nature and with other men is expressed in written and spoken symbols or signs which are both a result of that double interaction and a reflection of it. The association of the child's sensibility is with the language of his experience of life.

But there is more to it: communication between human beings is also the basis and process of evolving culture. In doing similar kinds of things and actions over and over again under similar circumstances, similar even in their mutability, certain patterns, moves, rhythms, habits, attitudes, experiences and knowledge emerge. Those experiences are handed over to the next generation and become the inherited basis for their further actions on nature and on themselves. There is a gradual accumulation of values which in time become almost self-evident truths governing their conception of what is right and wrong, good and bad, beautiful and ugly, courageous and cowardly, generous and mean in their internal and external relations. Over a time this becomes a way of life distinguishable from other ways of life. They develop a distinctive culture and history. Culture embodies those moral, ethical and aesthetic values, the set of spiritual eyeglasses, through which they come to view themselves and their place in the universe. Values are the basis of a people's identity, their sense of particularity as members of the human race. All this is carried by language. Language as culture is the collective memory bank of a people's experience in history. Culture is almost indistinguishable from the language that makes possible its genesis, growth, banking, articulation and indeed its transmission from one generation to the next.

Language as culture also has three important aspects. Culture is a product of the history which it in turn reflects. Culture in other words is a product and a reflection of human beings communicating with one another in the very struggle to create wealth and to control it. But culture does not merely reflect that history, or rather it does so by actually forming images or pictures of the world of nature and nurture. Thus the second aspect of language as culture is as an image-forming agent in the mind of a child. Our whole conception of ourselves as a people, individually and collectively, is based on those pictures and images which may or may not correctly correspond to the actual reality of the struggles with nature and nurture which produced them in the first place. But our capacity to confront the world creatively is dependent on how those images correspond or not to that reality, how they distort or clarify the reality of our struggles. Language as culture is thus mediating between me and my own self; between my own self and other selves; between me and nature. Language is mediating in my very being. And this brings us to the third aspect of language as culture. Culture transmits or imparts those images of the world and reality through the spoken and the written language, that is through a specific language. In other words, the capacity to speak, the capacity to order sounds in a manner that makes for mutual comprehension between human beings is universal. This is the universality of language, a quality specific to human beings. It corresponds to the universality of the struggle against nature and that between human beings. But the particularity of the sounds, the words, the word order into phrases and sentences, and the specific manner, or laws, of their ordering is what distinguishes one language from another. Thus a specific culture is not transmitted through language in its universality but in its particularity as the language of a specific community with a specific history. Written literature and orature are the main means by which a particular language transmits the images of the world contained in the culture it carries.

Language as communication and as culture are then products of each other. Communication creates culture: culture is a means of communication. Language carries culture, and culture carries, particularly through orature and literature, the entire body of values by which we come to perceive ourselves and our place in the world. How people perceive themselves affects how they look at their culture, at their politics and at the social production of wealth, at their entire relationship to nature and to other beings. Language is thus inseparable from ourselves as a community of human beings with a specific form and character, a specific history, a specific relationship to the world.

V

So what was the colonialist imposition of a foreign language doing to us children?

The real aim of colonialism was to control the people's wealth: what they produced, how they produced it, and how it was distributed; to control, in other words, the entire realm of the language of real life. Colonialism imposed its control of the social production of wealth through military conquest and subsequent political dictatorship. But its most important area of domination was the mental universe of the colonised, the control, through culture, of how people perceived themselves and their relationship to the world. Economic and political control can never be complete or effective without mental control. To control a people's culture is to control their tools of self-definition in relationship to others.

For colonialism this involved two aspects of the same process: the destruction or the deliberate undervaluing of a people's culture, their art, dances, religions, history, geography, education, orature and literature, and the conscious elevation of the language of the coloniser. The domination of a people's language by the languages of the colonising nations was crucial to the domination of the mental universe of the colonised.

Take language as communication. Imposing a foreign language, and suppressing the native languages as spoken and written, were already breaking the harmony previously existing between the African child and the three aspects of language. Since the new language as a means of communication was a product of and was reflecting the "real language of life" elsewhere, it could never as spoken or written properly reflect or imitate the real life of that community. This may in part explain why technology always appears to us as slightly external, *their* product and not *ours*. The word "missile" used to hold an alien far-away sound until I recently learnt its equivalent in Gĩkũyũ, *ngurukuhĩ* and it made me apprehend it differently. Learning, for a colonial child, became a cerebral activity and not an emotionally felt experience.

But since the new, imposed languages could never completely break the native languages as spoken, their most effective area of domination was the third aspect of language as communication, the written. The language of an African child's formal education was foreign. The language of the books he read was foreign. The language of his conceptualisation was foreign. Thought, in him, took the visible form of a foreign language. So the written language of a child's upbringing in the school (even his spoken language within the school compound) became divorced from his spoken language at home. There was often not the slightest relationship between the child's written world, which was also the language of his schooling, and the world of his immediate environment in the family and the community. For a colonial child, the harmony existing between the three aspects of language as communication was irrevocably broken. This resulted in the disassociation of the sensibility of that child from his natural and social environment, what we might call colonial alienation. The alienation became reinforced in the teaching of history, geography, music, where bourgeois Europe was always the centre of the universe.

This disassociation, divorce, or alienation from the immediate environment becomes clearer when you look at colonial language as a carrier of culture.

Since culture is a product of the history of a people which it in turn reflects, the child was now being exposed exclusively to a culture that was a product of a world external to himself. He was being made to stand outside himself to look at himself. *Catching Them Young* is the title of a book on racism, class, sex, and politics in children's literature by Bob Dixon. "Catching them young" as an aim was even more true of a colonial child. The images of his world and his place in it implanted in a child take years to eradicate, if they ever can be.

30   Since culture does not just reflect the world in images but actually, through those images, conditions a child to see that world a certain way, the colonial child was made to see the world and where he stands in it as seen and defined by or reflected in the culture of the language of imposition.

And since those images are mostly passed on through orature and literature it meant the child would now only see the world as seen in the literature of his language of adoption. From the point of view of alienation, that is of seeing oneself from outside oneself as if one was another self, it does not matter that the imported literature carried the great humanist tradition of the best Shakespeare, Goethe, Balzac, Tolstoy, Gorky, Brecht, Sholokhov, Dickens. The location of this great mirror of imagination was necessarily Europe and its history and culture and the rest of the universe was seen from that centre.

But obviously it was worse when the colonial child was exposed to images of his world as mirrored in the written languages of his coloniser. Where his own native languages were associated in his impressionable mind with low status, humiliation, corporal punishment, slow-footed intelligence and ability or downright stupidity, non-intelligibility and barbarism, this was reinforced by the world he met in the works of such geniuses of racism as a Rider Haggard or a Nicholas Monsarrat; not to mention the pronouncement of some of the giants of western intellectual and political establishment, such as Hume ("...The negro is naturally inferior to the whites..."), Thomas Jefferson ("...The blacks...are inferior to the whites on the endowments of both body and mind..."), or Hegel with his Africa comparable to a land of childhood still enveloped in the dark mantle of the night as far as the development of self-conscious history was concerned. Hegel's statement that there was nothing harmonious with humanity to be found in the African character is representative of the racist images of Africans and Africa such a colonial child was bound to encounter in the literature of the colonial languages. The results could be disastrous.

(1986)

QUESTIONS:

1. How do you feel the opening sentence affects the average Western reader? Why would Ngugi choose to write this, and to place it in such a prominent location in his essay?

2. What is the rhetorical purpose of paragraph 14? Is it effective?

3. In paragraph 15, Ngugi argues that a language has a communication function for all people who speak that language, but that it also serves as a carrier of culture for all those for whom that language is the mother-tongue. If you speak two or more languages, does this assertion meet with your own experience?

4. Discuss how the imposition of a foreign language breaks "the harmony previously existing between the African child and the three aspects of language" (paragraph 26).

5. Toward the end of his essay, Ngugi makes reference to the European-based writers of literature he was forced to study as a child, and how these stories did not match his own experiences. How do the poems, essays, plays and novels you are being asked to read in this course reflect your experiences? If you were the instructor of this course, how would you go about selecting a reading list?

ANNIE DILLARD

TERWILLIGER BUNTS ONE

This anecdotal piece by one of America's leading essayists focuses primarily on recollections of the writer's mother.

~~

One Sunday afternoon Mother wandered through our kitchen, where Father was making a sandwich and listening to the ball game. The Pirates were playing the New York Giants at Forbes Field. In those days, the Giants had a utility infielder named Wayne Terwilliger. Just as Mother passed through, the radio announcer cried—with undue drama—"Terwilliger bunts one!"

"Terwilliger bunts one?" Mother cried back, stopped short. She turned. "Is that English?"

"The player's name is Terwilliger," Father said. "He bunted."

"That's marvelous," Mather said. " 'Terwilliger bunts one.' No wonder you listen to baseball. 'Terwilliger bunts one.' "

For the next seven or eight years, Mother made this surprising string of syllables her own. Testing a microphone, she repeated, "Terwilliger bunts one"; testing a pen or a typewriter, she wrote it. If, as happened surprisingly often in the course of various improvised gags, she pretended to whisper something else in my ear, she actually whispered, "Terwilliger bunts one." Whenever someone used a French phrase, or a Latin one, she answered solemnly, "Terwilliger bunts one." If Mother had had, like Andrew Carnegie, the opportunity to cook up a motto for a coat of arms, hers would have read simply and tellingly, "Terwilliger bunts one." (Carnegie's was "Death to Privilege.")

She served us with other words and phrases. On a Florida trip, she repeated tremulously, "That...is a royal poinciana." I don't remember the tree; I remember the thrill in her voice. She pronounced it carefully, and spelled it. She also liked to say "portulaca."

The drama of the words "Tamiami Trail" stirred her, we learned on the same Florida trip. People built Tampa on one coast, and they built Miami on another. Then—the height of visionary ambition and folly—they piled a slow, tremendous road through the terrible Everglades to connect them. To build the road, men stood sunk in muck to their armpits. They fought off cottonmouth moccasins and six-foot alligators. They slept in boats, wet. They blasted muck with dynamite, cut jungle with machetes; they laid logs, dragged drilling machines, hauled dredges, heaped limestone. The road took fourteen years to build up by the shovelful, a Panama Canal in reverse, and cost hundreds of lives from tropical, mosquito-carried diseases. Then, capping it all, some genius thought of the word Tamiami: they called the road from Tampa to Miami, this very road under our spinning wheels, the Tamiami Trail. Some called it Alligator Alley. Anyone could drive over this road without a thought.

Hearing this, moved, I thought all the suffering of road building was worth it (it wasn't my suffering), now that we had this new thing to hang these new words on—Alligator Alley for those who liked things cute, and, for connoisseurs like Mother, for lovers of the human drama in all its boldness and terror, the Tamiami Trail.

Back home, Mother cut clips from reels of talk, as it were, and played them back at leisure. She noticed that many Pittsburghers confuse "leave" and "let." One kind relative brightened our morning by mentioning why she'd brought her son to visit: "He wanted to come with me, so I left him." Mother filled in Amy and me on locutions we missed. "I can't do it on Friday," her pretty sister told a crowded dinner party, "because Friday's the day I lay in the stores."

10 (All unconsciously, though, we ourselves used some pure Pittsburghisms. We said "tele pole," pronounced "telly pole," for that splintery sidewalk post I loved to climb. We said "slippy"—the sidewalks are "slippy." We said, "That's all the farther I could go." And we said, as Pittsburghers do say, "This glass needs washed," or "The dog needs walked"—a usage our father eschewed; he knew it was not standard English, nor even comprehensible English, but he never let on.)

"Spell 'poinsettia,'" Mother would throw out at me, smiling with pleasure. "Spell 'sherbet.' " The idea was not to make us whizzes, but, quite the contrary, to remind us—and I, especially, needed reminding—that we didn't know it all just yet.

"There's a deer standing in the front hall," she told me one quiet evening in the country.

"Really?"

"No, I just wanted to tell you something once without your saying, 'I know.' "

15 Supermarkets in the middle 1950s began luring, or bothering, customers by giving out Top Value Stamps or Green Stamps. Where, shopping with Mother, we got to the head of the checkout line, the checker, always a young man, asked, "Save stamps?"

"No," Mother replied genially, week after week, "I build model airplanes." I believe she originated this line. It took me years to determine where the joke lay.

Anyone who met her verbal challenges she adored. She had surgery on one of her eyes. On the operating table, just before she conked out, she appealed feelingly to the surgeon, saying, as she had been planning to say for weeks, "Will I be able to play the piano?" "Not on me," the surgeon said. "You won't pull that old one on me."

It was, indeed, an old one. The surgeon was supposed to answer, "Yes, my dear, brave woman, you will be able to play the piano after this operation," to which Mother intended to reply, "Oh, good, I've always wanted to play the piano." This pat scenario bored her; she loved having it interrupted. It must have galled her that usually her acquaintances were so predictably unalert; it must have galled her that, for the length of her life, she could surprise everyone so continually, so easily, when she had been the same all along. At any rate, she loved anyone who, as she put it, saw it coming, and called her on it.

She regarded the instructions on bureaucratic forms as straight lines. "Do you advocate the overthrow of the United States government by force or violence?" After some thought she wrote, "Force." She regarded children, even babies, as straight men. When Molly learned to crawl, Mother delighted in buying her gowns with drawstrings at the bottom, like Swee'-pea's, because, as she explained energetically, you could easily step on the drawstring without the baby's noticing, so that she crawled and crawled and crawled and never got anywhere except into a small ball at the gown's top.

20 When we children were young, she mothered us tenderly and dependably; as we got older, she resumed her career of anarchism. She collared us into her gags. If she answered the phone on a wrong number, she told the

caller, "Just a minute," and dragged the receiver to Amy or me, saying, "Here, take this, your name is Cecile," or, worse, just, "It's for you." You had to think on your feet. But did you want to perform well as Cecile, or did you want to take pity on the wretched caller?

During a family trip to the Highland Park Zoo, Mother and I were alone for a minute. She approached a young couple holding hands on a bench by the seals, and addressed the young man in dripping tones: "Where have you been? Still got those baby blue eyes; always did slay me. And this"—a swift nod at the dumbstruck young woman, who had removed her hand from the man's—"must be the one you were telling me about. She's not so bad, really, as you used to make out. But listen, you know how I miss you, you know where to reach me, same old place. And there's Ann over there—see how she's grown? See the blue eyes?"

And off she sashayed, taking me firmly by the hand, and leading us around briskly past the monkey house and away. She cocked an ear back, and both of us heard the desperate man begin, in a high-pitched wail, "I swear, I never saw her before in my life..."

On a long, sloping beach by the ocean, she lay stretched out sunning with Father and friends, until the conversation gradually grew tedious, when without forethought she gave a little push with her heel and rolled away. People were stunned. She rolled deadpan and apparently effortlessly, arms and legs extended and tidy, down the beach to the distant water's edge, where she lay at ease just as she had been, but half in the surf, and well out of earshot.

She dearly loved to fluster people by throwing out a game's rules at whim—when she was getting bored, losing in a dull sort of way, and when everybody else was taking it too seriously. If you turned your back, she moved the checkers around on the board. When you got them all straightened out, she denied she'd touched them; the next time you turned your back, she lined them up on the rug or hid them under your chair. In a betting rummy game called Michigan, she routinely played out of turn, or called out a card she didn't hold, or counted backward, simply to amuse herself by causing an uproar and watching the rest of us do double takes and have fits. (Much later, when serious suitors came to call, Mother subjected them to this fast card game as a trial by ordeal; she used it as an intelligence test and a measure of spirit. If the poor man could stay a round without breaking down or running out, he got to marry one of us, if he still wanted to.)

25   She excelled at bridge, playing fast and boldly, but when the stakes were low and the hands dull, she bid slams for the devilment of it, or raised her opponents' suit to bug them, or showed her hand, or tossed her cards in a handful behind her back in a characteristic swift motion accompanied by a vibrantly innocent look. It drove our stolid father crazy. The hand was over before it began, and the guests were appalled. How do you score it, who deals now, what do you do with a crazy person who is having so much fun? Or they were down seven, and the guests were appalled. "Pam!" "Dammit, Pam!" He groaned. What ails such people? What on earth possesses them? He rubbed his face.

    She was an unstoppable force; she never let go. When we moved across town, she persuaded the U.S. Post Office to let her keep her old address—forever—because she'd had stationery printed. I don't know how she did it. Every new post office worker, over decades, needed to learn that although the Doaks' mail is addressed to here, it is delivered to there.

    Mother's energy and intelligence suited her for a greater role in a larger arena—mayor of New York, say—than the one she had. She followed American politics closely; she had been known to vote for Democrats. She saw how things should be run, but she had nothing to run but our household. Even there, small minds bugged her, she was smarter than the people who designed the things she had to use all day for the length of her life.

    "Look," she said. "Whoever designed this corkscrew never used one. Why would anyone sell it without trying it out?" So she invented a better one. She showed me a drawing of it. The spirit of American enterprise never faded in Mother. If capitalizing and tooling up had been as interesting as theorizing and thinking up, she would have fired up a new factory every week, and chaired several hundred corporations.

    "It grieves me," she would say, "it grieves my heart," that the company that made one superior product packaged it poorly, or took the wrong tack in its advertising. She knew, as she held the thing mournfully in her two hands, that she'd never find another. She was right. We children wholly sympathized, and so did Father; what could she do, what could anyone do, about it? She was Samson in chains. She paced.

30   She didn't like the taste of stamps so she didn't lick stamps, she licked the corner of the envelope instead. She glued sandpaper to the sides of kitchen drawers, and under kitchen cabinets, so she always had a handy place to strike a match. She designed, and hounded workmen to build against all norms, doubly wide kitchen counters and elevated bathroom sinks. To splint a finger, she stuck it in a lightweight cigar tube. Conversely, to protect a

pack of cigarettes, she carried it in a Band-Aid box. She drew plans for an over-the-finger toothbrush for babies, an oven rack that slid up and down, and—the family favorite—Lendalarm. Lendalarm was a beeper you attached to books (or tools) you loaned friends. After ten days, the beeper sounded. Only the rightful owner could silence it.

She repeatedly reminded us of P.T. Barnum's dictum: You could sell anything to anybody if you marketed it right. The adman who thought of making Americans believe they needed underarm deodorant was a visionary. So, too, was the hero who made a success of a new product, Ivory soap. The executives were horrified, Mother told me, that a cake of this stuff floated. Soap wasn't supposed to float. Anyone would be able to tell it was mostly whipped-up air. Then some inspired adman made a leap: Advertise that it floats. Flaunt it. The rest is history.

She respected the rare few who broke through to new ways. "Look," she'd say, "here's an intelligent apron." She called upon us to admire intelligent control knobs and intelligent pan handles, intelligent andirons and picture frames and knife sharpeners. She questioned everything, every pair of scissors, every knitting needle, gardening glove, tape dispenser. Hers was a restless mental vigor that just about ignited the dumb household objects with its force.

Torpid conformity was a kind of sin; it was stupidity itself, the mighty stream against which Mother would never cease to struggle. If you held no minority opinions, or if you failed to risk total ostracism for them daily, the world would be a better place without you.

Always I heard Mother's emotional voice asking Amy and me the same few questions: Is that your own idea? Or somebody else's? "*Giant* is a good movie," I pronounced to the family at dinner. "Oh, really?" Mother warmed to these occasions. She all but rolled up her sleeves. She knew I hadn't seen it. "Is that your considered opinion?"

She herself held many unpopular, even fantastic, positions. She was scathingly sarcastic about the McCarthy hearings while they took place, right on our living-room television; she frantically opposed Father's wait-and-see calm. "We don't know enough about it," he said. "I do," she said. "I know all I need to know."

She asserted, against all opposition, that people who lived in trailer parks were not bad but simply poor, and had as much right to settle on beautiful land, such as rural Ligonier, Pennsylvania, as did the oldest of families in the finest of hidden houses. Therefore, the people who owned trailer parks, and sought zoning changes to permit trailer parks, needed our help. Her profound belief that the country-club pool sweeper was a person, and that the department-store saleslady, the bus driver, telephone operator, and housepainter were people, and even in groups the steelworkers who carried pickets and the Christmas shoppers who clogged intersections were people—this was a conviction common enough in democratic Pittsburgh, but not altogether common among our friends' parents, or even, perhaps, among our parents' friends.

Opposition emboldened Mother, and she would take on anybody on any issue—the chairman of the board, at a cocktail party, on the current strike; she would fly at him in a flurry of passion, as a songbird selflessly attacks a big hawk.

"Eisenhower's going to win," I announced after school. She lowered her magazine and looked me in the eyes: "How do you know?" I was doomed. It was fatal to say, "Everyone says so." We all knew well what happened. "Do you consult this Everyone before you make your decisions? What if Everyone decided to round up all the Jews?" Mother knew there was no danger of cowing me. She simply tried to keep us all awake. And in fact it was always clear to Amy and me, and to Molly when she grew old enough to listen, that if our classmates came to cruelty, just as much as if the neighborhood or the nation came to madness, we were expected to take, and would be each separately capable of taking, a stand.

(1987)

Questions:

1. What is the significance of the title? Is it an effective choice?

2. Describe, as succinctly as possible, the parenting philosophy of Dillard's mother.

3. This article appears to be simply a long string of anecdotes about the author's mother. What is Dillard trying to convey in this article? Do you think this structure is an effective way of doing so?

4. Is there any evidence in the article to suggest ways in which Dillard has been influenced by her mother?

5. We learn a lot about the mother's political views in this article. What connection, if any, does Dillard infer between her mother's political views and her unrelenting wit?

6. What role does Dillard's father play in this article?

W.H. GRAHAM

FOUR FARMS IN THE TENTH OF REACH

W.H. Graham's Greenbank *was acclaimed on publication as "a miracle of a book" (*Saturday Night Magazine*) and as evidence that local history could be "as good as any history now being written" (*The Globe and Mail*). "Four Farms in the Tenth of Reach" is the first chapter of this book.*

～∾～

THE PLACE

The landscape in which these people lived and worked lies on the north slope of the Oak Ridge moraine, a massive, arbitrary ridge of glacial drift stretching one hundred miles from southern Ontario's Niagara escarpment to the Trent River. Its width varies erratically from eight miles at its beginning and at Uxbridge to a few hundred yards near Manchester; it stands some eight hundred feet above the surrounding plain. Its size suggests the moraine's core was deposited by the earliest glaciers. The grinding and gouging of the later ice ages built up around it slopes which carry on their surfaces a fine sandy loam, known as Bondhead and described by physiographers as being a productive and durable soil of great benefit to farmers, and so it proved to the Greenbank settlers.

Rising above the surrounding countryside the ridge provides sweeping prospects, wide panoramas on every side. To the north and south lie little lakes, streams, swamps and woodlots, rich pasture and fertile cropland livened by powerfully composed groupings of farm buildings and by pleasing hamlets. It is a beautiful pastoral landscape, accented by dramatic vistas, and quite unnoticed, almost secret.

As Rupert Brooke remarked of another part of Canada, "No one is thinking of the lakes and hills you see before you…dumbly awaiting their Wordsworth or their Acropolis to give them a soul." Our perception of a landscape is strongly affected by what historians, painters, poets and others have told us. The view may be unremarkable in itself, but the moment we say, "Ah, Provence," or "the Plains of Abraham," or whatever, it becomes coloured and shaped by all the associations accumulated around its name. The windy plains of Troy are just that, but the scalp tingles as the mind sees the shadowy camp fires beside the hollow ships drawn up on the beach. The rolling grasslands of our western foothills shimmer with faint images of all the cowboy chases we have watched on the silver screen. When we look about us we see, not so much the place itself, as the legends that people it.

It is possible to see the landscape of Reach in the light of two suns, that of the nineteenth century and that of today. Under the older sun it is bleak and echoless, new and colourless, barely lived in. Under the sun of today it is resonant and evocative. A white, plaster-covered cottage on the Twelfth Line can never look insignificant when we know that in 1873 George Patterson, aged seventy, killed himself in bed with his shotgun, according to his wife, who was the only other person in the house at the time. The hill in the Eighth Concession that Highway 12 cuts through effortlessly, ceases to be a mere rise when we know that it was the infamous Bowles's Hill that no team could mount without stopping to draw breath. The image of the big barn, strong and noble in itself, acquires still more power when you know it was one of the two instruments that transformed the landscape from near wasteland, treeless and thistle-infested, to its present richness. This landscape is one profoundly affected by man, lived-in, nourishing and, in turn, nourished and cared-for, offering the careful observer its own account of the passage of the years.

If the history of these families indicates the decline of the agricultural interest in numbers and importance in the nineteenth century, the four farms themselves show us what has become of Ontario farmland in the twentieth. The automobile, urbanization, labour legislation and trade unions, centralization, growth of government at all levels, mechanization, the vast increase in the productivity of agriculture, the whole crowding host of phenomena peculiar to this century, has made a visible impact on the land, changing not only its occupation and use, even its very quality, but as much as anything, its look. The events that follow took place in a landscape more thoughtlessly scarred by man and more wretched than any to be seen today.

The bleakness of that landscape was the sign that the settler had completed the first essential, he had brought the land under the plow. A community could then be organized and the individual settler start to assume the role of citizen. This process, the way the people around Greenbank responded to the need for government, schools, churches, mills, shops, all the elements of an ordered society, is the theme of this account. The principal protagonists were not daily aware of their mighty task. The real achievement was never present in their intentions. They, as will emerge, were more deeply concerned with personal religion and the salvation of souls, with dynastic ambition, with the winning of wealth or the making of a comfortable subsistence. In only one case, the last, was the achieving of these aims permanently successful; all their stories have a dying fall, yet the society they built set the ethical and intellectual tone of Canada into the second half of the twentieth century.

The Sensibility

Our own times are best illuminated in the light thrown by the past. That light is generated, not by letting "observation with extensive view/Survey mankind from China to Peru," but by the minute examination of particular lives and places. The doings and sayings of political leaders, great divines and successful businessmen do not tell us much about their societies because such people are the exceptions. We need to hear from "the middle of humanity," but unhappily the voices of ordinary mortals of the past are muffled by mortality itself and the world they lived in is obscured by the accumulations of the years. What follows is an effort to hear some of those voices, and, like visitants from the future, to glimpse the speakers meeting the demands and the alterations of their own times and to see something of their world, for the light it throws on ours.

Other people's attitudes always seem a mixture of the reasonable and, at least, the peculiar and are seldom easy to understand. This should be remembered when reading this book, for while those who appear on these pages all belong to "the common people" with whom we might expect to have basic affinities, they are as well "other people," and they lived in a time with a social sensibility quite other than that of our own.

In the small town weekly newspapers of the last century the lofty sentiments of the obituaries and quirky snippets of local news combine to present a scene bustling with recognizable characters. Stories still told today of doughty great-grandparents and their eccentric children swell the crowd with additional familiar figures. It begins to seem as though Balzac or Dickens was the impresario, with yet another production on that great literary theme, the unchanging nature of the human comedy. The past, we begin to think, was filled with people just like ourselves.

10 But, from these same sources come other, brief yet revealing flashes, smoky flares of intelligence from this other time. We glimpse a picture, black and white, grainy, jerky, more like a Chaplin one-reeler than the opulent spectacle of great literature. It is lit by a sensibility different from ours, coarser and coloured by the insensitivity, even cruelty, that underlies Chaplin's slapstick. Even the language, while familiar, seems slightly skewed, as though our hearing were muffled. The characters in these scenes do not at all seem to be people just like ourselves.

Harsh attitudes are to be expected in a settler society, so it is not surprising that the Grand Jury in 1865 demanded "a good long probation in one of our Reformatories" for teenage horse thieves, nor that in the next year the warden of the Whitby jail considered two to three dozen lashes a very light sentence and the provincial inspector of prisons urged "really afflictive, thoroughly objectless labour" as a means of reducing the jail population and putting an end to the prevailing "jollity, amusement and exemption from labour." It is not entirely unexpected to hear, ten years later, Dr. Clark of the Toronto Insane Asylum deploring the attitude of the average citizen who looked upon the hospital "as a huge menagerie, erected for the purpose of gratifying his morbid curiosity"; nor that when Clark closed it to casual visitors the response was fierce opposition because the asylum was valued as "one of the 'sights' to be seen" by visitors to the city. These are known attitudes of that time, but how are we to respond to this cheerful, masculine treatment of a news story of 1882 about a man who "shot himself to death on the night of his marriage because the bride refused to pull off his boots?" It was headed, "Another Crank."

The same light-hearted callousness extended to spastics, who were not only considered to be idiots, but comic into the bargain. The overweight were admired. The *Ontario Observer* of Prince Albert acclaimed the "substantial" yeomen of the township, four of whom, weighing in at a grain merchant's in Manchester, tipped the scales at from 220 to 250 pounds, only to be topped by a bystander, a woman weighing 275 pounds. The editorial comment was, "Well done, Reach." The achievement was even more remarkable when we consider that almost certainly all of them were little over five feet tall.

Sudden death combined with an odd name did not need editorial comment to touch the nineteenth century funny-bone; this two-line news story stood out in a sea of white space that must have been deliberate: "On Friday last, Euphemia Drone of Beverely was struck by lightning." Hindsight makes it almost impossible to believe the triviality of a one-line editorial in the *Observer* in August of 1914: "Help wanted, apply at once to Kaiser William."

Death was closer and more familiar than it is today, and undertakers' advertising was direct and jaunty rather than unctuous and decorous. One boasted simply, "Funerals cheap and quick" with a double set of new plumes. A Prince Albert concern offered "Shrouds of all sizes in newest styles"; unfortunately there is no supporting illustration.

15   More distant death was regarded even more lightly. In 1895 the Turks slaughtered some 200,000 of their European subjects, and the "Armenian Atrocities" occupied the headlines of the newspapers of the west. A store in Uxbridge was quick to appropriate the story for a clearance sale advertisement with a cheerful piece of breakfast table dialogue:

SHE: …you reading about the Armenian slaughters, dear?
HE: No. I'm reading about the slaughter of prices at Brownscombe's department store.

A more direct experience of a smaller but similar horror was provided by a Toronto store in 1901 that promoted gramophone sales by playing a cylinder that recorded "the death cries of Henry Smith, the negro who was burned at the stake in Paris, Texas, some time ago."

This childlike attitude to violent death was of long standing. Dr. Knowllys, who practised in Prince Albert and Greenbank in the 1860s and was busy in politics, spoke his Tory, low-church Anglican mind with bluff levity, announcing at a nomination meeting that "he would prefer shooting Papists to pigeons." When he was charged with negligence in the death of a patient, he airily asked what all the commotion was about, after all, "Murphy was only a catholic."

In counterpoint to this easy-going attitude there ran a belief that modern life was too demanding. The same Dr Clark who banned sightseers from the Toronto asylum, in a later report of 1884 attributed the prevalence of insanity in Canada to the high tension under which so many people lived, and The Uxbridge *Journal* commented, "You can't get twenty-five horsepower out of a fifteen horsepower engine." Still later, in 1913, a report on rural life, prepared for the Methodist Church, declared that in contrast to the past, everyone lacked leisure.

The context of these remarks is not clear, but there is evidence from many sources of a high degree of tension among country people. It appeared at an early age, among children in school, where the line between discipline and disorder was fragile indeed as will be described in later pages. Older youths made the streets dangerous at night, according to accounts in both the Port Perry and Uxbridge papers in the early eighties. Reports of named men being beaten up are common, and there is more than one editorial on vigilantes not being the answer to public safety. An advertisement by a hardware store offering a selection of revolvers is unique, but it fits with several newspaper items from which the inference is clear that it was common for men to carry arms. Still, the greatest numbers of offences in the county Returns of Convictions reflect, not crimes of violence, but bad temper, malice and rowdyness. They include such charges as the use of abusive and threatening language, striking with eggs in the street, furious driving, disturbing the preaching in church, throwing snowballs at the plaintiff's house, using blasphemous language on the public highway, calling out improper names. They indicate rough but hardly violent conduct.

Reminiscences tell us that men who were at odds, when meeting on a one-track road, would get out of their sleighs and fight rather than make way. Refusing to yield half the road was a common charge in magistrates' courts. A newspaper complained of young men who, when driving with their girls, showed off by stopping at a narrow place in the road and standing up in the buggy to call to the drivers behind, "Are you in a hurry?" and laughing tauntingly as they drove slowly on.

Tales of theft and fraud and broken agreements among people who knew one another well are common in Greenbank and suggest it was almost a duty to get the better of your neighbour. Farmers regularly exchanged labour, but, for many, any excuse would do to get out of their part of the exchange. Boys frequently had to take their employers to court for their wages, employers who lived just down the road from the boys' parents. In the early days of automobiles it was customary to borrow licence plates when driving to Oshawa or Toronto where such things were taken seriously. There is a story of a Greenbank man with borrowed plates who knocked down a woman in Toronto. He gave the police the name of the owner of the plates. When the owner was charged, the borrower denied that he had been involved in any way, and his neighbour was convicted. A man, remembering the generation just departed and describing how a farmer cheated a neighbour of the promised use of some pasture in return for a week's work, concluded, "They were great Sunday Christians, but oh God, just watch them Monday morning."

There was a continuous conflict running through daily life. The society we are looking at was a small one, and its members were closely bound in many ways: by family connection, by acquaintanceship embracing generations and by a common occupation. There were few distractions to cushion the irritation of constant contacts with the same people. Like men in prison they saw each other every day. The tension of this closeness not only emphasized their community but exacerbated differences. Stress was ever present and found its most open expression in the brawling that was the almost ritual conclusion of raising bees, plowing matches, lodge meetings and, indeed, almost any assembly except church. Today, the mobility of people, the variety of occupations and of recreations that make society so dispersed and fluid, have had the further effect of making social relationships looser and, if not warmer, certainly more peaceful.

From the records that remain to us, we must infer that it was not only a rough world, but a man's world. The widely used book, *The Family Physician*, advises young men what to look for in a bride, namely, personal cleanliness and industrious habits rather than beauty or accomplishments. "No man of moderate means has ever dined off a piano solo." There is no corresponding advice for a young woman on what to look for in a man. It seems to have been assumed that she would do well to accept whatever came her way. Men's needs and ambitions were the motive power of society and women fitted in. This was so in Greenbank into the 1950s. Whenever a large purchase was made, such as a piano, an electric range or refrigerator, the shopping decisions were the man's affair.

The most visible evidence of the masculine quality of this world was the condition of public places. The indifference to appearances that marked the streets and stores, the mills and barnyards, was a trait of the country man, indeed of most men who put in long hours of physical labour and who consider what they do to be of overriding importance. It was particularly evident in a habit that has completely vanished. Within living memory signs were posted in streetcars and waiting rooms prohibiting spitting and quoting fines. The situation behind this prohibition is vividly described in an account of a trial in Port Perry in 1882.

The Magistrate interrupted the proceedings and, called attention to the disgusting condition of the floor of the hall which was already after a couple of hours sitting frescoed all over with tobacco spit of all shapes and sizes some of them as thick as treacle and others meandering among the feet of the operator like a river of amber and all contributing to render navigation dangerous and to fill the atmosphere with an unmitigated stench of tobacco almost suffocating. The Magistrate warned parties that the nuisance must be stopped.

Daniel Till, sometime constable of Greenbank and present at this trial, was driven from home by his adult sons for constant beating of his tiny wife, Mary Anne Cragg. He was briefly reinstated but finally turned out, according to legend, for spitting on the walls. He was among the last of the rough and wilful breed of the early comers for whom tension and defiance imbued the very air they breathed. When the House of Refuge was opened in Whitby he had himself admitted to shame his family. When he died there in 1918 he had already prepared his gravestone, which stands in Greenbank cemetery well apart from those of the rest of the family. The reproachful epitaph has defied the efforts of some unknown to edit it with a chisel:

> *God will call me home,*
> *He will think it best,*
> *Away from unkind friends,*
> *Away from sin and the world.*

Someone has chipped away at the "un" but no hammer can obliterate the rhythm.

25   While these anecdotes describe only the surface of daily life, the surface cannot be separated from the quality or nature of what lies beneath. The rural Victorian world seems, despite the high tone of its aspirations, to have been coarser and harsher than our own.

(1988)

QUESTIONS:

1. Unlike most local histories, *Greenbank* attempts to give the reader a broad sense of what life was like as well as a specific sense of a particular community. Discuss the organization of this passage (taken from the book's introductory chapter) with respect to its presentation of the general and the particular.

2. Discuss the use of metaphor in paragraph 11. At what distance does the author position himself from the world he is describing in the section on "the sensibility" of the time. How would you describe the tone of this section? Would it be more or less arresting if the author himself expressed more surprise?

3. More than once Graham refers to the degree to which the world he is describing was dominated by males. More than once as well he uses "man" or "men" to describe people generally at the time. Comment on this apparent contradiction, and on the degree to which it has come to be regarded as inappropriate to use "man" to refer to human beings generally.

STEVIE CAMERON

OUR DAUGHTERS, OURSELVES

In this newspaper essay, author and journalist Cameron addresses many of the central difficulties of growing up female in western society.

〜〜

They are so precious to us, our daughters. When they are born, we see their futures as unlimited and as they grow and learn, we try so hard to protect them: This is how we cross the street, hold my hand, wear your boots, don't talk to strangers, run to the neighbours if a man tries to get you in his car.

We tell our bright, shining girls that they can be anything: firefighters, doctors, policewomen, lawyers, scientists, soldiers, athletes, artists. What we don't tell them, yet, is how hard it will be. Maybe, we say to ourselves, by the time they're older it will be easier for them than it was for us.

But as they grow and learn, with aching hearts we have to start dealing with their bewilderment about injustice. Why do the boys get the best gyms, the best equipment and the best times on the field? Most of the school sports budget? Why does football matter more than gymnastics? Why are most of the teachers women and most of the principals men? Why do the boys make more money at their part-time jobs than we do?

And as they grow and learn we have to go on trying to protect them: We'll pick you up at the subway, we'll fetch you from the movie, stay with the group, make sure the parents drive you home from babysitting, don't walk across the park alone, lock the house if we're not there.

It's not fair, they say. Boys can walk where they want, come in when they want, work where they want. Not really, we say; boys get attacked too. But boys are not targets for men the way girls are so girls have to be more careful.

They plan for college and university and with wonder and pride we see them competing with the boys for spaces in engineering schools, medical schools, law schools, business schools.

We bite back the cautions that we feel we should give them; maybe by the time they've graduated things will have changed, we say to ourselves.

And then with aching hearts we take our precious daughters to lunch and listen to them talk about their friends: the one who was beaten by her boyfriend and then shunned by his friends when she asked for help from the dean, the one who was attacked in the parking lot, the one who gets obscene and threatening calls from a boy in the residence, the one who gets raped on a date, the one who was mocked by the male students in the public meeting.

They tell us about the sexism they're discovering in the adult world at university. Women professors who can't get jobs, who can't get tenure. Male professors who cannot comprehend women's stony silence after sexist jokes. An administration that only pays lip service to women's issues and refuses to accept the reality of physical danger to women on campus.

They tell us they're talking among themselves about how men are demanding rights over unborn children; it's not old dinosaurs who go to court to prevent a woman's abortion, it's young men. It's young men, they say with disbelief, their own generation, their own buddies with good educations, from "nice" families, who are abusive.

What can we say to our bright and shining daughters? How can we tell them how much we hurt to see them developing the same scars we've carried? How much we wanted it to be different for them? It's all about power, we say to them. Sharing power is not easy for anyone and men do not find it easy to share among themselves, much less with a group of equally talented, able women.

Now our daughters have been shocked to the core, as we all have, by the violence in Montreal.[1] They hear the women were separated from the men and meticulously slaughtered by a man who blamed his troubles on feminists. They ask themselves why nobody was able to help the terrified women, to somehow stop the hunter as he roamed the engineering building.

So now our daughters are truly frightened and it makes their mothers furious that they are frightened. They survived all the childhood dangers, they were careful as we trained them to be, they worked hard. Anything was possible and our daughters proved it. And now they are more scared than they were when they were little girls.

---

[1] On December 6, 1989, a male engineering student at l'Ecole Polytechnique in Montreal shot 27 women, killing 14 of them, before committing suicide. A note he left made it clear that he had conceived of this act of mass murder as an attack on feminists.

Fourteen of our bright and shining daughters won places in engineering schools, doing things we, their mothers, only dreamed of. That we lost them has broken our hearts; what is worse, is that we are not surprised.

(1989)

QUESTIONS:

1. Cameron uses the first person plural ("we," "us") throughout this essay, and the present tense. Discuss why each is appropriate to the tone and the message of the essay. Most pieces written in reaction to a horrific incident such as the Montreal Massacre or the Littleton, Colorado shooting begin with the incident itself and then move on to general reflections. This piece reverses that order. Discuss the effectiveness of the way in which Cameron has structured her essay.

2. What is the effect of the adverb "meticulously" in paragraph 12?

3. A good deal of discussion in the wake of the Montreal Massacre focused on the question of whether the shooter himself should be regarded as bearing the full responsibility, or society as a whole should accept some responsibility for fostering a climate discriminatory towards women. Cameron does not directly address this question; what attitude towards it is implied in her essay?

ANATOLE BROYARD

INTOXICATED BY MY ILLNESS

*In one of Anatole Broyard's last essays, the author describes how he was affected
by the discovery of his own terminal illness.*

～～

So much of a writer's life consists of assumed suffering, rhetorical suffering,
that I felt something like relief, even elation, when the doctor told me
that I had cancer of the prostate. Suddenly there was in the air a rich sense
of crisis, real crisis, yet one that also contained echoes of ideas like the crisis
of language, the crisis of literature, or of personality. It seemed to me that my
existence, whatever I thought, felt or did, had taken on a kind of meter, as
in poetry, or in taxis.

When you learn that your life is threatened, you can turn toward this
knowledge or away from it. I turned toward it. It was not a choice, but an
automatic shifting of gears, a tacit agreement between my body and my
brain. I thought that time had tapped me on the shoulder, that I had been
given a real deadline at last. It wasn't that I believed the cancer was going to
kill me, even though it had spread beyond the prostate—it could probably
be controlled, either by radiation or hormonal manipulation. No, what
struck me was the startled awareness that one day something, whatever it
might be, was going to interrupt my leisurely progress. It sounds trite, yet I
can only say that I realized for the first time that I don't have forever.

Time was no longer innocuous, nothing was casual any more. I
understood that living itself had a deadline. Like the book I had been
working on—how sheepish I would feel if I couldn't finish it. I had
promised it to myself and to my friends. Though I wouldn't say this out
loud, I had promised it to the world. All writers privately think this way.

When my friends heard I had cancer, they found me surprisingly cheerful and talked about my courage. But it has nothing to do with courage, at least not for me. As far as I can tell, it's a question of desire. I'm filled with desire—to live, to write, to do everything. Desire itself is a kind of immortality. While I've always had trouble concentrating, I now feel as concentrated as a diamond, or a microchip.

5   I remember a time in the 1950s when I tried to talk a friend of mine named Jules out of committing suicide. He had already made one attempt and when I went to see him he said "Give me a good reason to go on living." He was 30 years old.

I saw what I had to do. I started to sell life to him, like a real estate agent. Just look at the world, I said. How can you not be curious about it? The streets, the houses, the trees, the shops, the people, the movement and the stillness. Look at the women, so appealing, each in her own way. Think of all the things you can do with them, the places you can go together. Think of books, paintings, music. Think of your friends.

While I was talking I wondered, am I telling Jules the truth? He didn't think so, because he put his head in the oven a week later. As for me, I don't know whether I believed what I said or not, because I just went on behaving like everybody else. But I believe it now. When my wife made me a hamburger the other day I thought it was the most fabulous hamburger in the history of the world.

With this illness one of my recurrent dreams has finally come true. Several times in the past I've dreamed that I had committed a crime—or perhaps I was only accused of a crime, it's not clear. When brought to trial I refused to have a lawyer—I got up instead and made an impassioned speech in my own defense. This speech was so moving that I could feel myself tingling with it. It was inconceivable that the jury would not acquit me—only each time I woke before the verdict. Now cancer is the crime I may or may not have committed and the eloquence of being alive, the fervor of the survivor, is my best defense.

The way my friends have rallied around me is wonderful. They remind me of a flock of birds rising from a body of water into the sunset. If that image seems a bit extravagant, or tinged with satire, it's because I can't help thinking there's something comical about my friends' behavior, all these witty men suddenly saying pious, inspirational things.

10 They are not intoxicated as I am by my illness, but sobered. Since I refused to, they've taken on the responsibility of being serious. They appear abashed, or chagrined, in their sobriety. Stripped of their playfulness these pals of mine seem plainer, homelier—even older. It's as if they had all gone bald overnight.

Yet one of the effects of their fussing over me is that I feel vivid, multicolored, sharply drawn. On the other hand—and this is ungrateful—I remain outside of their solicitude, their love and best wishes. I'm isolated from them by the grandiose conviction that I am the healthy person and they are the sick ones. Like an existential hero, I have been cured by the truth while they still suffer the nausea of the uninitiated.

I've had eight-inch needles thrust into my belly where I could feel them tickling my metaphysics. I've worn Pampers. I've been licked by the flames and my sense of self has been singed. Sartre was right: you have to live each moment as if you're prepared to die.

Now at last I understand the conditional nature of the human condition. Yet, unlike Kierkegaard and Sartre, I'm not interested in the irony of my position. Cancer cures you of irony. Perhaps my irony was all in my prostate. A dangerous illness fills you with adrenaline and makes you feel very smart. I can afford now, I said to myself, to draw conclusions. All those grand generalizations toward which I have been building for so many years are finally taking shape. As I look back at how I used to be, it seems to me that an intellectual is a person who thinks that the classical clichés don't apply to him, that he is immune to homely truths. I know better now. I see everything with a summarizing eye. Nature is a terrific editor.

In the first stages of my illness, I couldn't sleep, urinate or defecate—the word ordeal comes to mind. Then when my doctor changed all this and everything worked again, what a voluptuous pleasure it was. With a cry of joy I realized how marvelous it is simply to function. My body, which in the last decade or two had become a familiar, no longer thrilling old flame, was reborn as a brand-new infatuation.

15   I realize of course that this elation I feel is just a phase, just a rush of consciousness, a splash of perspective, a hot flash of ontological alertness. But I'll take it, I'll use it. I'll use everything I can while I wait for the next phase. Illness is primarily a drama and it should be possible to enjoy it as well as to suffer it. I see now why the romantics were so fond of illness—the sick man sees everything as a metaphor. In this phase I'm infatuated with my cancer. It stinks of revelation.

As I look ahead, I feel like a man who has awakened from a long afternoon nap to find the evening stretched out before me. I'm reminded of D'Annunzio, the Italian poet, who said to a duchess he had just met at a party in Paris, "Come, we will have a profound evening." Why not? I see the balance of my life—everything comes in images now—as a beautiful paisley shawl thrown over a grand piano.

Why a paisley shawl, precisely? Why a grand piano? I have no idea. That's the way the situation presents itself to me. I have to take my imagery along with my medicine.

(1989)

QUESTIONS:

1. What is the meaning of the title of the essay?

2. Why does Broyard say, "Desire itself is a kind of immortality?"

3. Broyard uses a continual stream of imagery and metaphors in this essay. Describe some of them, and their effects.

4. Who is Broyard talking to in this essay? What is his ultimate point?

5. How does stress affect you? Describe a period in your life when you were under extreme stress and how you dealt with it. What, if any, lasting effect did it have on your life? How did it change you?

Bharati Mukherjee

A Four-Hundred-Year-Old Woman

In this essay an acclaimed writer of fiction discusses the connections between her life and her work.

∽

I was born into a class that did not live in its native language. I was born into a city that feared its future, and trained me for emigration. I attended a school run by Irish nuns, who regarded our walled-off school compound in Calcutta as a corner (forever green and tropical) of England. My "country"—called in Bengali *desh,* and suggesting more a homeland than a nation of which one is a citizen—I have never seen. It is the ancestral home of my father, and is now in Bangladesh. Nevertheless, I speak his dialect of Bengali, and think of myself as "belonging" to Faridpur, the tiny green-gold village that was his birthplace. I was born into a religion that placed me, a Brahmin, at the top of its hierarchy while condemning me, as a woman, to a role of subservience. The larger political entity to which I gave my first allegiance—India—was not even a sovereign nation when I was born.

My horoscope, cast by a neighborhood astrologer when I was a week-old infant, predicted that I would be a writer, that I would win some prizes, that I would cross "the black waters" of oceans and make my home among aliens. Brought up in a culture that places its faith in horoscopes, it never occurred to me to doubt it. The astrologer meant to offer me a melancholy future; to be destined to leave India was to be banished from the sources of true culture. The nuns at school, on the other hand, insinuated that India had long outlived its glories, and that if we wanted to be educated, modern women and make something of our lives, we'd better hit the trail westward.

All my girlhood, I straddled the seesaw of contradictions. *Bilayat,* meaning the scary, unknown "abroad," was both boom time and desperate loss.

I have found my way to the United States after many transit stops. The unglimpsed phantom Faridpur and the all too real Manhattan have merged as "desh." I am an American. I am an American writer, in the American mainstream, trying to extend it. This is a vitally important statement for me—I am not an Indian writer, not an exile, not an expatriate. I am an immigrant; my investment is in the American reality, not the Indian. I look on ghettoization—whether as a Bengali in India or a hyphenated Indo-American in North America—as a temptation to be surmounted.

It took me ten painful years, from the early seventies to the early eighties, to overthrow the smothering tyranny of nostalgia. The remaining struggle for me is to make the American readership, meaning the editorial and publishing industries as well, acknowledge the same fact. (As the reception of such films as *Gandhi* and *A Passage to India* as well as *The Far Pavillions* and *The Jewel in the Crown* shows, nostalgia is a two-way street. Americans can feel nostalgic for a world they never knew.) The foreign-born, the exotically raised Third World immigrant with non-Western religions and non-European languages and appearance, can be as American as any steerage passenger from Ireland, Italy or the Russian Pale. As I have written in another context (a review article in *The Nation* on books by Studs Terkel and Al Santoli), we are probably only a few years away from a Korean *What Makes Choon-li Run?* Or a Hmong *Call It Sleep.* In other words my literary agenda begins by acknowledging that America has transformed me. It does not end until I show how I (and the hundreds of thousands like me) have transformed America.

5 The agenda is simply stated, but in the long run revolutionary. Make the familiar exotic; the exotic familiar.

I have had to create an audience. I cannot rely on shorthand references to my community, my religion, my class, my region, or my old school tie. I've had to sensitize editors as well as readers to the richness of the lives I'm writing about. The most moving form of praise I receive from readers can be summed up in three words: *I never knew.* Meaning, I see these people (call them Indians, Filipinos, Koreans, Chinese) around me all the time and I never knew they had an inner life. I never knew they schemed and cheated, suffered, felt so strongly, cared so passionately. When even the forms of praise are so rudimentary, the writer knows she has an inexhaustible fictional population to enumerate. Perhaps even a mission, to appropriate a good colonial word.

I have been blessed with an enormity of material. I can be Chekhovian and Tolstoyan—with melancholy and philosophical perspectives on the breaking of hearts as well as the fall of civilizations—and I can be a brash and raucous homesteader, Huck Finn and Woman Warrior, on the unclaimed plains of American literature. My material, reduced to jacket-flap copy, is the rapid and dramatic transformation of the United States since the early 1970s. Within that perceived perimeter, however, I hope to wring surprises.

Yet (I am a writer much given to "yet") my imaginative home is also in the tales told by my mother and grandmother, the world of the Hindu epics. For all the hope and energy I have placed in the process of immigration and the accommodation—I'm a person who couldn't ride a public bus when she first arrived, and now I'm someone who watches tractor pulls on obscure cable channels—there are parts of me that remain Indian, parts that slide against the masks of newer selves. The form that my stories and novels take inevitably reflects the resources of Indian mythology—shape-changing, miracles, godly perspectives. My characters can, I hope, transcend the straitjacket of simple psychologizing. The people I write about are culturally and politically several hundred years old: consider the history they have witnessed (colonialism, technology, education, liberation, civil war, uprooting). They have shed old identities, taken on new ones, and learned to hide the scars. They may sell you newspapers, or clean your offices at night.

Writers (especially American writers, weaned on the luxury of affluence and freedom) often disavow the notion of a "literary duty" or "political consciousness," citing the all-too-frequent examples of writers ruined by their shrill commitments. Glibness abounds on both sides of the argument, but finally I have to side with my "Third World" compatriots: I do have a duty, beyond telling a good story or drawing a convincing character. My duty is to give voice to continents, but also to redefine the nature of *American* and what makes an American. In the process, work like mine and dozens like it will open up the canon of American literature.

10 It has not been an easy transition, from graduate student to citizen, from natural-born expatriate to the hurly-burly of immigration. My husband (Clark Blaise) and I spent fifteen years in his *desh* of Canada, and Canada was a country that discouraged the very process of assimilation. Eventually, it also discouraged the very presence of "Pakis" in its midst, and in 1980, a low point in our lives, we left, gave up our tenured, full-professor lives for the free-lancing life in the United States.

We were living in Iowa City in 1983 when Emory University called me to be writer-in-residence for the winter semester. My name, apparently, had been suggested to them by an old friend. I hadn't published a book in six years (two earlier novels, *The Tiger's Daughter* and *Wife*, as well as our joint nonfiction study, *Days and Nights in Calcutta*, were out of print) but somehow Emory didn't hold it against me.

Atlanta turned out to be the luckiest break of my life. For one of those mysterious reasons, stories that had been gathering in me suddenly exploded. I wrote nearly all the stories in *Darkness* (Penguin, 1985) in those three months. I finally had a glimpse of my true material, and that is immigration. In other words, transformation—not preservation. I saw myself and my own experience refracted through a dozen separate lives. Clark, who remained in Iowa City until our younger son finished high school, sent me newspaper accounts, and I turned them into stories. Indian friends in Atlanta took me to dinners and table gossip became stories. Suddenly, I had begun appropriating the American language. My stories were about the hurly-burly of the unsettled magma between two worlds.

Eventually—inevitably—we made our way to New York. My next batch of stories (*The Middleman and Other Stories*, Grove, 1988) appropriate the American language in ways that are personally most satisfying to me (one Chicago reviewer likened it to Nabokov's *Lolita*), and my characters are now as likely to be American as immigrant, and Chinese, Filipino, or Middle Eastern as much as Indian. That book has enjoyed widespread support both critically and commercially, and empowered me to write a new novel, *Jasmine*, and to contract for a major work, historical in nature, that nevertheless incorporates a much earlier version of my basic theme, due for completion in the next three years. *Days and Nights in Calcutta* is being made into a feature film.

My theme is the making of new Americans. Wherever I travel in the (very) Old World, I find "Americans" in the making, whether or not they ever make it to these shores. I see them as dreamers and conquerors, not afraid of transforming themselves, not afraid of abandoning some of their principles along the way. In *Jasmine*, my "American" is born in a Punjabi village, marries at fourteen, and is widowed at sixteen. Nevertheless, she is an American and will enter the book as an Iowa banker's wife.

Ancestral habits of mind can be constricting; they also confer one's individuality. I know I can appropriate the American language, but I can never be a minimalist. I have too many stories to tell. I am aware of myself as a four-hundred-year-old woman, born in the captivity of a colonial, pre-industrial oral culture and living now as a contemporary New Yorker.

My image of artistic structure and artistic excellence is the Moghul miniature painting with its crazy foreshortening of vanishing point, its insistence that everything happens simultaneously, bound only by shape and color. In the miniature paintings of India, there are a dozen separate foci, the most complicated stories can be rendered on a grain of rice, the corners are as elaborated as the centers. There is a sense of the interpenetration of all things. In the Moghul miniature of my life, there would be women investigating their bodies with mirrors, but they would be doing it on a distant balcony under fans wielded by bored serving girls; there would be a small girl listening to a bent old woman; there would be a white man eating popcorn and watching a baseball game; there would be cocktail parties and cornfields and a village set among rice paddies and skyscrapers. In a sense, I wrote that story, "Courtly Vision," at the end of *Darkness*. And in a dozen other ways I'm writing it today, and I will be writing, in the Moghul style, till I get it right.

(1990)

QUESTIONS:

1. What is the significance of Mukherjee referring to herself as (and titling her essay) "a four-hundred-year-old woman"?

2. In paragraph 14, Mukherjee positively characterizes those who hold American values as "conquerors" and as being unafraid of "abandoning some of their principles." Why does she see these traits as positive?

3. In paragraph 4, Mukherjee refers to the "ten painful" years of her life beginning in "the early seventies," and then in paragraph 7 refers to "the rapid and dramatic transformation of the United States since the early 1970s." How did the U.S. change in these years, and how (if at all) did this affect Mukherjee personally?

4. In paragraph 7, what rhetorical effect does the final sentence have upon the reader?

5. In paragraph 14, Mukherjee writes that she could "never be a minimalist." How would you describe her writing style?

EMILY MARTIN

THE EGG AND THE SPERM:

How Science has Constructed a Romance
Based on Stereotypical Male-Female Roles

In this 1991 scholarly article, anthropologist Emily Martin points out how our
society has portrayed the story of male reproductive biology as one of "remarkable
feats" and that of female reproductive biology as one of "passivity and decay."

∼∼

> The theory of the human body is always a part of a world-
> picture...The theory of the human body is always a part of a
> fantasy.
>
> [James Hillman, *The Myth of Analysis*][1]

A s an anthropologist, I am intrigued by the possibility that culture shapes how biological scientists describe what they discover about the natural world. If this were so, we would be learning about more than the natural world in high school biology class; we would be learning about cultural beliefs and practices as if they were part of nature. In the course of my research I realized that the picture of egg and sperm drawn in popular as well as scientific accounts of reproductive biology relies on stereotypes central to our cultural definitions of male and female. The stereotypes imply not only that female biological processes are less worthy than their male counterparts but also that women are less worthy than men. Part of my goal in writing this article is to shine a bright light on the gender stereotypes hidden within the scientific language of biology. Exposed in such a light, I hope they will lose much of their power to harm us.

---

[1] James Hillman, *The Myth of Analysis* (Evanston, Ill.: Northwestern University Press, 1972), 220. [Unless otherwise noted, all notes to this essay are from the author.]

EGG AND SPERM: A SCIENTIFIC FAIRY TALE

At a fundamental level, all major scientific textbooks depict male and female reproductive organs as systems for the production of valuable substances, such as eggs and sperm.[2] In the case of women, the monthly cycle is described as being designed to produce eggs and prepare a suitable place for them to be fertilized and grown—all to the end of making babies. But the enthusiasm ends there. By extolling the female cycle as a productive enterprise, menstruation must necessarily be viewed as a failure. Medical texts describe menstruation as the "debris" of the uterine lining, the result of necrosis, or death of tissue. The descriptions imply that a system has gone awry, making products of no use, not to specification, unsalable, wasted, scrap. An illustration in a widely used medical text shows menstruation as a chaotic disintegration of form, complementing the many texts that describe it as "ceasing," "dying," "losing," "denuding," "expelling."[3]

Male reproductive physiology is evaluated quite differently. One of the texts that sees menstruation as failed production employs a sort of breathless prose when it describes the maturation of sperm: "The mechanisms which guide the remarkable cellular transformation from spermatid to mature sperm remain uncertain....Perhaps the most amazing characteristic of spermatogenesis is its sheer magnitude: the normal human male may manufacture several hundred million sperm per day."[4] In the classic text *Medical Physiology*, edited by Vernon Mountcastle, the male/female, productive/destructive comparison is more explicit: "Whereas the female *sheds* only a single gamete each month, the seminiferous tubules *produce* hundreds of millions of sperm each day" (emphasis mine).[5] The female author of another text marvels at the length of the microscopic seminiferous tubules, which, if uncoiled and placed end to end, "would span almost one-third of a mile!" She writes, "In an adult male these structures produce millions of sperm cells each day." Later she asks, "How is this feat accom-

---

[2] The textbooks I consulted are the main ones used in classes for undergraduate premedical students or medical students (or those held on reserve in the library for these classes) during the past few years at Johns Hopkins University. These texts are widely used at other universities in the country as well.

[3] Arthur C. Guyton, *Physiology of the Human Body*, 6th ed. (Philadelphia: Saunders College Publishing, 1984), 624.

[4] Arthur J. Vander, James H. Sherman, and Dorothy S. Luciano, *Human Physiology: The Mechanisms of Body Function*, 3rd ed. (New York: McGraw Hill, 1980), 483–84.

[5] Vernon B. Mountcastle, *Medical Physiology*, 14th ed. (London: Mosby, 1980), 2:1624.

plished?"[6] None of these texts expresses such intense enthusiasm for any female processes. It is surely no accident that the "remarkable" process of making sperm involves precisely what, in the medical view, menstruation does not: production of something deemed valuable.[7]

One could argue that menstruation and spermatogenesis are not analogous processes and, therefore, should not be expected to elicit the same kind of response. The proper female analogy to spermatogenesis, biologically, is ovulation. Yet ovulation does not merit enthusiasm in these texts either. Textbook descriptions stress that all of the ovarian follicles containing ova are already present at birth. Far from being *produced*, as sperm are, they merely sit on the shelf, slowly degenerating and aging like overstocked inventory: "At birth, normal human ovaries contain an estimated one million follicles [each], and no new ones appear after birth. Thus, in marked contrast to the male, the newborn female already has all the germ cells she will ever have. Only a few, perhaps 400, are destined to reach full maturity during her active productive life. All the others degenerate at some point in their development so that few, if any remain by the time she reaches menopause at approximately 50 years of age."[8] Note the "marked contrast" that this description sets up between male and female, who has stockpiled germ cells by birth and is faced with their degeneration.

Nor are the female organs spared such vivid descriptions. One scientist writes in a newspaper article that a woman's ovaries become old and worn out from ripening eggs every month, even though the woman herself is still relatively young: "When you look through a laparoscope...at an ovary that has been through hundreds of cycles, even in a superbly healthy American female, you see a scarred, battered organ."[9]

To avoid the negative connotations that some people associate with the female reproductive system, scientists could begin to describe male and female processes as homologous. They might credit females with "producing" mature ova one at a time, as they're needed each month, and describe males as having to face problems of degenerating germ cells. This degenera-

---

[6]   Eldra Pearl Solomon, *Human Anatomy and Physiology* (New York: CBS College Publishing, 1983), 678.

[7]   For elaboration, see Emily Martin, *The Woman in the Body: A Cultural Analysis of Reproduction* (Boston: Beacon, 1987), 27–53.

[8]   Vander, Sherman, and Luciano, 568.

[9]   Melvin Konner, "Childbearing and Age," *New York Times Magazine* (December 27, 1987), 22–23, esp. 22.

tion would occur throughout life among spermatogonia, the undifferentiated germ cells in the testes that are the long-lived, dormant precursors of sperm.

But the texts have an almost dogged insistence on casting female processes in a negative light. The texts celebrate sperm production because it is continuous from puberty to senescence, while they portray egg production as inferior because it is finished at birth. This makes the female seem unproductive, but some texts will also insist that it is she who is wasteful.[10] In a section heading for *Molecular Biology of the Cell*, a best-selling text, we are told that "Oogenesis is wasteful." The text goes on to emphasize that of the seven million oogonia, or egg germ cells, in the female embryo, most degenerate in the ovary. Of those that do go on to become oocytes, or eggs, many also degenerate, so that at birth only two million eggs remain in the ovaries. Degeneration continues throughout a woman's life: by puberty 300,000 eggs remain, and only a few are present by menopause. "During the 40 or so years of a woman's reproductive life only 400 to 500 eggs will have been released," the authors write. "All the rest will have degenerated. It is still a mystery why so many eggs are formed only to die in the ovaries."[11]

The real mystery is why the male's vast production of sperm is not seen as wasteful.[12] Assuming that a man "produces" 100 million (10^8) sperm per day (a conservative estimate) during an average reproductive life of sixty years, he would produce well over two trillion sperm in his lifetime. Assuming that a woman "ripens" one egg per lunar month, or thirteen per year, over the course of her forty-year reproductive life, she would total five

---

[10]   I have found but one exception to the opinion that the female is wasteful: "Smallpox being the nasty disease it is, one might expect nature to have designed antibody molecules with combining sites that specifically recognize the epitopes on smallpox virus. Nature differs from technology, however: it thinks nothing of wastefulness. (For example, rather than improving the chance that a spermatozoon will meet an egg cell, nature finds it easier to produce millions of spermatozoa.)" (Niels Kaj Jerne, "The Immune System," *Scientific American* 229, no. 1 [July 1973]: 53). Thanks to a *Signs* reviewer for bringing this reference to my attention.

[11]   Bruce Alberts et al., *Molecular Biology of the Cell* (New York: Garland, 1983), 795.

[12]   In her essay "Have Only Men Evolved?" (in *Discovering Reality: Feminist Perspectives on Epistemology, Metaphysics, Methodology, and Philosophy of Science*, ed. Sandra Harding and Merrill B. Hintikka [Dordrecht: Reidel, 1983], 45–69, esp. 60–61), Ruth Hubbard points out that sociobiologists have said the female invests more energy than the male in the production of her large gametes, claiming that this explains why the female provides parental care. Hubbard questions whether it "really takes more 'energy' to generate the one or relatively few eggs than the large excess of sperms required to achieve fertilization." For further critique of how the greater size of eggs is interpreted in sociobiology, see Donna Haraway, "Investment Strategies for the Evolving Portfolio of Primate Females," in *Body/Politics*, ed. Mary Jacobus, Evelyn Fox Keller, and Sally Shuttleworth (New York: Routledge, 1990), 155–56.

hundred eggs in her lifetime. But the word "waste" implies an excess, too much produced. Assuming two or three offspring, for every baby a woman produces, she wastes only around two hundred eggs. For every baby a man produces, he wastes more than one trillion (10^{12}) sperm.

How is it that positive images are denied to the bodies of women? A look at language—in this case, scientific language—provides the first clue. Take the egg and the sperm.[13] It is remarkable how "femininely" the egg behaves and how "masculinely" the sperm.[14] The egg is seen as large and passive.[15] It does not *move* or *journey*, but passively "is transported," "is swept,"[16] or even "drifts"[17] along the fallopian tube. In utter contrast, sperm are small, "streamlined,"[18] and invariably active. They "deliver" their genes to the egg, "activate the developmental program of the egg,"[19] and have a "velocity" that is often remarked upon.[20] Their tails are "strong" and efficiently powered.[21] Together with the forces of ejaculation, they can "propel the semen into the deepest recesses of the vagina."[22] For this they need "energy," "fuel,"[23] so that

---

[13] The sources I used for this article provide compelling information on interactions among sperm. Lack of space prevents me from taking up this theme here, but the elements include competition, hierarchy, and sacrifice. For a newspaper report, see Malcolm W. Browne, "Some Thoughts on Self Sacrifice," *New York Times* (July 5, 1988), C6. For a literary rendition, see John Barth, "Night-Sea Journey," in his *Lost in the Funhouse* (Garden City, N.Y.: Doubleday, 1968), 3–13.

[14] See Carol Delaney, "The Meaning of Paternity and the Virgin Birth Debate," *Man* 21, no. 3 (September 1986): 494–513. She discusses the difference between this scientific view that women contribute genetic material to the fetus and the claim of long-standing Western folk theories that the origin and identity of the fetus comes from the male, as in the metaphor of planting a seed in soil.

[15] For a suggested direct link between human behavior and purportedly passive eggs and active sperm, see Erik H. Erikson, "Inner and Outer Space: Reflections on Womanhood," *Daedalus* 93, no. 2 (Spring 1964): 582–606, esp. 591.

[16] Guyton (n. 4 above), 619; and Mountcastle (n. 6 above), 1609.

[17] Jonathan Miller and David Pelham, *The Facts of Life* (New York: Viking Penguin, 1984), 5.

[18] Alberts et al., 796.

[19] Ibid., 796.

[20] See, e.g., William F. Ganong, *Review of Medical Physiology*, 7th ed. (Los Altos, Calif.: Lange Medical Publications, 1975), 322.

[21] Alberts et al. (n. 12 above), 796.

[22] Guyton, 615.

[23] Solomon (n. 7 above), 683.

with a "whiplashlike motion and strong lurches"[24] they can "burrow through the egg coat"[25] and "penetrate" it.[26]

10

At its extreme, the age-old relationship of the egg and the sperm takes on a royal or religious patina. The egg coat, its protective barrier, is sometimes called its "vestments," a term usually reserved for sacred, religious dress. The egg is said to have a "corona,"[27] a crown, and to be accompanied by "attendant cells."[28] It is holy, set apart and above, the queen to the sperm's king. The egg is also passive, which means it must depend on sperm for rescue. Gerald Schatten and Helen Schatten liken the egg's role to that of Sleeping Beauty: "a dormant bride awaiting her mate's magic kiss, which instills the spirit that brings her to life."[29] Sperm, by contrast, have a "mission,"[30] which is to "move through the female genital tract in quest of the ovum."[31] One popular account has it that the sperm carry out a "perilous journey" into the "warm darkness," where some fall away "exhausted." "Survivors" "assault" the egg, the successful candidates "surrounding the prize."[32] Part of the urgency of this journey, in more scientific terms, is that "once released from the supportive environment of the ovary, an egg will die within hours unless rescued by a sperm."[33] The wording stresses the fragility and dependency of the egg, even though the same text acknowledges elsewhere that sperm also live for only a few hours.[34]

In 1948, in a book remarkable for its early insights into these matters, Ruth Herschberger argued that female reproductive organs are seen as biologically interdependent, while male organs are viewed as autonomous, operating independently and in isolation:

---

[24] Vander, Sherman, and Luciano (n. 5 above), 4th ed. (1985), 580.

[25] Alberts et al., 796.

[26] All biology texts quoted above use the word "penetrate."

[27] Solomon, 700.

[28] A. Beldecos et al., "The Importance of Feminist Critique for Contemporary Cell Biology," Hypatia 3, no. 1 (Spring 1988): 61–76.

[29] Gerald Schatten and Helen Schatten, "The Energetic Egg," Medical World News 23 (January 23, 1984): 51–53, esp. 51.

[30] Alberts et al., 796.

[31] Guyton (n. 4 above), 613.

[32] Miller and Pelham (n. 18 above), 7.

[33] Alberts et al. (n. 12 above), 804.

[34] Ibid., 801.

At present the functional is stressed only in connection with women: it is in them that ovaries, tubes, uterus, and vagina have endless interdependence. In the male, reproduction would seem to involve "organs" only.

Yet the sperm, just as much as the egg, is dependent on a great many related processes. There are secretions which mitigate the urine in the urethra before ejaculation, to protect the sperm. There is the reflex shutting off of the bladder connection, the provision of prostatic secretions, and various types of muscular propulsion. The sperm is no more independent of its milieu than the egg, and yet from a wish that it were, biologists have lent their support to the notion that the human female, beginning with the egg, is congenitally more dependent than the male.[35]

Bringing out another aspect of the sperm's autonomy, an article in the journal *Cell* has the sperm making an "existential decision" to penetrate the egg: "Sperm are cells with a limited behavioral repertoire, one that is directed toward fertilizing eggs. To execute the decision to abandon the haploid state, sperm swim to an egg and there acquire the ability to effect membrane fusion."[36] Is this a corporate manager's version of the sperm's activities— "executing decisions" while fraught with dismay over difficult options that bring with them very high risk?

There is another way that sperm, despite their small size, can be made to loom in importance over the egg. In a collection of scientific papers, an electron micrograph of an enormous egg and tiny sperm is titled "A Portrait of the Sperm."[37] This is a little like showing a photo of a dog and calling it a picture of the fleas. Granted, microscopic sperm are harder to photograph than eggs, which are just large enough to see with the naked eye. But surely the use of the term "portrait," a word associated with the powerful and wealthy, is significant. Eggs have only micrographs or pictures, not portraits.

One depiction of sperm as weak and timid, instead of strong and powerful—the only such representation in western civilization, so far as I know—occurs in Woody Allen's movie *Everything You Always Wanted To Know About Sex* *But Were Afraid to Ask*. Allen, playing the part of an

---

[35] Ruth Herschberger, *Adam's Rib* (New York: Pellegrini & Cudaby, 1948), esp. 84. I am indebted to Ruth Hubbard for telling me about Herschberger's work, although at a point when this paper was already in draft form.

[36] Bennett M. Shapiro. "The Existential Decision of a Sperm," *Cell* 49, no. 3 (May 1987): 293–94, esp. 293.

[37] Lennart Nilsson, "A Portrait of the Sperm," in *The Functional Anatomy of the Spermatozoan*, ed. Bjorn A. Afzelius (New York: Pergamon, 1975), 79–82.

apprehensive sperm inside a man's testicles, is scared of the man's approaching orgasm. He is reluctant to launch himself into the darkness, afraid of contraceptive devices, afraid of winding up on the ceiling if the man masturbates.

15   The more common picture—egg as damsel in distress, shielded only by her sacred garments; sperm as heroic warrior to the rescue—cannot be proved to be dictated by the biology of these events. While the "facts" of biology may not *always* be constructed in cultural terms, I would argue that in this case they are. The degree of metaphorical content in these descriptions, the extent to which differences between egg and sperm are emphasized, and the parallels between cultural stereotypes of male and female behavior and the character of egg and sperm all point to this conclusion.

NEW RESEARCH, OLD IMAGERY

As new understandings of egg and sperm emerge, textbook gender imagery is being revised. But the new research, far from escaping the stereotypical representations of egg and sperm, simply replicates elements of textbook gender imagery in a different form. The persistence of this imagery calls to mind what Ludwig Fleck termed "the self-contained" nature of scientific thought. As he described it, "the interaction between what is already known, what remains to be learned, and those who are to apprehend it, go to ensure harmony within the system. But at the same time they also preserve the harmony of illusions, which is quite secure within the confines of a given thought style."[38] We need to understand the way in which the cultural content in scientific descriptions changes as biological discoveries unfold, and whether that cultural content is solidly entrenched or easily changed.

In all of the texts quoted above, sperm are described as penetrating the egg, and specific substances on a sperm's head are described as binding to the egg. Recently, this description of events was rewritten in a biophysics lab at Johns Hopkins University—transforming the egg from the passive to the active party.[39]

Prior to this research, it was thought that the zona, the inner vestments of the egg, formed an impenetrable barrier. Sperm overcame the barrier by

---

[38] Ludwig Fleck, *Genesis and Development of a Scientific Fact*, ed. Thaddeus J. Trenn and Robert K. Merton (Chicago: University of Chicago Press, 1979), 38.

[39] Jay M. Baltz carried out the research I describe when he was a graduate student in the Thomas C. Jenkins Department of Biophysics at Johns Hopkins University.

mechanically burrowing through, thrashing their tails and slowly working their way along. Later research showed that the sperm released digestive enzymes that chemically broke down the zona; thus, scientists presumed that the sperm used mechanical and chemical means to get through to the egg.

In this recent investigation, the researchers began to ask questions about the mechanical force of the sperm's tail. (The lab's goal was to develop a contraceptive that worked topically on sperm.) They discovered, to their great surprise, that the forward thrust of sperm is extremely weak, which contradicts the assumption that sperm are forceful penetrators.[40] Rather than thrusting forward, the sperm's head was now seen to move mostly back and forth. The sideways motion of the sperm's tail makes the head move sideways with a force that is ten times stronger than its forward movement. So even if the overall force of the sperm were strong enough to mechanically break the zona, most of its force would be directed sideways rather than forward. In fact, its strongest tendency, by tenfold, is to *escape* by attempting to pry itself off the egg. Sperm, then, must be exceptionally efficient at escaping from any cell surface they contact. And the surface of the egg must be designed to trap the sperm and prevent their escape. Otherwise, few if any sperm would reach the egg.

20   The researchers at Johns Hopkins concluded that the sperm and egg stick together because of adhesive molecules on the surfaces of each. The egg traps the sperm and adheres to it so tightly that the sperm's head is forced to lie flat against the surface of the zona, a little bit, they told me, "like Br'er Rabbit getting more and more stuck to tar baby the more he wriggles." The trapped sperm continues to wiggle ineffectually side to side. The mechanical force of its tail is so weak that a sperm cannot break even one chemical bond. This is where the digestive enzymes released by the sperm come in. If they start to soften the zona just at the tip of the sperm and the sides remain stuck, then the weak, flailing sperm can get oriented in the right direction and make it through the zona—provided that its bonds to the zona dissolve as it moves in.

Although this new version of the saga of the egg and the sperm broke through cultural expectations, the researchers who made the discovery

---

[40]   Far less is known about the physiology of sperm than comparable female substances, which some feminists claim is no accident. Greater scientific scrutiny of female reproduction has long enabled the burden of birth control to be placed on women. In this case, the researchers' discovery did not depend on development of any new technology: The experiments made use of glass pipettes, a manometer, and a simple microscope, all of which have been available for more than one hundred years.

continued to write papers and abstracts as if the sperm were the active party who attacks, binds, penetrates, and enters the egg. The only difference was that the sperm were now seen as performing these actions weakly.[41] Not until August 1987, more than three years after the findings described above, did these researchers reconceptualize the process to give the egg a more active role. They began to describe the zona as an aggressive sperm catcher, covered with adhesive molecules that can capture a sperm with a single bond and clasp it to the zona's surface.[42] In the words of their published account: "The innermost vestment, the *zona pellucida*, is a glycoprotein shell, which captures and tethers the sperm before they penetrate it....The sperm is captured at the initial contact between the sperm tip and the *zona*....Since the thrust [of the sperm] is much smaller than the force needed to break a single affinity bond, the first bond made upon the tip-first meeting of the sperm and *zona* can result in the capture of the sperm."[43]

Experiments in another lab reveal similar patterns of data interpretation. Gerald Schatten and Helen Schatten set out to show that, contrary to conventional wisdom, the "egg is not merely a large, yolk-filled sphere into which the sperm burrows to endow new life. Rather, recent research suggests the almost heretical view that sperm and egg are mutually active partners."[44] This sounds like a departure from the stereotypical textbook view, but further reading reveals Schatten and Schatten's conformity to the aggressive-sperm metaphor. They describe how "the sperm and egg first touch when, from the tip of the sperm's triangular head, a long, thin filament shoots out and harpoons the egg." Then we learn that "remarkably, the harpoon is not so much fired as assembled at great speed, molecule by

---

[41] Jay Baltz and Richard A. Cone, "What Force Is Needed to Tether a Sperm?" (abstract for Society for the Study of Reproduction, 1985), and "Flagellar Torque on the Head Determines the Force Needed to Tether a Sperm" (abstract for Biophysical Society, 1986).

[42] Jay M. Baltz, David F. Katz, and Richard A. Cone, "The Mechanics of the Sperm-Egg Interaction at the Zona Pellucida," *Biophysical Journal* 54, no. 4 (October 1988): 643–54. Lab members were somewhat familiar with work on metaphors in the biology of female reproduction. Richard Cone, who runs the lab, is my husband, and he talked with them about my earlier research on the subject from time to time. Even though my current research focuses on biological imagery and I heard about the lab's work from my husband every day, I myself did not recognize the role of imagery in the sperm research until many weeks after the period of research and writing I describe. Therefore, I assume that any awareness the lab members may have had about how underlying metaphor might be guiding this particular research was fairly inchoate.

[43] Ibid., 643, 650.

[44] Schatten and Schatten (n. 30 above), 51.

molecule, from a pool of protein stored in a specialized region called the acrosome. The filament may grow as much as twenty times longer than the sperm head itself before its tip reaches the egg and sticks."[45] Why not call this "making a bridge" or "throwing out a line" rather than firing a harpoon? Harpoons pierce prey and injure or kill them, while this filament only sticks. And why not focus, as the Hopkins lab did, on the stickiness of the egg, rather than the stickiness of the sperm?[46] Later in the article, the Schattens replicate the common view of the sperm's perilous journey into the warm darkness of the vagina, this time for the purpose of explaining its journey into the egg itself: "[The sperm] still has an arduous journey ahead. It must penetrate farther into the egg's huge sphere of cytoplasm and somehow locate the nucleus, so that the two cells' chromosomes can fuse. The sperm dives down into the cytoplasm, its tail beating. But it is soon interrupted by the sudden and swift migration of the egg nucleus, which rushes toward the sperm with a velocity triple that of the movement of chromosomes during cell division, crossing the entire egg in about a minute."[47]

Like Schatten and Schatten and the biophysicists at Johns Hopkins, another researcher has recently made discoveries that seem to point to a more interactive view of the relationship of egg and sperm. This work, which Paul Wassarman conducted on the sperm and eggs of mice, focuses on identifying the specific molecules in the egg coat (the zona pellucida) that are involved in egg-sperm interaction. At first glance, his descriptions seem to fit the model of an egalitarian relationship. Male and female gametes "recognize one another," and "interactions...take place between sperm and egg."[48] But the article in *Scientific American* in which those descriptions appear begins with a vignette that presages the dominant motif of their presentation: "It has been more than a century since Hermann Fol, a Swiss zoologist, peered into his microscope and became the first person to see a sperm penetrate an egg, fertilize it and form the first cell of a new embryo."[49] This portrayal of the sperm as the active party—the one that *penetrates* and *fertilizes* the egg and *produces* the embryo—is not cited as an example of an earlier, now out-

---

[45] Ibid, 52.

[46] Surprisingly, in an article intended for a general audience, the authors do not point out that these are sea urchin sperm and note that human sperm do not shoot out filaments at all.

[47] Schatten and Schatten, 53.

[48] Paul M. Wassarman, "Fertilization in Mammals," *Scientific American* 259, no. 6 (December 1988): 78–84, esp. 78, 84.

[49] Ibid., 78.

moded view. In fact, the author reiterates the point later in the article: "Many sperm can bind to and penetrate the zona pellucida, or outer coat, of an unfertilized mouse egg, but only one sperm will eventually fuse with the thin plasma membrane surrounding the egg proper (*inner sphere*), *fertilizing the egg and giving rise to a new embryo.*"[50]

The imagery of sperm as aggressor is particularly startling in this case: the main discovery being reported is isolation of a particular molecule *on the egg coat* that plays an important role in fertilization! Wassarman's choice of language sustains the picture. He calls the molecule that has been isolated, ZP3, a "sperm receptor." By allocating the passive, waiting role to the egg, Wassarman can continue to describe the sperm as the actor, the one that makes it all happen: "The basic process begins when many sperm first attach loosely and then bind tenaciously to receptors on the surface of the egg's thick outer coat, the zona pellucida. Each sperm, which has a large number of egg-binding proteins on its surface, binds to many sperm receptors on the egg. More specifically, a site on each of the egg-binding proteins fits a complementary site on a sperm receptor, much as a key fits a lock."[51] With the sperm designated as the "key" and the egg the "lock," it is obvious which one acts and which one is acted upon. Could this imagery not be reversed, letting the sperm (the lock) wait until the egg produces the key? Or could we speak of two halves of a locket matching, and regard the matching itself as the action that initiates the fertilization?

It is as if Wassarman were determined to make the egg the receiving partner. Usually in biological research, the protein member of the pair of binding molecules is called the receptor, and physically it has a pocket in it rather like a lock. As the diagrams that illustrate Wassarman's article show, the molecules on the sperm are proteins and have "pockets." The small, mobile molecules that fits into these pockets are called ligands. As shown in the diagrams, ZP3 on the egg is a polymer of "keys"; many small knobs stick out. Typically, molecules in the sperm would be called receptors and molecules on the egg would be called ligands. But Wassarman chose to name ZP3 on the egg the receptor and to create a new term, "the egg-binding

50 Ibid., 79.

51 Ibid., 78.

protein," for the molecule on the sperm that otherwise would have been called the receptor.[52]

Wassarman does credit the egg coat with having more functions than those of a sperm receptor. While he notes that "the zona pellucida has at times been viewed by investigators as a nuisance, a barrier to sperm and hence an impediment to fertilization," his new research reveals that the egg coat "serves as a sophisticated biological security system that screens incoming sperm, selects only those compatible with fertilization and development, prepares sperm for fusion with the egg and later protects the resulting embryo from polyspermy [a lethal condition caused by fusion of more than one sperm with a single egg]."[53] Although this description gives the egg an active role, that role is drawn in stereotypically feminine terms. The egg *selects* an appropriate mate, *prepares* him for fusion, and then *protects* the resulting offspring from harm. This is courtship and mating behavior as seen through the eyes of a sociobiologist: woman as the hard-to-get prize, who, following union with the chosen one, becomes woman as servant and mother.

And Wassarman does not quit there. In a review article for *Science*, he outlines the "chronology of fertilization."[54] Near the end of the article are two subject headings. One is "Sperm Penetration," in which Wassarman describes how the chemical dissolving of the zona pellucida combines with the "substantial propulsive force generated by sperm." The next heading is "Sperm-Egg Fusion." This section details what happens inside the zona after a sperm "penetrates" it. Sperm "can make contact with, adhere to, and fuse with (that is, fertilize) an egg."[55] Wassarman's word choice, again, is astonishingly skewed in favor of the sperm's activity, for in the next breath he says that sperm *lose* all motility upon fusion with the egg's surface. In mouse and sea urchin eggs, the sperm enters at the *egg's* volition, according to Wassarman's description: "Once fused with egg plasma membrane [the surface of the egg], how does a sperm enter the egg? The surface of both mouse and sea urchin eggs is covered with thousands of plasma mem-

---

[52] Since receptor molecules are relatively *immotile* and the ligands that bind to them relatively *motile*, one might imagine the egg being called the receptor and the sperm the ligand. But the molecules in question on egg and sperm are immotile molecules. It is the sperm as a *cell* that has motility, and the egg as a cell that has relative immotility.

[53] Wassarman, 78–79.

[54] Paul M. Wassarman, "The Biology and Chemistry of Fertilization," *Science* 235, no. 4788 (January 30, 1987): 553–60, esp. 554.

[55] Ibid., 557.

brane-bound projections, called microvilli [tiny 'hairs']. Evidence in sea urchins suggests that, after membrane fusion, a group of elongated microvilli cluster tightly around and interdigitate over the sperm head. As these microvilli are resorbed, the sperm is drawn into the egg. Therefore, sperm motility, which ceases at the time of fusion in both sea urchins and mice, is not required for sperm entry."[56] The section called "Sperm Penetration" more logically would be followed by a section called "The Egg Envelopes," rather than "Sperm-Egg Fusion." This would give a parallel—and more accurate—sense that both the egg and the sperm initiate action.

Another way that Wassarman makes less of the egg's activity is by describing components of the egg but referring to the sperm as a whole entity. Deborah Gordon has described such an approach as "atomism" ("the part is independent of and primordial to the whole") and identified it as one of the "tenacious assumptions" of Western science and medicine.[57] Wassarman employs atomism to his advantage. When he refers to processes going on within sperm, he consistently returns to descriptions that remind us from whence these activities came: they are part of sperm that penetrate an egg or generate propulsive force. When he refers to processes going on within eggs, he stops there. As a result, any active role he grants them appears to be assigned to the parts of the egg, and not to the egg itself. In the quote above, it is the microvilli that actively cluster around the sperm. In another example, "the driving force for engulfment of a fused sperm comes from a region of cytoplasm just beneath an egg's plasma membrane."[58]

SOCIAL IMPLICATIONS

All three of these revisionist accounts of egg and sperm cannot seem to escape the hierarchical imagery of older accounts. Even though each new account gives the egg a larger and more active role, taken together they bring into play another cultural stereotype: woman as a dangerous and aggressive threat. In the Johns Hopkins lab's revised model, the egg ends up as the female aggressor who "captures and tethers" the sperm with her sticky zona,

---

[56] Ibid, 557–58. This finding throws into question Schatten and Schatten's description (n. 30 above) of the sperm, its tail beating, diving down into the egg.

[57] Deborah R. Gordon, "Tenacious Assumptions in Western Medicine," in *Bio-medicine Examined*, ed. Margaret Lock and Deborah Gordon (Dordrecht: Kluwer, 1988), 19–56, esp. 26.

[58] Wassarman, "The Biology and Chemistry of Fertilization," 558.

rather like a spider lying in wait in her web.[59] The Schatten lab has the egg's nucleus "interrupt" the sperm's dive with a "sudden and swift" rush by which she "clasps the sperm and guides its nucleus to the center."[60] Wassarman's description of the surface of the egg "covered with thousands of plasma membrane-bound projections, called microvilli" that reach out and clasp the sperm adds to the spiderlike imagery.[61]

30

These images grant the egg an active role but at the cost of appearing disturbingly aggressive. Images of woman as dangerous and aggressive, the femme fatale who victimizes men, are widespread in Western literature and culture.[62] More specific is the connection of spider imagery with the idea of an engulfing, devouring mother.[63] New data did not lead scientists to eliminate gender stereotypes in their descriptions of egg and sperm. Instead, scientists simply began to describe egg and sperm in different, but no less damaging, terms.

Can we envision a less stereotypical view? Biology itself provides another model that could be applied to the egg and the sperm. The cybernetic model—with its feedback loops, flexible adaptation to change, coordination of the parts within a whole, evolution over time, and changing response to the environment—is common in genetics, endocrinology, and ecology and has a growing influence in medicine in general.[64] This model has the potential to shift our imagery from the negative, in which the female reproductive system is castigated both for not producing eggs after birth and for producing (and thus wasting) too many eggs overall, to something more positive. The female reproductive system could be seen as responding to the environment (pregnancy or menopause), adjusting to monthly changes (menstruation), and flexibly changing from reproductivity after puberty to nonreproductivity later in life. The sperm and egg's interaction could also be described in cybernetic terms. J.F. Hartman's research in reproductive

---

[59] Baltz, Katz, and Cone (n. 43 above), 643, 650.

[60] Schatten and Schatten, 53.

[61] Wassarman, "The Biology and Chemistry of Fertilization," 557.

[62] Mary Ellman, *Thinking about Women* (New York: Harcourt Brace Jovanovich, 1968), 140; Nina Auerbach, *Woman and the Demon* (Cambridge, Mass.: Harvard University Press, 1982), esp. 186.

[63] Kenneth Alan Adams, "Arachnophobia: Love American Style," *Journal of Psychoanalytic Anthropology* 4, no. 2 (1981): 157–97.

[64] William Ray Arney and Bernard Bergen, *Medicine and the Management of Living* (Chicago: University of Chicago Press, 1984).

biology demonstrated fifteen years ago that if an egg is killed by being pricked with a needle, live sperm cannot get through the zona.[65] Clearly, this evidence shows that the egg and sperm do interact on more mutual terms, making biology's refusal to portray them that way all the more disturbing.

We would do well to be aware, however, that cybernetic imagery is hardly neutral. In the past, cybernetic models have played an important part in the imposition of social control. These models inherently provide a way of thinking about a "field" of interacting components. Once the field can be seen, it can become the object of new forms of knowledge, which in turn can allow new forms of social control to be exerted over the components of the field. During the 1950s, for example, medicine began to recognize the psychosocial *environment* of the patient: the patient's family and its psychodynamics. Professions such as social work began to focus on this new environment, and the resulting knowledge became one way to further control the patient. Patients began to be seen not as isolated, individual bodies, but as psychosocial entities located in an "ecological" system: management of "the patient's psychology was a new entrée to patient control."[66]

The models that biologists use to describe their data can have important social effects. During the nineteenth century, the social and natural sciences strongly influenced each other: the social ideas of Malthus about how to avoid the natural increase of the poor inspired Darwin's *Origin of Species*.[67] Once the *Origin* stood as a description of the natural world, complete with competition and market struggles, it could be reimported into social science as social Darwinism, in order to justify the social order of the time. What we are seeing now is similar: the importation of cultural ideas about passive females and heroic males into the "personalities" of gametes. This amounts to the "implanting of social imagery on representations of nature so as to lay a firm basis for reimporting exactly that same imagery as natural explanations of social phenomena."[68]

Further research would show us exactly what social effects are being wrought from the biological imagery of egg and sperm. At the very least, the

---

[65]   J. F. Hartman, R. B. Gwatkin, and C. F. Hutchison, "Early Contact Interactions between Mammalian Gametes In Vitro," *Proceedings of the National Academy of Sciences* (U.S.) 69, no. 10 (1972): 2767–69.

[66]   Arney and Bergen, 68.

[67]   Ruth Hubbard, "Have Only Men Evolved?" (n. 13 above), 51–52.

[68]   David Harvey, personal communication, November 1989.

imagery keeps alive some of the hoariest old stereotypes about weak damsels in distress and their strong male rescuers. That these stereotypes are now being written in at the level of the cell constitutes a powerful move to make them seem so natural as to be beyond alteration.

35
The stereotypical imagery might also encourage people to imagine that what results from the interaction of egg and sperm—a fertilized egg—is the result of deliberate "human" action at the cellular level. Whatever the intentions of the human couple, in this microscopic "culture" a cellular "bride" (or femme fatale) and a cellular "groom" (her victim) make a cellular baby. Rosalind Petchesky points out that through visual representations such as sonograms, we are given "*images* of younger and younger, and tinier and tinier, fetuses being 'saved.'" This leads to "the point of visibility being 'pushed back' *indefinitely*."[69] Endowing egg and sperm with intentional action, a key aspect of personhood in our culture, lays the foundation for the point of viability being pushed back to the moment of fertilization. This will likely lead to greater acceptance of technological developments and new forms of scrutiny and manipulation, for the benefit of these inner "persons": court-ordered restrictions on a pregnant woman's activities in order to protect her fetus, fetal surgery, amniocentesis, and rescinding of abortion rights, to name but a few examples.[70]

Even if we succeed in substituting more egalitarian, interactive metaphors to describe the activities of egg and sperm, and manage to avoid the pitfalls of cybernetic models, we would still be guilty of endowing cellular entities with personhood. More crucial, then, than what *kinds* of personalities we bestow on cells is the very fact that we are doing it at all. This process could ultimately have the most disturbing social consequences.

One clear feminist challenge is to wake up sleeping metaphors in science, particularly those involved in descriptions of the egg and the sperm. Although the literary convention is to call such metaphors "dead," they are not so much dead as sleeping, hidden within the scientific content of

---

[69] Rosalind Petchesky, "Fetal Images: The Power of Visual Culture in the Politics of Reproduction," *Feminist Studies* 13, no. 2 (Summer 1987): 263–92, esp. 272.

[70] Rita Arditti, Renate Klein, and Shelley Minden, *Test-Tube Women* (London: Pandora, 1984); Ellen Goodman, "Whose Right to Life?" *Baltimore Sun* (November 17, 1987); Tamar Lewin, "Courts Acting to Force Care of the Unborn," *New York Times* (November 23, 1987), A1 and B10; Susan Irwin and Brigitte Jordan, "Knowledge, Practice, and Power: Court Ordered Cesarean Sections," *Medical Anthropology Quarterly* 1, no. 3 (September 1987): 319–34.

texts—and all the more powerful for it.[71] Waking up such metaphors, by becoming aware of when we are projecting cultural imagery onto what we study, will improve our ability to investigate and understand nature. Waking up such metaphors, by becoming aware of their implications, will rob them of their power to naturalize our social conventions about gender.

(1991)

Questions:

1. We tend to think of metaphor as the province of literary writing; by contrast, we think of scientific writing as purely descriptive. Is metaphor in fact a useful mode of description for scientific matters? Is it to some extent necessary to resort to metaphor in order to explain scientific processes adequately?

2. Why in Martin's view are the Johns Hopkins researchers (not named in the body of the article, but identified in the references as J. M. Baltz, David F. Catz, and Richard A. Cone) who carried out the work she discusses in paragraphs 10–14 not more deserving of praise for their ground-breaking research?

3. What effect might the use of the active or the passive voice have when used in scientific research to describe gendered processes or behaviours? Select (or make up) a sentence on this sort of topic written in the active voice, and then re-write the sentence in the passive voice.

4. Discuss the organization of Martin's essay. Is there an overall progression in the ideas she presents?

---

[71] Thanks to Elizabeth Fee and David Spain, who in February 1989 and April 1989, respectively, made points related to this.

Dionne Brand

On Poetry

*In this short piece a prominent poet and activist writes about the
nature and importance of poetry.*

〜

Every word turns on itself, every word falls after it is said. None of the
answers that I've given over the years is the truth. Those answers have all
been given like a guerrilla with her face in a handkerchief, her eyes still. She
is still, poised for quick movement, but still. Her boots sturdy, the gravel
under them dislodges and dusts. But her eyes are still. And I've answered like
the captive giving answers in an interrogation, telling just enough to appease
the interrogator and just enough to trace the story so she could repeat it
without giving anything away and without contradiction the next time she
has to tell it. I've told them the same things over and over again, and I'll tell
them again when they ask because they only ask certain questions, like where
I'm from and do I hate them.

But if I can give myself a moment, I would say it's been relief to write
poetry, it's been just room to live.

I've had moments when the life of my people has been so overwhelming
to bear that poetry seemed useless, and I cannot say that there is any moment
that I do not think that now. At times it has been more crucial to wield a
scythe over high grass in a field in Marigot; at times it has been more
important to figure out how a woman without papers in Toronto can have
a baby and not be caught and deported; at times it has been more helpful to
organise a demonstration in front of the police station at Bay and College
Streets. Often there's been no reason whatsoever to write poetry. There are
days when I cannot think of a single reason to write this life down.

There's a photograph of me when I was four. I'm standing next to my
little sister and my cousin. My big sister is in the picture, too. I do not

resemble myself except for my legs, which were bowed and still are. My little sister is crying, her fingers in her mouth, and my cousin looks stunned, as if she's been thrown into the picture. My big sister is tall and slender, heading for the glamour which will describe her life. She looks like Nancy Wilson. Black patent-leather shoes, white boat-necked dress. I am looking at the camera, my mouth open. I am holding a shac-shac, blurring in the picture, so that my little sister would stop crying. I look as if I'm trying to make this picture work. I remember the moment of consciously getting set, holding the shac-shac, being called upon to act, saying to my little sister don't cry, see, don't cry. My eyes in the picture are not those of a little girl; they seem knowledgeable, still. My little sister's eyes look teary, my cousin's, frightened, my big sister's, sad. Mine, still. Watching. I remember watching. Knowing that this was an occasion to watch out of ourselves and saying I'd hold the shac-shac so my little sister would not cry. I only recognise my legs and the eyes. Still. Watching out.

5   If I can take a second. Shaking the gravel from my shoes. Poetry is here, just *here*. Something wrestling with how we live, something dangerous, something honest.

(1994)

QUESTIONS:

1. What is the relation between Brand's political activism and the role of poetry in her life?

2. What does Brand mean when she writes, "Poetry is here, just *here*?"

3. Explain Brand's extended metaphor comparing herself to a guerrilla.

4. Identify the phrases that Brand repeats in this short article and speculate on why she does so.

5. Brand's older sister looks glamorous in the childhood photo, and she grows up to be glamorous. Why does Brand make this connection?

URSULA FRANKLIN

SILENCE AND THE NOTION OF THE COMMONS

In this essay a leading physicist discusses the implications of two changes
technology has wrought: separating sound from its source,
and making the sound permanent.

～

In a technological world, where the acoustic environment is largely artificial, silence takes on new dimensions, be it in terms of the human need for silence (perhaps a person's right to be free from acoustic assault), of communication, or of intentional modification of the environment.

This article is based on the text of a lecture given at the Banff Centre in August of 1993 as part of "The Tuning of the World" conference on acoustic ecology. It consists of two separate but interrelated parts: silence as spiritual experience (drawing largely, but not exclusively, on the Quaker tradition of religious worship) and silence as a common good. Silence is examined in terms of the general patterns of the social impact of modern technology. Silence possesses striking similarities with such aspects of life and community as unpolluted water, air, or soil, which once were taken for granted, but which have become special and precious in technologically mediated environments. The threat of a privatization of the soundscape is discussed and some immediate measures suggested.

I would like to thank everyone involved in this conference, and the organizers in particular, for inviting me to deliver this talk. I am very obviously an outsider and wish to come to this group to talk about something that is central to all the work that you people are doing. And so I come in a way as a friend and colleague, in a field where I am fully aware that silence has been the subject of many publications. It is the subject of more than a chapter in R. Murray Schafer's *The Tuning of the World* and John Cage and others have written books on it. I would like to examine how our concept—as well as our practice—of silence has been influenced by all the other things that have changed as our world has become what Jacques Ellul calls a "technological milieu," a world that is, in all its facets, increasingly mediated by technology.

Before we had a technologically mediated society, before we had electronics and electro-magnetic devices, sound was rightly seen as being ephemeral, sound was coupled to its source, and lasted only a very short time. This is very different from what we see in a landscape: however much we feel that the landscape might be modified, however much we feel that there is a horrible building somewhere in front of a beautiful mountain, on the scale of the soundscape, the landscape is permanent. What is put up is there. That's very different from the traditional soundscape. What modern technology has brought to sound is the possibility of doing two things: to separate the sound from the source and to make the sound permanent. In addition, modern devices make it possible to decompose, recompose, analyse and mix sounds, to change the initial magnitude and sustainability of sound, as well as to change all the characteristics that link the sound with its source. R. Murray Schafer called this "schizophonia," separating the sound from the source. We now have easy access to the multitude of opportunities that result from overcoming that coupling.

5   The social impact of this technology is significant. Prior to these developments there was a limitation to sound and sound penetration. If you heard a bagpipe band there was a limit to the amount of time it would play; if you found it displeasing you could patiently wait until the players got exhausted. But with a recording of a bagpipe band, you are out of luck. It's never going to be exhausted. Electronics, then, have altered the modern soundscape. While modern technology is a source of joy in modern composition, through the opening of many doors for expression, it is also the source of a good number of problems related to the soundscape, problems which society as a whole must adjust to, cope with, and possibly ameliorate.

But then there is not only sound, there is silence. Silence is affected by these same technological developments, the same means of separating sound from source and overcoming the ephemeral nature of a soundscape. I have attempted to define silence and to analyse the attributes that make it valuable. Defining silence as the absence of external or artificially generated sound is fine, but it's a little bit shallow, because silence in many ways is very much more than the absence of sound. Absence of sound is a condition necessary to silence but it is not sufficient in itself to define what we mean by silence. When one thinks about the concept of silence, one notices that there has to be somebody who listens before you can say there is silence. Silence, in addition to being an absence of sound, is defined by a listener, by hearing.

A further attribute, or parameter of silence, from my point of view, comes out of the question: *why is it that we worry about silence?* I feel that one comes to the root of the meaning and practice of silence only when one asks; *why is it that we value and try to establish silence?* Because silence is an enabling environment. This is the domain that we have traditionally associated with silence, the enabling condition in which unprogrammed and unprogrammable events can take place. That is the silence of contemplation; it is the silence when people get in touch with themselves; it is the silence of meditation and worship. The distinctive character of this domain of silence is that it is an enabling condition that opens up the possibility of unprogrammed, unplanned and unprogrammable happenings.

In this light we understand why, as Christians, traditional Quakers found it necessary in the seventeenth century, when they were surrounded by all the pomp and circumstance of the church of England, to reject it. We understand why they felt any ritual, in the sense of its programmed nature and predictability, to be a straitjacket rather than a comfort, and why they said to the amazement of their contemporaries: *we worship God in silence.* Their justification for the practice of silence was that they required it to hear God's voice. Beyond the individual's centering, beyond the individual effort of meditation, there was the need for *collective* silence. Collective silence is an enormously powerful event. There are contemporaneous accounts of Quaker meetings under heavy persecution in England, when thousands of people met silently on a hillside. Then out of the silence, one person—unappointed, unordained, unexpected, and unprogrammed—might speak, to say: *Out of the silence there can come a ministry.* The message is not essentially within that person, constructed in their intellect, but comes out of the silence to them. This isn't just history and theory. I think that if any one of you attended Quaker meetings, particularly on a regular basis, you would find that, suddenly, out of the silence, somebody speaks about something that had just entered *your* mind. It's an uncanny thing. The strength of collective silence is probably one of the most powerful spiritual forces.

Now, in order for something like this to happen, a lot of things are required. There is what Quakers call: *to be with heart and mind prepared.* But there is also the collective decision to be silent. And to be silent in order to let unforeseen, unforeseeable, and unprogrammed things happen. Such silence, I repeat, is the environment that enables the unprogrammed. I feel it is very much at risk.

10   I will elaborate on this, but first I want to say: there is another silence. There is the silence that enables a programmed, a planned, event to take place. There is the silence in which you courteously engage so that I might be heard: in order for one to be heard all the others have to be silent. But in many cases silence is not taken on voluntarily and it is this false silence of which I am afraid. It is not the silence only of the padded cell, or of solitary confinement; it is the silence that is enforced by the megaphone, the boom box, the PA system, and any other device that stifles other sounds and voices in order that a planned event can take place.

There is a critical juncture between the planned and the unplanned, the programmed and the unplannable that must be kept in mind. I feel very strongly that our present technological trends drive us toward a decrease in the space—be it in the soundscape, the landscape, or the mindscape—in which the unplanned and unplannable can happen. Yet silence has to remain available in the soundscape, the landscape, and the mindscape. Allowing openness to the unplannable, to the unprogrammed, is the core of the strength of silence. It is also the core of our individual and collective sanity. I extend that to the collectivity because, as a community, as a people, we are threatened just as much, if not more, by the impingement of the programmed over the silent, over that which enables the unprogrammed. Much of the impingement goes unnoticed, uncommented upon, since it is much less obvious than the intrusion of a structure into the landscape. While we may not win all the battles at City Hall to preserve our trees, at least there is now a semi-consciousness that this type of struggle is important.

Where can one go to get away from the dangers of even the gentle presence of programmed music, or Muzak, in our public buildings? Where do I protest that upon entering any place, from the shoe store to the restaurant, I am deprived of the opportunity to be quiet? Who has asked my permission to put that slop into the elevator I may have to use umpteen times every day? Many such "background" activities are intentionally manipulative. This is not merely "noise" that can be dealt with in terms of noise abatement. There are two aspects to be stressed in this context. One is that the elimination of silence is being done without anybody's consent. The other is that one really has to stop and think and analyse in order to see just how manipulative these interventions can be.

For instance, in the Toronto Skydome, friends tell me that the sound environment is coupled and geared to the game: if the home team misses, there are mournful and distressing sounds over the PA; when the home team scores there is a sort of athletic equivalent of the Hallelujah Chorus. Again, the visitor has no choice; the programmed soundscape is part of the event. You cannot be present at the game without being subjected to that mood manipulation. I wonder if music will soon be piped into the voter's booth, maybe an upbeat, slightly military tune: "*Get on with it. Get the votes in.*" Joking aside, soundscape manipulation is a serious issue. Who on earth has given anybody the right to manipulate the sound environment?

Now, I want to come back to the definition of silence and introduce the notion of the commons, because the soundscape essentially doesn't belong to anyone in particular. What we are hearing, I feel, is very much the privatization of the soundscape, in the same manner in which the enclosure laws in Britain destroyed the commons of old. There was a time when in fact every community had what was called "the commons," an area that belonged to everybody and where sheep could graze—a place important to all, belonging to all. The notion of the commons is deeply embedded in our social mind as something that all share. There are many "commons" that we take for granted and for millenia, clean air and clean water were the norm. Because of the ephemeral nature of sound in the past, silence was not considered part of the commons. Today, the technology to preserve and multiply sound and separate it from its source has resulted in our sudden awareness that silence, too, is a common good. Silence, which we need in order that unprogrammed and unprogrammable things can take place, is being removed from common access without much fuss and civic bother. It is being privatized.

This is another illustration of an often-observed occurrence related to the impact of technology: that things considered in the past to be normal or ordinary become rare or extraordinary, while those things once considered rare and unusual become normal and routine. Flying is no longer a big deal, but a handmade dress or a home-cooked meal may well be special. We essentially consider polluted water as normal now, and people who can afford it drink bottled water. It is hard to have bottled silence. But money still can buy distance from sound. Today, when there is civic anger, it is with respect to "noise"—like airport noise, etc. There is not yet such anger with respect to the manipulative elimination of silence from the soundscape.

There are those of us who have acknowledged and seen the deterioration of the commons as far as silence is concerned, who have seen that the soundscape is not only polluted by noise—so that one has to look for laws related to noise abatement—but also that the soundscape has become increasingly polluted through the private use of sound in the manipulative dimension of setting and programming moods and conditions. There is a desperate need for awareness of this, and for awareness of it in terms of the collectivity, rather than just individual needs. I feel very much that this is a time for civic anger. This is a time when one has to say: *town planning is constrained by by-laws on height, density, and other features; what are town planning's constraints in relation to silence?*

You may ask, what would I suggest? First of all, we must insist that, as human beings in a society, we have a right to silence. Just as we feel we have the right to walk down the street without being physically assaulted by people and preferably without being visually assaulted by ugly outdoor advertising, we also have the right not to be assaulted by sound, and in particular, not to be assaulted by sound that is there solely for the purpose of profit. Now is the time for civic rage, as well as civic education, but also for some action.

Think of the amount of care that goes into the regulation of parking, so that our good, precious, and necessary cars have a place to be well and safe. That's very important to society. I have yet to see, beyond hospitals, a public building that has a quiet room. Is not our sanity at least as important as the safety of our cars? One should begin to think: are there places, even in conferences like this, that are hassle-free, quiet spaces, where people can go? There were times when one could say to a kid: *"Where did you go?"*— *"Out."*— *"What did you do?"*—*"Nothing."* That sort of blessed time is past. The kid is programmed. We are programmed. And we don't even ask for a quiet space anymore.

One possible measure, relatively close at hand, is to set aside, as a normal matter of human rights, in those buildings over which we have some influence, a quiet room. Further, I highly recommend starting committee meetings with two minutes of silence, and ending them with a few minutes of silence, too. I sit on committees that have this practice, and find that it not only can expedite the business before the committee, but also contributes to a certain amount of peacefulness and sanity. One can start a lecture with a few minutes of silence, and can close it the same way. There can be a few minutes of silence before a shared meal. Such things help, even if they help only in small ways. I do think even small initiatives make silence "visible" as an ever-present part of life. I now invite you to have two minutes of silence before we go on into the question period. Let us be quiet together.

(1994)

QUESTIONS:

1. This article appeared in a journal (*Musicworks: The Journal of Sound Exploration*) that might appropriately be described as semi-scholarly; its audience consists primarily either of academics in music departments or those well-versed in the technical aspects of music and sound. How does Franklin position herself in paragraph 3 in relationship to this audience? In the remainder of the article, does Franklin invite a wider audience?

2. Using paragraph 6 of this essay as an example, comment on why it is often necessary to go beyond dictionary definitions in defining a term for technical or academic purposes.

3. How strong are the connections between silence and religion? Discuss with relation both to Franklin's argument in paragraph 8 and to whatever evidence you are able to assemble from outside this article about religious attitudes and practices.

4. How in Franklin's view is silence often "enforced" (paragraph 10)?

5. Explain in your own words the notion of "the commons" (paragraph 14).

6. Write up a plan of Franklin's argument, with a phrase or two summarizing each paragraph, and using headings and/or connector arrows as you feel appropriate.

7. Do technological developments inevitably tend towards a reduction in the level of silence in society?

8. Write a brief essay arguing for or against increased regulation in your community of the soundscape.

Lucy Grealy

Fear Itself

An award-winning poet writes about experiencing an
extraordinary physical ordeal.

∽

The streets in New York City are their own country. A knowledge of them gives one a sense of power. It makes no difference that for the most part New York is a giant grid, supremely traversable compared with such labyrinths as Paris or London. Its power heaves up from the pavement right in front of your eyes, steam escapes in fits and starts as if the whole place were going to blow any minute, people who have already blown apart lie crumpled in its crevasses, and all the while there is a thin promise, a slight wheedling tone, that something important, something drastic, is about to break.

I drove with my mother into the city five days a week, every week, for two years for radiation and chemotherapy treatments, and then once a week for another half year to finish out the chemotherapy, which was administered most Fridays, with periodic "vacations." My mother worked mornings in a local nursing home and would come to pick me up at our house at midday. We got into the car in our suburb, drove for just under an hour through the relative countryside of the Palisades Parkway, propelled ourselves across the Hudson via the George Washington Bridge, and found ourselves deposited smack in the middle of another world. Billboards advertised the good life in Spanish, ancient cobblestones emerged in patches from the tar, which shivered and smelled in summer and shone black and cruel in the winter. Grotesque figures loomed everywhere, but they didn't frighten me, nor did the filthy and the slobbering insane, the homeless and the drunk. I felt keenly the great expanses, the chasmal spaces between all of us, which one seemed prepared to reach across. Even as I was spooked, I was impressed by and admiring of the constant chord of toughness and strength, which acted to harmonize all the many and varied notes in the city, the thousand and one vignettes of overheard conversations, glimpsed lives.

My mother and I usually drove the miles to the city engulfed by our own private, inner travels, the radio's sound filling the front seat like an anesthetic. Once we got to the city and went through the customary parking ordeal, we walked the few blocks to the hospital in silence. This was the routine we fell into, and it seemed natural to both of us.

The Radiotherapy Department existed deep in the guts of the hospital in a specially built section with cement walls many feet thick. Chris, my "radiotherapist," explained that careful regulations made the walls so thick. She placed her hand on the otherwise innocuous, pale yellow plaster and told me in reverent tones about the care one had to take around radiation. She herself wore a thick green smock made of lead. She let me hold it once, and it seemed to weigh as much as I did.

On my first visit I could tell Chris was keen for me to see her "as a friend." Her hair was streaked blond and her arms were strong and athletic. Her uniform was an unbecoming yellow that clashed with the yellow walls. The entire department had a different feel from the rest of the hospital, set off by a cocoon quality and by genuine attempts to make something human of this lead and cement hole in the ground. The employees hung up family photos on the reception area walls, and if they didn't have kids of their own, they put up overly cute pictures of cats and dogs. Posters of orangutans proclaiming *Every time I figure out the rules, they change them* and of puppies thanking God it was Friday adorned the ceilings of the treatment rooms, demanding attention as I lay on my back.

Radiation treatment itself was a breeze, about as complicated as an x-ray. I'd get up on the table, and Chris would don her lead smock and turn out the lights. Bulbs inside the clunky machine hanging from tracks on the ceiling would shine down on my face, waiting to be aligned with the Magic Marker x's drawn on my neck and face. "Hold your breath!" the command would come from somewhere in the corner, and I'd inhale as deeply as I could, almost always thinking about a movie I'd seen, a maritime disaster in which the hero had to swim a long distance underwater in order to save everyone else. I'd held my breath along with him, wondering if I too had it in me to save the others. Believing that one should be prepared for any emergency, I went about trying to improve my breath-holding capacity, and lying there on the gurney in Radiotherapy seemed as good a place as any to practice for a disaster at sea. As the machines over my head clicked and whirred softly, my body swelled with air, trembling almost imperceptibly with the desire to let it all fall away from me, deflate back out to the place it had come from. Just when I was about to abandon all hope and let the salty water fill my lungs, Chris's voice would sound from the dark corner.

"Breathe!" The overhead lights came on, Chris appeared without her lead burden and helped me off the table, and it was all over until the next day.

If it was Monday, Tuesday, Wednesday, or Thursday, that was the whole procedure. I'd find my mother in the waiting room, and we'd take the long elevator ride back up to street level, get back in the car, and head home, hoping to avoid rush-hour traffic. Friday was different. Every Friday, usually around three o'clock, was my appointment with Dr. Woolf at the chemotherapy clinic.

I was already two weeks into the radiation treatment before I had my first appointment with Dr. Woolf, and despite Evan's father's early warning attempts, I went into it completely unprepared. Radiation at that point seemed like a good deal—all that time off from school, no pain, or at least not yet, the meditative drives into the city with my mother. The only thing that really worried me about chemo was the prospect of weekly injections, because that's all I thought it would be, an injection. If I had been blind to what the original operation would be like, and blind to warnings about chemo, once I entered the clinic I got my first intimations of what was about to happen.

10 In sharp contrast to the new Radiotherapy Department, the chemotherapy clinic was old-looking, drab. The main waiting area was on one side of a much-used hall, a main thoroughfare for the hospital. It was completely open, like a lounge, and on the walls hung dark oil portraits of men whose names I never bothered to learn. The couches and chairs were covered in dark green vinyl, the floor was black tile with white traces almost worn out of existence. My mother wasn't allowed to smoke, which drove her insane, especially since week after week for two and a half years we had to wait at least two hours past the scheduled time before my name was called.

The other people in the waiting room fascinated me. We all looked exhausted, though relative health seemed to vary widely. Over the years I became expert at diagnosing the drugs each child was receiving from his or her appearance. Some looked bloated and sluggish, others were thin as rakes, and almost everyone was in some stage of losing or growing in their hair. Hats, scarves, and wigs covered the naked scalps. On that first visit I felt apart from the rest of them, felt a million miles away.

When we were finally in Dr. Woolf's office, my mother ready to scream from the long wait, we encountered his telephone, apparently a permanent appendage. He could carry on a conversation with my mother, me, his nurse, his secretary down the hall, and someone on the phone simultaneously; he had it down to an art. My mother thought him incredibly rude, and she was right. Dr. Woolf's manner was gruff and unempathetic. The first time he examined me I could only flinch at his roughness as his large fingers pressed hard into my abdomen, pried open my still stiff mouth. His appearance didn't help. Tall, large-featured, and balding, he had a peculiar large white spot on his forehead, which caught the light in an unflattering, sinister way. His nose was tremendous, his lips invisible. He scared me.

His office was as drab as the waiting room but was saved by a large, multipaned window that looked out onto a well-tended courtyard with banks of blue flowers and ivy-clenched trees. I spent a lot of time looking out that window. I spent a lot of time forcing myself to look out that window, because even on that first visit I knew that this room was no place for me. The only thing I wanted to know about this particular interior was its implicit exterior, an existence that had nothing to do with me, Dr. Woolf, my mother, the treatment table, which was too tall for me to get onto by myself, or the two 60-cc syringes waiting patiently in their sterile packets.

This first examination was more thorough than the ones I would later receive. I was asked to strip down to my underwear, which I did, feeling humiliated and exposed. While the doctor talked to the nurse, my mother, and the person on the phone tucked beneath his chin, he prodded me with his hands, hit me just slightly too hard with his reflex hammer, and spoke far too loudly. When he touched me I could feel the vibrations of his voice in my own chest, feel them lapsing through my body's cavity the same way you feel a car passing too closely. He got out a tourniquet and wound it tightly around my arm, pinching the skin just like a kid on the playground giving an Indian burn, and despite every ounce of strength I could muster, I began to cry. Not loudly, not even particularly heartily, just a few simple tears, which were as accurate and prophetic as any I'd ever shed.

15 The butterfly needle, named for the winglike holds that fanned out from its short, delicate, bodylike cylinder, slipped into my arm, a slender pinch I barely felt. Because it was inserted into the crook of my arm, I had to sit with my arm rigidly straight, held up awkwardly and overly self-consciously. I began to grow warm, a caustic ache began settling into my elbow. For a split second, a split of a split second, the sensation was almost pleasurable, a glowing, fleshy sense of my body recognizing itself as a body, a thing in the

world. But immediately it was too much: I felt the lining of my stomach arc out and pull spastically back into itself like some colorful disturbed sea anemone.

It was an anatomy lesson. I had never known it was possible to *feel* your organs, feel them the way you feel your tongue in your mouth, or your teeth. My stomach outlined itself for me; my intestines, my liver, parts of me I didn't know the names of began heating up, trembling with their own warmth, creating friction and space by rubbing against the viscera, the muscles of my stomach, my back, my lungs. I wanted to collapse, to fall back onto the table or, better yet, go head first down onto the cold floor, but I couldn't. The injection had only begun; this syringe was still half full and there was a second one to go. My head began to hurt. Not sure if my brain was shrinking or swelling, I squinted around the office, not in the least bit surprised to see a yellow-green aura surrounding everyone, everything, like some macabre religious painting.

My body, wanting to turn itself inside out, made wave after wave of attempts to rid itself of this unseeable intruder, this overwhelming and noxious poison. I shook with heaves so strong they felt more like convulsions. Someone lifted a metal basin to my face, and I quickly deposited in it everything my digestive system owned, and when that wasn't enough I came up with the digestive juices themselves, pitiful spoonfuls of green bile, and then I just threw up air, breathing it down in deep gasps between bucking it back up in spasms that ached with fruitlessness. It was the emptiness that hurt the most. When my stomach had something to offer back it was happy to do so, but when it was empty, the convulsions still came, my stomach pressing inward with even greater self-spite, punishing its own lack by squeezing ever harder.

Gradually the waves of vomiting subsided, leaving behind an unacted-upon nausea that seemed to involve not just my stomach but all of me, even my feet, my scalp. As a result of the vomiting my sinuses swelled and ached, but knowing nothing about sinuses, I could only report that my nose hurt. Dr. Woolf looked puzzled but didn't follow up with any further questions. Someone helped me put my clothes back on; I don't remember the walk back to the car.

The sky was so blue it was almost transparent, and it moved seamlessly outside the window as I lay in the back seat. The trip home was straightforward, from the bridge onto the parkway, then off the parkway, down a few streets, and up the driveway. Once we were off the bridge, it was a half-hour trip, and I calculated there were only nine turns from start to finish. From this unfamiliar vantage point, without the normal visual landmarks, I stared at the sky and attempted to guess where we were. Each time the car turned I tried to visualize what it was turning toward: Exit 14, the supermarket, the stone house on the corner, our house. Somewhere along the way I messed up. I thought we were at least two more turns away, but suddenly I felt the rise of the driveway and knew I was wrong, but it would be the last time. Over the years I perfected the mental drive, could do it even when I was half asleep, even when the rhythm was interrupted by a sudden need to vomit into the kitchen mixing bowl my mother placed on the floor.

20   That first time I arrived home I remember feeling not quite so bad. I'd begun to feel less nauseous, or at least better able to control it. My father suggested I eat something, some ice cream perhaps. My head swimming, I sat at the kitchen table and ate several spoonfuls, my parents looking at me expectantly.

"It wasn't so bad, was it now, Lucinda Mag?" my father asked.

I shook my head no, purposefully bringing another spoonful of the vanilla, chocolate, and strawberry mixture up to my mouth. Speaking seemed like something one could grow tired of.

My stomach rebelled. I stood quickly and made my way over to the sink, where I threw up the now liquid ice cream, still cool and even soothing as it came up. For some reason I started to cry. My mother put her hand on my head and tried to soothe me, and when I was done began to explain that there was no need to cry, that everything would be all right, that I mustn't cry.

How could she know I would take her so seriously? She went on to explain how disappointed she was that I'd cried even before Dr. Woolf had put the needle into me, that crying was only because of fear, that I shouldn't be afraid, it would be all right. It was one thing to cry afterward, because she knew that it hurt, but why did I cry beforehand? Hadn't I always been so brave before?

25   I looked out of the kitchen window over the sink I had just thrown up into. Straggles of spider-plant cuttings had taken over most of it, the brown, tangled roots filling an assortment of drinking glasses placed on the ledges. There was also a collection of small ceramic houses, presents and mementos accumulated over the years. Immediately outside, the overgrown, sloppy fir trees prevented any clear view of the front lawn or street.

Sometimes the briefest moments capture us, force us to take them in, and demand that we live the rest of our lives in reference to them. What did my mother mean? Part of me knew then, and still knows, that she was afraid for me. If somehow she could convince me not to be afraid, we could rally around the truism she had grown up with: there was nothing to fear but fear itself. My mother didn't know how to conquer *what* I was afraid of, nor could she even begin to tell me how to do it for myself. Instead, out of her own fear, she offered her own philosophy, which meant in this instance that I should conquer the fear by not crying. It was a single brief sentence, a fleeting thought she probably did not mean and doesn't even remember saying but I, who would have done anything to find a way out of this pain, would never forget it. As I made my way downstairs to my room, I resolved to never cry again.

I kept my bedroom dark and watched the light from my television change color on the wall beside me. Every hour or so I felt a great urge to lean over and retch into the mixing bowl on the floor. I drank water constantly so as to have something to throw up. As soon as the vomiting was over I'd feel whole continents better, and the intense nausea that had been unendurable only moments before was suddenly bearable, exposed as a fake, something I'd only mistakenly thought I could not bear a second longer. I'd lie back on the pillow feeling both energized and exhausted. Gradually, over the next hour, the feeling of unbearableness would return, subtly, insidiously, until I again had to lift myself up and hang over the side of the bed, my intimate bowl beneath me. This went on all night.

The second day was better. The cycle between nausea and relief would gradually extend so that I was throwing up only every four hours, every six hours, only three times during the night. The third day was the breaking point. I could actually eat something innocuous like tapioca. I quickly learned to judge food not by what it tasted like in eating but how it tasted when I threw it back up. Vanilla pudding was best, though it turned an unfortunate color, making me opt for chocolate for purely aesthetic reasons. I'd try to leave it down long enough so that I could digest most, possibly even all, of it before my stomach rebelled yet again.

Sometime during the late afternoon, relief would come. A flicker at first, only a moment, but for that brief moment I understood I was going to get better, that this was going to end. I sat up in bed, felt the strength of my body support me. Another moment would go by and I'd feel ill again, my head beginning to throb, but an hour, maybe two hours later, the feeling would return, stay for just a few breaths longer before abandoning me. The next period of illness would be a few shades briefer, and so it would go on through the evening. When I woke up on the fourth day I felt only a little weak, a little washed out, but glorious and high, that sanguine, comfortable feeling one gets after performing some great physical feat. I had swum the Channel. I had climbed Mount Eiger.

30   I sat up, listening for the sounds of my mother's footsteps, the clicking of the dog's nails on the tiled floor. A tree obscured my window, shattering the light into patches on the dirty glass. I didn't understand how I could have overlooked the sheer joy of these things for so long, how the intricate message of their simplicity had escaped me until just this moment. This weightless now-ness, this ecstasy could sometimes last me all day, at least until that afternoon, when it was time to go back to the hospital for the radiation treatment, which, as I've said, didn't seem so bad, not really, anyway.

The fifth day was Tuesday, my favorite day of all. All but completely recovered, yet excused from the burden of school, I was free to wander about the still house, form intimate relationships with the cats and dogs, who regarded me nonjudgmentally as I tracked their movements over the living room floor, sleepily following the inexorable arc of the sun. Tuesday, still far away from Friday, was futureless, thoughtless, anxiety-free.

The house itself mothered me. With everyone else away at school or at work, I somehow thought my eavesdropping created a new meaning for the clock, the hot water heater, the cats growling over their food. I felt that my listening made for them, and for myself, a real home. The house empty was a different place from the house occupied.

With so many brothers and sisters, I'd never had many opportunities for privacy. I liked to go into my mother's closet and sit there in the dark for the sheer pleasure of smelling her, at the same time knowing how annoyed she'd be if she knew I'd invaded her privacy. I became a snoop, going through everyone's drawers, looking for clues to how other people lived their lives. I liked to lie on my sister's bed, look out her window, think to myself, *So this is what she sees when she wakes up in the morning.* What was it like to be somebody else? I went into my father's bedroom, dark and cluttered, and saw all the bits of paper, the stray ties, the dirty cups, as marks of how little he was touched by his personal surroundings, how little they, in return, touched him. It all seemed so random, so accidental. In my brother's room I found magazines with pictures of naked women, fascinating me for reasons I couldn't determine. His room seemed the most alien of all. Even when I lay down on his bed and saw what he saw, I knew I wasn't even close.

The long, elliptical mornings of invading other people's privacy while alone in the house seemed endless, but eventually I'd hear the car drive up to the house and know it was time to leave for the city. Except for Fridays,

I looked forward to the drive, counting groundhogs serenely eating grass along the highway, seemingly unaware of the danger a few feet away from them. I pretended I was riding alongside the road with great, graceful swiftness on a large black, gleaming horse, its sensual mane tangling in my face, the rhythm of its hooves a hypnotic lecture on how to arrive someplace entirely different.

Inexorably, Friday, or D-day, as we began calling it, would approach. Wednesday held anxiety at arm's length, but it was there on the edges, and I knew it. Thursday was almost unbearable. Friday morning I woke up early, as always, but I did not want to get out of bed, even to go lie on the floor with my best friends, the dogs, who I imagined understood my suffering and whose wet tongues licking my face weren't random or casual but pointed, intended, full of sympathy.

The second week of chemo was worse in that I knew what to expect. This presented a curious reversal of fear for me, because I already understood that with other types of pain the fear of not knowing about it usually brought about more suffering than the thing itself. This was different. This was dread. It wasn't some unknown black thing hovering and threatening in the shadows; it had already revealed itself to me and, knowing that I knew I couldn't escape, took its time stalking me. This was everything I ever needed to know about Fate.

We went through the whole routine again, the endless waiting, Dr. Woolf's eternal phone call, his strong hands on my body. I tried not to look at the syringes beside me, but when I looked out the window Dr. Woolf invariably passed in front of my line of vision, casually holding a syringe in the air. When I looked down at the floor, I somehow chanced to look at the exact time and the exact spot where Dr. Woolf would send a brief spurt of fluid out of the syringe to clear the needle of air. A graceful, thin arc of liquid would fall directly onto the tile I was concentrating on. I took it as a sign to cry, which I did, ashamed of myself, unable to meet my mother's eyes as she began telling me not to, to hold it back.

The tourniquet went on, and it began all over again, just like the week before, except that this time when I got home I went straight to bed. I didn't even try to sit up or to eat anything as grotesque as ice cream. I felt that my mother was disappointed with me. I hadn't gone straight to bed last time—why was I doing it this time? She came to my room and sat on the edge of my bed. She looked tired but beautiful, always beautiful to me, her makeup exact and perfect, the redness of her lips, the faint hue of her powder, the distinct, musky smell of her perfume.

"You can't let this get you down, you know. I know it's hard, but you can't get depressed by it. Don't give in to it. You were not so bad last time, so make sure that what you're feeling isn't just in your head."

40

She sat there a moment longer, staring at me sadly, before asking if there was anything else. When I said no, she stood up and left me alone with the television. My father had rigged up a buzzer to the kitchen, which I could press if I needed anything. For the first few weeks I pressed it every time I threw up, but as time passed and I failed, as I saw it, to not vomit too much, I began leaving the vomit in the bowl, even when it smelled awful, and only buzzed when the large vessel was full. I lay there in my room as if alone in the forest at night, dimly sensing something large breathing close by and feeling the eyes of something unfathomably lurid turning upon me.

My father bought me toys, not because he believed for a second that they would sufficiently compensate me but because it was as close a gesture as he could manage. He didn't really have the stomach for the treatments, and only on the rare days when my mother was ill or busy would he take me in for chemotherapy. His rhythm was entirely different from my mother's. We arrived late, so there was not as much waiting time, though he seemed happy to sit for as long as he could reading the paper. Once my name was called he'd accompany me into the office and exchange greetings with Dr. Woolf, but as soon as I was asked to take off my clothes he'd turn to me and say, "Right then, I'll go get the car." Perhaps in part he was embarrassed to see his daughter half naked, but I knew that he did not want to see me suffer.

He'd jangle the keys at me, just as he did with the dogs, for whom the level of excitement at that familiar sound approached heart attacks. He'd smile and announce, "I'll be right back," adding, "This way you won't have to walk so far when it's over. I'll double-park right outside and come get you."

I watched his back as he left and felt relief, because his embarrassment and awkwardness caused me as much pain as they did him. There was no blame in those moments, no regrets, no accusations, not even despair. Those things came later, when I learned to scrutinize and judge the past, but at the time his leaving was enabling. Knowing that my father had his own burdens, his own failings, allowed me to continue on through what would otherwise have been unbearable. As an adult, I wonder how he could have left me alone in there, but as a child I knew the answer to this clearly, and knew that as soon as he was out of the room I was, if nothing else, free to respond as *I* chose. My father's nervous whistling of Bobby Sherman's *Julie, Julie, do you love me* faded down the hall as Dr. Woolf turned to me with his tourniquet and I turned to him with my unfettered grief.

My moment of truth with my father was brief, followed mercifully by privacy and a sense of relief. It was harder to maintain a sense of transcendence during the appointments with my mother. She stayed in the room and still, despite my repeated failures, insisted that I not cry. But one summer day—it must have been summer because we were all hot and red-faced—I remember my mother bending beside me. The needle was in my arm, and I was feeling the first hot flushes in my stomach. I could smell her perfume, stronger than usual because of the heat. "Don't cry," she was whispering to me, as if it were a secret we were sharing. Dr. Woolf's voice was resonating over our heads, talking to neither one of us. Perhaps it was something in her voice that day, maybe it was the way everything shone and vibrated with the heat, but for the first time in a long time I lifted my eyes from the still empty basin and looked at her. Her own eyes were filling with water, tears that would never fall but hovered there, only inches from my own.

45 Suddenly my perception of the world shifted. I wasn't the only person in the world who suffered. I had always heard other children wailing from behind closed doors all along the corridor outside Dr. Woolf's door, so it would be false to say that I found myself hearing them for the first time or more clearly. What happened was more hallucinatory. My sense of space and self lengthened and transformed, extended itself out the door and down the corridor, while at the same time staying present with me, with my mother, who, to my profound discovery, was suffering not just because of, but also for, me.

Moments never repeat themselves exactly. Simply because I understood something important and urgent and graceful there on the examination table, looking at my mother's red-rimmed blue eyes, didn't mean that only seconds later I wasn't back in another moment in which I hated myself for crying, for not being strong enough. The beautifully simple revelation I had with my father in Dr. Woolf's office was followed by his parting, his footfalls dimming down the hall, leaving me alone to contemplate what I had just learned. My mother's very presence forced me to be present, disallowing me to dwell, and the comfort I gained from understanding her pain was both fleeting and insidious. Fleeting because that is the nature of all moments, and insidious because once I had tasted the freedom and transcendence of my epiphany, I wanted only to return to it. I confused that graceful state of mind with the attached solace it brought, so when the next injection came, the next bout of crying, and I *wasn't* able to not suffer I felt I had only myself to blame, felt that I had failed in some unknowable, spiritual way. In my mind I didn't have what it took: I didn't deserve to be comforted.

At night I dreamed that the children I was baby-sitting for had slipped down to the bottom of the pool we were standing by and had drowned. Try as I might, I could never fill my lungs with enough air to reach the bottom, where they lay struggling, the eerie light lapping over them. Afterward their useless corpses rose to the surface. I had to go to their parents, my empty arms outstretched toward them, my clothes soaking wet, and explain what had happened, how I had tried my best, really I had, but still, it wasn't enough.

(1994)

QUESTIONS:

1. How does the description of New York in the opening paragraph relate to the author's battle with cancer?

2. Analyze the author's various sensory experiences as the treatment for her cancer continues. Is there a shift toward or away from the use of any of her senses? If so, what reasons may account for this?

3. What does the reference to "Evan's father" in paragraph 9 indicate about the source of this essay?

4. In the dream described in the final paragraph, the author is unable to hold her breath long enough to save the children, imagery she had introduced earlier in her essay. In what way is this imagined or dreamed scenario connected with her real life?

Robert D. Putnam

Bowling Alone: America's Declining Social Capital

This article by a prominent social scientist has had a significant impact on American public policy debates of the past decade. In 2000 Putnam published an expanded version of these ideas in a book of the same title.

〜

Many students of the new democracies that have emerged over the past decade and a half have emphasized the importance of a strong and active civil society to the consolidation of democracy. Especially with regard to the postcommunist countries, scholars and democratic activists alike have lamented the absence or obliteration of traditions of independent civic engagement and a widespread tendency toward passive reliance on the state. To those concerned with the weakness of civil societies in the developing or postcommunist world, the advanced Western democracies and above all the United States have typically been taken as models to be emulated. There is striking evidence, however, that the vibrancy of American civil society has notably declined over the past several decades.

Ever since the publication of Alexis de Tocqueville's *Democracy in America*, the United States has played a cental role in systematic studies of the links between democracy and civil society. Although this is in part because trends in American life are often regarded as harbingers of social modernization, it is also because America has traditionally been considered unusually "civic" (a reputation that, as we shall later see, has not been entirely unjustified).

When Tocqueville visited the United States in the 1830s, it was the Americans' propensity for civic association that most impressed him as the key to their unprecedented ability to make democracy work. "Americans of all ages, all stations in life, and all types of disposition," he observed, "are forever forming associations. There are not only commercial and industrial associations in which all take part, but others of a thousand different types—religious, moral, serious, futile, very general and very limited, immensely large and very minute....Nothing, in my view, deserves more attention than the intellectual and moral associations in America."[1]

Recently, American social scientists of a neo-Tocquevillean bent have unearthed a wide range of empirical evidence that the quality of public life and the performance of social institutions (and not only in America) are indeed powerfully influenced by norms and networks of civic engagement. Researchers in such fields as education, urban poverty, unemployment, the control of crime and drug abuse, and even health have discovered that successful outcomes are more likely in civically engaged communities. Similarly, research on the varying economic attainments of different ethnic groups in the United States has demonstrated the importance of social bonds within each group. These results are consistent with research in a wide range of settings that demonstrates the vital importance of social networks for job placement and many other economic outcomes.

5   Meanwhile, a seemingly unrelated body of research on the sociology of economic development has also focused attention on the role of social networks. Some of this work is situated in the developing countries, and some of it elucidates the peculiarly successful "network capitalism" of East Asia.[2] Even in less exotic Western economies, however, researchers have

---

[1] Alexis de Tocqueville, *Democracy in America*, ed. J.P. Maier, trans. George Lawrence (Garden City, N.Y.: Anchor Books, 1969), 513–17. [Unless otherwise noted, all notes to this essay are from the author.]

[2] On social networks and economic growth in the developing world, see Milton J. Esman and Norman Uphoff, *Local Organizations: Intermediaries in Rural Development* (Ithaca: Cornell University Press, 1984), esp. 15–42 and 99–180; and Albert O. Hirschman, *Getting Ahead Collectively: Grassroots Experiences in Latin America* (Elmsford, N.Y.: Pergamon Press, 1984), esp. 42–77. On East Asia, see Gustav Papanek, "The New Asian Capitalism: An Economic Portrait," in Peter L. Berger and Hsin-Huang Michael Hsiao, eds., *In Search of an East Asian Development Model* (New Brunswick, N.J.: Transaction, 1987), 27–80; Peter B. Evans, "The State as Problem and Solution: Predation, Embedded Autonomy and Structural Change," in Stephan Haggard and Robert R. Kaufman, eds., *The Politics of Economic Adjustment* (Princeton: Princeton University Press, 1992), 139–81; and Gary G. Hamilton, William Zeile, and Wan-Jin Kim, "Network Structure of East Asian Economies," in Stewart R. Clegg and S. Gordon Redding, eds., *Capitalism in Contrasting Cultures* (Hawthorne, N.Y.: De Gruyter, 1990), 105–29. See also Gary G. Hamilton and Nicole Woolsey Biggart, "Market, Culture, and Authority: A Comparative Analysis of Management and Organization in the Far East," *American Journal of Sociology* (Supplement) 94 (1988): S52–S94; and Susan Greenhalgh, "Families and

discovered highly efficient, highly flexible "industrial districts" based on networks of collaboration among workers and small entrepreneurs. Far from being paleoindustrial anachronisms, these dense interpersonal and interorganizational networks undergrid ultramodern industries, from the high tech of Silicon Valley to the high fashion of Benetton.

The norms and networks of civic engagement also powerfully affect the performance of representative government. That, at least, was the central conclusion of my own 20-year, quasi-experimental study of subnational governments in different regions of Italy.[3] Although all these regional governments seemed identical on paper, their levels of effectiveness varied dramatically. Systematic inquiry showed that the quality of governance was determined by longstanding traditions of civic engagement (or its absence). Voter turnout, newspaper readership, membership in choral societies and football clubs—these were the hallmarks of a successful region. In fact, historical analysis suggested that these networks of organized reciprocity and civic solidarity, far from being an epiphenomenon of socioeconomic modernization, were a precondition for it.

No doubt the mechanisms through which civic engagement and social connectedness produce such results—better schools, faster economic development, lower crime, and more effective government—are multiple and complex. While these briefly recounted findings require further confirmation and perhaps qualification, the parallels across hundreds of empirical studies in a dozen disparate disciplines and subfields are striking. Social scientists in several fields have recently suggested a common framework for understanding these phenomena, a framework that rests on the concept of *social capital*.[4] By analogy with notions of physical capital and

Networks in Taiwan's Economic Development," in Edwin Winckler and Susan Greenhalgh, eds., *Contending Approaches to the Political Economy of Taiwan* (Armonk, N.Y.: M.E. Sharpe, 1987), 224–45.

[3] Robert D. Putnam, *Making Democracy Work: Civic Traditions in Modern Italy* (Princeton: Princeton University Press, 1993).

[4] James S. Coleman deserves primary credit for developing the "social capital" theoretical framework. See his "Social Capital in the Creation of Human Capital," *American Journal of Sociology* (Supplement) 94 (1988): S95–S120, as well as his *The Foundations of Social Theory* (Cambridge: Harvard University Press, 1990), 300–21. See also Mark Granovetter, "Economic Action and Social Structure: The Problem of Embeddedness," *American Journal of Sociology* 91 (1985): 481–510; Glenn C. Loury, "Why Should We Care About Group Inequality?" *Social Philosophy and Policy* 5 (1987): 249–71; and Robert D. Putnam, "The Prosperous Community: Social Capital and Public Life," *American Prospect* 13 (1993): 35–42. To my knowledge, the first scholar to use the term "social capital" in its current sense was Jane Jacobs, in *The Death and*

human capital—tools and training that enhance individual productivity—"social capital" refers to features of social organization such as networks, norms, and social trust that facilitate coordination and cooperation for mutual benefit.

For a variety of reasons, life is easier in a community blessed with a substantial stock of social capital. In the first place, networks of civic engagement foster sturdy norms of generalized reciprocity and encourage the emergence of social trust. Such networks facilitate coordination and communication, amplify reputations, and thus allow dilemmas of collective action to be resolved. When economic and political negotiation is embedded in dense networks of social interaction, incentives for opportunism are reduced. At the same time, networks of civic engagement embody past success at collaboration, which can serve as a cultural template for future collaboration. Finally, dense networks of interaction probably broaden the participants' sense of self, developing the "I" into the "we," or (in the language of rational-choice theorists) enhancing the participants' "taste" for collective benefits.

I do not intend here to survey (much less contribute to) the development of the theory of social capital. Instead, I use the central premise of that rapidly growing body of work—that social connections and civic engagement pervasively influence our public life, as well as our private prospects—as the starting point for an empirical survey of trends in social capital in contemporary America. I concentrate here entirely on the American case, although the developments I portray may in some measure characterize many contemporary societies.

Whatever Happened to Civic Engagement?

10   We begin with familiar evidence on changing patterns of political participation, not least because it is immediately relevant to issues of democracy in the narrow sense. Consider the well-known decline in turnout in national elections over the last three decades. From a relative high point in the early 1960s, voter turnout had by 1990 declined by nearly a quarter; tens of millions of Americans had forsaken their parents' habitual readiness to engage in the simplest act of citizenship. Broadly similar trends also characterize participation in state and local elections.

Life of Great American Cities (New York: Random House, 1961), 138.

It is not just the voting booth that has been increasingly deserted by Americans. A series of identical questions posed by the Roper Organization to national samples ten times each year over the last two decades reveals that since 1973 the number of Americans who report that "in the past year" they have "attended a public meeting on town or school affairs" has fallen by more than a third (from 22 percent in 1973 to 13 percent in 1993). Similar (or even greater) relative declines are evident in responses to questions about attending a political rally or speech, serving on a committee of some local organization, and working for a political party. By almost every measure, Americans' direct engagement in politics and government has fallen steadily and sharply over the last generation, despite the fact that average levels of education—the best individual-level predictor of political participation—haven risen sharply throughout this period. Every year over the last decade or two, millions more have withdrawn from the affairs of their communities.

Not coincidentally, Americans have also disengaged psychologically from politics and government over this era. The proportion of Americans who reply that they "trust the government in Washington" only "some of the time" or "almost never" has risen steadily from 30 percent in 1966 to 75 percent in 1992.

These trends are well known, of course, and taken by themselves would seem amenable to a strictly political explanation. Perhaps the long litany of political tragedies and scandals since the 1960s (assassinations, Vietnam, Watergate, Irangate, and so on) has triggered an understandable disgust for politics and government among Americans, and that in turn has motivated their withdrawal. I do not doubt that this common interpretation has some merit, but its limitations become plain when we examine trends in civic engagement of a wider sort.

Our survey of organizational membership among Americans can usefully begin with a glance at the aggregate results of the General Social Survey, a scientifically conducted, national-sample survey that has been repeated 14 times over the last two decades. Church-related groups constitute the most common type of organization joined by Americans; they are especially popular with women. Other types of organizations frequently joined by women include school-service groups (mostly parent-teacher associations), sports groups, professional societies, and literary societies. Among men, sports clubs, labor unions, professional societies, fraternal groups, veterans' groups, and service clubs are all relatively popular.

15   Religious affiliation is by far the most common associational membership among Americans. Indeed, by many measures America continues to be
(even more than in Tocqueville's time) an astonishingly "churched" society.
For example, the United States has more houses of worship per capita than
any other nation on Earth. Yet religious sentiment in America seems to be
becoming somewhat less tied to institutions and more self-defined.

How have these complex crosscurrents played out over the last three or
four decades in terms of Americans' engagement with organized religion?
The general pattern is clear: The 1960s witnessed a significant drop in
reported weekly churchgoing—from roughly 48 percent in the late 1950s to
roughly 41 percent in the early 1970s. Since then, it has stagnated or
(according to some surveys) declined still further. Meanwhile, data from the
General Social Survey show a modest decline in membership in all "church-
related groups" over the last 20 years. It would seem, then, that net
participation by Americans, both in religious services and in church-related
groups, has declined modestly (by perhaps a sixth) since the 1960s.

For many years, labor unions provided one of the most common
organizational affiliations among American workers. Yet union membership
has been falling for nearly four decades, with the steepest decline occurring
between 1975 and 1985. Since the mid-1950s, when union membership
peaked, the unionized portion of the nonagricultural work force in America
has dropped by more than half, falling from 32.5 percent in 1953 to 15.8
percent in 1992. By now, virtually all of the explosive growth in union
membership that was associated with the New Deal has been erased. The
solidarity of union halls is now mostly a fading memory of aging men.[5]

The parent-teacher association (PTA) has been an especially important
form of civic engagement in twentieth-century America because parental
involvement in the educational process represents a particularly productive
form of social capital. It is, therefore, dismaying to discover that participation in parent-teacher organizations has dropped drastically over the last
generation, from more than 12 million in 1964 to barely 5 million in 1982
before recovering to approximately 7 million now.

Next, we turn to evidence on membership in (and volunteering for) civic
and fraternal organizations. These data show some striking patterns. First,
membership in traditional women's groups has declined more or less steadily

---

[5] Any simplistically political interpretation of the collapse of American unionism would need
to confront the fact that the steepest decline began more than six years before the Reagan
administration's attack on PATCO. Data from the General Social Survey show a roughly 40-
percent decline in reported union membership between 1975 and 1991.

since the mid-1960s. For example, membership in the national Federation of Women's Clubs is down by more than half (59 percent) since 1964, while membership in the League of Women Voters (LWV) is off 42 percent since 1969.[6]

20   Similar reductions are apparent in the numbers of volunteers for mainline civic organizations, such as the Boy Scouts (off by 26 percent since 1970) and the Red Cross (off by 61 percent since 1970). But what about the possibility that volunteers have simply switched their loyalties to other organizations? Evidence on "regular" (as opposed to occasional or "drop by") volunteering is available from the Labor Department's Current Population Surveys of 1974 and 1989. These estimates suggest that serious volunteering declined by roughly one-sixth over these 15 years, from 24 percent of adults in 1974 to 20 percent in 1989. The multitudes of Red Cross aides and Boy Scout troop leaders now missing in action have apparently not been offset by equal numbers of new recruits elsewhere.

Fraternal organizations have also witnessed a substantial drop in membership during the 1980s and 1990s. Membership is down significantly in such groups as the Lions (off 12 percent since 1983), the Elks (off 18 percent since 1979), the Shriners (off 27 percent since 1979), the Jaycees (off 44 percent since 1979), and the Masons (down 39 percent since 1959). In sum, after expanding steadily throughout most of this century, many major civic organizations have experienced a sudden, substantial, and nearly simultaneous decline in membership over the last decade or two.

The most whimsical yet discomfiting bit of evidence of social disengagement in contemporary America that I have discovered is this: more Americans are bowling today than ever before, but bowling in organized leagues has plummeted in the last decade or so. Between 1980 and 1993 the total number of bowlers in America increased by 10 percent, while league bowling decreased by 40 percent. (Lest this be thought a wholly trivial example, I should note that nearly 80 million Americans went bowling at least once during 1993, *nearly a third more than voted in the 1994 congressional elections* and roughly the same number as claim to attend church

---

[6] Data for the LWV are available over a longer time span and show an interesting pattern: a sharp slump during the Depression, a strong and sustained rise after World War II that more than tripled membership between 1945 and 1969, and then the post-1969 decline, which has already erased virtually all the postwar gains and continues still. This same historical pattern applies to those men's fraternal organizations for which comparable data are available—steady increases for the first seven decades of the century, interrupted only by the Great Depression, followed by a collapse in the 1970s and 1980s that has already wiped out most of the postwar expansion and continues apace.

regularly. Even after the 1980s' plunge in league bowling, nearly 3 percent of American adults regularly bowl in leagues.) The rise of solo bowling threatens the livelihood of bowling-lane proprietors because those who bowl as members of leagues consume three times as much beer and pizza as solo bowlers, and the money in bowling is in the beer and pizza, not the balls and shoes. The broader social significance, however, lies in the social interaction and even occasionally civic conversations over beer and pizza that solo bowlers forgo. Whether or not bowling beats balloting in the eyes of most Americans, bowling teams illustrate yet another vanishing form of social capital.

COUNTERTRENDS

At this point, however, we must confront a serious counterargument. Perhaps the traditional forms of civic organization whose decay we have been tracing have been replaced by vibrant new organizations. For example, national environmental organizations (like the Sierra Club) and feminist groups (like the National Organization for Women) grew rapidly during the 1970s and 1980s and now count hundreds of thousands of dues-paying members. An even more dramatic example is the American Association of Retired Persons (AARP), which grew exponentially from 400,000 card-carrying members in 1960 to 33 million in 1993, becoming (after the Catholic Church) the largest private organization in the world. The national administrators of these organizations are among the most feared lobbyists in Washington, in large part because of their massive mailing lists of presumably loyal members.

These new mass-membership organizations are plainly of great political importance. From the point of view of social connectedness, however, they are sufficiently different from classic "secondary associations" that we need to invent a new label—perhaps "tertiary associations." For the vast majority of their members, the only act of membership consists in writing a check for dues or perhaps occasionally reading a newsletter. Few ever attend any meetings of such organizations, and most are unlikely ever (knowingly) to encounter any other member. The bond between any two members of the Sierra Club is less like the bond between any two members of a gardening club and more like the bond between any two Red Sox fans (or perhaps any two devoted Honda owners): they root for the same team and they share some of the same interests, but they are unaware of each other's existence. Their ties, in short, are to common symbols, common leaders, and perhaps common ideals, but not to one another. The theory of social capital argues that associational membership should, for example, increase social trust, but this prediction is much less straightforward with regard to membership in tertiary associations. From the point of view of social connectedness, the Environmental Defense Fund and a bowling league are just not in the same category.

25   If the growth of tertiary organizations represents one potential (but probably not real) counterexample to my thesis, a second countertrend is represented by the growing prominence of nonprofit organizations, especially nonprofit service agencies. This so-called third sector includes everything from Oxfam and the Metropolitan Museum of Art to the Ford Foundation and the Mayo Clinic. In other words, although most secondary associations are nonprofits, most nonprofit agencies are not secondary associations. To identify trends in the size of the nonprofit sector with trends in social connectedness would be another fundamental conceptual mistake.[7]

A third potential countertrend is much more relevant to an assessment of social capital and civic engagement. Some able researchers have argued that the last few decades have witnessed a rapid expansion in "support groups" of various sorts. Robert Wuthnow reports that fully 40 percent of all Americans claim to be "currently involved in [a] small group that meets regularly and provides support or caring for those who participate in it."[8] Many of these groups are religiously affiliated, but many others are not. For example, nearly 5 percent of Wuthnow's national sample claim to participate regularly in a "self-help" group, such as Alcoholics Anonymous, and nearly as many say they belong to book-discussion groups and hobby clubs.

The groups described by Wuthnow's respondents unquestionably represent an important form of social capital, and they need to be accounted for in any serious reckoning of trends in social connectedness. On the other hand, they do not typically play the same role as traditional civic associations. As Wuthnow emphasizes,

---

[7] Cf. Lester M. Salamon, "The Rise of the Nonprofit Sector," *Foreign Affairs* 73 (July–August 1994): 109–22. See also Salamon, "Partners in Public Service: The Scope and Theory of Government-Nonprofit Relations," in Walter W. Powell, ed., *The Nonprofit Sector: A Research Handbook* (New Haven: Yale University Press, 1987), 99–117. Salamon's empirical evidence does not sustain his broad claims abut a global "associational revolution" comparable in significance to the rise of the nation-state several centuries ago.

[8] Robert Wuthnow, *Sharing the Journey: Support Groups and America's New Quest for Community* (New York: The Free Press, 1994), 45.

Small groups may not be fostering community as effectively as many of their proponents would like. Some small groups merely provide occasions for individuals to focus on themselves in the presence of others. The social contract binding members together asserts only the weakest of obligations. Come if you have time. Talk if you feel like it. Respect everyone's opinion. Never criticize. Leave quietly if you become dissatisfied.... We can imagine that [these small groups] really substitute for families, neighborhoods, and broader community attachments that may demand lifelong commitments, when, in fact, they do not.[9]

All three of these potential countertrends—tertiary organizations, nonprofit organizations, and support groups—need somehow to be weighed against the erosion of conventional civic organizations. One way of doing so is to consult the General Social Survey.

Within all educational categories, total associational membership declined significantly between 1967 and 1993. Among the college-educated, the average number of group memberships per person fell from 2.8 to 2.0 (a 26-percent decline); among high-school graduates, the number fell from 1.8 to 1.2 (32 percent); and among those with fewer than 12 years of education, the number fell from 1.4 to 1.1 (25 percent). In other words, at *all* educational (and hence social) levels of American society, and counting *all* sorts of group memberships, *the average number of associational memberships has fallen by about a fourth over the last quarter-century.* Without controls for educational levels, the trend is not nearly so clear, but the central point is this: *more Americans than ever before are in social circumstances that foster associational involvement (higher education, middle age, and so on), but nevertheless aggregate associational membership appears to be stagnant or declining.*

Broken down by type of group, the downward trend is most marked for church-related groups, for labor unions, for fraternal and veterans' organizations, and for school-service groups. Conversely, membership in professional associations has risen over these years, although less than might have been predicted, given sharply rising educational and occupational levels. Essentially the same trends are evident for both men and women in the sample. In short, the available survey evidence confirms our earlier conclusion: American social capital in the form of civic associations has significantly eroded over the last generation.

---

[9] Ibid., 3–6.

Good Neighborliness and Social Trust

30 I noted earlier that most readily available quantitative evidence on trends in social connectedness involves formal settings, such as the voting booth, the union hall, or the PTA. One glaring exception is so widely discussed as to require little comment here: the most fundamental form of social capital is the family, and the massive evidence of the loosening of bonds within the family (both extended and nuclear) is well known. This trend, of course, is quite consistent with—and may help to explain—our theme of social decapitalization.

A second aspect of informal social capital on which we happen to have reasonably reliable time-series data involves neighborliness. In each General Social Survey since 1974 respondents have been asked, "How often do you spend a social evening with a neighbor?" The proportion of Americans who socialize with their neighbors more than once a year has slowly but steadily declined over the last two decades, from 72 percent in 1974 to 61 percent in 1993. (On the other hand, socializing with "friends who do not live in your neighborhood" appears to be on the increase, a trend that may reflect the growth of workplace-based social connections.)

Americans are also less trusting. The proportion of Americans saying that most people can be trusted fell by more than a third between 1960, when 58 percent chose that alternative, and 1993, when only 37 percent did. The same trend is apparent in all educational groups; indeed, because social trust is also correlated with education and because educational levels have risen sharply, the overall decrease in social trust is even more apparent if we control for education.

Our discussion of trends in social connectedness and civic engagement has tacitly assumed that all the forms of social capital that we have discussed are themselves coherently correlated across individuals. This is in fact true. Members of associations are much more likely than nonmembers to participate in politics, to spend time with neighbors, to express social trust and so on.

The close correlation between social trust and associational membership is true not only across time and across individuals, but also across countries. Evidence from the 1991 World Values Survey demonstrates the following:[10]

---

[10] I am grateful to Ronald Inglehart, who directs this unique cross-national project, for sharing these highly useful data with me. See his "The Impact of Culture on Economic Development: Theory, Hypotheses, and Some Empirical Tests" (unpublished manuscript, University of Michigan, 1994).

1. Across the 35 countries in this survey, social trust and civic engagement are strongly correlated; the greater the density of associational membership in a society, the more trusting its citizens. Trust and engagement are two facets of the same underlying factor—social capital.

2. America still ranks relatively high by cross-national standards on both these dimensions of social capital. Even in the 1990s, after several decades' erosion, Americans are more trusting and more engaged than people in most other countries of the world.

3. The trends of the past quarter-century, however, have apparently moved the United States significantly lower in the international rankings of social capital. The recent deterioration in American social capital has been sufficiently great that (if no other country changed its position in the meantime) another quarter-century of change at the same rate would bring the United States, roughly speaking, to the midpoint among all these countries, roughly equivalent to South Korea, Belgium, or Estonia today. Two generations' decline at the same rate would leave the United States at the level of today's Chile, Portugal, and Slovenia.

WHY IS U.S. SOCIAL CAPITAL ERODING?

35 As we have seen, something has happened in America in the last two or three decades to diminish civic engagement and social connectedness. What could that "something" be? Here are several possible explanations, along with some initial evidence on each.

The movement of women into the labor force. Over these same two or three decades, many millions of American women have moved out of the home into paid employment. This is the primary, though not the sole, reason why the weekly working hours of the average American have increased significantly during these years. It seems highly plausible that this social revolution should have reduced the time and energy available for building social capital. For certain organizations, such as the PTA, the League of Women Voters, the Federation of Women's Clubs, and the Red Cross, this is almost certainly an important part of the story. The sharpest decline in women's civic participation seems to have come in the 1970s; membership in such "women's" organizations as these has been virtually halved since the late 1960s. By contrast, most of the decline in participation in men's organizations occurred about ten years later; the total decline to date has been approximately 25 percent for the typical organization. On the other hand, the survey data imply that the aggregate declines for men are virtually as great as those for women. It is logically possible, of course, that the male declines might represent the knock-on effect of women's liberation, as dishwashing crowded out the lodge, but time-budget studies suggest that most husbands of working wives have assumed only a minor part of the housework. In short, something besides the women's revolution seems to lie behind the erosion of social capital.

Mobility: The "re-potting" hypothesis. Numerous studies of organizational involvement have shown that residential stability and such related phenomena as home ownership are clearly associated with greater civic engagement. Mobility, like frequent re-potting of plants, tends to disrupt root systems, and it takes time for an uprooted individual to put down new roots. It seems plausible that the automobile, suburbanization, and the movement to the Sun Belt have reduced the social rootedness of the average American, but one fundamental difficulty with this hypothesis is apparent: the best evidence shows that residential stability and homeownership in America have risen modestly since 1965, and are surely higher now than during the 1950s, when civic engagement and social connectedness by our measures was definitely higher.

Other demographic transformations. A range of additional changes have transformed the American family since the 1960s—fewer marriages, more divorces, fewer children, lower real wages, and so on. Each of these changes might account for some of the slackening of civic engagement, since married, middle-class parents are generally more socially involved than other people. Moreover, the changes in scale that have swept over the American economy in these years—illustrated by the replacement of the corner grocery by the supermarket and now perhaps of the supermarket by electronic shopping at home, or the replacement of community-based enterprises by outposts of distant multinational firms—may perhaps have undermined the material and even physical basis for civic engagement.

The technological transformation of leisure. There is reason to believe that deep-seated technological trends are radically "privatizing" or "individualizing" our use of leisure time and thus disrupting many opportunities for social-capital formation. The most obvious and probably the most powerful instrument of this revolution is television. Time-budget studies in the 1960s showed that the growth in time spent watching television dwarfed all other changes in the way Americans passed their days and nights. Television has made our communities (or, rather, what we experience as our communities) wider and shallower. In the language of economics, electronic technology enables individual tastes to be satisfied more fully, but at the cost of the positive social externalities associated with more primitive forms of entertainment. The same logic applies to the replacement of vaudeville by the movies and now of movies by the VCR. The new "virtual reality" helmets that we will soon don to be entertained in total isolation are merely the latest extension of this trend. Is technology thus driving a wedge between our individual interests and our collective interests? It is a question that seems worth exploring more systematically.

What Is to Be Done?

40 The last refuge of a social-scientific scoundrel is to call for more research. Nevertheless, I cannot forbear from suggesting some further lines of inquiry.

- We must sort out the dimensions of social capital, which clearly is not a unidimensional concept, despite language (even in this essay) that implies the contrary. What types of organizations and networks most effectively embody—or generate—social capital, in the sense of mutual reciprocity, the resolution of dilemmas of collective action, and the broadening of social identities? In this essay I have emphasized the density of associational life. In earlier work I stressed the structure of networks, arguing that "horizontal" ties represented more productive social capital than vertical ties.[11]

- Another set of important issues involves macrosociological cross-currents that might intersect with the trends described here. What will be the impact, for example, of electronic networks on social capital? My hunch is that meeting in an electronic forum is not the equivalent of meeting in a bowling alley—or even in a saloon—but hard empirical research is needed. What about the development of social capital in the workplace? Is it growing in counterpoint to the decline of civic engagement, reflecting some social analogue of the first law of thermodynamics—social capital is neither created nor

---

[11] See my *Making Democracy Work*, esp. ch. 6.

destroyed, merely redistributed? Or do the trends described in this essay represent a deadweight loss?

- A rounded assessment of changes in American social capital over the last quarter-century needs to count the costs as well as the benefits of community engagement. We must not romanticize small-town, middle-class civic life in the America of the 1950s. In addition to the deleterious trends emphasized in this essay, recent decades have witnessed a substantial decline in intolerance and probably also in overt discrimination, and those beneficent trends may be related in complex ways to the erosion of traditional social capital. Moreover, a balanced accounting of the social-capital books would need to reconcile the insights of this approach with the undoubted insights offered by Mancur Olson and others who stress that closely knit social, economic, and political organizations are prone to inefficient cartelization and to what political economists term "rent seeking" and ordinary men and women call corruption.[12]

- Finally, and perhaps most urgently, we need to explore creatively how public policy impinges on (or might impinge on) social-capital formation. In some well-known instances, public policy has destroyed highly effective social networks and norms. American slum-clearance policy of the 1950s and 1960s, for example, renovated physical capital, but at a very high cost to existing social capital. The consolidation of country post offices and small school districts has promised administrative and financial efficiencies, but full-cost accounting for the effects of these policies on social capital might produce a more negative verdict. On the other hand, such past initiatives as the county agricultural-agent system, community colleges, and tax deductions for charitable contributions illustrate that government can encourage social-capital formation. Even a recent proposal in San Luis Obispo, California, to require that all new houses have front porches illustrates the power of government to influence where and how networks are formed.

The concept of "civil society" has played a central role in the recent global debate about the preconditions for democracy and democratization.

---

[12] See Mancur Olson, *The Rise and Decline of Nations: Economic Growth, Stagflation, and Social Rigidities* (New Haven: Yale University Press, 1982), 2.

In the newer democracies this phrase has properly focused attention on the need to foster a vibrant civic life in soils traditionally inhospitable to self-government. In the established democracies, ironically, growing numbers of citizens are questioning the effectiveness of their public institutions at the very moment when liberal democracy has swept the battlefield, both ideologically and geopolitically. In America, at least, there is reason to suspect that this democratic disarray may be linked to a broad and continuing erosion of civic engagement that began a quarter-century ago. High on our scholarly agenda should be the question of whether a comparable erosion of social capital may be under way in other advanced democracies, perhaps in different institutional and behavioral guises. High on America's agenda should be the question of how to reverse these adverse trends in social connectedness, thus restoring civic engagement and civic trust.

COMMENTARY AND WRITINGS ON RELATED TOPICS:

- Nicholas Lemann, Kicking in Groups, *The Atlantic Monthly* (April 1996).
- Mary Ann Zehr, Getting Involved in Civic Life, *Foundation News and Commentary* (May/June 1996). *The* Foundation News and Commentary *is a publication of The Council on Foundations.*

(1995)

QUESTIONS:

1. Putnam argues that "social capital" is greater in groups such as the PTA than it is for groups such as Alcoholics Anonymous. Note his reasons for this distinction and then argue for or against his position.

2. What rhetorical function does the "Countertrends" section play in the strength of Putnam's argument?

3. Under the heading "Why is U.S. Social Capital Eroding?" Putnam lists four possible reasons. Which of these four would you argue is the most significant? Can you think of other reasons that Putnam does not list?

4. Who do you think Putnam's intended audience is? What clues lead you to draw this conclusion? Pick another plausible audience and discuss how Putnam would need to alter his style in addressing it.

5. Discuss the importance of "social trust" to a democracy.

6. In what ways do you feel the Internet is increasing or decreasing social capital?

7. The ideas Putnam first presented here were revised and greatly expanded in the book published in 2000, *Bowling Alone: The Collapse and Revival of American Community*. Look up the book in your library and write two or three paragraphs discussing some of the respects in which the arguments as presented in the book have been extended and revised. Comment as well on the tone and the style of Putnam's writing in the book. How does it differ from that of the article?

ALICE BECK KEHOE

TRANSCRIBING INSIMA, A BLACKFOOT "OLD LADY"[1]

In this long essay, a well-known anthropologist recovers a lost voice in Native American History.

～

Sue Sommers[2] had completed only one year of graduate work in anthropology at New York's Columbia University when she arrived in Browning, Montana, on the Blackfeet Indian Reservation early in the summer of 1939. Ruth Benedict, her professor and organizer of the

---

[1] David Reed Miller and Susan Miller introduced me to Sue Sommers Dietrich. After procrastinating for a couple of years I telephoned her home in south-suburban Chicago in August 1993 and made an appointment to interview her about the 1939 Blackfoot project. Sue was a delightful interviewee and a gracious hostess. She lent me three folders of her typed interviews with Insima so that the fragile sheets could be copied and archived by Mark Thiel, Marquette University archivist, and she invited me to return. Less than two months later, Sue Dietrich was killed by a car near her home.

The estate of Susan Dietrich has consented to the use of these interviews for this volume. [Unless otherwise noted, all notes to this essay are from the author.]

[2] Sylvia Sue Roma Sommers, named after the women's rights activist Sylvia Pankhurst and Susan B. Anthony, was born in 1914 in Trenton, New Jersey, where her parents had immigrated from Russia. She earned a Bachelor of Arts in sociology from Hunter College in 1936, worked as a social worker in Harlem, and in 1938 enrolled in Columbia University's graduate program in anthropology. The following summer, at Ruth Benedict's invitation, she joined the Laboratory project on the Blackfeet Reservation.

Sommers served in World War II and afterward married Donald Dietrich, a psychoanalyst who, in 1948 and 1949, accompanied by Sue, did comparative psychology field research on three Plains reservations (one of them the Blackfeet). Sue Dietrich devoted herself to activities related to Quaker missions to promote peace, particularly a series of trips to Viet Nam and China. She visited the Blackfeet Reservation several times after the 1949 fieldwork with her husband, remaining in contact with the Yellow Kidney family.

Columbia University Laboratory for ethnography, was already there, living in a tent. Sommers recalled that Professor Benedict had her sleeping bag on the ground, and was grateful when the young woman lent her an air mattress. Several other graduate students enrolled in the Laboratory project later became well-known anthropologists, including Oscar and Ruth Lewis, Esther Goldfrank, and Lucien Hanks and Jane Richardson, who later married (Goldfrank 1978:128). Benedict planned that they would divide and cover the four Blackfoot reserves, the North Blackfoot, Blood, and North Piegan in Alberta, Canada, and the Blackfeet (South Piegan[3]) in Montana, comparing the four societies and investigating their histories. Sue Sommers joined fellow student Gitel Steed and her painter husband, Bob, at Two Medicine River on the Montana reservation. Benedict gave the inexperienced students the simplest of instructions: "See if you can establish contact with a family and live with them."

Sommers arrived on the reservation during the South Piegans' annual reunion, the North American Indian Days powwow. She dressed in jeans and commercial moccasins, twisted her long, thick hair into two braids, and went into the campground. A group of women, noticing her, exclaimed over her braids. A middle-aged man, Jim Little Plume, came over and escorted Sommers to the tipi of Yellow Kidney, then about 70 years old, where she was invited to sit beside the fire hospitably burning in the tipi. A tourist from Connecticut came in with his two sons, saying that he wanted his boys adopted into the tribe and given Indian names. The tourist took out a notebook and asked each person's name, writing down the replies. When he came to Sommers, Jim Little Plume spoke up, "She is Long Braids, she is my wife." As soon as the man departed, everyone in the tipi laughed heartily at the joke. Little Plume showed up daily to escort Sommers around the reservation, and every morning he placed a bouquet of wildflowers at her tent.

Yellow Kidney and his wife Insima (*I'nssimaa*, "Gardener, Planter") agreed to set up a large tipi next to their house for the Steeds and Sommers. Tipis are often erected in the summer to shelter a family's guests, and this tipi was so comfortable that Benedict preferred it to the accommodations of the other students on the Canadian reserves. In the evenings, the Steeds and Sommers often joined the Yellow Kidney family in their home. Officially, Yellow Kidney spoke only Blackfoot and required anthropologists to hire interpreters at 25 cents an hour, but after hours, his English proved adequate

---

[3] Piegan and Peigan are variants of Pikuni, the closest English spelling for the Blackfoot term *Piikani*. The South Piegan in Montana are the *Aamsskaapipiikani*.

if not fluent, and he would comment on the day's interpreter. Yellow Kidney's neighbor and long-time comrade (*itakkaa*, "buddy," "partner") was Jappy Takes Gun On Top, who had been stepfather to D.C. Duvall, the half-Piegan collaborator with Clark Wissler on the American Museum series of ethnographies of the Blackfoot (Wissler and Duvall 1908). Yellow Kidney was half-brother to Jim's deceased father, the original Little Plume, and their families had been neighbors on Two Medicine River early in the century. Cuts Different, widow of that Little Plume, remained close to her brother-in-law.

Sommers wanted to interview the three women in the family: Insima, her daughter Agnes Chief All Over, and Cuts Different. Although she obediently recorded extended interviews with Yellow Kidney, Philip Wells, and other respected older men throughout July, in mid-August she began interviewing Agnes Chief All Over and her fascinating mother. Jim Little Plume had interpreted at first, but he was killed on 9 July when Bob Steed's roadster, in which he was a passenger, overturned rounding a dangerous curve. Agnes took over the task of interpreting, and gave Sommers pages of her own life history as well.

Insima was 72, the same age as her husband Yellow Kidney, and had the Christian name Cecile. She had formerly been married to Yellow Wolf, more than 20 years her senior, who died at 82 about ten years before the Laboratory project. Insima was listed as "Cecile" in the 1907–08 Allotment Census, where her father is given as Isadore Sanderville, son of a non-Indian supposedly of the same name and a Piegan woman called Catch For Nothing. He had married Margaret, daughter of the Piegans Red Bird Tail and Twice Success. Cecile had two older brothers, Oliver and Richard (Dick), and a sister Louise (Mrs. John Crow in 1908). Dick Sanderville served on the Blackfeet Tribal Council as early as 1909.

Sue Sommers found Insima captivating. "Five by five feet," energetic and funny, and "really controlling, of the men, of everybody," Sommers recalled her. (One day, Insima picked up Sommers and threw her down, just in fun.) Insima much enjoyed imitating men, putting a pillow under her skirt to appear as a man's big paunch belly (see Appendix for one story of her joking). Her serious side was as a midwife and herb doctor. Sommers remembered her "running up and down the hills" picking medicinal herbs on one occasion while Sommers labored to get a car out of a stream crossing. Told of his wife's energy, Yellow Kidney remarked, "That's how she keeps in shape for when she wants to chase after men."

Ruth Benedict expected Sommers to take down Indians' life histories. Yellow Kidney's was an obvious choice, since he was a prominent elder in the community. Sue learned that as a young man Yellow Kidney had been in a circus, doing stunts on a horse, but the thick folder of typescript from days of interviews with him mentions nothing of this; instead, the practised informant retold a list of Piegan bands, details of the All-comrades' societies, of the Sun Dance, of bison hunting. Trying to take a life history, Sommers found that Yellow Kidney veered off into what she called "folktales," well-known stories of battles and the foundation myths for medicine bundles and their rituals (Wissler 1912). Yellow Kidney had become familiar with what anthropologists wanted, from George Bird Grinnell (e.g., 1892, 1901) in the late 1880s through Walter McClintock, Clark Wissler and Duvall (1908), and James Willard Schultz, who married into Yellow Kidney's community. Salvage ethnography was the task, recording from the last generation to have lived as independent nations, experiencing the bison hunting, ceremonies, and warfare they lost when they settled upon the reservation in 1884. Personal histories were considered idiosyncratic, unscientific in the effort to obtain *the* culture of *the* tribe, and Yellow Kidney's circus exploits were definitely not subjects for a respected elder's recorded life history (cf. DeMallie 1984).

In accordance with the classic ethnographers' expectations that each "primitive" society had "a culture," whose tribal members hewed unthinking to a tradition passed on by their forebears over thousands of years,[4] Yellow Kidney told how it was supposed to have been. For example, "In buffalo days [there was] never a woman who vowed [the Sun Dance] and wasn't pure. Have that just lately. Only being very bad to family" (8-4-39:33). The technical word for Yellow Kidney's accounts is "normative." Wissler (1971 [1938]:206) understood that Indians collaborated, for their own reasons, with their ethnographers in this skewed model: "The old people I knew came to adult life before reservation days and so saw the breakdown of tribal life and independence. Some of them were discouraged as to the future, but by living in the past and capitalizing their ancestral pride, they carried on."

---

[4] One might term this the Holiday Fruitcake paradigm: firmly moulded, dark, studded with traits, infused with spirits, ritually bestowed and hardly nibbled at until, at last, Civilization came and, by the hand of Acculturation, discarded it.

Men's and Women's Business

Yellow Kidney and Insima were each requested to dictate life histories to young "Long Braids." Sommers collected her interview material into one thick folder labeled "Yellow Kidney," another labeled "Insema," and thinner transcripts from other Piegans. With one small exception, the July interviews were all with men. On 1 August 1939, Sommers got five pages of typescript from Short Chief (Good Leader Woman?), identified only as a woman over 80 whose first husband had been Heavy Gun. After another week with Yellow Kidney, on 11 August Sommers interviewed Agnes Chief All Over. At last, from 16 to 18 August, she could work with Insima, Agnes Chief All Over interpreting.

10 In contrast to her husband's didactic presentations of "Plains Indian culture," Insima said nothing of battles and myths. Her reminiscences focused on who married whom, and how good, or bad, the husbands were. Both she and her daughter Agnes recalled their childhoods and especially their relationships to women and girls. Notably absent from Insima's interviews are data on midwifery or herb doctoring, the specialties for which she was well known in her community, or on how she managed her professional and familial commitments. Insima seems to have offered "women's business," that is, marital concerns and childrearing (Goldfrank 1978:140), in complement to the "men's business" of warfare and ritual performance presented by her husband.

"Insema Interviews" is the heading on the folder of typescripts. Immediately we are engrossed in a woman's account of coping with the actuality of reservation life. Men recited the glories of the "buffalo days"; for Insima, the real battles lay in surviving her nation's economic and political collapse. Sommers, if she had followed other mid-century anthropologists, might have labeled her recording of Insima's history a study of "acculturation," or how the Indian adopted a more Western style of life. Perhaps one factor in Sommers's neglect of publishing these field data was her inchoate understanding that the popular term was a biased, ethnocentric distortion of the indigenous nations' protracted contests with the invaders. From a First Nations' perspective, the Blackfoot adopted substitutes for their principal economic resource, the bison, and accepted opportunities to learn English, reading, and other means of dealing with the conquerors. To call these strategies "acculturation"—that is, moving *toward* Western culture—misses the essential point that indigenous people were struggling to *retain* as much of their heritage as possible under the much altered circumstances of the reservation.

Sommers's informants were members of a community formed out of the Grease Melters (translated "Fries" by Agnes Chief All Over; McClintock [1910:57] gives it as *Ich-poch-semo*), a band that dispersed onto farms around 1896, in Yellow Kidney's recollection (7/7/39:1). Sets of brothers formed its core: Yellow Kidney's father was a brother of the Three Suns (Big Nose), respected chief of the Grease Melters at the formation of the reservation in 1884. Yellow Kidney's half-brother was Little Plume, and Yellow Kidney had brought up his brother's son, Jim Little Plume, who became "Long Braids's" friend and guide. A young boy Sommers met, Buster Yellow Kidney, said to be *minipoka*, favorite child, to his maternal grandfather Yellow Kidney, today occupies the place of knowledgeable elder once held by that grandfather.

Insima's notion of a life history was a history of lives. She began the first lengthy interview with stories about her neighbor Running Owl (born 1859). Running Owl's daughter Susie and Insima's Agnes were close friends and they got married at the same time:

> When Agnes was 15 she wanted to get married and she did [to Sam Middle Calf]. Gave her a house. Had a bed on the floor. At same time Susie married [John] Calf Tail. Running Owl didn't like to see this. Running Owl would follow both girls. First night they went to bed he went in and sat and smoked and smoked. Had lamp lit and watched them all night for several nights. Johnny [Calf Tail] told Susie, "Since your Father doesn't want you to marry me, I'm going to leave you," and he did. Not long after that Susie was killed by Jim Little Plume. Agnes' husband left her also.

This is both personal and social history, documenting the early age and instability of marriage among the Blackfoot of the early reservation period. Sommers' experience as a social worker in Harlem had prepared her to listen to accounts of lives quite different from those of most Columbia University students. Sommers's kind, gentle and attentive friend, Jim Little Plume, had, she was told at his funeral that July, "got up drunk one morning and shot his wife, child, and seven other people. He had been in prison for twenty years [but] he had gotten out before [Sommers] arrived and no one spoke of it to her; [she] was impressed at how accepting Indians are" (interview, 8/29/93). Sommers recalled, in 1993, that she and the Steeds attended Jim Little Plume's funeral, conducted by a priest. Two hundred people were there, she estimated, and Insima and Yellow Kidney "went over and gave prayers" in addition to the priest's service. Sommers went with a man named Yellow

Owl to dig Jim's grave along the Two Medicine river (interview, 8/29/93). Half a century later, Sommers remembered Jim Little Plume fondly, and like the Indians, in our interview preferred not to dwell on the tragedies of his life. She had said to Insima at his wake, "Why hadn't you told me about his past?" Insima answered, "Would it have made a difference?" "That was one of the most important lessons I had ever learned," Sommers believed, "of great importance to my life."

Insima's Reminiscences

15 Sommers's typescript for 16 August 1939 launched into "Indian's [Insima's] life." (Apparently Sommers initially misheard *I'nssimaa* as "Indian.") The young woman's transcription style of writing as rapidly as she could in English has the virtue of recording the stream of tale-telling. Sommers did not realize the importance of including her own queries in the text, so we can only guess where she asked for clarification or more information. Minor problems arise from Sommers's unfamiliarity with the dramatis personae of the Reservation, and from Agnes's occasional tendency to give a literal but inappropriate translation: for example, saying "daughter" for what Insima likely termed *itan*. As Sommers's fellow students Hanks and Richardson [1945:31] noted for the North Blackfoot, the term *itan* also includes "(female speaker) daughter of sister; daughter of comrade...first generation female descendant of husband's senior," and extends to *otanimm*, "emotionally attached as to a daughter, adopted as a daughter." Her linguistic naïvetè led Sommers to write (8/16/39, p. 28) that Fine Shield Woman, Pikuni first wife of James Willard Schultz, was Agnes's "daughter," although elsewhere Insima noted that Agnes was a year younger than Fine Shield Woman's son Hart; in English terminology, Fine Shield Woman was Agnes's first cousin. Occasionally, Agnes was careless using "he" versus "she," a common slip stemming from the fact that gender in the Blackfoot language distinguishes animate from inanimate, but not masculine from feminine.

Here is part of Insima's response—translated as she spoke by Agnes Chief All Over—to the ethnographer's request for her life history:

> Yellow Wolf [Insima's first husband] told father that he was going to Browning's Willow Creek to see if it was a good place to build a home. Moved with another family.

Moved. Camped right where Browning is now.[5] Rode and looked Willow Creek over and decided on a place on which they can settle down, and soon to get cattle and cut hay.[6]

Next day, moved to mountains to cut house logs…and poles for corrals. When through, hauled them down as far as Browning on wagons. Build houses there. Finished. From there used to go to Old Agency for rations. Yellow Wolf got mowing machine, rake, and grindstone from government. Bear Paw joined them and asked, Why they didn't let them know they were going to move. Yellow Wolf thought, I wouldn't want to move. After [he] bought machinery a white man came—Mr. Stuart, he married an Indian woman. Told Yellow Wolf, "I heard about this place and you're going to have a lot of hay. Come to put it up for you so you can give me some." Agreed. First time [that] they learned how to cut hay and put it up. When through, put up corral and barn. Then heard some cattle was to be issued to them.

Black Bear said, they should winter cattle at Cut Bank because here, there isn't much shelter. "We'll take hay down there."

Yellow Wolf went to Old Agency. Each family got four cows and four calves regardless of size of families. They told him about milk and he knew how to milk and so did it right away, but didn't know how to make butter.

North of Browning, they found a place [to winter cattle]—thick trees for good shelter. All three—yet—Black Bear and Bear Paw had hayracks and in no time had half the hay there. Sometimes made 3 trips a day. When enough hay there, they moved there. Made house there of cotton[wood] trees.

[Insima] left Agnes because grandmother took Agnes and would[n't] let her go. Father agreed to let her stay and they go ahead. Will build house for them and then send for them.

Yellow Wolf went to agency and when he returned told wife to tell Mother [mother-in-law and son-in-law traditionally did not speak directly to one another] he wanted Agnes to go to school. Grandmother had Agnes—same story as for daughter. Didn't even know when she was brought to school. Policemen come around and collect children. Finally caught. Crying but taken to the school. Told that all children under six had to go to school, even if they were five or three—if older, whites claimed they were younger than they were.

When it occurred to Insima that Sommers would be unfamiliar with Blackfoot custom, she interjected explanations. For example, after mention-

---

[5] The Blackfeet Agency was transferred to Willow Creek, near Joe Kipp's trading post, in 1895, and the town of Browning grew up around Kipp's by 1900 (Farr 1984:40–42).

[6] Cattle were issued to the Piegans beginning in 1890, as part of the 1886 treaty negotiations (Ewers 1958:307; Farr 1984:98).

ing how closely her second pregnancy followed Agnes's birth, she described methods of avoiding too-frequent pregnancies:

> Usually don't have intercourse with husband a month or six weeks after that [childbirth]. Afraid of husband then—don't want to have another child right away but they usually do have a child every two years. After tenth day [after childbirth], going to get out of bed, they put entirely new clothes on. Mother gets any old lady [telling her] that her girl is getting out of bed and to go help her put them on. When old lady gets there, takes all the clothes off. Makes sweet smoke—blankets, moccasins, stocking, etc., and hold them over smoke and then puts the clothes on her. Paints girl's face. Not paid for this. This lady must be old enough to no longer have children. Take all the girl's old clothes that she wore in bed, blanket, and she keeps these. This is to keep the girl from being caught [pregnant] right away.
>
> Agnes' "daughter" [that is, her *nitan. 'a*, Fine Shield Woman] was married to Mr. Schultz [James Willard Schultz]. Almost died when she gave birth to Hart Schultz. Potato [Fine Shield Woman's mother] went to Mother and asked her to help her daughter so she wouldn't have any more children. We almost lost her. Father agreed that something should be done. There was a round copper bracelet with a hole—put a buckskin string through it and put it on the woman's neck. Told her, if a dog has puppies don't pick up or take one (it's all right if they're older and running around) or you'll be caught then. Never did have another child.
>
> [Insima's] Mother also fixed up Louis Champagne's wife for birth control. Mother didn't like to do it anymore—only helped—felt it was killing. Doesn't know where she learned how. She only had one child.

Later in the interviews, Insima indulged in reminiscences of her childhood:

> Insema went hunting when she was very small. In winter went with Boy Chief and Louis Champagne [Yellow Wolf's nephews] and her far away husband [the term for sister's husband (Hanks and Richardson 1945:31)], Morning Plume. A far away husband never says anything out of the way before girl marries and girl does not know how to treat a far away husband.
>
> It was a cold but a nice day. Before she knew how to ride, her Mother used to tie her on the horse. Boy Chief and Morning Plume and Yellow Wolf chased a buffalo. The sky was clear—not a cloud. After each killed a buffalo, they started to cut them up. Then the clouds started to come up like a smoke. Hurried because it looked bad. Insema had an extra horse with her and Morning Plume had four extra horses and so did Yellow Wolf. She had just followed Morning Plume to the hunt. As fast as they cut meat and packed on

horses, the cloud was traveling fast. We started back. Blizzard came and it sure was cold. Many had gone buffalo hunting but in all different directions.

While going, her moccasin ripped on heel—all at once felt a sting—didn't know but her heel had frozen. Got lost and way above the camps and stood around and heard dogs barking down below. When they came home—they—Mother and Father—were sure mad at her. When I got off horse I just fell backwards. They had told me not to go but I wanted to go and pick out my own meat. When I go inside tipi, my heel started to thaw and burn badly but I was ashamed to say anything. Went to another old lady and told her, my heel froze. She took a dried gut, cooked it in a fire until brown. Chewed it and put it on the frozen heel. Didn't sting anymore. Next morning, my heel blistered. Put more gut on. Blisters broke—put more gut on.

Next day, heard one boy missing, never returned and many men went on hunt. Blizzard was over. It was the equinox and storm. Boy had frozen to death. His blanket coat was raggy and leggings torn. Horse was right by him.

[Insima] got a lot of meat from men, hind legs, ribs, heart, liver, kidney, and some guts and ribs. Men didn't mind that she had come. Many times she went in the summer—followed the men. Never went with Father. He would never get chance to go because he had two fast buffalo horses and some one would ask to borrow them and they would bring him meat.

Remembering hunting brought to mind the early reservation period when the bison herds disappeared:

People claimed they were being starved....That was when they first learned to make a garden. Potatoes, rutabagas and carrots—about 57 years ago [1882]. Men plowed and women put in seeds. When first issued rations—flour, meat, bacon, rice, crackers, coffee, tobacco—big long plug, salt, tapioca—called it fish eggs. In fall when garden ready, issued it to them like rations. Have a great big slab of bacon. Scared of the flour because they found bones in it. Claim it was ghost bones—bones from human skeleton.[7] Had to use it but would pick bones out. When we started to eat it, two or three died every morning complaining of their stomachs. White man there [at Old Agency] with Indian wife who talked English and acted as interpreter [probably Malenda Wren (Farr 1984:29)].

Woman would tell them what husband dreamt last night, that he made two or three coffins and sure enough next morning he have to make that many coffins. Then buffalo all gone—no other way to live—not permitted

---

[7] Rodent bones may have occurred in the flour. The necessity of shipping food long distances without refrigeration, the government practice of accepting the lowest bids, and chicanery from suppliers all contributed to the likelihood of contamination in flour and other rations.

to roam—had to stay right there. Think flour poisoned them. Didn't like smell of cows and so didn't like to eat them and didn't like so many different colored animals.

At Old Agency, women did all the work. Agent, Grey Beard, put out two saws and two axes and when he'd open up tool house all the women rush over. Hand out saw and tallest would grab, and same with rest. Pick out best friend to help her with the saw. Be 4 women with 2 axes. Usual to pay them paper money and white paper. The white paper was for sugar. Saw and axes would put up a cordwood and get $4 for one cordwood. Green paper—a dollar. Each get $4, and $1 for sugar.

Men would go up to mountains and haul timber for the agency. One with big load—get $7—way up to mountains. In those days wagons very scarce. Build little log houses. Wouldn't stand long and roofs broke in. Took men a long time to [learn how to] guide a team and how to put harness on. Put harness on up side down. An old man when first learning how to cut hay—didn't know he had to oil it [the machine]. Started to get hot and smoke. Had wife follow with a bucket of water to pour on it. Stand awhile till wife returned with water.

Horses and cattle increased fast. Had over 510 heads of cattle. Father have over 480 horses; he had no cattle. Agency didn't issue cattle to old people. Insema had 22 head of horses.

Insema's fourth daughter was Molly. Molly was born one year after Yellow Wolf's fourth wife had left the family. Katie was the fifth child. She was born three years later. A third daughter had died when she was nine years. (Couldn't remember her name—she had no Indian name.) She had died of pneumonia. Her clothes and toys were buried with her. Molly died when Fannie [Molly's daughter] was very small and Insema raised her. Fannie went to school, staying in dormitory, [and got pregnant by] the principal. Blamed it on young Indian man because she didn't want to get the principal in trouble. He sent Fannie to Minot, N.D. and he paid all expenses and hospital fees there.

Husband [Yellow Wolf] got a salary as a policeman, but the amount was forgotten. He was paid every month. He never actually quit, nor was he fired, but he just didn't return to work. He wasn't paid after he failed to return to work. The salary was stopped after they had moved to Willow Creek. They were living at Willow Creek when Yellow Wolf died. At the time of Yellow Wolf's death, they had both a house and a tent. Yellow Wolf and Insema lived in the tent. Emma and her husband John Little Plume [not related to Yellow Wolf's brother] lived in the house, with Emma's husband's father and mother. Katie and her husband ([Paul] Home Gun), Agnes, her second husband James Big Top and her daughter Mary, lived in Yellow Wolf's tent.

Everyone was there because Yellow Wolf was very rich, and he knew he was going to die. Those who lived there all the time were Insema, Yellow

Wolf and Mary, with Emma and her husband in their own house. (No one lived in Yellow Wolf's house throughout the summer.) Yellow Wolf died at 82 [c. 1927]. He did not die of any illness. He had been shot in war, a little below the shoulder, and the bullet had never been removed. It had swelled and finally burst inside. He [Insima?] cut her hair.[8]

She kept everything. All Yellow Wolf's clothes were put in a sack and buried with him, together with all his little things, pipe, tobacco, matches. He had given his saddle away while he was still alive, and had refused to ride again. Insema gave it to her father. Mrs. Powell—a white woman married to a fullblood—took her to Browning. She stayed with the woman less than a year. She did nothing at all. The woman's daughter-in-law did all the cooking and called them when food was ready. Her other two daughters came after them to eat. Insema did not pay anything for her keep during the time she was there. When father was living, Insema did a lot of work for her, beading and making repairs for her. This woman asked to take Insema home with her because she was older and felt Insema would be happier with her than with her children, who were young and often went out. Insema took only [her granddaughter] Mary with her.

When Agnes had her baby, Insema was nearby but not present. Every time Agnes suffered, she had to run out and cry. Thus she was constantly running in and out. However, she was present at the second birth. (It is always like this—mothers hate to be present at the first birth their daughter has. Mother might stay if she felt others are not helping enough and she can do more for her daughter, everyone thinks she is brave in such a case.) There was no medicine smoke at that time, it had been stopped by the [blank: agent or priest?]. If the girl suffers for two or three days, they make a [blank] to bring child right away. Medicine man and wife called on Agnes to change clothes and make medicine so that she does not have another child soon. His wife took care of changing her clothes, and he painted her face yellow. Gave her no medicine or anything to wear. Told her that if she let no one wear her shawl she would not have another baby right away. He lied, for she had one three years later, and she so informed him. He was paid with a work horse.

Insema adopted Mary after Agnes left her husband. She left in the summer and remarried in the fall. Agnes' new husband told Agnes to let Mother and Father keep Mary since they already had her. "Sometimes we'll take her home with us." Mary got used to her grandparents. Agnes got her clothes and shoes. Insema cared very little when Agnes left her first husband, because she knew he drank and gambled away the cattle and horses; he would never gather wood or go to work. Glad to be rid of him.

---

[8] It was Blackfoot custom that close family members, particularly widows, cut off their hair as a sign of grief and mourning. (Note Agnes's slip in choosing the English pronoun, since Blackfoot uses one animate form for both masculine and feminine.)

If grandparents love their grandchildren and feel that they can take better care of them than their parents, the mother cannot object. Nowadays, it is not necessary to go to court in order to adopt grandchildren. However, to adopt an unrelated orphan, it is necessary to go to court and pay $25.00. The child is then registered in your name and when you die, your property goes to adopted children.

Glad she picked out second husband because he was known as a good man. Agnes knew the second husband [James Big Top] when he was married to Minnie. They would come and stay several nights. Minnie's mother came down for a week. Minnie used to say he was good to her, but his mother was mean to her. Agnes didn't speak much to him. Heard later that Minnie had quit him.

Agnes met him in town, Browning, one day and he asked if she was going back to her husband. When she told him she was not, he asked her to marry him. She said nothing. He asked her again every time he met her. Told mother first time he asked. She finally said yes but said she had heard his mother was mean. He said she acted that way to Minnie because Minnie was running around with his brothers.

When Agnes married her second husband, Insema stopped the taboo [against mother- and son-in-law speaking]. Agnes and husband would visit her, but son-in-law and mother-in-law never spoke to each other. Agnes told her, "You should stop avoiding your son-in-law, it's unusual, you should think of your son-in-law as your son." She was glad not to have to avoid her son-in-law because now he could visit her. She thought of how she had had to avoid her first son-in-law and she would have to go out—only one place in tipi and both couldn't be present. Liked the new arrangement.

Mary [Middle Calf, Agnes' daughter, born 1902] got married that year. Agnes' first husband picked the man for her. Agnes knew nothing about it. She lived quite a distance from Mary. Nobody told Insema about it—she found out about it from others. When Yellow Wolf died, Mary's father came and took her home, and it was during that time that she was married.

Jack, Mary's husband, had given no gifts when he married. (That is not done anymore, Mary got nothing from anyone until later on. Insema started getting bedding, furnishing and tent for her.) Mary did not know Jack before they were married. They were both young.

Six years after Yellow Wolf died, Yellow Kidney's wife died. Insema had not known Yellow Kidney before she married him. His wife was the same age as Insema. Insema went to Browning and while there went to visit an old lady, Mrs. Bird. While she was visiting, Walter McGee and John Mountain Chief, policemen, came in and told her she was wanted at the Indian Agency. She wondered whether she had done something wrong and was under arrest. Decided to go and find out what it was about. Mrs. Bird told her that she would go there with her when Mrs. Bird had finished her cooking. They both went. They found a place, a small room, and Yellow Kidney waiting there. Yellow Kidney didn't know either what they wanted with him. They had just brought them together there.[9] "Wonder if they came after me over that man." They gave me a chair and told me to sit down. They placed her on one side of the desk and Yellow Kidney on the other.

Another policeman, Mr. Tevenus, started to talk to her. He said, "We sent for you because you are going to marry that man." She didn't wish to marry him—she had never know him before (she was very young at the time of her first marriage, and hadn't known any better). They said she wouldn't have to be rustling for herself, and she'd have someone to help her and do things for her. She didn't answer. Walter McGee started to talk kindly to her. Asked her if she had made up her mind. She told them, "The reason I am saying nothing is that I have children and grandchildren and Yellow Kidney might not like them." They said, "The reason we brought you together was that we thought you two would get along together. You are both good workers and will have a nice home soon." They wouldn't let her go until she said yes. Yellow Kidney had been listening to all this. His wife had died only two weeks before.

She said, "It's up to him to say whether he wants to marry me." They started to talk to him. Yellow Kidney said he'd marry her.

I went home but not with him. After I went out they told him to go where I was staying. He came there in a rig. He brought lots of grub, dress goods, a blanket and a shawl. When she got home she explained to Mary and Jack. They told her to marry him.

"I'd like to marry him but he's stranger and I feel ashamed."

Yellow Kidney: "I have some things for you and you can take all that's in the rig." When Yellow Kidney's wife had died they had taken everything that belonged to his wife. Mary Little Plume took all the cooking utensils. Stayed with Mary and Jack quite a while, when finally Yellow Kidney suggested they fix up his place for their own. They came here and cleaned up the place.

20   We can leave Insima here. She went on to tell of the marriage of her youngest daughter Katie to Paul Home Gun, "a good worker" who "never drinks or gambles," and Agnes's marriage to George Chief All Over after Agnes's second husband died. She also told stories of jealous husbands, and of the adventure of a mistreated Blackfoot youth and his orphaned comrade, who went over the mountains to the Flathead Valley and returned with two Salish Flathead women escaping from cruel husbands. This story resembles

---

[9] This passage shows the paternalism of the reservation Agent, treating mature widowed men and women as if they were too feckless to make suitable living arrangements.

men's standard tales of war exploits, except that Insima emphasized the Salish women's active participation in the escape.

Insima's reminiscences are first-hand accounts of the early reservation period that in recent years has increasingly drawn historians' interest. Because scholars during that time were engaged in salvage ethnography, there was little contemporary description outside official documents and newspapers, and particularly little directly and candidly from Indians. The memoir Sommers transcribed is doubly rare because it is from a woman speaking freely and at length.

How valid is this document? Discourse analysis, formerly confined to linguistics, has entered general anthropology and made us more sensitive to the parameters of ethnographic work, to "issues of power and perspective, questions of how authoritative knowledge is legitimated, of self-awareness and authenticity of voice in the presentation of data, and of the constraints of the historical and cultural contexts within which knowledge develops" (Rubinstein 1991:12–13). In 1939, these issues were stuff for the researcher to grapple with before reaching the final draft of a monograph: it was unseemly to expose one's struggles. The persona one presented in print, to the public, was the aloof observer before whose magisterial gaze the events of the field fell into orderly categories. Sommers, who had been a social worker before entering graduate school, could not maintain such an objective analytical stance. World War II pre-empted her personal crisis over a career decision, and after the war she engaged herself in international social activism. Her 1939 typescripts remained raw data.

Rubinstein identifies a "folktale" (as Sommers would have called it) told within the profession of American anthropology, about naive graduate students supposedly cast into the field with only a blank notebook, to flounder about, shiver and shake, until a kind Native adopted them and taught them what they ought to know. Fifty years later, Sommers remembered herself as such a stereotypical innocent. But as Rubinstein points out (1991:14), all those graduate students who *felt*, as they arrived in a strange land, like babes cast adrift, had in fact been prepared by years of academic study of scientific observation and social analysis. They had all read the classics of ethnography *and* heard their professors informally tell their own field experiences. Benedict's instruction, as Sommers recalled it, seemed maddeningly simplistic, yet Sommers knew, from the seminars she took, what an ethnographer was expected to do once he or she "establishes contact with a family and lives with them." Her professor was on the reservation, ready to listen to her students' experiences and suggest how they might proceed. Sommers's fellow student Jane Richardson recalled that they

> sought out the tribal elders to obtain their recollections of Blackfoot life in more free-spirited times. The old ones liked to talk for hours about war deeds, or the sadly vanishing religion of the medicine bundles (Hoffman 1988:118).

This was, Richardson explained, "the formal method of anthropological research [she] had learned…at Columbia" (Hoffman 1988:118).

In Sommers's typescripts we have admired a Blackfoot's matron's *story*, in every sense of that word, told to a young woman who showed herself respectful, empathetic, and fascinated by the lively "Old Lady." Insima, who had listened for too many years to men's stories of war and prescriptions of correct ritual, wanted young Long Braids to hear and record the affairs of real life, how Blackfoot people *lived*. *I'nssimaa*, the Gardener, would plant, would cultivate, a text on women's business—the business of maintaining life. Sommers had paid her dues for more than a month, dutifully recording the standard accounts of men; now, the feminist consciousness nourished in her childhood could resonate with her hostess's Blackfoot pride in womanly accomplishments. Sommers's transcript is perhaps naive in that she made no effort to learn the Blackfoot language (which is difficult for English speakers), she put on paper only the translated formal interviews with no minutiae of context, and she left out her own presence, her queries, her reactions.

25   As a straightforward narrative, however, Sommers's "Insema" folder documents both Blackfoot history and women's history. Its particulars reverberate against dry official archives and sweeping summaries. It is only *a* text, one woman's selected memories, but we owe gratitude to Ruth Benedict who let her student work in a much less-travelled way; to Sue Sommers who persisted; and especially to Insima and her daughter Agnes who wanted their stories to be history.

CONCLUSION

Insima's narratives convey the spirit with which the Piegans adapted to the new economy, carefully selecting ranch land and moving into cabins once they could no longer obtain sturdy bison skins for tipis. Insima partnered her husband in hauling wood and ranching while her mother, according to

Blackfoot custom, cared for Insima's young child. It was hard for Insima's mother to see the granddaughter constrained by dresses, shoes, school buildings, kept from the outdoor exercise and work that make women strong. The older woman's fears of sickness were well founded, for mortality rates, especially among children, were appalling in the early reservation period. Yet, in spite of the terrible toll taken by malnutrition and diseases after the collapse of their indigenous economy, the Piegans maintained their communities throughout the radical step of becoming ranchers in widely separated hamlets along the prairie streams.

Clark Wissler (1971[1938]:239) remarked, "so far as I could see, the morale of the women was far less shattered [by reservation life] and it was they who saved tribal life from complete collapse." Wissler may very well have met Insima; his collaborator Duvall commissioned her in 1904 to make a cradleboard for the American Museum collections.[10] His evaluation of women's business on the reservation seems well borne out by Sommers's transcript of her interviews with Insima.

APPENDIX: INSIMA PLAYS THE DIRTY WHITE MAN

[Interview of 8–17–39 or 8–18–39, Insima speaking, Agnes Chief All Over interpreting]

> She [Insima] was picking [choke]cherries. There was an old lady "Steals Good" heard that another old lady had almost been raped. She got mad and said "I wish I had been there with my butcher knife." She was grinding cherries as she spoke. As she spoke she shook her big butcher knife. Insima thought "I'll see what you can do." Mary and Jack were camping there too. Told Mary "I'm going to play a trick on her. When you see me go to her out of the brush you tell her you're going to the house to put the baby to sleep." Insima went in the tent and put Yellow Kidney's pants on. Cut the fur off a pair of old chaps. Rubbed syrup all over her chin and pasted the fur all over chin and cheeks. Put coat on and dish towel around her head. Put her hair up under an old hat.
>
> Went way around and from east walked up to camp. When Mary saw her she said her piece. She [Steals Good] was facing the grinding. Insima said

[10] Duvall wrote Wissler, "Mrs. Yellow Wolf is making the Baby Board and her mother is making the dog travois" (letter of 12 October 1904), then on 10 November "Mrs. Yellow Wolf, and Boy, also failed to make some of the things" (Wissler papers, American Museum of Natural History). (author's note)

"Hello." She looked up and said "Hello." Made signs "Eat some of these cherries, they're good." Took some and spit them out and said "No good."

"They're good." Stopped grinding and started backing away. She moved near her and drew her near and said "Lot of fat, lot of fat." "No, no, I haven't any meat." Insima grabbed her any place—kept yelling, "No good, no good." She kept hollering for Insima to come—half crying. She kept calling for Mary. Insima had her around the waist and reached under her dress and she cried out. She hollered and hollered. Insima held her tight and pushed her. She cried. Mary finally came running. Insima had an old axe over her shoulder and had dropped it. Insima was holding her under one leg to lift her. Mary was pushing them apart, talking English.

She grabbed the axe and said to Mary "Here's his axe—that dirty white man. I'm going to give it to Jack so he'll know."

Insima circled around to her tent and washed and changed. "What's wrong? I was picking cherries across the river and heard you screaming." Steals Good bawled her out. Asked her which way did white man go? Mary said "Down that way?"

Insima: "Why didn't you grab your knife?" "Well, right from the start he grabbed me and threw me down, and I never thought of my knife. There's his axe, I'm going to give it to my son."

"It was me. I wanted to see if you'd use your knife."

Old lady took after her and did grab her.

References

Benedict, Ruth
    1939   Letter to Oscar and Ruth Lewis. Unpublished, in possession of Ruth M. Lewis, Urbana, IL.

DeMallie, Raymond J., ed.
    1984   *The Sixth Grandfather: Black Elk's Teachings Given to John G. Neihardt.* Lincoln: University of Nebraska Press.

Dietrich, Sue Sommers
    1939   Field Notes, Blackfeet Indian Reservation, Montana. Typescript in author's possession.
    1993   Interview with Alice B. Kehoe, 29 August 1993, in Dietrich's home in Olympia Fields, IL.

Ewers, John C.
    1958   *The Blackfeet: Raiders on the Northwestern Plains.* Norman: University of Oklahoma Press.

Farr, William E.
    1984   *The Reservation Blackfeet, 1882–1945.* Seattle: University of Washington Press.

Goldfrank, Esther S.

    1978   *Notes on an Undirected Life*. Flushing, NY: Queens College Publications in Anthropology, no. 3.

Grinnell, George Bird

    1892   *Blackfoot Lodge Tales*. New York: Charles Scribner's Sons. See *American Anthropologist* o.s., 1896, 9:286–87; n.s. 1899, 1:194–96; 1901, 3:650–68 ("The Lodges of the Blackfoot").

Hanks, Lucien M., Jr., and Jane Richardson

    1945   *Observations on Northern Blackfoot Kinship*. Monograph 9, American Ethnological Society. Seattle: University of Washington Press.

Hoffman, Edward

    1988   *The Right to be Human: A Biography of Abraham Maslow*. Los Angeles: Jeremy P. Tarcher.

McClintock, Walter

    1910   *The Old North Trail*. Lincoln: University of Nebraska Press (1968 Bison Book facsimile reprint).

Rubinstein, Robert A.

    1991   Introduction. In *Fieldwork: The Correspondence of Robert Redfield & Sol Tax*. Boulder, CO: Westview Press.

Schultz, James Willard (Apikuni)

    1907   *My Life as an Indian*. New York: Forest and Stream.

    1962   *Blackfeet and Buffalo*. Keith C. Seele, ed. Norman: University of Oklahoma Press.

    1974   *Why Gone Those Times? Blackfoot Tales*. Eugene Lee Silliman, ed. Norman: University of Oklahoma Press.

Wissler, Clark

    1911   *The Social Life of the Blackfoot Indians*. Anthropological Papers, vol. 7, pt. 1, 1–64. New York: American Museum of Natural History.

    1912   *Ceremonial Bundles of the Blackfoot Indians. Anthropological Papers, vol. 7*, pt. 2, 65–289. New York: American Museum of Natural History.

    1971   [1938] *Red Man Reservations*. New York: Collier. (Originally published 1938 as *Indian Cavalcade or Life on the Old-Time Indian Reservations* by Sheridan House.)

Wissler, Clark, and D.C. Duvall

    1908   *Mythology of the Blackfoot Indians*. Anthropological Papers, vol. 2, pt. 1, 1–163. New York: American Museum of Natural History.

(1996)

QUESTIONS:

1. Kehoe presents a series of long excerpts from Sommers's transcription of Insima's account. Is this a more appropriate way of presenting the material than shaping it for the reader and presenting it in much shorter snippets?

2. Why were researchers at the time of the 1939 Blackfoot project not very interested in personal narratives of this sort? What were their priorities? In what way does Kehoe suggest that the priorities of the researchers dovetailed with the desires of the Blackfoot at the time?

3. For what reasons does Kehoe suggest that Sommers's transcription is a relatively reliable document?

4. Summarize in a paragraph the story of how Insima married Yellow Kidney.

5. What is suggested about the relative importance of men and women in Blackfoot society? What evidence can you point to in Insima's account itself that supports the generalizations made by Kehoe in the section "Men's and Women's Business," and by Wissler (quoted in the final paragraph of the essay)?

6. In their introduction to the volume in which this essay first appeared, Jennifer S. H. Brown and Elizabeth Vibert suggest that Insima's account of her life "counters the 'braves and buffalo' stereotypes of classic plains anthropology and imagery." What are some of the ways in which these stereotypes are undermined in Insima's account? To what extent might this be the result of Insima herself being an extraordinary individual (as opposed to being the result of a failure on the part of historians and anthropologists to take the point of view of women adequately into consideration)?

Henry Louis Gates, Jr.

The Passing of Anatole Broyard

*One of present-day America's leading cultural critics comments on the life and
death of a leading critic of the past generation.*

～～

In 1982, an investment banker named Richard Grand-Jean took a
summer's lease on an eighteenth-century farmhouse in Fairfield, Connecticut; its owner, Anatole Broyard, spent his summers in Martha's Vineyard.
The house was handsomely furnished with period antiques, and the
surrounding acreage included a swimming pool and a pond. But the
property had another attraction, too. Grand-Jean, a managing director of
Salomon Brothers, was an avid reader, and he took satisfaction in renting
from so illustrious a figure. Anatole Broyard had by then been a daily book
reviewer for the *Times* for more than a decade, and that meant that he was
one of literary America's foremost gatekeepers. Grand-Jean might turn to the
business pages of the *Times* first, out of professional obligation, but he
turned to the book page next, out of a sense of self. In his Walter Mittyish
moments, he sometimes imagined what it might be like to be someone who
read and wrote about books for a living—someone to whom millions of
readers looked for guidance.

Broyard's columns were suffused with both worldliness and high culture.
Wry, mandarin, even self-amused at times, he wrote like a man about town,
but one who just happened to have all of Western literature at his fingertips.
Always, he radiated an air of soigné self-confidence: he could be amiable in
his opinions or waspish, but he never betrayed a flicker of doubt about what
he thought. This was a man who knew that his judgment would never falter
and his sentences never fail him.

Grand-Jean knew little about Broyard's earlier career, but as he
rummaged through Broyard's bookshelves he came across old copies of

intellectual journals like *Partisan Review* and *Commentary*, to which Broyard had contributed a few pieces in the late forties and early fifties. One day, Grand-Jean found himself leafing through a magazine that contained an early article by Broyard. What caught his eye, though, was the contributor's note for the article—or, rather, its absence. It had been neatly cut out, as if with a razor.

A few years later, Grand-Jean happened on another copy of that magazine, and decided to look up the Broyard article again. This time, the note on the contributor was intact. It offered a few humdrum details—that Broyard was born in New Orleans, attended Brooklyn College and the New School for Social Research, and taught at New York University's Division of General Education. It also offered a less humdrum one: the situation of the American Negro, the note asserted, was a subject that the author "knows at first hand." It was an elliptical formulation, to be sure, but for Anatole Broyard it may not have been elliptical enough.

5   Broyard was born black and became white, and his story is compounded of equal parts pragmatism and principle. He knew that the world was filled with such snippets and scraps of paper, all conspiring to reduce him to an identity that other people had invented and he had no say in. Broyard responded with X-Acto knives and evasions, with distance and denials and half-denials and cunning half-truths. Over the years, he became a virtuoso of ambiguity and equivocation. Some of his acquaintances knew the truth; many more had heard rumours about "distant" black ancestry (wasn't there a grandfather who was black? a great-grandfather?). But most were entirely unaware, and that was as he preferred it. He kept the truth even from his own children. Society had decreed race to be a matter of natural law, but he wanted race to be an elective affinity, and it was never going to be a fair fight. A penalty was exacted. He shed a past and an identity to become a writer—a writer who wrote endlessly about the act of shedding a past and an identity.

Anatole Paul Broyard was born on July 16, 1920, in New Orleans to Paul Broyard and Edna Miller. His father was a carpenter and worked as a builder, along with his brothers; neither parent had graduated from elementary school. Anatole spent his early years in a modest house on St. Ann Street, in a colored neighborhood in the French Quarter. Documents in the Louisiana state archives show all Anatole's ancestors, on both sides, to have been Negroes, at least since the late eighteenth century. The rumor about a distant black ancestor was, in a sense, the reverse of the truth: he may have had one distant white ancestor. Of course, the conventions of color stratification within black America—nowhere more pronounced than in New Orleans—meant that light-skinned blacks often intermarried with other light-skinned blacks, and this was the case with Paul and his "high yellow" wife, Edna. Anatole was the second of three children; he and his sister Lorraine, two years older, were light-skinned, while Shirley, two years younger, was not so light-skinned. (The inheritance of melanin is an uneven business.) In any event, the family was identified as Negro, and identified itself as Negro. It was not the most interesting thing about them. But in America it was not a negligible social fact. The year before Anatole's birth, for example, close to a hundred blacks were lynched in the South and anti-black race riots claimed the lives of hundreds more.

While Anatole was still a child, the family moved to the Bedford-Stuyvesant area of Brooklyn, thus joining the great migration that took hundreds of thousands of Southern blacks to Northern cities during the twenties. In the French Quarter, Paul Broyard had been a legendary dancer, beau, and *galant*; in the French Quarter, the Broyards—Paul was one of ten siblings—were known for their craftsmanship. Brooklyn was a less welcoming environment. "He should never have left New Orleans, but my mother nagged him into it," Broyard recalled years later. Though Paul Broyard arrived there a master carpenter, he soon discovered that the carpenters' union was not favorably inclined toward colored applicants. A stranger in a strange city, Paul decided to pass as white in order to join the union and get work. It was strictly a professional decision, which affected his work and nothing else.

For Paul, being colored was a banal fact of life, which might be disguised when convenient; it was not a creed or something to take pride in. Paul did take pride in his craft, and he liked to boast of rescuing projects from know-nothing architects. He filled his home with furniture he had made himself—flawlessly professional, if a little too sturdily built to be stylish. He also took pride in his long legs and his dance-hall agility (an agility Anatole would share). It was a challenge to be a Brooklyn *galant*, but he did his best.

"Family life was very congenial, it was nice and warm and cozy, but we just didn't have any sort of cultural or intellectual nourishment at home," Shirley, who was the only member of the family to graduate from college, recalls. "My parents had no idea even what *The New York Times* was, let alone being able to imagine that Anatole might write for it." She says, "Anatole was different from the beginning." There was a sense, early on, that

Anatole Broyard—or Buddy, as he was called then—was not entirely comfortable being a Broyard.

Shirley has a photograph, taken when Anatole was around four or five, of a family visit back to New Orleans. In it you can see Edna and her two daughters, and you can make out Anatole, down the street, facing in the opposite direction. The configuration was, Shirley says, pretty representative.

After graduating from Boys High School, in the late thirties, he enrolled in Brooklyn College. Already, he had a passion for modern culture—for European cinema and European literature. The idea that meaning could operate on several levels seemed to appeal to him. Shirley recalls exasperating conversations along those lines: "He'd ask me about a Kafka story I'd read or a French film I'd seen and say, 'Well, you see that on more than one level, don't you?' I felt like saying 'Oh, get off it.' Brothers don't say that to their sisters."

Just after the war began, he got married, to a black Puerto Rican woman, Aida, and they soon had a daughter. (He named her Gala, after Salvador Dali's wife.) Shirley recalls, "He got married and had a child on purpose—the purpose being to stay out of the Army. Then Anatole goes in the Army anyway, in spite of this child." And his wife and child moved in with the Broyard family.

Though his military records were apparently destroyed in a fire, some people who knew him at this time say that he entered the segregated Army as a white man. If so, he must have relished the irony that after attending officers' training school he was made the captain of an all-black stevedore battalion. Even then, his thoughts were not far from the new life he envisioned for himself. He said that he joined the Army with a copy of Wallace Stevens in his back pocket; now he was sending money home to his wife and asking her to save it so that he could open a bookstore in the Village when he got back. "She had other ideas," Shirley notes. "She wanted him to get a nice job, nine to five."

Between Aida and the allure of a literary life there was not much competition. Soon after his discharge from the Army, at war's end, he found an apartment in the Village, and he took advantage of the G.I. bill to attend evening classes at the New School for Social Research, on Twelfth Street. His new life had no room for Aida and Gala. (Aida, with the child, later moved to California and remarried.) He left other things behind, too. The black scholar and dramatist W. F. Lucas, who knew Buddy Broyard from Bed-Stuy, says, "He was black when he got into the subway in Brooklyn, but as soon as he got out at West Fourth Street he became white."

15   He told his sister Lorraine that he had resolved to pass so that he could be a writer, rather than a Negro writer. His darker-skinned younger sister, Shirley, represented a possible snag, of course, but then he and Shirley had never been particularly close, and anyway she was busy with her own life and her own friends. (Shirley graduated Phi Beta Kappa from Hunter College, and went on to marry Franklin Williams, who helped organize the Peace Corps and served as ambassador to Ghana.) They had drifted apart: it was just a matter of drifting farther apart. Besides, wasn't that why everybody came to New York—to run away from the confines of family, from places where people thought they knew who and what you were? Whose family *wasn't* in some way unsuitable? In a *Times* column in 1979 Broyard wrote, "My mother and father were too folksy for me, too colorful....Eventually, I ran away to Greenwich Village, where no one had been born of a mother and father, where the people I met had sprung from their own brows, or from the pages of a bad novel....Orphans of the avant-garde, we outdistanced our history and our humanity." Like so much of what he wrote in this vein, it meant more than it said; like the modernist culture he loved, it had levels.

In the Village, where Broyard started a bookstore on Cornelia Street, the salient thing about him wasn't that he was black but that he was beautiful, charming, and erudite. In those days, the Village was crowded with ambitious and talented young writers and artists, and Broyard—known for calling men "Sport" and girls "Slim"—was never more at home. He could hang out at the San Remo bar with Dwight Macdonald and Delmore Schwartz, and with a younger set who yearned to be the next Macdonalds and the next Schwartzes. Vincent Livelli, a friend of Broyard's since Brooklyn College days, recalls, "Everybody was so brilliant around us—we kept dueling with each other. But he was the guy that set the pace in the Village." His conversation sparkled—everybody said so. The sentences came out perfectly formed, festooned with the most apposite literary allusions. His high-beam charm could inspire worship but also resentment. Livelli says, "Anatole had a sort of dancing attitude toward life—he'd dance away from you. He had people understand that he was brilliant and therefore you couldn't hold him if you weren't worthy of his attention."

    The novelist and editor Gordon Lish says, "Photographs don't suggest in any wise the enormous power he had in person. No part of him was ever for a moment at rest." He adds, "I adored him as a man. I mean, he was really in a league with Neal Cassady as a kind of presence." But there was, he says, a fundamental difference between Broyard and Kerouac's inspiration and muse: "Unlike Cassady, who was out of control, Anatole was *exorbitantly* in control. He was fastidious about managing things."

Except, perhaps, the sorts of things you're supposed to manage. His bookstore provided him with entrée to Village intellectuals—and them with entrée to Anatole—yet it was not run as a business, exactly. Its offerings were few but choice: Céline, Kafka, other hard-to-find translations. The critic Richard Gilman, who was one of its patrons, recalls that Broyard had a hard time parting with the inventory: "He had these books on the shelf, and someone would want to buy one, and he would snatch it back."

Around 1948, Broyard started to attract notice not merely for his charm, his looks, and his conversation but for his published writings. The early pieces, as often as not, were about a subject to which he had privileged access: blacks and black culture. *Commentary*, in his third appearance in its pages, dubbed him an "anatomist of the Negro personality in a white world." But was he merely an anthropologist or was he a native informant? It wasn't an ambiguity that he was in any hurry to resolve. Still, if all criticism is a form of autobiography (as Oscar Wilde would have it), one might look to these pieces for clues to his preoccupations at the time. In a 1950 *Commentary* article entitled "Portrait of the Inauthentic Negro," he wrote that the Negro's embarrassment over blackness should be banished by the realization that "thousands of Negroes with 'typical' features are accepted as whites merely because of light complexion." He continued:

> The inauthentic Negro is not only estranged from whites—he is also estranged from his own group and from himself. Since his companions are a mirror in which he sees himself as ugly, he must reject them; and since his own self is mainly a tension between an accusation and a denial, he can hardly find it, much less live in it.…He is adrift without a role in a world predicated on roles.

20 A year later, in "Keep Cool, Man: The Negro Rejection of Jazz," he wrote, just as despairingly, that the Negro's

> contact with white society has opened new vistas, new ideals in his imagination, and these he defends by repression, freezing up against the desire to be white, to have normal social intercourse with whites, to behave like them.… But in coolness he evades the issue…he becomes a pacifist in the struggle between social groups—not a conscientious objector, but a draft-dodger.

These are words that could be read as self-indictment, if anybody chose to do so. Certainly they reveal a ticklish sense of the perplexities he found himself in, and a degree of self-interrogation (as opposed to self-examination) he seldom displayed again.

In 1950, in a bar near Sheridan Square, Broyard met Anne Bernays, a Barnard junior and the daughter of Edward L. Bernays, who is considered the father of public relations. "There was this guy who was the handsomest man I have ever seen in my life, and I fell madly in love with him," Bernays, who is best known for such novels as *Growing Up Rich* and *Professor Romeo*, recalls. "He was physically irresistible, and he had this dominating personality, and I guess I needed to be dominated. His hair was so short that you couldn't tell whether it was curly or straight. He had high cheekbones and very smooth skin." She knew that he was black, through a mutual friend, the poet and Blake scholar Milton Klonsky. (Years later, in a sort of epiphany, she recognized Anatole's loping walk as an African-American cultural style: "It was almost as if this were inside him dying to get out and express itself, but he felt he couldn't do it.")

After graduation, she got a job as an editor at the literary semi-annual *Discovery*. She persuaded Broyard to submit his work, and in 1954 the magazine ran a short story entitled "What the Cystoscope Said"—an extraordinary account of his father's terminal illness:

> I didn't recognize him at first, he was so bad. His mouth was open and his breathing was hungry. They had removed his false teeth, and his cheeks were so thin that his mouth looked like a keyhole. I leaned over his bed and brought my face before his eyes. "Hello darlin'," he whispered, and he smiled. His voice, faint as it was, was full of love, and it bristled the hairs on the nape of my neck and raised goose flesh on my forearms. I couldn't speak, so I kissed him. His cheek smelled like wax.

Overnight, Broyard's renown was raised to a higher level. "Broyard knocked people flat with 'What the Cystoscope Said,'" Lish recalls. One of those people was Burt Britton, a bookseller who later co-founded Books & Co. In the fifties, he says, he read the works of young American writers religiously: "Now, if writing were a horse race, which God knows it's not, I would have gone out and put my two bucks down on Broyard." In *Advertisements for Myself*, Norman Mailer wrote that he'd buy a novel by Broyard the day it appeared. Indeed, Bernays recalls, on the basis of that story the Atlantic Monthly Press offered Broyard a twenty-thousand-dollar advance—then a staggeringly large sum for a literary work by an unknown—for a novel of which "Cystoscope" would be a chapter. "The whole literary world was waiting with bated breath for this great novelist who was about to arrive," Michael Vincent Miller, a friend of Broyard's since the late fifties, recalls. "Some feelings of expectation lasted for years."

Rumor surrounded Broyard like a gentle murmur, and sometimes it became a din. Being an orphan of the avant-garde was hard work. Among the black literati, certainly, his ancestry was a topic of speculation, and when a picture of Broyard accompanied a 1958 *Time* review of a Beat anthology it was closely scrutinized. Arna Bontemps wrote to Langston Hughes, "His picture…makes him look Negroid. If so, he is the only spade among the Beat Generation." Charlie Parker spied Broyard in Washington Square Park one day and told a companion, "He's one of us, but he doesn't want to admit he's one of us." Richard Gilman recalls an awkwardness that ensued when he stumbled across Anatole with his dark-skinned wife and child: "I just happened to come upon them in a restaurant that was not near our usual stomping grounds. He introduced me, and it was fine, but my sense was that he would rather not have had anyone he knew meet them." He adds, "I remember thinking at the time that he had the look of an octoroon or a quadroon, one of those—which he strenuously denied. He got into very great disputes with people."

One of those disputes was with Chandler Brossard, who had been a close friend: Broyard was the best man at Brossard's wedding. There was a falling out, and Brossard produced an unflattering portrait of Broyard as the hustler and opportunist Henry Porter in his 1952 novel, *Who Walk in Darkness*. Brossard knew just where Broyard was most vulnerable, and he pushed hard. His novel originally began, "People said Henry Porter had Negro blood," as does the version published in France. Apparently fearing legal action, however, Brossard's American publisher, New Directions, sent it to Broyard in galley form before it was published.

Anne Bernays was with Broyard when the galleys arrived. Broyard explained to her, "They asked me to read it because they are afraid I am going to sue." But why would he sue, she wanted to know. "Because it says I'm a Negro," he replied grimly. "Then," Bernays recalls, "I said, 'What are you going to do?' He said, 'I am going to make them change it.' And he did."

The novel went on to be celebrated as a groundbreaking chronicle of Village hipsters; it also—as a result of the legal redactions—reads rather oddly in places. Henry Porter, the Broyard character, is rumored to be not a Negro but merely an illegitimate:

> I suspect [the rumor] was supposed to explain the difference between the way he behaved and the way the rest of us behaved. Porter did not show that he knew people were talking about him this way. I must give him credit for maintaining a front of indifference that was really remarkable.
>
> Someone both Porter and I knew quite well once told me the next time he saw Porter he was going to ask him if he was or was not an illegitimate. He said it was the only way to clear the air. Maybe so. But I said I would not think of doing it....I felt that if Porter ever wanted the stories about himself cleared up, publicly, he would one day do so. I was willing to wait.

And that, after all, is the nature of such secrets: they are not what cannot be known but what cannot be acknowledged.

Another trip wire seems to have landed Broyard in one of the masterpieces of twentieth-century American fiction, William Gaddis's *The Recognitions*. Livelli explains, "Now, around 1947 or '48, William Gaddis and Anatole were in love with the same gal, Sheri Martinelli. They were rivals, almost at each other's throats. And Willie was such a sweetheart that he had a mild approach to everything, and Anatole was sort of a stabber: he injected words like poison into conversations." When *The Recognitions* came out, in 1955, "Anatole caught on to it right away, and he was kind of angry over it." The Broyard character is named Max, and Gaddis wrote that he "always looked the same, always the same age, his hair always the same short length," seemingly "a parody on the moment, as his clothes caricatured a past at eastern colleges where he had never been." Worse is his "unconscionable smile," which intimates "that the wearer knew all of the dismal secrets of some evil jungle whence he had just come."

Broyard's own account of these years—published in 1993 as *Kafka Was the Rage*—is fueled by the intertwined themes of writing and women. Gaddis says, "His eyes were these great pools—soft, gentle pools. It was girls, girls, girls: a kind of intoxication of its own. I always thought, frankly, that that's where his career went, his creative energies."

Anne Bernays maintains, "If you leave the sex part out, you're only telling half the story. With women, he was just like an alcoholic with booze." She stopped seeing him in 1952, at her therapist's urging. "It was like going cold turkey off a drug," she says, remembering how crushing the experience was, and she adds, "I think most women have an Anatole in their lives."

Indeed, not a few of them had Anatole. "He was a pussy gangster, really," Lucas, a former professor of comparative literature, says with Bed-Stuy bluntness. Gilman recalls being in Bergdorf Goodman and coming across Broyard putting the moves on a salesgirl. "I hid behind a pillar—otherwise he'd know that I'd seen him—and watched him go through every stage of seduction: 'What do you think? Can I put this against you? Oh, it looks great against your skin. You have the most wonderful skin.' And then he quoted Baudelaire."

Quoting Baudelaire turns out to be key. Broyard's great friend Ernest van den Haag recalls trolling the Village with Broyard in those days: "We obviously quite often compared our modus operandi, and what I observed about Anatole is that when he liked a girl he could speak to her brilliantly about all kinds of things which the girl didn't in the least understand, because Anatole was really vastly erudite. The girl had no idea what he was talking about, but she loved it, because she was under the impression, rightly so, that she was listening to something very interesting and important. His was a solipsistic discourse, in some ways." Indeed, the narrator of "What the Cystoscope Said" tells of seducing his ailing father's young and ingenuous nurse in a similar manner:

> "Listen," I said, borrowing a tone of urgency from another source, "I want to give you a book. A book that was written for you, a book that belongs to you as much as your diary, that's dedicated to you like your nurse's certificate."...My apartment was four blocks away, so I bridged the distance with talk, raving about *Journey to the End of the Night*, the book she needed like she needed a hole in her head.

Broyard recognized that seduction was a matter not only of talking but of listening, too, and he knew how to pay attention with an engulfing level of concentration. The writer Ellen Schwamm, who met Broyard in the late fifties, says, "You show me a man who talks, and I'll show you a thousand women who hurl themselves at his feet. I don't mean just talk, I mean dialogues. He *listened*, and he was willing to speak of things that most men are not interested in: literature and its effect on life." But she also saw another side to Broyard's relentless need to seduce. She invokes a formulation made by her husband, the late Harold Brodkey: "Harold used to say that a lot of men steal from women. They steal bits of their souls, bits of their personalities, to construct an emotional life, which many men don't have. And I think Anatole needed something of that sort."

It's an image of self-assemblage which is very much in keeping with Broyard's own accounts of himself. Starting in 1946, and continuing at intervals for the rest of his life, he underwent analysis. Yet the word "analysis" is misleading: what he wanted was to be refashioned—or, as he told his first analyst, to be *transfigured*. "When I came out with the word, I was like someone who sneezes into a handkerchief and finds it full of blood," he wrote in the 1993 memoir. "I wanted to discuss my life with him not as a patient talking to an analyst but as if we were two literary critics discussing a novel....I had a literature rather than a personality, a set of fictions about myself." He lived a lie because he didn't want to live a larger lie: and Anatole Broyard, Negro writer, was that larger lie.

35   Alexandra Nelson, known as Sandy, met Broyard in January of 1961. Broyard was forty, teaching the odd course at the New School and supporting himself by freelancing: promotional copy for publishers, liner notes for Columbia jazz records, blurbs for the Book-of-the-Month Club. Sandy was twenty-three and a dancer, and Broyard had always loved dancers. Of Norwegian descent, she was strikingly beautiful, and strikingly intelligent. Michael Miller recalls, "She represented a certain kind of blonde, a certain kind of sophisticated carriage and a way of moving through the world with a sense of the good things. They both had marvelous taste."

    It was as if a sorcerer had made a list of everything Broyard loved and had given it life. At long last, the conqueror was conquered: in less than a year, Broyard and Sandy were married. Sandy remembers his aura in those days: "Anatole was very hip. It wasn't a pose—it was in his sinew, in his bones. And, when he was talking to you, you just felt that you were receiving all this radiance from him." (Van den Haag says, "I do think it's not without significance that Anatole married a blonde, and about as white as you can get. He may have feared a little bit that the children might turn out black. He must have been pleased that they didn't.")

    While they were still dating, two of Broyard's friends told Sandy that he was black, in what seemed to be a clumsy attempt to scare her off. "I think they really weren't happy to lose him, to see him get into a serious relationship," she says. "They were losing a playmate, in a way." Whatever the cultural sanctions, she was unfazed. But she says that when she asked Broyard about it he proved evasive: "He claimed that he wasn't black, but he talked about 'island influences,' or said that he had a grandmother who used to live in a tree on some island in the Caribbean. Anatole was like that—he was very slippery." Sandy didn't force the issue, and the succeeding years only fortified his sense of reserve. "Anatole was very strong," she says. "And he said about certain things, 'Just keep out. This is the deal if you get mixed up with me.'" The life that Broyard chose to live meant that the children did not meet their Aunt Shirley until after his death—nor, except for a couple of brief visits in the sixties, was there any contact even with Broyard's light-skinned mother and older sister. It was a matter of respecting the ground rules. "I would try to poke in those areas, but the message was very direct and strong," Sandy explains. "Oh, when I got angry at him, you know, one always pushes the tender points. But over time you grow up about these things and realize you do what you can do and there are certain things you can't."

In 1963, just before their first child, Todd, was born, Anatole shocked his friends by another big move—to Connecticut. Not only was he moving to Connecticut but he was going to be commuting to work: for the first time in his life, he would be a company man. "I think one of his claims to fame was that he hadn't had an office job—somehow, he'd escaped that," Sandy says. "There had been no real need for him to grow up." But after Todd was born—a daughter, Bliss, followed in 1966—Anatole spent seven years working full-time as a copywriter at the Manhattan advertising agency Wunderman Ricotta & Kline.

Over the next quarter century, the family lived in a series of eighteenth-century houses, sometimes bought on impulse, in places like Fairfield, Redding, Greens Farms, and Southport. Here, in a land of leaf-blowers and lawnmowers, Bed-Stuy must have seemed almost comically remote. Many of Broyard's intimates from the late forties knew about his family; the intimates he acquired in the sixties did not, or else had heard only rumors. Each year, the number of people who knew Buddy from Bed-Stuy dwindled; each year, the rumors grew more nebulous; each year, he left his past further behind. Miller says, "Anatole was a master at what Erving Goffman calls 'impression management.'" The writer Evelyn Toynton says, "I remember once going to a party with Sandy and him in Connecticut. There were these rather dull people there, stockbrokers and the usual sorts of people, and Anatole just knocked himself out to charm every single person in the room. I said to him, 'Anatole, can't you ever *not* be charming?'" Miller observes, "He was a wonderful host. He could take people from different walks of life—the president of Stanley Tools or a vice-president of Merrill Lynch, say, and some bohemian type from the Village—and keep the whole scene flowing beautifully. He had perfect pitch for the social encounter, like Jay Gatsby."

It was as if, wedded to an ideal of American self-fashioning, he sought to put himself to the ultimate test. It was one thing to be accepted in the Village, amid the Beats and hipsters and émigrés, but to gain acceptance in Cheever territory was an achievement of a higher order. "Anatole, when he left the Village and went to Connecticut, was able not only to pass but even to be a kind of influential presence in that world of rich white Wasps," Miller says. "Maybe that was a shallower part of the passing—to be accepted by Connecticut gentry."

Broyard's feat raised eyebrows among some of his literary admirers: something borrowed, something new. Daphne Merkin, another longtime friend, detected "a 'country-squire' tendency—a complicated tendency to want to establish a sort of safety through bourgeoisness. It was like a Galsworthy quality."

Even in Arcadia, however, there could be no relaxation of vigilance: in his most intimate relationships, there were guardrails. Broyard once wrote that Michael Miller was one of the people he liked best in the world, and Miller is candid about Broyard's profound influence on him. Today, Miller is a psychotherapist, based in Cambridge, and the author, most recently, of *Intimate Terrorism*. From the time they met until his death, Broyard read to him the first draft of almost every piece he wrote. Yet a thirty-year friendship of unusual intimacy was circumscribed by a subject that they never discussed. "First of all, I didn't *know*," Miller says. "I just had intuitions and had heard intimations. It was some years before I'd even put together some intuition and little rumblings—nothing ever emerged clearly. There was a certain tacit understanding between us to accept certain pathways as our best selves, and not challenge that too much." It was perhaps, he says a little sadly, a limitation on the relationship.

In the late sixties, Broyard wrote several front-page reviews for the *Times Book Review*. "They were brilliant, absolutely sensational," the novelist Charles Simmons, who was then an assistant editor there, says. In 1971, the *Times* was casting about for a new daily reviewer, and Simmons was among those who suggested Anatole Broyard. It wasn't a tough sell. Arthur Gelb, at the time the paper's cultural editor, recalls, "Anatole was among the first critics I brought to the paper. He was very funny, and he also had that special knack for penetrating hypocrisy. I don't think he was capable of uttering a boring sentence."

You could say that his arrival was a sign of the times. Imagine: Anatole Broyard, downtown flaneur and apostle of sex and high modernism, ensconced in what was, literarily speaking, the ultimate establishment perch. "There had been an awful lot of very tame, very conventional people at the *Times*, and Broyard came in as a sort of ambassador from the Village and Village sophistication," Alfred Kazin recalls. Broyard had a highly developed appreciation of the paper's institutional power, and he even managed to use it to avenge wrongs done him in his Village days. Just before he started his job at the daily, he published a review in the *Times Book Review* of a new novel by one Chandler Brossard. The review began, "Here's a book so transcendently bad it makes us fear not only for the condition of the novel in this country, but for the country itself."

45 Broyard's reviews were published in alternation with those of Christopher Lehmann-Haupt, who has now been a daily reviewer at the *Times* for more than a quarter century, and who readily admits that Broyard's appointment did not gladden his heart. They hadn't got along particularly well when Lehmann-Haupt was an editor at the *Times Book Review*, nor did Lehmann-Haupt entirely approve of Broyard's status as a fabled libertine. So when A. M. Rosenthal, the paper's managing editor, was considering hiring him, Lehmann-Haupt expressed reservations. He recalls, "Rosenthal was saying, 'Give me five reasons why not.' And I thoughtlessly blurted out, 'Well, first of all, he is the biggest ass man in town.' And Rosenthal rose up from his desk and said, 'If that were a disqualification for working for *The New York Times*'—and he waved— 'this place would be empty!'"

Broyard got off to an impressive start. Lehmann-Haupt says, "He had a wonderful way of setting a tone, and a wonderful way of talking himself through a review. He had good, tough instincts when it came to fiction. He had taste." And the jovial Herbert Mitgang, who served a stint as a daily reviewer himself, says, "I always thought he was the most literary of the reviewers. There would be something like a little essay in his daily reviews."

Occasionally, his acerbic opinions got him in trouble. There was, for example, the storm that attended an uncharitable review of a novel by Christy Brown, an Irish writer who was born with severe cerebral palsy. The review concluded:

> It is unfortunate that the author of "A Shadow on Summer" is an almost total spastic—he is said to have typed his highly regarded first novel, "Down All the Days," with his left foot—but I don't see how the badness of his second novel can be blamed on that. Any man who can learn to type with his left foot can learn to write better than he has here.

Then, there was the controversial review of James Baldwin's piously sentimental novel of black suffering, *If Beale Street Could Talk*. Broyard wrote:

If I have to read one more description of the garbage piled up in the streets of Harlem, I may just throw protocol to the winds and ask whose garbage is it? I would like to remind Mr. Baldwin that the City Health Code stipulates that garbage must be put out in proper containers, not indiscriminately "piled."

No one could accuse Broyard of proselytizing for progressive causes. Jason Epstein, for one, was quick to detect a neoconservative air in his reviews, and Broyard's old friend Ernest van den Haag, a longtime contributing editor at *National Review*, volunteers that he was available to set Broyard straight on the issues when the need arose. Broyard could be mischievous, and he could be tendentious. It did not escape notice that he was consistently hostile to feminist writers. "Perhaps it's naïve of me to expect people to write reasonable books about emotionally charged subjects," one such review began, irritably. "But when you have to read and review two or three books each week, you do get tired of 'understanding' so much personal bias. You reach a point where it no longer matters that the author's mistakes are well meant. You don't care that he or she is on the side of the angels: you just want them to tell the truth."

Nor did relations between the two daily reviewers ever become altogether cordial. Lehmann-Haupt tells of a time in 1974 when Broyard said that he was sick and couldn't deliver a review. Lehmann-Haupt had to write an extra review in less than a day, so that he could get to the Ali-Frazier fight the next night, where he had ringside seats. Later, when they discussed the match, Broyard seemed suspiciously knowledgeable about its particulars; he claimed that a friend of his had been invited by a television executive to watch it on closed-circuit TV. "I waited about six months, because one of the charming things about Anatole was that he never remembered his lies," Lehmann-Haupt says, laughing. "And I said, 'Did you see that fight?' And he said, 'Oh, yeah—I was there as a guest of this television executive.' *That's* why he couldn't write the review!"

Broyard had been teaching off and on at the New School since the late fifties, and now his reputation as a writing teacher began to soar. Certainly his fluent prose style, with its combination of grace and clarity, was a considerable recommendation. He was charismatic and magisterial, and, because he was sometimes brutal about students' work, they found it all the more gratifying when he was complimentary. Among his students were Paul Breslow, Robert Olen Butler, Daphne Merkin, and Hilma Wolitzer. Ellen

Schwamm, who took a workshop with him in the early seventies, says, "He had a gourmet's taste for literature and for language, and he was really able to convey that: it was a very sensual experience."

These were years of heady success and, at the same time, of a rising sense of failure. An arbiter of American writing, Broyard was racked by his inability to write his own magnum opus. In the fifties, the Atlantic Monthly Press had contracted for an autobiographical novel—the novel that was supposed to secure Broyard's fame, his place in contemporary literature—but, all these years later, he had made no progress. It wasn't for lack of trying. Lehmann-Haupt recalls his taking a lengthy vacation in order to get the book written. "I remember talking to him—he was up in Vermont, where somebody had lent him a house—and he was in agony. He banished himself from the Vineyard, was clearly suffering, and he just couldn't do it." John Updike, who knew Broyard slightly from the Vineyard, was reminded of the anticipation surrounding Ellison's second novel: "The most famous non-book around was the one that Broyard was not writing." (The two non-book writers were in fact quite friendly: Broyard admired Ellison not only as a writer but as a dancer—a high tribute from such an adept as Broyard.)

Surrounded by analysts and psychotherapists—Sandy Broyard had become a therapist herself by this time—Broyard had no shortage of explanations for his inability to write his book. "He did have a total writer's block," van den Haag says, "and he was analyzed by various persons, but it didn't fully overcome the writer's block. I couldn't prevent him from going back to 'The Cystoscope' and trying to improve it. He made it, of course, not better but worse." Broyard's fluency as an essayist and a reviewer wasn't quite compensation. Charles Simmons says, "He had produced all this charming criticism, but the one thing that mattered to him was the one thing he hadn't managed to do."

As the seventies wore on, Miller discussed the matter of blockage with his best friend in relatively abstract terms: he suggested that there might be something in Broyard's relationship to his family background that was holding him back. In the eighties, he referred Broyard to his own chief mentor in gestalt therapy, Isador From, and From became perhaps Broyard's most important therapist in his later years. "In gestalt therapy, we talk a lot about 'unfinished business': anything that's incomplete, unfinished, haunts the whole personality and tends, at some level, to create inhibition or blockage," Miller says. "You're stuck there at a certain point. It's like living with a partly full bladder all your life."

55   Some people speculated that the reason Broyard couldn't write his novel was that he was living it—that race loomed larger in his life because it was unacknowledged, that he couldn't put it behind him because he had put it beneath him. If he had been a different sort of writer, it might not have mattered so much. But Merkin points out, "Anatole's subject, even in fiction, was essentially himself. I think that ultimately he would have had to deal with more than he wanted to deal with."

Broyard may have been the picture of serene self-mastery, but there was one subject that could reliably fluster him. Gordon Lish recalls an occasion in the mid-seventies when Burt Britton (who was married to a black woman) alluded to Anatole's racial ancestry. Lish says, "Anatole became inflamed, and he left the room. He snapped, like a dog snapping—he *barked* at Britton. It was an ugly moment." To people who knew nothing about the matter, Broyard's sensitivities were at times simply perplexing. The critic Judith Dunford used to go to lunch with Broyard in the eighties. One day, Broyard mentioned his sister Shirley, and Dunford, idly making conversation, asked him what she looked like. Suddenly, she saw an extremely worried expression on his face. Very carefully, he replied, "Darker than me."

There was, finally, no sanctuary. "When the children were older, I began, every eighteen months or so, to bring up the issue of how they needed to know at some point," Sandy Broyard says. "And then he would totally shut down and go into a rage. He'd say that at some point he would tell them, but he would not tell them now." He was the Scheherazade of racial imposture, seeking and securing one deferral after another. It must have made things not easier but harder. In the modern era, children are supposed to come out to their parents: it works better that way around. For children, we know, can judge their parents harshly—above all, for what they understand as failures of candor. His children would see the world in terms of authenticity; he saw the world in terms of self-creation. Would they think that he had made a Faustian bargain? Would they speculate about what else he had not told them—about the limits of self-invention? Broyard's resistance is not hard to fathom. He must have wondered when the past would learn its place, and stay past.

Anatole Broyard had confessed enough in his time to know that confession did nothing for the soul. He preferred to communicate his truths on higher frequencies. As if in exorcism, Broyard's personal essays deal regularly with the necessary, guilt-ridden endeavor of escaping family history: and yet the feelings involved are well-nigh universal. The thematic elements of passing—fragmentation, alienation, liminality, self-fashioning—echo the great themes of modernism. As a result, he could prepare the way for exposure without ever risking it. Miller observes, "If you look at the writing closely enough, and listen to the intonations, there's something there that is like no writer from the completely white world. Freud talked about the repetition compulsion. With Anatole, it's interesting that he was constantly hiding it and in some ways constantly revealing it."

Sandy speaks of these matters in calmly analytic tones; perhaps because she is a therapist, her love is tempered by an almost professional dispassion. She says, "I think his own personal history continued to be painful to him," and she adds, "In passing, you cause your family great anguish, but I also think, conversely, do we look at the anguish it causes the person who is passing? Or the anguish that it was born out of?"

60   It may be tempting to describe Broyard's self-positioning as arising from a tortured allegiance to some liberal-humanist creed. In fact, the liberal pieties of the day were not much to his taste. "It wasn't about an ideal of raceless-ness but something much more complex and interesting," Miller says. "He was actually quite anti-black," Evelyn Toynton says. She tells of a time when she was walking with him on a street in New York and a drunken black man came up to him and asked for a dollar. Broyard seethed. Afterward, he remarked to her, "I look around New York, and I think to myself, If there were no blacks in New York, would it really be any loss?"

No doubt this is a calculation that whites, even white liberals, sometimes find themselves idly working out: How many black muggers is one Thelonious Monk worth? How many Willie Hortons does Gwendolyn Brooks redeem? In 1970, Ellison published his classic essay "What America Would Be Like Without Blacks," in *Time*; and one reason it is a classic essay is that it addresses a question that lingers in the American political uncon-scious. Commanding as Ellison's arguments are, there remains a whit of defensiveness in the very exercise. It's a burdensome thing to refute a fantasy.

And a burdensome thing to be privy to it. Ellen Schwamm recalls that one of those houses Broyard had in Connecticut had a black jockey on the lawn, and that "he used to tell me that Jimmy Baldwin had said to him, 'I can't come and see you with this crap on your lawn.'" (Sandy remembers the lawn jockey—an antique—as having come with the house; she also recalls that it was stolen one day.) Charles Simmons says that the writer Herbert Gold, before introducing him to Broyard, warned him that Broyard was prone to make comments about "spades," and Broyard did make a few such comments. "He personally, on a deeper level, was not enamored of blacks," van den Haag says. "He avoided blacks. There is no question he did." Sandy is gingerly in alluding to this subject. "He was very short-tempered with the behavior of black people, the sort of behavior that was shown in the news. He had paid the price to be at liberty to say things that, if you didn't know he was black, you would misunderstand. I think it made him ironical."

Every once in a while, however, Broyard's irony would slacken, and he would speak of the thing with an unaccustomed and halting forthrightness. Toynton says that after they'd known each other for several years he told her there was a "C" (actually, "col," for "colored") on his birth certificate. "And then another time he told me that his sister was black and that she was married to a black man." The circumlocutions are striking: not that *he* was black but that his birth certificate was; not that *he* was black but that his family was. Perhaps this was a matter less of evasiveness than of precision.

"Some shrink had said to him that the reason he didn't like brown-haired women or dark women was that he was afraid of his own shit," Toynton continues. "And I said, 'Anatole, it's as plain as plain can be that it has to do with being black.' And he just stopped and said, 'You don't know what it was like. It was horrible.' He told me once that he didn't like to see his sisters, because they reminded him of his unhappy childhood." (Shirley's account suggests that this unhappy childhood may have had more to do with the child than with the hood.)

65 Ellen Schwamm remembers one occasion when Broyard visited her and Harold Brodkey at their apartment, and read them part of the memoir he was working on. She says that the passages seemed stilted and distant, and that Brodkey said to him, "You're not telling the truth, and if you try to write lies or evade the truth this is what you get. What's the real story?" She says, "Anatole took a deep breath and said, 'The real story is that I'm not who I seem. I'm a black.' I said, 'Well, Anatole, it's no great shock, because this rumor has been around for years and years and years, and everyone assumes there's a small percentage of you that's black, if that's what you're trying to say.' And he said, 'No, that's not what I'm trying to say. My father could pass, but in fact my mother's black, too. We're black as far back as I know.' We never said a word of it to anybody, because he asked us not to."

Schwamm also says that she begged him to write about his history: it seemed to her excellent material for a book. But he explained that he didn't want notoriety based on his race—on his revealing himself to be black—rather than on his talent. As Toynton puts it, Broyard felt that he had to make a choice between being an aesthete and being a Negro. "He felt that once he said, 'I'm a Negro writer,' he would have to write about black issues, and Anatole was such an aesthete."

All the same, Schwamm was impressed by a paradox: the man wanted to be appreciated not for being black but for being a writer, even though his pretending not to be black was stopping him from writing. It was one of the very few ironies that Broyard, the master ironist, was ill equipped to appreciate.

Besides, there was always his day job to attend to. Broyard might suffer through a midnight of the soul in Vermont; but he was also a working journalist, and when it came to filing his copy he nearly always met his deadlines. In the late seventies, he also began publishing brief personal essays in the *Times*. They are among the finest work he did—easeful, witty, perfectly poised between surface and depth. In them he perfected the feat of being self-revelatory without revealing anything. He wrote about his current life, in Connecticut: "People in New York City have psychotherapists, and people in the suburbs have handymen. While anxiety in the city is existential, in the country it is structural." And he wrote about his earlier life, in the city: "There was a kind of jazz in my father's movements, a rhythm compounded of economy and flourishes, functional and decorative. He had a blues song in his blood, a wistful jauntiness he brought with him from New Orleans." (Wistful, and even worrisome: "I half-expected him to break into the Camel Walk, the Shimmy Shewobble, the Black Bottom or the Mess Around.") In a 1979 essay he wrote about how much he dreaded family excursions:

> To me, they were like a suicide pact. Didn't my parents know that the world was just waiting for a chance to come between us?
> Inside, we were a family, but outside we were immigrants, bizarre in our differences. I thought that people stared at us, and my face grew hot. At any moment, I expected my father and mother to expose their tribal rites, their eccentric anthropology, to the gape of strangers.
> Anyone who saw me with my family knew too much about me.

These were the themes he returned to in many of his personal essays, seemingly marking out the threshold he would not cross. And if some of his colleagues at the *Times* knew too much about him, or had heard the rumors, they wouldn't have dreamed of saying anything. Abe Rosenthal (who did know about him) says that the subject never arose. "What was there to talk about? I didn't really consider it my business. I didn't think it was proper or polite, nor did I want him to think I was prejudiced, or anything."

But most people knew nothing about it. C. Gerald Fraser, a reporter and an editor at the *Times* from 1967 until 1991, was friendly with Broyard's brother-in-law Ambassador Franklin Williams. Fraser, who is black, recalls that one day Williams asked him how many black journalists there were at the *Times*. "I listed them," he says, "and he said, 'You forgot one.' I went over the list again, and I said, 'What do you mean?' He said, 'Shirley's brother, Anatole Broyard.' I was dumbstruck, because I'd never heard it mentioned at the *Times* that he was black, or that the paper had a black critic."

70 In any event, Broyard's colleagues did not have to know what he was to have reservations about *who* he was. He cultivated his image as a trick-ster—someone who would bend the rules, finesse the system—and that image only intensified his detractors' ire. "A good book review is an act of seduction, and when he did it there was nobody better," John Leonard says, but he feels that Broyard's best was not always offered. "I considered him to be one of the laziest book reviewers to come down the pike." Soon a running joke was that Broyard would review only novels shorter than two hundred pages. In the introduction to *Aroused by Books*, a collection of the reviews he published in the early seventies, Broyard wrote that he tried to choose books for review that were "closest to [his] feelings." Lehmann-Haupt says dryly, "We began to suspect that he often picked the books according to the attractiveness of the young female novelists who had written them." Rosenthal had shamed him for voicing his disquiet about Broyard's reputation as a Don Juan, but before long Rosenthal himself changed his tune. "Maybe five or six years later," Lehmann-Haupt recalls, "Rosenthal comes up to me, jabbing me in the chest with a stiffened index finger and saying, 'The trouble with Broyard is that he writes with his cock!' I bit my tongue."

Gradually, a measure of discontent with Broyard's reviews began to make itself felt among the paper's cultural commissars. Harvey Shapiro, the editor of the *Book Review* from 1975 to 1983, recalls conversations with Rosenthal in which "he would tell me that all his friends hated Anatole's essays, and I would tell him that all my friends loved Anatole's essays, and that would be the end of the conversation." In 1984, Broyard was removed from the daily *Times* and given a column in the *Book Review*.

Mitchel Levitas, the editor of the *Book Review* from 1983 to 1989, edited Broyard's column himself. He says, "It was a tough time for him, you see, because he had come off the daily book review, where he was out there in the public eye twice a week. That was a major change in his public role." In addition to writing his column, he was put to work as an editor at the *Book Review*. The office environment was perhaps not altogether congenial to a man of his temperament. Kazin recalls, "He complained to me constantly about being on the *Book Review*, because he had to check people's quotations and such. I think he thought that he was superior to the job."

Then, too, it was an era in which the very notion of passing was beginning to seem less plangent than preposterous. Certainly Broyard's skittishness around the subject wasn't to everyone's liking. Brent Staples, who is black, was an editor at the *Book Review* at the time Broyard was there. "Anatole had it both ways," Staples says. "He would give you a kind of burlesque wink that seemed to indicate he was ready to accept the fact of your knowing that he was a black person. It was a real ambiguity, tacit and sort of recessed. He jived around and played with it a lot, but never made it express the fact that he was black." It was a game that tried Staples's patience. "When Anatole came anywhere near me, for example, his whole style, demeanor, and tone would change," he recalls. "I took that as him conveying to me, 'Yes, I am like you. But I'm relating this to you on a kind of recondite channel.' Over all, it made me angry. Here was a guy who was, for a long period of time, probably one of the two or three most important critical voices on literature in the United States. How could you, actively or passively, have this fact hidden?"

Staples pauses, then says, "You know, he turned it into a joke. And when you change something basic about yourself into a joke, it spreads, it metastasizes, and so his whole presentation of self became completely ironic. *Everything* about him was ironic."

There were some people who came to have a professional interest in achieving a measure of clarity on the topic. Not long before Broyard retired from the *Times*, in 1989, Daphne Merkin, as an editor at Harcourt Brace Jovanovich, gave him an advance of a hundred thousand dollars for his memoirs. (The completed portion was ultimately published, as *Kafka Was the Rage* by Crown.) Merkin learned that "he was, in some ways, opaque to himself," and her disquiet grew when the early chapters arrived. "I said, 'Anatole, there's something odd here. Within the memoir, you have your family moving to a black neighborhood in Brooklyn. I find that strange—unless they're black.' I said, 'You can do many things if you're writing a memoir. But if you squelch stuff that seems to be crucial about you, and pretend it doesn't exist...'" She observes that he was much attached to aspects of his childhood, but "in a clouded way."

When Broyard retired from the *Times*, he was nearly sixty-nine. To Sandy, it was a source of some anguish that their children still did not know the truth about him. Yet what was that truth? Broyard was a critic—a critic who specialized in European and American fiction. And what was race but a European and American fiction? If he was passing for white, perhaps he understood that the alternative was passing for black. "But if some people are light enough to live like white, mother, why should there be such a fuss?" a girl asks her mother in "Near-White," a 1931 story by the Harlem Renaissance author Claude McKay. "Why should they live colored when they could be happier living white?" Why, indeed? One could concede that the passing of Anatole Broyard involved dishonesty; but is it so very clear that the dishonesty was mostly Broyard's?

To pass is to sin against authenticity, and "authenticity" is among the founding lies of the modern age. The philosopher Charles Taylor summarizes its ideology thus: "There is a certain way of being human that is *my* way. I am called upon to live my life in this way, and not in imitation of anyone else's life. But the notion gives a new importance to being true to myself. If I am not, I miss the point of my life; I miss what being human is for *me*." And the Romantic fallacy of authenticity is only compounded when it is collectivized: when the putative real me gives way to the real us. You can say that Anatole Broyard was (by any juridical reckoning) "really" a Negro, without conceding that a Negro is a thing you can really be. The vagaries of racial identity were increased by what anthropologists call the rule of "hypodescent"—the one-drop rule. When those of mixed ancestry—and the majority of blacks are of mixed ancestry—disappear into the white majority, they are traditionally accused of running from their "blackness." Yet why isn't the alternative a matter of running from their "whiteness"? To emphasize these perversities, however, is a distraction from a larger perversity. You can't get race "right" by refining the boundary conditions.

The act of razoring out your contributor's note may be quixotic, but it is not mad. The mistake is to assume that birth certificates and biographical sketches and all the other documents generated by the modern bureaucratic state reveal an anterior truth—that they are merely signs of an independently existing identity. But in fact they constitute it. The social meaning of race is established by these identity papers—by tracts and treatises and certificates and pamphlets and all the other verbal artifacts that proclaim race to be real and, by that proclamation, make it so.

So here is a man who passed for white because he wanted to be a writer and he did not want to be a Negro writer. It is a crass disjunction, but it is not his crassness or his disjunction. His perception was perfectly correct. He *would* have had to be a Negro writer, which was something he did not want to be. In his terms, he did not want to write about black love, black passion, black suffering, black joy; he wanted to write about love and passion and suffering and joy. We give lip service to the idea of the writer who happens to be black, but had anyone, in the postwar era, ever seen such a thing?

80

Broyard's friend Richard A. Shweder, an anthropologist and a theorist of culture, says, "I think he believed that reality is constituted by style," and ascribed to Broyard a "deeply romantic view of the intimate connection between style and reality." Broyard passed not because he thought that race wasn't important but because he knew that it was. The durable social facts of race were beyond reason, and like Paul Broyard's furniture, their strength came at the expense of style. Anatole Broyard lived in a world where race had, indeed, become a trope for indelibility, for permanence. "All I *have* to do,"a black folk saying has it, "is stay black and die."

Broyard was a connoisseur of the liminal—of crossing over and, in the familiar phrase, getting over. But the ideologies of modernity have a kicker, which is that they permit no exit. Racial recusal is a forlorn hope. In a system where whiteness is the default, racelessness is never a possibility. You cannot opt out; you can only opt in. In a scathing review of a now forgotten black author, Broyard announced that it was time to reconsider the assumption of many black writers that "'whitey' will never let you forget you're black." For his part, he wasn't taking any chances. At a certain point, he seems to have decided that all he had to do was stay white and die.

In 1989, Broyard resolved that he and his wife would change their life once more. With both their children grown, they could do what they pleased. And what they pleased—what he pleased, anyway—was to move to Cambridge, Massachusetts. They would be near Harvard, and so part of an intellectual community. He had a vision of walking through Harvard Square, bumping into people like the sociologist Daniel Bell, and having conversations about ideas in the street. Besides, his close friend Michael Miller was living in the area. Anne Bernays, also a Cambridge resident, says, "I remember his calling several times and asking me about neighborhoods. It was important for him to get that right. I think he was a little disappointed when he moved that it wasn't to a fancy neighborhood like Brattle or Channing Street. He was on Wendell Street, where there's a tennis court across the street and an apartment building and the houses are fairly close together." It wasn't a matter of passing so much as of positioning.

Sandy says that they had another the-children-must-be-told conversation shortly before the move. "We were driving to Michael's fiftieth-birthday party—I used to plan to bring up the subject in a place where he couldn't walk out. I brought it up then because at that point our son was out of college and our daughter had just graduated, and my feeling was that they just absolutely needed to know, as adults." She pauses. "And we had words. He would just bring down this gate." Sandy surmises, again, that he may have wanted to protect them from what he had experienced as a child. "Also," she says, "I think he needed still to protect himself." The day after they moved into their house on Wendell Street, Broyard learned that he had prostate cancer, and that it was inoperable.

Broyard spent much of the time before his death, fourteen months later, making a study of the literature of illness and death, and publishing a number of essays on the subject. Despite the occasion, they were imbued with an almost dandyish, even jokey sense of incongruity: "My urologist, who is quite famous, wanted to cut off my testicles....Speaking as a surgeon, he said that it was the surest, quickest, neatest solution. Too neat, I said, picturing myself with no balls. I knew that such a solution would depress me, and I was sure that depression is bad medicine." He had attracted notice in 1954 with the account of his father's death from a similar cancer; now he recharged his writing career as a chronicler of his own progress toward death. He thought about calling his collection of writings on the subject "Critically Ill." It was a pun he delighted in.

Soon after the diagnosis was made, he was told that he might have "in the neighborhood of years." Eight months later, it became clear that this prognosis was too optimistic. Richard Shweder, the anthropologist, talks about a trip to France that he and his wife made with Anatole and Sandy not long before Anatole's death. One day, the two men were left alone. Shweder says, "And what did he want to do? He wanted to throw a ball. The two of us just played catch, back and forth." The moment, he believes, captures Broyard's athleticism, his love of physical grace.

Broyard spent the last five weeks of his life at the Dana Farber Cancer Institute, in Boston. In therapy sessions, the need to set things straight before the end had come up again—the need to deal with unfinished business and, most of all, with his secret. He appeared willing, if reluctant, to do so. But by now he was in almost constant pain, and the two children lived in different places, so the opportunities to have the discussion as a family were limited. "Anatole was in such physical pain that I don't think he had the wherewithal," Sandy says. "So he missed the opportunity to tell the children himself." She speaks of the expense of spirit, of psychic energy, that would have been required. The challenge would have been to explain why it had remained a secret. And no doubt the old anxieties were not easily dispelled: would it have been condemned as a Faustian bargain or understood as a case of personality overspilling, or rebelling against, the reign of category?

It pains Sandy even now that the children never had the chance to have an open discussion with their father. In any event, she felt that they needed to know before he died, and, for the first time, she took it upon herself to declare what her husband could not. It was an early afternoon, ten days before his death, when she sat down with her two children on a patch of grass across the street from the institute. "They knew there was a family secret, and they wanted to know what their father had to tell them. And I told them."

The stillness of the afternoon was undisturbed. She says carefully, "Their first reaction was relief that it was only this, and not an event or circumstance of larger proportions. Only following their father's death did they begin to feel the loss of not having known. And of having to reformulate who it was that they understood their father—and themselves—to be."

At this stage of his illness, Anatole was moving in and out of lucidity, but in his room Sandy and the children talked with humor and irony about secrets and about this particular secret. Even if Anatole could not participate in the conversation, he could at least listen to it. "The nurses said that hearing was the last sense to go," Sandy says.

It was not as she would have planned it. She says, gently, "Anatole always found his own way through things."

The writer Leslie Garis, a friend of the Broyards' from Connecticut, was in Broyard's room during the last weekend of September, 1990, and recorded much of what he said on his last day of something like sentience. He weighed perhaps seventy pounds, she guessed, and she describes his jaundice-clouded eyes as having the permanently startled look born of emancipation. He was partly lucid, mostly not. There are glimpses of his usual wit, but in a mode more aleatoric than logical. He spoke of Robert Graves, of Sheri Martinelli, of John Hawkes interpreting Miles Davis. He told Sandy that he needed to find a place to go where he could "protect his

90

irony." As if, having been protected by irony throughout his life, it was now time to return the favor.

"I think friends are coming, so I think we ought to order some food," he announced hours before he lapsed into his final coma. "We'll want cheese and crackers, and Faust."

"Faust?" Sandy asked.

Anatole explained, "He's the kind of guy who makes the Faustian bargain, and who can be happy only when the thing is revealed."

95   A memorial service, held at a Congregationalist church in Connecticut, featured august figures from literary New York, colleagues from the *Times*, and neighbors and friends from the Village and the Vineyard. Charles Simmons told me that he was surprised at how hard he took Broyard's death. "You felt that you were going to have him forever, the way you feel about your own child," he said. "There was something wrong about his dying, and that was the reason." Speaking of the memorial service, he says, marveling, "You think that you're the close friend, you know? And then I realized that there were twenty people ahead of me. And that his genius was for close friends."

Indeed, six years after Broyard's death many of his friends seem to be still mourning his loss. For them he was plainly a vital principle, a dancer and romancer, a seducer of men and women. (He considered seduction, he wrote, "the most heartfelt literature of the self.") Sandy tells me, simply, "You felt more alive in his presence," and I've heard almost precisely the same words from a great many others. They felt that he lived more intensely than other men. They loved him—perhaps his male friends especially, or, anyway, more volubly—and they admired him. They speak of a limber beauty, of agelessness, of a radiance. They also speak of his excesses and his penchant for poses. Perhaps, as the bard has it, Broyard was "much more the better for being a little bad."

And if his presence in American fiction was pretty much limited to other people's novels, that is no small tribute to his personal vibrancy. You find him reflected and refracted in the books of his peers, like Anne Bernays (she says there is a Broyard character in every novel she's written) and Brossard and Gaddis, of course, but also in those of his students. His own great gift was as a feuilletonist. The personal essays collected in *Men, Women and Other Anticlimaxes* can put you in mind of *The Autocrat of the Breakfast-Table*, by Oliver Wendell Holmes, Sr. They are brief impromptus, tonally flawless. To read them is to feel that you are in the company of someone who is thinking things through. The essays are often urbane and sophisticated, but not unbearably so, and they can be unexpectedly moving. Literary culture still fetishizes the novel, and there he was perhaps out of step with the times. Sandy says, "In the seventies and eighties, the trend, in literature and film, was to get sparer, and the flourish of Anatole's voice was dependent on the luxuriance of his language." Richard Shweder says, "It does seem that Anatole's strength was the brief, witty remark. It was aphoristic. It was the critical review. He was brilliant in a thousand or two thousand words." Perhaps he wasn't destined to be a novelist, but what of it? Broyard was a Negro who wanted to be something other than a Negro, a critic who wanted to be something other than a critic. Broyard, you might say, wanted to be something other than Broyard. He very nearly succeeded.

Shirley Broyard Williams came to his memorial service, and many of his friends—including Alfred Kazin, who delivered one of the eulogies—remember being puzzled and then astonished as they realized that Anatole Broyard was black. For Todd and Bliss, however, meeting Aunt Shirley was, at last, a flesh-and-blood confirmation of what they had been told. Shirley is sorry that they didn't meet sooner, and she remains baffled about her brother's decision. But she isn't bitter about it; her attitude is that she has had a full and eventful life of her own—husband, kids, friends—and that if her brother wanted to keep himself aloof she respected his decision. She describes the conversations they had when they did speak: "They always had to be focused on something, like a movie, because you couldn't afford to be very intimate. There had to be something that would get in the way of the intimacy." And when she phoned him during his illness it was the same way. "He never gave that up," she says, sounding more wistful than reproachful. "He never learned how to be comfortable with me." So it has been a trying set of circumstances all around. "The hypocrisy that surrounds this issue is so thick you could chew it," Shirley says wearily.

Shirley's husband died several months before Anatole, and I think she must have found it cheering to be able to meet family members who had been sequestered from her. She says that she wants to get to know her nephew and her niece—that there's a lot of time to make up. "I've been encouraging Bliss to come and talk, and we had lunch, and she calls me on the phone. She's really responded very well. Considering that it's sort of last-minute."

100   Years earlier, in an essay entitled "Growing Up Irrational," Anatole Broyard wrote, "I *descended* from my mother and father. I was *extracted* from

them." His parents were "a conspiracy, a plot against society," as he saw it, but also a source of profound embarrassment. "Like every great tradition, my family had to die before I could understand how much I missed them and what they meant to me. When they went into the flames at the crematorium, all my letters of introduction went with them." Now that he had a wife and family of his own, he had started to worry about whether his children's feelings about him would reprise his feelings about his parents: "Am I an embarrassment to them, or an accepted part of the human comedy? Have they joined my conspiracy, or are they just pretending? Do they understand that, after all those years of running away from home, I am still trying to get back?"

(1997)

QUESTIONS:

1. Gates opens his essay with the story of investment banker Richard Grand-Jean. Do you feel this is an effective method of introducing us to Broyard's story?

2. Write a brief essay either for or against "passing," whether it be passing for another race, another sexual orientation, or another social class. Is it essential for a person to be "authentic," or should a person be entitled to "reinvent" him or herself in the manner that Broyard did?

3. The story of Broyard is one of considerable irony. Write the best definition of irony that you can, and then list examples of irony in Broyard's life.

4. What do the would-be title of Broyard's essays on coping with cancer, *Critically Ill*, and the title of this essay have in common? Why are they appropriate titles for someone such as Broyard, who considered himself, and was considered by others, an "aesthete"?

5. Gates quotes heavily from those who knew Broyard for most of this essay rather than gathering information and then writing solely in his own voice. What are the effects of this technique? Is there a certain tone (pathetic, comic, ironic, sympathetic, detached, or other) toward Broyard that Gates adopts when he is not quoting?

MALCOLM GLADWELL

THE SPORTS TABOO

*Do some groups innately possess on average greater potential to excel in certain
fields? This "taboo" subject is here explored by a noted journalist.*

The education of any athlete begins, in part, with an education in the
racial taxonomy of his chosen sport—in the subtle, unwritten rules
about what whites are supposed to be good at and what blacks are supposed
to be good at. In football, whites play quarterback and blacks play running
back; in baseball whites pitch and blacks play the outfield. I grew up in
Canada, where my brother Geoffrey and I ran high-school track, and in
Canada the rule of running was that anything under the quarter-mile
belonged to the West Indians. This didn't mean that white people didn't run
the sprints. But the expectation was that they would never win, and, sure
enough, they rarely did. There was just a handful of West Indian immigrants
in Ontario at that point—clustered in and around Toronto—but they
owned Canadian sprinting, setting up under the stands at every major
championship, cranking up the reggae on their boom boxes, and then
humiliating everyone else on the track. My brother and I weren't from
Toronto, so we weren't part of that scene. But our West Indian heritage
meant that we got to share in the swagger. Geoffrey was a magnificent
runner, with powerful legs and a barrel chest, and when he was warming up
he used to do that exaggerated, slow-motion jog that the white guys would
try to do and never quite pull off. I was a miler, which was a little outside the
West Indian range. But, the way I figured it, the rules meant that no one
should ever outkick me over the final two hundred metres of any race. And
in the golden summer of my fourteenth year, when my running career
prematurely peaked, no one ever did.

When I started running, there was a quarter-miler just a few years older than I was by the name of Arnold Stotz. He was a bulldog of a runner, hugely talented, and each year that he moved through the sprinting ranks he invariably broke the existing four-hundred-metre record in his age class. Stotz was white, though, and every time I saw the results of a big track meet I'd keep an eye out for his name, because I was convinced that he could not keep winning. It was as if I saw his whiteness as a degenerative disease, which would eventually claim and cripple him. I never asked him whether he felt the same anxiety, but I can't imagine that he didn't. There was only so long that anyone could defy the rules. One day, at the provincial championships, I looked up at the results board and Stotz was gone.

Talking openly about the racial dimension of sports in this way, of course, is considered unseemly. It's all right to say that blacks dominate sports because they lack opportunities elsewhere. That's the "Hoop Dreams" line, which says whites are allowed to acknowledge black athletic success as long as they feel guilty about it. What you're not supposed to say is what we were saying in my track days—that we were better because we were black, because of something intrinsic to being black. Nobody said anything like that publicly last month when Tiger Woods won the Masters or when, a week later, African men claimed thirteen out of the top twenty places in the Boston Marathon. Nor is it likely to come up this month, when African-Americans will make up eighty per cent of the players on the floor for the N.B.A. playoffs. When the popular television sports commentator Jimmy (the Greek) Snyder did break this taboo, in 1988—infamously ruminating on the size and significance of black thighs—one prominent N.A.A.C.P. official said that his remarks "could set race relations back a hundred years." The assumption is that the whole project of trying to get us to treat each other the same will be undermined if we don't all agree that under the skin we actually are the same.

The point of this, presumably, is to put our discussion of sports on a par with legal notions of racial equality, which would be a fine idea except that civil-rights law governs matters like housing and employment and the sports taboo covers matters like what can be said about someone's jump shot. In his much heralded new book "Darwin's Athletes," the University of Texas scholar John Hoberman tries to argue that these two things are the same, that it's impossible to speak of black physical superiority without implying intellectual inferiority. But it isn't long before the argument starts to get ridiculous. "The spectacle of black athleticism," he writes, inevitably turns into "a highly public image of black retardation." Oh, really? What, exactly, about Tiger Woods's victory in the Masters resembled "a highly public image of black retardation"? Today's black athletes are multimillion-dollar corporate pitchmen, with talk shows and sneaker deals and publicity machines and almost daily media opportunities to share their thoughts with the world, and it's very hard to see how all this contrives to make them look stupid. Hoberman spends a lot of time trying to inflate the significance of sports, arguing that how we talk about events on the baseball diamond or the track has grave consequences for how we talk about race in general. Here he is, for example, on Jackie Robinson:

> The sheer volume of sentimental and intellectual energy that has been invested in the mythic saga of Jackie Robinson has discouraged further thinking about what his career did and did not accomplish....Black America has paid a high and largely unacknowledged price for the extraordinary prominence given the black athlete rather than other black men of action (such as military pilots and astronauts), who represent modern aptitudes in ways that athletes cannot.

5   Please. Black America has paid a high and largely unacknowledged price for a long list of things, and having great athletes is far from the top of the list. Sometimes a baseball player is just a baseball player, and sometimes an observation about racial difference is just an observation about racial difference. Few object when medical scientists talk about the significant epidemiological differences between blacks and whites—the fact that blacks have a higher incidence of hypertension than whites and twice as many black males die of diabetes and prostate cancer as white males, that breast tumors appear to grow faster in black women than in white women, that black girls show signs of puberty sooner than white girls. So why aren't we allowed to say that there might be athletically significant differences between blacks and whites?

According to the medical evidence, African-Americans seem to have, on the average, greater bone mass than do white Americans—a difference that suggests greater muscle mass. Black men have slightly higher circulating levels of testosterone and human-growth hormone than their white counterparts, and blacks over all tend to have proportionally slimmer hips, wider shoulders, and longer legs. In one study, the Swedish physiologist Bengt Saltin compared a group of Kenyan distance runners with a group of Swedish distance runners and found interesting differences in muscle composition: Saltin reported that the Africans appeared to have more blood-carrying capillaries and more mitochondria (the body's cellular power plant) in the fibres of their quadriceps. Another study found that, while black South African distance runners ran at the same speed as white South African runners, they were able to use more oxygen—eighty-nine per cent versus eighty-one per cent—over extended periods: somehow, they were able to exert themselves more. Such evidence suggested that there were physical differences in black athletes which have a bearing on activities like running and jumping, which should hardly come as a surprise to anyone who follows competitive sports.

To use track as an example—since track is probably the purest measure of athletic ability—Africans recorded fifteen out of the twenty fastest times last year in the men's ten-thousand-metre event. In the five thousand metres, eighteen out of the twenty fastest times were recorded by Africans. In the fifteen hundred metres, thirteen out of the twenty fastest times were African, and in the sprints, in the men's hundred metres, you have to go all the way down to the twenty-third place in the world rankings—to Geir Moen, of Norway—before you find a white face. There is a point at which it becomes foolish to deny the fact of black athletic prowess, and even more foolish to banish speculation on the topic. Clearly, something is going on. The question is what.

2.

If we are to decide what to make of the differences between blacks and whites, we first have to decide what to make of the word "difference," which can mean any number of things. A useful case study is to compare the ability of men and women in math. If you give a large, representative sample of male and female students a standardized math test, their mean scores will come out pretty much the same. But if you look at the margins, at the very best and the very worst students, sharp differences emerge. In the math portion of an achievement test conducted by Project Talent—a nationwide survey of fifteen-year-olds—there were 1.3 boys for every girl in the top ten per cent, 1.5 boys for every girl in the top five per cent, and seven boys for every girl in the top one per cent. In the fifty-six-year history of the Putnam Mathematical Competition, which has been described as the Olympics of college math, all but one of the winners have been male. Conversely, if you look at people with the very lowest math ability, you'll find more boys than girls there, too. In other words, although the average math ability of boys and girls is the same, the distribution isn't: there are more males than females at the bottom of the pile, more males than females at the top of the pile, and fewer males than females in the middle. Statisticians refer to this as a difference in variability.

This pattern, as it turns out, is repeated in almost every conceivable area of gender difference. Boys are more variable than girls on the College Board entrance exam and in routine elementary-school spelling tests. Male mortality patterns are more variable than female patterns; that is, many more men die in early and middle age than women, who tend to die in more of a concentrated clump toward the end of life. The problem is that variability differences are regularly confused with average differences. If men had higher average math scores than women, you could say they were better at the subject. But because they are only more variable the word "better" seems inappropriate.

10   The same holds true for differences between the races. A racist stereotype is the assertion of average difference—it's the claim that the typical white is superior to the typical black. It allows a white man to assume that the black man he passes on the street is stupider than he is. By contrast, if what racists believed was that black intelligence was simply more variable than white intelligence, then it would be impossible for them to construct a stereotype about black intelligence at all. They wouldn't be able to generalize. If they wanted to believe that there were a lot of blacks dumber than whites, they would also have to believe that there were a lot of blacks smarter than they were. This distinction is critical to understanding the relation between race and athletic performance. What are we seeing when we remark black domination of élite sporting events—an average difference between the races or merely a difference in variability?

This question has been explored by geneticists and physical anthropologists, and some of the most notable work has been conducted over the past few years by Kenneth Kidd, at Yale. Kidd and his colleagues have been taking DNA samples from two African Pygmy tribes in Zaire and the Central African Republic and comparing them with DNA samples taken from populations all over the world. What they have been looking for is variants—subtle differences between the DNA of one person and another—and what they have found is fascinating. "I would say, without a doubt, that in almost any single African population—a tribe or however you want to define it—there is more genetic variation than in all the rest of the world put together," Kidd told me. In a sample of fifty Pygmies, for example, you might find nine variants in one stretch of DNA. In a sample of hundreds of people from around the rest of the world, you might find only a total of six variants in that same stretch of DNA—and probably every one of those six variants would also be found in the Pygmies. If everyone in the world was wiped out except Africans, in other words, almost all the human genetic diversity would be preserved.

The likelihood is that these results reflect Africa's status as the homeland of Homo sapiens: since every human population outside Africa is essentially a subset of the original African population, it makes sense that everyone in such a population would be a genetic subset of Africans, too. So you can expect groups of Africans to be more variable in respect to almost anything that has a genetic component. If, for example, your genes control how you react to aspirin, you'd expect to see more Africans than whites for whom one aspirin stops a bad headache, more for whom no amount of aspirin works, more who are allergic to aspirin, and more who need to take, say, four aspirin at a time to get any benefit—but far fewer Africans for whom the standard two-aspirin dose would work well. And to the extent that running is influenced by genetic factors you would expect to see more really fast blacks—and more really slow blacks—than whites but far fewer Africans of merely average speed. Blacks are like boys. Whites are like girls.

There is nothing particularly scary about this fact, and certainly nothing to warrant the kind of gag order on talk of racial differences which is now in place. What it means is that comparing élite athletes of different races tells you very little about the races themselves. A few years ago, for example, a prominent scientist argued for black athletic supremacy by pointing out that there had never been a white Michael Jordan. True. But, as the Yale anthropologist Jonathan Marks has noted, until recently there was no black Michael Jordan, either. Michael Jordan, like Tiger Woods or Wayne Gretzky or Cal Ripken, is one of the best players in his sport not because he's like the other members of his own ethnic group but precisely because he's not like them—or like anyone else, for that matter. Élite athletes are élite athletes because, in some sense, they are on the fringes of genetic variability. As it happens, African populations seem to create more of these genetic outliers than white populations do, and this is what underpins the claim that blacks are better athletes than whites. But that's all the claim amounts to. It doesn't say anything at all about the rest of us, of all races, muddling around in the genetic middle.

3.

There is a second consideration to keep in mind when we compare blacks and whites. Take the men's hundred-metre final at the Atlanta Olympics. Every runner in that race was of either Western African or

Southern African descent, as you would expect if Africans had some genetic affinity for sprinting. But suppose we forget about skin color and look just at country of origin. The eight-man final was made up of two African-Americans, two Africans (one from Namibia and one from Nigeria), a Trinidadian, a Canadian of Jamaican descent, an Englishman of Jamaican descent, and a Jamaican. The race was won by the Jamaican-Canadian, in world-record time, with the Namibian coming in second and the Trinidadian third. The sprint relay—the 4 x 100—was won by a team from Canada, consisting of the Jamaican-Canadian from the final, a Haitian-Canadian, a Trinidadian-Canadian, and another Jamaican-Canadian. Now it appears that African heritage is important as an initial determinant of sprinting ability, but also that the most important advantage of all is some kind of cultural or environmental factor associated with the Caribbean.

15   Or consider, in a completely different realm, the problem of hypertension. Black Americans have a higher incidence of hypertension than white Americans, even after you control for every conceivable variable, including income, diet, and weight, so it's tempting to conclude that there is something about being of African descent that makes blacks prone to hypertension. But it turns out that although some Caribbean countries have a problem with hypertension, others—Jamaica, St. Kitts, and the Bahamas—don't. It also turns out that people in Liberia and Nigeria—two countries where many New World slaves came from—have similar and perhaps even lower blood-pressure rates than white North Americans, while studies of Zulus, Indians, and whites in Durban, South Africa, showed that urban white males had the highest hypertension rates and urban white females had the lowest. So it's likely that the disease has nothing at all to do with Africanness.

The same is true for the distinctive muscle characteristic observed when Kenyans were compared with Swedes. Saltin, the Swedish physiologist, subsequently found many of the same characteristics in Nordic skiers who train at high altitudes and Nordic runners who train in very hilly regions—conditions, in other words, that resemble the mountainous regions of Kenya's Rift Valley, where so many of the country's distance runners come from. The key factor seems to be Kenya, not genes.

Lots of things that seem to be genetic in origin, then, actually aren't. Similarly, lots of things that we wouldn't normally think might affect athletic ability actually do. Once again, the social-science literature on male and female math achievement is instructive. Psychologists argue that when it comes to subjects like math, boys tend to engage in what's known as ability attribution. A boy who is doing well will attribute his success to the fact that he's good at math, and if he's doing badly he'll blame his teacher or his own lack of motivation—anything but his ability. That makes it easy for him to bounce back from failure or disappointment, and gives him a lot of confidence in the face of a tough new challenge. After all, if you think you do well in math because you're good at math, what's stopping you from being good at, say, algebra, or advanced calculus? On the other hand, if you ask a girl why she is doing well in math she will say, more often than not, that she succeeds because she works hard. If she's doing poorly, she'll say she isn't smart enough. This, as should be obvious, is a self-defeating attitude. Psychologists call it "learned helplessness"—the state in which failure is perceived as insurmountable. Girls who engage in effort attribution learn helplessness because in the face of a more difficult task like algebra or advanced calculus they can conceive of no solution. They're convinced that they can't work harder, because they think they're working as hard as they can, and that they can't rely on their intelligence, because they never thought they were that smart to begin with. In fact, one of the fascinating findings of attribution research is that the smarter girls are, the more likely they are to fall into this trap. High achievers are sometimes the most helpless. Here, surely, is part of the explanation for greater math variability among males. The female math whizzes, the ones who should be competing in the top one and two percent with their male counterparts, are the ones most often paralyzed by a lack of confidence in their own aptitude. They think they belong only in the intellectual middle.

The striking thing about these descriptions of male and female stereotyping in math, though, is how similar they are to black and white stereotyping in athletics—to the unwritten rules holding that blacks achieve through natural ability and whites through effort. Here's how Sports Illustrated described, in a recent article, the white basketball player Steve Kerr, who plays alongside Michael Jordan for the Chicago Bulls. According to the magazine, Kerr is a "hard-working overachiever," distinguished by his "work ethic and heady play" and by a shooting style "born of a million practice shots." Bear in mind that Kerr is one of the best shooters in basketball today, and a key player on what is arguably one of the finest basketball teams in history. Bear in mind, too, that there is no evidence that Kerr works any harder than his teammates, least of all Jordan himself, whose work habits are legendary. But you'd never guess that from the article. It concludes, "All over America, whenever quicker, stronger gym rats see Kerr in action, they must wonder, How can that guy be out there instead of me?"

There are real consequences to this stereotyping. As the psychologists Carol Dweck and Barbara Licht write of high-achieving schoolgirls, "[They] may view themselves as so motivated and well disciplined that they cannot entertain the possibility that they did poorly on an academic task because of insufficient effort. Since blaming the teacher would also be out of character, blaming their abilities when they confront difficulty may seem like the most reasonable option." If you substitute the words "white athletes" for "girls" and "coach" for "teacher," I think you have part of the reason that so many white athletes are underrepresented at the highest levels of professional sports. Whites have been saddled with the athletic equivalent of learned helplessness—the idea that it is all but fruitless to try and compete at the highest levels, because they have only effort on their side. The causes of athletic and gender discrimination may be diverse, but its effects are not. Once again, blacks are like boys, and whites are like girls.

4.

20   When I was in college, I once met an old acquaintance from my high-school running days. Both of us had long since quit track, and we talked about a recurrent fantasy we found we'd both had for getting back into shape. It was that we would go away somewhere remote for a year and do nothing but train, so that when the year was up we might finally know how good we were. Neither of us had any intention of doing this, though, which is why it was a fantasy. In adolescence, athletic excess has a certain appeal—during high school, I happily spent Sunday afternoons running up and down snow-covered sandhills—but with most of us that obsessiveness soon begins to fade. Athletic success depends on having the right genes and on a self-reinforcing belief in one's own ability. But it also depends on a rare form of tunnel vision. To be a great athlete, you have to care, and what was obvious to us both was that neither of us cared anymore. This is the last piece of the puzzle about what we mean when we say one group is better at something than another: sometimes different groups care about different things. Of the seven hundred men who play major-league baseball, for example, eighty-six come from either the Dominican Republic or Puerto Rico, even though those two islands have a combined population of only eleven million. But then baseball is something that Dominicans and Puerto Ricans care about—and you can say the same thing about African-Americans and basketball, West Indians and sprinting, Canadians and hockey, and Russians and chess. Desire is the great intangible in performance, and unlike genes or psychological affect we can't measure it and trace its implications.

This is the problem, in the end, with the question of whether blacks are better at sports than whites. It's not that it's offensive, or that it leads to discrimination. It's that, in some sense, it's not a terribly interesting question; "better" promises a tidier explanation than can ever be provided.

I quit competitive running when I was sixteen—just after the summer I had qualified for the Ontario track team in my age class. Late that August, we had travelled to St. John's, Newfoundland, for the Canadian championships. In those days, I was whippet-thin, as milers often are, five feet six and not much more than a hundred pounds, and I could skim along the ground so lightly that I barely needed to catch my breath. I had two white friends on that team, both distance runners, too, and both, improbably, even smaller and lighter than I was. Every morning, the three of us would run through the streets of St. John's, charging up the hills and flying down the other side. One of these friends went on to have a distinguished college running career, the other became a world-class miler; that summer, I myself was the Canadian record holder in the fifteen hundred metres for my age class. We were almost terrifyingly competitive, without a shred of doubt in our ability, and as we raced along we never stopped talking and joking, just to prove how absurdly easy we found running to be. I thought of us all as equals. Then, on the last day of our stay in St. John's, we ran to the bottom of Signal Hill, which is the town's principal geographical landmark—an abrupt outcrop as steep as anything in San Francisco. We stopped at the base, and the two of them turned to me and announced that we were all going to run straight up Signal Hill backward. I don't know whether I had more running ability than those two or whether my Africanness gave me any genetic advantage over their whiteness. What I do know is that such questions were irrelevant, because, as I realized, they were willing to go to far greater lengths to develop their talent. They ran up the hill backward. I ran home.

(1997)

QUESTIONS:

1. Is this essay primarily about race or about sports? Why do you think this?

2. Do you agree with Gladwell that there is in fact a taboo about discussing racial differences in sport? Why?

3. Using textual evidence, argue whether Gladwell believes physiological advantages or desire is the greater factor in separating great athletes from the very best athletes.

4. In your own words, what is Gladwell's thesis statement?

5. How do you think Gladwell might account for Tiger Woods's dominance in the sport of golf, which has historically excluded blacks (both actively and passively)? Genetics? Work habits? Confidence? Desire? How do you account for it?

6. Assume that Gladwell's claims are true, and also that Steven Jay Gould's claims are true in "Entropic Homogeneity Isn't Why No One Hits .400 Anymore." Who, then, will be the dominant athletes in 200 years?

7. Malcolm Gladwell makes much of his writing available through his website, www.gladwell.com. Read at least two other essays by him, and then write two or three paragraphs on Gladwell as a writer—the themes he addresses, the ways in which he typically approaches a topic, his writing style, etc.

THOMAS HURKA

PHILOSOPHY, MORALITY, AND
The English Patient

In this article, a leading philosopher compares the moral perspective implicit in the film The English Patient *with that implied in* Casablanca, *and argues that each reflects the spirit of its time.*

～

The movie *The English Patient*, based on the novel by Michael Ondaatje, won nine Academy Awards this year, including Best Picture. This last award normally goes only to serious movies, ones that address important themes. But looked at this way, *The English Patient* is a disturbing choice. It has a moral perspective on the events it describes, but it is a me-centred and immoral one. Philosophy can help explain why.

In saying this, I don't assume that all art is subject to moral critique, a common view in the nineteenth century. At that time, people believed that even landscape painting and instrumental music have as their main function to morally improve their audience, and should be evaluated for how well they do so. I think it's obvious that many works of art have no moral content, so a moral commentary on them is irrelevant. But other works, especially of literature and drama, raise and explore moral issues. And when they do, we can ask how well they do so.

The English Patient has a moral issue at the center of its plot. In an Italian villa at the end of the Second World War, a burn victim is slowly dying. His face is scarred beyond recognition, and he claims not to know his own identity. But one character, Caravaggio, has figured out who the patient is. He is Count Laszlo de Almasy, a Hungarian desert explorer who just before the war gave the German army crucial desert maps that enabled them to attack Tobruk and almost win the war in North Africa. Caravaggio himself was captured and tortured in that offensive. He thinks Almasy is guilty of betrayal and wants to bring him to account. Caravaggio has killed everyone else responsible for his capture and torture, and he now wants to kill Almasy. So a key question is: *did Almasy act wrongly in handing over the maps?* The rest of the movie addresses this question by showing what led to his choice.

Before the war Almasy was deeply in love with a married woman, Katherine Clifton. Much of the movie describes their passionate and all-consuming affair. But just before the outbreak of hostilities, Katherine was seriously injured in a desert plane crash that also killed her husband. Almasy, who was present, carried her to shelter in a cave and promised to return with help. His first attempt to get that help, from the British army, was rebuffed. Confronted by someone with no identification papers and a foreign accent, they instead arrested him as a spy. After escaping from the British, Almasy went to the German army. But to get their help he needed to offer them something in return. As the only way to keep his promise to Katherine, and from profound love for her, he gave the Germans the maps.

5 When he hears this story Caravaggio says he no longer has any desire to punish Almasy. The "poison," he says, has left him. And the movie's treatment of Almasy is now overwhelmingly sympathetic. Its emotional high point comes when Almasy, finding he has returned to Katherine too late, emerges from the cave carrying her dead body. Tears stream down his face; the photography is lush and gorgeous; the background music swells. As portrayed here Almasy is an entirely romantic figure. There is an equally sympathetic treatment as Almasy, having requested a morphine overdose, dies at the movie's end. Again both the camera and his nurse surround him with unqualified love.

After his escape from the British, Almasy faced a choice between a political end, resisting Nazism or at least not colluding with it, and a personal end, keeping his promise to Katherine. And the movie's treatment implies that his preference for the personal end was understandable and even right. This is implicit in the movie's most important line, a remark of Katherine's that it emphasizes by repeating: "Betrayals in war are childlike compared to our betrayals in peace." Loyalty in love, this line says, is more important than loyalty to political ends such as those fought for in war. Whatever its consequences for politics, any action done from love is right.

It is this utter denigration of the political that makes *The English Patient* immoral. There was not just some political end at stake in the Second World War; there was resistance to Nazism, a movement threatening millions of innocent people. Yet the movie treats even this end as morally inconsequential. Its attitude is therefore the opposite of that taken in *Casablanca,* a movie likewise set in North Africa in the Second World War. In *Casablanca* Humphrey Bogart's character Rick sacrifices his love for Ilsa in order to join the fight against Nazism. As he tells her and her husband, "The problems of three little people don't amount to a hill of beans in this crazy world." In *The English Patient,* by contrast, the fight against Nazism is blithely sacrificed for love. The problems of the world, the movie says, and of the millions of people threatened by Nazism don't amount to a hill of beans beside those of two love-crazed people.

This critique of *The English Patient* is most compelling given a certain assumption about its plot; that given the time it took Almasy to reach the British army, escape from them, and reach the Germans, he should have known there was no chance Katherine would be alive when he reached the cave. He was keeping a promise to someone dead, and however romantic that may be, it has little moral weight beside a duty not to collude with Nazism.

This assumption may be challenged, however. Maybe Almasy got to the Germans fast enough that he did have a reasonable chance of saving Katherine. Then his choice was fraught in a way that Rick's in *Casablanca* is not. Whatever Rick does, he knows Ilsa will be safe. But for Almasy to honour the political demand is to consign his loved one to death. Given this circumstance, is his choice so obviously wrong?

10 *The English Patient,* revealingly, doesn't bother to settle this morally crucial detail of plot. But let's grant that Katherine might still have been alive. A movie could then portray Almasy as caught between two powerful but conflicting moral demands, one personal and one political, with some horrible violation inevitable whichever choice he makes. If he resists Nazism he fails the woman he loves; if he saves her he colludes with moral evil. This possible movie has the structure some find in classical Greek tragedies such as Aeschylus's *Agamemnon,* where the protagonist faces a tragic conflict between two competing moral duties and cannot avoid doing something morally wrong. Whichever duty he chooses, he is guilty of violating the other and must pay for that guilt. But this possible movie is not *The English Patient,* which gives Almasy's political duty no serious attention at all. Here, when love is at stake, its demands not only outweigh the competing demands of politics but render them trivial.

This is certainly Almasy's view. Before the war he thought the coming conflict was just one between silly nationalisms. In the Italian villa, after his story has been told, he thinks his choice about the maps was not just right but obviously so. Told that his explorer friend Madox killed himself when he learned of Almasy's betrayal, he is simply and entirely surprised: *why would anyone react like that?* And he offers excuses for his choice that are morally pathetic. One is that his action did not mean that any extra people were killed; it only changed which people were killed. But even if this is true (and how does Almasy know it?), he couldn't have known it at the time. His transfer of the maps could easily have led to a Nazi victory in North Africa, with incalculable effects on the future course of the war. And doesn't it matter whether the people killed in war are guilty Nazi aggressors or morally innocent defenders?

Almasy's view is also the movie's. As I have said, its treatment of him, especially in its most emotionally loaded scenes, is entirely sympathetic. And this sympathy is almost inevitable given the way the movie frames the moral issue Almasy faces.

In a recent moral defence of the movie, Ondaatje has borrowed from that central line of Katherine's. Its theme, he says, is "love, desire, betrayals in war and betrayals in peace." This is indeed how the movie presents Almasy's choice, as one between conflicting loyalties and different possible betrayals. But the concepts of loyalty and betrayal are essentially personalized or me-centred: *I can be loyal to a person I love or to the nation I belong to or to a group of people specially connected to ME. But I can't be loyal to a stranger, and I can't betray a stranger.* In framing the moral issue as it does, the movie frames it in an essentially me-centred way. Almasy is to ask himself which of the people specially connected to him he should care most about, or which attachment to him, that of his lover or of his nation, is morally most important.

But this approach entirely ignores a more impersonal type of moral demand. This demand is impersonal not in the sense that it is not about people but in that it is about people independently of any special connection to oneself, or just as human beings. Other people matter morally in themselves and we have duties to care about them whatever their relation to us. This impersonal type of duty was utterly central in the Second World War. Nazism threatened the lives of millions of innocent people and regardless of their nationality those people needed protection. This is clearly recognized in *Casablanca*. In that movie Rick has no reason of loyalty to join the fight against Nazism; he is an American and the U.S. is not yet in the war. But he sees that, loyalties aside, Nazism is an evil that must be resisted. His reason for fighting is therefore not me-centred but in the sense I am using impersonal. And this kind of reason is given no place in *The English Patient*. By recognizing only the concepts of loyalty and betrayal, that movie leaves no room for a demand to care about people only as people.

15   That is why the movie inevitably sympathizes with Almasy's choice. If the alternatives are loyalty to a particular person one loves and loyalty to something as abstract as a nation, of course the former is more important. It's the same with E. M. Forster's famous remark that if he had to choose between betraying his country and betraying his friend, he hoped he would have the guts to betray his country. As described, that choice again seems correct. But in each case this is only because the choice is described in a tendentiously incomplete way, one leaving out impersonal considerations. And those considerations are often morally decisive. Consider: if you had to choose between betraying your friend and colluding in the murder of millions of innocent people, would you hope you had the guts to murder those people?

     This is the central immorality of *The English Patient*: its reduction of all moral demands to me-centred demands, those based on other people's relationships to oneself. The reduction appears in many places in the movie.

     One is its taking seriously another of Almasy's pathetic excuses. He wasn't guilty of betrayal in handing over the maps, he says, because the British betrayed him first in refusing him help to save Katherine. Set aside the question of whether the British really did mistreat Almasy at all. With the world on the brink of war, he was in disputed territory with no papers; he was abusive in his manners and gave no satisfactory explanation for his request. But that aside, why should one little betrayal by the British license him to collude with Nazis? That conclusion would only follow if the coming war were, as Almasy thought, just another conflict between silly nationalisms. But of course in this war one side, whatever the other's failings, was incomparably morally worse. That is why Elizabeth Pathy Salett was entirely correct to say, in the *Washington Post* article to which Ondaatje responded, that the movie's "presentation of a moral equivalency between the Germans and Allies trivializes the significance of the choices men like Almasy made."

     Even the voice against Almasy in the movie speaks in me-centred terms. That voice is Caravaggio, and what does Caravaggio want? He above all wants revenge, and revenge is again a personalized concept: *I can want revenge only for a wrong done to me or someone closely connected to me, and I get revenge only if I inflict it myself.* In both respects a desire for revenge contrasts with a desire for justice, which can be aroused by wrongdoing against anyone and can be satisfied when punishment is imposed by anyone, including the impersonal state. But expressing the moral challenge to Almasy in terms of revenge again has a trivializing effect. It reduces that challenge to a "poison" that can be easily extracted when Almasy's story is told. And it utterly underdescribes the subject of that challenge. As part of his torture Caravaggio had his thumbs cut off. This means that he can no longer do sleight of hand tricks—when he tries one with an egg he drops it—and can no longer ply his former trade as a pickpocket. It is hard to think of a less adequate representation of the threat posed by Nazism.

Here are, then, three levels of moral critique of *The English Patient*. First, the movie sympathizes with a choice that is simply morally wrong. Second, it sees nothing at all problematic about a choice that, even if not simply wrong, violates an important political duty. Third, the movie casts its moral considerations entirely in the me-centred terms of loyalty and betrayal, never recognizing the impersonal demands that were so central in its setting of the Second World War. Of these critiques the second and especially the third are philosophical. Moral philosophy does not consider issues that are completely different from those of ordinary moral thought. It considers the same issues but at a higher level of abstraction, identifying the principles and structures of principles that underlie and explain particular moral judgements. In this, as in many cases, it is the most philosophical critique that is most important. It is because it recognizes only me-centred and no impersonal moral duties that *The English Patient* sees nothing troubling in and even sympathizes with a highly questionable choice.

20 *Casablanca* was very much a product of its time. Its impersonal moral vision expresses the experience of people who were fighting to resist aggression on another continent. *The English Patient* is, unfortunately, also a product of its time, one in which many people have abandoned concern for those in other countries or even for less fortunate members of their own society. It is a time of withdrawal from the impersonal concerns of politics into a smaller realm focused on the self and its few chosen intimates. It is no surprise that *The English Patient* won its Academy Awards. The movie has the kind of high-minded tone that Academy voters find impressive. And its substance fits the depressing tenor of our time.

(1997)

Questions:

1. Hurka concludes that *The English Patient* is "a product of its time, one in which many people have abandoned concern for those in other countries or even for less fortunate members of their own society." To what extent do you believe this to be true? Do you think it was any more or less true in 1997 when this article appeared than it is today?

2. This article is unusual in that it was written in two different versions. Hurka originally published a newspaper column on this topic in *The Globe and Mail*; that piece is posted on the website for *The Broadview Anthology of Expository Prose*. The column ignited a storm of controversy, and in the wake of many letters to the editor Hurka was asked by *Queen's Quarterly* to write a longer version for publication in that journal (an academic publication, but one that aims for an audience outside the academy as well as within it). After reading the original newspaper version, compare the two. What elements in particular does Hurka expand on in writing the longer version?

3. Comment on the difference in paragraphing between the two versions. Are there indications in the writing style that a somewhat different audience is being addressed? (Note in answering that the same individuals may constitute a different audience when glancing at a morning newspaper and when reading a semi-scholarly journal.)

4. What if any grounds do you feel may justify intervention by a nation or a group of nations in the affairs of another country? What practical or pragmatic considerations (if any) should also be taken into consideration? Write a brief essay on this topic, either in the abstract or using a particular current issue as your focus.

5. A key principle that Hurka espouses when he talks about writing is that the writer should devote space in an essay to the different ideas being presented that is commensurate with the importance placed by the writer on each of those ideas. On those grounds, what can be said about which of Hurka's ideas he feels to be most important?

JUDITH RICH HARRIS

WHERE IS THE CHILD'S ENVIRONMENT? A GROUP SOCIALIZATION THEORY OF DEVELOPMENT[1]

This article is one of the most controversial and influential academic research papers of the past decade. In it, Harris calls into question both the prevailing theory on which much of modern parenting has been based and the ground on which the nature/nurture debate has been conducted.

∽

In 1983, after many dozens of pages spent reviewing the literature on the effects parents have on children, Eleanor Maccoby and John Martin paused for a critical overview of the field of socialization research. They questioned the size and robustness of the effects they had just summarized; they wondered whether the number of significant correlations was greater than that expected by chance. They cited other research indicating that biological or adoptive siblings do not develop similar personalities as a result of being reared in the same household. This was their conclusion:

> These findings imply strongly that there is very little impact of the physical environment that parents provide for children and very little impact of parental characteristics that must be essentially the same for all children in a family...Indeed, the implications are either that parental behaviors have no effect, or that the only effective aspects of parenting must vary greatly from

---

[1] I thank the following people, who do not necessarily agree with the views presented here, for their helpful comments on earlier versions of this work: William A. Corsaro, Judith L. Gibbons, Charles S. Harris, Neil J. Salkind, Sandra Scarr, and Naomi Weisstein. [Unless otherwise noted, all notes to this essay are from the author.]

one child to another within the same family. (Maccoby & Martin, 1983, p. 82)

Since 1983, many developmental psychologists have focused on the second of Maccoby and Martin's two possible implications, "that the only effective aspects of parenting must vary greatly from one child to another." The other possibility, "that parental behaviors have no effect," has never been considered as a serious alternative.

This article examines both alternatives. I begin by showing why "must vary greatly from one child to another" cannot explain the results that puzzled Maccoby and Martin. Then I consider the possibility "that parental behaviors have no effect." The conclusion reached is that, within the range of families that have been studied, parental behaviors have no effect on the psychological characteristics their children will have as adults. To explain this outcome, I propose a theory of group socialization (GS theory), based on the findings of behavioral genetics, on sociological views of intra- and intergroup processes, on psychological research showing that learning is highly context-specific, and on evolutionary considerations.

Does the Family Environment Matter?

By the time they are adults, adoptive siblings who were reared in the same home will, on average, bear no resemblance to each other in personality. Biological siblings who were reared in the same home will be somewhat more alike, but still not very similar. Even identical (monozygotic) twins reared in the same home will not be identical in personality. They will not be noticeably more alike than identical twins reared in separate homes (Bouchard, Lykken, McGue, Segal, & Tellegen, 1990; Plomin & Daniels, 1987; Scarr, 1992).

These are some of the findings of the field of developmental behavioral genetics. The data on which they are based consist of correlations between pairs of people who share all, some, or none of their genes, and who did or did not grow up in the same home. Two conclusions—one surprising and the other not—emerged from the analysis of such data. The unsurprising conclusion was that about half of the variance in the measured psychological characteristics was due to differences in heredity. The surprising conclusion involved the other half of the variance: Very little of it could be attributed to differences in the home environments in which the participants in these studies were reared (Loehlin & Nichols, 1976; Plomin, Chipuer, & Neider-hiser, 1994; Plomin & Daniels, 1987; Scarr, 1992).

Behavioral Genetic Methods and Results

Behavioral genetic studies begin by collecting data—for example, scores on personality or intelligence tests—from pairs of people. Ideally, data from two or more types of subject pairs, such as twins and adoptive siblings, are combined in the data analysis. That makes it possible to test different mathematical models, based on slightly different assumptions, to see which provides the best fit for the data. The winning model is then used to divide up the variance calculated from the test scores—the individual differences among the subjects—into three, or sometimes four, sectors.

The first sector consists of variance that can be attributed to shared genes; this is called *heritability*. Heritability generally accounts for 40% to 50% of the variance in personality characteristics, if the measurements are made in adulthood (McGue, Bouchard, Iacono, & Lykken, 1993; N.L. Pedersen, Plomin, Nesselrode, & McClearn, 1992; Plomin, Owen & McGuffin, 1994).

The second sector consists of variance that can be attributed to *shared environmental influence*—the home in which a given pair of people were reared. This sector is very small if the measurements are made in adulthood: from 0 to 10% in most studies (Bouchard, 1994; Loehlin, 1992; Plomin & Daniels, 1987). The implication of this finding is that resemblances between siblings are due almost entirely to shared genes. Their shared environment has not made them more alike.

The third sector consists of measurement error, which is around 20% for personality tests (Plomin, 1990). Some analyses do not produce an estimate for this component of the variance, in which case it is included in the last sector, which consists of variance that can be attributed neither to shared genes nor to shared rearing environment (Goldsmith, 1993a). This sector of the variance is usually referred to as *nonshared environmental influence*, but a more accurate label for it is *unexplained environmental variance*. On the average, from 40% to 50% of the variance in adult personality characteristics falls into the unexplained or nonshared sector.

10   If heredity can account for only about half of the reliable variation among adults, then environmental influences must account for the rest. The challenge is to find the source of these influences. Behavioral genetic studies have demonstrated which aspects of the environment are *not* likely to be

important. The aspects that are not likely to be important are all those that are shared by children who grow up in the same home: the parents' personalities and philosophies of child rearing, their presence or absence in the home, the number of books or TV sets or guns the home contains, and so on. In short, almost all of the factors previously associated with the term *environment*, and associated even more closely with the term *nurture*, appear to be ineffective in shaping children's personalities.

Within-Family Environmental Differences

This outcome went against the deeply held beliefs of many developmental psychologists. But, unlike the socialization research that was judged by Maccoby and Martin (1983) to be lacking in robustness, the findings of behavioral genetics are quite reliable. The results are consistent within and between studies and cannot readily be explained away (Scarr, 1993). Children reared in the same home by the same parents do not, on average, turn out to be similar unless they share genes, and even if they share all of their genes, they are not as similar as one might expect. For identical twins reared in the same home, correlations of personality characteristics are seldom above .50, which leaves at least 30% of the variance unexplained by shared genes plus a shared home environment.[2]

Faced with these results, most behavioral geneticists and many socialization theorists turned to Maccoby and Martin's (1983) second alternative, "that the only effective aspects of parenting must vary greatly from one child to another within the same family" (p. 82). The unexplained variance was attributed to *within-family environmental differences* (Daniels and Plomin, 1985; Dunn, 1992; Hoffman, 1991). According to this concept, each child in a family inhabits his or her unique niche in the ecology of the family, and it is within these niches, or *microenvironments* (Braungart, Plomin, DeFries, & Fulker, 1992; Dunn & Plomin, 1990), that the formative aspects of development are presumed to occur.

In the past decade, much attention has been focused on these microenvironments. That they exist is unquestionable; the question is whether they can account for almost half the variance in personality characteristics. The next section summarizes the evidence that has led one

---

[2] A correlation of .50 between twins means that .50 of the variance covaries between them; therefore the correlation accounts for 50% of the variance in that measure (for a detailed explanation, see Plomin, 1990). Allowing 20% for measurement error leaves 30% of the variance unaccounted for.

behavioral geneticist to admit that the matter "remains largely a mystery" (Bouchard, 1994, p. 1701) and another to conclude that the family environment (macro- and micro-) may, in fact, "exert little influence on personality development over the life course" (Rowe, 1994, p. 1).

* * *

WHO SOCIALIZES THE CHILD?

In the days when psychoanalytic theory was an influential force in developmental psychology, a child learned how to behave by identifying with his father or her mother. Identification, around age 4 or 5, led to the formation of a superego; good behavior was then enforced by the superego. Fraiberg (1959) used this theory to account for the fact that most children learn family rules and become less likely to violate them as they get older. As an illustration she offered the story of Julia and the eggs:

> Thirty-month-old Julia finds herself alone in the kitchen while her mother is on the telephone. A bowl of eggs is on the table. An urge is experienced by Julia to make scrambled eggs....When Julia's mother returns to the kitchen, she finds her daughter cheerfully plopping eggs on the linoleum and scolding herself sharply for each plop, "NoNoNo. Mustn't dood it. NoNoNo. *Mustn't dood it!*" (Fraiberg, 1959, p. 135)

15 Fraiberg attributed this lapse to the fact that Julia had not yet acquired a superego, presumably because she had not yet identified with her mother. But notice what Julia was doing: By making "scrambled eggs" and yelling "NoNoNo!" she was behaving exactly like her mother. What Julia must learn is that she is not allowed to behave like her mother. Children in our society spend their early years discovering that they cannot do most of the things they see their parents doing—making messes, telling other people how to behave, and engaging in many other activities that look like fun to those who are not allowed to do them.

Cross-Cultural Considerations

Julia's dilemma is not unique to our society; there are many societies in which the distinction between acceptable adult behavior and acceptable child behavior is greater than in our own. In the Marquesas Islands of Polynesia, children must learn two different sets of rules for social behavior: one for interacting with other children, the other for interacting with parents and other adults. The adult is expected to initiate and control interactions; the child is expected to be restrained and compliant (Martini, 1994). Polynesian children cannot learn the rules of social interaction by observing their parents' behavior. Furthermore, in most traditional societies, parents do not act either as playmates or as teachers to their children. The kind of parental instruction we take for granted in the United States is by no means universal. The Kaluli of Papua, New Guinea do not help children learn language by rephrasing a toddler's poorly formed sentence into proper grammar; they believe it is the responsibility of the child to make the listener understand what she or he wants to say (Snow, 1991). In the Embu District of Kenya, parents and toddlers have few verbal interactions of any sort: "Almost all sustained social interactions and most verbal interchanges of toddlers in this culture involve other children" (McDonald, Sigman, Espinosa, & Neumann, 1994, p. 411).

Fortunately, children can learn things in a variety of ways; even a creature as simple as a honeybee has more than one mechanism for getting to a flower (Gould, 1992). Many kinds of learning do not require the presence of a model, and for those that do, such as language learning, every society provides some kind of a model. In most traditional societies, the models are older children, especially siblings (Zukow, 1989). A common pattern in such societies is that toddlers are given over to the care of an older sister or brother when they are 2 or 2½, and the older sibling—who may be no more than 4 or 5—carries the younger one along to the children's play group. There the toddler might be allowed to participate as a sort of living doll or be left to watch or to whine on the sidelines (Martini, 1994; Whiting & Edwards, 1988). Thus, siblings are a part—often a major part—of the young child's social group. Outside-the-home socialization begins, according to GS theory, in this mixed-age, mixed-sex group. By preadolescence, children in most present-day societies are able to form age- and sex-segregated groups (Edwards, 1992).

Is the Family a Group?

In urbanized societies, school-age children spend most of their time outside the home in age- and sex-segregated groups that do not ordinarily include a sibling. Most of their interactions with their siblings and parents occur within the home. Does the family function like a group? Does the child identify with this group?

In some societies—particularly Asian societies—the answer appears to be yes. Chinese, Japanese, and Indian cultures emphasize the importance of the family group or social group and deemphasize the importance of the individual; independence and autonomy are not considered virtues in a child (Cole, 1992; Guisinger & Blatt, 1994; Miller, 1987; H. W. Stevenson, Chen, & Lee, 1992). In precolonial China, if a man committed a serious crime, his siblings, parents, and children were executed along with him, the idea being that the whole family shared in the responsibility (Heckathorn, 1992).

20   In contrast, Western culture puts the emphasis on the individual rather than the group (Guisinger & Blatt, 1994; Miller, 1987). Only in certain situations—for example, when they are traveling together in an unfamiliar area—are the members of North American or European families likely to function as a group. When they are at home together, I believe that they function as individuals, each with her own agenda, his own patch of turf to defend. They are not a group because the social category *our family* is not salient. It is not salient because no other social categories are present, either actually or symbolically (Turner, 1987), in the privacy of the contemporary Western home.

Within-Family Effects

When group identity is not salient, differentiation is likely to predominate over assimilation. If siblings see themselves as separate individuals rather than as part of the family group, status hierarchies and social comparisons may increase the differences among them. Dominance hierarchies would tend to make older siblings dominant over younger ones, which happens as a matter of course in most societies and which North American parents try very hard, and not very successfully, to prevent (Whiting & Edwards, 1988). However, there is little or no resemblance between children's relationships with their siblings and their relationships with their peers (Abramovitch et al., 1986; Stocker & Dunn, 1990), which is consistent with the finding that birth order has no reliable effects on personality (Ernst & Angst, 1983; Reiss et al., 1994).

Social comparisons between siblings may have more interesting consequences. Tesser's (1988) self-evaluation maintenance theory predicts that siblings should each develop specialties of their own—areas that they consider important to their self-definition and in which they are willing to compete. If one sibling is an excellent pianist, for example, the other sibling may avoid playing the piano for fear of being bested in the comparison. Note that this "niche-picking" process does not require any parental intervention or labeling: it involves only the two individuals in question. Nor is there need to postulate a special motivator; within-group jockeying for status, found in most human and nonhuman primate groups, is sufficient to do the job.

Within-family social comparisons should also widen personality differences between siblings—a within-family contrast effect. If this effect occurs, it must be small in magnitude. Schachter (1982) asked college students to judge how similar they were to their siblings and found a tendency toward polarization of personality attributes that was significant only between firstborns and secondborns. Loehlin (1992) investigated the possibility that a contrast effect might occur between twins who are reared together; he assumed that if such an effect existed, it would make twins reared together less similar in personality than twins reared apart. He found that twins reared together were somewhat *more* similar than those reared apart[3] and concluded that no contrast effect had occurred. However, twins reared together also share an environment outside the home; they go to the same school and often belong to the same peer group. According to GS theory, the shared outside-the-home environment should make twins reared together more alike than twins reared apart; thus, if they are not more alike, a within-family contrast effect may be reducing their similarity. Notice that this prediction—that inside-the-family effects will make twins more different and outside-the-family effects will make them more alike—is exactly the opposite of the assumption made by behavioral geneticists.

Parental Influence Versus Peer Influence

In a number of studies, researchers have asked children and adolescents questions of the form, "What would you do if your friends wanted you to do something that your parents told you not to do?" (e.g., Berndt, 1979; Bowerman & Kinch, 1969). Depending on the precise wording of the question, the results generally show that parents' influence is high during the early school years and then gradually declines, and that peers' influence is low at first and gradually increases, reaching a peak in early adolescence.

---

[3] Although Loehlin found that identical twins reared together were more similar in personality than those reared apart, other researchers (e.g., Bouchard et al., 1990) have found reared-apart and reared-together identical twins to be equally similar.

25   Such experiments are misleading or irrelevant for several reasons. First, the questions are asked by a researcher who is an adult. Given the context-sensitivity of social behavior, the replies might be different if the questioner were a child. Second, replies to questions of the type "What would you do if…?" have low validity, as shown by the lack of correspondence between tests of moral judgment and tests of moral behavior (see Perry & Bussey, 1984). Third, the questions tend to focus on emotionally charged relationships, rather than on behavior; in effect, the child is being asked, "Whom do you love more, your parents or your friends?" Finally, children generally belong to peer groups that share their attitudes and, in many cases, their parents' attitudes. They may know that their friends would not ask them to do something dangerous or illegal.

When researchers observe, rather than ask questions, peer influence is found to be potent, even at ages and in circumstances where parental influence would be expected to have priority. For example, it is well known that preschoolers are loath to eat certain foods, despite much favorable propaganda or forceful urging from their parents. As Birch (1987) discovered, the best way to induce children of this age to eat a disliked food is to put them at a table with a group of children who like it.

Absence of Parents Versus Absence of Peers

No one can question the fact that, without parents, babies and young children are bitterly unhappy (Bowlby, 1969); in fact, an early attachment to a caregiver appears to be a requirement for normal social development (Rutter, 1979), just as early exposure to light and pattern is a requirement for normal development of the visual system (Mitchell, 1980). However, case studies involving deprivation of one kind or another suggest that the absence of peers may have more serious long-term consequences than the absence of parents. Rhesus monkeys reared without peers are more abnormal as adults than those reared without a mother (Harlow & Harlow, 1962/1975). The case of the Jewish children who spent their first 3 years together in a Nazi concentration camp (Freud & Dann, 1951) suggests that the same may be true for humans. The six children had been cared for in the concentration camp by an everchanging series of adults, none of whom survived. When the children arrived in England and came to the attention of Anna Freud, they were found to be completely indifferent—if not hostile—to all adults; they cared only about each other. According to Hartup

(1983), these children grew up to become normal adults and at last report were leading "effective lives" (pp. 157–158).

Cases like Victor, the wild boy of Aveyron (Lane, 1976), and Genie, the locked-up girl of California (Curtiss, 1977), do not have happy endings. Note, though, that these children were deprived not only of normal parent-child relationships but of normal peer relationships as well. There is a case in which two children—twins—were isolated but were locked up together; these children were completely rehabilitated after a few years in which they lived with a foster family and attended school (Koluchová, 1972, 1976).

Dyadic Relationships Versus Group Processes

The view that early relationships with parents are of central importance in personality development is a legacy from psychoanalytic psychology. Among the modern adherents to this view are the attachment theorists (Ainsworth, Blehar, Waters, & Wall, 1978; Bowlby, 1969). According to attachment theory, infants whose mothers care for them in a sensitive, responsive way are likely to become securely attached to their mothers; secure attachments increase the chances of success in later undertakings, especially those that are social in nature. Security of attachment is assessed by observing a child's behavior, generally at age 12 or 13 months, when the mother leaves the child in an unfamiliar laboratory room and then returns a short time later. Children who greet their mothers with unalloyed joy are adjudged securely attached (Ainsworth et al., 1978; Belsky, Rovine, & Taylor, 1984; Sroufe, 1985).

There are two major problems that make most socialization research, including the attachment literature, difficult to interpret. First is the nature-or-nurture problem. Behavioral geneticists have pointed out clearly and repeatedly (e.g., Plomin & Daniels, 1987; Scarr, 1993) that most socialization studies lack an essential control: If all the pairs of research participants share 50% of their genes, as do mothers and their biological children, there is no way of factoring out the effects of heredity from those of environment. There is no way of telling whether the observed resemblances between the mothers and their children (in friendliness, nervousness, competence, etc.) are due to heredity, environment, or both.

Second is the cause-or-effect problem. A mother-child relationship, like all dyadic relationships, involves two people who each play a role in the success of the relationship (Hartup & Laursen, 1991; Hinde & Stevenson-Hinde, 1986). Just as some adults are better than others at caring for infants, some infants are better than others at evoking sensitive, responsive parenting. Because infants who are particularly appealing to their mothers are also likely to be appealing to other people, a child who does well in one relationship is likely to do well in others (Jacobson & Wille, 1986).

Thus, it is surprising to discover that the correlations among a child's various relationships are actually quite low. A child who is securely attached to Mother is not necessarily securely attached to Father (Fox, Kimmerly, & Schafer, 1991; Main & Weston, 1981) or to other caregivers (Goossens & van Ijzendoorn, 1990). Efforts to link parent-child relationships with child-peer relationships have had inconsistent results; some studies (Pastor, 1981; Waters, Wippman, & Sroufe, 1979) find a correlation, others do not (Howes, Matheson, & Hamilton, 1994). Sometimes correlations are found that are "counterintuitive" (Youngblade, Park, & Belsky, 1993, p. 564). As mentioned previously, there is also little or no correlation between the nature of children's sibling relationships and their relationships with their peers (Abramovitch et al., 1986; Stocker & Dunn, 1990). These findings are surprising because it is the same child, with the same genes, who participates in all of these relationships.

The most reasonable explanation of why these correlations are so low is that behaviors, emotions, and cognitions acquired in a dyadic relationship are specific to that relationship (Hinde & Stevenson-Hinde, 1986; MacKinnon-Lewis et al., 1994). There may be, as Bowlby (1969) proposed, a "working model" of the mother-child relationship in the child's mind, but if so, it is trotted out only when Mother is around. A child discovers very early in life that learning what to expect from Mother is of limited usefulness for dealing with Father or Sister. A child who has learned through hard experience to avoid the school bully does not avoid all of the other children on the playground (Asendorpf & van Aken, 1994).

Evolutionary considerations discussed earlier led to the view that dyadic relationships and group affiliation are driven by separate adaptive mechanisms. Consistent with this view is the finding that children's group relationships are to a large extent independent of their dyadic relationships. Although there are children who get along poorly in every social context, many children who have low status in the group are able to form successful friendships (Bukowski & Hoza, 1989; Parker & Asher, 1993a, 1993b).

According to GS theory, identification with a group, not participation in dyadic relationships, is responsible for environmental modifications of personality characteristics. If two people are a dyad and three are a group, this distinction may appear to be splitting hairs. However, the difference between group processes and dyadic relationships is not just a matter of number. The important point about human groups is that they are social categories. When children categorize themselves as members of a group, they take on its norms of behavior (Turner, 1987). A child who says, "Oh Mom, I can't wear that, the kids will laugh at me," is not worrying about the reaction of her best friend—she is worried about the consequences of violating group norms.

In dyadic relationships, children learn how to behave with Person A, with Person B, and with Person C. In the peer group they learn how to behave in public.

The Transient Effects of the Home Environment

Behavioral genetic data indicate that any transient effect of the home environment on personality fades by adulthood—shared environment accounts for little or no variance in adult characteristics. According to GS theory, the reason the home environment has no lasting effects is that children are predisposed to favor the outside-the-home behavioral system over the one they acquired at home. Children who learn one language at home and a different one outside the home become increasingly reluctant to speak the home language, even at home (Baron, 1992). The language they speak with their peers will become their "native language" when they are adults (Bickerton, 1983).

Some researchers have claimed that the reason the immigrant child drops the home language is that it lacks economic and cultural prestige; it is not valued by the community (Umbel, Pearson, Fernandez, & Oller, 1992). Evidence against this view comes from deaf children born to hearing parents during the era when sign language was not valued by the community—in fact, the community tried hard to suppress it. This misguided effort failed. When these children went to schools where, for the first time, they met other deaf children, they picked up sign language in the dormitories. Sign language was brought into the schools by the deaf children of deaf parents, and all the children used it surreptitiously to converse among themselves (Meier, 1991; Newport, 1990). It became their "native language" despite earnest efforts by their teachers to give them a language that had greater economic and cultural prestige.

There are good evolutionary reasons why children might be biologically predisposed to discard what they learned in their first few years of life. First, their parental home is not where they are likely to spend their future. As

Erikson (1963) noted about the school-age child, "There is no workable future within the womb of his family" (p. 259). In order to survive and reproduce, children must be able to function successfully in the world outside their home. They must form alliances that go beyond the nuclear family.

Second, children are already similar to their parents for genetic reasons—the 40% or 50% of the variance that is attributable to heritability. If environmental influences added to and increased these similarities, children would be so much like their parents and siblings that the family might lack sufficient variability. This would decrease the number and variety of ecological niches the members of the family could fit into and reduce the likelihood that at least one child would survive.

There is a biological mechanism that reduces the chances of incest: In humans and other animals, the sex drive tends to be dampened by stimuli that are too familiar. Members of the opposite sex who are familiar from infancy and early childhood are generally not regarded as sexually stimulating (Tooby & Cosmides, 1990; Wilson & Daly, 1992). I suggest that a similar mechanism may operate in regard to socialization: When there is a choice, children do not choose what they learned in infancy and early childhood.

References

Abramovitch, R., Corter, C., Pepler, D.J., & Stanhope, L. (1986). Sibling and peer interaction: A final follow-up and a comparison. *Child Development, 57,* 217–229.

Ainsworth, M.D.S., Blehar, M.C., Waters, E., & Wall, S. (1978) *Patterns of attachment: A psychological study of the Strange Situation.* Hillsdale, NJ: Erlbaum.

Asendorpf, J.B., & van Aken, M.A.G. (1994). Traits and relationship status: Stranger versus peer group inhibition and test intelligence versus peer group competence as early predictors of later self-esteem. *Child Development, 65,* 1786–1798.

Baron, N.S. (1992). *Growing up with language: How children learn to talk.* Reading, MA: Addison-Wesley.

Belsky, J., Rovine, M., & Taylor, D.G. (1984). The Pennsylvania Infant and Family Development Project: III. The origins of individual differences in infant-mother attachment: Maternal and infant contributions. *Child Development, 55,* 718–728.

Berndt, T.J. (1979). Developmental changes in conformity to peers and parents. *Developmental Psychology, 15,* 606–616.

Bickerton, D. (1983, July). Creole languages. *Scientific American, 249,* 116–122.

Birch, L.L. (1987). Children's food preferences: Developmental patterns and environmental influences. *Annals of Child Development, 4,* 171–208.

Bouchard, T.J., Jr. (1994, June 17). Genes, environment, and personality. *Science, 264,* 1700–1701.

Bouchard, T.J., Jr., Lykken, D.T., McGue, M., Segal, N.L., & Tellegen, A. (1990, October 12). Sources of human psychological differences: The Minnesota Study of Twins Reared Apart. *Science, 250,* 223–228.

Bowerman, C.E., & Kinch, J.W. (1969). Changes in family and peer orientation of children between the fourth and tenth grades. In M. Gold & E. Douvan (Eds.), *Adolescent development* (pp. 137–141). Boston: Allyn & Bacon.

Bowlby, J. (1969). *Attachment and loss: Vol. 1. Attachment.* New York: Basic Books.

Braungart, J.M., Plomin, R., DeFries, J.C., & Fulker, D.W. (1992). Genetic influence on tester–rated infant temperament as assessed by Bayley's Infant Behavior Record: Nonadoptive and adoptive siblings and twins. *Developmental Psychology, 28,* 40–47.

Bukowski, W.M., & Hoza, B. (1989). Popularity and friendship: Issues in theory, measurement, and outcome. In T. J. Berndt & G. W. Ladd (Eds.), *Peer relationships in child development* (pp. 15–45). New York: Wiley.

Cole, M. (1992). Culture in development. In M.H. Bornstein & M.E. Lamb (Eds.), *Developmental psychology: An advanced textbook* (pp. 731–789). Hillsdale, NJ: Erlbaum.

Curtiss, S.R. (1977). *Genie: A linguistic study of a modern day "wild child."* New York: Academic Press.

Daniels, D., & Plomin, R. (1985). Differential experience of siblings in the same family. *Developmental Psychology, 21,* 747–760.

Dunn, J. (1992). Siblings and development. *Current Directions in Psychological Science, 1,* 6–9.

Dunn, J., & Plomin, R. (1990). *Separate lives: Why siblings are so different.* New York: Basic Books.

Edwards, C.P. (1992). Cross-cultural perspectives on family-peer relations. In R.D. Parke & G.W. Ladd (Eds.), *Family-peer relationships: Modes of linkage* (pp. 285–316). Hillsdale, NJ: Erlbaum.

Erikson, E.H. (1963). *Childhood and society* (2nd ed.). New York: Norton.

Ernst, C., & Angst, J. (1983). *Birth order: Its influence on personality.* Berlin, Germany: Springer-Verlag.

Fox, N.A., Kimmerly, N.L., & Schafer, W.D. (1991). Attachment to mother/attachment to father: A meta-analysis. *Child Development, 62,* 210–225.

Fraiberg, S. (1959). *The magic years.* New York: Scribner's.

Freud, A., & Dann, S. (1951). An experiment in group upbringing. *Psychoanalytic Study of the Child, 6,* 127–168.

Goldsmith, H.H. (1993a). Nature-nurture issues in the behavioral genetics context: Overcoming barriers to communication. In R. Plomin & G.E. McClearn (Eds.), *Nature, nurture, and psychology* (pp. 325–339). Washington, DC: American Psychological Association.

Goossens, F.A., & van Ijzendoorn, M.H. (1990). Quality of infants' attachments to professional caregivers: Relation to infant-parent attachment and day-care characteristics. *Child Development, 61,* 550–567.

Gould, J.L. (1992). Interpreting the honeybee's dance. *American Scientist, 80,* 278–279.

Guisinger, S., & Blatt, S.J. (1994). Individuality and relatedness: Evolution of a fundamental dialectic. *American Psychologist, 49,* 104–111.

Harlow, H.F., & Harlow, M.K. (1975). Social deprivation in monkeys. In R.C. Atkinson (Ed.), *Readings from Scientific American: Psychology in progress* (pp. 225–233). San Francisco: Freeman. (Original work published 1962).

Hartup, W.W. (1983). Peer relations. In P.H. Mussen (Series Ed.) & E.M. Hetherington (Vol. Ed.), *Handbook of child psychology: Vol. 4. Socialization, personality, and social development* (4th ed., pp. 103–196). New York: Wiley.

Hartup, W.W., & Laursen, B. (1991). Relationships as developmental contexts. In R. Cohen & A.W. Siegel (Eds.), *Context and development* (pp. 253–279). Hillsdale, NJ: Erlbaum.

Heckathorn, D.D. (1992). Collective sanctions and group heterogeneity: Cohesion and polarization in normative systems. In E.J. Lawler, B. Markovsky, C. Ridgeway, & H.A. Walker (Eds.), *Advances in group processes* (Vol. 9, pp. 41–63). Greenwich, CT: JAI Press.

Hinde, R.A., & Stevenson-Hinde, J. (1986). Relating childhood relationships to individual characteristics. In W.W. Hartup & Z. Rubin (Eds.), *Relationships and development* (pp. 27–50). Hillsdale, NJ: Erlbaum.

Hoffman, L.W. (1991). The influence of the family environment on personality: Accounting for sibling differences. *Psychological Bulletin, 110,* 187–203.

Howes, C., Matheson, C.C., & Hamilton, C.E. (1994). Maternal, teacher, and child care history correlates of children's relationships with peers. *Child Development, 65,* 264–273.

Jacobson, J.L., & Wille, D.E. (1986). The influence of attachment pattern on developmental changes in peer interaction from the toddler to the preschool period. *Child Development, 57,* 338–347.

Koluchová, J. (1972). Severe deprivation in twins: A case study. *Journal of Child Psychology and Psychiatry, 13,* 107–114.

Koluchová, J. (1976). The further development of twins after severe and prolonged deprivation: A second report. *Journal of Child Psychology and Psychiatry, 17,* 181–188.

Lane, H. (1976). *The wild boy of Aveyron.* Cambridge, MA: Harvard University Press.

Loehlin, J. C. (1992). *Genes and environment in personality development.* Newbury Park, CA: Sage.

Loehlin, J.C., & Nichols, R.C. (1976). *Heredity, environment, and personality.* Austin: University of Texas Press.

Maccoby, E.E., & Martin, J.A. (1983). Socialization in the context of the family: Parent-child interaction. In P.H. Mussen (Series Ed.) & E.M. Hetherington (Vol. Ed.), *Handbook of child psychology: Vol. 4. Socialization, personality, and social development* (4th ed., pp. 1–101). New York: Wiley.

MacKinnon-Lewis, C., Volling, B.L., Lamb, M.E., Dechman, K., Rabiner, D., & Curtner, M.E. (1994). A cross-contextual analysis of boys' social competence from family to school. *Developmental Psychology, 30,* 325–333.

Main, M., & Weston, D.R. (1981). The quality of the toddler's relationship to mother and to father: Related to conflict behavior and the readiness to establish new relationships. *Child Development, 52,* 932–940.

Martini, M. (1994). Peer interactions in Polynesia: A view from the Marquesas. In J.L. Roopnarine & J.E. Johnson (Eds.), *Children's play in diverse cultures* (pp. 73–103). Albany: State University of New York Press.

McDonald, M.A., Sigman, M., Espinosa, M.P., & Neumann, C.G. (1994). Impact of a temporary food shortage on children and their mothers. *Child Development, 65,* 404–415.

McGue, M., Bouchard, T.J., Jr., Iacono, W.G., & Lykken, D.T. (1993). Behavioral genetics of cognitive ability: A life-span perspective. In R. Plomin & G.E. McClearn (Eds.), *Nature, nurture, and psychology* (pp. 59–76). Washington, DC: American Psychological Association.

Meier, R.P. (1991). Language acquisition by deaf children. *American Scientist, 79,* 60–70.

Miller, J.G. (1987). Cultural influences on the development of conceptual differentiation in person description. *British Journal of Developmental Psychology, 5,* 309–319.

Mitchell, D.E. (1980). The influence of early visual experience on visual perception. In C.S. Harris (Ed.), *Visual coding and adaptability* (pp. 1–50). Hillsdale, NJ: Erlbaum.

Newport, E.L. (1990). Maturational constraints on language learning. *Cognitive Science, 14,* 11–28.

Parker, J.G., & Asher, S.R. (1993a). Beyond group acceptance: Friendship and friendship quality as distinct dimensions of children's peer adjustment. In D. Perlman and W.H. Jones (Eds.), *Advances in personal relationships* (Vol. 4, pp. 261–294). London: Jessica Kingsley Publishers.

Parker, J.G., & Asher, S.R. (1993b). Friendship and friendship quality in middle childhood: Links with peer group acceptance and feelings of loneliness and social dissatisfaction. *Developmental Psychology, 29,* 611–621.

Pastor, D. (1981). The quality of mother-infant attachment and its relationship to toddlers' initial sociability with peers. *Developmental Psychology, 17,* 326–335.

Pedersen, N.L., Plomin, R., Nesselroade, J.R., & McClearn, G.E. (1992). A quantitative genetic analysis of cognitive abilities during the second half of the life span. *Psychological Science, 3,* 346–353.

Perry, D.G., & Bussey, K. (1984). *Social development.* Englewood Cliffs, NJ: Prentice-Hall.

Plomin, R. (1990). *Nature and nurture: An introduction to human behavioral genetics.* Pacific Grove, CA: Brooks/Cole.

Plomin, R., Chipuer, H.M., & Neiderhiser, J.M. (1994). Behavioral genetic evidence for the importance of nonshared environment. In E.M. Hetherington, D. Reiss, & R. Plomin (Eds.), *Separate social worlds of siblings: The impact of nonshared environment on development* (pp. 1–31). Hillsdale, NJ: Erlbaum.

Plomin, R., & Daniels, D. (1987). Why are children in the same family so different from one another? *Behavioral and Brain Sciences, 10,* 1–60.

Plomin, R., Owen, M.J., & McGuffin, P. (1994, June 17). The genetic basis of complex human behaviors. *Science, 264,* 1733–1739.

Reiss, D., Plomin, R., Hetherington, E.M., Howe, G.W., Rovine, M., Tryon, A., & Hagan, M.S. (1994). The separate worlds of teenage siblings: An introduction to the study of the nonshared environment and adolescent development. In E.M. Hetherington, D. Reiss, & R. Plomin (Eds.), *Separate social worlds of siblings: The impact of nonshared environment on development* (pp. 63–109). Hillsdale, NJ: Erlbaum.

Rowe, D. C. (1994). *The limits of family influence: Genes, experience, and behavior.* New York: Guilford Press.

Rutter, M. (1979). Maternal deprivation, 1972–1978: New findings, new concepts, new approaches. *Child Development, 50,* 283–305.

Scarr, S. (1992). Developmental theories for the 1990s: Development and individual differences. *Child Development, 63,* 1–19.

Scarr, S. (1993). Biological and cultural diversity: The legacy of Darwin for development. *Child Development, 64,* 1333–1353.

Schachter, F.F. (1982). Sibling deidentification and split-parent identification: A family tetrad. In M.E. Lamb & B. Sutton-Smith (Eds.), *Sibling relationships: Their nature and significance across the life-span* (pp. 123–151). Hillsdale, NJ: Erlbaum.

Snow, C. (1991). A new environmentalism for child language acquisition. *Harvard Graduate School of Education Bulletin, 36* (1), 15–16.

Sroufe, L.A. (1985). Attachment classification from the perspective of infant-caregiver relationships and infant temperament. *Child Development, 56,* 1–14.

Stevenson, H.W., Chen, C., & Lee, S. (1992). Chinese families. In J.L. Roopnarine & B. Carter (Eds.), *Parent-child relations in diverse cultures* (pp. 17–33). Norwood, NJ: Ablex.

Stocker, C., & Dunn, J. (1990). Sibling relationships in childhood: Links with friendships and peer relationships. *British Journal of Developmental Psychology, 8,* 227–244.

Tesser, A. (1988). Toward a self-evaluation maintenance model of social behavior. In L. Berkowitz (Ed.), *Advances in experimental social psychology* (Vol. 21, pp. 81–227). San Diego, CA: Academic Press.

Tooby, J., & Cosmides, L. (1990). The past explains the present: Emotional adaptations and the structure of ancestral environments. *Ethology and Sociobiology, 11,* 375–424.

Turner, J.C., (with Hogg, M.A., Oakes, P.J., Reicher, S.D., & Wetherell, M.S.). (1987). *Rediscovering the social group: A self-categorization theory.* Oxford, England: Basil Blackwell.

Umbel, V.M., Pearson, B.Z., Fernández, M.C., & Oller, D.K. (1992). Measuring bilingual children's receptive vocabulary. *Child Development, 63,* 1012–1020.

Waters, E., Wippman, J., & Sroufe, L.A. (1979). Attachment, positive affect, and competence in the peer group: Two studies in construct validation. *Child Development, 50,* 821–829.

Whiting, B.B., & Edwards, C.P. (1988). *Children of different worlds: The formation of social behavior.* Cambridge, MA: Harvard University Press.

Wilson, M., & Daly, M. (1992). The man who mistook his wife for a chattel. In J. Barkow, L. Cosmides, & J. Tooby (Eds.), *The adapted mind: Evolutionary psychology and the generation of culture* (pp. 289–322). New York: Oxford University Press.

Youngblade, L.M., Park, K.A., & Belsky, J. (1993). Measurement of young children's close friendship: A comparison of two independent assessment systems and their associations with attachment security. *International Journal of Behavioral Development, 16,* 563–587.

Zukow, P. G. (1989). Siblings as effective socializing agents: Evidence from Central Mexico. In P.G. Zukow (Ed.), *Sibling interaction across cultures: Theoretical and methodological issues* (pp. 79–104). New York: Springer-Verlag.

(1997)

QUESTIONS:

1. As Harris points out, as soon as one casts the debate as to the respective influence of heredity and environment in terms of "nature/nurture" one has already implicitly concluded that the one important element in a child's environment is the "nurture" of parents. What evidence is presented here to suggest that the influence of environmental factors *other than* style of parenting are more important?

2. What implications for parenting do Harris' arguments have?

3. Explain in your own words the difference between correlation and cause.

4. Are there elements of Harris' argument that to you seem counter-intuitive? To what extent does your own experience and knowledge support Harris' line of argument?

5. Why are studies involving twins important to issues of the sort that Harris is discussing?

ADAM GOPNIK

SAVING THE BALZAR

In this essay a noted New Yorker *writer recounts the struggle to preserve a Paris restaurant.*

∽

The Balzar, on the Rue des Écoles, in the Fifth Arrondissement of Paris, happens to be the best restaurant in the world. It is the best restaurant in the world not because it has the best food—though the food is (or used to be) excellent—and not because it is "hot," or even particularly fashionable, but because of a hundred small things that make it a uniquely soulful and happy place.

The Balzar is a brasserie, which means that it is Alsatian in origin, serves beer, and stays open late. Over the years, it has added a full dinner menu, so that it has become indistinguishable from a restaurant. For more than a hundred years, the Balzar has been a family business, and each of the families has managed to keep it constant without making it stale. It's a one-story, one-room spot, small by brasserie standards—with only ninety or so covers—and has a glass front that looks out onto the street; you can see with one eye people boarding the No. 63 bus in the twilight, and with the other a pretty little park dedicated to Montesquieu, with plane trees and pink-flowering chestnuts.

The Balzar is a democratic place. You are greeted at the door with a handshake and a quick squint of crinkled, harried warmth, by the two maîtres d'hotel—one always in a tuxedo, the other in a suit—and are shown to your table with a few pensive words about families, children and the weather. There's not a trace of unctuousness or forced familiarity, no appraisal of your wallet, your last review, or your weekend gross. There are long banquettes covered with dark-brown leather along the walls, and a T-shaped banquette in the middle of the room. On the tables are white linen and glasses and silver. The light—from eight round globe lamps, high above—is warm and bright, gay without being harsh. The *carte* is a long printed card with the dishes listed on the front and the wines on the back, and it never changes. There are leeks and tomato salad and herring for starters—foie gras if you're in an expansive mood—and then the same six or so *plats*: steak au poivre, roast chicken, grilled sole or salmon, calf's liver, *gigot* with white and green beans. The wine list is short, and usually the best thing on it is the Réserve Balzar, a pleasant red Bordeaux. The only sauces are the sauce au poivre on the steak and a béarnaise for the grilled salmon. The *pommes frites* are fine, the crème caramel is good, the profiteroles the best in Paris.

It is the waiters—or *serveurs*, as they're called—who give the Balzar its soul. A team of the same ten men has been in place for decades: they are courteous, warm-hearted, ironic (able to warn a client off a dubious *plat* with an eyebrow), and mildly lubricious. (They have been known to evaluate, sotto voce, the size and shape of a woman's rear even as they pull out the table to make way for it.) They work hard. By tradition at the Balzar, the *plats* arrive beautifully arranged on an oval platter and then are carefully transferred by the waiter to a round plate. This doubles the work but creates an effect. Whenever I am feeling blue, I like to go to the Balzar and watch a waiter gravely transfer a steak au poivre and its accompaniments from an oval platter to a plate, item by item. It reaffirms my faith in the sanity of superfluous civilization.

5   The other famous Left Bank brasserie, the Lipp, is known as a canteen for the men of power in the Fifth Republic, but when Lionel Jospin, the virtuous socialist who is trying to transform French politics, was running for President three years ago he made an event of being photographed, for *Paris Match*, having dinner at the Balzar. Everyone got the point.

On a Sunday night in April, my wife and I, with our three-year-old son, were sitting at a table in the back, just finishing one in a long line of good dinners, and were once again refining our long-term plan to be buried at the Balzar—or, more precisely, to have the urns containing our ashes placed on the dessert counter just above the mille-feuilles and the lemon tart, and on either side of the flowers. The plaques, we decided, should read "A Faithful Client" or, better, should repeat the words of those inscriptions you see all over Paris: "Here, fallen for France…"

Just then, Jean-Claude, the maître d' in the tuxedo, came over to our table. His gravelly *sud-ouest* voice was pitched low and to my amazement, his eyes were glistening. "I'd like to introduce you to someone who'll be working with us," he said graciously, and he summoned a melancholy-faced, lantern-jawed man, buttoned up in a good suit, whom I had idly noticed standing by the door earlier in the evening. "This is M. Delouche," he said. I shook hands with M. Delouche and raised my eyebrows at Jean-Claude.

"The Balzar has been sold," he said. "M. Delouche is here representing the new management." He walked away quickly, and M. Delouche followed.

I grabbed our waiter as he came by the table. "The restaurant has been sold?" I said. "To whom was it sold?"

"To the Flo Group," he answered, in a strangled voice.

The Flo Group! I felt as I imagined I would feel if I had been stabbed: first surprise, then nothing, then pain. The Flo Group is the creation of an Alsatian waiter turned restaurant tycoon named Jean-Paul Bucher, and in Paris it is often referred to as the *"rouleau-compresseur Flo,"* the Flo steamroller. It is for many people the symbol of the forces of restaurant consolidation, globalization, standardization, and even Disneyfication—Flo runs five restaurants at Disneyland Paris. Over the past thirty years, Bucher has bought up some of the oldest and most famous brasseries and bistros in Paris, while also running a chain of lesser Flos, a catering business, and a chain of cheap restaurants called Hippopotamus. Some of the Flo Group restaurants—Julien, Le Boeuf sur le Toit—are actually pretty good. But even the good places have a processed, overwrought quality, and the food at one is pretty much like the food at the others. They lack all the things that the Balzar possesses so effortlessly: distinctiveness, eccentricity, and a sense of continuity.

A few moments later, one of the waiters, whom I had known for a long time, and whom I'll call Thierry, came up to me and suggested, under his breath, that we meet for coffee the next day. When we met, Thierry told me the history of the Balzar, seen from below. He was in mufti, wearing jeans and a jean jacket, a standard uniform for off-duty waiters, like blue windbreakers on off-duty New York cops. The Balzar had never been a perfectly happy place, he maintained, and the *syndicat*, the union, had suffered a good deal even under the old owners. Nonetheless, the *garçons* loved the work, because they like the clients and the clients like them. (I noticed that he referred to the waiters by the usually forbidden, old-fashioned word *"garçons,"* or boys, and that he also referred to their métier as *"restauration,"* or restaurant work. The two words together gave their profession blue-collar integrity.) He outlined their fears. The Flo people, he said, might close the Balzar "for restoration" and dispense the waiters to other Flo restaurants, all over Paris, never to be reassembled. "They express a savoir-faire that dates from 1968," he said. "Ours dates from 1894." It was said that the Flo people had arranged to have American tour groups brought to the Balzar; it was also said that they were standardizing the kitchen produce, bringing it in line with the rest of the Flo Group. More immediately, the *garçons* were appalled because the new man, M. Delouche, had been put "on the service," drawing his salary from their tips—the fifteen-per-cent service charge that is added to all French restaurant bills. (Thierry explained to me that the service charge was real and sacrosanct: before Flo took over, one of the *garçons* collected it at the end of every evening and put it in a drawer, to which each of them had a key. Now they have to wait five weeks for the same money.) It also turned out that the suit-tuxedo distinction among the greeters was a deeply significant code: a maître d' in a suit was aligned with the owner, one in a tuxedo with the staff.

Within a week or so, a group of Balzar regulars, mostly editors and publishers and professors—the Balzar is around the corner from the Sorbonne—arranged to meet at the apartment of one of the staunchest clients on the Quai Anatole-France, to think about what we could do. It was a beautiful day, but ominous reports were coming in from all sides. Someone had had a doubtful sole; someone else had noticed that *oeufs crevettes*, hard-boiled eggs with shrimp, had been sneaked onto the menu. (No, no, someone else said, reassuringly, the *oeufs crevettes* were there twenty years ago; it was really a restoration.) More seriously, it was said that the waiters were being forced to rush checks to the table. It is a Balzar tradition that you can nurse even a cup of coffee and a plate of cold cuts for as long as you like. Now, it was said, after seventy minutes the waiters were forced to put the check on the table. This was—well, there was no other word for it—so *American*. You see this in California, someone said; he had eaten once in Santa Monica, and the young woman slapped the bill on the table after an hour and a half. (I could only imagine the waitress, on her way to her Tai Chi or acting class, dying on the vine while a couple of Frenchmen sat polishing off a bottle and solving the world's problems.) More horror stories were told: a keen-eyed regular claimed to have spotted a Flo Group camion parked outside the Balzar at six o'clock one morning, bringing in Flo produce.

It was obvious that something had to be done, but what? One person suggested a boycott; another person a sit-in; someone else a campaign of letter writing. We had a left, a right, and a center even before we had a party. Finally, a leader emerged, a handsome, round-faced young publisher named

Lorenzo Valentin. He had an excellent plan: why not invite all the regulars we could find to reserve tables on the same night, occupy the restaurant, make a scene, and demand that Bucher meet with us? Fine, someone else said, but added that if we did it we had to be sure not to leave the waiters, on whose behalf we were acting, "in an ambiguous position." If we sat in, occupied the restaurant, and didn't order anything, they would be the ones to suffer. Therefore, we also had to order and eat dinner. Good, one woman said, but we had to be sure to hold on to the tables for the entire evening. "Eat, but eat slowly" would be our motto. Why not order foie gras on toast, she suggested; that could be spread very slowly. She mimed just how to do it, like a veteran of many a foie-gras slowdown on the barricades. We all watched her studiously.

15   During the next two weeks, as I helped to organize the occupation, I felt exhilarated, though I recognized in my exhilaration a certain hypocrisy. Like every American in France, I had spent a fair amount of time being exasperated by the French because of the inability to accept change, their refusal to accept the inevitable logic of the market, and their tendency to blame Americans for everything. As I raged against the changes at the Balzar, I began to hear people repeating to me the same tiresome and sensible logic that I had been preaching so long myself: that nothing stays the same; change must be welcomed; one must choose to live in the world as it is or live in a museum whose walls increasingly recede inward…It was all true, and, when it came to the Balzar, I didn't care. I would like to say that the difference was that my concern was now attached to particular people—to Thierry and Jean-Claude and the rest. But that would be giving myself too much credit for disinterestedness. The difference was not that it was happening to the Balzar. The difference was that it was happening to me. I was being asked to give up the continuity of a thousand small associations and pleasures—the night we went after we signed the lease, the night we went, still jet-lagged, after a summer away—and I didn't see why I should.

    "Can't repeat the past?" says Gatsby. "Why of course you can!" And every American schoolchild is taught that in this belief lies Gatsby's tragedy. But why should the thought be so absurd? Can't repeat the past? We do it every day. We build a life, or try to, of pleasures and duties that will become routine, so that every day will be the same day, or nearly so, "the day of our life," Randall Jarrell called it. There seemed to me nothing stranger about my wanting to eat forever at an unchanged Balzar than about my wanting to stay married to the same wife or be father of the same kid. ("M. Bucher has now bought your family, and will be adding a new child to the staff on the same terms. Change is good. Here, try Ralphie for a while. He comes from the centralized nursery and only speaks German, but you'll soon find that…") On the day of my life, I eat dinner at the Balzar—the Balzar as it is and was, and not some improved, Flo Group version. I realize that one of the tricks of capitalism is to lure you into a misleadingly unreciprocated love with a cash register, but what impressed me about my friends in the Balzar was that they weren't prepared to treat their attachment as somehow less real than the cash register.

June 25th was picked as the day for our occupation of the Balzar. We carefully arranged to stagger our phone calls to reserve tables for that Thursday night, to avoid tipping our hand. When my turn came, I was so nervous that I had to dial twice and then, in a high-pitched quaver, I reserved my table. ("*Oui*, Madame," said an obviously bemused maître d'.) On the night, I arrived with a couple of American friends. The tables filled up with regulars, gaily overacting the part of ordinary diners——Oh how *sympa*, you're here, too, we said to each other, exchanging meaty, significant winks. We ordered apéritifs and made nervous conversation. Finally at nine o'clock, the last regular sat down, and, with two taps on a glass, Lorenzo Valentin rose. The revolution was under way.

"We are here tonight," he said, "to demonstrate our sympathy with the waiters, clients, and tradition of the Balzar." Valentin stepped away from his table and addressed Bucher's man, M. Delouche, directly. Delouche clasped his hands behind his back and thrust out his chin, both obsequious and defiant. When I saw him like that, bearing the brunt of a sudden wave of disapproval—and, surely, thinking, I'm the working stiff here, these people are rich *gauchistes*, easy for them—I have to admit that a small whitecap of sympathy for him rose in my mind.

"This is not a personal assault on anyone," Lorenzo declared. "We have gathered here tonight as, shall we say, an opportunity to discuss the issue at the heart of our concerns about the recent purchase of the Balzar by the Flo Group. Our question is: Is this merely a place to eat or is it something more—and, if it is something more, what is it? Our organization, Les Amis du Balzar, is here to safeguard the quality and, what's more, to defend the spirit and the staff of a place that we believe offers a respite from time itself." This was grandly said, and he got a big hand.

20   M. Delouche attempted to defend his position, but his voice was mostly inaudible: all you could make out was "logic," "safeguard," "continuity."

"But what about the staff?" Lorenzo demanded. "What of their continuity?"

"*Les serveurs! Les serveurs!*" The cry went up from around the room as we pounded the tables and hit cutlery against glasses. The waiters, their eyes fixed studiously on the floor or on the tables, continued to serve.

"Why can't this place be different from other places bought by Flo?" another protester said, rising to his feet. "We all know what Flo does. How many people here are former clients of La Coupole?"

"*Anciens! Anciens!*" we chanted in unison, pounding the tables some more, and meaning that we used to go to La Coupole and didn't anymore.

25   We were building up to an impressive pitch of indignation, but at that point the waiters began to serve the dinners that we had ordered while we were waiting to begin our protest, and this weakened the revolutionary spirit a little. There was, I sensed, a flaw in our strategy: if you take over a restaurant as an act of protest and then order dinner at the restaurant, what you have actually done is gone to the restaurant and had dinner, since a restaurant is, by definition, always occupied, by its diners. Having come to say that you just won't take it anymore, you have to add sheepishly that you will take it, *au point* and with béarnaise sauce. It was as if, at the Boston Tea Party, the patriots had boarded the ship, bought up all the boxes of tea, and then brewed them.

Nonetheless, we carried on. We loudly criticized the fish; we angrily demanded a meeting with Bucher; we rose and offered memories of the Balzar, and vowed that we would fight for the Balzar yet to be.

We were hoping for a little *médiatisation*, and we got it. Pieces about the protest appeared in the magazine *Marianne* and in *Le Figaro*. Then, unfortunately, Jean-Pierre Quelin, the food critic of *Le Monde*, who is a kind of Jonathan Yardley of French restaurant writing, weighed in, announcing that the food at the Balzar had always been terrible—but that he had eaten there since the Flo Group took over and now it was even worse, so to hell with everybody. Lorenzo thought that this might actually be a useful article for our cause: by defining the Balzar radical fringe, Quelin was allowing us to occupy the rational center.

To the surprise of my American self, Bucher sent back word that he would be delighted to meet with our association—to have breakfast with what amounted to our Directorate at the Balzar itself. At nine on a recent Saturday morning, we assembled at the Café Sorbon, across the street, and then trooped over to meet the enemy. Bucher turned out to be a simple round Alsatian, wearing an open shirt, and he spoke with the guttural accent of Alsace. We all shook hands—he had a couple of his P.R. people sitting behind him at a second table—and then Lorenzo Valentin, with quiet dignity, began his speech.

"We are here," he said, "as representatives of our association, to argue that your regime is not compatible with the spirit of the Balzar. This is not meant to be offensive to you—"

"Not at all," Bucher said politely.

"But, without denying your right of property, we claim for ourselves a kind of right of usage." And, from that premise, Valentin carefully outlined our thesis and what mattered was the *esprit* of the Balzar, and that the *esprit* of the Flo Group was, on the evidence, not compatible with that *esprit* we were defending. We asked him to keep the Balzar an autonomous brasserie, outside the Flo Group proper, and to make no changes in the staff, in the décor, or in the spirit of the place. After stating these demands, Lorenzo looked at him squarely.

I don't think any of us were prepared for what happened next. Bucher looked us over, up and down the table. "No problem," he said, a friendly, gap-toothed smile creasing his face. "No problem. Tell me, my friends, why would I want to change something that is working so well right now, something that works so effectively? I bought the Balzar because it's the crown jewel of Parisian brasseries. I bought the Balzar because I love it. What motive would I have to want it to be different? I'm here because if I weren't McDonald's would be—and that would be too bad. I sincerely think that we are defending the same thing."

Our committee exchanged glances. Lorenzo pressed his point. "It's not just the cuisine," he said. "It's something more. A certain relaxation, the feeling of time suspended, the spirit of a place. You see, five hundred and fifty people have already joined Les Amis du Balzar."

Bucher nodded emphatically. "I know—you are to be congratulated," he said. "What an accomplishment!" After some more conversation about the cooking—he had brought out the chef de cuisine, who was understandably upset about the piece in *Le Monde*—he said, "I am sixty years old. I give you a guarantee that I will keep the Balzar as it is. This wasn't a good buy for me. My accountants advised against it. My heart and my soul told me to do it, and they're with you. A restaurant this small—it makes no sense for my chain. A hundred covers. It makes no sense for me except as the jewel in the crown of my Parisian brasseries, whose quality and values I'm going to defend."

35   We mumbled something and, after more handshaking, withdrew to the sidewalk. We had not anticipated the strategic advantage to Bucher of total, enthusiastic assent. We wanted to save the steak au poivre on the oval plate and the waiter serving it, but you couldn't argue with the man when he pointed to the steak, the plate, and the waiter and said nothing's changed. (Thierry, when he heard of our breakfast with Bucher, said, "It is the old technique of the kings of France: treat your worst enemy like your best friend.")

I did not doubt that Bucher was being perfectly sincere, as far as it went, and that in his case as-far-as-it-went went as far it could. The Balzar would stay the same, until it changed. The waiters seem encouraged by our actions. When I go to the Balzar now, Thierry, bringing a coupe champagne, slips by and, under his breath, makes a toast: "*À la santé de l'association*—to the health of the association!" We repeat the toast, under our breath. It is like being in the Resistance. (But when M. Delouche comes over we shake his hand, too. Perhaps that is also like being in the Resistance.)

Les Amis du Balzar has sent an eloquent new letter to Bucher, written by Lorenzo Valentin, and describing the "*objet de nos préoccupations*": that no dish will come from a centralized kitchen, and that there will be real autonomy for the staff, and real autonomy in the management. My Parisian self is prepared to defend the Balzar to the end, whatever it takes. My American self suspects that the Balzar will stay the same, and then it will change, and that we will love it as long as we can.

(1998)

QUESTIONS:

1. What does the Balzar provide, or at least represent, to its regular patrons? What is it about the restaurant that makes them feel compelled to preserve it?

2. Why does Gopnik choose, in paragraph 12, to compare the off-duty clothes of the Paris waiters to the off-duty clothes of New York police officers?

3. The flaws in the clients' occupation are comic, but there is also a trace of irony in their ineptitude. Discuss this instance of irony, and any others you can locate in the essay.

4. Near the end of the essay, Gopnik concludes, "The Balzar would stay the same, until it changed." Broadly stated, what does Gopnik mean?

5. This essay encourages you to compare the "Resistance" Gopnik describes with the French Resistance of WWII. What is Gopnik's aim in encouraging such a comparison?

Philip Gourevitch

from We Wish to Inform You That
Tomorrow We Will Be Killed
with Our Families

*Surprised by his own conflicting responses to the genocidal horrors he has
witnessed in Rwanda, the author inquires into how ordinary people can be
capable of extraordinary crimes.*

~

In the Province of Kibungo, in eastern Rwanda, in the swamp- and
pastureland near the Tanzanian border, there's a rocky hill called
Nyarubuye with a church where many Tutsis were slaughtered in mid-April
of 1994. A year after the killing I went to Nyarubuye with two Canadian
military officers. We flew in a United Nations helicopter, traveling low over
the hills in the morning mists, with the banana trees like green starbursts
dense over the slopes. The uncut grass blew back as we dropped into the
center of the parish schoolyard. A lone soldier materialized with his
Kalashnikov, and shook our hands with stiff, shy formality. The Canadians
presented the paperwork for our visit, and I stepped up into the open
doorway of a classroom.

At least fifty mostly decomposed cadavers covered the floor, wadded in
clothing, their belongings strewn about and smashed. Macheted skulls had
rolled here and there.

The dead looked like pictures of the dead. They did not smell. They did
not buzz with flies. They had been killed thirteen months earlier, and they
hadn't been moved. Skin stuck here and there over the bones, many of
which lay scattered away from the bodies, dismembered by the killers, or by
scavengers—birds, dogs, bugs. The more complete figures looked a lot like

people, which they were once. A woman in a cloth wrap printed with flowers lay near the door. Her fleshless hip bones were high and her legs slightly spread, and a child's skeleton extended between them. Her torso was hollowed out. Her ribs and spinal column poked through the rotting cloth. Her head was tipped back and her mouth was open: a strange image—half agony, half repose.

I had never been among the dead before. What to do? Look? Yes. I wanted to see them, I suppose; I had come to see them—the dead had been left unburied at Nyarubuye for memorial purposes—and there they were, so intimately exposed. I didn't need to see them. I already knew, and believed, what had happened in Rwanda. Yet looking at the buildings and the bodies, and hearing the silence of the place, with the grand Italianate basilica standing there deserted, and beds of exquisite, decadent, death-fertilized flowers blooming over the corpses, it was still strangely unimaginable. I mean one still had to imagine it.

Those dead Rwandans will be with me forever, I expect. That was why I had felt compelled to come to Nyarubuye: to be stuck with them—not with their experience, but with the experience of looking at them. They had been killed there, and they were dead there. What else could you really see at first? The Bible bloated with rain lying on top of one corpse or, littered about, the little woven wreaths of thatch which Rwandan women wear as crowns to balance the enormous loads they carry on their heads, and the water gourds, and the Converse tennis sneaker stuck somehow in a pelvis.

The soldier with the Kalashnikov—Sergeant Francis of the Rwandese Patriotic Army, a Tutsi whose parents had fled to Uganda with him when he was a boy, after similar but less extensive massacres in the early 1960s, and who had fought his way home in 1994 and found it like this—said that the dead in this room were mostly women who had been raped before being murdered. Sergeant Francis had high, rolling girlish hips, and he walked and stood with his butt stuck out behind him, an oddly purposeful posture, tipped forward, driven. He was, at once, candid and briskly official. His English had the punctilious clip of military drill, and after he told me what I was looking at I looked instead at my feet. The rusty head of a hatchet lay beside them in the dirt.

A few weeks earlier, in Bukavu, Zaire, in the giant market of a refugee camp that was home to many Rwandan Hutu militiamen, I had watched a man butchering a cow with a machete. He was quite expert at his work, taking big precise strokes that made a sharp hacking noise. The rallying cry to the killers during the genocide was "Do your work!" And I saw that it *was* work, this butchery; hard work. It took many hacks—two, three, four, five hard hacks—to chop through the cow's leg. How many hacks to dismember a person?

Considering the enormity of the task, it is tempting to play with theories of collective madness, mob mania, a fever of hatred erupted into a mass crime of passion, and to imagine the blind orgy of the mob, with each member killing one or two people. But at Nyarubuye, and at thousands of other sites in this tiny country, on the same days of a few months in 1994, hundreds of thousands of Hutus had worked as killers in regular shifts. There was always the next victim, and the next. What sustained them, beyond the frenzy of the first attack, through the plain physical exhaustion and mess of it?

The pygmy in Gikongoro said that humanity is part of nature and that we must go against nature to get along and have peace. But mass violence, too, must be organized; it does not occur aimlessly. Even mobs and riots have a design, and great and sustained destruction requires great ambition. It must be conceived as the means toward achieving a new order, and although the idea behind that new order may be criminal and objectively very stupid, it must also be compellingly simple and at the same time absolute. The ideology of genocide is all of those things, and in Rwanda it went by the bald name of Hutu Power. For those who set about systematically exterminating an entire people—even a fairly small and unresisting subpopulation of perhaps a million and a quarter men, women, and children, like the Tutsis in Rwanda—blood lust surely helps. But the engineers and perpetrators of a slaughter like the one just inside the door where I stood need not enjoy killing, and they may even find it unpleasant. What is required above all is that they want their victims dead. They have to want it so badly that they consider it a necessity.

So I still had much to imagine as I entered the classroom and stepped carefully between the remains. These dead and their killers had been neighbors, schoolmates, colleagues, sometimes friends, even in-laws. The dead had seen their killers training as militias in the weeks before the end, and it was well known that they were training to kill Tutsis; it was announced on the radio, it was in the newspapers, people spoke of it openly. The week before the massacre at Nyarubuye, the killing began in Rwanda's capital, Kigali. Hutus who opposed the Hutu Power ideology were publicly denounced as "accomplices" of the Tutsis and were among the first to be killed as the extermination got under way. In Nyarubuye, when Tutsis asked the Hutu Power mayor how they might be spared, he suggested that they seek sanctuary at the church. They did, and a few days later the mayor came to kill them. He came at the head of a pack of soldiers, policemen, militiamen, and villagers; he gave out arms and orders to complete the job well. No more was required of the mayor, but he was also said to have killed a few Tutsis himself.

The killers killed all day at Nyarubuye. At night they cut the Achilles tendons of survivors and went off to feast behind the church, roasting cattle looted from their victims in big fires, and drinking beer. (Bottled beer, banana beer—Rwandans may not drink more beer than other Africans, but they drink prodigious quantities of it around the clock.) And, in the morning, still drunk after whatever sleep they could find beneath the cries of their prey, the killers at Nyarubuye went back and killed again. Day after day, minute to minute, Tutsi by Tutsi: all across Rwanda, they worked like that. "It was a process," Sergeant Francis said. I can see that it happened, I can be told how, and after nearly three years of looking around Rwanda and listening to Rwandans, I can tell you how, and I will. But the horror of it—the idiocy, the waste, the sheer wrongness—remains uncircumscribable.

Like Leontius, the young Athenian in Plato, I presume that you are reading this because you desire a closer look, and that you, too, are properly disturbed by your curiosity. Perhaps, in examining this extremity with me, you hope for some understanding, some insight, some flicker of self-knowledge—a moral, or a lesson, or a clue about how to behave in this world: some such information. I don't discount the possibility, but when it comes to genocide, you already know right from wrong. The best reason I have come up with for looking closely into Rwanda's stories is that ignoring them makes me even more uncomfortable about existence and my place in it. The horror, as horror, interests me only insofar as a precise memory of the offense is necessary to understand its legacy.

The dead at Nyarubuye were, I'm afraid, beautiful. There was no getting around it. The skeleton is a beautiful thing. The randomness of the fallen forms, the strange tranquillity of their rude exposure, the skull here, the arm bent in some uninterpretable gesture there—these things were beautiful, and their beauty only added to the affront of the place. I couldn't settle on any meaningful response: revulsion, alarm, sorrow, grief, shame, incomprehension, sure, but nothing truly meaningful. I just looked, and I took photographs, because I wondered whether I could really see what I was seeing while I saw it, and I wanted also an excuse to look a bit more closely.

We went on through the first room and out the far side. There was another room and another and another and another. They were all full of bodies, and more bodies were scattered in the grass and there were stray skulls in the grass, which was thick and wonderfully green. Standing outside, I heard a crunch. The old Canadian colonel stumbled in front of me, and I saw, though he did not notice, that his foot had rolled on a skull and broken it. For the first time at Nyarubuye my feelings focused, and what I felt was a small but keen anger at this man. Then I heard another crunch, and felt a vibration underfoot. I had stepped on one, too.

15   Rwanda is spectacular to behold. Throughout its center, a winding succession of steep, tightly terraced slopes radiates out from small roadside settlements and solitary compounds. Gashes of red clay and black loam mark fresh hoe work; eucalyptus trees flash silver against brilliant green tea plantations; banana trees are everywhere. On the theme of hills, Rwanda produces countless variations: jagged rain forests, round-shouldered buttes, undulating moors, broad swells of savanna, volcanic peaks sharp as filed teeth. During the rainy season, the clouds are huge and low and fast, mists cling in highland hollows, lightning flickers through the nights, and by day the land is lustrous. After the rains, the skies lift, the terrain takes on a ragged look beneath the flat unvarying haze of the dry season, and in the savannas of the Akagera Park wildlife blackens the hills.

One day, when I was returning to Kigali from the south, the car mounted a rise between two winding valleys, the windshield filled with purple-bellied clouds, and I asked Joseph, the man who was giving me a ride, whether Rwandans realize what a beautiful country they have. "Beautiful?" he said. "You think so? After the things that happened here? The people aren't good. If the people were good, the country might be OK." Joseph told me that his brother and sister had been killed, and he made a soft hissing click with his tongue against his teeth. "The country is empty," he said. "Empty!"

It was not just the dead who were missing. The genocide had been brought to a halt by the Rwandese Patriotic Front, a rebel army led by Tutsi refugees from past persecutions, and as the RPF advanced through the country in the summer of 1994, some two million Hutus had fled into exile at the behest of the same leaders who had urged them to kill. Yet except in some rural areas in the south, where the desertion of Hutus had left nothing but bush to reclaim the fields around crumbling adobe houses, I, as a newcomer, could not see the emptiness that blinded Joseph to Rwanda's beauty. Yes, there were grenade-flattened buildings, burnt homesteads, shot-up facades, and mortar-pitted roads. But these were the ravages of war, not of genocide, and by the summer of 1995, most of the dead had been buried. Fifteen months earlier, Rwanda had been the most densely populated country in Africa. Now the work of the killers looked just as they had intended: invisible.

From time to time, mass graves were discovered and excavated, and the remains would be transferred to new, properly consecrated mass graves. Yet even the occasionally exposed bones, the conspicuous number of amputees and people with deforming scars, and the superabundance of packed orphanages could not be taken as evidence that what had happened to Rwanda was an attempt to eliminate a people. There were only people's stories.

"Every survivor wonders why he is alive," Abbé Modeste, a priest at the cathedral in Butare, Rwanda's second-largest city, told me. Abbé Modeste had hidden for weeks in his sacristy, eating communion wafers, before moving under the desk in his study, and finally into the rafters at the home of some neighboring nuns. The obvious explanation of his survival was that the RPF had come to the rescue. But the RPF didn't reach Butare till early July, and roughly seventy-five percent of the Tutsis in Rwanda had been killed by early May. In this regard, at least, the genocide had been entirely successful: to those who were targeted, it was not death but life that seemed an accident of fate.

"I had eighteen people killed at my house," said Etienne Niyonzima, a former businessman who had become a deputy in the National Assembly. "Everything was totally destroyed—a place of fifty-five meters by fifty meters. In my neighborhood they killed six hundred and forty-seven people. They tortured them, too. You had to see how they killed them. They had the number of everyone's house, and they went through with red paint and marked the homes of all the Tutsis and of the Hutu moderates. My wife was at a friend's, shot with two bullets. She is still alive, only"—he fell quiet for a moment—"she has no arms. The others with her were killed. The militia left her for dead. Her whole family of sixty-five in Gitarama were killed." Niyonzima was in hiding at the time. Only after he had been separated from his wife for three months did he learn that she and four of their children had survived. "Well," he said, "one son was cut in the head with a machete. I don't know where he went." His voice weakened, and caught. "He disappeared." Niyonzima clicked his tongue, and said, "But the others are still alive. Quite honestly, I don't understand at all how I was saved."

Laurent Nkongoli attributed his survival to "Providence, and also good neighbors, and old woman who said, 'Run away, we don't want to see your corpse.'" Nkongoli, a lawyer, who had become the vice president of the National Assembly after the genocide, was a robust man, with a taste for double-breasted suit jackets and lively ties, and he moved, as he spoke, with a brisk determination. But before taking his neighbor's advice, and fleeing Kigali in late April of 1994, he said, "I had accepted death. At a certain moment this happens. One hopes not to die cruelly, but one expects to die anyway. Not death by machete, one hopes, but with a bullet. If you were willing to pay for it, you could often ask for a bullet. Death was more or less normal, a resignation. You lose the will to fight. There were four thousand Tutsis killed here at Kacyiru"—a neighborhood of Kigali. "The soldiers brought them here, and told them to sit down because they were going to throw grenades. And they sat.

"Rwandan culture is a culture of fear," Nkongoli went on. "I remember what people said." He adopted a pipey voice, and his face took on a look of disgust: "'Just let us pray, then kill us,' or 'I don't want to die in the street, I want to die at home.'" He resumed his normal voice. "When you're that resigned and oppressed you're already dead. It shows the genocide was prepared for too long. I detest this fear. These victims of genocide had been psychologically prepared to expect death just for being Tutsi. They were being killed for so long that they were already dead."

I reminded Nkongoli that, for all his hatred of fear, he had himself accepted death before his neighbor urged him to run away. "Yes," he said. "I got tired in the genocide. You struggle so long, then you get tired."

Every Rwandan I spoke with seemed to have a favorite, unanswerable question. For Nkongoli, it was how so many Tutsis had allowed themselves to be killed. For François Xavier Nkurunziza, a Kigali lawyer, whose father was Hutu and whose mother and wife were Tutsi, the question was how so many Hutus had allowed themselves to kill. Nkurunziza had escaped death only by chance as he moved around the country from one hiding place to another, and he had lost many family members. "Conformity is very deep, very developed here," he told me. "In Rwandan history, everyone obeys authority. People revere power, and there isn't enough education. You take a poor, ignorant population, and give them arms, and say, 'It's yours. Kill.' They'll obey. The peasants, who were paid or forced to kill, were looking up to people of higher socio-economic standing to see how to behave. So the people of influence, or the big financiers, are often the big men in the genocide. They may think they didn't kill because they didn't take life with their own hands, but the people were looking to them for their orders. And, in Rwanda, an order can be given very quietly."

25   As I traveled around the country, collecting accounts of the killing, it almost seemed as if, with the machete, the *masu*—a club studded with nails—a few well-placed grenades, and a few bursts of automatic-rifle fire, the quiet orders of Hutu Power had made the neutron bomb obsolete.

"Everyone was called to hunt the enemy," said Theodore Nyilinkwaya, a survivor of the massacres in his home village of Kimbogo, in the southwestern province of Cyangugu. "But let's say someone is reluctant. Say that guy comes with a stick. They tell him, 'No, get a *masu*.' So, OK, he does, and he runs along with the rest, but he doesn't kill. They say, 'Hey, he might denounce us later. He must kill. Everyone must help to kill at least one person.' So this person who is not a killer is made to do it. And the next day it's become a game for him. You don't need to keep pushing him."

At Nyarubuye, even the little terracotta votive statues in the sacristy had been methodically decapitated. "They were associated with Tutsis," Sergeant Francis explained.

(1999)

Questions:

1. What is the author's conclusion at the end of his journey? What message is Gourevitch trying to convey to us about Rwanda's experience, and how it may relate to us?

2. How does Gourevitch communicate the horror of the scene of the corpses in the schoolroom?

3. How can you explain Gourevitch's use of the word "beautiful" in reference to the massacred bodies he sees? Why does he use it, and what effect does it have on the reader?

4. The first part of the essay deals with how Gourevitch dealt personally with confronting the facts of the massacre. The second part deals in a more objective way with the politics underlying the massacre. How does the first part of the essay affect the reading of the second part?

GWYNNE DYER

HOW PEOPLE POWER TOPPLES THE TYRANT

A political analyst traces the roots of the 1990's upheavals in Europe to earlier events on another continent.

∿

In 15 years, we have gone from a world where two-thirds of the people lived under tyrannies to one where more than two-thirds live in more or less democratic societies. We have done so without the explosions of violence that historically accompany change on this scale.

Ten years ago this weekend, I sat in a stuffy office arguing about the possibility of German unification with Sergei Plekhanov, then a star researcher at the Institute for the Study of the USA and Canada. He thought it might happen in 20 years or so. I said it could well happen before the end of the century. And we both thought ourselves quite daring and farsighted to be having such a conversation right in the heart of Moscow.

I had been far-sighted, in a sense, for after a 1987 visit to Moscow I had persuaded the CBC (which was both bolder and richer in those days) to give me a travel budget on the grounds that *something* big was going to happen, and I would give them a radio series when it did.

I had spent the summer of 1989 travelling all over the Soviet bloc from Berlin to Baku, talking to everyone from Andrei Sakharov to Boris Yeltsin, and by now I was sure that some kind of democratization was coming soon in the satellites and in the Soviet Union itself.

But I did not imagine how much, how soon. And then, a couple of weeks later, I got on a plane to Budapest.

5   You could see that it had started (whatever "it" was going to be) on the way in from the airport. Trabants, the pathetic two-stroke East German excuse for a people's car, were abandoned everywhere in the streets.

On Sept. 10, the Hungarian government, which was still formally Communist but with "reformers" in the majority, had abolished exit controls on its border with Austria. On Sept. 11, East Germans realized they could travel visa-free to the fraternal People's Republic of Hungary, and thence defect via Austria to West Germany without having to brave the mines and machine guns of the inter-German border.

On Sept. 12, the hemorrhage began: as many as 10,000 East Germans a day travelling to Hungary for "holidays" and then fleeing west.

By Sept. 13, when I arrived, the Hungarian government had opened a refugee camp—with the world's fastest turnover—in a Young Pioneer facility in the hills behind Buda. East Germans mostly arrived by taxi from the city centre, and convoys of coaches bore them away to West Germany within hours of arrival. I stood outside the gates for a couple of hours, interviewing them as they arrived—they were mostly young couples with good academic or technical qualifications—and it suddenly became clear that the jig was up *now*.

I remember writing a piece on the plane back to Canada about how East Germany's Communist regime was like one of those Disney characters that runs straight off a cliff but doesn't fall until he looks down. As soon as I landed, I booked a ticket back to Berlin. It was frankly a bit frightening, because, in Europe, revolutions have traditionally been served with buckets of blood.

10   The question was not whether the Communist regimes of the continent were finished. They were obviously at the end of their tether, utterly outperformed economically by the West and politically discredited in the eyes of their own people. But nobody knew how to get rid of them safely, and as late as 1956 in Hungary the Communists had shown their willingness to kill large numbers of people to defend their power.

There was one slightly more hopeful precedent—the "Prague spring" of 1968. But apart from the discouraging fact that it had been easily suppressed by a show of force, you couldn't depend on everybody else to be as moderate and patient as the Czechs had been. This time, it was going to start with the Germans, not exactly a historical model of moderation, and they would be going up against the most unequivocallly Stalinist regime left in Europe. (It came out later that Erich Honecker's Socialist Unity Party had distributed about half a million weapons to party members to fight off the counter-revolution, if it came.)

There was good reason to worry that the Communists would take a lot of their fellow countrymen with them on the way down—and maybe lots of other people as well, given that this would be happening in a divided and hugely militarized country with six foreign armies on its soil. The Cold War, after all, was still officially on.

I think that's why most of the analysts employed by Western governments simply denied that the wholesale collapse of communism could happen: It seemed unthinkably dangerous. Even those of us who did believe it was coming were thoroughly scared. We were all wrong. It was fast and smooth and almost completely peaceful: The demonstrations against the East German regime in October, the opening of the Berlin Wall followed by the Velvet Revolution in Prague in November, practically all of Eastern Europe free of Communist rule by New Year's Day, and scarcely a life lost in the entire process except in Romania.

It was the biggest and best surprise of modern history.

Ten years later, though we know all the details of what happened, there is still no consensus on why it happened as it did: Not just the abrupt collapse of communism in Europe but the overwhelmingly *non-violent* character of the change. It was young East Germans who solved the problem and I would argue that they did it mostly by watching television pictures from Asia.

A little genealogy here. Non-violent political protest has a long pedigree in the 20th century, and its two most distinguished proponents, Mohandas Gandhi and Martin Luther King, enjoy the status of secular saints. Both Gandhi and King were struggling against essentially democratic and law-bound governments. All discussions of non-violence's potential for effecting real political change down to the 1970s tended to end with the observation that it wouldn't have worked against Hitler or Stalin. But then, in 1986, the Filipinos successfully used it against a dictator.

The Philippines was a good place to start, because it was a media-wise country whose opposition leaders were well aware of both the Asian and the American traditions of non-violence. Moreover, the "people power" revolution in Manila was the first popular uprising where there was television coverage with live satellite up-links, and its leaders brilliantly exploited their direct access to a global audience to deter Ferdinand Marcos from a violent response. If a dictatorship loses its will to resort to force, it is finished: Get on the helicopter quick, and to hell with Imelda's shoes.

The methodology of Manila was broadcast around the world, and other Asians were quick to pick it up. In the next three years, there were successful copycat non-violent revolutions against dictators in Bangladesh, Thailand and South Korea (plus a tragic failure in Burma in 1988, where the media coverage was sparse and the generals were not deterred). And then, in May and June of 1989, the Chinese students tried the same tactics.

They failed in the end, but for three weeks they hovered on the brink of some sort of success while the world watched. Subsequently, I interviewed a number of the students who led the Tiananmen Square occupation, and most confirmed that, in 1988 and early 1989, they were conducting what amounted to clandestine seminars in non-violence at Beijing University. They were deliberately studying Gandhi, King and videotapes of the events in Manila and elsewhere with the idea that the same tactics might work in a Chinese context. Then they took them out and road-tested them.

20 We will not know how close they came to success until the archives of the Chinese Communist Party are opened, years or even decades from now. For the purposes of the present argument, that doesn't matter. The point is that the whole world saw these tactics apparently coming close to success in a *Communist* capital—including, most important, the East Germans, a majority of whom lived in easy reach of West German television signals.

Less than six months later, having taken note of their own regime's isolation and inability to stop the mass exodus through Hungary, the East Germans got out on the streets of Leipzig and Berlin and used the same tactics with total success. They correctly calculated that local Communists, unlike the Chinese variety, had lost the will to massacre their own citizens—and once that was clear, the game was quickly over, not only in East Germany but all over the Soviet bloc. Three hundred and seventy-five million people in what are now two dozen countries removed their rulers and dismantled an empire with hardly a shot fired.

There have been quite a few shots fired subsequently, mostly in the mountainous and ethnically tangled southern borderlands of the former empire, but that is just the usual post-imperial turmoil. The revolution itself was bloodless almost everywhere, and despite the economic miseries that the transition has brought to many people, the planet is a much better and safer place as a result. No more gulags, no more obsessive discussions of nuclear throw-weight, no more bipolar world where to reject the local orthodoxy was to "defect."

It was the first time that Asia has led the way politically for at least several hundred years, and the expanded scope for non-violent action in a media-saturated world has continued to show its power throughout the past decade in new democratic revolutions from South Africa to Indonesia. In 15 years, we have gone from a world where two-thirds of the people lived under tyrannies to a world where more than two-thirds of the people live in more or less democratic societies, and we have done so without the great explosions of violence that historically accompanied change on this scale.

Even as I write this, I can sense a million lips curling in scorn at my naiveté, a million myopic quibbles being composed about the highly imperfect nature of these new democracies and the wickedness of the new global economy and the thousand other things that are still wrong with the world. If historical ingratitude were a crime, then the entire chattering classes of the West would be serving life sentences at hard labour.

Never mind. It was a miracle created by millions of other people whose imagination and courage triumphed over their natural cynicism. They have given the world a powerful new political strategy that tilts the scales in favour of human rights, and in a sense they have freed us all.

(1999)

QUESTIONS:

1. What assumptions does the author make about his audience?

2. Summarize the role that media played in the revolutions of 1989, and discuss the role that media plays in political matters today.

3. In what ways do newspaper articles (such as this one) differ from most of the other essays and articles in this anthology? For each difference you identify, try to come up with a plausible explanation.

4. In paragraph 23, the author asserts that the 1989 revolutions represented "the first time that Asia has led the way politically for at least several hundred years." Can you think of any events that would counter this claim?

5. The author's second last paragraph is devoted to speculating about those who are likely to disagree with him. Discuss the rhetorical strengths or weaknesses of the approach taken in this paragraph. Why do you think Dyer begins this argumentative essay with several paragraphs written in narrative mode?

LARISSA LAI

POLITICAL ANIMALS AND THE BODY OF HISTORY[1]

An accomplished young writer explores issues of politics, literature and identity—including racial and sexual identity.

～～

Entranceways are the most difficult because you have to pass through them alone. I wanted to bring someone with me, someone who in this moment might function as a translator, not from some other language into English but from one English to another. Because I already know this entranceway is not where I come from, and yet I must say I do, in order for you to understand me.

Ashok Mathur, a writer, critic and activist, but mostly a trusted friend was here first, keeping watch over the literary/academic entranceway, asking the leading question. I did not want to come in the door like that. And yet it seemed to be the main entrance. He thought it was important that I enter the dialogue, and so asked the question—a door-opening kind of question, a come-right-this-way sort of question to lead the sniff-sniffing fox out of her lair onto the green. Not to assume she'd be hunted, but no sense denying the possibility.

The question was this: How could you or would you describe your writing as coming from a racialized space?[2]

A question from the middle of a conversation, begun in some other place, long ago and far away. Which is to say right here and now, but of

---

[1] This piece was originally produced for the conference *Making History, Constructing Race* at the University of Victoria, October 23–25, 1998. [author's note]

[2] E-mail interview with Ashok Mathur, July 1998. Available at http://www.acs.ucalgary.ca/~amathur/. [author's note]

another root, another wellspring. An awkward question because it demands a starting point apart from the self. A question that assumes one already knows how she is looked at from someplace that is by definition outside of her, and yet familiar at the same time.

It took me a long time to answer. I kept turning the question around in my head, asking myself what he meant when he asked it, and how he perceived his own work in that regard. We'd talked about the question before, so I knew he understood my ambivalence. How can a person write from a place constructed for her, pejoratively, by someone else? Why would she want to? But then, does she have a choice? My racialization is a historical fact, begun in Europe centuries before I was born, and perpetuated in a sometimes friendly Canadian sort of way through the social, bureaucratic and corporate structures of this society. I still live with the hope that the body exists prior to race, that experience exists prior to race. Living in a country that could not and does not exist without the concept of race, and for that matter, why be polite, white superiority, it is often hard to maintain this hope. When I say pejorative, I mean, you know, I didn't *ask* for this. And when Ashok asks me how I see my work coming from a racialized space, he is implicitly acknowledging that we both know this. He is asking me, faced with this recognition, what I intend to do about the injustice of it. He is asking me whether I see this othering of my body and my work by the mainstream as my responsibility to undo. If it is not my responsibility, are there reasons why I would choose to do it? He is asking me whether or not I think I have a choice. He is asking me because he faces similar questions.

These questions rise from the context this country has handed me. They are not the centre of my world. What I mean to say is, I didn't want to come in the door like this, nor dressed in these clothes, these shackles. But would you, white or brown, content or discontent, have recognized me otherwise? Perhaps. But I am not yet a creature of great faith.

My work comes from many places at once. There is an aspect in recent years that has been about trying, Houdini-like to break from the box which allows only two possibilities—to understand and work from the racialized position this society allots to the likes of us, or to work from a "colour-blind" liberal position which actively denies the way we have been racialized even as it perpetuates the very racial interests it claims not to see.

Growing up in Canada in the seventies, and eighties, I was very much crammed inside the racism-was-terrible-but-now-it's-over box—a quick-fix product of official Multiculturalism that did precious little materially except sweep the problem of white racism under the carpet. This liberal position, so seemingly loaded with good intentions, had a pale, clammy underside that merely masked existing power imbalances while doing little to rectify them. For those of us who grew up in that era, it meant knowing something was wrong but never being able to put your finger on it.

In the late eighties/early nineties, I was drawn to the anti-oppression movements, which, though they had been growing for years, were currently flowering on the West Coast and in other parts of the country. It was and continues to be incredibly empowering to embrace a confrontative politic that refuses to accept the historically rooted racism of this country and to call it into question wherever it rears its ugly head. I was and am very interested in questions of strategy—How can people of colour and First Nations people empower ourselves and one another given the colonial and neo-colonial contexts we live with? In a collective sense, this means taking particular stands on issues such as appropriation and affirmative action as a means of pushing white liberals to look at the hypocrisies of colour-blindness, multiculturalism and other stances that seemed so liberal in the seventies. It means forcing the hand of those who would like credit for a belief in equality without having to put that belief into practice by giving up the ill-gotten gains of racially endowed power.

I took a particular interest in questions of history for a number of reasons. I think part of what is so aggravating about the reactionary racism that is so often the knee-jerk response to an anti-racist critique is the way in which it denies this country's ugly histories—the histories of the residential schools, the Japanese Internment, the Chinese Exclusion Act, the Komagata Maru incident as well as larger international histories of colonialism and exploitation which shaped and continue to shape the globe. It was particularly empowering to be introduced to works by marginalised people that addressed these histories from our own points of view. There was an urgency around their production and reading which I still feel. Gloria Anzaldua and Cherie Moraga's *This Bridge Called My Back* was seminal, as much as a presence as a test. I remember being thrilled by the publication of *Piece of My Heart: A Lesbian of Colour Anthology* put out by Sister Vision Press in 1990. Trinh's *Woman, Native, Other* was also important, as was bell hooks' *Ain't I a Woman*. There were also numerous cultural projects and special issues of periodicals that while problematic in their tokenized status were, nonetheless, affirming and thought-provoking. Although very few of these things became institutionalized or regularized, each served as a form to move dialogue forward. In some ways the ad hoc nature of these projects was liberating in that they allowed various communities different ways of entering the discussions and validated a variety of voices in a variety of media.

I began to take note, however, of how certain texts became rapidly fetishized by critics, academics and the general public in ways comparable to the way anthropologists and missionaries address field notes. I attended many readings and I can't count the number of times audience members have asked writers of colour, referring to the main character of any particular writer's text: "Is that you?" Or of my own work, which at moments actively resists that question: "Did you get these stories from your grandmother?" The suggestion is, of course, that we are not creative agents capable of constructing nuanced fictions which address historical situations, but rather mere native informants reconstructing, as accurately as our second-rate minds allow, what actually happened. Not, I might add, that I am trying to create a hierarchy of genres that inadvertently favours narrative fiction—I think it is very important that those who remember "what actually happened" write about it, and I have faith that they have written and will continue to write it well. It is rather the reception of the work, and the assumptions around that reception, that I wish to critique.

I understand that these questions may well be addressed to novel writers across race, class, gender and sexuality lines; however, their anthropological resonance with regard to marginalized peoples can not be denied. (I betcha no one ever asked Dickens if he was really Tiny Tim.) I feel a certain ambivalence here. My authority as an author is of no great importance or interest to me. My one great wish for readers is that they understand writing as a practice rather than as the production of an inert, consumable text. In some ways, the question "Is that you?" affirms this wish.

There are other genres that have a tradition of foregrounding within the body of their texts questions about how we read, that have a history of resisting readings that would consume them. These are the same texts that within many circles, both progressive and conservative, get labelled as too intellectual, too academic, incomprehensible. They are circulated within certain small if thoughtful circles, but do not reach the audiences which novels reach. I do not wish to address the question of whether their "elitism" is inherent or constructed. I am conscious of my choice to write fiction as a strategy chosen because it reaches people. On the other hand, in this age of steroid-enhanced capitalism, the tension between engaging those technologies which enable one to reach large numbers of people, and opening oneself and one's work to quick fix consumption, is no easy thing to resolve. Indeed, the quick fix consumptive scrutiny itself is all too easily transmuted into a kind of surveillance which generates new stereotypes, dangerous ones if their sources can be traced to a semblance of native reportage. This is the editorial power of capital.

And yet the fact remains that narrative compels me. What is history, after all, but narrative? And she who inhabits that narrative truly has ground to stand on. That grounding is necessary when her belonging to the land she lives on is so contested.

15   My second interest in the question of history is a more personal one, tied to my own historical situation. It is also very much caught up in questions of strategy: How do we diasporized types make a homespace for ourselves given all the disjunctures and discontinuities of our histories, and for that matter, the co-temporalities of some of them? It is also about the second box, if you were following my Houdini metaphor. The paradox of claiming a racialized space as a space from which to work is an uncomfortable one. To claim a racialized space is empowering in that it demands acknowledgement of a history of racism to which the mainstream does not want to admit. It demands acknowledgement of the continued perpetuation of that racism often, though not always, in new forms in the present. On the other hand, to claim that space also confirms and validates that eurocentric racist stance by placing ourselves in opposition to it, enforcing a binarism which itself is a Western social construct. So how to break from the second box without falling back into the first one, the one which denies a history or race and racialization as shaping our lives?

My strategy in recent years has been to make a project of constructing a consciously artificial history for myself and others like me—a history with women identified women of Chinese descent living in the West at its centre. (I eschew the term "lesbian" because of its eurocentric roots, and because it does not necessarily connote community or social interdependence.) It must be artificial because our history is so disparate, and also because it has been so historically rare for women to have control over the means of recording and dissemination. The writing and rewriting of history has always been the prerogative of men and of the upper classes. I have the added disadvantage— the result of an unfortunate combination of my own childhood foolishness and the pressures of assimilation—of not being able to read Chinese. So my readings of history are bleached not only by the ideological interests of gender and class but also of race and culture.

As a quick example, my research into the life of Yu Hsuan-chi, the courtesan and poet on whom the "Poetess" character in *When Fox is a*

Thousand is based, turned up two records of her. One described her as a woman with many lovers, hence lascivious, hence immoral, hence capable of murder. The second suggested she might have been framed for the murder of a young maidservant by an official who did not like her strong ideas about the role of women in Chinese society. Although she is supposed to have left a sizable body of poetry, very little of it appears in anthologies of Chinese poetry in translation, which tend to favour sanctioned male heavyweights.

The history I'm going to write, I told myself, may be ideologically interested, but no more so than what's already out there.

Several queer Asian theorists caution against projecting the needs and contexts of the present onto the past (see Shah, Lee). How can we understand, for instance, temple images in South Asia in the same terms that the makers of those images understood them, regardless of what we think we see? At the same time, without claiming those histories what are we? Shah suggests that the fact that we are here now in the present should be enough. But it isn't. In the everyday discussions of politically active people of colour, lesbian, gay or straight, I hear this nostalgic referring back to a homeland that no longer exists, indeed, one that never did. I don't think this practice originates so much with naiveté as with a burning desire for that past; that it should have form, that it should have a body. Sometimes I feel our very survival in this country depends on the articulation of this form, the construction and affirmation of this body.

20   Animals at last. The myth and the tall tale. The secret and the subterranean. The dark, the feminine, the yin. All allies in this task. For, if diasporic cultures in the West are to be living breathing things they must change. We must have the power of construction, as long, of course, as we behave as responsibly as we know how in the act of construction. (By "responsibly" I mean that the ideas I have discussed above do matter. I do not hold the ideal of freedom of speech, or freedom of the imagination above other freedoms and other ideals, especially at a historical moment when these freedoms are regularly invoked in order to justify the reproduction of tired stereotypes and the perpetuation of historically unjust power imbalances. I do not believe in censorship, because I think it solves nothing. I do believe in integrity, and expect it of myself and of other writers.) This project obviously can not be one of creating a totalizing history; it is rather one of uninhibited, zany invention for the sheer joy of it.

My interest in the archetype of the fox began with my stumbling across Pu Songling's *Strange Tales of Liaozhai*, a well-known text of the sixteenth century. Pu is supposed to have collected these various tales of the supernatural from ordinary people and compiled them into this anthology. The preface to one translation (which comes out of the PRC) talks about these tales as proto-socialist in their critiques of class structure, corruption and abuse of power. A reason to love them—or is this merely a pretext to circulate an old text that has been such a pleasurable read for so many years? There are stories in the compilation which are obviously allegorical in their intentions. And then there are the fox stories, which certainly have their allegorical aspects, but I like to think that there is more to them than that. Some are not so politically palatable at all, such as the one about a wily supernatural fox woman who leads an innocent man from his pious life into debauchery, sickness and death. There is another about an unsavory young man who leers at a beautiful woman; the woman turns out to be a fox, and the fox trounces him. There is yet another about how a fox and a young man fall in love—star-crossed love, of course, because the human and the divine are not supposed to have carnal dealings with one another. I suppose this one could be read as a comment on class or a critique of the repression of romantic love.

But what is more compelling in many ways is the figure of the fox herself, as a creature of darkness, death, germination and sexuality. The fox has the power to travel both above the earth and below it. In order to work her mischief she needs human form, which she achieves by entering the graveyard late at night and finding the corpse of some poor young girl who has died before her time. She breathes life into it. In this form, her power over men (and perhaps women too?) is the power of seduction. I find these stories very rich and very visceral. They are also politically compelling for a number of reasons. The first is contemporary feminism's struggle with questions of sexual representation. What does it mean for a feminist to embrace the power of seduction? And am I a feminist, or is that also a colonized space? The second is the question of how to deal with sexual representations of Asians in the West where we have been so much exoticized and/or de-sexualized in a society which insists on pathologizing the sexuality of the other. I was compelled to find out what kind of warrior the fox could be in that battle. The third is the possibility of employing the fox as a new trope of lesbian representation, or, if that term and its history reeks too much of its western origins, then as a trope of Asian women's community and power.

I have been much influenced by the work of the Vancouver collective Kiss and Tell, and by much of the sex-positive work that has come out of Canada and the United States in recent years. The work is valuable in that it makes sex a site of resistance as well as a site of pleasure. I can't help thinking, however, that much as using one's racialization as a point of entry into political and philosophical discussions shapes what one can say and learn, so using sex as a point of departure shapes the way one thinks about women's community, and how one goes about looking for echoes of it in the past. My concern here, I hope, is not one of prudery or reaction, but one of wanting a little more give in the technologies we use to tap history. Elsewhere I have spoken about my interest in a tradition of spinsterhood, which became radicalized in Shundak (my father's long-ago county of origin, in Guandong Province) at the turn of the last century. Although my sources on this tradition are entirely and problematically anthropological, I was struck by the argument (see Sankar) that the act that clinched this practice for women was not sex but the acceptance of the idea that younger generations of spinsters could feed, through ancestral worship, the souls of the older generation. This practice is normally reserved for the members of patriarchal families only.

That said, I must also add that it is extremely difficult to find historical materials on Chinese lesbians. I suspect this is not because they did not exist, but because for a long time sexual practice was not considered as a focal point for identity. It could be argued, in fact, that the notion of identity arose from Western philosophical traditions, and from the needs of Western colonial practices. Later, the absence of such texts could be ascribed to the fact that women's lives were not deemed important enough to write about, or if worthy of writing, not deemed worthy of translation. The only scholarship on lesbian history in China that I could find in English was an appendix to a book called *Passions of the Cut Sleeve,* which dealt in its main body with the history of gay men. That appendix, perhaps ten pages long, focussed exclusively on the question of sexual practice, which felt empty and unsatisfying in its narrowness.

25   Insofar as *When Fox is a Thousand* concerns anti-racism—and it does, although I think it also goes much further than that—I think issues of the body are primary. There are the obvious metaphors—the Fox breathing life into the bodies of the dead is like an Asian woman trying to breathe life into the assimilated almost-white self required by the social pressures of liberalism. She can never do it perfectly. There are always moments where the synapses don't connect, where there are understandings missing. But for the Fox, these moments of breathing life into the dead are also moments of passion. This is something she is compelled to do. It is her nature. The work of Calgary writer Yasmin Ladha is compelling in that it talks about

colonialism and its effect in terms of romance. A very messy and dangerous romance, rife with the abuse of power, but also tinged with hope. I think in doing so she takes a great risk, particularly as the spectres of Pocahontas, Suzy Wong, Madame Butterfly and their ilk loom above us. But to engage in this way also opens up possibilities for living here that might not otherwise exist.

It did not occur to me until well after completing the book that the notion of transformation through breath is both a Taoist and a Buddhist notion. Or perhaps, indeed, it is a remnant of some earlier indigenous religion that has since disappeared or become subsumed by these more organized forms. Breath, like writing, is stilling and insistent. It moves and it sustains life. To engage the breath is to disrupt the binary opposition of Houdini's two boxes, to break from what Judith Butler refers to as "the discursive site of injury." What happens for me in the process of writing, at certain electric moments, is a contacting of the past that resonates with something akin to truth and belonging. A bit metaphysical perhaps but in a country built on denial, I am used to ghosts and not frightened of things that are only half apparent. These are not moments that sing of hurt but rather compel my interest in Taoist and pre-Taoist cosmologies. Here again, there are dangers. My compunction towards home-making belongs to the realm of the feminine in a way of which some branches of feminism might not approve. I think it is important to remember, to get back to the question of racialization, that there are entire knowledge systems and ways of living in our historical pasts that pre-date white racist modes of identification and their reclamations. How to touch those systems and practices may not be obvious, and the dangers of naïve idealization are far from negligible. For me, the consciously artificial narrative construction of history that acknowledges the desires of the present but also resonates with the past, seems a very useful possibility.

Thanks to Rita Wong, Ashok Mathur and Debora O for their support and feedback on this piece.

WORKS CITED

Butler, Judith. "Subjection, Resistance, Resignification: Between Freud and Foucault." *Psychic Life of Power: Theories on Subjection.* Stanford: Stanford UP, 1997, 83–105.
Eng, David L. and Alice Y. Hom, ed. *Q&A: Queer in Asian America.* Philadelphia: Temple UP, 1998.

Hinsch, Bret. *Passions of the Cut Sleeve: The Male Homosexual Tradition in China*. Los Angeles: U of California P, 1992.

Ladha, Yasmin. *Lion's Granddaughter and Other Stories*. Edmonton: NeWest Press, 1992.

Lai, Larissa. "The Heart of the Matter: Interview with Yasmin Ladha," *Kinesis*. Vancouver, February 1993. 15.

_____. *When Fox is a Thousand*. Vancouver: Press Gang, 1995.

Lee, JeeYeun. "Toward a Queer Korean American Diasporic History." Eng and Hom. 185–209.

Sankar, Andrea. "Sisters and brothers, lovers and enemies: marriage resistance in southern Kwangtung." *Journal of Homosexuality*. 11.3/4 (1985): 69–81.

Pu, Songling, *Selected Tales of Liaozhai*. Trans. Yang Xianyi and Gladys Yang. Beijing: Panda Books, 1981.

_____. *Strange Tales of Liaozhai*. Trans. Lu Yunzhong et al. Hong Kong: The Commercial Press, 1988.

P'u Sung-ling. *Strange Stories from a Chinese Studio*. Trans. Herbert A. Giles. Hong Kong: Kelly and Walsh, 1968.

Shah, Nayan. "Sexuality, Identity and the Uses of History." Eng and Hom. 141–56.

(1999)

QUESTIONS:

1. What does Lai mean in paragraph 5 when she writes, "I still live with the hope that the body exists prior to race, that experience exists prior to race"?

2. Why does Lai wish to construct a consciously artificial history in her writing?

3. In paragraph 9, Lai refers to "pushing white liberals to look at the hypocrisies of colour-blindness." According to Lai, how has racism in Canada changed over the decades?

4. The article was originally published in *Canadian Literature*, a scholarly journal. Discuss the ways in which Lai has geared her article toward this particular audience.

5. In what ways is publishing an essay such as this one effective in the fight against racism? Compare the effect of such an essay with that of writing an article in a popular magazine, demonstrating in an anti-racism rally, or standing up to racism when you see it in practice.

Witold Rybczynski

One Good Turn
Why the Robertson Screwdriver is the Biggest Little Invention of the Twentieth Century

A leading writer on cultural and architectural history addresses the unlikely topic of the screwdriver.

～

Take a close look at a modern screw. It is a remarkable little object. The thread begins at the gimlet point, sharp as a pin. This point gently tapers into the body of the screw, whose core is cylindrical. At the top, the core tapers into a smooth shank, the thread running out to nothing.

From the time of their invention in the Middle Ages until the beginning of the twentieth century, all screws had either square or octagonal heads, or slots. The former were turned by a wrench, the latter by a screwdriver. There is no mystery as to the origin of the slot. A square head had to be accurate to fit the wrench; a slot was a shape that could be roughly filed or cut by hand. Screws with slotted heads could also be countersunk so that they would not protrude beyond the surface.

Yet a slotted screw has several drawbacks. It is easy to "cam out," that is, to push the screwdriver out of the slot; the result is often damage to the material that is being fastened or injury to one's fingers—or both. The slot offers a tenuous purchase on the screw, and it is not uncommon to strip the slot when trying to tighten a new screw or loosen an old one. Finally, there are awkward situations—balancing on a stepladder, for example, or working in confined quarters—when one has to drive the screw with one hand. This is almost impossible to do with a slotted screw. The screw wobbles, the screwdriver slips, the screw falls to the ground and rolls away, the handyman curses—not for the first time—the inventor of this maddening device.

American screw manufacturers were well aware of these shortcomings. Between 1860 and 1890, there was a flurry of patents for magnetic screwdrivers, screw-holding gadgets, slots that did not extend across the face of the screw, double slots, and a variety of square, triangular, and hexagonal sockets or recesses. The last held the most promise. Replacing the slot by a socket held the screwdriver snugly and prevented cam-out. The difficulty—once more—lay in manufacturing. Screw heads are formed by mechanically stamping a cold-steel rod; punching a socket sufficiently deep to hold the screwdriver tended to either weaken the screw or deform the head.

5   The solution was discovered by a twenty-seven-year-old Canadian, Peter L. Robertson. Robertson was a so-called "high-pitch man" for a Philadelphia tool company, a travelling salesman who plied his wares on street corners and at country fairs in eastern Canada. He spent his spare time in his workshop, dabbling in mechanical inventions. He invented and promoted "Robertson's 20th Century Wrench-Brace," a combination tool that could be used as a brace, a monkey wrench, a screwdriver, a bench vise, and a rivet-maker. He vainly patented an improved corkscrew, a new type of cufflink, even a better mousetrap. Then, in 1906, he applied for a patent for a socket-head screw.

Robertson later said that he got the idea for the socket head while demonstrating a spring-loaded screwdriver to a group of sidewalk hawkers in Montreal—the blade slipped out of the slot and injured his hand. The secret of his invention was the exact shape of the recess, which was square with chamfered edges, slightly tapering sides, and a pyramidal bottom. Later, he rather grandly explained his invention: "It was discovered early by the use of this form of punch, constructed with the exact angles indicated, cold metal would flow to the sides, and not be driven ahead of the tools, resulting beneficially in knitting the atoms into greater strength, and also assisting in the work of lateral extension, and without a waste or cutting away of any of the metal so treated, as is the case in the manufacture of the ordinary slotted head screw."

An enthusiastic promoter, Robertson found financial backers, talked a small Ontario town, Milton, into giving him a loan and other concessions, and established his own screw factory. "The big fortunes are in the small inventions," he trumpeted to prospective investors. "This is considered by many as the biggest little invention of the twentieth century so far." In truth, the square socket really was a big improvement. The special square-headed screwdriver fitted snugly—Robertson claimed an accuracy within one one-thousandth of an inch—and never cammed out. Craftsmen, especially furniture-makers and boat builders, appreciated the convenience of screws that were self-centring and could be driven with one hand. Industry liked socket-head screws, too, since they reduced product damage and speeded up production. The Fisher Body Company, which made wood bodies in Canada for Ford cars, became a large Robertson customer; so did the new Ford Model T plant in Windsor, Ontario, which soon accounted for a third of Robertson's output. Within five years, he was employing seventy-five workers and had built his own powerhouse and a plant to draw the cold-steel rod used in making the screws.

In 1913, Robertson decided to expand his business outside Canada. His father had been a Scottish immigrant, so Robertson turned his attention to Britain. He established an independent English company to serve as a base for exporting to Germany and Russia. The venture was not a success. He was thwarted by a combination of undercapitalization, the First World War, the defeat of Germany, and the Russian Revolution. Moreover, it proved difficult to run businesses on two continents. After seven years, unhappy English shareholders replaced Robertson as managing director. The English company struggled along until it was liquidated in 1926.

Meanwhile, Robertson turned to the United States. Negotiations with a large screw manufacturer in Buffalo broke down after it became clear that Robertson was unwilling to share control over production decisions. Henry Ford was interested, since his Canadian plants were reputedly saving as much as $2.60 per car using Robertson screws. However, Ford, too, wanted a measure of control that the stubborn Robertson was unwilling to grant. They met, but no deal was struck. It was Robertson's last attempt to export his product. A life-long bachelor, he spent the rest of his life in Milton, a big fish in a decidedly small pond.

Meanwhile, American automobile manufacturers followed Ford's lead and stuck to slotted screws. Yet the success of the new Robertson screw did not go unnoticed. In 1936 alone, there were more than twenty American patents for improved screws and screwdrivers.

Several of these were granted to Henry F. Phillips, a forty-six-year-old businessman in Portland, Oregon. Like Robertson, Phillips had been a travelling salesman. He was also a promoter of new inventions and acquired patents from a Portland inventor, John P. Thompson, for a socket screw. Thompson's socket was too deep to be practicable, but Phillips incorporated its distinctive shape—a cruciform—into an improved design of his own. Like Robertson, Phillips claimed that the socket was "particularly adapted for firm engagement with a correspondingly shaped driving tool or screwdriver, and in such a way that there will be no tendency of the driver to cam out of the recess." Unlike Robertson, however, Phillips did not start his own company but planned to license his patent to screw manufacturers.

All the major screw companies turned him down. "The manufacture and marketing of these articles do not promise sufficient commercial success," was a typical response. Phillips did not give up. Several years later the president of the giant American Screw Company agreed to undertake the industrial development of the innovative socket screw. In his patents, Phillips emphasized that the screw was particularly suited to power-driven operations, which at the time chiefly meant automobile assembly lines. The American Screw Company convinced General Motors to test the new screw; it was first used in the 1936 Cadillac. The trial proved so effective that within two years all automobile companies save one had switched to socket screws, and by 1939 most screw manufacturers produced what were now called Phillips screws.

The Phillips screw has many of the same benefits as the Robertson screw (and the added advantage that it can be driven with a slotted screwdriver if necessary). "We estimate that our operators save between thirty and sixty percent of their time by using Phillips screws," wrote a satisfied builder of boats and gliders. "Our men claim they can accomplish at least seventy-five percent more work than with the old-fashioned type," maintained a manufacturer of garden furniture. Phillips screws—and the familiar cross-tipped screwdrivers—were now everywhere. The First World War had stymied Robertson; the Second World War ensured that the Phillips screw became an industry standard as it was widely adopted by wartime manufacturers. By the mid-1960s, when Phillip's patents expired, there were more than 160 domestic, and eighty foreign, licensees.

The Phillips screw became the international socket screw; the Robertson screw is used only in Canada and by a select number of American woodworkers. (Starting in the 1950s, Robertson screws began to be used by some American furniture manufacturers, by the mobile-home industry, and eventually by a growing number of craftsmen and hobbyists. The Robertson company itself was purchased by an American conglomerate in 1968.) A few years ago, *Consumer Reports* tested Robertson and Phillips screwdrivers. "After driving hundreds of screws by hand and with a cordless drill fitted with a Robertson tip, we're convinced. Compared with slotted and Phillips-head screwdrivers, the Robertson worked faster, with less cam-out."

The explanation is simple. Although Phillips designed his screw to have "firm engagement" with the screwdriver, in fact a cruciform recess is a less perfect fit than a square socket. Paradoxically, this very quality is what attracted automobile manufacturers to the Phillips screw; the point of an automated driver turning the screw with increasing force would pop out of the recess when the screw was fully set, preventing overscrewing. Thus, a certain degree of cam-out was incorporated into the design from the beginning. However, what worked on the assembly line has bedevilled handymen ever since. Phillips screws are notorious for slippage, cam-out, and stripped sockets (especially if the screw or the screwdriver is improperly made).

Here I must confess myself to be a confirmed Robertson user. The square-headed screwdriver sits snugly in the socket; you can shake a Robertson screwdriver, and the screw on the end will not fall off; drive a Robertson screw with a power drill and the fully set screw simply stops the drill dead; no matter how old, rusty, or painted over, a Robertson screw can always be unscrewed. The "biggest little invention of the twentieth century"? Why not.

(2000)

QUESTIONS:

1. Although the author purports the Robertson to be a superior screw to the Phillips, it has not had the commercial success of the Phillips. What role did the differing business philosophies of the two inventors play in this result?

2. This article is an excerpt from a book rather than a self-contained essay. How is the effectiveness of the article limited because of this? With this in mind, what changes would you make to the article to strengthen it?

3. In the final sentence of paragraph 9, why does the author reveal that Robertson was a life-long bachelor? Why does he choose this moment to do so? Why does he then employ an often used metaphor instead of simply stating that Robertson was an important man in an otherwise unimportant town? Other than the bare facts, what, if anything, is the author trying to infer in this sentence?

4. Rybczynski is often described as an "engaging" writer. Through what means does he effectively engage the interest of his readers?

TIM DEVLIN

DOES WORKING FOR WELFARE WORK?

In this article from a general interest magazine, an Alberta writer evaluates a government program of which he has personal experience.

≈

"I've led an interesting life, in the Chinese sense of the word interesting. I was almost 42 when I returned to Canada penniless and applied for welfare for the first time in my life—after spending 18 months in a Bangkok prison. I have no trade skills, so Calgary's booming construction industry was not an option for me. I began applying for simple labouring positions, unloading trucks, factory production lines—jobs I would have had no trouble getting 20 years earlier. Nobody wanted to hire me, and after years of drug addiction and a trip through a surreal Third World death camp, I was terrified of life in all of its jangling chords. I fully accept responsibility for the situation I found myself in, but it was frightening nevertheless, and I eagerly grasped at the hope that Alberta Job Corps purported to represent."

Marianne (all names have been changed) is a single mother of two teenage children. After a serious illness she lost her job and became a statistic on the provincial welfare rolls. She was drafted into Alberta Job Corps, the Alberta government's work-for-welfare program, and has since found an office job—a "stepping stone." She says the program provided motivation at the "right time" in her life. Marianne is a true success story, but she looked decidedly out of place at Alberta Job Corps. An intelligent and well-read 41-year-old, she was hardly a typical recruit. Given the mandate of the program it's difficult to understand why she was drafted in the first place.

Alberta Job Corps (AJC), or "the Corps" as some of the troops laughingly refer to it, was ostensibly set up to get the chronically unemployed back to work. The program was launched in 1995 with plenty of fanfare. It is administered by Supports for Independence (SFI), which falls under the Ministry of Human Resources and Employment.

According to internal SFI documents, the Job Corps is intended for welfare recipients who are poor candidates for "academic upgrading or formal skill development." They have "issues" ruling them out of other government programs because "they would not be hired or would drop out of jobs after short stints." These "issues" include alcoholism, drug addiction and mental illness. While acknowledging the client group in question is unsuitable for "pre-employment training" or "training on the job," the document warns they are in danger of being cut off financial support: "For these clients Alberta Job Corps is the last opportunity."

Cecelia is in her early 40s and she wants to work, but has been diagnosed as suffering from bipolar disorder. Mathew is 32 years old and able bodied, but he was in a car crash in 1994, suffers from severe brain scarring, seizures, alcoholism and serious anger management issues. Subsisting on welfare since the crash, living in a seedy downtown hotel, Mathew says when he was referred to AJC, he was interested "right off the bat."

After interviews, Cecelia and Mathew were asked to sign documents and congratulated as new recruits making $5.65 an hour, the minimum wage at the time. Both were told they would be learning marketable skills directly transferable into the workplace, supplemented with training courses including the handling of dangerous goods and first aid. If they had the right stuff for the Corps they would move into lead hand positions and receive $7.50 an hour. They were also told that 80 per cent of the people in the AJC program were off financial assistance one year later. "She (the employment development worker) glorified it and made it sound like I was going to come out with something, and it sounded like a real good program," says Mathew. But instead, he discovered "it's a joke."

He says all he did during his time at AJC was paint, and "not very well." Mathew complains he found the experience, "very, very disorganized" and "confusing," and says he learned very little in the way of marketable skills. Mathew "flipped out" on several occasions and says his anger problems grew worse because of the frustration he felt. He was taking an expensive medication to control seizures. Before AJC, Mathew's prescriptions were covered by SFI. He maintains he couldn't afford to buy his medication working at minimum wage, and he quit after SFI refused to help pay for it.

Mathew didn't have enough hours for Employment Insurance benefits and was refused welfare because he had quit AJC. He later approached the Southern Alberta Brain Injury Society, which is helping him with a claim under the Assured Income for the Severely Handicapped program. Mathew adds that paying minimum wage to people who have been trapped in the system is not enough incentive to motivate anyone. He feels that raising the wage "even a dollar" would be enough to stimulate people to "get something going with their life."

Cecelia has also found it hard to pay for her medication at minimum wage and no benefits. "It's a catch 22" Cecelia sighs, "I'm so fed up." She has stopped taking one medication, which costs $150 per month.

Alberta Job Corps operates in Calgary, Edmonton and the two northern corners of the province. According to a government spokesman the program cost $8.8-million last year. Province-wide, 938 welfare clients were hired. The Regional Income and Employment Program Management Committee, composed of the managers from district SFI offices, meets monthly. Attached to the minutes from a meeting held in 1999 are statistics circulated by Donna Daniluck, the manager of Alberta Job Corps. The numbers show that even with pressure to keep the program supplied with bodies, it was only operating at "about 60 per cent of capacity." Highlights from a study by the Social Research and Demonstration Corporation were also attached to the minutes. The study notes that while successfully enforcing a work-for-benefits approach, "workfare programs have not reduced caseloads or led to unsubsidized employment." More disturbing is another "key lesson" the document identifies: "Welfare-to-work programs have not usually increased the overall incomes to families," because "increased earnings have largely been offset by reductions in benefits."

A confidential source who works for Supports for Independence explains that the province's galloping economy and tightened eligibility requirements have led to a big drop in the number of welfare recipients in recent years. He says that while AJC draws its employees from a diminished client base, pressure at the district welfare offices ensures clients are referred to AJC. Social workers try to screen those who are obviously unsuitable, but others are directed to the program simply to find out what is wrong. He agrees it's an expensive way to weed out the unemployable and says part of the screening problem lies in the fact the provincial government has "de-skilled" the profession. He points out that in the last few years, people with no training, some with "nothing more than Grade 10," were promoted from secretarial jobs into front line positions as financial benefit workers.

10   Single mothers make up a significant percentage of recruits at AJC. Many have children under school age; some have children under the age of one. The SFI source explains that once a baby is six months old, mothers are required to look for work, some type of job preparation program or school "even if the woman is breastfeeding." In some cases he says, women are forced into low paying jobs, and the daycare bill, which SFI picks up, means the government actually loses money on the deal. He calls the guidelines a "harsh, harsh policy," and describes as hypocritical the cries of "family values" from members of the Klein government. He feels that women "should not be referred to Job Corps because the chance of their being able to support their families is slim to none."

In Calgary AJC operates out of a building in a busy northeast warehouse district. The comprehensive program claims to develop basic plumbing, electrical, automotive, carpentry and painting skills. The schedule is laid out in week-by-week modules which combine training with on-site work experience. In the last weeks of what is supposed to be a six-month program, the emphasis shifts and participants begin actively searching for a full-time job.

Eight Employment Development Workers (EDWs) oversee the clients daily. Four of them are social workers. The rest are skilled tradesmen or journeymen who have abandoned the volatile construction industry for the questionably more secure bosom of the Alberta government. Ministry spokesman Tom Neufeld says that to qualify to work at AJC tradesmen have to possess proven supervisory experience. He says they are encouraged to take "human services training" but that is not a mandatory requirement.

Serious ethical questions arise when construction workers are placed in charge of welfare clients. Three women interviewed say they saw inappropriate behaviour that would not have been tolerated in the private sector, let alone in a situation where "vulnerable people" are involved. One AJC trades supervisor was suspended for two weeks after complaints about his behaviour, but returned to work with no explanation offered, not even to the woman who laid the complaint.

Emily was recently referred to Alberta Job Corps. She is in her 50s and entered the job market a few years ago following a marriage breakdown. Although she has upgraded her clerical skills, and is intelligent and warm, Emily continues to have difficulty finding full-time, continuous employment because of her age. You would be hard pressed to find anyone more ill suited to the Job Corps experience. An AJC employee who painted on various projects with Emily says it was "like trying to work on a construction site with your mom." Of the initial referral, Emily says "I didn't want to go; I just went because I had to." How appropriate is it to refer women like Emily and mothers with babies to Job Corps? The trades are seasonal. Women usually don't work out in the trades and they can run into a lot of discrimination.

15   The universal complaint from people attending AJC is that while they are initially told they will be learning a variety of construction skills, nearly all of the projects are painting jobs. Despite that, everyone interviewed (more than 20 people) maintains that no one really has any idea of how to paint to a professional standard. For the most part crews are dropped off at job sites in the morning and the supervisor doesn't return until the end of the day. "We weren't taught anything," according to Emily, "the trades people were not out there." Mathew didn't find the supervisors much help either: "They just dropped you off and you had your lead hands come and show you what to do."

Lead hands don't necessarily lead. Emily says it didn't matter if people had the necessary skills or leadership ability. Lead hand appointments were "based on attendance and being on time." Emily relates how four lead hands, working together because hardly anyone else showed up that day, were suspended after they were caught drinking. Another employee became the poster boy for new recruits, even though he freely admits to drinking on the job. Jerry agrees he has a serious alcohol problem but he was able to drag himself to work in the morning and that was all it took to advance at AJC. He was appointed lead hand and was twice lauded for his flawless attendance—at an awards presentation held each month when new clients join the program. During his time as lead hand Jerry was in charge of a crew painting a Government of Alberta office. He says that was his favourite project because the place was like "a maze. You could disappear and nobody knew where you were. And there was a liquor store across the street."

Marianne had no experience with addiction. She immediately noticed that most of the people had alcohol or other drug problems, but trained social workers seemed blind to the fact. Marianne was "quite surprised they were not helping these people in that way," and says the root problem, addiction, was ignored except in the most obvious cases.

Alberta Job Corps attempts to educate clients in a number of life skills areas, but Emily calls the one-day seminars on topics like household budgeting a waste of time, "just information." She observes that other people didn't pay much attention in class, nor did they apply any of the lessons offered. "They still would have no money. They still were doing the things they were doing before." Attendance at morning muster is usually lowest after payday (sometimes half the workforce stays home) and Emily says there are "suspensions constantly, letters, written warnings." Emily believes that most of the people cannot survive in the real world because "they're having a hard time in a place where they are given so many chances. A real employer is not going to take that."

Employees at AJC attend abbreviated courses in a number of areas including the transportation of dangerous goods, first aid and bobcat training. Marianne says none of the workshops offered at the Corps were "long enough or in-depth enough." She feels not enough attention is paid to individual needs and likens it to a "school where there's not enough teachers compared to kids."

20 From a practical point of view, the most valuable training offered at Alberta Job Corps is the St. John's Ambulance First Aid course. Marianne says the teacher was professional and helpful, but she estimates only half the people in her class of 10 would be competent in an emergency. When asked how she would feel about someone from AJC performing first aid on her, Emily laughs, "Thanks but no thanks."

Despite taking minimal certification courses in the handling and transport of dangerous goods, and passing, Emily still doesn't feel confident about working with toxic substances. She believes there should be more supervision on the projects because there has been carelessness and the supervisors don't really inspect the job sites at the end of the day. She says that job is often left up to the lead hand and "God only knows what kind of mind frame the lead hand is in."

The bobcat course at AJC is an example of wasted dollars. A small skid-steer front-end loader, a bobcat is expensive to maintain and transport. Three hours are spent on classroom instruction, followed by a short written test. Each person operates the bobcat for roughly ten minutes, sometimes simply driving up and down the back alley behind AJC headquarters. Everyone who passes the written exam (and people are given more than one chance) is issued a meaningless certificate. In the real working world it takes 300 hours of training and practice before someone is considered proficient in operating a bobcat.

An African immigrant, who calls himself a "citizen of the world," says that the social workers at AJC are totally out of touch. Frank, who instantly passes from street-smart wise guy into charming offbeat philosopher, feels the staff doesn't understand the people directed to Job Corps. He grins as he describes how one individual told him she knew what it was like to be a visible minority because she'd been to Barbados on a two-week vacation. The EDW couldn't understand why Frank found her comments so amusing. Although Frank received the training and accompanying certificates provided by AJC, he says the "pieces of paper" haven't helped him get a job, because "in the real world nobody wanted to see them." He is collecting Employment Insurance and points to his list of employer contacts as evidence he is still looking for a job. "I played the game the way they wanted me to play it," Frank laughs ruefully.

In literature distributed to potential employers, mostly church and community groups, AJC is described as an "effective program" which broadens job skills and allows welfare clients to break free from government assistance. It promises "hands-on" skill development that approximates "actual work" situations. On an average day, however, less than five hours is actually spent on the job. Mathew says that sometimes crews sat around at the rear of the building until 9:30, and after driving to the job site, in some cases 40 minutes traveling time, it was nearly coffee time. "You work a bit till coffee time. Then by the time you figure out what you're supposed to be doing again, there's more time wasted. It's almost lunchtime." Emily says with another coffee break, cleanup and a pickup time around 3:30, on a good day there was four hours of "actual work."

The SFI source says sometimes people hang onto low paying seasonal jobs for a few months, but for the most part "it's a revolving door." For a majority of the clients, all that is accomplished is a temporary shift from the welfare rolls over to the federal Employment Insurance program. He says attending AJC takes individuals out of the Alberta system briefly but it never relieves the pressure on the public purse.

Nonetheless, Clint Dunford, the minister responsible, says that overall he is happy with AJC, claiming he has had nothing but positive feedback and has no knowledge of any problems. Dunford has toured a couple of AJC work sites and says, "actually we're pretty proud of the program. I've just been moving merrily along, saying OK, of all the things that I'm responsible for I guess I don't have to worry about that one."

Dunford caused a flap when he took over as Minister of Human Resources and Employment last spring. Asked at the time to comment on statistics that indicate a large number of working families in Alberta were forced to rely on food banks, the Lethbridge West MLA implied that those people were taking advantage of the system.

When asked if tradespeople at AJC had received training that would prepare them to work with SFI clients, many of whom are emotionally damaged and easily manipulated, the minister laughed. Dunford said the working world isn't "a cocoon," and that the program is set up that way. "Clients have to have some sort of mentor and somebody with some skills so who should it be but a tradesman?"

Dunford says that roughly 70 per cent of the people initially hired by AJC are off social assistance one year later. He did not know how many people that figure represented, the cost per individual or the total cost of the program. According to ministry statistics, on a year-to-year basis, the number is closer to 65 percent. By any standard the figures quoted are a poor measure of true success. Although the program is nearly five years old, no reliable follow-up studies have been done. Ministry spokesman Tom Neufeld says that after clients leave they are never contacted directly. Instead, results are measured by checking the SFI rolls six months after a person leaves Job Corps and again at the one-year mark. If someone is not receiving welfare benefits at that point they are considered a success story. Most telling, in fact, is that the ministry stops monitoring clients after one year. No figures are available at the two-year mark, when an individual's Employment Insurance benefits would be exhausted and the program could be more accurately assessed.

30   Forcing people with serious psychiatric and emotional problems, often combined with crippling addictions, to participate in a program that neither improves their lot in life nor saves money seems pointless. Many of the clients at Alberta Job Corps are frankly unsympathetic characters, but they are still people. If conservative ideology demands that individuals considered unemployable in the private sector work for a subsistence existence, perhaps the Klein government should fully and honestly embrace the concept. A percentage of the clients, and the non-profit groups that make use of free labour provided by AJC, benefit from the program. Perhaps an ongoing workfare system could be developed that accepts the failings of these people and offers them continuous employment, to say nothing of a raise and some basic medical benefits.

What brings individuals to the brink of the abyss? In every case the reasons are different, but one thing is certain: no one chooses the streets or the welfare shuffle or the food bank because the experiences are fun, invigorating or financially rewarding. The human beings in question are damaged, and if there is a time in history and a place on the planet where we can afford to take care of such lost souls in a meaningful way, surely it is Alberta.

"Both the minister and a senior government official have suggested I am simply someone with a 'grudge' because I'd had a 'bad experience' in a program. In fact, I enjoyed my time at AJC and I liked most of the people I met there. The social workers and the majority of the tradespeople are trying to make a difference, and there is a much different attitude than I've encountered at most welfare offices. Unfortunately the program is fatally flawed. Except for first aid, I did not learn anything of value and I would suggest, given my background and education, I had a better chance than most of the clients directed to AJC.

"Alberta Job Corps did help restore my confidence, and in an ironic twist the AJC experience got me back into the field of journalism. It also filled me with disgust that the government of the province I was born in would use damaged people to make a political point."

(2000)

QUESTIONS:

1. This essay relies on personal anecdote for much of its effect. To what extent do you think an anecdotal approach is helpful in exploring public policy issues?

2. Though this article addresses the specific situation in the province of Alberta, it has relevance to many other geographical areas; "workfare" has been a popular concept throughout much of North America over the last few years. Does this essay alter in any way your own opinions about "workfare"?

3. The quotations appearing at the beginning and the end of this article recount the author's own experiences—though they are not identified as being by the author. Do you find that they help to set the article in an appropriate context? Or do they seem to you largely irrelevant to the article itself? Do you think it would have been more appropriate for the author to have made clear who is speaking?

4. In the nineteenth century it was commonly believed that if someone was poor it was their own fault rather than a matter of bad luck or of the structure of society. That view had almost died out by the late 1970s, but is now again held by significant numbers of people. Is it in fact possible to generalize on such matters? Make a list of as many possible causes of individual poverty and individual wealth as you can think of. Compare your list with those of others, and then write a brief essay on the topic.

NAOMI KLEIN

THE SWOOSH

In this selection from her enormously influential bestseller No Logo: Taking
Aim at the Brand Bullies, *a leading social activist discusses "the most inflated of
all the balloon brands."*

～

Nike CEO Phil Knight has long been a hero of the business schools.
Prestigious academic publications such as *The Harvard Business Review*
have lauded his pioneering marketing techniques, his understanding of
branding and his early use of outsourcing. Countless MBA candidates and
other students of marketing and communications have studied the Nike
formula of "brands, not products." So when Phil Knight was invited to be
a guest speaker at the Stanford University Business School—Knight's own
alma mater—in May 1997, the visit was expected to be one in a long line of
Nike love-ins. Instead, Knight was greeted by a crowd of picketing students,
and when he approached the microphone he was taunted with chants of
"Hey Phil, off the stage. Pay your workers a living wage." The Nike
honeymoon had come to a grinding halt.

No story illustrates the growing distrust of the culture of corporate
branding more than the international anti-Nike movement—the most
publicized and tenacious of the brand-based campaigns. Nike's sweatshop
scandals have been the subject of over 1,500 news articles and opinion
columns. Its Asian factories have been probed by cameras from nearly every
major media organization, from CBS to Disney's sports station, ESPN. On
top of all that, it has been the subject of a series of Doonesbury cartoon strips
and the butt of Michael Moore's documentary *The Big One*. As a result,
several people in Nike's PR department work full time dealing with the
sweatshop controversy—fielding complaints, meeting with local groups and
developing Nike's response—and the company has created a new executive

position: vice president for corporate responsibility. Nike has received hundreds and thousands of letters of protest, faced hundreds of both small and large groups of demonstrators, and is the target of a dozen critical Web sites.

For the last two years, anti-Nike forces in North America and Europe have attempted to focus all the scattered swoosh bashing on a single day. Every six months they have declared an International Nike Day of Action, and brought their demands for fair wages and independent monitoring directly to Nike's customers, shoppers at flagship Nike Towns in urban centers or the less glamorous Foot Locker outlets in suburban malls. According to Campaign for Labor Rights, the largest anti-Nike event so far took place on October 18, 1997: eighty-five cities in thirteen countries participated. Not all the protests have attracted large crowds, but since the movement is so decentralized, the sheer number of individual anti-Nike events has left the company's public-relations department scrambling to get its spin onto dozens of local newscasts. Though you'd never know it from its branding ubiquity, even Nike can't be everywhere at once.

Since so many of the stores that sell Nike products are located in malls, protests often end with a security guard escorting participants into the parking lot. Jeff Smith, an activist from Grand Rapids, Michigan, reported that "when we asked if private property rights ruled over free speech rights, the [security] officer hesitated and then emphatically said YES!" (Though in the economically depressed city of St. John's, Newfoundland, anti-Nike campaigners reported that after being thrown out of a mall, "they were approached by a security guard who asked to sign their petition."[1]) But there's plenty that can be done on the sidewalk or in the mall parking lot. Campaigners have dramatized Nike's labor practices through what they call "sweatshop fashion shows," and "The Transnational Capital Auction: A Game of Survival" (the lowest bidder wins), and a global economy treadmill (run fast, stay in the same place). In Australia, anti-Nike protestors have been known to parade around in calico bags painted with the slogan "Rather wear a bag than Nike." Students at the University of Colorado in Boulder dramatized the difference between the legal minimum wage and a living wage by holding a fundraising run in which "participants pay an entrance fee of $1.60 (daily wages for a Nike worker in Vietnam) and the winner will

---

[1] Memo, 4 May 1998, from Maquila Solidarity Network, "Nike Day of Action Canada Report & Task Force Update." [Unless otherwise noted, all notes to this essay are from the author.]

receive $2.10 (the price of three square meals in Vietnam)."[2] Meanwhile, activists in Austin, Texas, made a giant papier-mâché Nike sneaker piñata, and a protest outside a Regina, Saskatchewan, shopping center featured a deface-the-swoosh booth. The last stunt is something of a running theme in all the anti-Nike actions: Nike's logo and slogan have been jammed so many times—on T-shirts, stickers, placards, banners and pins—that the semiotic bruises have turned them black and blue.

5   Tellingly, the anti-Nike movement is at its strongest inside the company's home state of Oregon, even though the area has reaped substantial economic benefits from Nike's success (Nike is the largest employer in Portland and a significant local philanthropist). Phil Knight's neighbors, nonetheless, have not all rushed to his defense in his hour of need. In fact, since the *Life* magazine soccer-ball story broke, many Oregonians have been out for blood. The demonstrations outside the Portland Nike Town are among the largest and most militant in the country, sometimes sporting a menacing giant Phil Knight puppet with dollar signs for eyes or a twelve-foot Nike swoosh dragged by small children (to dramatize child labor). And in contravention of the principles of nonviolence that govern the anti-Nike movement, one protest in Eugene, Oregon, led to acts of vandalism including the tearing-down of a fence surrounding the construction of a new Nike Town, gear pulled off shelves at an existing Nike store and, according to one eyewitness, "an entire rack of clothes...dumped off a balcony into a fountain below."[3]

Local papers in Oregon have aggressively (sometimes gleefully) followed Knight's sweatshop scandals, and the daily paper *The Oregonian* sent a reporter to Southeast Asia to do its own lengthy investigation of the factories. Mark Zusman, editor of the Oregon newspaper *The Willamette Week*, publicly admonished Knight in a 1996 "memo": "Frankly, Phil, it's time to get a little more sophisticated about this media orgy...Oregonians already have suffered through the shame of Tonya Harding, Bob Packwood and Wes Cooley. Spare us the added humiliation of being known as the home of the most exploitative capitalist in the free world."[4]

Even Nike's charitable donations have become controversial. In the midst of a critical fundraising drive to try to address a $15 million shortfall,

---

[2] "Nike protest update," *Labour Alerts*, 18 October 1997.

[3] "Nike Mobilization: Local Reports," *Labor Alerts*, Campaign for Labor Rights, 26 October 1998.

[4] Mark L. Zusman, "Editor's Notebook," *Willamette Week*, 12 June 1996.

the Portland School Board was torn apart by a debate about whether to accept Nike's gift of $500,000 in cash and swooshed athletic gear. The board ended up accepting the donation, but not before looking their gift horse publicly in the mouth. "I asked myself," school board trustee Joseph Tam told *The Oregonian*, "Nike contributed this money so my children can have a better education, but at whose expense? At the expense of children who work for six cents an hour?...As an immigrant and as an Asian I have to face this moral and ethical dilemma."[5]

Nike's sponsorship scandals have reached far beyond the company's home state. In Edmonton, Alberta, teachers, parents and some students tried to block Nike from sponsoring a children's street hockey program because "a company which profits from child labor in Pakistan ought not to be held up as a hero to Edmonton children."[6] At least one school involved in the city-wide program sent back its swooshed equipment to Nike headquarters. And when Nike approached the City of Ottawa Council in March 1998 to suggest building one of its swooshed gymnasium floors in a local community center, it faced questions about "blood money." Nike withdrew its offer and gave the court to a more grateful center, run by the Boys and Girls Clubs. The dilemma of accepting Nike sponsorship money has also exploded on university campuses.

At first, much of the outrage stemmed from the fact that when the sweatshop scandal hit the papers, Nike wasn't really acting all that sorry about it. While Kathie Lee Gifford and the Gap had at least displayed contrition when they got caught with their sweatshops showing, Phil Knight had practically stonewalled: denying responsibility, attacking journalists, blaming rogue contractors and sending out flacks to speak for the company. While Kathie Lee was crying on TV, Michael Jordan was shrugging his shoulders and saying that his job was to shoot hoop, not play politics. And while the Gap agreed to allow a particularly controversial factory in El Salvador to be monitored by local human-rights groups, Nike was paying lip service to a code of conduct that its Asian workers, when interviewed, had never heard of.

10   But there was a critical difference between Nike and the Gap at this stage. Nike didn't panic when its scandals hit the middle-American mall, because the mall, while it is indeed where most Nike products are sold, is not

---

[5] *Oregonian*, 16 June 1996.

[6] Campaign for Labor Rights Web site, regional reports.

where Nike's image was made. Unlike the Gap, Nike has drawn on the inner cities, merging, as we've seen, with the styles of poor black and Latino youth to load up on imagery and attitude. Nike's branding power is thoroughly intertwined with the African-American heroes who have endorsed its products since the mid-eighties: Michael Jordan, Charles Barkley, Scottie Pippen, Michael Johnson, Spike Lee, Tiger Woods, Bo Jackson—not to mention the rappers who wear Nike gear on stage. While hip-hop style was the major influence at the mall, Phil Knight must have known that as long as Nike was King Brand with Jordan fans in Compton and the Bronx, he could be stirred but not shaken. Sure, their parents, teachers and church leaders might be tut-tutting over sweatshops, but as far as Nike's core demographic of thirteen- to seventeen-year-old kids was concerned, the swoosh was still made of Teflon.

By 1997, it had become clear to Nike's critics that if they were serious about taking on the swoosh in an image war, they would have to get at the source of the brand's cachet—and as Nick Alexander of the multicultural *Third Force* magazine wrote in the summer of that year, they weren't even close. "Nobody has figured out how to make Nike break down and cry. The reason is that nobody has engaged African Americans in the fight....To gain significant support from communities of color, corporate campaigns need to make connections between Nike's overseas operations and conditions here at home."[7]

The connections were there to be made. It is the cruelest irony of Nike's "brands, not products" formula that the people who have done the most to infuse the swoosh with cutting-edge meaning are the very people most hurt by the company's pumped-up prices and nonexistent manufacturing base. It is inner-city youth who have most directly felt the impact of Nike's decision to manufacture its products outside the U.S., both in high unemployment rates and in the erosion of the community tax base (which sets the stage for the deterioration of local public schools).

Instead of jobs for their parents, what the inner-city kids get from Nike is the occasional visit from its marketers and designers on "bro-ing" pilgrimages. "Hey, bro, what do you think of these new Jordans—are they fresh or what?" The effect of high-priced cool hunters whipping up brand frenzy on the cracked asphalt basketball courts of Harlem, the Bronx and Compton has already been discussed: kids incorporate the brands into gang-wear uniforms; some want the gear so badly they are willing to sell drugs,

---

[7] Nick Alexander, "Sweatshop Activism: Missing Pieces," *Z Magazine*, September 1997, 14–17.

steal, mug, even kill for it. Jessie Collins, executive director of the Edenwald-Gun Hill Neighborhood Center in the northeast Bronx, tells me that it's sometimes drug or gang money, but more often it's the mothers' minimum-wage salary or welfare checks that are spent on disposable status wear. When I asked her about the media reports of kids stabbing each other for their $150 Air Jordans she said dryly, "It's enough to beat up on your mother for…$150 is a hell of a lot of money."[8]

Shoe-store owners like Steven Roth of Essex House of Fashion are often uncomfortable with the way so-called street fashions play out for real on the postindustrial streets of Newark, New Jersey, where his store is located:

> I do get weary and worn down from it all. I'm always forced to face the fact that I make my money from poor people. A lot of them are on welfare. Sometimes a mother will come in here with a kid, and the kid is dirty and poorly dressed. But the kid wants a hundred-twenty-buck pair of shoes and that stupid mother buys them for him. I can feel that kid's inner need—this desire to own these things and have the feelings that go with them—but it hurts me that this is the way things are.[9]

It's easy to blame the parents for giving in, but that "deep inner need" for designer gear has grown so intense that it has confounded everyone from community leaders to the police. Everyone pretty much agrees that brands like Nike are playing a powerful surrogate role in the ghetto, subbing for everything from self-esteem to African-American cultural history to political power. What they are far less sure about is how to fill that need with empowerment and a sense of self-worth that does not necessarily come with a logo attached. Even broaching the subject of brand fetishism to these kids is risky. With so much emotion invested in celebrity consumer goods, many kids take criticism of Nike or Tommy as a personal attack, as grave a transgression as insulting someone's mother to his face.

15 Not surprisingly, Nike sees its appeal among disadvantaged kids differently. By supporting sports programs in Boys and Girls Clubs, by paying to repave urban basketball courts and by turning high-performance sports gear into street fashions, the company claims it is sending out the inspirational message that even poor kids can "Just Do It." In its press material and ads, there is an almost messianic quality to Nike's portrayal of its role in the inner cities: troubled kids will have higher self-esteem, fewer

---

[8] Personal interview, 6 October 1997.

[9] Katz, *Just Do It*, 271. [author's note]

unwanted pregnancies and more ambition—all because at Nike "We see them as athletes." For Nike, its $150 Air Jordans are not a shoe but a kind of talisman with which poor kids can run out of the ghetto and better their lives. Nike's magic slippers will help them fly—just as they made Michael Jordan fly.

A remarkable, subversive accomplishment? Maybe. But one can't help thinking that one of the main reasons black urban youth can get out of the ghetto only by rapping or shooting hoops is that Nike and the other multinationals are reinforcing stereotypical images of black youth and simultaneously taking all the jobs away. As U.S. Congressman Bernie Sanders and Congresswoman Marcy Kaptur stated in a letter to the company, Nike has played a pivotal part in the industrial exodus from urban centers. "Nike has led the way in abandoning the manufacturing workers of the United States and their families....Apparently, Nike believes that workers in the United States are good enough to purchase your shoe products, but are no longer worthy enough to manufacture them."[10]

And when the company's urban branding strategy is taken in conjunction with this employment record, Nike ceases to be the savior of the inner city and turns into the guy who steals your job, then sells you a pair of overpriced sneakers and yells, "Run like hell!" Hey, it's the only way out of the ghetto, kid. Just do it.

That's what Mike Gitelson thought, anyway. A social worker at the Bronx's Edenwald-Gun Hill Neighborhood Center, he was unimpressed with the swoosh's powers as a self-help guru in the projects and "sick of seeing kids wearing sneakers they couldn't afford and which their parents couldn't afford."[11] Nike's critics on college campuses and in the labor movement may be fueled largely by moral outrage, but Mike Gitelson and his colleagues simply feel ripped off. So rather than lecturing the kids on the virtues of frugality, they began telling them about how Nike made the shoes that they wanted so badly. Gitelson told them about the workers in Indonesia who earned $2 a day, he told them that it cost Nike only $5 to make the shoes they bought for between $100 and $180, and he told them about how Nike didn't make any of its shoes in the U.S.—which was part of the reason their parents had such a tough time finding work. "We got really angry," says Gitelson, "because they were taking so much money from us here and then

---

[10]   Letter dated 24 October 1997.

[11]   Personal interview.

going to other countries and exploiting people even worse....We want our kids to see how it affects them here on the streets, but also how here on the streets affects people in Southeast Asia." His colleague at the center, youth worker Leo Johnson, lays out the issue using the kids' own lingo. "Yo, dude," he tells his preteen audiences, "you're being suckered if you pay $100 for a sneaker that costs $5 to make. If somebody did that to you on the block, you know where it's going."[12]

The kids at the center were upset to learn about the sweatshops but they were clearly most pissed off that Phil Knight and Michael Jordan were playing them for chumps. They sent Phil Knight a hundred letters about how much money they had spent on Nike gear over the years—and how, the way they figured it, Nike owed them big time. "I just bought a pair of Nikes for $100," one kid wrote. "It's not right what you're doing. A fair price would have been $30. Could you please send me back $70?" When the company answered the kids with a form letter, "That's when we got really angry and started putting together the protest," Gitelson says.

20 They decided the protest would take the form of a "shoe-in" at the Nike Town at Fifth Avenue and Fifty-seventh Street. Since most of the kids at the center are full-fledged swooshaholics, their closets are jam-packed with old Air Jordans and Air Carnivores that they would no longer even consider wearing. To put the obsolete shoes to practical use, they decided to gather them together in garbage bags and dump them on the doorstep of Nike Town.

When Nike executives got wind that a bunch of black and Latino kids from the Bronx were planning to publicly diss their company, the form letters came to an abrupt halt. Up to that point, Nike had met most criticism by attacking its critics as members of "fringe groups," but this was different: if a backlash took root in the inner cities, it could sink the brand at the mall. As Gitelson puts it, "Our kids are exactly who Nike depends upon to set the trends for them so that the rest of the country buys their sneakers. White middle-class adults who are fighting them, well, it's almost okay. But when youth of color start speaking out against Nike, they start getting scared."[13]

The executives in Oregon also knew, no doubt, that Edenwald was only the tip of the iceberg. For the past couple of years, debates have been raging

---

[12] David Gonzalez, "Youthful Foes Go Toe to Toe with Nike," *New York Times*, 27 September 1997, B1.

[13] Personal interview.

in hip-hop scenes about rappers "label whoring for Nike and Tommy" instead of supporting black-owned clothing companies like FUBU (For Us By Us). And rapper KRS-One planned to launch the Temple of Hip Hop, a project that promised to wrest the culture of African-American youth away from white record and clothing labels and return it to the communities that built it. It was against this backdrop that, on September 10, 1997—two weeks before the shoe-in protest was scheduled to take place—Nike's chief of public relations, Vada Manager, made the unprecedented move of flying in from Oregon with a colleague to try to convince the center that the swoosh was a friend of the projects.

"He was working overtime to put the spins on us," says Gitelson. It didn't work. At the meeting, the center laid out three very concrete demands:

1. Those who work for Nike overseas should be paid a living wage, with independent monitoring to ensure that it is happening.
2. Nike sneakers should be sold less expensively here in America with no concessions to American workforce (i.e. no downsizing, or loss of benefits)
3. Nike should seriously re-invest in the inner city in America, especially New York City since we have been the subject of much of their advertising.[14]

Gitelson may have recognized that Nike was scared—but not *that* scared. Once it became clear that the two parties were at an impasse, the meeting turned into a scolding session as the two Nike executives were required to listen to Edenwald director Jessie Collins comparing the company's Asian sweatshops with her experience as a young girl picking cotton in the sharecropping South. Back in Alabama, she told Manager, she earned $2 a day, just like the Indonesians. "And maybe a lot of Americans can't identify with those workers' situation, but I certainly can."[15]

Vada Manager returned to Oregon defeated and the protest went off as planned, with two hundred participants from eleven community centers around New York. The kids—most of whom were between eleven and thirteen years old—hooted and hollered and dumped several clear garbage

---

[14] Minutes from 10 September meeting between Nike executives and the Edenwald-Gun Hill Neighborhood Center.

[15] Personal interview.

bags of smelly old Nikes at the feet of a line of security guards who had been brought in on special assignment to protect the sacred Nike premises. Vada Manager again flew to New York to run damage control, but there was little he could do. Local TV crews covered the event, as did an ABC news team and *The New York Times*.

In a harsh bit of bad timing for the company, the *Times* piece ran on a page facing another story about Nike. Graphically underlining the urgency of the protest, this story reported that a fourteen-year-old boy from Crown Heights had just been murdered by a fifteen-year-old boy who beat him and left him on the subway tracks with a train approaching. "Police Say Teenager Died for His Sneakers and Beeper," the headline read. And the brand of his sneakers? Air Jordans. The article quoted the killer's mother saying that her son had got mixed up with gangs because he wanted to "have nice things." A friend of the victim explained that wearing designer clothes and carrying a beeper had become a way for poor kids to "feel important."

The African-American and Latino kids outside Nike Town on Fifth Avenue—the ones swarmed by cameras and surrounded by curious onlookers—were feeling pretty important, too. Taking on Nike "toe to toe," as they said, turned out to be even more fun than wearing Nikes. With the Fox News camera pointed in his face, one of the young activists—a thirteen-year-old boy from the Bronx—stared into the lens and delivered a message to Phil Knight: "Nike, we made you. We can break you."

What is perhaps most remarkable about the Nike backlash is its durability. After four solid years in the public eye, the Nike story still has legs (so too, of course, does the Nike brand). Still, most corporate scandals are successfully faced down with a statement of "regret" and a few glossy ads of children playing happily under the offending logo. Not with Nike. The news reports, labor studies and academic research documenting the sweat behind the swoosh have yet to slow down, and Nike critics remain tireless at dissecting the steady stream of materials churned out by Nike's PR machine. They were unmoved by Phil Knight's presence on the White House Task Force on Sweatshops—despite his priceless photo op standing beside President Clinton at the Rose Garden press conference. They sliced and diced the report Nike commissioned from civil-rights leader Andrew Young, pointing out that Young completely dodged the question of whether Nike's factory wages are inhumanely exploitative, and attacking him for relying on translators provided by Nike itself when he visited the factories in Indonesia and Vietnam. As for Nike's other study-for-hire—this one by a group of

Dartmouth business students who concluded that workers in Vietnam were living the good life on less than $2 a day—well, everyone pretty much ignored that one altogether.

Finally, in May 1998, Phil Knight stepped out from behind the curtain of spin doctors and called a press conference in Washington to address his critics directly. Knight began by saying that he had been painted as a "corporate crook, the perfect corporate villain for these times." He acknowledged that his shoes "have become synonymous with slave wages, forced overtime and arbitrary abuse." Then, to much fanfare, he unveiled a plan to improve working conditions in Asia. It contained some tough new regulations on factory air quality and the use of petroleum-based chemicals. It promised to provide classes inside some Indonesian factories and promised not to hire anyone under eighteen years old in the shoe factories. But there was still nothing substantial in the plan about allowing independent outside monitors to inspect the factories, and there were no wage raises for the workers. Knight did promise, however, that Nike's contractors would no longer be permitted to appeal to the Indonesian government for a waiver on the minimum wage.

It wasn't enough. That September the San Francisco human-rights group Global Exchange, one of the company's harshest critics, released an alarming report on the status of Nike's Indonesian workers in the midst of the country's economic and political crisis. "While workers producing Nike shoes were low paid before their currency, the rupiah, began plummeting in late 1997, the dollar value of their wages has dropped from $2.47/day in 1997 to 80 cents/day in 1998." Meanwhile, the report noted that with soaring commodity prices, workers "estimated that their cost of living had gone up anywhere from 100 to 300 per cent."[114] Global Exchange called on Nike to double the wages of its Indonesian workforce, an exercise that would cost it $20 million a year—exactly what Michael Jordan is paid annually to endorse the company.

Not surprisingly, Nike did not double the wages, but it did, three weeks later, give 30 percent of the Indonesian workforce a 25 percent raise.[115] That, too, failed to silence the crowds outside the superstores, and five months later Nike came forward again, this time with what vice president of corporate responsibility Maria Eitel called "an aggressive corporate responsi-

30

---

[114] "Wages and Living Expense for Nike Workers in Indonesia," report released by Global Exchange, 23 September 1998.

[115] "Nike Raises Wages for Indonesian Workers," *Oregonian*, 16 October 1998.

bility agenda at Nike."[18] As of April 1, 1999, workers would get another 6 percent raise. The company had also opened up a Vietnamese factory near Ho Chi Minh City to outside health and safety monitors, who found conditions much improved. Dara O'Rourke of the University of California at Berkeley reported that the factory had "implemented important changes over the past 18 months which appear to have significantly reduced worker exposures to toxic solvents, adhesives and other chemicals." What made the report all the more remarkable was that O'Rourke's inspection was a genuinely independent one: in fact, less than two years earlier, he had enraged the company by leaking a report conducted by Ernst & Young that showed that Nike was ignoring widespread violations at that same factory.

O'Rourke's findings weren't all glowing. There were still persistent problems with air quality, factory overheating and safety gear—and he had visited only the one factory.[19] As well, Nike's much-heralded 6 percent pay raise for Indonesian workers still left much to be desired; it amounted to an increase of one cent an hour and, with inflation and currency fluctuation, only brought wages to about half of what Nike paychecks were worth before the economic crisis. Even so, these were significant gestures coming from a company that two years earlier was playing the role of the powerless global shopper, claiming that contractors alone had the authority to set wages and make the rules.

The resilience of the Nike campaign in the face of the public-relations onslaught is persuasive evidence that invasive marketing, coupled with worker abandonment, strikes a wide range of people from different walks of life as grossly unfair and unsustainable. Moreover, many of those people are not interested in letting Nike off the hook simply because this formula has become the standard one for capitalism-as-usual. On the contrary, there seems to be a part of the public psyche that likes kicking the most macho and extreme of all the sporting-goods companies in the shins—I mean *really* likes it. Nike's critics have shown that they don't want this story to be brushed under the rug with a reassuring bit of corporate PR; they want it out in the open, where they can keep a close eye on it.

In large part, this is because Nike's critics know the company's sweatshop scandals are not the result of a series of freak accidents: they know

---

[18] "Nike to Improve Minimum Monthly Wage Package for Indonesian Workers," Nike press release, 19 March 1999.

[19] Steven Greenhouse, "Nike Critic Praises Gains in Air Quality at Vietnam Factory," *New York Times*, 12 March 1999.

that the criticisms leveled at Nike apply to all the brand-based shoe companies contracting out to a global maze of firms. But rather than this serving as a justification, Nike—as the market leader—has become a lightning rod for this broader resentment. It has been latched on to as the essential story of the extremes of the current global economy: the disparities between those who profit from Nike's success and those who are exploited by it are so gaping that a child could understand what is wrong with this picture and indeed it is children and teenagers who most readily do.

So, when does the total boycott of Nike products begin? Not soon, apparently. A cursory glance around any city in the world shows that the swoosh is still ubiquitous; some athletes still tattoo it on their navels, and plenty of high-school students still deck themselves out in the coveted gear. But at the same time, there can be little doubt that the millions of dollars that Nike has saved in labor costs over the years are beginning to bite back, and take a toll on its bottom line. "We didn't think that the Nike situation would be as bad as it seems to be," said Nikko stock analyst Tim Finucane in *The Wall Street Journal* in March 1998.[20] Wall Street really had no choice but to turn on the company that had been its darling for so many years. Despite the fact that Asia's plummeting currencies meant that Nike's labor costs in Indonesia, for instance, were a quarter of what they were before the crash, the company was still suffering. Nike's profits were down, orders were down, stock prices were *way* down, and after an average annual growth of 34 percent since 1995, quarterly earnings were suddenly down by 70 percent. By the third quarter, which ended in February 1999, Nike's profits were once again up 70 percent—but by the company's own account, the recovery was not the result of rebounding sales but rather of Nike's decision to cut jobs and contracts. In fact, Nike's revenues and future orders were down in 1999 for the second year in a row.[21]

35   Nike has blamed its financial problems on everything *but* the human-rights campaign. The Asian currency crisis was the reason Nikes weren't selling well in Japan and South Korea; or it was because Americans were buying "brown shoes" (walking shoes and hiking boots) as opposed to big white sneakers. But the brown-shoe excuse rang hollow. Nike makes plenty of brown shoes—it has a line of hiking boots, and it owns Cole Haan (and

---

[20]   Shanthi Kalathil, "Being Tied to Nike Affects Share Price of Yue Yuen," *Wall Street Journal*, 25 March 1998.

[21]   "Third quarter brings 70 percent increase in net income for sneaker giant," Associated Press, 19 March 1999.

recently saved millions by closing down the Cole Haan factory in Portland, Maine, and moving production to Mexico and Brazil).[22] More to the point, Adidas staged a massive comeback during the very year that Nike was free-falling. In the quarter when Nike nose-dived, Adidas sales were up 42 percent, its net income was up 48 percent, to $255 million, and its stock price had tripled in two years. The German company, as we have seen, turned its fortunes around by copying Nike's production structure and all but Xeroxing its approach to marketing and sponsorships. In 1997–98, Adidas even redesigned its basketball shoes so they looked just like Nikes: big, white and ultra high tech. But unlike Nikes, they sold briskly. So much for the brown-shoe theory.

Over the years Nike has tried dozens of tactics to silence the cries of its critics, but the most ironic by far has been the company's desperate attempt to hide behind its product. "We're not political activists. We are a footwear manufacturer," said Nike spokeswoman Donna Gibbs, when the sweatshop scandal first began to erupt.[23] A footwear manufacturer? This from the company that made a concerted decision in the mid-eighties not to be about boring corporeal stuff like footwear—and certainly nothing as crass as manufacturing. Nike wanted to be about sports, Knight told us, it wanted to be about the idea of sports, then the idea of transcendence through sports; then it wanted to be about self-empowerment, women's rights, racial equality. It wanted its stores to be temples, its ads a religion, its customers a nation, its workers a tribe. After taking us all on such a branded ride, to turn around and say, "Don't look at us, we just make shoes" rings laughably hollow.

Nike was the most inflated of all the balloon brands, and the bigger it grew, the louder it popped.

(2000)

---

[22] "Cole Haan Joins Ranks of Shoe Companies Leaving Maine," Associated Press, 23 April 1999.

[23] Zusman, "Editor's Notebook."

QUESTIONS:

1. What is a "balloon brand"?

2. Summarize in no more than two paragraphs the case against Nike as Klein presents it.

3. In Klein's view, why is it particularly pernicious for Nike to have drawn on the ethos of black inner-city culture in shaping the image of its brand?

4. To what extent does it trouble you to buy products that were made under exploitive conditions? To what degree are your purchasing decisions likely to be altered by information such as that provided by Klein?

5. Legible clothing makes a statement about the values and self-image of the wearer. But it also provides free advertising. Do you wear legible clothing? Why?

6. How would you describe the tone of Klein's writing? With particular reference to paragraphs 26–28, comment on how this tone is created.

7. Klein refers elsewhere in her book to the loss of "unmarketed space" in modern Western society. Comment on this phenomenon as you perceive it.

MARGARET ATWOOD

FIRST JOB

In this short piece written for The New Yorker, *a famous poet and novelist tells the story of her first "real job."*

~~

I'll pass over the mini-jobs of adolescence—the summer-camp stints that were more like getting paid for having fun. I'll pass over, too, the self-created pin-money generators—the puppet shows put on for kids at office parties, the serigraph posters turned out on the Ping-Pong table—and turn to my first real job. By "real job," I mean one that had nothing to do with friends of my parents or parents of my friends but was obtained in the adult manner, by looking through the ads in newspapers and going in to be interviewed—one for which I was entirely unsuited, and that I wouldn't have done except for the money. I was surprised when I got it, underpaid while doing it, and frustrated in the performance of it, and these qualities have remained linked, for me, to the ominous word "job."

The year was 1962, the place was Toronto. It was summer, and I was faced with the necessity of earning the difference between my scholarship for the next year and what it would cost me to live. The job was in the coffee shop of a small hotel on Avenue Road; it is now in the process of being torn down, but at that time it was a clean, well-lighted place, with booths along one side and a counter—possibly marble—down the other. The booths were served by a waitressing pro who lipsticked outside the lines, and who thought I was a mutant. My job would be serving things at the counter—coffee I would pour, toast I would create from bread, milkshakes I would whip up in the obstetrical stainless-steel device provided. ("Easy as pie," I was told.) I would also be running the customers' money through the cash register—an opaque machine with buttons to be pushed, little drawers that shot in and out, and a neurotic system of locks.

I said I had never worked a cash register before. This delighted the manager, a plump, unctuous character out of some novel I hadn't yet read. He said the cash register, too, was easy as pie, and I would catch on to it in no time, as I was a smart girl with an M.A. He said I should go and get myself a white dress.

I didn't know what he meant by "white dress." I bought the first thing I could find on sale, a nylon afternoon number with daisies appliquéd onto the bodice. The waitress told me this would not do: I needed a dress like hers, a *uniform*. ("How dense can you be?" I overheard her saying.) I got the uniform, but I had to go through the first day in my nylon daisies.

5   This first humiliation set the tone. The coffee was easy enough—I just had to keep the Bunn filled—and the milkshakes were possible; few people wanted them anyway. The sandwiches and deep-fried shrimp were made at the back: all I had to do was order them over the intercom and bin the leftovers.

But the cash register was perverse. Its drawers would pop open for no reason, or it would ring eerily when I swore I was nowhere near it; or it would lock itself shut, and the queue of customers waiting to pay would lengthen and scowl as I wrestled and sweated. I kept expecting to be fired for incompetence, but the manager chortled more than ever. Occasionally, he would bring some man in a suit to view me. "She's got an M.A.," he would say, in a proud but pitying voice, and the two of them would stare at me and shake their heads.

An ex-boyfriend discovered my place of employment, and would also come to stare and shake his head, ordering a single coffee, taking an hour to drink it, leaving me a sardonic nickel tip. The Greek short-order cook decided I would be the perfect up-front woman for the restaurant he wanted to open: he would marry me and do the cooking, I would speak English to the clientele and work—was he mad?—the cash register. He divulged his bank balance, and demanded to meet my father so the two of them could close the deal. When I declined, he took to phoning me over the intercom to whisper blandishments, and to plying me with deep-fried shrimp. A girl as scrawny as myself, he pointed out, was unlikely to get such a good offer again.

Then the Shriners hit town, took over the hotel, and began calling for buckets of ice, or for doctors because they'd had heart attacks: too much tricycle-riding in the hot sun was felling them in herds. I couldn't handle the responsibility, the cash register had betrayed me once too often, and the short-order cook was beginning to sing Frank Sinatra songs to me. I gave notice.

Only when I'd quit did the manager reveal his true stratagem: they'd wanted someone inept as me because they suspected their real cashier of skimming the accounts, a procedure I was obviously too ignorant to ever figure out. "Too stunned," as the waitress put it. She was on the cashier's side, and had me fingered as a stoolie all along.

(2001)

Questions:

1. Describe as concisely as you can Atwood's tone in this essay.

2. What are some of the sources of humor in this piece? To what extent do you think it would be amusing to readers unfamiliar with North American culture?

3. Say as much as you can about the unusual use of words in the following phrases in paragraph 2; what is going on in each case, and what effect does it have on the reader?

   "lipsticked outside the lines"
   "toast I would create from bread"
   "an opaque machine"

4. Comment on the choice of the verb "pointed out" in the last sentence of paragraph 7.

5. Write a short and light-hearted essay about a job you have worked at; in writing it try out some of the same stylistic devices that Atwood employs.

BIOGRAPHICAL NOTES

～～

ADDAMS, JANE (1860–1935)

American reformer and founder in 1889 of Hull-House, a Chicago settlement-house. Through her activities here, she created a strong social reform movement and was instrumental in the passage of several child labour and education laws. Written works include *Democracy and Social Ethics* (1902), *Twenty Years at Hull-House* (1910), and *A New Conscience and an Ancient Evil* (1912). In recognition of her reform efforts, Addams was awarded the 1931 Nobel Peace Prize.

ATWOOD, MARGARET (1939–)

Atwood's collection of poetry *The Circle Game* won the 1966 Governor General's Award, and her critical book *Survival: A Thematic Guide to Canadian Literature* (1972) led to the entrenchment of Canadian Literature as a legitimate field of study in Canadian universities. Despite these lofty achievements, Atwood is perhaps best known for her novels, including *The Edible Woman* (1969), *The Handmaid's Tale* (1985) and *The Blind Assassin*, which won the 2000 Booker Prize.

BACON, FRANCIS (1561–1626)

English statesman and philosopher. During the reign of Queen Elizabeth I, Bacon was a member of British Parliament, and advanced to the position of Lord Chancellor during the reign of King James I. Bacon lost political favour in 1621, when he was convicted of accepting bribes and was imprisoned for a short duration. Bacon's written works include *Essays* (1597), *The Advancement of Learning* (1605) and *Novum Organum* (1620).

BARTHES, ROLAND (1915–1980)

French social and literary critic known for his writings on semiotics and structuralism. Written works include *Mythologies* (1957), *Elements of Semiology* (1967), *The Empire of Signs* (1970) and *The Luminous Room* (1980).

BENNETT, JONATHAN (1930–)

Bennett's wide-ranging research has included work in the history of philosophy, philosophical psychology, and the philosophy of language. His books include *Kant's Analytic* (1966), *Locke, Berkeley, Hume: Central Themes* (1971) and *The Act Itself* (1995).

BRAND, DIONNE (1953–)

Canadian author, film maker and social activist known for her work in Canadian Black women's history and in fighting against racism. Written works include *Chronicles of the Hostile Sun* (1984), *Another Place, Not Here* (1996), and *A Land to Light On* (1997).

BROYARD, ANATOLE (1920–1990)

An essayist and book reviewer for the *New York Times*, Broyard was also a writer of fiction. *Intoxicated by My Illness and Other Writings on Life and Death* was written mainly in the period between being diagnosed with metastatic prostate cancer in 1989, and his death the following year.

CAMERON, STEVIE (1943–)

Former Editor-in-Chief of *Elm Street* magazine and a former host of *The Fifth Estate* for the Canadian Broadcasting Corporation. Written works include *On The Take: Crime, Corruption and Greed in the Mulroney Years* (1995) and *The Blue Trust: The Lawyer, The Author, The Wife and Her Money* (1999).

CAVENDISH, MARGARET (DUCHESS OF NEWCASTLE) (1623–1673)

The first English woman to write mainly for publication, she was both widely criticized and celebrated for her public disregard of social and literary conventions, particularly with regard to her views on the education of women. Works include *Poems and Fancies* (1653), *Philosophical and Physical Opinions* (1656), *Observations upon Experimental Philosophy* (1666), and a work of science fiction entitled *The Description of a New World, called The Blazing World* (1668).

Copway, George (1818–1863)

Native-American preacher and writer on Indian affairs, Copway was among the first Native-Americans to publish an autobiography. Books include *The life, history and travels of Kah-ge-ga-gah-bowh (George Copway): a young Indian Chief of the Ojebwa nation* (1847), *The Ojibway conquest, a tale of the Northwest by Kah-ge-ga-gah-bowh* (1850), and *The traditional history and characteristic sketches of the Ojibway nation* (1850).

Darnton, Robert C. (1939–)

Professor of European History at Princeton University specializing in eighteenth-century French history. His books include *The Great Cat Massacre and Other Episodes in French Cultural History* (1984), *The Kiss of Lamourette: Reflections in Cultural History* (1989) and *The Corpus of Clandestine Literature in France, 1769–1789* (1995).

Darwin, Charles (1809–1882)

Born the son of an English doctor, Darwin himself attended medical school at the University of Edinburgh from 1825–1827. During his later service as a naturalist aboard *H M S Beagle*, 1831–1836, he observed the similarities and differences of various species, and was led to question the established position that species remained as God had first created them. Darwin delayed publishing his theory, but eventually did so when he published *Origin of Species* in 1859.

Devlin, Tim (1954–)

Tim Devlin has more than twenty years experience as a journalist and broadcaster, with a special focus on social activism. He has recently served as Director of TRUCK, an artist-run gallery in Calgary, Alberta, and is currently at work on his first novel, which will examine the war on drugs.

DIDION, JOAN (1934–)

Didion is an American novelist, essayist, journalist and screenwriter known for her minimalist style. Her novels include *A Book of Common Prayer* (1977), *Democracy* (1984) and *The Last Thing He Wanted* (1996). Her novel *Play It as It Lays* (1970) was nominated for a National Book Award. Didion's essay compilations include *The White Album* (1979) and *After Henry* (1992).

DILLARD, ANNIE (1945–)

American essayist and poet and recipient of the Pulitzer Prize for *Pilgrim at Tinker Creek* (1974). Other works include *Tickets for a Prayer Wheel* (1974), *Teaching a Stone to Talk* (1982), *The Writing Life* (1989), *The Annie Dillard Reader* (1994) and *Mornings Like This: Found Poems* (1995).

DONNE, JOHN (1572–1631)

Donne is widely considered to be the greatest of the metaphysical poets, and his poems are characterized by the use of elaborate conceits in examination of man's mortality and capacity to love. He was also a priest at St. Paul's Cathedral, and his celebrated sermons led him to be perhaps the most famous preacher of his age.

DU BOIS, W.E.B. (1868–1963)

Du Bois was an African-American educator and historian, the founder of the Niagra Movement and the National Association for the Advancement of Colored People, and the editor of the NAACP journal *Crisis* from 1910 to 1934. Written works include *The Philadelphia Negro* (1899) and *The Souls of Black Folk* (1903).

DYER, GWYNNE (1943–)

Gwynne Dyer is a London-based independent journalist whose articles are published in 45 countries, as well as a broadcaster, author and film maker. Dyer was producer and host of CBC Television's seven-part series *War*, and is the collaborative author (with Tina Viljoan) of *The Defense of Canada* (1980).

ELIOT, GEORGE (1819–1880)

Eliot (born Mary Anne Evans) was an English writer best known for her novels, which include *Adam Bede* (1859), *The Mill on the Floss* (1860), *Silas Marner* (1861), *Felix Holt* (1866) and *Middlemarch* (1871). One hundred years after her death, Eliot was memorialized in Westminster Abbey's celebrated Poet's Corner.

FLANNER, JANET (1892–1978)

Although an American, Flanner lived in Paris for most of her life. As a journalist, she provided reports and commentary on European culture and political affairs for five decades. Some of her most famous work includes her "Letter from Paris" column for *The New Yorker* and her important articles on Hitler's rise to power.

FRANKLIN, URSULA M. (1921–)

Franklin, an experimental physicist and University Professor Emeritus at the University of Toronto, is the author of many scholarly articles and several books, including *The Real World of Technology* (1989). She has served on both the National Research Council and the Science Council of Canada and is the recipient of more than ten honorary degrees.

GATES (JR.), HENRY LOUIS (1950–)

American scholar specializing in African-American literature and culture. Books include *Figures in Black: Words, Signs and the "Racial Self"* (1987), *The Signifying Monkey: A Theory of African-American Literary Criticism* (1988) and *Thirteen Ways of Looking at a Black Man* (1997). Gates is currently head of Afro-American Studies at Harvard University.

GLADWELL, MALCOLM (1963–)

Malcolm Gladwell was born in England and raised in Canada. Since 1996 he has been a staff writer for *The New Yorker* magazine, and is the author of *The Tipping Point: How Little Things Can Make a Big Difference* (2000).

Gopnik, Adam (1956–)

Adam Gopnik has been a contributor to *The New Yorker* since 1986. He has received the National Magazine Award for Essay and Criticism as well as the George Polk Award for Magazine Reporting. He is also a regular broadcaster for the Canadian Broadcasting Corporation, and is the author of *Paris to the Moon* (2000).

Gould, Stephen Jay (1941–)

Paleontologist, professor of geology and author of several books including *Ever Since Darwin: Reflections in Natural History* (1977), *The Panda's Thumb: More Reflections in Natural History* (1980) and *The Flamingo's Smile* (1985). In opposition to the gradualist theory of evolution, Gould originated the "punctuated equilibrium" theory, which proposes that the evolution of a species occurs through rapid changes in isolated populations, followed by long stable periods.

Gourevitch, Philip (1961–)

A staff writer for *The New Yorker*, Philip Gourevitch was initially sent by that magazine to Rwanda in 1995 to study the aftermath of the genocide of the Tutsi minority. He stayed nine months in Rwanda and in neighbouring Congo, and published the book *We Wish To Inform You That Tomorrow We Will Be Killed With Our Families* (1998).

Graham, W.H. (1912–1997)

Born and raised in Manitoba, William Hugh Graham distinguished himself as a soldier and Staff Officer in World War II and later as Chairman of the Board of the National Theatre School. He is the author of *The Tiger of Canada West: The Biography of William Dunlop* (1962) and *Greenbank* (1988), which won The Canadian Historical Association Best Regional History Award.

Grealy, Lucy (1963–)

Lucy Grealy is an award-winning poet who has attended the Iowa Writer's Workshop. Born in Ireland, she grew up in New York and currently lives in New York City, where she teaches writing at Sarah Lawrence and Amherst colleges.

Harris, Judith Rich (1938–)

American author of numerous articles on the subject of childhood development. Senior author of *The Child* (1984) and *Infant and Child* (1992) and author of *The Nurture Assumption: Why Children Turn Out the Way They Do* (1998).

Harris, Marvin (1927–)

American anthropologist and theoretician known for his research in cultural materialism. Author of *The Rise of Anthropological Theory* (1968), *Cannibals and Kings: The Origins of Cultures* (1977) and *Cultural Anthropology* (1983).

Hurka, Thomas (1952–)

Educated at the University of Toronto and Oxford University, Hurka has been a professor in the Department of Philosophy at the University of Calgary since 1979. In 2002 he will take up an appointment at the University of Toronto. He is the author of *Perfectionism* (1993) and *Virtue, Vice and Value* (2001). He is a frequent radio and television commentator and a regular contributor to *The Globe and Mail* newspaper.

Johnson, Samuel (1709–1784)

English writer, lexicographer and publisher of the periodicals *The Rambler* (1750–1752) and *The Idler* (1758–1760). A prolific writer, Johnson's major contributions to eighteenth-century literature were his *Dictionary of the English Language* (1755) and *The Lives of the English Poets* (1781). Johnson is the subject of one of English literature's most significant biographies, James Boswell's *Life of Samuel Johnson* (1791).

Kehoe, Alice Beck (1936–)

Alice Beck Kehoe, a professor of anthropology at Marquette University in Milwaukee, is the author of *The Ghost Dance: Ethnohistory and Revitalization* (1989) and of *North American Indians: A Comprehensive Account* (1992).

King (Jr.), Martin Luther (1929–1968)

African-American minister and leader of the American civil-rights movement in the 1950s and 1960s. King received the 1964 Nobel Peace Prize for his leadership of nonviolent civil-rights demonstrations. A charismatic speaker and author, King's books include *Stride Toward Freedom* (1958), *Why We Can't Wait* (1964) and *Where Do We Go From Here: Chaos or Community?* (1967). King was assassinated by James Earl Ray in Memphis, Tenn.

KLEIN, NAOMI (1970–)

Klein was born in Montreal and now makes her home in Toronto. She is a journalist whose work has appeared in such magazines as *The Village Voice, The Nation*, and *Ms.* Her book *No Logo: Taking Aim at the Brand Bullies* (2000) has been translated into 13 languages.

LAI, LARISSA (1967–)

Larissa Lai is a Vancouver-based writer and cultural organizer. Her novel *When Fox is a Thousand* (Press Gang, 1995) was nominated for the Chapters/Books in Canada First Novel Award in 1996. In 1997–98 she was the Markin-Flanagan Canadian Writer-in-Residence at the University of Calgary. In 1999 she organized a national touring project, "Writers for Change."

LAURENCE, MARGARET (1926–1987)

Raised in Manitoba, Margaret Laurence lived in Ghana for some years in the 1950s before settling in Ontario. Her novels include *A Jest of God* (1966) and *The Diviners* (1974), both of which received a Governor General's Award, although *The Stone Angel* (1965) is often regarded as her finest novel. Her memoir, *Dance on the Earth*, appeared posthumously in 1989.

LEACOCK, STEPHEN (1869–1944)

Born in England and raised in Canada, Leacock earned a PhD in Economics at the University of Chicago, and then worked as a professor of economics at McGill University; his writings on political economy were widely read by academics and the general public. He began to publish humourous stories and sketches in 1899, and achieved enormous popularity with the publication of the collections *Literary Lapses* (1910) and *Sunshine Sketches of a Little Town* (1912).

Lebowitz, Fran (1950–)

American journalist known for her satirical observations of urban living and irreverent humor. In addition to numerous magazine contributions, she is the author of *Metropolitan Life* (1978), *Social Studies* (1981) and the children's book *Mr. Chas and Lisa Sue Meet the Pandas* (1994).

Lyell, Sir Charles (1797–1875)

Lyell was a Scottish geologist and developer of uniformitarianism (the theory that changes in the earth's form result from gradual and continual natural processes). Author of *Principles of Geology* (1830), Lyell and his theories influenced the work of Charles Darwin. Lyell is also considered a founder of stratigraphy, a method of classifying layers in the earth's surface.

Martin, Emily (1944–)

Anthropology and ethnography professor at Princeton University. Her work studies the effects that race, gender and class have on the historical and ethnographic study of science and medicine as forms of knowledge about the body and the world. Her books include *The Cult of the Dead in a Chinese Village* (1973) and *The Anthropology of Taiwanese Society* (1981).

Martineau, Harriet (1802–1876)

English writer, social critic and feminist. Her written works include *Poor Laws and Paupers* (1833), *Society in America* (1837), and *Letters on the Laws of Man's Nature and Development* (1851). A friend of economist Thomas Malthus, and writers George Eliot and Thomas Carlyle, Martineau was frequently the subject of controversy due to her public views on various social and religious subjects.

Marx, Groucho (Julius) (1895–1977)

Born in New York City, Groucho and his brothers appeared in vaudeville and films including *Animal Crackers* (1930), *Duck Soup* (1933) and *A Night at the Opera* (1935). Groucho's written works include *Groucho and Me* (1959) and *Memoirs of a Shaggy Lover* (1964).

MILGRAM, STANLEY (1933–1984)

Milgram is regarded as one of the most important psychologists of the twentieth century, based mainly on his human obedience experiments at Yale University (1961–62). He is also noted for the small-world method, which became the inspiration for John Guare's *Six Degrees of Separation*, and for an experiment on the effects of televised antisocial behaviour. His books include *Obedience to Authority: An Experimental View* (1983).

MOMADAY, N(AVARRE) SCOTT (1934–)

Born in Oklahoma, Momaday was educated at Augusta Military Academy, The University of New Mexico, and Stanford University. His novel *House Made Dawn* (1968) won a Pulitzer prize and was followed the next year by *The Way to Rainy Mountain*, a book which combines reflections on native history and folklore with Momaday's own reminiscences. Momaday has taught at the University of Arizona since 1982.

DE MONTAIGNE, MICHEL EYQUEM (1533–1592)

French thinker and developer of the essay as a literary form. Montaigne's essays can be found in three volumes entitled *Essais* (vols. I & II, 1580, vol. III, 1588). Montaigne also published a translation of Spanish theologian Raymond the Second's *Theologia Naturalis* (1569).

MUKHERJEE, BHARATI (1940–)

Indian-born novelist and short story writer known for her observations of Indian culture and the experiences of immigrants. Novels include *The Tiger's Daughter* (1972), *Wife* (1975), *Jasmine* (1989) and *The Holder of the World* (1993). Other works include *The Middleman and Other Stories* (1988) and *Wanting America: Selected Stories* (1995).

MUMFORD, LEWIS (1895–1990)

Through the middle decades of the twentieth century, Lewis Mumford was one of the most articulate American social critics. In a wide variety of articles and in books such as *The Culture of Cities* (1938) and *The Condition of Man* (1944) he argued forcefully against the dehumanizing tendencies of modern technological society.

Munro, Alice (1931–)

Award-winning Canadian writer known primarily for short stories characteristically containing themes of interest to women. Her short story collections include the Governor General's Award winning *Dance of the Happy Shades* (1968), and *Who Do You Think You Are?* (1978), as well as *The Moons of Jupiter* (1982) and *The Love of a Good Woman* (1998).

Ngugi, wa Thiong'o (1938–)

Ngugi is East Africa's leading novelist and social critic. Originally named James Thiong'o Ngugi, the author changed his name in reaction to the effects of colonialism in Africa. His novels include *Weep Not, Child* (1964), *The River Between* (1965), *Petals of Blood* (1977) and *Devil on the Cross* (1980). Other works include *Homecoming* (1972), *Moving the Centre* (1993) and *Decolonising the Mind: The Politics of Language in African Literature* (1986).

Nowlan, Alden (1933–1983)

Nowlan was a Canadian poet, fiction writer, playwright and journalist, whose writing often reflects his interest in ordinary citizens. Nowlan, who received only a grade four education, won the Governor General's Award for his collection of poetry *Bread, Wine and Salt* (1967), and then spent the remaining fifteen years of his life as the writer-in-residence at the University of New Brunswick.

Orwell, George (1903–1950)

Pseudonym of English political journalist and satirist Eric Blair; served with the Indian Imperial Police in Burma, 1922–27, fought with the Republicans in Spain, describing the experience in *Homage to Catalonia* (1938); author of *Animal Farm* (1945) and *Nineteen Eighty-Four* (1949).

Putnam, Robert D. (1941–)

Professor of American politics, international relations and public policy at Harvard University. Author of *Double-Edged Diplomacy: International Bargaining and Domestic Politics* (1993), *Making Democracy Work: Civic Traditions in Modern Italy* (1993) and *Bowling Alone: America's Declining Social Capital* (1995).

Rich, Adrienne (1929–)

American poet and essayist best-known for her written exploration of women's issues and women's roles in society. She is the author of nearly twenty volumes of poetry, including *Diving into the Wreck* (1974), which was awarded the National Book Award, *Dark Fields of the Republic: Poems 1991–1995* (1995), and *Midnight Salvage: Poems 1995–1998* (1999). Her works of prose include *Of Woman Born* (1976; 1986) and *What is Found There* (1993).

Royko, Mike (1932–1997)

Syndicated columnist for the *Chicago Tribune*, known for his sympathy for the working-class, Royko won the Pulitzer Prize in 1972. He was also the author of an unauthorized biography of Mayor Richard J. Daley (1971) and collections of his own written work.

Rybczynski, Witold (1943–)

Rybczynski is a Scottish-born architect and planner. His written works include *Home: A Short History of an Idea* (1986), *The Most Beautiful House in the World* (1989) and *City Life: Urban Expectations in a New World* (1995).

Showalter, Elaine (1941–)

Showalter, a professor in the English department of Princeton University, is one of the founders of contemporary feminist criticism. Her works include *A Literature of Their Own* (1977), *The Female Malady: Women, Madness, and English Culture 1830–1980* (1985) and *Hystories: Historical Epidemics and Modern Culture* (1997).

Singer, Peter (1946–)

Singer is a controversial Australian bioethicist with a utilitarian (the idea that an action is ethically correct if it satisfies those affected and is best for the greatest number of people) approach to ethical issues involved in genetic engineering, abortion, euthanasia and embryo experimentation. Singer has authored several books including *Animal Liberation* (1975), *Practical Ethics* (1979) and *How Are We to Live?* (1993).

Swift, Jonathan (1667–1745)

Swift was an Irish poet, fiction writer, essayist and political pamphleteer, best known for his satire aimed at political hypocrisy, literary pretension and the folly of human society. Key works include *Tale of a Tub* (1704), *A Modest Proposal* (1729) and *Gulliver's Travels* (1726).

Thoreau, Henry David (1817–1862)

American naturalist and writer known for his individualist and transcendental philosophies. His most popular works include *A Week on the Concord and Merrimack Rivers* (1849) and *Walden; or, Life in the Woods* (1854). His posthumously published works include *Excursions* (1863), *Cape Cod* (1865), and *Faith in a Seed* (1993).

Twain, Mark (1835–1910)

Born Samuel Langhorne Clemens, Twain grew up in Missouri, and at 22 became a Mississippi river pilot. Five years later he began writing for a living, and was soon publishing humorous tales and delivering public lectures. After he married and moved to Hartford in 1870, Twain began to write the works for which he is now most famous, including *The Adventures of Tom Sawyer* (1876), *Life on the Mississippi* (1883) and *The Adventures of Huckleberry Finn* (1884).

White, E.B. (1899–1985)

White was a journalist, essayist, and a regular contributor to *The New Yorker* magazine for over half a century. He is perhaps best known as the author of the renowned children's books *Stuart Little* (1945) and *Charlotte's Web* (1952).

Wilde, Oscar (1854–1900)

Born and raised in Ireland, Wilde attended Oxford University and then settled in London. His works include the novel *The Picture of Dorian Gray* (1890) and the plays: *Lady Windermere's Fan*, *A Woman of No Importance*, *An Ideal Husband*, and *The Importance of Being Ernest* (all 1892–1895). In 1895 he was tried, convicted, and imprisoned on charges of homosexual behaviour. After his release from Reading Jail, he left England for France, never to return.

WILLIAMS, RAYMOND (1921–1988)

Prodigious Welsh author and pioneer in the field of cultural studies, Williams originated the concept of "cultural materialism." His written works include *Culture and Society* (1958), *The Long Revolution* (1961) and *Marxism and Literature* (1977).

WILSON, J. TUZO (1908–1993)

Wilson was a Canadian geologist and geophysicist whose research in plate tectonics helped revolutionize geophysical science. A professor of geophysics at the University of Toronto from 1946 to 1974, Wilson then became Director of the Ontario Science Center. Major publications include *A Revolution in Earth Science* (1967) and *Continents Adrift and Continents Aground* (1977). There is a mountain range in Antarctica named for him.

WOLF, SUSAN (1952–)

Wolf was a professor at Harvard University and the University of Maryland before becoming Chair of the Department of Philosophy at Johns Hopkins University. She is the author *Freedom Within Reason* (1990) and numerous articles on ethics and the philosophy of mind, which include "Morality and Partiality," "Two Levels of Pluralism," "Self-Interest and Interest in Selves," "Moral Saints" and "Asymmetrical Freedom."

WOLLSTONECRAFT, MARY (1759–1797)

Wollstonecraft was an English writer and early advocate of women's rights, best known for her feminist work *A Vindication of the Rights of Woman* (1792). She was married to English philosopher William Godwin and was the mother of *Frankenstein* author Mary Wollstonecraft Shelley.

WOOLF, VIRGINIA (1882–1941)

Woolf was an innovative and influential English writer, whose novels include *Mrs. Dalloway* (1925), *To the Lighthouse* (1927) and *The Waves* (1931). She was also a literary critic, and an early advocate of feminism, most notably in her book *A Room of One's Own* (1929).

ACKNOWLEDGEMENTS

Margaret Atwood, "First Job," from *The New Yorker Magazine*, April 23 & 30, 2001. Copyright © 2001 by Margaret Atwood.

Roland Barthes, "The World of Wrestling," from *Mythologies* by Roland Barthes, translated by Annette Lavers. Copyright © 1972 by Roland Barthes.

Jonathan Bennett, "The Conscience of Huckleberry Finn." Originally published in *Philosophy* 49, April 1974. Copyright © 1974 by the Royal Institute of Philosophy. Reprinted with the permission of Cambridge University Press.

Dionne Brand, "On Poetry," from *Bread Out of Stone* by Dionne Brand. Copyright © 1994 by Dionne Brand.

Anatole Broyard, "Intoxicated by My Illness." Originally published in *The New York Times Magazine*, Nov. 12, 1989. Copyright © 1989 by The New York Times Company. Reprinted by permission.

Stevie Cameron, "Our Daughters, Ourselves," from *The Montreal Massacre*, edited by Louise Malett and Marie Chalouh, translated by Marlene Wildeman. Originally appeared in *The Globe and Mail*, December 8, 1989. Reprinted by permission of Women's Press, www.womenspress.ca.

Robert Darnton, "Workers Revolt: The Great Cat Massacre of the Rue Saint-Séverin," from *The Great Cat Massacre and Other Essays in French Cultural History* by Robert Darnton. Copyright ©1984 by Basic Books, Inc. Reprinted by permission of Basic Books, a member of Perseus Books, L.L.C.

Tim Devlin, "Does Working For Welfare Work?" Originally published in *Alberta Views*, May/June 2000. Reprinted by permission of the author.

Joan Didion, "On Going Home," from *Slouching Towards Bethlehem* by Joan Didion. Copyright © 1966, 1968, renewed 1996 by Joan Didion. Reprinted by permission of Farrar, Strauss and Giroux, LLC.

Annie Dillard, "Terwilliger Bunts One," from *An American Childhood* by Annie Dillard. Copyright © 1987 by Annie Dillard. Reprinted by permission of HarperCollins Publishers, Inc.

Gwynne Dyer, "How People Power Topples the Tyrant." Originally published in *The Globe and Mail*, August 28, 1999. Copyright © 1999 by Gwynne Dyer. Reprinted by permission of the author.

Janet Flanner, "Mme. Marie Curie." Originally published in *The New Yorker Magazine*. Reprinted by permission. "Pablo Picasso," from *Janet Flanner's World: Uncollected Writings 1932-1975*, edited by Irving Drutman. Copyright © 1979 by Natalia Danesi Murray.

Ursula Franklin, "Silence and the Notion of the Commons." Originally published in *Musicworks* 59, Summer 1994. Copyright © 1994 by Ursula Franklin. Reprinted by permission of the author.

Henry Louis Gates, Jr., "The Passing of Anatole Broyard," from *Thirteen Ways of Looking at a Black Man* by Henry Louis Gates, Jr. Copyright © 1997 by Henry Louis Gates, Jr. Originally published in the *New Yorker Magazine*. Used by permission of Random House, Inc.

Malcolm Gladwell, "The Sports Taboo: Why Blacks Are Like Boys and Whites Are Like Girls." Originally published in *The New Yorker Magazine*, May 19, 1997. Copyright © 1997 by Malcolm Gladwell. Reprinted by permission of the author.

Adam Gopnik, "Saving the Balzar," from *The New Yorker Magazine* 74:22, August 3, 1998. Copyright © 1998 by Adam Gopnik.

Stephen Jay Gould, "Entropic Homogeneity Isn't Why No One Hits .400 Any More." Originally published in *Discover Magazine*, August, 1986. Reprinted by permission of the author.

Philip Gourevitch, "We Wish To Inform You That Tomorrow We Will Be Killed With Our Families," from *We Wish To Inform You That Tomorrow We Will Be Killed With Our Families* by Philip Gourevitch. Copyright © 1998 by Philip Gourevitch.

W.H. Graham, "Four Farms in the Tenth of Reach," from *Greenbank* by W.H. Graham. Copyright © 1988 by W.H. Graham, renewed by Hugh Graham, Heir to W.H. Graham. Reprinted by permission of Hugh Graham.

Lucy Grealy, "Fear Itself" from *Autobiography of a Face* by Lucy Grealy. Copyright © 1994 by Lucy Grealy. Reprinted by permission of Houghton Mifflin Co. All rights reserved.

Judith Rich Harris, "Where Is the Child's Environment? A Group Socialization Theory of Development." Originally published in *Psychological Review* 102:3, 1995. Copyright © 1995 by the American Psychological Association. Adapted by permission of the author.

Marvin Harris, "Pig Lovers and Pig Haters," from *Cows, Pigs, Wars, and Witches* by Marvin Harris. Copyright © 1974 by Marvin Harris. Used by permission of Random House, Inc.

Thomas Hurka, "Philosophy, Morality, and *The English Patient*." Originally published in *Queens Quarterly* 104:1, Spring 1997. Copyright © 1997 by Thomas Hurka. Reprinted by permission of the author.

Alice Beck Kehoe, "Transcribing Insima, A Blackfoot 'Old Lady'," from *Reading Beyond Words: Contexts For Native History*, edited by Jennifer S.H. Brown and Elizabeth Vibert. Copyright © 1996 by Alice Beck Kehoe. Reprinted by permission of the author.

Martin Luther King, Jr., "Letter From Birmingham Jail," from *Why We Can't Wait* by Martin Luther King, Jr. Copyright © 1963 by Martin Luther King, Jr., copyright © renewed 1991 by Coretta Scott King. Reprinted by arrangement with The Heirs to the Estate of Martin Luther King, Jr., c/o Writers House Inc., as agent for the proprietor.

Naomi Klein, " The Swoosh," from *No Logo: Taking Aim at the Brand Bullies* by Naomi Klein. Vintage Canada Edition, 2000. Copyright © 2000 by Naomi Klein. Reprinted by permission of Alfred A. Knopf Canada, a division of Random House of Canada Limited.

Larissa Lai, "Political Animals and the Body of History," originally published in *Canadian Literature* 163, Winter 1999. Copyright © 1999 by Larissa Lai. Reprinted by permission.

Margaret Laurence, "Where the World Began." Copyright © 1976 by Margaret Laurence. Reprinted by permission of The Estate of Margaret Laurence.

Fran Lebowitz, "Children: Pro or Con?" from *The Fran Lebowitz Reader* by Fran Lebowitz. Copyright © 1974, 1975, 1976, 1977, 1978, 1979, 1980, 1981, 1994 by Fran Lebowitz.

Emily Martin, "The Egg and the Sperm: How Science Has Constructed a Romance Based on Stereotypical Male-Female Roles," from *Signs: Journal of Women and Culture in Society* 16:3, 1991. Copyright © by The University of Chicago. Reprinted by permission of The University of Chicago Press.

Groucho Marx, "Dinner With My Celebrated Pen Pal, T.S. Eliot," from *The Groucho Letters* by Groucho Marx. Copyright © 1967 by Groucho Marx. Copyright renewed © 1995 by Miriam Marx, Arthur Marx, and Melinda Marx. Reprinted by permission of Simon & Schuster.

Stanley Milgram, "Behavioral Study of Obedience," from *Journal of Abnormal and Social Psychology*. Vol. 67 No. 4, 1963, pp. 371-378. Copyright © by The Estate of Stanley Milgram. Reprinted by permission of Alexandra Milgram.

N. Scott Momaday, "The Way to Rainy Mountain," from *The Way to Rainy Mountain* by N. Scott Momaday. Copyright © 1969 by The University of New Mexico Press. First published in *The Reporter*, January 26, 1967. Reprinted by permission of The University of New Mexico Press.

Bharati Mukherjee, "A Four-Hundred-Year-Old Woman," from *The Writer on Her Work*, Vol. II, edited by Janet Sternburg. Copyright © 1991 by Bharati Mukherjee.

Lewis Mumford, "The Highway and the City," from *The Highway and the City* by Lewis Mumford. Copyright © 1953, 1956, 1958, 1959, 1960, 1961, 1962, 1963 by Lewis Mumford.

Alice Munro, "What is Real?" from *What is Real?* Copyright © 1982 by Methuen Publishing Ltd. Originally appeared in *Making It New: Contemporary Canadian Stories*, edited by John Metcalf. Reprinted by permission of Methuen Publishing Ltd.

Ngugi wa Thiong'o, "Decolonising the Mind," from *Decolonising the Mind: The Politics of Language in African Literature* by Ngugi wa Thiong'o. Copyright © 1986 by Ngugi wa Thiong'o. Published in North America by Heinemann, a division of Reed Elsevier Inc., Portsmouth, NH. Reprinted by permission.

Alden Nowlan, "Ladies and Gentlemen, Stompin' Tom Connors!" from *Double Exposure* by Alden Nowlan. Originally published in *Macleans*, August 1972. Copyright © 1978 by Alden Nowlan. Reprinted by permission of the Estate of Alden Nowlan.

George Orwell, "Politics and the English Language," from *Shooting an Elephant and Other Essays* by George Orwell. Copyright © George Orwell 1946, and "Lear, Tolstoy and the Fool," Copyright © 1947. Reprinted by permission of Bill Hamilton as the Literary Executor of the Estate of the Late Sonia Brownell Orwell and Secker & Warburg Ltd.

Robert D. Putnam, "Bowling Alone: America's Declining Social Capital," from *Journal of Democracy* 6:1, January, 1995. This article has been revised and expanded in *Bowling Alone: The Collapse and Revival of American Community* by Robert D. Putnam. Copyright © 2000 by Robert D. Putnam. Reprinted by permission of the author.

Adrienne Rich, "Invisibility in Academe," from *Blood, Bread, and Poetry: Selected Prose 1978-1985* by Adrienne Rich. Copyright © 1986 by Adrienne Rich. Used by permission of the author and W. W. Norton & Company, Inc. "Taking Women Students Seriously," from *On Lies, Secrets, and Silence: Selected Prose 1966-1978* by Adrienne Rich. Copyright © 1979 by W. W. Norton & Company, Inc. Used by permission of the author and W. W. Norton & Company, Inc.

Mike Royko, "Another Accolade For Charter Arms Corp." Originally published in *The Chicago Tribune*, 1980. Reprinted by permission of *The Toronto Star Syndicate*. Copyright © Tribune Media Services.

Witold Rybcynski, "One Good Turn: Why the Robertson Screwdriver is the Biggest Little Invention of the Twentieth Century," from *Saturday Night*, July 29, 2000. This article has been revised and expanded in *One Good Turn: The Natural History of the Screwdriver and the Screw* by Witold Rybcynski. Copyright © 2000 by Witold Rybcynski.

Elaine Showalter, "Representing Ophelia: Women, Madness, and the Responsibilities of Feminist Criticism," from *Shakespeare and the Question of Theory*, edited by Patricia Parker and Geoffrey Hartman. Copyright © 1985 by Methuen Publishing Ltd. Reprinted by permission of Methuen Publishing Ltd.

Peter Singer, "Speciesism and the Equality of Animals," from *Animal Liberation*, (New York: Avon Books). Copyright © 1977 by Peter Singer. Reprinted by permission of the author.

E.B. White, "Once More to the Lake," from *One Man's Meat*. Text copyright © 1941 by E. B. White. Reprinted by permission of Tilbury House, Publishers, Gardiner, Maine.

Raymond Williams, "Correctness and the English Language," from *The Long Revolution* by Raymond Williams. Copyright © 1961, 2001 by The Estate of Raymond Williams. Reprinted by permission.

J. Tuzo Wilson, "Did the Atlantic Close and Then Re-Open?" from *Nature* 211, pp. 676-681. Copyright © 1966 by Macmillan Magazines Ltd. Reprinted by permission.

INDEX